THIR

Adult Development and Aging

Diane E. Papalia

Harvey L. Sterns

Ruth Duskin Feldman

Cameron J. Camp

Mc
Graw
Hill

Boston   Burr Ridge, IL   Dubuque, IA   Madison, WI   New York   San Francisco   St. Louis
Bangkok   Bogotá   Caracas   Kuala Lumpur   Lisbon   London   Madrid   Mexico City
Milan   Montreal   New Delhi   Santiago   Seoul   Singapore   Sydney   Taipei   Toronto

The McGraw·Hill Companies

Higher Education

ADULT DEVELOPMENT AND AGING

This book is printed on acid-free paper.

1 2 3 4 5 6 7 8 9 0 DOC/DOC 0 9 8 7 6

ISBN-13: 978-0-07-111287-1
ISBN-10:   0-07-111287-1

www.mhhe.com

About the Authors

As a professor, Diane E. Papalia taught thousands of undergraduates at the University of Wisconsin-Madison. She received her bachelor's degree, majoring in psychology, from Vassar College and both her master's degree in child development and family relations and her Ph.D. in lifespan developmental psychology from West Virginia University. She has published numerous articles in such professional journals as *Human Development, International Journal of Aging and Human Development, Sex Roles, Journal of Experimental Child Psychology* and *Journal of Gerontology.* Most of these papers have dealt with her major research focus, cognitive development from childhood through old age. She is especially interested in intellectual development and factors that contribute to the maintenance of intellectual functioning. She is a Fellow in the Gerontological Society of America. She is the coauthor of *A Child's World,* now in its ninth edition, with Sally Wendkos Olds and Ruth Duskin Feldman; of *Human Development,* now in its tenth edition, with Sally Wendkos Olds and Ruth Duskin Feldman; of *Psychology* with Sally Wendkos Olds; and of *Child Development: A Topical Approach* with Dana Gross and Ruth Duskin Feldman.

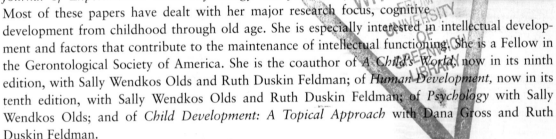

Harvey L. Sterns has three decades of experience in teaching undergraduate and graduate students lifespan development and adult development and aging. He received his bachelor's degree from Bard College with a double major in biology and psychology, his master's degree in experimental psychology from the State University of New York at Buffalo, and a Ph.D. in lifespan developmental psychology from West Virginia University. Additional training in gerontology was received at the University of Southern California and the Pennsylvania State University. He is Professor of Psychology and Director of the Institute for Life-Span Development and Gerontology at The University of Akron. Dr. Sterns is also Research Professor of Gerontology and served as Co-Director of the Western Reserve Geriatric Education Center at the Northeastern Ohio Universities College of Medicine. He has published over 100 book chapters and articles in professional journals including the *Journal of Gerontology, Journal of Vocational Behavior, Developmental Psychology, Experimental Aging Research,* and *Applied Psychology: An International Review.* He is a licensed psychologist in Ohio and is a Fellow of the American Psychological Association, American Psychological Society, Gerontological Society of America, and the Association for Gerontology in Higher Education. He served as president in 2002–2003 of Division 20, Adult Development and Aging, of the American Psychological Association. He is coauthor, editor/co-editor of four books.

Dr. Sterns's research has focused on improving older adult learning and problem solving; improving skills related to older adult driving; family and friends' intervention with older drivers; maintaining professional competence; training and career development; personality and housing choices by older adults; and life planning research and curriculum development for adults and older adults with MR/DD as part of the Rehabilitation Research and Training Center on Aging and Mental Retardation. In 2005, he received the Outstanding Gerontological Educator Award in Ohio from the Ohio Association of Gerontology and Education. In 2004, he received the M. Powell Lawton Distinguished Contribution Award in Applied Gerontology from Division 20 of the American Psychological Association and the Retirement Research Foundation.

Ruth Duskin Feldman is an award-winning writer and educator. With Diane E. Papalia and Sally Wendkos Olds, she coauthored the Fourth, Seventh, Eighth, Ninth, and Tenth Editions of *Human Development* and the Eighth, Ninth, and Tenth Editions of *A Child's World.* She is also coauthor of *Adult Development and Aging* and of *Child Development: A Topical Approach.* A former teacher, she has developed educational materials for all levels from elementary school through college and has prepared ancillaries to accompany the Papalia-Olds books. She is author or coauthor of four books addressed to general readers, including *Whatever Happened to the Quiz Kids? Perils and Profits of Growing Up Gifted* (republished in 2000 by iuniverse.com). She has written for numerous newspapers and magazines and has lectured extensively and made national and local media appearances throughout the United States on education and gifted children. She received her bachelor's degree from Northwestern University, where she was graduated with highest distinction and was elected to Phi Beta Kappa.

Cameron J. Camp is a noted psychologist specializing in applied research in gerontology. He received a bachelor's degree in psychology from the University of Houston, where he graduated summa cum laude, and master's and doctoral degrees in experimental psychology from the same institution. For 16 years, he taught undergraduate courses in adult development and aging, as well as in memory, general psychology, child development, and experimental design, first at Fort Hays University in Kansas, and then at the University of New Orleans. He is the author of numerous articles in professional journals such as *Psychology and Aging, Journal of Gerontology, The Gerontologist, Experimental Aging Research, Human Development,* and *Clinical Gerontologist.* He has contributed chapters to books on memory and aging, problem solving, and lifespan development and is coauthor of a college textbook, *Human Sexuality Today.* Currently he is Director and Senior Research Scientist at the Myers Research Institute of Menorah Park Center for the Aging in Cleveland, Ohio. Much of his research involves the development of behavioral and cognitive interventions to help persons with dementia live more independent and fulfilling lives and to reduce burdens on caregivers. He is a member of the Gerontological Society of America and is a Fellow of the American Psychological Association's division on adult development and aging.

Contents

Preface

To write a textbook about adult development and aging is an exciting challenge. This rapidly growing field of study about a vital, diverse, and expanding population draws on the findings of many academic disciplines. This book takes a topical rather than a chronological approach. We discuss each aspect of development—physical, cognitive, social, and personality development—in relation to all periods of the adult life span, with special emphasis on late adulthood.

By combining the talents and experience of the author of a leading textbook on lifespan development, noted researchers in adult development and aging who have extensive teaching experience in the field, and a professional writer who has written textbooks and peripherals in developmental psychology, we believe we have achieved not only a high degree of accuracy and thoroughness, but also a tone and a writing style that are fresh, lively, clear, engaging, thought-provoking, and accessible.

Every book is written by real people, whose selection of subject matter, examples, and interpretations is inevitably colored by their experiences and attitudes. We four authors make up a diversified team. Our ages range from the forties to the seventies; our combined life experience encompasses the periods from the Great Depression of the 1930s to the present. Our ethnic origins are Italian, eastern European Jewish, Irish, Norwegian, and Native American. All of us are parents, and two of us are grandparents.

What sets this book apart from others in the field? What were our aims in writing it?

- We believe that central to the study of adult development and aging is that people have the potential to develop as long as they live. In this vein we try to present adult development as a very human story. Each chapter begins with a biographical vignette about a real person. The subjects are well-known men and women (such as Betty Friedan and Nelson Mandela) of varying racial, national, and ethnic origin, whose lives dramatize important themes in the chapter. Students will enjoy and identify with these stories, which lead directly and smoothly into the body of each chapter.

- We believe that adults live in a wide array of cultures that exhibit the richness and complexity of human aspirations and experience. Hence, we take a consistently cross-cultural perspective. Extensive multicultural and multiethnic material is woven into topical discussions throughout the book. In addition, a series of boxes called "The Multicultural Context" focuses on specific topics such as how traditional beliefs influence the course of disease, whether intelligent behavior is the same in all cultures, and how rural Malaysians cope with economic change. Photographs reinforce the themes of diversity and demographic balance.

- We believe that adults help to shape their own development, and to this effect, we discuss contemporary trends and lifestyles in a complex, changing world. The introductory chapter sets the tone for current, issue-oriented coverage. As an integral part of our discussions of relationships and family life, we deal with such topics as single parenting, dual-earner families, homosexuality, and caregiving grandparents.

- We take a positive yet realistic view of aging; a natural process of development that includes both losses and gains. We believe that all periods of adulthood are equally important and provide opportunities for growth. Throughout the book, we point out insights to be gained from a lifespan developmental perspective and a multidisciplinary approach.

- We balance theoretical, empirical, and practical concerns. To emphasize the evolving nature of scientific knowledge and its applications, a series of boxes called "Applied Approaches" describe groundbreaking research, past and present. Another series of boxes, "The Art of Aging," feature specific research issues such as environmental adaptations to meet the needs of an aging population. Where controversy exists, we explore it. We present the field of adult development as it is: a developing field whose practitioners still have much to discover.

Designed primarily for undergraduates—sophomores or juniors—taking courses in adult development and aging, *Adult Development and Aging* may also be used for advanced and graduate level courses. It is also appropriate for lifespan developmental courses, in conjunction with a text on child and adolescent development. No prior knowledge of psychology is necessary, because basic concepts and methods are explained as needed.

In this third edition, we have incorporated new demographic material while at the same time maintaining material on issues that are still current and relevant today. We group the thirteen chapters as follows: Chapters 1 and 2 include an introductory overview of the field and a chapter on metatheories and research methods. Chapters 3–7 cover physical, cognitive, and moral development. Chapters 8–10 explore education, work, retirement, and leisure; relationships and lifestyles; and living arrangements, caregiving, and community support. Chapters 11–13 turn to personality development, mental health and coping, and death and bereavement. We believe that this organization provides a clear, logical treatment of the most salient topics in the study of adult development and aging. Augmenting the material in the text is an epilogue, which summarizes contemporary topics in the field of adult development and aging.

LEARNING AIDS

As in the first and second editions, this book contains a number of pedagogical aids for the student:

- *Chapter openers.* Each chapter continues to open with a chapter outline that previews the major topics, and a short biographical vignette that brings those topics into focus.
- *Critical thinking questions.* Marginal questions in each chapter challenge the student to think more critically about the subject matter.
- *Chapter summaries.* Each chapter offers brief statements organized around the main topics in the chapter that review the important concepts.
- *Boxes.* Existing boxed material [Art of Aging, Applied Approaches, Multicultural Context] has been replaced with more contemporary examples. For example, material on Work and Retirement in Japan has been included in Chapter 8.
- *Illustrations, figures, and tables.* Drawings, graphs, charts and photographs are carefully chosen to underscore important points in the text.
- *Key terms.* As each important new term is introduced, it is highlighted and defined in the text. Key terms and the pages on which they first appear, are listed at the end of each chapter.
- *Glossary.* Key terms and their definitions appear in alphabetical order in an end-of-book glossary.
- *Bibliography.* A complete listing of references appears alphabetically by author at the end of the book.

SUPPLEMENTARY MATERIALS

Adult Development and Aging is accompanied by a complete learning and teaching package consisting of a combined Instructor's Manual and Test Bank prepared by Rita M. Curl, Minot State University, North Dakota, and Dean Blevins of the Center for Mental Healthcare & Outcomes Research, Central Arkansas Veterans Healthcare System. The Instructor's Manual contains interesting new features such as a *chapter introduction;* a *total teaching package outline* directing instructors to all the MGH resources available that correlate to material in each chapter; *scenarios/vignettes* that include key points from the chapter to aid identification of concepts in applied contexts and to promote class discussion; *class activities* incorporating use of the Web; *critical thinking exercises* based on those in the new edition; and a list of *recommended popular films.* A Computerized Test Bank is also available with full editing and selection capabilities, for use on either Mac or IBM systems. Please consult your McGraw-Hill representative for availability of these and other supplements.

ACKNOWLEDGMENTS

We would like to thank all the people who graciously reviewed the third edition manuscript including the following: S. Craig Campbell, Weber State University; Celia Wolk Gershenson, University of Minnesota; Leslee Pollina, Southeast Missouri State University; Jeannine M. Taylor, Kent State University; and Susan M. Troy, Northeast Iowa Community College.

We appreciate the strong support we have had from our publisher. We would like to express our special thanks to Mike Sugarman, senior sponsoring editor; Kate Russillo, editorial coordinator, whose constant editorial support helped guide the revision; and Rick Hecker, project manager, who has been instrumental in making this project run smoothly. Most especially we would like to thank Kelly Zacharias for all of her extensive work on the revision of this third edition. We also want to thank Greta Lax and Kristen Granata for their contributions to specific chapters. All are from the Institute for Life-Span Development and Gerontology, at The University of Akron, and have offered much support throughout the revision process.

Our sincere hope for this edition is that it fosters an appreciation of the study of adult development and aging, that is, the study of changing individuals in an ever-changing world. As always, we welcome and appreciate comments from readers, which help us continue to improve *Adult Development and Aging.*

Diane E. Papalia

Harvey L. Sterns

Ruth Duskin Feldman

Cameron J. Camp

CHAPTER 1

Adult Development and Aging in a Changing World

◈ FOCUS: BETTY FRIEDAN

There is nothing permanent except change.
　　　—Heraclitus, fragment (sixth century B.C.)

© Shelley Gazin/Corbis Images

BETTY FRIEDAN* STOOD a feisty 5 feet 2 inches tall and did not shrink from a fight. At age 42, she wrote *The Feminine Mystique* (1963), a call to arms for the women's movement in the United States. Three decades later, Friedan became a standard-bearer for another crusade with *The Fountain of Age* (1993), aimed at freeing older adults from a restrictive image of aging. Recently, Friedan wrote her memoir, *A Life So Far* (2000), which recounts the hardships and triumphs she experienced as an active leader in these movements. Friedan's involvement

*Sources for biographical information about Betty Friedan are Carlson & Crowley (1992), Friedan (1963, 1976, 1981, 1993, 1994, 2000), Klagsbrun (1993), and *Who's Who in America* (2002).

in both causes was deeply rooted in her own experience.

Friedan's odyssey from her beginnings in Peoria, Illinois, a small town in the American heartland, tells much, not only about her personal development as an adult but about the changing social context of adult development and aging. Not wanting to be like her mother, who always regretted having given up her career for marriage, the bright, energetic young woman went east to Smith College, a prestigious women's school. She majored in psychology, graduated summa cum laude, and later did postgraduate work with such leaders in the field as Kurt Lewin and Erik Erikson. She also worked as a reporter for a labor news service but was bumped by a returning World War II veteran—a common experience for working women who had been recruited to fill in for fighting men, only to be told, after the war, to go home where they "belonged."

In 1947, Friedan was married. Two years later, fired from a newspaper job for being pregnant, she (like most other young women of her time and place) became a self-described housewife, seeking the feminine fulfillment her mother had failed to achieve. But somehow she wanted more. During the 1950s, while raising her three children in a New York suburb, she wrote articles for national women's magazines and secretly began work on her myth-shattering book, *The Feminine Mystique*.

"I never set out to write a book to change women's lives, to change history," Friedan recalls in *A Life So Far*. "To get behind the facade of the feminine mystique, to dig out its origins and the base of its appeal, I had to go beyond that women's magazine world. I had to dig deep into my intellectual roots in psychology, and into the misery, the mystery, of my own flight from it" (Friedan, 2000, pp. 106, 111).

The Feminine Mystique—which has so far sold more than 3 million copies—expressed Friedan's growing frustration with her role in a male-dominated society in which a woman's "place" was in the home and her sole identity was "wife and mother." It articulated the unacknowledged rage, emptiness, and desperation of millions of women who chafed under the bonds of domesticity yet succumbed to societal pressures against having lives and careers of their own. The message was threatening to many women but liberating to many others.

Friedan became an organizer of the women's movement, the founder and first president of the National Organization for Women (NOW), and the convener of the National Women's Political Caucus. On August 26, 1970, a year after she divorced her husband, she called a "Women's Strike for Equality" and led an estimated 50,000 marchers down Manhattan's Fifth Avenue. Friedan (1976, 1981) gradually broadened her sights, pressing for new approaches to divorce, abortion reform, housing, employment, and education; for equality within marriage as well as in the workplace; and for societal supports for women who wanted to balance a career and children.

In her eighties, the woman who raised the consciousness of a generation of young and middle-aged women was determined to do the same for older adults. Before starting 10 years of research for *The Fountain of Age*, she had to break through her psychological denial of her own aging. Ultimately, Friedan (who had six grandchildren and two step-granddaughters, and was a visiting professor at New York University) set out "to debunk the 'age mystique' that defines older people as passive objects of care and . . . denies them their 'personhood,' just as the feminine mystique denied women theirs" (Carlson & Crowley, 1992, pp. 20, 15).

The Fountain of Age has been hailed by some critics, but dismissed by others as too upbeat. It seeks to change the prevalent view of aging as a process of inevitable deterioration, helplessness, and disease, and of older adults as a burden and a drain on society—an image that does not match the real lives of vast numbers of older adults. Instead of defining old age merely as a loss of youth, Friedan saw it as another stage of devel-opment with its own, as yet largely untested, pos-sibilities and strengths—"an adventure, not a problem" (Carlson & Crowley, 1992). "I was de-termined to break through the view of age only as deny-at-all-cost deterioration and decline-from-youth-as-peak-of-life to the new years of life that so many Americans were in fact living so well" (Friedan, 2000, p. 321). Ms. Friedan died on February 4, 2006, on her 85th birthday.

BETTY FRIEDAN'S ADULT LIFE AND work demonstrated what she learned from her teachers of psychology: that human beings develop in a context. Her story dramatizes how an individual adult can affect and be affected by changing social conditions. Friedan's dissatisfaction with her role as a suburban wife and mother in the 1950s sparked a movement that changed the lives of many Amer-ican women—and her own as well. Now, with the "baby boom" generation—fully one-third of the nation's population—approaching later life, a major shift is occurring in how adults think about and deal with their own development.

This shift is reflected in a growing interest in the study of adult develop-ment and aging. In introducing you to that study, we start with basic ques-tions and concepts: What does it mean for an adult to develop? Is aging more than a process of decline? How has adult development been studied? Does age have more than one meaning? Why do some people seem to age differently than others? What kinds of influences can alter the course of adult develop-ment? We go on to discuss changing views and realities of aging. We briefly describe the diverse composition of a graying population in the United States and worldwide, and the challenges and dilemmas it presents.

APPROACHING THE STUDY OF ADULT DEVELOPMENT AND AGING: AN OVERVIEW

Before beginning a study of adult development and aging, we need to raise a basic question: Do adults actually *develop,* or do human beings reach maturity in their early twenties and then decline? Until the middle of the twentieth cen-tury, most psychologists would have given the second answer. Sigmund Freud, the father of psychoanalysis, saw puberty as the end point of development. Re-searchers limited their attention to children; even adolescence was not consid-ered a separate stage of life until the turn of the twentieth century. Only during the past 50 years has there been serious, scientific study of adult development. That study is still in an early phase, and many of its discoveries are still quite tentative; but developmentalists are asking and exploring important questions.

CRITICAL THINKING

What evidence can you give to support the conclusion that devel-opment continues across the life span?

What Is Adult Development?

We've been speaking about *development* but what, precisely, does this term mean? In ordinary speech, forms of the word are used in many contexts. For example:

- Horace is developing a cold.
- Flowers develop from buds.
- Many developing nations are rapidly becoming industrialized.
- Lindsay took a roll of film to be developed.
- Detectives reported a new development in the murder case.

Obviously, development involves change. But not all change is developmental. If a person changes clothes, or changes the bedsheets, we hardly would call that *development*.

Change is simply a difference in something or someone from one time to another. Changes in a human being over the course of adult life are too numerous, too diverse, and often too random to study usefully. **Development** is a systematic process of adaptive change in behavior in one or more directions. Development is *systematic* in that it is coherent and organized. It is *adaptive* in that it is aimed at dealing with the ever-changing internal and external conditions of existence. Development tends to progress from simple to complex forms (as in the development of language from simple words, to phrases, to grammatical sentences). It may take more than one route and may or may not have a definite goal; but there is some connection between the often-imperceptible changes of which it is composed. The child you were shaped the adult you have become, and the adult you are today will shape the adult you become tomorrow. Developmentalists study how people change—and also how they do *not* change—throughout the life span.

Development may involve **learning**: long-lasting changes in behavior as a result of experience. Or it may be the result of **maturation** of the brain and other physical systems and structures of the body. This unfolding of a biologically determined sequence of behavior patterns includes readiness to master new abilities. More often, development involves a complex interaction between maturation and learning, as when a young child says the first word or the first sentence. While children pass such milestones at pretty much the same ages, individual differences widen as people grow older and experience becomes more of a factor. Adult development may not be as rapid or as obvious as childhood development and may involve losses as well as gains; but even older adults can continue to develop new skills, such as learning to use computers.

Bettmann/Corbis Images

The psychologist G. Stanley Hall (1846–1924) was a pioneer in the study of aging, as well as of childhood and adolescence. He was a founder and the first president of the American Psychological Association, and he established the nation's first professional psychology journal and its first psychology laboratory.

How the Study of Adult Development and Aging Evolved

The first major work on aging in the United States was published in the second decade of the twentieth century. In 1922, at age 78, G. Stanley Hall, who had been a pioneer in the study of childhood and adolescence, published

Senescence: The Last Half of Life. Six years later, Stanford University opened the first major scientific research unit devoted to aging. But not until a generation later did this area of study blossom. By 1946, the National Institutes of Health (NIH) had established a large-scale research unit, and specialized organizations and journals were reporting the latest findings.

Since the late 1930s, a number of long-term studies have focused on adults. The Grant Study of Adult Development followed Harvard University students through adulthood. In the mid 1950s Bernice Neugarten and her associates at the University of Chicago began studies of middle-aged people, and K. Warner Schaie launched the still-ongoing Seattle Longitudinal Study of adult intelligence. Paul Costa and Robert McCrae have conducted a study of personality traits based on data collected beginning in the late 1950s to mid 1960s on thousands of adults of all ages in Boston and Baltimore.

Full lifespan studies in the United States grew out of programs designed to follow children through adulthood. The Stanford Studies of Gifted Children (begun in 1921 under the direction of Lewis Terman) continue to trace the development of people who were identified as unusually intelligent in childhood. Other major studies that began around 1930—the Berkeley Growth Study, the Oakland Growth Study, and the Fels Research Institute Study—have yielded information on long-term development.

These and other studies we discuss in this book have drawn on a variety of research tools and have added much to our understanding of adulthood. However, we still know much more about children and older adults than we do about those in between. A growing emphasis on studies about young and middle-aged adults is evident in research being conducted by the MacArthur Foundation Research Network on Successful Midlife Development.

CRITICAL THINKING

What arguments would you present to support long-term studies across the life span versus research that focuses on adults and aging persons?

A Lifespan Developmental Approach

Today, most psychologists accept the idea that human development goes on throughout life. This concept of development as a lifelong process of adaptation is known as **lifespan development**. Scientific study of lifespan development is the primary task of **lifespan developmental psychology**.

Paul B. Baltes (1987; Baltes & Smith, 2004; Baltes, Lindenberger, & Staudinger, 1998), a leader in the study of lifespan developmental psychology, has identified key principles of a lifespan developmental approach, a framework for the study of lifespan development (summarized in Table 1.1). They include these:

- *Development is lifelong.* Each period of the life span is influenced by what happened before and will affect what is to come. Each period has its own unique characteristics and value; none is more or less important than any other.
- *Development depends on history and context.* Each person develops within a specific set of circumstances or conditions defined by time and place. Human beings influence, and are influenced by, their historical and social context. They not only respond to their physical and social environments but also interact with and change them.

CRITICAL THINKING

What historical and contextual circumstances are you experiencing that will influence your own aging?

TABLE 1.1

Key Features of a Lifespan Developmental Approach

Feature	Explanation
Multidirectionality	Development can result in both increases and decreases, at varying rates, within the same person, age period, or category of behavior.
Multidimensionality	Development can affect multiple capacities or aspects of a person. Personality, intelligence, and perception can be changing at the same time.
Plasticity	It is possible to improve functioning throughout the life span, though there are limits on how much a person can improve at any age.
History and context	People develop within a physical and social context, which differs at different points in history. Individuals not only respond to their context but also interact with and actively influence it.
Multiple causality	Development has multiple causes. Because no single perspective can adequately describe or explain the complexities of development, the study of lifespan development requires cooperative, multidisciplinary efforts of scholars from many fields.

SOURCE: Adapted from Baltes, 1987.

- *Development is multidimensional and multidirectional.* Development throughout life involves a balance of growth and decline. As people gain in one area, they may lose in another, and at varying rates. Children grow mostly in one direction—up—both in size and in abilities. In adulthood the balance gradually shifts. Some capacities, such as vocabulary, continue to increase; others, such as the ability to solve unfamiliar problems, may diminish; and some new attributes, such as expertise, may emerge. People seek to maximize gains and to minimize losses by learning to manage or compensate for them.
- *Development is pliable, or plastic.* **Plasticity** means modifiability of performance. Many abilities, such as memory, strength, and endurance, can be significantly improved with training and practice, even late in life. However, even children are not infinitely pliable; the potential for change has limits.

The idea that development goes on throughout the life span has several important implications. It suggests that each phase of a person's life is influenced by what has already occurred and will affect what is to come. Thus each part of the life span has its own unique characteristics and value. No part of life is more or less important than any other.

Basic Concepts

An extremely useful way to visualize adult development is as a product of *multiple concurrent forces acting on a complex system*. This concept allows us to look at several aspects of the same person, who may be—for example—growing intellectually while experiencing some physical decline. We can view a person as having not one but several different ages: not only chronological but also functional, biological, psychological, and social. And we can measure the effects of many kinds of factors that influence development.

CRITICAL THINKING

How do you think adults maintain a high quality of life as aspects of their development show decline? How will you do it?

Aspects of Development

One reason adult development is complex is that changes occur in several aspects of the self. In this book, we speak of physical, intellectual, personality, and social development. Changes in *physical* systems and structures of the body include sensory capacities, organ and nervous systems, health and fitness, and motor skills. All of these are aspects of *physical* development. To some extent, physical development may be genetically programmed; but research now suggests that people can control their own physical development to a much greater extent than once was thought possible. Changes in mental functioning—such as memory, intelligence, practical problem solving, moral reasoning, and wisdom—are aspects of *intellectual,* or *cognitive,* development. *Personality* development involves the unique way each person deals with the world and expresses thoughts and emotions. *Social development* refers to changes in an individual's social world—the world of relationships, living arrangements, work, and leisure.

Both rates and results of development vary widely. Individuals differ in height, weight, and body build, in such constitutional factors as health and energy level, and in how their bodies adapt to aging. They differ in intellectual abilities and in emotional reactions; in the work they do, how well they do it, and how much they like it; in the homes and communities they live in, the people they see, and the relationships they have; and in how they use their leisure.

Although we talk separately about physical, intellectual, social, and personality development, these domains are interrelated, and each aspect of development affects the others. Physical and intellectual capacities, for example, contribute greatly to self-esteem and can affect choice of occupation—important elements of personality and social development. Decisions about work and retirement can affect physical and intellectual functioning. Anxiety about taking a test can impair physical or intellectual performance. And grief can literally make a bereaved person ill.

Periods of Adulthood

CRITICAL THINKING

Taking Baltes's lifespan developmental approach into consideration, what value would you identify in each period of adulthood?

When does a person become an adult? When does an adult reach middle or old age? These questions are not as simple as they may seem. The demarcation of periods of the life span varies in different times and in different societies. Still, most research divides adulthood into three periods: young adulthood (approximately ages 20 to 40), middle age (ages 40 to 65), and late, or older, adulthood (age 65 or more). At least in most western societies today, each of these periods has characteristic events and concerns (see Table 1.2).

Young adults are generally at the height of their physical powers and many aspects of their intellectual powers. During these years, they make career choices and form intimate relationships that may be lifelong.

Middle-aged adults might see some decline in health and physical abilities but develop more mature patterns of thinking based on practical experience. Some middle-aged people are at the height of their careers; others have reached dead ends. Some dust off mothballed dreams or pursue new goals. Many have children who are leaving the nest. A growing consciousness of the inevitability of death may bring on personality changes and exploration of new opportunities for growth.

Most *older adults* are physically active, relatively healthy, independent, and mentally alert, though they may be having changes in health. Chronic conditions may develop, but these can be controlled by medical intervention. Many older adults have more time for personal relationships. But they must deal with the decline of some faculties, the loss of friends and loved ones, and the prospect of death.

Meanings of Age

A number of common sayings suggest that there can be discrepancies between chronological age and how old a person feels and acts:

"Act your age!"
"You're only as old as you feel."
"He is wise beyond his years."
"She's old before her time."

Just as most Americans identify themselves as "middle-class," many adults think of themselves as "thirtysomething." Young adults generally feel just about their own age, but middle-aged and older adults tend to feel younger than they are (Montepare & Lachman, 1989). Older people often tend to feel younger and have a positive view of their own health status. The older adult population is relatively healthy and independent (Rowe & Kahn, 1998). One anthropologist, on the basis of interviews with older adults in a California

TABLE 1.2

Major Developments in the Three Periods of Adulthood

Age Period	Physical Developments	Cognitive Developments	Psychosocial Developments
Young Adulthood (20 to 40 years)	Physical condition peaks, then declines slightly. Lifestyle choices influence health.	Cognitive abilities and moral judgments assume more complexity. Educational and career choices are made.	Personality traits and styles become relatively stable, but changes in personality may be influenced by life stages and events. Decisions are made about intimate relationships and personal lifestyles. Most people marry, and most become parents.
Middle Adulthood (40 to 65 years)	Some deterioration of sensory abilities, health, stamina, and prowess may take place. Women experience menopause.	Most basic mental abilities peak; expertise and practical problem-solving skills are high. Creative output may decline but improve in quality. For some, career success and earning powers peak; for others, burnout or career change may occur.	Sense of identity continues to develop; stressful midlife transition may occur. Double responsibilities of caring for children and elderly parents may cause stress. Launching of children leaves empty nest.
Late Adulthood (65 years and older)	Most people are healthy and active, although health and physical abilities decline somewhat. Slowing of reaction time affects some aspects of functioning.	Most people are mentally alert. Although intelligence and memory may deteriorate in some areas, most people find ways to compensate.	Retirement may offer new options for use of time, including new full- or part-time work. People need to cope with personal losses and impending death. Relationships with family and close friends can provide important support. Search for meaning in life assumes central importance.

metropolitan area, coined the term **ageless self** to capture this perception that the self remains the same despite chronological aging and physical change (Kaufman, 1986). Some very old people feel like young people inhabiting an old body. One man, at age 84, was still working as an engineer and talking about putting money aside for his "twilight years." A 94-year-old man does not like to go to the senior center because "too many old people show up."

All this suggests that a person can age in a number of ways, which are not necessarily "in sync."* **Chronological age** is simply a count of how many times an inhabitant of this planet has orbited the sun. Minimum age limits for drinking, driving, voting, and the like assume that chronological age is a barometer of the ability to perform certain functions. However, that assumption is not necessarily accurate. The mere passage of time does not cause development. Not only can the pace of development differ among individuals, the same person may also develop more quickly or more slowly in certain areas. For example, a college student who is physically and sexually mature may be immature when it comes to knowing how to act in a social situation.

Functional age is a measure of how well a person can function in a physical and social environment as compared with other people of the same chronological age. A 70-year-old who is "young at heart" may be functionally younger than a 50-year-old who finds life's challenges overwhelming. **Gerontologists,** scientists who study aged people and the aging process, sometimes divide today's older people into two categories. The *young-old* (55 to 75), the majority, are those who—regardless of chronological age—are vital, vigorous, and active. The *old-old* (75 and above) experience more changes in health and may become more frail or experience major health and psychological changes (Neugarten & Neugarten, 1987). So, while this book—for convenience and consistency with much of the research literature—refers to adults as falling into conventional categories based on chronological age, in actuality these divisions are approximate and arbitrary.

Three components of functional age are biological age, psychological age, and social age, and these may differ greatly. **Biological age** is a measure of how far a person has progressed along a potential life span; it is predicted by the person's physical condition. We can measure biological age by examining how well vital organ systems, such as the respiratory and circulatory systems, are functioning. A 50-year-old who has exercised regularly is likely to be biologically younger than a 40-year-old whose most strenuous exercise is clicking a remote control. To some extent, it's possible to reverse the march of biological age by making healthful changes in lifestyle, such as quitting smoking. Giving up cigarettes can add years to life expectancy; taking up smoking (a disturbing trend among teenagers and young adults today) increases a person's biological age.

The ability to deal with the demands of the environment, such as an unexpected pregnancy, an accident, a move, or a change in job, depends on **psychological age:** how well, in comparison with same-aged peers, a person

---

*This discussion is indebted to Birren & Cunningham (1985), Birren & Renner (1977), and Birren & Schroots (1996).

can cope with environmental challenges. A 50-year-old who lives with his or her parents, has no job, and cannot form a meaningful personal relationship may be psychologically younger than a 20-year-old who is independent and exerts control over life choices.

Social age depends on how closely behavior conforms to the norms, expectancies, and roles a person of a certain chronological age is expected to play in society. A woman having her first child in her mid-forties is adopting the role of parent later than most of her peers; she thus has a younger social age. Likewise, older adults who sign up for a college course in archaeology are socially younger than most of their peers. A 23-year-old widow is relatively advanced in social age.

The concept of social age assumes that social development follows a typical pattern based on a particular society's set of expectations. (Box 1.1 on p. 12 describes the meaning of social age in two African tribes.) As the lifespan developmental approach points out, history too is a factor in development. Social roles differ markedly at different periods of time. For example, in the not-too-distant past, Americans typically married at an earlier age than they do today. Such a historical role shift exemplifies one of the major kinds of influences on the course of adult development, which we look at now.

Influences on the Course of Adult Development and Aging

Development is subject to many influences. Some originate with **heredity**—the inborn genetic endowment that human beings receive from their biological parents. Others come from the external **environment**—the world outside the person. But this distinction soon blurs: people change their world even as their world changes them.

In discussing how adults develop, we look at influences that affect many or most people and also at those that affect people differently: gender, race, ethnicity, culture, socioeconomic status (social class, education, occupation, and income), lifestyles, family constellations, and the presence or absence of physical or mental disabilities. Some influences are purely individual, while others are common to certain groups—age groups, generations, or people who live in or were raised in particular societies.

NORMATIVE AND NONNORMATIVE INFLUENCES

Some researchers distinguish between normative and nonnormative influences on development (Baltes, Reese, & Lipsitt, 1980).

An event is *normative* when it occurs in a similar way for most people in a given group. **Normative age-graded influences** are very similar for people in a particular age group. They include biological events (such as menopause and diminution of sexual potency) and cultural events (such as retirement). **Normative history-graded influences** are common to a particular **cohort**: a group of people who share a similar experience, in this case growing up at the same time in the same place. Some examples are the worldwide economic depression of the 1930s,

> CRITICAL THINKING
>
> How do normative and nonnormative influences, contexts of influence, and the role of culture overlap to affect development? Do you think it is possible for these influences to act independently?

Meanings of Age and Family in the Kalahari Desert

In the Kalahari Desert of Botswana in southwest Africa live two very different neighboring tribes: the !Kung San Bushmen and the Herero.

Since the 1960s, the !Kung have given up their traditional nomadic ways and settled down in encampments beside government-dug wells, storing the food they hunt and gather. Each family has a low hut of branches and grass, not so much to live in as to mark its territory and to keep its food, skins, and tools dry.

The Herero, by contrast, are literate and relatively prosperous; they keep cattle, goats, and sheep. The women dress in bright colors with ruffles and flounces, and they build thatched mud houses, with smooth white walls decorated with painted flowers. The village patriarch owns all the houses and cattle and children and has several wives.

In 1987, a husband-and-wife team—Patricia Draper and Henry Harpending of Pennsylvania State University—moved their family to Botswana to live with these tribes and find out what each of the two peoples thought about the meaning of age (Brown, 1990). Both Draper and Harpending had lived among the !Kung before. This time they went as part of a team of anthropologists working on four continents. Each researcher was to interview 200 people, including 50 older adults.

It soon became apparent that a question such as "How old are you?" does not make sense to the !Kung. In this culture, people do not count the number of years they have been alive. They do not even count their children or how many times they have moved. A mother would recount having had a child at a certain place and time; she could recall each birth perfectly, and what had happened to each child. But she left it to the researcher to figure out how many children this recital added up to.

In fact, the !Kung do not regard age as useful information. They know only who is older or younger than someone else, not how old specific people are. When asked what they call people of different ages, the !Kung name individuals. Although they do have words for *teenaged* and *middle-aged*, they rarely respond by using them.

Furthermore, social roles of adults are not determined by age. Women in their twenties and their sixties do the same things: tending gardens, drawing water from wells, and taking care of children (their own or other women's).

The Herero, on the other hand, are quite age-conscious. They fear old age, which they equate with inability to work—inability to replace a rotten gatepost, say, or to water cattle. Like many people in western countries, they prepare for retirement by arranging for a place to move to and for children to help them.

the Vietnam war, the massive famines in Africa during the 1980s, the Persian Gulf war of the early 1990s, and the violent conflicts in eastern Europe in the late 1990s and 2000. Also in this category are such cultural developments as the changing roles of women and the impact of television and computers.

Nonnormative life events are unusual events that have a major impact on individual lives. They are either (1) typical events that occur at an atypical

Age can have different meanings in different cultures. The !Kung San of Botswana in southwest Africa do not keep track of their age and do not consider it important. Social roles such as hunting, gathering, and preparing food are performed by adults of all ages.

© Marjorie Shostak/Anthro–Photo

But while the Herero concept of age is more like that in western countries than that of the !Kung, their concept of family is quite foreign to ours. In their culture, the care of older adults is valued the way Americans value the care and nurture of children; high praise for a woman would be not "Look how well she takes care of her children" but "Look how well she takes care of her mother!" Young children are expected to take care of adults, rather than the other way around—doing errands, fetching wood and water, cooking, and helping with other everyday chores.

Most Herero men and women do not marry for love, and many women return to their own families after some years of marriage. A wife who has had no children may arrange for someone else's daughter to take her place. When unmarried women become pregnant, older people who have no children of their own place "orders" for them. Many Americans would consider this buying and selling of children shocking, but the system seems to work for the Herero.

Clearly, the meanings of age and family, and the way a society deals with older adults, are strongly influenced by culture. Looking at cultures different from our own allows us to see the values and customs of our own culture from a fresh perspective. That is one of the benefits of cross-cultural research.

time of life, such as becoming a father at age 60, or (2) atypical events, such as being in an airplane crash or winning a lottery. Whether such an event is positive or negative, it is likely to cause stress when a person does not expect it, is not prepared for it, and might need special help in adapting to it. People often create their own nonnormative life events—by, say, applying for a challenging job or taking up a risky hobby like skydiving—and thus participate actively in their own development.

CONTEXTS OF INFLUENCES: A BIOECOLOGICAL APPROACH

Another way of classifying influences is by immediacy of impact. Urie Bronfenbrenner's (1979, 1994, 2000) **bioecological approach** to development identifies five levels of environmental influence, ranging from very intimate to very broad: microsystem, mesosystem, exosystem, macrosystem, and chronosystem (see Figure 1.1). To understand the complexity of influences on development, we must see a person within the context of these multiple environments.

A *microsystem* is the everyday environment of home, school, work, or neighborhood, including face-to-face relationships with spouse, children, friends, classmates, teachers, employers, or colleagues. How does a new baby affect the parents' lives? How do male professors' attitudes affect a young woman's performance in college?

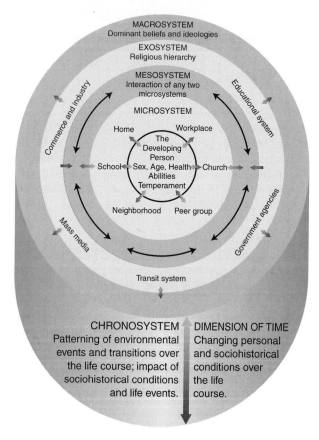

FIGURE 1.1 *Bronfenbrenner's bioecological theory.* Concentric circles show four levels of environmental influence on the individual, from the most intimate environment (innermost circle) to the broadest—all within the dimension of time. *SOURCE:* Adapted from Cole & Cole, 1989.

The *mesosystem* is the interlocking of various microsystems—linkages between home and school, work and neighborhood. How does a bitterly contested divorce affect a person's performance at work? How does unhappiness on the job affect a parent-child relationship?

The *exosystem* consists of linkages between a microsystem and outside systems or institutions that affect a person indirectly. How does a community's transit system affect job opportunities? In what ways does the federal government play a role in health care and services assisting older adults?

The *macrosystem* consists of overarching cultural patterns, such as dominant beliefs, ideologies, and economic and political systems. How is an individual affected by living in a capitalist or socialist society?

Finally, the *chronosystem* adds the dimension of time: change or constancy in the person and the environment. This can include changes in family structure, place of residence, or employment, as well as larger cultural changes such as wars and economic cycles. Emphasis is on the patterning of environmental events and transitions in the course of a life span.

By looking at systems that affect individuals in and beyond the family, this ecological approach helps us to see the variety and complexity of influences on adult development. The relative importance of each system may vary from one society to another and from one cultural group to another within the same society. This is one reason for doing cross-cultural research. In this book, these levels of analysis will be used to focus on important influences on changing individuals in a changing world.

THE ROLE OF CULTURE

When adults in the Kpelle tribe in central Liberia were asked to sort 20 objects, they consistently sorted on the basis of functional categories (that is, they matched a knife with an orange, or a potato with a hoe). Western psychologists associate functional sorting with a low level of thought; but since the participants kept saying that this was how a "wise man" would do it, the experimenter finally asked, "How would a fool do it?" He then received the "higher-order" categories he had originally expected—four neat piles with food in one, tools in another, and so on (J. Glick, 1975, p. 636).

By conducting research among various cultural groups, developmental scientists can recognize biases that often go unquestioned—"as with the fish who reputedly is unaware of water until removed from it" (Rogoff & Morelli, 1989, p. 343). Cross-cultural research can tell us which aspects of development are universal (and thus seem to be intrinsic to the human condition) and which are cultural. This book discusses several influential theories developed from research on western subjects that do not hold up when tested in other cultures—theories about gender roles, abstract thinking, moral reasoning, and a number of other concepts. In each chapter, we look at adults in cultures other than the dominant one in the United States, to show how closely adult development is tied to society and culture and to understand normal development in a variety of settings.

Changing Images and Realities of Aging

Imagine that you are listening to the radio in the year 2030 and you hear the following commercial message:

> Are you tired of looking younger than you feel? Do you want to get the respect that you deserve? Are other people being promoted ahead of you, even when you know they are no older than you? What do they have that you don't? They may be using GRAY DAYS. Yes, GRAY DAYS is a natural product, used by millions, which gradually puts that look of wisdom into your hair. Used once a day, this colorless, odorless formula will make you look like the experienced, level-headed person you know you are. Of course you could wait until the gray came naturally to your hair, but remember this: some people don't start to show the color of prestige until their fifties or even later! Don't take that chance. Start now. Make the changes in your life that will put you at the head of the line. Don't be embarrassed by the doorman at the seniors' bar who keeps asking you to prove you're old enough to get in. Let GRAY DAYS give you a start toward great days—TODAY!
>
> And, for that "I've been alive a long time" look, try our new WRINK-AID. Just rub it in at bedtime. In the morning your skin will show the lines and wrinkles of maturity. WRINK-AID's "natural look of aging" lasts all day. Use WRINK-AID every day, and you'll never again be called a "baby face." Show the world you've been around and have what it takes. Why wait? Get WRINK-AID and wrink it up, NOW!

It may seem implausible that any such switch in attitudes could take place in the United States. Yet a look at portraits of George Washington and our other founding fathers tells us that there was a time when men in this country wore powdered wigs as a mark of distinction (in fact, barristers and judges in Great Britain still wear wigs today). The men who wrote our Constitution also set minimum age limits for candidates for public office. For example, a person under 35 years of age cannot serve as president of the United States.

In the year 2030, more than half of the population in the United States will be over age 40, and one in five people will be age 65 or older (Older Americans, 2000). Is it unreasonable to predict that age may again be valued more highly than youth?

Cultural Views of Aging

In most western countries, it is considered rude to ask a person's age. But in Japan, where old age has high status, it is traditional for travelers checking into hotels to be asked their age to ensure that they receive proper deference. A man celebrating his sixtieth birthday wears a red vest, symbolizing rebirth into an advanced phase of life (Kimmel, 1988).

In American culture today, aging is seen as undesirable—unless one considers the alternative. Try browsing through a rack of greeting cards. Do most cards express positive or negative sentiments about arriving at a fortieth, fiftieth, or sixtieth birthday? Although everybody wants to live long, hardly anybody wants to be *old*, a word that connotes physical frailty, narrow-mindedness, incompetence, and loss of attractiveness. People of advanced years are called "senior citizens," "golden-agers," "the elderly," "older Americans," or even "chronologically gifted." Such language is an effort to counteract **ageism:** prejudice or discrimination, usually against older persons, based on age. Ageism has been said to arise from a "deep and profound dread of growing old" (Butler, 1987a, p. 22)—a need to distance oneself from older people and from one's own future self.

The media are full of stereotypes about aging. An article in *Time* magazine on detective programs built around older stars such as Angela Lansbury was titled "Murder, They Wheezed." The central characters of "these arthritic whodunits" were described as "old codgers" or as "easygoing dilettantes" who "would rather be napping." The illustration accompanying the article depicted these crime fighters as doddering and decrepit (Zoglin, 1994).

Such stereotypes reflect widespread misconceptions about aging: that older people are usually tired, poorly coordinated, and prone to infections; that they have many accidents and spend most of their time in bed; that they live in institutions; that they can neither remember nor learn; that they have no interest in sexual relationships; that they are isolated from others and depend on television or radio; that they do not use their time productively; and that they are grouchy, self-pitying, touchy, and cranky. These negative stereotypes do real harm. A physician who does not bring up sexual issues with a 75-year-old heart patient may deny the patient an important source of fulfillment. An overprotective adult child may encourage an aging parent to become infantile. A social worker who considers depression "to be expected" in old age may in effect abandon an elderly client.

Evidence of ageism showed up in an analysis of forty-three studies. Older people were judged more negatively than younger people on all characteristics studied, especially on competence and attractiveness (Kite & Johnson, 1988). However, negative stereotyping of older adults is reduced when contextual information about the elderly is provided, particularly information about their work-related roles (Kite, Stockdale, Whitley & Johnson, 2005). Negative stereotypes can have practical effects, as pervasive as unwillingness of younger adults to listen to an older person's opinions and as serious as loss of a job. Positive stereotypes, which picture old age as a "golden age" of peace and relaxation when people harvest the fruits of their lifelong labors, or as a carefree second childhood spent idly on the golf course or at the card table, are no more accurate or helpful.

Ageism affects middle-aged adults, too. It is during this period that anxiety over slipping faculties and loss of attractiveness often sets in, especially among women. One of the most prized compliments for a woman is to be told that she looks younger than her age. In men, gray hair, coarsened skin, and "crow's feet" are indicators of experience and mastery; in women, they are signs of being "over the hill."

According to evolutionary psychology, this traditional double standard of aging goes back to the universal drive to perpetuate the species. Because women lose their reproductive capacity earlier than men, loss of youthful appearance may have warned a man that a woman was no longer desirable as a mate (Katchadourian, 1987). Today, when the value of relationships is not measured only by the biological mandate to reproduce, a societal standard "that regards beauty as the exclusive preserve of the young ... makes women especially vulnerable to the fear of aging. . . . The relentless social pressures to retain a slim 'girlish' figure make women self-conscious about their bodies ... [and] can be detrimental to the midlife woman's personal growth and sense of self-worth" (Lenz, 1993, pp. 26, 28).

Efforts to combat ageism are making headway, in part thanks to such writers as Betty Friedan and Gail Sheehy and in part because of the visibility of a growing cadre of active, healthy, middle-aged and older Americans. Sheehy (1995, 1998), for example, has suggested a radical restructuring of the adult life course in graphic terms. Her most recent model describes phases as the Tryout Twenties, Turbulent Thirties, Flourishing Forties, Flaming Fifties, Serene Sixties, Sage Seventies, Uninhibited Eighties, Noble Nineties, and Celebratory Centenarians.

CRITICAL THINKING

Why are generalities about the aging population more difficult to support than in the past?

On television, older people are less frequently portrayed as "comical, stubborn, eccentric, and foolish" and more often as "powerful, affluent, healthy, active, admired, and sexy" (Bell, 1992, p. 305; Rowe & Kahn, 1998). But negative stereotypes persist; and even positive stereotypes fail to acknowledge diversity among older adults. Furthermore, older women still are rarely shown, and when they are shown, they are generally subordinate to men. Meanwhile, "the media continue to bombard us with advertising for cosmetic surgery, hair coloring, anti-wrinkle creams, pills, potions, tonics and diet programs that, they assure us, will make it possible to maintain our youthful attractiveness forever" (Lenz, 1993, p. 26). In 2002, U.S. consumers spent $30 billion on anti-aging products. Between 1997 and 2002, cosmetic plastic surgery increased by 1,125 prcent. In the past, older adults were more apt to have plastic surgery, but it has become increasingly more common among middle-aged people ages 45 to 54 (Weiss, 2002).

We need to look beyond distorted images of age to its true, multifaceted reality, gazing neither through rose-colored glasses nor through dark ones. Aging adults are an extremely diverse lot, with individual strengths and weaknesses. And they are becoming more so as they grow increasingly numerous.

CRITICAL THINKING

If you had a choice, would you prefer to live a long life? How would you feel if you were no longer able to do certain things physically? How would you react to major changes in your cognitive abilities?

The Shifting Demographics of Aging

There are no 45-year-olds being born today—nor 28-year-olds, nor 67-year-olds. Thus we can count a definite number of people of a given age group who are now alive and, on the basis of that figure, project how many will be alive in 2010, 2020, 2030, and so on. Using census data, international population studies, and other sources, we can obtain fairly accurate descriptions of the current population and predict (barring famines or other disasters) how many people will be of a certain age at a certain date. It is much harder, of course, to predict how it will feel to be alive at that time, or what quality of life people of different ages will experience. One thing, however, is clear: both as a nation and as a global population, we are growing older.

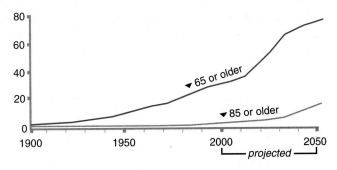

FIGURE 1.2 *Total number of persons age 65 or older, by age group, 1900 to 2050, in millions.*
There are more than ten times as many older Americans today as there were in 1900; in 2030 there
will be twice as many as today. The percentage of the population age 65 and older is growing too—
from 4 percent at the turn of the twentieth century to nearly 13 percent at the turn of the twenty-first.
The size of the older population is projected to double over the next 30 years, growing to 70 million
by 2030. *SOURCE:* Older Americans, 2000.

The population of the United States in the first half of the twenty-first century will look quite different from today's (Figure 1.2). By 2030, the median
age will rise from 34 to 42, and fully one-third of the people will be 55 or older.
By 2050, 1 in 5 Americans—more than 80 million in all, and more than twice
the present number—will be age 65 and above (Older Americans, 2000).

As startling as these predictions might seem, our population has been aging for quite some time. In 2000, there were 35 million people age 65 or older
in the United States, accounting for almost 13 percent of the total population.
The number of older Americans has increased tenfold since 1900, when there
were 3 million people age 65 or older (4 percent of the total population)
(Older Americans, 2000).

The graying of the population has several causes: the high birthrates of the
late 1800s and the early to mid 1900s, the high immigration rates of the twentieth century, and longer life due to medical progress (see Chapter 3). The increase in life expectancy during the twentieth century has been an extraordinary
achievement. If mortality rates remain constant, persons age 65 in 2000 are expected to live another 18 years, on average, compared with persons age 65 in
1990, who had a remaining life expectancy of 12 years. In 2011, the "baby
boom" generation (the 78 million Americans born between 1946 and 1964)
will begin to turn 65, and by 2030, it is projected that one in five people will be
age 65 or older (Older Americans, 2000). In 2003, 4 million adults turned 21.
They are part of a group (Generation Y) made up of 72 million people born between 1977 and 1994 who will reach late adulthood starting in 2042.

Not only is the population aging, the population of older adults is itself getting older. Between 1990 and 2000 there was a 35 percent increase in the
number of centenarians (people ages 100 and over), from 37,306 to 50,545.
The number of centenarians is projected to grow so rapidly that there may be
as many as 381,000 of them by 2030. In 2000, an estimated 2 percent of the

population (4 million) were age 85 and older. It has been projected that by 2050 this age group will be almost 5 percent of the U.S. population (around 19 million) (Older Americans, 2000).

Today's young adults, then, can expect to spend a much larger portion of their adult lives in old age than their grandparents did. The "aging avalanche" may bring significant changes in the physical and social environment in which all of us live (see Box 1.2). It is raising serious questions about our ability to support a graying population. Similar trends worry policymakers in other parts of the world. For these reasons, and because more data are available on people age 65 and over than on any other adult age group, let's take a closer look at our own older adult population and then at the global picture.

The Aging Population: A Profile of Diversity

> It is useful, maybe even necessary, to imagine that there is a definable group called "the elderly." But all such conceptions inevitably fail. It is accurate only to say that a certain part of the population has lived longer than other parts of the population, and that they differ widely. (Kidder, 1993, p. 53)

Are there more older men or more older women? Do men or women have a better quality of life in old age? What percentage of older Americans are members of minority groups, and does their experience of aging differ from that of white people? How likely are older adults to live in nursing homes? To be employed? To be poor? To have finished high school? To be in ill health? We discuss such questions in more depth later in this book. For now, let's take a snapshot of our aging population.

GENDER

Because women typically live longer than men, there are more older women than older men in the United States, and the proportion of the population that is female increases with age (see Figure 1.3 on p. 22). In 2000, women made up 58 percent of the population age 65 or older, and 70 percent of the population age 85 and older (Older Americans, 2000).

Older women are more likely than older men to be widowed, to remain unmarried afterward, and to have more years of poor health and fewer years of active life and independence. Older women are much more likely than older men to be poor, to live alone, and to need help with such necessities of daily living as eating, dressing, bathing, preparing meals, managing money, and getting outside (Older Americans, 2000).

RACE AND ETHNICITY

The United States began as a nation of immigrants. Since 1980, because of tight immigration laws, the flow has slowed to a trickle. But as a result of shifting *patterns* of immigration, high minority birthrates, and declining births among

New Environments for an Aging Population

As the population ages, we can expect many changes in our physical environment and in the products we use. Already, pain relievers, previously packaged in childproof bottles that stymied arthritic adults, are being repackaged in easier-to-open containers.

The gerontologist Ken Dychtwald, in *Age Wave* (Dychtwald & Flower, 1990) and *Age Power* (Dychtwald, 1999), predicted ways in which the environment of the twenty-first century will be redesigned to accommodate physical changes that often accompany aging. Here are examples, some already in place.

Aids to Vision

Signals now given visually will be spoken as well. There will be talking exit signs, talking clocks, talking appliances that tell you when they get hot, talking cameras that warn you when the light is too low, and talking automobiles that caution you when you're about to collide with something. Windshields will adjust their tint automatically to varying weather and light conditions and will be equipped with large, liquid-crystal displays of speed and other information (so that older drivers need not take their eyes off the road and readjust their focus). Reading lights will be brighter, and books will have larger print. Floors will be carpeted or textured, not waxed to a smooth, glaring gloss.

Aids to Hearing

Public address systems and recordings will be engineered to an older adult's auditory range. Park benches and couches will be replaced by angled or clustered seating so that older adults can communicate face-to-face.

Aids to Manual Dexterity

To compensate for stiff, aging joints, it will become increasingly common to find such items as comb and brush extenders, stretchable shoelaces, Velcro tabs instead of buttons, lightweight motorized pot-and-pan scrubbers and garden tools, tap turners on faucets, foot mops that eliminate bending, voice-activated telephone dialers, long-handled easy-grip zippers, and contoured eating utensils.

Aids to Mobility and Safety

Ramps will become more common, levers will replace knobs, street lights will change more slowly, and traffic islands will let slow walkers pause and rest. Closet shelves and bus platforms will be lower, as will windows, for people who sit a lot. Regulators will keep tap water from scalding. "Soft tubs" will prevent slips, add comfort, and keep bath water from cooling too fast. Automobiles will be programmed to operate windows, radio, heater, lights, wipers, and even the ignition by verbal commands.

Temperature Adjustments

Because older bodies take longer to adjust to temperature changes and have more trouble keeping warm, homes and hotels will have heated furniture and thermostats in each room. Some people will wear heated clothing and eat foods that promote warmth.

Such innovations will make life easier and more convenient for everyone. An environment designed for older rather than younger adults can be more user-friendly for all age groups.

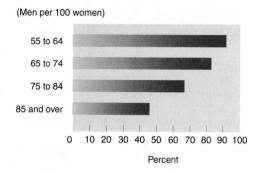

(Men per 100 women)

55 to 64

65 to 74

75 to 84

85 and over

0   10 20 30 40 50 60 70 80 90 100

Percent

FIGURE 1.3 *As the population ages, the proportion of men for every 100 women declines.* One result is that older women are more likely than older men to live alone and to need help from their families and from society. *SOURCE:* U.S. Census Bureau, Annual Demographic Supplement to the March 2002 Current Population Survey; Smith, 2003.

the white majority, the American population is becoming far more racially and ethnically diverse. In 2002 non-Hispanic whites accounted for 69 percent of the total population. However, this proportion varied with age: 66 percent of the population under age 55 as compared with 81 percent of those 55 and over (see Figure 1.4 for a detailed breakdown by age and ethnicity). It has been projected that by 2050, non-Hispanic whites will constitute only 64 percent of older Americans, whereas the percentage of Hispanic older persons will more than double to 16 percent, with smaller increases for non-Hispanic blacks (to 12 percent) and Asian and Pacific Islanders (to 7 percent). Thus, the older population will increase among all racial and ethnic groups; the Hispanic older population is projected to grow the fastest. In fact, it has been projected that by 2028, the Hispanic population age 65 and older will outnumber the non-Hispanic black population in that age group (Older Americans, 2000).

Many aging members of minority groups are at great risk because of poverty, spotty histories of work and education, and inadequate health care. Older African Americans and Hispanics tend to be less educated and to have lower incomes than white people (American Association of Retired Persons [AARP], 1994). They are also likely to die younger (see Chapter 3). Although their need for social and medical services is greater, they often live in areas where services are least available. Older people in various ethnic groups, especially those born in other countries, often fail to take advantage of community and government services because they lack information about these services, because they are too proud to accept help, or because they feel uncomfortable dealing with agency staff members who do not understand their way of life (Gelfand, 1982). Instead, adults in minority groups often turn to family members. African American and Hispanic American families have large kinship networks, with high levels of interaction and strong emotional bonds (Taylor & Chatters, 1991). The generations commonly help each other with money, child care, advice, and other forms of support (Gibson, 1986; Mindel, 1983).

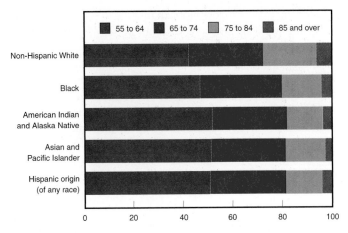

| | 55 to 64 | 65 to 74 | 75 to 84 | 85 and over |

FIGURE 1.4 *Percent distribution of people 55 years and over by race, Hispanic origin, and age: 2002.* Non-Hispanic whites had the oldest age distribution in 2002 with 42.1 percent in the 55 to 64 age group and 6.2 percent who were 85 and over. American Indian and Alaska Natives, Asian and Pacific Islanders, and Hispanics had the youngest age distribution with 51.7 percent, 51.1 percent, and 50.6 percent respectively in the 55 to 64 age group, and only 3.6 percent, 2.9 percent, and 4.1 percent in the group 85 and older. *SOURCE:* U.S. Census Bureau, Annual Demographic Supplement to the March 2002 Current Population Survey, Smith, 2003.

LIVING ARRANGEMENTS

Negative images of aging suggest that most older adults live alone or in nursing homes. Actually, in 2000 only 4.5 percent of the U.S. population aged 65 or older (about 1.56 million persons) lived in nursing homes. This is a lower percentage than in the mid 1980s and is due to a greater emphasis on home-care services. However, those who were in nursing homes were more likely to have serious functional limitations, such as incontinence, difficulty eating, or limited mobility (Older Americans, 2004). Women are much more likely than men to live in nursing homes (AARP, 1999). About 3 out of 10 older adults outside of institutions* live alone—39.7 percent of older women, but only 18.8 percent of older men (Older Americans, 2004).

SOCIOECONOMIC STATUS AND WORK

Stereotypes depict older adults either as too infirm to work or as mindlessly enjoying a life of idleness. In reality, a significant proportion of older Americans are in the workforce. While 64 percent of people age 65 and over report being completely retired, 14 percent describe themselves as not retired, and 13 percent describe themselves as retired and working (Cutler, Whitelaw, & Beattie,

---

*Unless otherwise noted, data on living arrangements, socioeconomic status, education, and health refer to noninstitutionalized older adults.

2002). Men aged 55 and over are more likely than women to be in the labor force; the proportion declines with age for both sexes. In 2002, 77 percent of men ages 55 to 59 were in the labor force compared to 63 percent of women. Among people ages 60 to 64, these proportions were 57 percent for men and 44 percent for women. Among people age 65 and over, 18 percent of men and 10 percent of women were working. Among people 55 and over, 3.8 percent were unemployed (Smith, 2003). Although most older adults are defined as retired, many of them have active, productive lifestyles. Retired older adults also make valuable contributions to other generations, such as taking care of grandchildren.

CRITICAL THINKING

How does poverty exemplify the impact of normative and nonnormative influences, contexts of influence, and the role of culture on human development?

Other images of older adults suggest that most are poor and live solely on Social Security. Actually, in 2002, Social Security benefits constituted the majority of income for only one-third of adults 65 and over. Assets, pensions, and earnings accounted for the other income (Older Americans, 2004). For persons age 85 or older, Social Security and assets account for a larger proportion of total income, and earnings and pensions a smaller proportion, than for persons aged 65 to 69 (Older Americans, 2000).

Most older adults are relatively secure financially and have more assets than younger adults. Between 1984 and 1999, the median net worth among households headed by persons age 65 or older increased by 69 percent, while the median net worth for households headed by persons ages 45 to 54 declined by 23 percent. In 1999, median net worth among older black households was estimated to be about $13,000, compared with about $181,000 for older white households (Older Americans, 2000).

In 2005, about 10.2 percent of older persons lived in poverty (Older Americans, 2004); in 1959, 35 percent were poor. Social Security provided more than 80 percent of income for older Americans with the lowest levels of income. For those in the highest income category, Social Security accounted for approximately 20 percent of total income. Most likely to be impoverished are women (especially widows), blacks, Hispanics, single people, people living alone or with nonrelatives, people who did not finish high school, former unskilled laborers, and the ill or disabled (AARP, 1994; Hurd, 1989; U.S. Bureau of the Census, 1992b, 1995; Older Americans 2000).

Individuals who have multiple risk factors are most likely to be poor. For example, 44 percent of older black women who live alone are poor (AARP, 1994). Thus, while most older adults do not live in poverty, some elements of the older population are at extreme risk.

EDUCATION

The current generation of older Americans is more highly educated than previous cohorts of older persons, and this trend will continue. In 1998, about 11 percent of older women and 20 percent of older men were college graduates (Older Americans, 2000). Despite the overall increase in educational attainment among older Americans, there are still substantial educational differences among racial and ethnic groups. In 1998, about 72 percent of the non-Hispanic white population age 65 and older had finished high school, compared with 65 percent of the non-Hispanic Asian and Pacific Islander older population, 44 percent of the non-Hispanic black older population, and 29 percent of the Hispanic older population. In 1998, 16 percent of non-Hispanic white older Americans had a bachelor's degree or higher, compared with 22 percent of older non-Hispanic Asian and Pacific Islanders (Older Americans, 2000).

HEALTH

Older adults age 65 and over asked to provide an assessment of their own health report being evenly distributed between excellent to very good health (47 percent) and good-fair-poor health (53 percent). Twenty-nine percent of community residing adults report being limited in daily activities due to health reasons or disability (Cutler, Whitelaw, & Beattie, 2002). The prevalence of chronic conditions varies by race and ethnicity. African Americans are more likely to have diabetes, stroke, and hypertension than either non-Hispanic white or Hispanic persons (Older Americans, 2000). Most older people have one or more chronic conditions, such as arthritis, hypertension, heart disease, cataracts, sinusitis, diabetes, tinnitus, and visual, hearing, or orthopedic impairments. About 3 out of 4 older adults can manage without help; the proportion falls steeply with age (AARP, 1994; see Figure 4.1 in Chapter 4).

© Erika Stone/Photo Researchers

Most older Americans consider themselves to be in good to excellent health. This makes possible a wide range of activities including time with grandchildren. Increased longevity allows many families to have interactions across four or more generations.

Because many adults remain vigorous and active into their seventies, eighties, and beyond, it is becoming harder to tell where middle age leaves off and old age begins. In fact, one author has called the years between 50 and 75 a "second middle age" (Bronte, 1993). As we discuss in Chapter 4, many problems of the "old old" are due to lifestyle factors or health problems that may or may not accompany aging. Research in gerontology and **geriatrics,** the branch of medicine concerned with treating and managing diseases related to aging, has underlined the need for support services for the frail elderly, many of whom have outlived their savings and cannot pay for their own care. (We take a look at the "oldest old" in Box 1.3 on p. 26.)

Clearly, older adults are a heterogeneous group. Like people of all ages, they are individuals with varying needs, desires, abilities, lifestyles, and cultural backgrounds. As we move into the twenty-first century and our society becomes increasingly older and more diverse, dealing with this aging population will require a great deal of knowledge, sophistication, and flexibility.

Challenges and Dilemmas of a Graying World

The graying of the population is far from unique to the United States (Kinsella & Velkoff, 2001). Worldwide, the older adult population is growing faster than any other age group and nearly twice as fast as the population as a whole (see

The Oldest Old

Since the number of healthy, vigorous people over age 65 is growing rapidly, we may soon begin to talk of old age as starting at 85. This age group, the fastest-growing segment of the United States population, numbered 4 million in 2000 (Vierck & Hodges, 2003). This figure represented a whopping increase of 274 percent since 1960, a period in which the total population grew by only 45 percent. By the middle of the twenty-first century, these "oldest old" could be nearly one-fourth of the elderly population (Older Americans, 2000).

Who are the oldest old? Where and how do they live? How healthy are they? What do they like to do? Some of the answers, according to 1990 census data, are predictable, but others are unexpected.

© PhotoDisc

Active older adults are a dramatically increasing group. Some of them are continuing lifelong patterns of participation; others are starting new activities later in life.

Because of men's lower life expectancy, there are fewer than 46 men for every 100 women age 85 and over (Older Americans, 2000; see Figure 1.3). Women are three times as likely as men to be poor, mainly because their husbands have died. When wives die, widowers tend to remarry quickly, an option rarely available to women because there are fewer men.

Most people over 85 live in their own homes, and 30 percent live alone. One-fourth are in nursing homes, hospitals, or other institutions, and 1 in 6 is poor. Many never went beyond eighth grade. Future generations, though, will be both better educated and more affluent (Longino, 1988; Older Americans, 2000).

Most people in the 85 and older age group spend time with other people. More than half of an Iowa sample belong to professional, social, recreational, or religious groups and go to religious services at least once a week. More than 3 out of 4 see their children or other close relatives once a month (Meer, 1987).

A surprisingly large number of these oldest citizens need little medical care, but many do have health problems. Almost 10 percent of those outside institutions are disabled and isolated—unable to use public transportation—and 50 percent need assistance with everyday activities (Older Americans, 2000). Costs of health care for the "oldest old" are expected to soar; by 2040 Medicare costs may increase sixfold (Schneider & Guralnik, 1990). Cost containment will depend on the ability to prevent or cure disorders of old age that entail the greatest need for long-term care.

Even at the last stage of life, then, it is misleading to generalize about people. What emerges is a picture not of "the elderly" but of individual human beings—some needy and frail, but most independent, healthy, and involved.

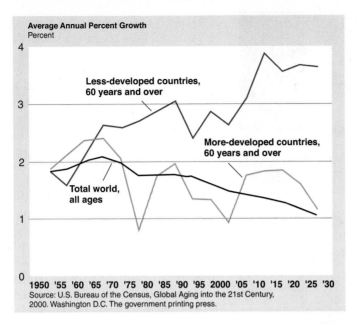

Average Annual Percent Growth
Percent

Less-developed countries,
60 years and over

More-developed countries,
60 years and over

Total world,
all ages

1950 '55 '60 '65 '70 '75 '80 '85 '90 '95 2000 '05 '10 '15 '20 '25 '30
Source: U.S. Bureau of the Census, Global Aging into the 21st Century,
2000. Washington D.C. The government printing press.

FIGURE 1.5 *Population growth in developed and developing countries.* The rate of growth in the world's elderly population has shifted dramatically. In developing countries the growth rate of the elderly has sharply increased and is substantially higher than that of the world's population of all ages. Developing nations as a whole are aging much faster than more developed nations.

Figure 1.5). The number of adults age 60 and over—about 550 million in 1996—is expected to approach 1.2 billion by the year 2025. Due to declines in fertility and increased life expectancy, in most countries the older population is growing faster than the population as a whole.

However, the trend toward population aging is most advanced in developing countries. In absolute numbers, the older adult populations of today's economically developed regions (North America, Japan, Europe, Australia, New Zealand, and the former Soviet Union) will not be as large. Still, by 2025 the 60-plus age group will amount to fully one-quarter of the people in those parts of the world, as compared with 12 percent in the developing regions (Chawla, 1993).

This demographic explosion poses serious challenges to both developed and developing countries. As an example, let's look at the changing situation in Asia; we'll then consider some economic issues.

AGING IN ASIA

It is hard to generalize about Asian countries. Life expectancy at birth in Japan and Singapore has reached 80 years, the highest of all the world's major countries (life expectancy at birth in the United States is 77.1) (Kinsella & Velkoff,

© Dave Bartruff/Image Works

Respect for elders is traditional in Asian cultures. Here we see three generations of a family in Okinawa, Japan, dressing for a party.

2001). In Nepal, a very poor nation, the average woman lives to only 52 and the average man to 55 (Central Bureau of Statistics, 1992). There is at least one link among the diverse Asian nations: a great respect for elders and an expectation that when old people can no longer care for themselves, their families will care for them. But today, while both patterns remain more prevalent than in the west, they are disintegrating under the pressure of a rising older population.*

Since the 1940s, Asia has been the most successful region of the world in reducing fertility. In China, for example, the government has introduced policies that encourage a later age at marriage and smaller family size. If China maintains its present, relatively low fertility levels, its birthrate will continue to decline and its growth rate should continue to fall, from about 1 percent in 1998 to about a fifth of this rate 25 years from now (U.S. Bureau of the Census, 1999).

Meanwhile, higher standards of living, better sanitation, and immunization programs have extended the adult life span. As a result, it is projected that by 2025, the elderly in China, Hong Kong, Singapore, and Sri Lanka will constitute more than 10 percent of the population; in Japan, they will make up more than 20 percent.

Although about three-quarters of elderly Asians live with their children, they are less likely to do so than older people were in the past. Along with the shifting balance between old and young, such trends as urbanization, migration, and an increase in the proportion of women in the workforce make home care of elderly relatives less feasible. While most Asians want to help care for aging family members, doing this is becoming a difficult challenge. In Korea, a survey taken in 1981 found that only 7 percent of adults thought their children would care for them in old age; 64 percent expected to care for themselves.

To halt this erosion in care of the aged, China, Japan, and Singapore have passed laws obliging people to care for elderly relatives, and Japan and Singapore provide tax relief to those who give older relatives financial help. In Japan, lotteries for tenancy in public housing give households with a member age 60 or older a 10 times greater chance of winning. Institutionalization is still seen as a last resort, only for those who are destitute or without families—in part because few such homes exist. The proportion of older adults living in homes for the aged ranges from 0.33 percent in China to 2.5 percent in Singapore.

---

*Unless otherwise indicated, this discussion is based on Martin (1998).

Such limited access to institutional care places severe strains on the traditional family. In Japan, where suicide among older women is more prevalent than anywhere else in the world (MacAdam, 1993), older adults living in three-generation households are more likely to take their lives than those living alone.

A major controversy in Asia, as in the west, is whether housing, health care, and other social services should be offered on the basis of age. Young adults with small children worry that, in order to fund services for the old, governments may have to cut back what little social welfare exists for the young. In Japan, Korea, Indonesia, the Philippines, Singapore, and Thailand, older adults are joining senior citizens' clubs, which may strengthen their political clout. The establishment of Respect for the Aged Day (September 15) in Japan and National Aging Day (April 13) in Thailand reflects this growing "gray power." But the need for such symbolism underlines a decline in the tradition of reverence for age.

In some ways, however, this tradition continues to set Japan apart from other advanced industrial nations. Only 10 percent of older adults in Japan live alone (5.2 percent of men and 14.8 percent of women), as compared with 23.9 to 42.3 percent in the four western countries (Kinsella & Velkoff, 2001). Older adults in the United States and Canada are least likely to get help from their families when they are ill or need money. Still, about 6 out of 10 older adults in those two countries are very satisfied with their lives, as compared with only 28 percent in Japan (Commonwealth Fund Commission on Elderly People Living Alone, 1992). Another way to look at how people are satisfied with their lives is by studying subjective well-being. How one feels (affective) and thinks (cognitive) about one's life experience is what many researchers mean by subjective well-being. Diener and Associates (1999) looked at pleasant affect, unpleasant affect and satisfaction. A survey of 60,000 adults from 40 nations (Diener & Suh, 1998) reported that pleasant affect declined with age, whereas life satisfaction and unpleasant affect did not change. These findings did not appear to be influenced by periods of rapid economic growth (Diener, Suh, Lucas, & Smith, 1999).

ECONOMIC DEVELOPMENT AND AGING

The issues presented by a graying population are somewhat different in developed and developing nations. Planners and politicians in almost all industrialized nations fear that the cost of supporting a growing contingent of retirees will place an insupportable burden on a shrinking group of working adults (Crown, 1993). In the United States, some analysts fear that the cost of medical care for older adults will bankrupt the health care system and reduce the quality of care available to younger adults and their families (Binstock, 1993). A drastic solution, suggested in some quarters, would be a "renegotiation" of the implied "social contract" that has called for younger, able-bodied adults to support retired and disabled workers (Adamchak, 1993, p. 6).

The key to supporting an aging population may be an economy capable of meeting the demographic challenge. If incomes go up faster than the taxes needed to fund social programs for the elderly, the actual burden on workers may not increase: "The affordability of an aging population will be dictated largely by future economic growth" (Crown, 1993).

That is likely to be true in the developing world as well. In such countries as the Dominican Republic, Sri Lanka, and Thailand, where large numbers of older adults must continue to work for a bare subsistence (Kaiser, 1993), worries about retirement benefits and government-funded health care, though still down the road, are likely to arise in the not-too-distant future (MacAdam, 1993). Certain observers predict that as labor loses its ties to the land and becomes dependent on a market economy, some form of western-style welfare state will be necessary (Schulz, 1993a). Others call for developing countries to find solutions rooted in their traditional, family-centered cultures.

In developing countries, issues of economic development and aging are closely linked. The graying of the population is a direct result of economic improvement and the amelioration of widespread deprivation, hunger, and disease. But this "success story" is often seen as a burden rather than a boon: Will older adults drain scarce resources, impeding further development (Chawla, 1993; Kaiser, 1993)?

The United Nations General Assembly observed the year 1999 as the International Year of Older Persons "in recognition of humanity's demographic coming of age" and the promise that holds for "maturing attitudes and capabilities in social, economic, cultural and spiritual undertakings" (United Nations General Assembly, 1992). As international planners begin to stress the human dimension of economic development, developing societies need to find ways to diminish dependency by expanding the productive abilities of older adults. This concept of **productive aging** "views older persons as potentially unlimited human resources contributing to the goods, services, and products available for themselves and society" (Kaiser, 1993, p. 66). In Zambia, destitute older adults learn basic farming skills and then are given small farms on which they can raise grain and poultry to feed their families (Kerschner, 1992). In Bogotá, Colombia, a group of older adults opened a bakery and used the proceeds to provide medical and other services to the poor and institutionalized elderly (Checkoway, 1992). Such examples suggest ways in which a growing older population can present "an opportunity rather than a crisis, a solution rather than a problem, an asset rather than a burden, a resource rather than a drain on resources" (Kerschner, 1992, p. 4).

New Roles for Older Adults

An emphasis on productive aging, whether in developed or developing countries, may help solve the economic dilemmas posed by an aging global population. It also fits in with current thinking on adult development and aging.

Social roles for younger and middle-aged adults, though more flexible now than they were in the past, generally remain fairly clear: spouse, worker, parent, grandparent. But as the life span increases and more years stretch out after retirement, what new expectations will society have for older adults? Will there be greater freedom for them to play a variety of social roles and to maximize control of their own lives?

Ken Dychtwald, the gerontologist who wrote *Age Wave,* has divided the human life span, and human history, into three "ages" (Dychtwald & Flower, 1990). The first age, from birth to about age 25, represents nearly the full average life span in premodern times, when the primary tasks of life were physical development, basic learning, and survival. The second age, from about 26 to 60, represents the normal life span before the mid-twentieth century, when adult concerns were centered on work, family, and parenting. The third age, only now coming into its own, is the period from the sixties on, a period when many of the tasks of the second age are already done. This can be a time of less external pressure and more internal development—a time "for giving back to society the lessons, resources, and experiences accumulated and articulated over a lifetime" (p. 347).

SUMMARY AND KEY TERMS

Approaching the Study of Adult Development and Aging: An Overview

- The idea that adults develop is relatively recent. Today most psychologists believe that human development goes on throughout life.
- The lifespan developmental approach of Paul Baltes emphasizes multidirectionality, multidimensionality, plasticity, historical and cultural influences, and multidisciplinary research.

change (p. 4)	**lifespan development (p. 5)**
development (p. 4)	**lifespan developmental**
learning (p. 4)	**psychology (p. 5)**
maturation (p. 4)	**plasticity (p. 6)**

Basic Concepts

- A useful way to visualize adult development is as a product of multiple concurrent forces acting on a complex system. Each aspect of development encompasses a wide range of individual differences.
- The periods of adulthood—young adulthood, middle age, and late adulthood or old age—are somewhat arbitrarily demarcated, but most people go through a fairly typical sequence of development.
- Chronological age is not necessarily an indicator of functional age. Functional age has three dimensions—biological, psychological, and social. They are not necessarily synchronized.
- Both heredity and environment influence development. Some investigators distinguish among normative age-graded influences, normative history-graded influences, and nonnormative life events. Bronfenbrenner's bioecological approach identifies levels of environmental influence.
- Cross-cultural research can indicate whether certain aspects of development are universal or cultural.

ageless self (p. 10)

chronological age (p. 10)

functional age (p. 10)

gerontologists (p. 10)

biological age (p. 10)

psychological age (p. 10)

social age (p. 11)

heredity (p. 11)

environment (p. 11)

normative age-graded influences (p. 11)

normative history-graded influences (p. 11)

cohort (p. 11)

nonnormative life events (p. 12)

bioecological approach (p. 14)

Changing Images and Realities of Aging

- Cultural attitudes toward aging contrast markedly across both time and space.
- Both the United States and the world are experiencing a "graying of the population."
- In the United States, women live longer than men and tend to have more difficulties in old age. The adult population is becoming more racially and ethnically diverse.
- Only 5 percent of older adults are in institutions. Many older adults work, and most are relatively secure financially. Still, about 1 in 5 older adults is poor or near poor.
- Older Americans today are increasingly well-educated, and most (the "young old") have good to excellent health. The "old old" are the frail, infirm minority who need support services.
- Worldwide, the most dramatic growth in the older adult population is in developing regions. This growth, which can place great strains on societal institutions such as the family, and on the economy, has led to an emphasis on productive aging. In developed nations, concerns center on retirement and health benefits for an aging population.

ageism (p. 17)

geriatrics (p. 25)

productive aging (p. 30)

CHAPTER 2

Metatheoretical Perspectives and Research Methods

◈ FOCUS: ERIK H. ERIKSON

There is one thing even more vital to science than intelligent methods; and that is, the sincere desire to find out the truth, whatever it may be.

—Charles Sanders Peirce, Collected Papers, vol. 5

UPI/Corbis Images

Erik H. Erikson,* one of the first investigators to extend the systematic study of personality development into adulthood, wrote: "I have . . . learned from life histories that everything that is new and worth saying . . . has a highly personal aspect" (Erikson, personal communication, in Coles, 1970, p. 181). Erikson's own life and work demonstrate his point.

One of the key concepts Erikson introduced was the

---

*Sources of bibliographical material on Erikson are Coles (1970), Hall & Lindzey (1978), P. H. Miller (1983), Roazen (1976), Stevens (1983), and Erikson's obituary in the *New York Times*, May 13, 1994, p. C16.

identity crisis—an unsettling period, usually in adolescence or young adulthood, in which people search for a sense of self and of meaning in their lives. In his research, Erikson repeatedly found echoes of his own prolonged identity crisis, which included coping with his father's absence, growing up among peers who regarded him as a stranger, stumbling onto his career path in his mid twenties and then, in his mid thirties, resettling in a new land and learning a new language.

Themes of "identity confusion" and alienation run through Erikson's life story, beginning with the dubious circumstances of his birth. He was born in 1902 near Frankfurt, Germany, to a Danish-Jewish woman; he never knew his father. His mother's Danish husband apparently left her before the child's birth, after discovering that the father was another man. Her second husband, a Jewish doctor named Theodor Homburger, gave the child his name and raised him as a Jew.

An outsider among both his anti-Semitic German schoolmates and his non-Nordic Jewish peers, the youth left school at the age of 18, dabbled in art, and wandered around Europe for seven years, "trying to come to grips with himself" (Coles, 1970, p. 15). At 25, he was hired as a children's tutor in Vienna and helped found a small progressive school for children whose parents were involved in Sigmund Freud's growing psychoanalytic movement. (*Psychoanalysis* is a therapeutic method designed to free patients from emotional disturbances traced to long-buried memories of early, traumatic experiences.) "Herr Erik" eventually took psychoanalytic training (though he lacked the usual medical background, having only a high school diploma) and became a member of Freud's circle.

In 1933, when Hitler came to power, the young psychoanalyst, his Canadian-born wife, and their two sons moved to the United States. In 1939, when he became an American citizen, he took the name Erikson (son of Erik), perhaps identifying with the Norwegian discoverer of his adopted country, but also suggesting that he was the child of himself—that his identity was his own creation.

Although Erikson was a child psychiatrist by training and profession, his greatest contributions may well have been in illuminating the inner world of adulthood. His own experiences of rootlessness and immigration as a young adult convinced him that Freud was wrong in believing that personality development stops at puberty. Erikson's wide-ranging research among American combat veterans, normal and disturbed adolescents, Native Americans, and Hindus in India, as well as his studies of the lives of Martin Luther and Mahatma Gandhi, led him to place more importance on the influences of society and culture than Freud, whose psychoanalytic theory grew out of clinical work with a limited Viennese clientele. In his later years Erikson, in the belief that development continues throughout life, sought a deeper understanding of middle and old age—unlike Freud, who saw no point in working with older adults at all. Erikson's last works, written in his eighties with his wife, Joan, elaborated on his view that people in late life achieve wisdom based on the positive resolution of earlier emotional crises.

Erikson died in 1994 at age 91. He had, as the *New York Times* reported, "profoundly reshaped" our view of human—and particularly of adult—development.

The STORY OF ERIK H. ERIKSON underlines several important points about the study of adult development and aging. First, research on human beings is not dry, abstract, or esoteric. It deals with the substance of real life.

Second, theory and research are interwoven strands in the seamless fabric of scientific study. A **theory** is a coherent set of related concepts, which seeks to organize and explain **data,** the information gathered from research. As painstaking research adds, bit by bit, to the body of knowledge, theoretical concepts, such as Erikson's "identity crisis," help us make sense of, and see connections between, these isolated pieces of data. Theories, in turn, inspire further research and predict its results. Research can indicate whether a theory is accurate in its predictions but cannot conclusively prove a theory. Scientists must always be ready to change their theories to account for new and unexpected data.

Finally, developmental science cannot be completely objective. Theories and research about human behavior are products of very human individuals, whose inquiries and interpretations are inevitably influenced by their own values and experience. As Erikson observed, this personal dimension can yield enriching insights; but it can also produce blind spots. In striving for greater objectivity, researchers must scrutinize how they and their colleagues conduct their work, the assumptions on which it is based, and how they arrive at their conclusions.

Throughout this book, we examine many, often conflicting, theories. In assessing them, it is important to keep in mind that they reflect the outlooks of the human beings who originated them. In the first part of this chapter, we present three basic perspectives that underlie much of the theoretical and research work in adult development and aging, as well as in other fields of science. In the remainder of the chapter, we look at how researchers gather information, so that you will be better able to judge whether or not it is on solid ground.

METATHEORIES

Imagine that a shaman (spiritual healer) from India wanders into a convention where an American university professor is presenting a paper on how age affects recall of stories. The professor reports that older and younger adults are equally able to remember the main points of a story, but younger adults recollect many more details than older adults do. She suggests that perhaps memory aids can ameliorate this problem. On hearing this, the shaman says: "I understand your concern, but your own numbers give you cause for hope. Some day the young will simply outgrow their affliction."

Why do the professor and the shaman give opposite interpretations of the same data, and which interpretation is correct? The fact is that the shaman and the professor view adult development from different perspectives, both of which may be equally valid because they start from different assumptions and focus on different problems.

The professor emphasizes **quantitative development**—changes in number or amount. The problem she sees is a decrease in the number of details that older adults can extract from a story and remember. She views aging as a

> CRITICAL THINKING
>
> Why do you think it is valuable to have several metatheories and the respective individual theories to support investigations in specific domains of human research?

time of decline; an older adult cannot remember as much as a younger adult. She assumes that older people need help to compensate for this quantitative deficiency.

The shaman, on the other hand, emphasizes **qualitative development**—changes in the *kinds* of things older and younger adults can do, or how they do them. He sees the problem in terms of ability to *retell* a story. Concentration on recalling details can get in the way; fresh details drawn from personal experience lend vividness and immediacy. The shaman views aging as one of a series of progressive developments throughout life. He assumes that experience will eventually make a young adult a more effective storyteller.

In the shaman's eyes, the professor is inexplicably trying to make older adults act like younger adults. To the professor, the shaman has an overly rosy view of aging.

The perspectives from which people, including scientists, view phenomena such as aging are called *metatheories*. A **metatheory** is a broad hypothesis, or tentative explanation, about how the world works (Pepper, 1942, 1961). It is like a lens through which a person looks at the universe: a set of assumptions and values that filter perceptions and focus one's view of reality. A metatheory is a "supertheory." Operating in various branches of science, it embraces a family of theories that take a similar approach (though some theories seem to fall into more than one metatheoretical camp). Metatheory can critically influence a research design. It can shape the questions researchers ask, the topics they think it important to study, the methods they use, the kinds of evidence they look for, and the way they interpret their results.

At the heart of differences among theories of adult development and aging are fundamental issues concerning how human beings change as they go through life and interact with their environment. Is development primarily quantitative or qualitative? Is it continuous, or does it start and stop? Does it progress in a series of universal stages, or is it idiosyncratic? Does it move in one direction or more than one? The positions investigators take on these issues reflect their metatheoretical orientation. Different thinkers, looking through different lenses, come up with different explanations for how people behave. And these scientists may have as much trouble communicating with one another as the shaman and the professor.

Three Metatheories: Mechanistic, Organismic, and Contextual

Let's look at three metatheories and some developmental theories and models that flow from them. (A **model** is a concrete image or structural representation of theoretical relationships.) None of these metatheories is necessarily better or truer than any of the others. Each offers a singular perspective that can shed light on adult development and aging, as well as on other natural phenomena. Each has a basic metaphor—a central image or analogy that captures its essential character. Table 2.1 summarizes major features of the three metatheories: mechanistic, organismic, and contextual.

TABLE 2.1

Comparison of Three Metatheories

	Mechanistic	**Organismic**	**Contextual**
Basic metaphor	Machine	Developing organism (e.g., embryo)	Development as an ongoing act in context
View of development	Continuous (no stages)	Discontinuous (stages)	Continuous and discontinuous (shifting goals and contexts)
Type of change emphasized	Quantitative	Qualitative	Quantitative and qualitative
View of causality	Internal and external environment	Internal; directed to optimal endpoint	Individual goals within contextual opportunities and constraints
Predictability	Very high	Moderate to high	Low to moderate
Direction of change	Unidirectional; decline or decline with compensation	Unidirectional; ever more integrated and adaptive	Multidirectional; gains and losses at each point of life
Value of old age	Low	Neutral to high	Neutral

THE MECHANISTIC PERSPECTIVE

The **mechanistic perspective** views all things in nature, including adult human beings, as if they were machines (Pepper, 1942, 1961). A machine is the sum of its parts. To understand it, we can break it down into its smallest components and then reassemble it.

Machines do not operate of their own volition; they react automatically and passively to physical forces or inputs. Fill a car with gas, turn the ignition key, press the accelerator, and the vehicle will move. In the mechanistic view, human behavior is much the same: it results from the operation of biological parts in response to external or internal stimuli. In principle, if we know enough about how the human "machine" is put together and about the forces impinging upon it, behavior is perfectly predictable. Of course, just as a car may not start in subzero temperatures or a part may break down under excessive stress, special external or internal conditions can affect human responses.

Mechanistic theorists (like the professor in our story) deal with quantitative development—for example, how much or how quickly a person can remember, rather than what memory is or how it operates. They see development as continuous and as moving in one direction at a time. One unidirectional view of development is the traditional view of adulthood and aging as unbroken physical and intellectual decline—the idea that people, like flowers, develop in a steadily positive direction until maturity and then undergo unremitting decay. Another view of development supports the idea that behavior can be modified by intervention approaches which may prevent decline or improve performance of those who have declined.

Information-processing theory, representing the mechanistic view, explains how the human mind works. It breaks the complex processes of thinking and remembering into their component parts. Information-processing researchers study the processes people go through in manipulating information and solving problems. In this model, human beings, like computers, register incoming information, code and store it, and then retrieve it when the right "keys" are pushed. Much as the parts of a machine wear down, information processing seems to become slower with age. The human "machine" reaches peak efficiency in young adulthood and then declines. Thus information-processing researchers design *interventions*—techniques to boost older adults' functioning. However, information-processing theories are not necessarily purely mechanistic. Many psychologists who study information processing believe that nonmechanical characteristics such as emotions and motivations play a part in thought and memory.

While the mechanist analyzes phenomena by breaking them down into simpler elements, the other two perspectives synthesize data. For them, a phenomenon is more than the sum of its parts. The meaning of a family relationship, for example, goes beyond what can be learned from studying its individual members and their day-to-day interactions. Also, in the other two metatheories people play a more active role in their own development.

THE ORGANISMIC PERSPECTIVE

The **organismic perspective** sees people as developing organisms (Pepper, 1942, 1961). Like embryos, they are growing, maturing beings with internally generated patterns of development. They initiate events; they do not just react. Environmental influences do not cause or significantly alter development, though they might speed it up or slow it down.

For organicists, development has an underlying, orderly structure, though it may not be obvious from moment to moment. As a fertilized egg cell develops into an embryo and then into a fetus, it goes through a series of qualitative changes not overtly predictable from what came before. Swellings on the head become eyes, ears, mouth, and nose. The brain begins to coordinate breathing, digestion, and elimination. Sex organs form. Similarly, organicists describe development after birth as a progressive sequence of stages, moving in one direction: toward full maturation.

A **stage** is a pattern of behavior typical of a certain period of development, which leads to a different, usually more advanced pattern. (As with a teenager's sulky moods, what may appear to be a reversion to less mature behavior prepares the way for a resumption of forward movement.) At each stage, people cope with different kinds of problems and develop different kinds of abilities. Transitions between stages tend to be abrupt, but there is continuity, too; each stage builds on the previous one and lays the foundation for the next. Organicists see this unfolding structure of development as universal: everyone goes through the same stages in the same order, though the precise timing varies.

It might seem logical that organicists would view old age as the climax of development rather than a time of decline. However, classic stage theories, such as those of Freud and the Swiss cognitive theoretician Jean Piaget, placed the normal endpoint of maturation around puberty. Erikson was one of the first influential thinkers to view adulthood and old age as unique stages of life with their own issues to be resolved. (Table 2.2 lists the stages in each of these

TABLE 2.2

Stages of Human Development: Three Major Theories

Psychosexual Stages (Freud)	Psychosocial Stages (Erikson)	Cognitive Stages (Piaget)
Oral (birth to 12–18 months). Baby's chief source of pleasure is mouth-oriented activities like sucking and eating.	*Basic trust versus mistrust (birth to 12–18 months).* Baby develops sense of whether world can be trusted. Virtue: hope.	*Sensorimotor (birth to 2 years).* Infant changes from a being who responds primarily through reflexes to one who can organize activities in relation to the environment. Uses sensory and motor abilities to comprehend world.
Anal (12–18 months to 3 years). Child derives sensual gratification from withholding and expelling feces.	*Autonomy versus shame and doubt (12–18 months to 3 years).* Child develops a balance of independence over doubt and shame. Virtue: will.	*Preoperational (2 to 7 years).* Child develops a representational system and uses symbols such as words to represent people, places, and events.
Phallic (3 to 6 years). Child becomes attached to parent of other sex; later identifies with same-sex parent.	*Initiative versus guilt (3 to 6 years).* Child develops initiative when trying out new things and is not overwhelmed by failure. Virtue: purpose.	
Latency (6 years to puberty). Time of relative calm between more turbulent stages.	*Industry versus inferiority (6 years to puberty).* Child must learn skills of the culture or face feelings of inferiority. Virtue: skill.	*Concrete operations (7 to 12 years).* Child can solve problems logically if they are focused on the here and now.

(continued)

TABLE 2.2

Stages of Human Development: Three Major Theories (Continued)

Psychosexual Stages (Freud)	Psychosocial Stages (Erikson)	Cognitive Stages (Piaget)
Genital (puberty through adulthood). Time of mature adult sexuality.	*Identity versus identity confusion (puberty to young adulthood).* Adolescent must determine own sense of self. Virtue: fidelity.	*Formal operations (12 years through adulthood).* Person can think in abstract terms, deal with hypothetical situations, and think about possibilities.
	Intimacy versus isolation (young adulthood). Person seeks to make commitments to others; if unsuccessful, may suffer from sense of isolation and self-absorption. Virtue: love.	
	Generativity versus stagnation (middle adulthood). Mature adult is concerned with establishing and guiding the next generation or else feels personal impoverishment. Virtue: care.	
	Integrity versus despair (old age). Elderly person achieves a sense of acceptance of own life, allowing the acceptance of death, or else falls into despair. Virtue: wisdom.	

NOTE: All ages are approximate.

theories.) Today, many theorists believe that new stages of development occur across the adult life span, especially in cognition and personality.

Erikson's theory of personality development illustrates an important feature of organismic development: integration driven by conflict. At each stage, resolution of a "crisis" or turning point depends on achieving a healthy balance between opposing traits (such as intimacy versus isolation); this resolution results in development of a "virtue" (such as love). Without satisfactory resolution of a crisis, a person will continue to struggle with it, impeding healthy development.

THE CONTEXTUAL PERSPECTIVE

The central image of the **contextual perspective** is the ongoing act in its context—a dynamic event in a setting that is always in flux. An act is never isolated. Its immediate context grows out of the past and affects the future. For purposes of study, we can look at an event at a given moment in time, but this is an artificial separation that distorts reality.

In contextualism, as in organicism, people actively shape their own development. But contextualists place more emphasis on interaction with the environment. Every act is produced by and irrevocably changes, both the actor and the context, creating new conditions for development—much as, in a price war, each round of price reductions alters the circumstances within which the next round occurs. The changing person acts on and changes the environment, and the changing environment acts on and changes the person.

Individuals set goals within a particular context as they perceive it, and then select new goals within the new context that they seek out or that then presents itself. Thus, although development is continuous from one moment to the next, it is also discontinuous, as goals and contexts shift. Furthermore, the context is not just "out there." It includes a person's own aspirations, beliefs, and interpretations. Individuals influence and are influenced by the context of which they are a part.

Charlotte Bühler (1933, 1968a, 1968b) was one of the first theorists to talk about development as focused on setting and attaining personal goals. On the basis of more than 200 biographical studies and years of intensive interviews, she concluded that self-fulfillment is the key to healthy development and depends on the achievement of self-defined goals—though people may not always be conscious of them at the time.

Contextualists view development as both quantitative and qualitative; they look at changes in what people do as well as in how much they can do. Unlike organicists, contextualists do not see development as directed toward any particular endpoint. Instead, they emphasize individual differences. People develop in many directions, and no path is intrinsically superior. Success hinges on how appropriate behavior is to its context. For example, making fishing boats may be highly adaptive on an island until the coming of a factory whose polluted discharge kills the fish.

In the "activated lifespace" model (Sansone & Berg, 1993), a current example of the contextualist perspective, each person has a unique set of experiences and abilities; and each activity occurs within a unique context, which may include physical setting, social pressures, rewards, feedback, and other features. In trying to solve a problem, a person "activates" (uses) only those personal resources and contextual features within his or her "lifespace" that seem relevant at the moment. At different times of life, a person may bring different experiences and abilities to bear on a task in different contexts. An older adult who can't solve a math problem on a timed test may be able to solve a similar problem while shopping.

Although the lifespan developmental approach (Baltes, 1987; Baltes & Graf, 1996) discussed in Chapter 1 blends aspects of all three metatheories, many of its key features—history and context, multiple avenues of research, and multidirectional development—fit within contextualism. The lifespan approach is coming to the fore at a time when older adults are becoming more numerous and diverse, and when technological innovations allow researchers in different fields to communicate rapidly and effectively.

Indeed, from a contextual perspective, metatheories themselves are grounded in particular social, political, and economic conditions (Riegel, 1977). The mechanistic perspective was developed chiefly in the United States and Great Britain, highly competitive societies in which "the main criterion for intellectual and personal excellence was the amount of information accumulated, just as the criterion for social respectability was the amount of wealth and property acquired" (p. 71). The organismic perspective emerged in stratified continental European societies in which different age groups had their own special roles. Contextualism seems to reflect a contemporary world in which notions of orderly progress have broken down, the universe (science tells us) is in flux, the planet Earth is becoming an interdependent global village, and people's life choices are dynamic, ever-changing, and highly individual.

Applying Metatheories

CRITICAL THINKING

Do you think each metatheory is equally valuable in explaining human development during middle age and late adulthood?

How would representatives of the three metatheoretical perspectives approach the same research problem? Think back to the professor and the shaman. The professor represents a mechanistic perspective. She focuses on quantitative differences in the amount of detail that older and younger adults can recall. Since an older adult's "machinery" appears to be functioning less efficiently, she proposes interventions to bring it up to speed. The shaman represents an organismic perspective. He sees the professor's findings as reflecting a natural course of qualitative development requiring no intervention. Each age group is acting as it should and must.

A contextual researcher in the audience might comment that the study was incomplete. He might suggest further research to compare older and younger adults in a variety of situations: working alone, working with another person, or working with a group of people. Since remembering often takes place in a social context, he might predict that some older individuals would be more motivated and better able to recall details in cooperation with others.

As you read this book, keep asking yourself: Which metatheoretical perspective does this theory, research finding, or interpretation represent? What is *my* metatheoretical perspective on this issue? Everyone uses metatheories. Your attitude toward your own development, the way you deal with the inevitable process of growing older, will depend on the metatheory under which you operate. Remember that no metatheory has an exclusive claim to truth. You may choose one metatheoretical approach toward one type of problem and a different approach toward another. Indeed, some developmentalists maintain that the ability to select the most appropriate metatheoretical perspective on a particular situation is a sign of mature thought.

BASIC RESEARCH METHODS

The purpose of research is to draw valid, reliable conclusions about the world and the human beings who inhabit it—**valid** in that the conclusions appropriately apply to the phenomena and populations being studied, and **reliable** in that the results are reasonably consistent across time. For example, an intelligence test is valid if it actually measures the abilities it claims to measure. It is reliable if a person's scores do not vary greatly from one testing to another.

Let's look now at the basic methods researchers use; then, in the next section, at some basic research plans, or designs. In the final section of this chapter, we'll turn to special problems in doing research on adult development and aging.

Two key issues at the outset of any investigation are how the participants will be chosen and how the data will be collected. These decisions often depend on what questions the research is intended to answer. All these issues play a part in a research plan or design.

Researchers in adult development work within two methodological traditions: *quantitative* and *qualitative*.***Quantitative research** deals with "hard," objectively measurable data; for example, how much fear or anxiety patients feel before surgery, as measured by standardized tests, physiological changes, or statistical analysis. **Qualitative research** deals with "soft" data about the nature or quality of participants' subjective experiences, feelings, or beliefs—for instance, how patients describe their emotions before surgery (Morse & Field, 1995).

Quantitative research is based on the **scientific method**, an overall process that generally characterizes scientific inquiry in any field. Careful use of the scientific method enables researchers to come to sound conclusions about human development. The usual steps in the method are

- *Identifying a problem* to be studied, often on the basis of a theory or of previous research.
- *Formulating hypotheses* to be tested by research.
- *Collecting data.*
- *Analyzing the data* to determine whether or not they support the hypothesis.
- *Disseminating findings* so that other observers can check, learn from, analyze, repeat, and build on the results.

Qualitative research takes a more open-ended, exploratory route. Instead of generating hypotheses from previous research, qualitative researchers gather data and then examine it to see what hypotheses or theories may emerge. Qualitative

*Unless otherwise indicated, the discussion in this section and the next is based on Papalia, Olds, & Feldman (2003).

CRITICAL THINKING

Why do you think information gathered through the scientific method is superior to that gathered through observations of people in natural settings?

research is highly interpretive; it cannot yield general conclusions, but it can be a rich source of insights into individuals' attitudes and behavior.

The selection of quantitative or qualitative methods depends on a number of factors: the topic for study, how much is already known about it, the researcher's expertise and theoretical orientation, and the setting. Quantitative research is often done in laboratory settings, where controlled conditions can produce replicable (repeatable) results. Qualitative research is most appropriate in everyday social settings, for investigating topics about which little is currently known. Qualitative research can be extremely time consuming and expensive.

Investigators may combine the two methods. Often qualitative research yields findings that point the way to quantitative research. For example, patients' descriptions of their experience may suggest means of reducing stress before surgery, which can then be tested and compared for effectiveness (Morse & Field, 1995; Shadish, Cook, & Campbell, 2002).

Sampling

How similar are you to the other members of your family? To your neighbors? To people you go to school with, or work with? To people who have more money than you do? To people who have less money than you do? To people from the same ethnic background? To people from different ethnic backgrounds? To people of your gender? To people of the other gender? How comfortable would you feel if the results of a study about you were applied to each of these groups? How comfortable would you be if their results were applied to you?

Your answers may depend in part on the kinds of questions being studied and on the research design. But a way to make *sure* that the results of a study have **external validity**—that they can be generalized to people other than those in the study—is to control who gets into the study. Of course, if an entire population (all members of the group being studied) could take part, any findings would be valid for them; but studying an entire population is usually too costly and time consuming. Therefore, quantitative investigators select a **sample,** a smaller group within the population. Only if the sample is truly representative can the results be properly generalized to the population as a whole.

Researchers ensure representativeness by **random selection,** which gives every person in a population an equal chance of being chosen. The result of random selection is a **random sample**. One way to select a random sample of the students in an adult development class, for example, would be to put all their names into a hat, shake it, and then draw out a certain number of names. A random sample, especially a large one, is likely to represent the population well—that is, to show relevant characteristics and behavior in the same proportion in which they are found in the entire population.

A recent example of random sampling in research comes from work assessing some of the effects of the September 11, 2001 tragedies. To find out how the September 11 terrorist attacks affected the mental health of Manhattan residents, researchers reached 1,008 households by random digit dialing and conducted telephone interviews with the adult in the household whose birthday was most recent. In the interviews, which were conducted within two months after the attacks, 9.7 percent of the sample reported current symptoms of depression, and 7.5 percent appeared to suffer from post-traumatic stress disorder (PTSD). Among adults living near the World Trade Center, 20 percent reported symptoms of PTSD. The researchers then generalized the findings to estimate the extent of those disorders among the population of Manhattan (Galea et a., 2002).

To make sure that a sample includes representative percentages of certain subgroups, such as women, minorities, and older adults, polling organizations often randomly select within each of these subgroups. This type of sample is sometimes called a *stratified random sample.*

Although precise stratification is not always necessary, it is important that a sample does not leave out or greatly underrepresent major segments of the population. For example, in Box 2.1 on p. 46 we discuss sampling problems in Alfred Kinsey's pioneering studies of sexuality.

Similarly, we must be careful about generalizing the results of studies done in one culture to other cultures that may have different characteristics (see Box 2.2 on p. 48 and Figure 2.1 on p. 49). Also, if a significant proportion of a randomly chosen sample refuse to participate, the sample's representativeness may be compromised.

In qualitative research, samples tend to be small and need not be random. Participants in this kind of research may be chosen for their ability to communicate the nature of their experience—say, what it feels like to go through surgery—or because they have undergone a particular type of surgery.

Data Collection

Common ways of gathering data include self-reports (verbal reports of a person's own thoughts, feelings, or actions); tests and other behavioral measures; and observation. Researchers may use one or more of these data-collection techniques in any research design.

SELF-REPORTS: DIARIES, INTERVIEWS, AND QUESTIONNAIRES

The simplest form of self-report is a diary or log. People may be asked, for example, to record their daily diet, times when they feel depressed, or times when they forget something. Other types of self-reports are interviews and questionnaires.

In an *interview,* a researcher asks questions about a person's attitudes, opinions, or behavior. The questioning may be face to face or by telephone; telephone interviews can reach a greater number of people more efficiently. In a *structured interview,* every participant gets the same fixed set of questions or tasks. In an *open-ended interview,* the interviewer has more flexibility with regard to determining topics and order of questions and asking follow-up questions based on the responses. Some interviews

CRITICAL THINKING
Which data collection method would give you the greatest confidence if you were deciding how to reduce the isolation of older adults?

Early Studies of Sexuality

What percentages of American men and women have had homosexual experiences? What percentages have engaged in sex outside of marriage? What percentages are impotent or infertile?

Answers to such questions are widely available today. But scientific data about human sexual behavior were virtually nonexistent in 1938, when Alfred C. Kinsey, a zoology professor at Indiana University, began to survey students about what kinds of sexual activities they had engaged in, when, and how often. Kinsey soon switched from questionnaires to in-person interviews, which allowed more flexibility and detail. Ultimately, he and his colleagues interviewed 5,300 men and nearly 6,000 women nationwide and produced two eye-opening reports: *Sexual Behavior in the Human Male* (1948) and *Sexual Behavior in the Human Female* (1953). The latter, which found, among other things, that 62 percent of women masturbate, was especially controversial. At a time when women's sexual needs were neither widely recognized nor openly discussed, the report was attacked as "offensive . . . amoral, antifamily, and even tainted with communism" (Masters, Johnson, & Kolodny, 1988, p. 20).

Critics were quick to point out methodological flaws. The most serious problem was that Kinsey's *sample*, the group of participants chosen to represent the population, was in fact unrepresentative. For example, the original sample contained very few black people; the elderly, too, were underrepresented. And the fact that the participants were volunteers could have distorted the findings.

Bettmann/Corbis Images

Alfred C. Kinsey and his wife arrive in Paris in October 1955, carrying a French translation of his groundbreaking book, Sexual Behavior in the Human Female. *Despite some methodological flaws, Kinsey's work became the foundation for scientific study of human sexuality.*

Still, a committee of the American Statistical Association gave the Kinsey reports a favorable overall rating (Cochran, Mosteller, & Tukey, 1953). In retrospect, William H. Masters and Virginia E. Johnson attribute methodological "quibbles" about Kinsey's work largely to "an attempt to discredit the credibility of Kinsey's 'shocking' findings" (Masters et al., 1988, p. 31).

combine the two approaches. For example, an interviewer may ask a group of adults to complete a series of sentences such as: "The thing I dislike most about my job is . . . " Then the interviewer may probe further: "You said you don't like your boss. What is it about him or her that you

Although Masters and Johnson's own study of the physical processes of human sexual arousal, *Human Sexual Response* (1966), appeared at a time when societal attitudes toward sexuality were becoming more liberal, it, too, aroused furious controversy. If concerns about Kinsey's methodology may have masked outrage at the subject matter of his research, objections to Masters and Johnson's work centered on the methods themselves. In a marked departure from Kinsey's relatively tame interviews, Masters and Johnson for 11 years directly observed and recorded the physical responses of 382 women and 312 men engaging in various types of sexual activity in their laboratory at Washington University Medical School in St. Louis. In addition to machinery to measure heart rate and rhythm and muscular tension and contractions, their equipment included an artificial penis that could film vaginal changes during simulated intercourse.

One criticism was that people who would agree to be in such studies would not be typical of the population. However, Masters and Johnson did interview prospective participants to assess emotional stability and motivations. Besides, they argued, a true cross-section of the population is not generally required in research on normal bodily functions, "as long as the sample is both diverse and healthy" (Masters et al., 1988, p. 40). The sample included a modest number of older people, and some of the findings addressed sexual capacity in older men and women.

Another criticism was that the participants' responses might have been affected by the artificiality of the setting. But to help the couples feel at ease, the researchers first had them engage in an unobserved "practice session," without the equipment. In addition, the investigators soundproofed the laboratory and shifted sessions to the evening, when fewer curiosity seekers would be hanging around.

Ultimately, Masters and Johnson rest their case for the value of their work on its successful application to contraceptive design, infertility counseling, sex education, and particularly to sex therapy, a profession that grew out of their clinical studies reported in *Human Sexual Inadequacy* (1970).

These groundbreaking forays into the field of human sexuality demonstrate the importance of methodology in scientific research. The progression of methods used by Kinsey and then by Masters and Johnson, from questionnaires to interviews to laboratory observation to clinical treatment, shows how research can evolve to meet changing goals or unforeseen problems and outcomes. And the controversy over these reports demonstrates how methodological weaknesses can endanger the acceptance of research that delves into culturally "taboo" subjects or uses unorthodox methods.

NOTE: Unless otherwise indicated, this discussion of early investigations of human sexuality is based on Masters et al. (1988).

don't like?" Groups of people can be interviewed and research questions discussed in *focus groups*. Such groups can clarify issues, determine reactions to issues or products, or provide the basis for more structured questionnaire research.

Avoiding Cultural Bias in Research

Many studies have found that as people get older, their hearing—especially for high-pitched sounds—gradually deteriorates, necessitating the use of hearing aids. Is hearing loss entirely a physiological phenomenon of aging, or do environmental and cultural factors make a difference?

To find out, one group of researchers (Baltes, Reese, & Nesselroade, 1977) compared samples of older adults in rural and urban American areas and also among the Mabaans, a tribe in the African nation of Sudan who live in an especially noise-free environment (see Figure 2.1). Older Mabaans showed less hearing loss than *any* of the American samples, male or female. Men in the United States showed more hearing loss than women; and, among men, the degree of hearing impairment was related to how much noise they heard in their everyday environments. Rural men, who heard less noise throughout their lives than urban factory workers, experienced less hearing loss in late adulthood than the factory workers did.

Findings like these illustrate how cross-cultural research can provide *external validity*. A study using only an American sample (especially a sample using only American males, or American urban males) could overestimate the amount of hearing loss associated with normal physiological aging. Clearly, such a study could not be generalized to American women or to Mabaans in Sudan—or perhaps to other cultures as well. By looking at people from various cultural and ethnic groups, researchers can learn which aspects of development seem to be universal (and thus a part of the aging process everywhere), and which are cultural.

Just as travelers returning from abroad may see familiar aspects of their own world in a new light, learning about the ideas and practices of other cultures can give us a new perspective on our own. Throughout this book, we present many examples of cross-cultural research. These studies demonstrate how closely adult development is tied to society and culture and how greatly "normal" development can vary in different cultural settings.

Questionnaires are written instruments, given either in person or by mail. Because questionnaires are easier than interviews to tabulate and summarize, they are often used in large-scale surveys.

Any kind of self-report can be prone to inaccuracy. Participants' memory may be faulty, or a respondent may consciously or unconsciously edit replies to make them more acceptable. The wording of a question can affect the answer. One example was a Roper survey published by the American Jewish Committee in 1993. The original results were startling: 22 percent of the adult respondents said it seemed "possible" rather than "impossible" that the Holocaust (the Nazis' annihilation of Jews during World War II) had never happened (Siano, 1993; T. W. Smith, 1995; "Testing Awareness of the Holocaust," 1993). However, when the survey was repeated twice using a more

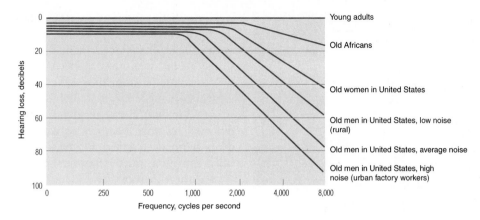

FIGURE 2.1 Cross-cultural differences in hearing loss showed up in a study that compared American men and women exposed to varying noise levels in their everyday environment, with older people in a Sudanese tribe exposed to unusually low noise levels. These findings suggest that hearing loss is not purely physiological but is environmentally influenced. *SOURCE:* Baltes, Reese, & Nesselroade, 1977.

clearly worded question, only 1 to 3 percent said it seemed possible that the Holocaust had not occurred (T. W. Smith, 1995). Sometimes the identity of the questioner makes a difference. In a Northwestern University survey, men were twice as likely to admit to having engaged in sexual harassment in the workplace when questioned by a man as by a woman (Secter, 1995).

Self-reports have an important place in psychological investigation but are limited by their subjectivity. They depend on awareness of processes that may be less than fully conscious; and they are inevitably filtered through each participant's interpretive screen. For many kinds of research, investigators seek greater objectivity through measures that do not depend on verbal reports.

BEHAVIORAL METHODS: TESTS AND OTHER MEASURES

A behavioral measure such as an intelligence test *shows* something about a person rather than asking the person to *tell* about it. Tests and other behavioral and neuropsychological measures, including mechanical and electronic devices, may be used to assess abilities, skills, knowledge, comptencies, or physiological responses.

OBSERVATION

A scientist must ... be absolutely like a child. If he sees a thing, he must say that he sees it, whether it was what he thought he was going to see or not. See first, think later, then test. But always see first. Otherwise you will only see what you were expecting. (D. Adams, 1985, pp. 164–165)

Seeing is a common word for what scientists call *observation*. Observation can take two forms: naturalistic observation and laboratory observation.

> **CRITICAL THINKING**
>
> What strategies would you use to make naturalistic observation as systematic and unbiased as possible?

© Joel Gordon

Many caregivers have observed the "mirror phenomenon," in which a person with Alzheimer's disease reacts to his or her own reflection as if it were another person. Such naturalistic observations can suggest questions for further study.

Naturalistic observation takes place in real-life settings. Researchers do not manipulate the environment or the participants' activities. They simply record what they observe.

Systematic, sustained observation can reveal information missed by casual observation. In one study of nursing home residents who had been reported by staff members to wander, the residents wore electronic ankle tags that automatically activated video recorders. Staff members viewed the videotapes and identified patterns of movement. About 81 percent of the movement of residents reported to be "wanderers" (compared with 94 percent for "nonwanderers") turned out to be direct travel from one place to another. Apparently, much of what staff members ordinarily saw as aimless wandering was actually efficient movement (Martino-Saltzman, Blasch, Morris, & McNeal, 1991).

Sometimes naturalistic observation raises questions that it cannot conclusively answer. A 68-year-old woman with Alzheimer's disease became agitated and refused to enter the bathroom, claiming there was a stranger inside. Her daughter gently led her into the bathroom and said, "Show me the stranger." The mother hesitantly went to the mirror and pointed to her own reflection. A number of caregivers have reported this "mirror phenomenon," in which demented patients react to their own reflection as if it were another person. Might particular features of the situation, or degree of dementia, have something to do with this phenomenon? Answers can come from **laboratory observation**—which may or may not take place in an actual laboratory—in which researchers observe a group of people under identical, controlled conditions. By manipulating the environment, the investigators can observe any differences in behavior.

In one study in a French geriatric center (Biringer, Anderson, & Strubel, 1988), eighteen women at three discrete, progressively advanced stages of Alzheimer's disease (stages 5, 6, and 7) sat, by turns, before a mirror. The researchers observed each woman from the next room for 5 minutes to see whether she would act as if she knew that she was facing her own reflection. Next, an investigator entered the room and, while rearranging the woman's hair (a common procedure at the center), smudged her forehead with soot from a burnt cork. The investigator again left the room and observed the woman for 5 minutes. Finally, the investigator again returned and put a mark on the woman's hand, where she could see it without looking in the mirror, and then observed her for 5 more minutes.

Most of the women at a less advanced stage of the disease (stage 5) recognized themselves in the mirror during the first observation period, and every one of them showed an understanding that the mark on the forehead of the reflection in the mirror was actually on her own forehead. Some of the women at stage 6 could recognize themselves and respond appropriately to the marks on their foreheads, and some could not. However, all these women responded appropriately to the marks on their hands, suggesting that lack of response to a mark on the forehead was not due simply to lack of interest in strange marks on the body. At stage 7, all the women failed to respond to marks on their reflections, and all but one failed to respond to marks on their hands.

Observation can yield much useful descriptive information. But even under controlled laboratory conditions, observation by itself cannot explain behavior. The studies described above do not tell us why patients with advanced Alzheimer's disease seem to lose the ability to recognize themselves before they lose the ability to notice a mark on their hands. Two additional cautions: First, an observer's presence may affect behavior. If adults know they are being observed, they may act differently. Researchers may be able to obtain a clear, accurate picture only through long-term observation in which they gradually fade into the background, or when the observation is made so unobtrusively that the person being observed is unaware of it. Second, the value of observation may be limited by **observer bias:** a tendency to misinterpret or distort observed data to fit the observer's expectations, perhaps by emphasizing some aspects and minimizing others.

BASIC RESEARCH DESIGNS

A research design is a plan for conducting a scientific investigation: what questions are to be answered, how participants are to be selected, how data are to be collected and interpreted, and how valid conclusions can be drawn. Three basic designs used in developmental research are case studies, correlational studies, and experiments. Each design has advantages and drawbacks, and each is appropriate for certain kinds of research problems (see Table 2.3).

Case Studies

A **case study** is a study of a single case or individual. A number of theories, such as those of Freud and Erikson, have grown out of clinical case studies—some later modified or fleshed out by other types of research. Both Freud and Erikson also did historical case studies, using biographical, autobiographical, and documentary materials. Case studies can achieve great depth and breadth in exploring sources of behavior and developing and testing treatments for problems.

One advantage of a case study is flexibility. The researcher is free to explore avenues of inquiry that arise during the course of the study. One of the authors of this textbook (R. D. Feldman, 1982) conducted open-ended interviews with several middle-aged men and women who, like her, had been frequent panelists on *Quiz Kids,* a popular radio and television quiz show

TABLE 2.3

Basic Research Designs

Type	Main Characteristics	Advantages	Disadvantages
Case study	Study of single individual in depth.	Flexibility; provides detailed picture of one person's behavior and development; can generate hypotheses.	May not generalize to others; conclusions not directly testable; cannot establish cause and effect.
Ethnographic study	In-depth study of a culture or subculture.	Can help overcome culturally based biases in theory and research; can test universality of developmental phenomena.	Subject to observer bias.
Correlational study	Attempt to find a positive or negative relationship between variables.	Enables predication of one variable on basis of another; can suggest hypotheses about causal relationships.	Cannot establish cause and effect.
Experiment	Controlled procedure in which an experimenter controls the independent variable to determine its effect on the dependent variable; may be conducted in the laboratory or field.	Establishes cause-and-effect relationships; is highly controlled and can be repeated by another investigator; degree of control is greatest in the laboratory experiment.	Findings, especially when derived from laboratory experiments, may not generalize to situations outside the laboratory.

featuring precocious youngsters. One, Claude Brenner, was a 52-year-old engineer with a varied career ranging from space technology to energy conservation. After reflecting at length on the effects of *Quiz Kids* on his personal and professional life, Brenner concluded:

So the question comes back to the extent to which we were influenced, controlled, governed and shaped by the Quiz Kids experience. I would say strongly, but not exclusively. Perhaps I was laying all my emotional difficulties on that experience, and that is unfair. There were other factors going on in our lives. Our families—but our families themselves were inevitably shaped by our Quiz Kids experience. There's an interweaving of

In the 1940s, Claude Brenner (far right) was a panelist on Quiz Kids, a popular radio quiz show featuring bright children. At age 52, Brenner was one of several former Quiz Kids who participated in case studies by their fellow panelist Ruth Duskin Feldman (center), one of the authors of this textbook. Another former Quiz Kid, James Dewey Watson (second from left), won a Nobel prize in 1962 for the discovery of the structure of DNA, the substance that determines hereditary characteristics.

cause and effect that becomes a seamless web . . . We will never know whether we were Quiz Kids because of the kind of people we were or whether we're the kind of people we are because we were Quiz Kids. (R. D. Feldman, 1982, p. 135)

Brenner's comment illuminates an important limitation of case studies: they do not yield unequivocal information about causal relationships because there is no way to test the validity of an explanation. Also, case studies are particularly prone to observer bias. In one notorious case, Freud rebuked an 18-year-old girl, who complained of a family friend's sexual advances, for her "hysterical" refusal to follow what Freud maintained was her true desire to have sex with the man (Lakoff & Coyne, 1993). Finally, while a case study may offer a rich description of a single individual, it is questionable how the information applies to people in general.

Despite their limitations, however, case studies can provide valuable information about individual personality and behavior and can suggest hypotheses to be tested by other research. In one famous case study, an epileptic known as H. M. lost his memory of recent events but not his ability to learn new skills—such as solving puzzles—after his hippocampus and neighboring brain structures were removed in an attempt to stop his seizures (Kalat, 1992). Case studies such as this one have stimulated research about distinctions between memory for facts and for skills, and the brain structures that seem to be involved in each.

Correlational Studies

Suppose we want to see whether blood pressure has something to do with the risk of heart attack. By carefully measuring both phenomena, we might find that people with high blood pressure are more likely to have heart attacks than people with low blood pressure. If so, we have found a *correlation*, or relationship, between blood pressure and heart attacks.

Researchers are often interested in identifying relationships among **variables**—phenomena that change or vary among people. (*Constants* are things that do not change or vary.) Researchers are particularly interested in finding variables (such as blood pressure and risk of heart attack) that change together, that is, are related to one another.

A **correlational study** is designed to find out whether a statistical correlation can be calculated showing the direction and strength of a relationship between variables. It can show whether two variables are related *positively* (that is, both increase or decrease together, like blood pressure and heart attacks) or *negatively* (as one increases, the other decreases), and to what degree. A negative correlation does *not* mean "no correlation." It means that the two factors change in opposite directions. For example, studies in a number of countries show a negative correlation between educational level and the risk of dementia due to Alzheimer's disease. In Shanghai, people over age 75 with little or no education are twice as likely to become demented as those who have had some schooling. In other words, *less* schooling is associated with *more* dementia (Katzman, 1993).

Numerical correlations range from +1.0 (a perfect positive, or direct, relationship) to −1.0 (a perfect negative, or inverse, relationship). Of course, perfect correlations are rare. The closer a correlation comes to +1 or −1, the stronger the relationship, either positive or negative. A correlation of zero means that the variables have no relationship (see Figure 2.2).

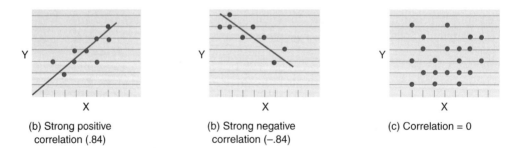

(b) Strong positive correlation (.84)

(b) Strong negative correlation (−.84)

(c) Correlation = 0

FIGURE 2.2 *Correlational studies may find positive or negative correlations or no correlation.* (a) In a positive correlation, data plotted on a graph cluster around a line showing that one variable (X) increases as the other variable (Y) increases. (b) In a negative correlation, one variable (X) increases as the other variable (Y) decreases. (c) No correlation—zero correlation—exists when increases and decreases in two variables show no consistent relationship (that is, data plotted on a graph show no pattern).

Correlations allow researchers to make predictions but not to draw conclusions about cause and effect. A rooster's crow heralds, but does not bring, the dawn. A strong positive correlation suggests, but cannot tell us with certainty, that high blood pressure causes heart attacks. Heart disease (and, perhaps, high blood pressure as well) might result from an unknown third factor. Similarly, the negative correlation between education and dementia might be due to another variable, such as socioeconomic status, which might explain *both* lower levels of schooling *and* higher levels of dementia. Compared with people who can afford advanced schooling, people who cannot afford it may have poorer diets, more exposure to environmental toxins, less adequate health care, or other deprivations that may contribute to a greater likelihood of mental deterioration. If a study found a correlation between education and brain development, it would be a strong indication that intellectual activity can protect against dementia, but it still could not definitively establish a causal connection. Only an experiment could do that. (In this case, however, for both practical and ethical reasons that will become clear later, such an experiment could not be conducted.)

Experiments

An **experiment** is a rigorously controlled procedure in which the experimenter systematically manipulates one or more variables to see whether this manipulation causes change in other, uncontrolled variables. This manipulation is what permits experimenters to establish cause and effect. Experiments must be conducted and reported in such a way that other investigators can replicate (repeat) them to verify the results and conclusions.

DESIGNING AN EXPERIMENT

Let's imagine that we see an advertisement for a pill that is supposed to improve eyesight. How might we design an experiment to test that claim?

Variables and Groups The first step is to identify the variables. An **independent variable** is something over which the experimenter has direct control—in this case, ingestion of vision pills. A **dependent variable**—in this case, visual acuity—is something that may or may not change as a result of changes in the independent variable; that is, it may or may not depend on the independent variable. The experimenter manipulates the independent variable (the pills) to see whether and how it affects the dependent variable (eyesight). This manipulation of the independent variable—the thing the experimenter wants to study—is called the **treatment**.

After identifying the variables, the experimenter must divide the participants into two groups: an **experimental group,** which will be given the treatment, and a **control group,** which will not. A control group is an essential element; it consists of people similar to the experimental group who are exposed to everything that group experiences except the treatment. A control group shows what the people who got the treatment would have been like without it.

In our experiment, the experimental group would take the vision pills, while the control group would take a placebo, which looked exactly like the vision pill but had no active ingredients. None of the participants would know which type of pill they were getting. This is called a *single-blind test*. Ideally, the person who gave out the pills also would be unaware of the purpose of the study and would not know which participants got the vision pills and which got the placebo. Such a procedure is commonly called a *double-blind test*.

Before giving the experimental group the treatment, we could test both groups to make sure that their visual acuity was approximately equal. After both groups had taken equal numbers of pills, we would test them again, once or more, to measure the effect of the treatment. (Again, ideally the person administering the test would not know who had taken which pill, or even why the test was being given.) We would compare any changes in average performance of the groups and determine whether they were statistically significant, that is, whether the difference was greater than that attributable to chance.

CRITICAL THINKING

Why is it impractical to establish experimental control through random assignment in research of adult development?

Random Assignment   In our vision pill experiment, if a significant difference emerged in the performance of the experimental and control groups, could we validly conclude that the pills were the cause? Not necessarily. We would have to be sure that initially the two groups were similar in all relevant ways, not just in visual acuity.

We have already discussed how random sampling can ensure external validity: generalizability of results beyond the study sample. The question here is one of **internal validity** for the sample itself—assurance that the outcome was due to the treatment and only to the treatment. How can we be sure that the vision pills and not some other factor (such as physical changes that might coincidentally have occurred during the course of the study) caused the difference in performance of the two groups?

The answer hinges on control of who gets the treatment. Experimenters achieve this control through **random assignment** of participants to experimental and control groups. This means that all members of a sample have an equal chance of being in the group that receives the treatment. If the sample is large enough, random assignment ensures that differences in such factors as age, sex, race, and socioeconomic status will be evenly distributed by chance, so that the experimental and control groups are as alike as possible in every way but one: receipt of the treatment. Random assignment controls for all other variables; it prevents these other variables from affecting the results, so that the outcome of the experiment will reflect only the impact of the independent variable (the treatment).

In our vision pill study, we could achieve internal validity if, after selecting the sample, we alternately drew names for the experimental and control groups. Of course, we could instead attempt to deliberately match the experimental and control groups for any and all factors that might have an effect. But no matter how carefully we matched groups for certain characteristics, we would probably miss others that might turn out to be just as important. The best way to control for such unforeseen factors is to assign participants randomly to experimental and control groups. Together, random sampling and random assignment can give an experiment both external and internal validity.

What makes scientific research so fascinating is that investigators can never be sure of the outcome of a study in advance. Although scientists often have hunches or hypotheses about what might occur in an experiment, nature seems ever ready to hand out surprises. For example, the experiment outlined above, if actually conducted, might show that the vision pills *decreased* visual acuity. Then we would have to look for, and test, a new hypothesis to explain that unexpected result.

LABORATORY, FIELD, AND NATURAL EXPERIMENTS

CRITICAL THINKING

What kinds of research seem most suitable to a laboratory setting and what kinds to a field setting? Give examples.

Methods such as random assignment are most easily used in *laboratory experiments,* in which researchers have full control and can isolate groups and variables for study. Not all studies can be neatly confined within a laboratory, but it's possible to achieve internal validity in experiments outside the laboratory—if researchers control who gets the treatment. A *field experiment* is a controlled study conducted in a setting (such as a supermarket, singles bar, or nursing home) that is part of everyday life.

Sometimes, for practical or ethical reasons, it is impossible to conduct a true experiment (though, as we discuss at the end of this chapter, scientists have at times done experiments that today would be considered unethical). For example, an experiment testing whether education has a protective effect against dementia would have to deprive the control group of education.

However, nature may provide the raw materials for a *natural experiment.* Here the investigator compares people who were divided into different groups by circumstances of life—one group who were exposed to, say, famine, venereal disease, a birth defect, or advanced education; and another group who were not. Natural experiments, because they do not permit manipulation of variables or control of assignment to groups, are actually correlational studies.

ISSUES OF CONSTRUCT VALIDITY AND FACTORIAL INVARIANCE

A boy received a voice-activated toy car for his fifth birthday. The car would careen across the floor when the boy said "Go!" After awhile, the boy decided to pull the wheels off the car and see what would happen. When he said "Go!" the car stood still. "Look," said the boy to his mother, "If you pull off all of a car's wheels, it goes deaf."

What is wrong with the boy's statement? Clearly, the treatment (removing the wheels) produced the effect he identified (failure to move when commanded). If he were to check his conclusion experimentally by removing the wheels of a randomly selected and assigned experimental group of voice-activated toy cars and not those of a control group, the cars in the control group would move on command, and those in the experimental group would not. Thus the experiment would have internal and external validity. Furthermore, the results should be easy to replicate.

The problem is that the boy was not studying the thing he thought he was studying. He thought he was studying hearing loss when he was actually studying physical mobility. His experiment lacked **construct validity** because the manipulations and measures he used were not pertinent to the *construct,* the phenomenon under study.

Researchers ensure construct validity in two ways: first, by precisely defining the construct; second, by finding more than one way to produce or measure it. The boy used only one criterion: the car's failure to move when commanded. Another measure (such as observing whether the axles still turned when the boy said "Go!") might suggest a different conclusion.

A related problem in research on adult development and aging is **factorial invariance**. It may not be appropriate to use the same instrument to measure a construct (phenomenon) in different age groups. For example, affirmative responses to such statements as "I feel a lot of aches and pains" and "I don't have as much energy as I used to" may be a valid index of depression in young adults. But those statements may be true for many older adults who are *not* depressed. One way to check for factorial invariance is to find out whether two or more items in a questionnaire show similar correlations in all age groups. For example, items about pains and energy may be positively related to items about feeling sad in almost all young adults, but not in almost all older adults.

QUASI-EXPERIMENTAL DESIGNS: THE PROBLEM OF INTERNAL VALIDITY

If we want to know how age affects some aspect of development, we are asking a question about a causal relationship; thus the appropriate research design would seem to be an experiment. Unfortunately, a true experiment on the effects of aging can't be done because the "treatment" under study is chronological age, and age is not subject to control.

Actually, the passage of time in itself does not change anything. When researchers set out to study effects of age, they are really studying the effects of processes associated with aging, such as long-term exposure to sunlight, which may cause wrinkles. But these processes vary among individuals, and investigators cannot randomly assign people to age groups so as to control for the variations; an experimenter cannot tell a participant, "Today you will be 45 years old." Without random assignment, we cannot be sure that age is the *only* relevant difference between groups. Therefore, most studies of age effects (as well as studies of other unalterable conditions, such as gender) use a special type of correlational design called a *quasi experiment*.

A **quasi experiment** looks something like an experiment. It may measure differences between groups, or changes following a treatment. But (like a natural experiment) it lacks a critical feature of all true experiments: control based on random assignment. Without the ability to randomly assign who

CRITICAL THINKING

What personal observations have you made that exemplify the statement "The passage of time in itself does not change anything"?

gets a treatment, the researcher cannot confi-
dently rule out alternative explanations for
the outcome. Quasi experiments, then, have
problems of internal validity. Let's look at
several types of quasi-experimental design
used in research on adult development and
aging.

Cross-Sectional Studies

Investigators who want to study effects of aging on, say, memory or physical strength typically compare the ability of groups of younger
and older adults to recall a string of numbers
or lift a certain weight. This research design,
in which people of different ages are assessed
on one occasion, is a **cross-sectional study**—
the design most commonly used in research on
adult development and aging.

Advantages of cross-sectional research include speed and economy; data can be gathered fairly quickly from large numbers of
people. A cross-sectional study can measure
age differences between groups of younger
and older adults, but, lacking random assignment of ages, a researcher cannot conclude that aging *causes* those differences.

A researcher has to consider threats to internal validity, including selective sampling
(people selected might be more capable or less

© Edward Holub/Corbis Images

*Going to a cafe takes on
new meaning with the ap-
pearance of Cyber Cafes.
Opportunities for new ex-
periences are available for
people of all ages, but
may be more influential
for a particular cohort.*

capable), selective survival (people who live longer might differ from people
who have died), and terminal change (people close to death might show declines in ability). Another threat to internal validity is that participants of different ages belong to different *cohorts*. A **cohort** is a group of people who have
shared a common experience, in this case, the experience of growing up at approximately the same time. People in different cohorts are affected by different formative cultural events (such as war, a stock market crash, the
assassination of a president, or the advent of computers). For example, the war
in Vietnam was a formative influence for the cohort growing up in the mid
1960s to the mid 1970s, just as the Great Depression was for the cohort growing up in the 1930s.

When we try to compare younger and older groups, then, how do we know
whether to attribute our observations to age differences or to cohort (generational) differences, or both? The effects of age and cohort may be *confounded*
(mixed together). This confounding, or confusion, of age and cohort effects is
an intrinsic flaw of cross-sectional research. Another challenge is the issue of

external validity (generalizing to other cross-sectional studies). Will the outcomes involving ages and cohorts be the same as the outcomes for the same ages with different cohorts? Understanding issues of internal and external validity has been important in lifespan research. This makes us more sensitive to what are real differences due to chronological age and what are sociocultural factors related to cohort specific (historical) experiences.

Cross-sectional studies are sometimes misinterpreted as yielding information about developmental changes—information that may be misleading, as the gerontologist Robert Kastenbaum suggests in this tongue-in-cheek observation:

> Occasionally I have the opportunity to chat with elderly people who live in the communities near Cushing Hospital. I cannot help but observe that many of these people speak with an Italian accent. I also chat with young adults who live in these same communities. They do *not* speak with an Italian accent. As a student of human behavior and development . . . I indulge in some deep thinking and come up with the following conclusion: as people grow older they develop Italian accents. (Quoted in Botwinick, 1984, p. 381)

What if, instead of observing a difference in accents, Kastenbaum had noted more rigid personality traits among elderly people than among younger adults? Could he validly attribute that difference to aging? Such an inference may seem more reasonable, and sometimes is made; but it still may be false. Older adults who are more rigid than younger adults may also have been more rigid in their youth. We cannot know unless they were studied then—and that would have required a longitudinal design.

Longitudinal Studies

Whereas cross-sectional research provides information about *differences* among age groups, a **longitudinal study** shows *changes* in the same person or persons (see Figure 2.3 and Box 2.3). In longitudinal research, the participants are studied more than once over a period of time, sometimes years apart. Researchers may measure one characteristic—such as IQ, height, aggressiveness, or size of vocabulary—or several characteristics. Longitudinal studies, then, can track long-term individual development. However, they are more time consuming and expensive than cross-sectional studies and are subject to internal validity issues such as attrition—participants may die (selective survival) or leave the study (drop out). Another likely shortcoming is sampling bias (selective sampling): people who volunteer for such studies (and especially those who stay with them) tend to be above average in intelligence and socioeconomic status. Still another problem is testing effects (practice effects): people who are tested repeatedly tend to do better because of practice with the questions or familiarity with the procedures. An additional threat to internal validity is terminal change.

Longitudinal studies also may have problems of external validity. Conclusions from a study of a particular cohort (say, people born in 1930) may not apply to other cohorts (say, people born in 1980).

CRITICAL THINKING

How might research results on the topic "strength and flexibility in adulthood" differ if data were collected using a cross-sectional versus a longitudinal study?

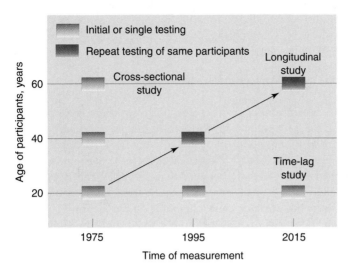

FIGURE 2.3 *Three designs for studying adult development.* In a *cross-sectional study*, adults of different ages are measured at the same time to obtain data about age-related *differences* in performance. Here, groups of 20-, 40-, and 60-year-olds were tested in 1975. In a *longitudinal study*, a group of adults is measured more than once to show age-related *changes* in individual performance. Here, young adults were first measured in 1975, when they were 20 years old. They were retested in 1995 at age 40 and are to be tested again in 2015 at age 60. In a *time-lag comparison*, which shows historical influences, different groups of people are measured at different times when they are the same age. Here, a group of 20-year-olds was tested in 1975; another group of 20-year-olds was tested in 1995; and a third group will be tested in 2015.

Furthermore, just as cross-sectional studies confound age effects and cohort effects, longitudinal studies confound age effects and time-of-measurement effects: cultural changes that occur between the times when measurements are taken. For example, intelligence test scores in the United States increased between World War I and World War II. Was this because people became smarter as they grew older, or because of a widening of educational opportunity? Lacking a control group that does not age, a longitudinal study cannot establish with certainty that the changes it reveals are effects of aging.

Time-Lag Studies

Erland Nelson (1954), in a longitudinal study of college students, attempted to untangle age from time-of-measurement effects. First, he tested students' attitudes toward a wide variety of issues. When he retested the participants 14 years later, he found their attitudes more liberal. Did this mean that liberalism increases during young adulthood? Such a conclusion might have seemed likely— except that, at the same time he retested his original sample, Nelson tested a *new* sample of college students the same age as the original sample had been

What Longitudinal Studies Can Tell Us

In 1932, Stuart Campbell, age 11, became one of more than 500 children recruited for three studies known collectively as the Berkeley Longitudinal Studies. Stuart had been effectively orphaned at age 6 (his mother died and his alcoholic father abandoned him) and was being raised in near-poverty by a stern but loving grandmother. The study in which Stuart was enrolled was the (Oakland) Adolescent Growth Study, which was designed to assess social and emotional development through the senior high school years. Twenty years later, a full-scale follow-up study began. A succession of interviews and tests enabled investigators to track Stuart's life through age 63.

Measures

All participants had medical examinations, and their family histories and current living situations were recorded. They took periodic intelligence and psychological tests, including personality inventories (instruments that yield psychometric, or quantitative, ratings of certain traits or groupings of traits). On the basis of recorded data and interviews, the researchers developed detailed life histories (case studies) of 60 participants.

Eventually the research began to focus on a theoretical construct (phenomenon) which the personality inventories called *planful competence*, a combination of self-confidence, intellectual commitment, and dependable effectiveness. Of the 60 participants for whom case studies were developed, Stuart Campbell had the highest score for planful competence.

Findings

The sociologist John A. Clausen (1993), analyzing the results of this longitudinal study, concluded that planful competence helps people mobilize resources and cope with difficulties. Planful competence did not *guarantee* success, nor did its absence ensure failure. But it did turn out to be the most powerful influence on the course of a person's life. Competent people made good choices in adolescence and early adulthood, which often led to promising opportunities (scholarships, good jobs, and competent spouses); less competent teenagers made

when first tested. This new sample was just as liberal as the retested sample and more liberal than the original group had been 14 years earlier—not surprisingly since the years from 1940 to 1954 had been a period of growing liberalism in American society. Nelson concluded that this historical change was probably the major influence on the change in the original participants' attitudes.

A **time-lag study**—what Nelson did in comparing the two groups of students—measures different cohorts at different times, when they are the same age (refer to Figure 2.3). Parents often make informal time-lag comparisons ("When I was your age . . . "). Although time-lag comparisons avoid confounding age with other effects, they do confound cohort and time of measurement. Both effects result from important cultural influences at particular times in history; but cohort effects, unlike time-of-measurement effects, may

poorer early decisions and then tended to lead crisis-ridden lives.

Stuart Campbell, for example, knew by age 17 that he wanted to be a doctor. He became a pediatrician, married early in life, went through an amicable divorce, married again (this time happily), had five children, and established a home and a solid professional and civic reputation in an upper-middle-class community. He was a strong family man, a man who could be counted on. At age 61, he was self-confident, intellectually involved, and dependable, as well as outgoing, warm, agreeable, and modestly assertive—all qualities he had shown since early adolescence.

Methodological Issues

"Longitudinal studies do not approach the neat precision of a well-conceived research design," said Clausen. "In some ways, they are messy and have loose ends. . . . Human lives are that way too" (p. 35).

For example, planful competence initially was a dependent variable. Researchers wanted to see whether and to what extent it was influ-enced by such independent variables as parenting practices, intelligence test scores, and social class. Later, during the adult phase of the study, planful competence became an independent variable; researchers measured its influence on success in life.

The report of these studies is entitled *American Lives*, but it is actually a report of only *some* American lives. The participants were a cohort born in the 1920s in one part of the country (the San Francisco Bay area). The sample (reflecting the population living there at the time) was almost entirely white, mostly native-born, Christian, and middle-class. Thus, the findings may lack external validity. Also, of the approximately 200 participants who dropped out, a disproportionate number were from families with financial or interpersonal problems, skewing the ultimate sample toward those with fewer problems.

Still, with these caveats, the findings can be useful as an indication of the persistence of personality traits throughout adulthood and of how human beings can help shape their own lives.

have occurred before the period under study. (Table 2.4 compares time-lag with cross-sectional and longitudinal designs.)

Sequential Designs

Some researchers might wish for a time machine, which would allow them to regress a representative sample of older adults to their younger selves and test them on, say, cognitive functioning. Then the machine would transport them back to the present. If a second test showed improvement or decline, it would be clear that age was the cause, since nothing else would have changed. In reality, of course, it is impossible to test the same group of people on the same day at different ages; and "experiments we perform in real life are efforts to

TABLE 2.4

Three Quasi-Experimental Designs

Design	Measures	Holds Constant	Internal Validity Confounds
Cross-sectional	Differences between age groups	Time of measurement	Cohort effects with age, selective sampling, selective survival, and terminal change
Longitudinal	Changes with age	Cohort	Time of measurement with age, practice effects, selective dropout, selective sampling, selective survival, and terminal change
Time-lag	Historical influences	Age	Time of measurement and cohort

approximate, as closely as possible, this nearly ideal state of affairs" (Lachman, Lachman, & Taylor, 1982, p. 282).

K. Warner Schaie (1965) provided a new methodological approach to the analysis of developmental data. Building on the cross-sectional, longitudinal, and time-lag designs, he combined these three approaches into three sequential designs. The *cohort-sequential design* separates age and cohort effects and their interactions by replicating a longitudinal study with two or more cohorts. Time-of-measurement effects are assumed to be minimal. The *time-sequential design* separates age and time of measurement and their interaction. This design involves replicating a cross-sectional study at one or more times of measurement. Cohort effects are assumed to be minimal. The *cross-sequential design* separates cohort and time of measurement and their interactions by using the time-lag method. Age effects are assumed to be minimal.

Suppose we start with a cross-sectional comparison in 1975, when five cohorts (age groups) ranging from ages 15 to 55 take an intelligence test (see Figure 2.4). We then test these people every 10 years through 2015, providing longitudinal data for each cohort. In addition, we make time-lag comparisons between cohorts; for example, we can compare 25-year-olds born in 1950 and tested in 1975 with 25-year-olds born in 1960 and tested in 1985. At each retesting, we add new participants from each cohort to detect improvements due to testing (practice) effects. For example, we can compare the scores of people tested for the second (or third or fourth or fifth) time in, say, 1995 with scores of people from the same cohort who are tested for the first time that same year.

CRITICAL THINKING

What differences in personal characteristics can you identify between you, a parent, and a grandparent that might result from cohort effects? What data, collected in a sequential design, would you compare to investigate your hypothesis with groups of people in these age groups?

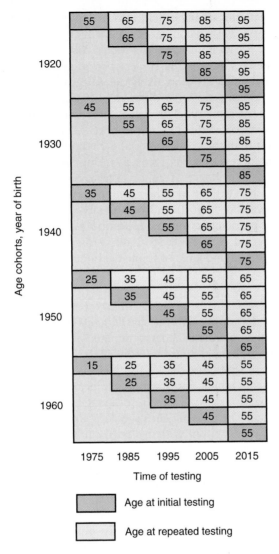

FIGURE 2.4 Schaie's "most efficient" sequential study design combines cross-sectional, longitudinal, and time-lag designs. Participants in five age cohorts are measured five successive times, 10 years apart. Each time, new participants in each cohort are added, to control for testing effects (improvements in performance with repeated testing). Comparisons among cohorts at the same time of testing show cross-sectional differences. Each cohort is also followed longitudinally, showing change through time. Time-lag comparisons are made possible by comparing, for example, 55-year-olds tested in 1975 with 55-year-olds (in other cohorts) tested in 1985, 1995, 2005, and 2015.

Such a design permits many other kinds of comparisons that help sort out effects. For example, we can compare changes in one cohort's scores between, say, ages 55 and 65 with changes in another cohort's scores between these same ages. If changes during this 10-year period are similar for the two cohorts, then such changes are more likely due to age differences than to cohort differences. But if cross-sectional differences (differences between scores of cohorts tested at the same time) are larger than longitudinal changes (differences in successive scores for the same cohort), then age-related effects may be less significant than the cross-sectional data alone would suggest.

Most sequential research has focused on intelligence. Sequential studies have provided clear evidence of cohort effects on intellectual performance (Schaie, 1990a; see Chapter 6). Their major drawbacks—and these can be daunting—involve time, effort, and complexity. Sequential designs require large numbers of participants and the collection and analysis of huge amounts of data over a period of many years. Interpreting their findings and conclusions can demand a high degree of sophistication.

ETHICS OF RESEARCH

Should research that might harm its participants ever be undertaken? How can we balance the possible benefits to humanity against the risk of intellectual, emotional, or physical injury to individuals?

Between the late 1940s and the 1970s, the United States government sponsored experiments in which unsuspecting adults and children were fed or injected with radioactive substances to test the effects of radiation in the event of a nuclear attack. The government's shocking disclosure of these studies in late 1993 elicited comparisons with the "medical" experiments the Nazis had perpetrated on Jews during World War II. The radiation research was also chillingly reminiscent of another infamous American government-supported study during approximately the same period: a 40-year study of the effects of untreated syphilis in black males (Jones, 1981).

In 1932, when that study began, syphilis—a progressive, sexually transmitted disease that eventually can produce paralysis, blindness, insanity, and major heart damage, leading to death—was spreading rapidly among the poor, mostly black population in rural Macon County, Alabama. Methods of treatment in existence at that time were of dubious safety and effectiveness. Officials of the U.S. Public Health Service, in cooperation with the respected Tuskegee Institute (which was located in the area) and state and county health agencies, took the opportunity to study the natural evolution of the disease in 399 black men who had never been treated. Free blood tests and medical examinations, hot lunches, and promises of free burial benefits induced the participants to submit to periodic painful spinal taps intended to determine how the disease was progressing.

The sponsors concealed the nature and purpose of the study from the mostly illiterate participants, who were falsely told that the spinal taps were treatments. Nor were they informed that they would be excluded from any future treatment that became available. The goal was "bringing them to autopsy" (Jones, 1981, p. 132). After the discovery of penicillin in the 1940s, information about the drug was withheld from them, and those who found out about it were actively discouraged from taking it. In the view of the sponsors, the growing use of this "wonder drug" made the Tuskegee study a final opportunity to study an untreated group of syphilitics. In reality, methodological defects, such as lack of any control group of treated syphilitics—and the fact that many of the participants did manage to get treatment on their own—made the study's findings worthless.

Although reports of the Tuskegee study were published from time to time in medical journals, no objection was raised until the mid 1960s. After the press broke the story in 1972, there was a congressional investigation that led to the termination of the study. Survivors sued the federal government and won an out-of-court settlement.

Today it is almost inconceivable that such a study would be conducted. Since the 1970s, federally mandated committees have been set up at colleges, universities, and other institutions to review proposed research from an ethical standpoint. The American Psychological Association's guidelines cover such points as protection of research participants from harm and loss of dignity, guarantees of privacy and confidentiality, informed consent, avoidance of deception, the right to decline or withdraw from an experiment at any time, and the responsibility of investigators to correct any undesirable effects (APA, 2002). Still, researchers may face troubling ethical questions.

CRITICAL THINKING
What steps should be taken to protect older adults and other vulnerable persons from harm due to participation in human research?

National Archive, Southeast Region

Home visits by a nurse, Eunice Rivers, were part of the Tuskegee study of the course of untreated syphilis, a classic illustration of the need for informed consent in research. The participants were mostly poor, illiterate black men in rural Macon County, Alabama, like this cotton farmworker. When safe, effective treatment became available, it was withheld from them. The study, which began in 1932, was ended 40 years later, after a congressional investigation. Ethical standards in effect today would prohibit such research on human beings.

One of the most disturbing aspects of both the radiation studies and the Tuskegee study is lack of informed consent. Informed consent exists when participants voluntarily agree to participate and are fully aware of risks as well as potential benefits. Ethical standards require that participants are competent to give consent and are not being exploited. But studies that seek causes and treatments for Alzheimer's disease, for example, need participants whose mental status may preclude their being fully or even partially aware of what is involved. When, if ever, is it appropriate for a demented person to be part of a study that may be beneficial to people with that condition? (An example would be the study cited earlier involving women with Alzheimer's disease who were tested to see if they could recognize smudges on their foreheads.) What if a person gives consent and later forgets having done so? If caregivers give consent, how can we be sure that they are acting in the patient's best interest? Current practice, to be on the safe side, is to ask *both* participants and caregivers for consent.

Obviously, informed consent cannot exist when participants are deceived about the nature of a study. In a controversial experiment at Yale University, Stanley Milgram (1963) probed how far ordinary Americans would go in obeying orders to hurt an innocent person. Participants who were recruited for a "learning experiment" were actually tested on their willingness to follow instructions to inflict apparently painful, increasingly strong "electric shocks" on an unsuccessful "learner" hidden behind a screen. In retrospect, the moral theorist Lawrence Kohlberg (1974b), who observed the study, called it "a morally dubious experiment" (p. 42) because of its effect on the participants' moral sensibilities. Research like this, which is intrinsically deceptive, may add to knowledge, but at the cost of participants' right to know what they are getting involved in.

It may be that precautions regarding informed consent have gone so far as to work *against* a patient's welfare in some instances. In recent tests, a new plunger-like pump was proving more effective than traditional methods in restoring blood circulation immediately after cardiac arrest. But since the unconscious patients were in no position to give informed consent, the U.S. Food and Drug Administration discontinued the study, even though the technique appeared to boost survival and recovery rates significantly (Hurley, 1994).

Should adults be subjected to research that may harm their self-esteem? Studies on limits of memory, for example, have a built-in "failure factor": the researcher keeps asking questions until the participant cannot answer. Might this inevitable failure affect a participant's self-confidence? Might the publication of studies in which younger adults score higher than older adults create self-fulfilling prophecies, affecting societal expectations and older adults' performance?

What about the right to privacy? Is it ethical to use one-way mirrors and hidden cameras to observe people without their knowledge? How can we protect the confidentiality of personal information that participants may reveal in interviews or questionnaires (for example, about income or family relationships or even about illegal activities, such as smoking marijuana or shoplifting)?

Despite the stringent rules and vastly improved ethical climate that prevail today, specific situations often call for hard judgments. Everyone in the field of adult development and aging must accept the responsibility to try to do good and, at the very least, to do no harm.

Summary and Key Terms

Metatheories

- A metatheory embraces theories and models with similar features in various branches of science. Scientists with different metatheoretical perspectives may study different problems, use different methods, and interpret data differently.
- Three important metatheories are the mechanistic, organismic, and contextual perspectives.
- The mechanistic perspective views behavior as machinelike and analyzes phenomena by breaking them down into simpler parts. Mechanists view development as quantitative and see aging as a time of decline. An example is information-processing theory.
- The organismic perspective views adults as organisms developing in a systematic, internally controlled order. Development occurs in a universal series of qualitative stages. An example is Erikson's theory of personality development.
- The contextual perspective views behavior as an ongoing act in a fluid context. Contextualists emphasize individual differences and see development as adaptive, as produced by interaction between the individual and the environment. Bühler's theory of setting goals and Sansone and Berg's "activated lifespace" model are examples.
- The lifespan developmental approach draws upon all three metatheories, particularly the contextual.

theory (p. 35)	**mechanistic perspective (p. 37)**
data (p. 35)	**information-processing theory**
quantitative development (p. 35)	**(p. 38)**
qualitative development (p. 36)	**organismic perspective (p. 38)**
metatheory (p. 36)	**stage (p. 38)**
model (p. 36)	**contextual perspective (p. 41)**

Basic Research Methods

- Research can be quantitative or qualitative.
- Research based on the scientific method can draw valid, reliable conclusions about the world and its inhabitants.
- Random selection of a research sample can ensure external validity. Stratification of a random sample can ensure representation of subgroups within the population.
- Cross-cultural research can check for generalizability of experimental results from one culture to another.
- Forms of data collection include self-reports (diaries, structured or open-ended interviews, and questionnaires), tests and other behavioral measures, and naturalistic or laboratory observation. The value of self-reports is limited by subjectivity; the value of observation is limited by observer bias.

valid (p. 43)	**quantitative research (p. 43)**
reliable (p. 43)	**qualitative research (p. 43)**

Basic Research Designs

- Three basic designs used in developmental research are case studies, correlational studies, and experiments.

- Only experiments can establish causal relationships. Case studies and correlational studies can provide hypotheses or predictions to be tested by experimental research.

- Experiments must be rigorously controlled so as to be valid and reliable. Random assignment of participants to experimental or control groups ensures internal validity.

- In laboratory experiments, researchers have full control and can isolate variables for study. However, controlled field experiments also can achieve internal validity.

- Natural experiments, which are actually correlational studies, may be useful in situations where true experiments would be impractical or unethical.

- To ensure construct validity, a researcher must precisely define the phenomenon being studied and should use more than one way to measure it.

Quasi-Experimental Designs: The Problem of Internal Validity

- Because age is beyond the researcher's control, most studies of age effects are quasi experiments, which present problems of internal validity.

- Cross-sectional designs confound age with cohort effects. Longitudinal studies confound age with time-of-measurement effects. Time-lag comparisons confound cohort with time of measurement. Sequential designs combine the quasi-experimental designs.

Ethics of Research

- Ethical issues in research on development include informed consent, deception, self-esteem, and privacy of participants.

Longevity and Physiological Aging

◈ **FOCUS: JOHN GLENN, SPACE PIONEER**

The truth is the old stereotypes no longer fit, if ever they did. Older people are increasingly active. While the processes I was going to study in space do tend to slow people down as they age, increased longevity and better health mean more people are doing more things than ever before.

—*John Glenn,* John Glenn: A Memoir, *1999.*

WHEN JOHN H. GLENN, Jr.* (b. 1921) blasted off from the Kennedy Space Center at Cape Canaveral on October 29, 1998 as a payload specialist on the shuttle *Discovery*, he became a space pioneer for the second time. In 1962, at the age of 40, Glenn had been the first American to orbit the earth. What made him a pioneer in 1998, when he next donned the orange jumpsuit, was that he was 77

NASA

*Sources of information about John Glenn were Cutler (1998), Eastman (1965), and articles from the *New York Times* and other newspapers.

years old—the oldest person ever to go into outer space.

Throughout his adult life, Glenn has won medals and set records. As a fighter pilot during the Korean War, he earned five Distinguished Flying Crosses. In 1957 he made the first cross-country supersonic jet flight. In 1962, when his *Friendship 7* one-man space capsule circled the globe three times in less than 5 hours, he instantly became a national hero.

Glenn was elected a U.S. senator from Ohio in 1974 and served four terms. As a member of the Senate Special Committee on Aging and a grandfather of two, his interest in the subject of aging prompted him to offer himself as a human guinea pig on the 9-day *Discovery* mission.

As Glenn discovered while browsing through a medical textbook, the zero-gravity conditions of space flight mimic at accelerated speed what normally happens to the body as it ages. Thus, Glenn reasoned, sending an older man into space might give scientists a thumbnail glimpse of processes of aging. By studying how weightlessness affected Glenn's bones, muscles, blood pressure, heart rates, balance, immune system, and sleep cycles, as well as his ability to bounce back after the flight as compared with younger astronauts, medical researchers could obtain information that might ultimately have broader applications. The data would not, of course, provide conclusive findings; but, as in any good case study, the findings could generate hypotheses to be tested by further research with larger groups of participants. The flight also would

have an important side effect: to demolish common stereotypes about aging.

Space travel is a challenge even for the youngest and most physically fit adults. Not everyone can be an astronaut; candidates have to pass stringent physical and mental tests. Because of his age, Glenn was held to even tougher physical standards. An avid weightlifter and power-walker, he was in superb physical condition. He passed the examinations with flying colors and then spent nearly 500 hours in training.

It was a clear, cloudless October day when, after two suspenseful delays, the shuttle *Discovery* lifted off with what the countdown commentator called "a crew of six astronaut heroes and one American legend." Three hours and 10 minutes later, 342 miles above Hawaii, a beaming Glenn repeated his own historic words broadcast 36 years before: "Zero G, and I feel fine." On November 7, *Discovery* touched down at Cape Canaveral, and John Glenn, though weak and wobbly, walked out of the shuttle on his own two feet. Within 4 days he had fully recovered his balance and was completely back to normal.

Glenn's achievement proved that, at 77, he still had "the right stuff." His heroic exploit captured public imagination around the world. As Stephen J. Cutler, president of the Gerontological Society of America, put it, " . . . it's hard to imagine a better demonstration of the capabilities of older persons and of the productive contributions they can make" (Cutler, 1998, p. 1).

JOHN GLENN EPITOMIZES A NEW view of aging, challenging the formerly pervasive picture of old age as a time of inevitable physical and mental decline. On the whole, people today are living longer and better than at any other time in history. In the United States, older adults as a group are healthier, more numerous, and younger at heart than ever before. With improved health habits and medical care, it is becoming harder to draw the line between the end of middle adulthood and the beginning of late adulthood. Many 70-year-olds act, think, and feel much as 50-year-olds did a decade or two ago.

Today, with medical advances allowing many people to live longer and better than at any previous time in human history, more and more ordinary adults are defying age by running marathons, lifting weights, climbing mountains, playing competitive sports, and living active and productive lives through their eighties and beyond. Of course, not all older adults are models of vigor and zest. Indeed, Glenn's achievement is impressive precisely because it is unusual. As we will see throughout this book, older adults vary greatly in health, education, income, occupation, and living arrangements. Like people of all ages, they are individuals with differing needs, desires, abilities, lifestyles, and cultural backgrounds.

In this chapter and Chapter 4, we look at physical development throughout adulthood. We start with influences on length of life and theories of why bodies age. We describe physiological changes often associated with aging: gradual changes in appearance, sensory and motor abilities, and sexual and reproductive capacities. In Chapter 4, we discuss changes in internal body systems and factors that contribute to health and disease.

LIFE SPAN AND THE AGING PROCESS

How long will I live? Why do I have to grow old? Would I want to live forever? Human beings have been wondering about these questions for thousands of years.

The first question involves two different but related concepts: **life expectancy**, the age to which a person born at a certain time and place is statistically likely to live; and **longevity**, how long a particular person actually does live. Life expectancy is based on the average longevity, or life span, of members of a population. The second question expresses an age-old theme: a yearning for a fountain or potion of youth. Behind this yearning is a fear, not so much of chronological age, as of biological aging: loss of health and physical powers. Similarly, the third question expresses a concern not just with how long but with how well we live.

CRITICAL THINKING

What evidence supports the argument that our culture is shifting from a fascination with youth to an appreciation of middle age and older adulthood?

Trends in Life Expectancy

Today, most people can expect to grow old, often very old. A person born in the United States in 2000 could expect to live 76.9 years, about 30 years longer than a person born in 1900 (Vierck & Hodges, 2003). Worldwide, average life expectancy has risen 37 percent since 1955—from 48 years to 66 years—and is projected to reach 73 years by 2025 (World Health Organization [WHO], 1998). Such longevity, unprecedented in human history (see Figure 3.1), is directly related to the graying of the population. It reflects a sharp decline in mortality rates (the proportions of a total population, or of certain age groups, who die in a given year). Today's longer life span stems largely from a dramatic reduction in infant and child deaths; fewer young

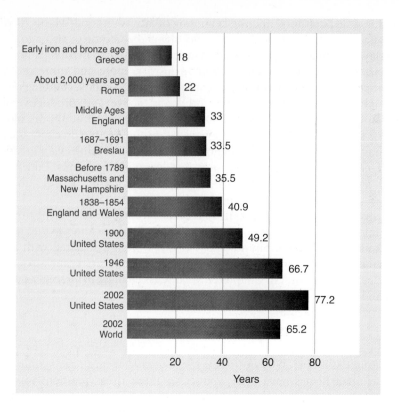

FIGURE 3.1 *Changes in life expectancy from ancient to modern times.* *SOURCE:* Adapted from Katchadourian, 1987; 1998 data from Martin et al., 1999, and WHO, 1998, 2003.

adult deaths, particularly of women in childbirth; new treatments for many once-fatal illnesses; and a better-educated, more health-conscious population who are receiving more effective health care in the middle and later years (Rowe & Kahn, 1998).

In the United States, death rates from heart disease (the leading cause of death in late adulthood) have been cut in half since 1970 among 65- to 84-year-olds and have dropped 21 percent among those 85 and older (National Center for Health Statistics [NCHS], 1999a). The other leading causes of death in late life, in descending order, are cancer, stroke, lung disease, accidents, diabetes, influenza, pneumonia, and Alzheimer's disease (CDC, 2006).

The longer people live, the longer they are likely to continue living. Americans who made it to age 65 in 1998 could expect to reach nearly 83—about 6 years more than the life expectancy of an infant born in 1998 (R. N. Anderson, 1999). If mortality rates remain constant, persons age 65 and older in 2000 will live an average of 18 more years—6 years longer than persons aged 65 in 1900, who had a remaining life expectancy of 12 years (Older Americans, 2000). Life expectancy at birth is lower in the United States than in many other industrialized countries that have lower infant mortality rates, but the gap closes by very old age, possibly because of more education or greater expenditures on health care in the United States (Manton & Vaupel, 1995). Less-educated people tend to have more serious diseases and disabilities, and therefore higher mortality rates (Amaducci et al., 1998).

Race and gender are factors in life expectancy. White Americans made up 84 percent of the population aged 65 and older in 2000, a proportion that is expected to decline to 64 percent by 2050. On average, white Americans live about 6 years longer than African Americans, and women live about 5 to 6 years longer than men (Martin et al., 1999). It has been estimated that in the year 2000, 58 percent of persons aged 65 and older, and 70 percent of persons 85 and older, were women (Older Americans, 2000).

How Far Can the Human Life Span Be Extended?

In 1986, a Japanese man named Shigechiyo Izumi died of pneumonia at age 120, and in 1997 Jeanne Calment of France died at the age of 122. The oldest known living person is in Brazil and she is 125 (see photo on p. 76). As far as we know, theirs are the longest authentically documented human lives. Many gerontologists long maintained that 110 to 120 years was the upper limit of human longevity, but research on various organisms is challenging the idea of a genetically unalterable limit for each species. Scientists have extended the healthy life span of worms, fruit flies, and mice through slight genetic mutations (Ishii et al., 1998; T. E. Johnson, 1990; Kolata, 1999; Lin, Seroude, & Benzer, 1998; Parkes et al., 1998; Pennisi, 1998). In human beings, genetic control of a biological process may be far more complex. Today, however, scientists are reconsidering the idea of a fixed limit of life. Is it possible for a human being to live to 130, 150, or even 200? With continued medical progress, is there any limit to how long people could live?

At least part of the key to the maximum life span for each species appears to be in the *genes*: bits of deoxyribonucleic acid (DNA), strung on chromosomes, which govern the inherited characteristics of every living thing. DNA carries the "program"—unique to each individual—that tells each cell what functions to perform and how.

Leonard Hayflick (1974; 2003) studied cells of various animals and found a limit on the number of times a cell would divide—about 50 times for human cells; this is called the **Hayflick limit**. Cells divide by duplicating their DNA and associated proteins, including chromosomes. When the chromosomes have doubled, the cell divides. Each chromosome has a telomere (a DNA sequence that caps chromosomes) at the end, and the telomere is what researchers currently believe to be the critical element in determining when a cell will stop dividing. With each cell division, the telomere shortens and when it becomes too short, the cell can no longer divide. Thus, there seems to be a biological clock that limits the life span of human cells and therefore of human life. According to Hayflick, if all diseases and causes of death were eliminated, humans would remain healthy until about 110 years of age. Then the cellular clock would run out and they would die, much as the biological clock that controls the female menstrual cycle turns off, typically between ages 45 and 55.

© George Gobet/AFP/Getty Images

Maria Olivia da Silva of Astorga, Brazil, is the world's oldest known living person. Born in 1880, she celebrated her 125th birthday on February 28, 2005.

Recent research calls that idea into question. Researchers have isolated genes that affect longevity in yeast, worms, and fruit flies. A mutant gene has been identified that extends the life span of roundworms by 60 percent—from 26 days to 60—while they remain biologically young (T. E. Johnson, 1990). Fruit flies have been selectively bred to nearly double their normal life span (Rose, cited in National Institute on Aging [NIA], 1993).

Perhaps the most promising line of research is on calorie restriction (CR), strictly limiting caloric intake to lengthen life span (see Box 3.1 on p. 78). Studies of CR have been done on worms, mice, rats, and dogs and have extended life in each species. In studies of rats and mice, CR extended life up to 40 percent, while decreasing the incidence of cardiovascular disease, cancer, diabetes, osteoporosis, and neurological decline (Okie, 2001).

What, if anything, might such research tell us about the human life span? In 1987, the National Institute on Aging (NIA) began a long-term study (which is still continuing) on primates to determine whether CR will be effective in higher-order species. Primates on CR have elevated levels of good cholesterol, decreased levels of triglycerides, and lower blood pressure, all of which reduce the risk of cardiovascular disease, as well as lower risk for developing diabetes (Goddard, 2002; NIH, 1997). These findings fit in with theories that view the rate of metabolism, or energy use, as the crucial determinant of aging (Masoro, 1985, 1988, 1992; Sohal & Weindruch, 1996). Caloric restriction also seems to reduce production of free radicals, facilitate DNA repair, and preserve the immune system's ability to fight disease (Walford, quoted in Couzin, 1998).

Research on the exploding centenarian population is shattering long-established beliefs about health and aging and about the limits of human life. **Survival curves**—the percentages of members of a species that live to various ages—have supported the idea of a biological limit to the life span, with more and more members dying each year as they approach it (see Figure 3.2). Internationally, average life expectancies in industrialized countries hover between 74 and 83 despite differences in diet and lifestyle (see Figure 3.3). However, it now appears that the pattern changes after age 100: mortality rates begin to decrease. People at 110 are no more likely to die in a given year than people in their eighties. The same thing is true of fruit flies, wasps, and parasitic worms: at a certain point late in the life span, death rates peak and then drop (Vaupe et al., 1998). In other words, individuals hardy enough to reach a certain age are likely to go on living a while longer. But how much longer? That is the question life-extension research seeks to answer.

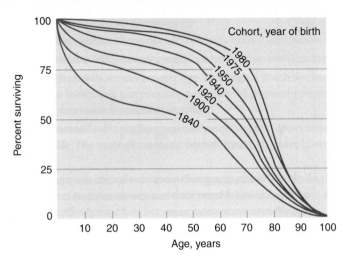

FIGURE 3.2 Survival curves show the percentage of persons born in the United States in selected years who survived, or are expected to survive, to each age. Survival curves have become increasingly "rectangularized" as life expectancy has increased owing to medical advances. But while a larger percentage of the population is surviving to more advanced ages, the curves still drop to zero by about age 100, suggesting that there may be a genetically determined limit to human life. *SOURCE: Katchadourian, 1987.*

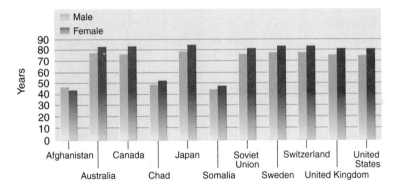

FIGURE 3.3 People in wealthy, industrialized countries, such as Switzerland and Japan, live longer than people in developing countries, such as Afghanistan and Somalia, where more people die prematurely of infectious diseases, starvation, and other ailments. But there is little variance in life expectancy *among* industrialized countries. For example, the Japanese (who have a low-fat diet) and the Swiss (who eat a good deal of fat) have virtually the same life expectancy—suggesting that there may be a limit to the life-extending potential of diet, health care, and other lifestyle factors. *SOURCE: People Facts-Population Life Expectancy (April 9, 2001) http://www.os-connect.com/pop/p1.htm.*

Can We Push Out the Boundaries of Life?

A 100-year-old man was asked, "What can people do to help them live as long as you have?" The centenarian thought for a moment and then responded, "Well, first make sure that you don't die."

Are there ways to slow down the aging process and delay death? The novelist Tom Robbins, in *Jitterbug Perfume* (1984), gives some fanciful but research-based answers to that question. The novel revolves around two characters who find a way to live hundreds of years without aging. Their secret is based on principles related to the four ancient "elements": *air* (breathing deeply and steadily), *fire* (frequent sex), *water* (hot baths, followed by cooling off), and *earth* (eating small portions and fasting periodically). To what extent does research support Robbins's four points?

The first life-extending technique, deep and rhythmic breathing, is supposed to lessen the ravages of stress and of free radicals produced during the metabolism of oxygen, which damage cell tissue. The characters in *Jitterbug Perfume* believe that proper breathing will reduce the level of free radicals in the body. Research to support that idea is scanty or inconclusive. However, deep, rhythmic breathing *is* widely used in yoga and other meditation or relaxation techniques to ward off stress. And stress (as we discuss in Chapter 4) is a special threat to older adults.

As for the second life-extending technique, frequent sexual intercourse, most research has found a direct relationship between sexual activity and health; and people who are sexually active in middle age are more likely to remain sexually active in old age (Katchadourian, 1987). But can sexual activity actually lengthen the normal life span? Such an effect is not well documented—though perhaps the emotional aspects of a healthy sex life with a willing and understanding partner create psychological benefits, such as reduced stress, which might influence longevity.

In an aging body, the autoimmune system tends to attack the body's own cells because it confuses them with invading organisms (see Chapter 4). The third life-extension technique is based on the belief that a sudden contrast be-

The potential implications of research on human systematic life extension are staggering. Life-extension studies have raised hopes for eventual realization of the age-old dream of a "fountain of youth"; but they also raise ethical questions about the propriety of "tinkering" with human life and worries about the costs of supporting an elderly population far more numerous than currently projected.

A key question is whether increased longevity would be accompanied by the disappearance or postponement of age-related diseases (Banks & Fossel, 1997). The motto of the Gerontological Society of America is "To Add Life to Years, Not Just Years to Life." The goal of research is not just to lengthen life but also to lengthen the vigorous and productive years. However, given

tween hot and cold will check this tendency by cooling the blood and decreasing body temperature. Accordingly, the technique consists of a series of hot baths, each followed by getting out and cooling off. However, no research as yet supports this idea.

That leaves Robbins's fourth technique: eating less. Here he may be on somewhat firmer ground. As reported in this chapter, drastically reducing the caloric intake of rodents, fish, worms, and other species, while giving them necessary vitamins and other nutrients, dramatically increases their life span while they retain youthful appearance and health.

Roy Walford was one of the forerunners in studying the effects of a calorie restrictive (CR) diet and how it may lengthen and improve quality of life. He began his research on rats and then began following CR himself. He began by cutting his average daily food intake to 1,500 to 2,000 calories (largely vegetables and grains), as compared with 2,500 for the average man, and reduced his weight by 25 percent. He also took many vitamins, and kept physically active to stay in shape.

"There is no doubt at all that the life span of animals can be extended by more than 50 percent by dietary means, corresponding to humans living to be 150 or 160 years old," Walford wrote (1986, p. 18). He predicted that people who adopt a lifestyle like his might double their remaining life expectancy (Angier, 1990) while retaining more youthful appearance and vigor (Weindruch & Walford, 1988). Born in 1925, Walford hoped to continue his experiment until 2065, when, if his hypothesis was borne out, he would have lived to be 140.

But in April of 2004, Walford died from amyotrophic lateral sclerosis (ALS, also known as Lou Gehrig's disease) at age 79, thus ending his experiment on himself. ALS is a genetic disease with no known cure, making death inevitable, and is unrelated to CR. Advocates suggest that CR helped Walford live well past the considerably shortened life span of someone with ALS, but this conjecture cannot be proven. Currently, a small group of life exentionists practice CR in hopes of staving off the effects of aging and living longer lives.

the rising rates of chronic conditions such as obesity, high blood pressure, diabetes, and asthma among younger generations, economists suggest that expanded life spans will increase these risks, as well as the cost of caring for the elderly (Lehrman, 2001).

Even if science conquers all diseases and all older adults stay healthy until they reach their genetically predetermined end, will society have a place for all of them? According to one estimate, by the year 2050 retirees will outnumber workers 100 to 36 (Lehrman, 2001). Can national economies grow fast enough to meet these challenges without placing an insupportable burden on a shrinking number of working adults (Binstock, 1993; Crown, 1993; WHO, 1998)?

CRITICAL THINKING

What elements do you believe are essential to maintain a high quality of life for the aging individual? What elements are essential to society as a whole?

Theories of Biological Aging

CRITICAL THINKING

What explanations seem to account for differences between people who age well versus those who seem to deteriorate quickly?

Questions of longevity and quality of life are intimately connected with what happens to our bodies as we age. A typical young adult is a fine physical specimen. Strength, energy, agility, endurance, and health are at their peak. The senses are sharpest, and body systems work at top efficiency. From young adulthood through midlife, physical losses are typically so small and so gradual as to be barely noticed. But as people age, their physical differences increase. The onset of **senescence**—the period of the life span marked by obvious declines in body functioning generally associated with aging—varies greatly. One 80-year-old man can hear every word of a whispered conversation; another cannot hear the doorbell. One 70-year-old woman runs marathons; another cannot walk around the block.

Why does senescence come earlier for some people than for others? For that matter, why do people age biologically at all? Most theories about biological aging fall into two general categories: *genetic-programming theories* and *variable-rate theories* (see Table 3.1).

GENETIC-PROGRAMMING THEORIES

Genetic-programming theories hold that bodies age according to a normal developmental timetable built into the genes. Since each species has its own life expectancy and pattern of aging, this pattern must be predetermined and inborn, subject to only minor modifications.

Genetic-programming theory is consistent with the idea of a genetically decreed maximum life span. Hayflick's (1981; 2003) suggestion that human cells in a laboratory culture go through the same aging process as within the body implies that environmental influences play little or no role in aging (Gerhard & Cristofalo, 1992; Hayflick, 2003). And that the human body, like a machine, is biologically programmed to fail at a certain point, even if kept in tip-top condition. Failure may come through *programmed senescence*, in which specific genes "switch off" at times when age-related losses (for example, in vision, hearing, and motor control) become evident. Or the biological clock may act through genes which control *hormonal changes*, or which cause problems in the *immune system*, leaving the body vulnerable to infectious disease.

A variant of genetic-programming theory is that genes are programmed to enable humans to live long enough to reproduce. Like a booster stage, which has no further function after putting a satellite into orbit and eventually burns out, adults may continue to live past the childbearing years, but the genetic program no longer can help them and may even hurt them.

If genes control aging, could tinkering with the genetic program overcome programmed biological declines and extend life? We need to remember that genetic control of a biological process can be extremely complex. Approximately 200 genes seem to be involved in regulating human aging (Schneider, 1992), with specific genes controlling different processes, such as those in the endocrine and immune systems. **Gene therapy** (replacement or insertion of genes to correct a defect, improve functioning, or delay senescence) is not rec-

TABLE 3.1

Theories of Biological Aging

Genetic-Programming Theories

Programmed senescence. Aging is the result of the sequential switching on and off of certain genes, with senescence being defined as the time when age-associated deficits are manifested.

Endocrine theory. Biological clocks act through hormones to control the pace of aging.

Immunological theory. A programmed decline in immune system functions leads to an increased vulnerability to infectious disease and thus to aging and death.

Variable-Rate Theories

Wear and tear. Cells and tissues have vital parts that wear out.

Free radicals. Accumulated damage caused by oxygen radicals causes cells and eventually organs to stop functioning.

Rate of living. The greater an organism's rate of oxygen basal metabolism, the shorter its life span.

Error catastrophe. Damage to mechanisms that synthesize proteins results in faulty proteins, which accumulate to a level that causes catastrophic damage to cells, tissues, and organs.

Somatic mutation. Genetic mutations occur and accumulate with increasing age, causing cells to deteriorate and malfunction.

Crosslinking. An accumulation of crosslinked proteins damages cells and tissues, slowing down bodily processes.

SOURCE: Adapted from NIH/NIA, 1993, p. 2.

ommended at present, as clinical studies have not been effective. Several factors have prevented gene therapy from becoming a successful treatment, including the short life span of the treated gene, the automatic response of the immune system to attack foreign objects, the lack of a reliable carrier of the treated gene, and the fact that the most common diseases are not all from the same gene (Human Genome Project, 2003).

VARIABLE-RATE THEORIES

Variable-rate theories, sometimes called *error theories*, view aging as a result of processes that vary from person to person and are influenced by both the internal and the external environments. In most variable-rate theories, aging involves damage due to chance errors in, or environmental assaults on, people's biological systems. Other variable-rate theories focus on internal processes such as metabolism (the process by which the body turns food and oxygen into energy), which may more directly and continuously influence the rate of aging (NIA, 1993; Schneider, 1992).

Wear-and-tear theory holds that the body ages as a result of accumulated damage to the system, like a car that develops one problem after another as its parts wear out. This wearing-out process occurs more swiftly under stress. Today, most theorists do not believe that normal wear and tear is an adequate explanation for aging. For one thing, a human being (unlike a car) is capable of self-repair and can compensate for damage to the system.

Free-radical theory focuses on the harmful effects of **free radicals**—highly unstable atoms or molecules formed during metabolism, which react with and can damage cell membranes, cell proteins, fats, carbohydrates, and even DNA. Damage from free radicals accumulates with age and has been associated with such diverse diseases as arthritis, muscular dystrophy, cataracts, and cancer (Stadtman, 1992). It has been suggested that defective molecules (possibly the result of injury induced by free radicals) may cause late-onset diabetes and neurological disorders such as Parkinson's disease (Wallace, 1992). "Antioxidant" supplements of vitamins C and E and beta-carotene are popularly believed to stop free-radical activity, but research on their effects is inconclusive. Also, it is not clear whether accumulation of free radicals (or other "errors") is a *cause* or an *effect* of aging.

Rate-of-living theory suggests that the body can do just so much work, and that's all; the faster it works, the faster it wears out. According to this theory, speed of metabolism determines length of life. For example, fish whose metabolism is lowered by putting them in cooler water live longer than they would in warm water (Schneider, 1992). The research on dietary restriction in rodents also appears to support this theory. A low-calorie diet seems to temper the long-term harmful effects of glucose, or blood sugar (including free-radical formation), and lower the rate of metabolism (Masoro, 1985).

Error-catastrophe theory and *somatic-mutation theory* are based on the fact that as body cells divide, errors (destruction or changes in cellular structure) occur. External and internal stressors, such as exposure to toxic substances and ultraviolet light, may alter the composition of cells and tissues in the brain, liver, and other organs; and as they grow older, they are less able to repair themselves. Eventually, according to this theory, an accumulation of these erroneous occurrences causes deterioration of body parts, malfunctioning, and death.

Cross-linking theory attributes errors to bonds, or links, that form between cellular proteins. For example, cross-linking of the protein collagen makes the skin less flexible. There is some recent evidence that high levels of blood sugar, as in diabetes, cross-link proteins in the lens of the eye and in the kidneys and blood vessels, causing disease (Schneider, 1992).

COMPARING GENETIC-PROGRAMMING
AND VARIABLE-RATE THEORIES

If human beings are programmed to age at a certain rate, they can do little to retard the process except, perhaps, look for controlling genes and attempt to alter them. But if aging is variable, then lifestyle and health practices may influence it.

Variable-rate theories seem better able to explain the wide variations in physiological aging. It may be, though, that each of these perspectives offers part of the truth. Genetic programming may limit the maximum length of life, but environmental and lifestyle factors may affect how closely a person approaches the maximum and in what condition. For example, people who limit their exposure to the sun may be able to minimize wrinkling and avoid skin cancer.

Some gerontologists make a distinction between *primary* and *secondary* aging. **Primary aging** is a gene-coded gradual, inevitable process of bodily deterioration that begins early in life and continues through the years. **Secondary aging** consists of results of disease, abuse, and disuse—factors that are often avoidable and within people's control (Busse, 1987; Horn & Meer, 1987). By eating sensibly and keeping physically fit, many older adults can and do stave off secondary effects of aging.

Predicting Individual Longevity

Is it possible to predict how long a particular person—you, for example—will live? Life insurance companies make such predictions when they set premium rates on the basis of variables that appear to be correlated with longevity. For example, before the practice was outlawed as discriminatory, men generally paid higher rates than women because women tend to live longer.

Good health is positively correlated with long life. So are exercise, nutrition, education, intelligence, socioeconomic status, satisfaction with work, long-lived parents and grandparents, a positive attitude toward life, and the ability to cope with adversity. Variables that are negatively correlated with long life include being overweight, poor, illiterate, chronically ill, or unmarried; smoking; bearing children after age 35; and having high blood pressure, many children, psychiatric disturbances such as schizophrenia or depression, or a family history of diseases such as cancer or diabetes (Botwinick, 1984).

But while these variables predict life expectancy for certain classes of people, they cannot predict an individual's life span. Furthermore, correlational analyses cannot tell us what *causes* long life. The fact that it tends to run in families, for example, doesn't indicate whether the cause is hereditary, environmental, or both. Some predictors of longevity tend to cluster together. People with high-paying jobs are also likely to have higher education and income and better access to medical care than people with low-paying jobs. But do any of these factors actually cause people to live longer? Again, we don't know.

Some scientists, in an attempt to identify biological processes that actually determine an individual life span, are searching for **biomarkers** of aging: specific, universally valid measures of biological age. No single biomarker is likely to predict a person's life span. Investigators look for a set of physical attributes, such as lung capacity, size of heart, strength of grip, and reaction time, which together may be reasonably accurate in predicting how long a person has left to live (Sprott & Roth, 1992; Walford, 1986). Most of the data collected so far have been cross-sectional and therefore cannot measure changes in the same individual. Longitudinal studies of various physiological changes in nonhuman primates are now in progress.

Although it would be premature to draw any conclusions, at least two possible biomarkers seem to be good candidates: declines in immune system functioning and in blood levels of the hormone dehydroepiandrosterone (DHEA), which is produced by the adrenal glands (Sprott & Roth, 1992). Most 70-year-olds have only one-tenth as much DHEA as they did at 25 (August, 1995). Low levels of DHEA have been associated with immune dysfunction, inflammation, increased risk of some cancers, heart disease (in men), and osteoporosis (Greenwell, 2001).

Keep in mind that biomarkers of aging and biomarkers of longevity are not necessarily the same. For example, a widely observed drop in cognitive functioning before death (see Chapters 6 and 13) may indicate that a person will soon die but not how rapidly the body is aging (Sprott & Roth, 1992). And increasing the length of life is not identical with increasing the length of time the body remains biologically young. Still, in research on caloric restriction, the long-lived rodents do appear to maintain their vitality and to develop age-related diseases later than normal.

CRITICAL THINKING
What age do you predict that you will reach, based on key variables identified through correlational analyses?

We are a long way from being able to point to biological markers that can accurately predict an individual human life span. Even if scientists succeed in finding these markers, to what use should such information be put? Would it affect the cost and availability of health insurance and pension benefits? Would you want to know how long you are likely to live? Would that knowledge change the way you live?

PHYSICAL APPEARANCE

There is no "typical adult." At any age, adults come in many sizes and shapes. They differ in strength, stamina, and other physical abilities. They have different lifestyles. Their body systems age at different rates, and their health varies. Outward appearance also varies; a 30-year-old may look more like 40, and some older adults look middle-aged. Still, we can sketch changes in physical appearance that typically take place with age—changes that can affect how adults are treated and how they feel about themselves.

Young adults normally have smooth, taut skin, and their hair has color, fullness, and sheen. Today's 20-year-olds tend to be taller than their parents because of a *secular trend* in growth that has taken place during the past century in developed countries. Young people in the United States, western Europe, and Japan reach adult height and sexual maturity earlier than in past generations, apparently because of better nourishment and health care (Chumlea, 1982; Eveleth & Tanner, 1976).

Most young adults are quite appearance conscious. The ideal of a slim, lean physique fuels the diet industry and fosters such eating disorders as anorexia (self-starvation) and bulimia (binging and purging). Still, many young adults are too fat; the risk of being overweight, which threatens not only appearance but health, is highest from ages 25 to 34 (Williamson,

Kahn, Remington, & Anda, 1990). (We discuss diet, obesity, and exercise in Chapter 4.)

"Middle age," said the comedian Bob Hope, "is when your age starts to show around your middle." Especially in men who lead sedentary lives, middle-age spread increases markedly until about age 55 to 60, as fat replaces muscle. Habitual facial expressions set into "character" lines (Katchadourian, 1987).

By late adulthood, physical changes become more obvious. The skin tends to become paler and splotchier; it takes on a parchmentlike texture, loses elasticity, and hangs in folds and wrinkles. Varicose veins of the legs are more common. In both men and women, the hair on the head turns white and becomes thinner, and sometimes it sprouts in new places—on a woman's chin, or out of a man's ears. People may become shorter as the disks between their spinal vertebrae atrophy, and they may look even smaller because of stooped posture. In some women a thinning of the bone (see Chapter 4) may cause a "widow's hump" at the back of the neck.

Because our society places a premium on youth, middle-aged and older adults spend a great deal of time, effort, and money trying to maintain a youthful appearance. Although many "anti-aging" treatments are useless, emollient creams and lotions offer temporary improvement in skin tone and moisture. Damage to the skin, such as wrinkles and age spots, which are thought to be associated with aging, actually results from a lifetime of exposure to sunlight. The best way to protect skin from such damage is to minimize time in the sun and always use sunscreen (NIA, 2000).

The popularity of anti-aging treatments is an indication of the widespread desire to hide the appearance of aging. If your "ideal self" has the body of a 20-year-old, then with each passing year it takes more and more effort—whether by cosmetics, by plastic surgery, or by taking a young lover—to deny what is occurring. Self-esteem suffers when people devalue their physical being. But even in the face of powerful social forces that reinforce a worship of youth, many adults can and do learn to accept the changes taking place in themselves.

SENSORIMOTOR FUNCTIONING

From the mid-twenties until about age 50, changes in sensory and motor capacities are gradual and generally imperceptible and highly individual. A 45-year-old who has never worn glasses discovers that she cannot read the telephone book and needs reading glasses. Another who has worn glasses since youth needs a major change in his prescription. A 55-year-old woman must admit that her tennis game is not as quick as it used to be. Another player her age is just about as limber as she was in earlier years.

Most middle-aged people compensate well for any changes they experience, and some actively pursue interventions, such as exercise programs to increase strength and prevent muscle loss. Other middle-aged persons do nothing to compensate for the changes they are experiencing from aging.

CRITICAL THINKING
How might expected changes in adult sensorimotor function influence services provided by community businesses and other agencies?

© Bob Daemmrich/Stock Boston

Sensorimotor abilities are the outcome of complex processes involving the nervous system. Each person has a unique level of ability in each area of sensory and motor activity, and even a person with a disability may develop ways to compensate so as to pursue a favorite activity.

Sensorimotor abilities typically decline in late adulthood. Again, though, there is much individual variation.

Most aging adults do worry about sensory losses. And no wonder! From the ring of the alarm clock and the aroma of freshly brewed coffee to the softness of the pillow as we shut our eyes at night, our senses are the primary means by which we know our world. Many people also regret declines in muscular strength, endurance, coordination, and reaction time (Digiovanna, 2000).

Because sensorimotor abilities are the outcome of a complex series of processes involving the nervous system, they may be affected by developmental changes in that system (discussed in Chapter 4). It may take longer for the brain to assess a situation and decide what to do. Slowed reflex responses can result in accidental injuries. Slowed information processing can result in requests to repeat information that has been presented too quickly or not clearly enough. Remember, though, as we describe changes typical with advancing age,* that each person has a unique level of ability in each area of sensory and motor activity.

Vision

Ted Williams, a baseball player who is in the Hall of Fame, gave a batting exhibition when he was middle-aged. At that time, it is said, he could still see with the naked eye exactly where his bat met a spinning fast ball when he hit it.

As with all aspects of aging, there are great individual differences in visual ability. Some people in their eighties or older do not need glasses, while some young adults do. Most age-related visual problems occur in five areas: dynamic vision (reading moving signs), near vision, sensitivity to light, visual search (for example, locating a sign), and speed of processing visual information (Kline et al., 1992; Kosnick, Winslow, Kline, Rasinski, & Sekuler, 1988; Schieber, 2006). Corrective lenses or medical or surgical treatment—including some new technologies (see Box 3.2 on p. 88 and Figure 3.4)—can often help people with moderate visual problems.

CHANGES IN EYE STRUCTURE AND FUNCTION

Aging usually brings a loss of **visual acuity**, ability to distinguish detail. Visual acuity, which is measured when you look at an eye chart in the doctor's office

---

*The discussion of sensory changes in the following sections is based largely on Spence (1989).

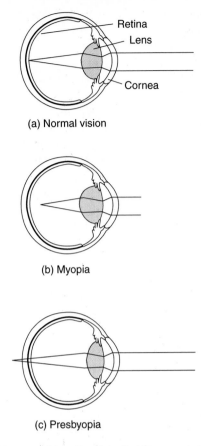

Retina
Lens
Cornea

(a) Normal vision

(b) Myopia

(c) Presbyopia

FIGURE 3.4 *Normal vision, myopia, and presbyopia.* (*a*) In normal vision, light rays focus on the retina at the rear of the eye. (*b*) In myopia (nearsightedness), the eyeball is too long, or the curvature of the lens or cornea is too great, so the light rays focus in front of the retina. (*c*) In presbyopia, a form of farsightedness that often develops with aging, the lens becomes thickened and loses elasticity, so that it cannot curve enough to focus light from nearby objects on the retina; instead, the image focuses behind the retina. *SOURCE:* Adapted from Donn, 1985, p. 649.

or when you apply for a driver's license, is keenest at about age 20 and begins to decline by about age 50. By age 85, some adults have lost as much as 80 percent of the visual acuity they had in young adulthood. However, despite the dramatic decline in average acuity, the majority of older adults maintain "good" corrected vision through their mid-eighties (Schieber & Baldwin, 1996).

Dynamic visual acuity is the ability to see moving objects clearly. This ability—even more than acuity for stationary objects—declines with age. Thus information presented in motion, such as credits scrolled down or across a movie or television screen, is much harder for older adults to follow than for younger adults (Kline & Scialfa, 1996).

New Ways to Better Vision and Hearing

Recent advances in technology have made possible new surgical treatments for nearsightedness, astigmatism, and cataracts and new methods to aid hearing.

Vision

Laser eye surgery has become a popular choice in recent years to correct certain visual problems. These operations are also called refractive surgeries because they attempt to correct refractive errors in the cornea. To create an image on the retina, light must first pass through the cornea, then, with help from the lens, focuses the image on the photosensitive tissue at the back of the eye, made up of rods and cones. Errors in refraction (bending and focusing of light) occur when the cornea, lens, or the eye is not perfectly shaped. As a result, images on the retina are blurred or out of focus.

LASIK (laser-assisted in situ keratomileusis) eye surgery involves the use of a laser to remove part of the cornea to change its shape, thus improving the ability to focus light. LASIK surgery is used to correct myopia, hyperopia, and astigmatism. New surgical techniques recently have been approved to treat presbyopia; long-term outcomes are currently being evaluated. The precursors to LASIK surgery were Photorefractive Keratectomy (PRK) and Radial Keratotomy (RK). The same laser technique can be used for all three surgeries, to operate on different parts of the cornea (FDA, 2004).

After surgery some people may experience mild pain and discomfort, burning or scratchiness, or tearing or watery eyes for a couple of days. Sensitivity to light, hazy or blurred vision, dry eyes, glare, or difficulty driving at night may persist longer and, in some instances, may require further surgery. Fluctuation in vision may last for 3 to 6 months (FDA, 2004). Despite the potential adverse side effects, success rates of laser surgery are good; according to The American Academy of Ophthalmology 70 percent of patients attain 20/20 vision (FTC, 2000).

Corrective surgery for cataracts is now commonplace. Various surgical techniques are used to remove the clouded lens and replace it with an artificial one. Because the stitches required to close the incision made in the bag holding the cornea may cause astigmatism, a one-stitch (or no-stitch) method is gaining popularity. Other advances such as topical anesthesia, LASIK surgery to correct astigmatism, and new lens designs have contributed to the 98 percent success rate for cataract surgery (NEI, 2006). The outpatient procedure usually lasts about 30 minutes and produces very little discomfort. Generally, normal activities may be resumed within 1 to 7 days (Brint, 1989).

Probably the most common visual problem after about age 40 is a form of farsightedness called **presbyopia** (see figure 3.4), which makes many people put on reading glasses or switch to blended or bifocal glasses. Presbyopia stems from structural changes in the lens of the eye. The lens, unlike most body structures, keeps growing throughout life. As new cells accumulate on

Hearing

When older adults complain that people around them are mumbling, it's generally because they have lost their hearing for high-frequency consonants, though they can still hear vowels, which are lower in frequency. Hearing aids are the most common tool used to improve the quality of hearing, and users can choose from several types. The type of hearing aid chosen may depend on the severity of hearing loss, as well as the size of the aid and the level of sophistication desired. Hearing aids can be placed in the ear canal, in the ear, or behind the ear or worn on the body. Hearing aids worn inside the ear canal must be very small and therefore not very powerful. As size increases, power and available options also increase. Analog/adjustable aids are typically the least expensive and are built to the user's hearing needs in a laboratory. An analog/programmable hearing aid is set by a computer and can be programmed with different settings to accommodate different listening environments. This type may come with a remote control to allow the user to change the settings as the need arises. A third type is digital/programmable; it uses a computer chip to give the user the greatest amount of flexibility. In this case, the individual is tested by an automated program. The audiologist then uses the computer output to program the hearing aid to exactly match the person's audiological profile. It is highly individualized and tends to be the most expensive of the three types (NIDCD, 2004).

For people with profound hearing loss, **cochlear implants** can make a dramatic difference. These electronic devices transform sound into electrical signals and deliver them to the receptor nerve cells of the *cochlea* in the inner ear, which then channels the impulses to the *auditory cortex* of the brain. The electrodes must be surgically implanted in the cochlea. The patient wears a speech processor, which analyzes and encodes sounds before transmitting them to the implant. People who undergo cochlear implantation should participate in aural rehabilitation programs, which include fitting and adjusting the speech processor, training in speech production, and informational or personal counseling (Gagné, Parnes, LaRocque, Hassan, & Vidas, 1991; ASHA, 2004).

Most implant recipients improve in the ability to read lips, and two-thirds to three-fourths can understand speech without visual clues. With daily activities easier to perform and conversation less stressful, many experience improvements in psychological, social, and emotional health as well (Gagné, 1992). As with any surgery, there are possible complications, including temporary injury to the facial nerve, but surgeons experienced in cochlear implantation generally do not encounter such problems (Cohen et al., 1993; NIDCD, 2004).

the outer part of the lens, the older lens fibers (cells) are squeezed together and pushed toward the center. By age 70, the lens may be at least 3 times thicker than it was originally. Meanwhile, it hardens, flattens, and becomes less elastic—less able to change shape to focus on nearby objects (refer to Figure 3.4). This continuous lifelong process usually becomes noticeable for the first time in middle age, when the eye's ability to accommodate, or adjust its focus, also slows (Schieber & Baldwin, 1996). Women usually develop presbyopia about 3 to 5 years earlier than men do (Kline & Schieber, 1985).

Initially, most people try to compensate for presbyopia by holding books, newspapers, or whatever they are reading farther and farther away from the face—until it is so far away that the letters are too small to make out. Some people at this age need nothing more than magnifying lenses. Others need bifocals, which have one focal length for reading and another for distant vision. Presbyopia usually stabilizes at about age 60, and, with corrective lenses, most older people can see fairly well.

The lens also may begin to turn yellow and filter out green, blue, and violet light (Kline & Scialfa, 1996). Thus these colors should not be used for objects, such as medicines, that older adults need to be able to distinguish. An older person might easily mix up two pills of the same shape if the only apparent difference was that one was violet and the other blue.

Another change is in the size of the *pupil*, the dark opening in the center of the *iris*, the colored portion of the eye. If you look at the eyes of a 5- or 6-year-old child, you will notice that the pupils are larger than in a young adult. If you look at a 75-year-old's pupils, they are likely to be smaller than a young adult's. That is because the muscles in the iris that dilate the pupil in dark places (such as movie theaters) to let in more light become weaker in middle age, and the pupil no longer dilates as much. As a result, middle-aged adults need about one-third more brightness than young adults to compensate for the loss of light reaching the retina (Schieber & Baldwin, 1996). This tendency may increase in old age, so older adults need even more light to read or make out objects. Partly for the same reason, the visual function of older adults may be slower and less able to adapt to darkness.

Depth perception may diminish with advancing age, which is why some older people tend to run into or trip over things, or to miss their footing on steps or curbs. Older adults also become more sensitive to glare. And because they lose visual contrast sensitivity, they have trouble reading either very small or very large characters (Akutsu, Legge, Ross, & Schuebel, 1991; Kline & Scialfa, 1996).

VISUAL DISORDERS AND DISEASES

Some of the visual impairments discussed above, such as sensitivity to glare and contrast, are aggravated by **cataracts**. More than half of older adults develop these cloudy or opaque areas in the lens, which prevent light from passing through, causing blurred vision (USDHHS, 1993a). Surgery to remove cataracts (refer to Box 3.2) is the most common operation among Americans over 65 (Steinberg et al., 1993); more than 1.3 million cataract operations were performed in 1993 (Research to Prevent Blindness, 1994). Eating foods high in vitamin A (broccoli, carrots, and spinach) at least five times a week can greatly lower the risk of cataracts, according to a large-scale 8-year study. Taking vitamin A supplements did not necessarily have the same effect (Hankinson et al., 1992).

Cataracts are the most frequent cause of preventable blindness in the world as a whole; but **age-related macular degeneration** (AMD), in which the *macula*, the central part of the retina, gradually loses the ability to distinguish fine details, is the leading cause of *functional blindness* in Americans over 60 years old (NEI, 2004a). It affects 10 million Americans over age 65 (NEI, 2004a), especially white women, smokers, and those with light eye color (Stuen & Faye, 2003). Though not limited entirely to older adults, this disorder is more common with advancing age; a diet high in carotenoids such as spinach, collard greens, and carrots apparently reduces the risk.

There are 2 types of AMD: dry and wet. Dry AMD is much more common; it accounts for approximately 90 percent of all AMD cases (Mezger, 2000). Dry AMD is the result of a gradual breakdown of the light-sensitive cells in the macula, leaving a person with slightly blurred vision that may continue to worsen with time (NEI, 2004a). There are 3 stages of dry AMD: early, intermediate, and advanced. The only treatment options available in the early and intermediate stages are special glasses and magnifiers (Mezger, 2000). A study done by The National Eye Institute (2004a) found that high doses of antioxidants and zinc slowed the progression of the disease and reduced the risk of advanced stage AMD.

Wet AMD is more severe than dry AMD and can occur suddenly as a result of the breakage of tiny, abnormal blood vessels under the retina. Two treatments are available to those with wet AMD: laser surgery and photodynamic therapy. Laser surgery, also called photocoagulation, uses a laser to destroy the abnormal blood vessels. However, very few people can be treated with this method and more damage and vision loss may occur as a result of the surgery. In photodynamic therapy, a light-sensitive drug is injected into the body, and the affected eye is treated with a laser. This treatment slows the growth of the abnormal blood vessels, and this helps prevent further vision loss (NEI, 2004a; Stuen & Faye, 2003).

Glaucoma occurs when fluid pressure builds up within the eye because of inadequate drainage, which damages the optic nerve. The disease affects 3 million Americans, many of whom are unaware of it until it causes severe damage to their vision. Glaucoma can be called the "silent" or "sneak" thief of vision because at first there usually are no symptoms or pain, and vision is normal (NEI, 2004b). As symptoms begin to appear (after significant damage to the optic nerve), they may include blurred vision, seeing rings of color around light sources (such as a halo of red around a light bulb), severe headache, and pain and watering of the eye. An early symptom of the most common form of glaucoma (open-angle glaucoma) is a gradual loss of peripheral vision. Angle-closure glaucoma is a more serious form of the disease and accounts for about 10 percent of all cases. It comes on suddenly, and total blindness may occur within hours if not treated immediately (Rosenfeld, 2002).

When detected early, glaucoma can be treated and controlled with eye drops, medicine, laser treatments, or surgery. Each of these treatments is designed to help drain fluid from the eye. Eye exams are recommended every 2 years for adults over the age of 40, especially African Americans. The risk of glaucoma increases for all races after the age of 60, in particular for Mexican Americans. Other risk factors include family history, being diabetic, or having a previous injury to the eyes (NEI, 2004b; Rosenfeld, 2002).

Corneal disease occurs when the cornea, the front surface of the eye, becomes clouded, scarred, or distorted by injury, disease, or hereditary defects. Artificial corneal implants have become a common procedure as success rates have improved due to technological advances. The National Eye Institute (2001) has funded research, including genetic studies and cell transplants, to help physicians understand and treat corneal disease.

DEALING WITH VISUAL LOSSES

When the French painter Edgar Degas began to lose his vision in his late sixties, he switched to making wax sculptures, taking advantage of the sense of touch (McMullen, 1984). But even those older adults who do not have serious disorders often have trouble doing things that depend on vision and need to find ways to compensate. Reduced ability to adapt to dim light, tolerate glare, and locate and read signs can make driving (especially at night) particularly difficult and even dangerous. It may also be hard for older adults to read or do close work and even to do such everyday tasks as shopping and cooking. After 65, serious visual problems not only may curtail everyday activities but sometimes cause accidents both inside and outside the home (Branch, Horowitz, & Carr, 1989; Tideiksaar, 2002). Loss of visual abilities can have serious psychological consequences when it deprives older people of activities, social life, and independence.

There are simple ways to help people remain safely active and self-reliant. Make sure lighting in work and reading areas is bright enough and directed efficiently. A good fluorescent lamp (yellowish, not blue) can provide a high level of illumination with low glare. Get rid of unnecessary items in cupboards and bookshelves, and highlight often-used items with bright-colored markers. Helpful accessories include sunglasses, so that less adjustment is necessary when coming indoors; a pocket flashlight for reading menus and theater programs; a magnifying glass to put in a pocket or hang on a chain; and large-type reading matter. Since older eyes need sharper contrasts, make stair treads a different color from risers, and edges of counters and tables a different color from the tops; paint bathroom grab bars to contrast with the walls. Carpeting and other textured materials can prevent distracting glare. (Table 3.2 lists additional suggestions for preventing falls.)

Hearing

CRITICAL THINKING

Which theory of biological aging best explains the developmental processes observed in vision and hearing?

Hearing, like vision, is at its best at about age 20. A gradual hearing loss typically begins before age 25 and becomes more apparent after that age. Most people do not notice their hearing loss during young adulthood and middle age because it does not affect frequencies used in normal speech. It is not until the seventies that most adults begin to miss words in conversation (Katchadourian, 1987). Adults should have their hearing checked if they find it hard to understand words; complain that other people are "mumbling"; cannot hear a dripping faucet or high notes in music; have a hissing or ring-

TABLE 3.2

Safety Checklist for Preventing Falls in the Home

Stairways, hallways, and pathways	Free of clutter
	Good lighting, especially at top of stairs
	Light switches at top and bottom of stairs
	Tightly fastened handrails on both sides and full length of stairs
	Carpets firmly attached and not frayed; rough-textured or abrasive strips to secure footing
Bathrooms	Grab bars conveniently located inside and outside of tubs and showers and near toilets
	Nonskid mats, abrasive strips, or carpet on all surfaces that may get wet
	Night lights
Bedrooms	Telephones and night lights or light switches within easy reach of beds
All living areas	Electrical cords and telephone wires out of walking paths
	Rugs well secured to floor
	Inspect for hazards, such as exposed nails and loose threshold trim
	Furniture and other objects in familiar places and not in the way; rounded or padded table edges
	Couches and chairs proper height to get into and out of easily

SOURCE: Tideiksaar, 2002.

ing noise in the ears; or do not enjoy parties, television, or concerts because they miss much of what goes on (NIA, 1993; Weinstein, 2003).

CAUSES OF HEARING LOSS

Hearing loss is the third most common chronic condition, exceeded only by arthritis and hypertension (Schneider & Pichora-Fuller, 2000). Most age-related hearing impairment is due to degeneration of structures in the inner ear. There are several patterns of loss, depending on which parts of the inner ear are affected.

Sensorineural hearing loss is the number one type of hearing loss in people over the age of 65. It involves damage to the nerves in the inner ear, the auditory nerve, or hearing pathways in the brain. This type of hearing loss can be caused by aging, infection, exposure to loud noise, heredity, tumors, circulatory problems, or head trauma (NIA, 2002a). This type of hearing loss is permanent and can be treated only through the use of a hearing aid.

The most common type of sensorineural hearing loss is **presbycusis**. At first, hearing loss is limited to high-pitched sounds and progresses more rapidly in men than in women (Schieber & Baldwin, 1996; NIDCD, 2004). Presbycusis is very common in late life, though usually not severe; about 30 to 35 percent of people between ages 65 and 74, and about half of those 75 and older have it to some degree. Whereas a young child can hear frequencies as high as 20,000 cycles per second, an older adult is unlikely to hear anything above 8,000 cycles per second. Some high frequency sounds can be critically important. An older adult might be unable to hear a high pitched smoke alarm, no matter how loud it is—just as blowing hard on a dog whistle whose sound is above the frequency range of the human ear will not make it easier for a person to hear it.

Conductive hearing loss is another common type of hearing loss caused by a blockage of sound in the outer or middle ear. Blockage can occur as a result of buildup of ear wax, abnormal bone growth, a punctured ear drum, or an infection in the middle ear. As a result of conductive hearing loss, a person may experience a reduction in overall sound levels and have difficulty hearing faint sounds. This type of hearing loss is usually treated medically or surgically. A combination of sensorineural and conductive hearing loss is called **mixed hearing loss**. As when the types of hearing loss occur separately, conductive loss can be treated, but the sensorineural loss cannot.

Hearing also can be damaged by constant exposure to loud noise. People who are especially at risk for noise-induced hearing loss are those with careers in farming, mining, construction, manufacturing, transportation, the military, and music (NIOSH, 2004). Where a person lives does not make a difference in rates of hearing loss; people in both rural and urban areas are exposed to noise on a daily basis that has the potential to cause hearing loss (NIDCD, 2004).

About 10 percent of older adults have **tinnitus**, a persistent ringing or buzzing in the ears. Tinnitus can occur at any point in adulthood, but the number of cases increases with increasing age. It is uncertain exactly why tinnitus occurs, but it may be caused by loud noise, hearing loss, or certain medications or health problems. It may be permanent, or it may come and go (NIA, 2002a). It seems to occur more frequently in women. A person who takes large doses of aspirin may have this symptom temporarily, along with a temporary hearing loss. Chronic tinnitus can be extremely stressful. It can be treated medically or through the use of a masker, which makes the ringing less noticeable (NIA, 2002a).

DEALING WITH HEARING LOSS

Hearing aids, which amplify sound, can compensate for mild hearing loss to some degree. However, they can be hard to adjust to, since they magnify background noises as well as sounds the wearer wants to hear. Furthermore, many people feel that wearing a hearing aid is like wearing a sign saying "I'm getting old." Newer hearing aids using microchip technology provide improved sound quality (refer to Box 3.2). Medical treatment, special training, and surgery are other ways to deal with hearing impairment.

People who talk to hearing-impaired older adults can take some simple steps to improve communication (Hull, 1980; NIDCD 2002). When speaking to someone with a hearing problem, make sure you are in good light, where the other person can see you, so that your lip movements and gestures can be used as clues to your words. Speak from a distance of 3 to 6 feet, never right into the person's ear. Don't chew, eat, or cover your mouth while speaking, and turn off the radio and television. Speak somewhat more loudly than usual, but don't shout. Speak clearly and not too quickly. Don't exaggerate articulation—exaggeration can distort both sounds and visual cues. If the listener doesn't understand what you say, don't just repeat it; rephrase it in short, simple sentences.

Taste and Smell

Taste and smell generally begin to decline in midlife, but individual differences are great.

Because the taste buds become less sensitive, foods that may be quite flavorful to a younger person can seem bland to the same person in middle age (Troll, 1985; Saxon & Etton, 2002). A woman might lose her sweet tooth, her husband might find his martinis not sour enough. One person could become less sensitive to salty foods, another to sweet, bitter, or sour foods. And the same person may remain more sensitive to some of these tastes than to others (Stevens, Cruz, Hoffman, & Patterson, 1995; Whitbourne, 1999). Many people compensate for losses in taste by eating foods that are more highly seasoned. Some oversalt their food, possibly contributing to high blood pressure. Others eat less and may become undernourished. Research is attempting to gain a better understanding of basic taste mechanisms and of ways to enhance older people's taste (Schiffman, 1995; Saxon & Etton, 2002).

Taste often depends upon smell. When older people find that their food doesn't taste good anymore, this could be not only because they have fewer taste buds in the tongue, but also because they have fewer olfactory receptors to transmit smells to the brain. As with taste, the loss of olfactory receptors occurs more rapidly in some older adults than in others (Stevens, Cain, Demarque, & Ruthruff, 1991), and the ability to detect certain odors tends to decline faster in some than in others (Wysocki & Gilbert, 1989). Some older adults may have difficulty in detecting by smell whether food is spoiled.

These changes might be related to illness, aging, smoking, medications, or environmental pollution (American Academy of Otolaryngology, 1986). Individuals also may differ in their cognitive ability to recognize odors and tastes (Whitbourne, 1999).

Touch, Pain, and Temperature

The skin at the fingertips may become less sensitive with age (Stevens, 1992). For most people, this lessening of tactile acuity has little impact, but for the visually disabled it can interfere with the ability to read braille.

Do older people become less sensitive to pain? Studies have been inconclusive (Harkins, 1995). Some older people seem to become less sensitive to pain, but they also may become less able to tolerate it. As a result, many older adults find pain more distressing than before (Katchadourian, 1987). Still, though chronic pain is a major challenge in geriatric care, people over age 70 tend to be underrepresented at pain treatment clinics. Intervention and pain control have now become a major focus of geriatric care.

An older person's body adjusts more slowly to cold and becomes chilled more easily than that of a younger person. Exposure to outdoor cold and to poorly heated interiors may lower body temperature—a serious risk for the very old. Older adults cannot cope as well with heat, either. The body's normal cooling mechanisms—sweating and pumping blood to the skin—don't perform as well as in younger persons. During hot weather, or after exercise, older people need to drink plenty of water to replace lost body fluids (M. J. Holland, 1990).

Motor Functions

CRITICAL THINKING

Do you believe that genetics or environment has the greatest impact on motor function during adulthood? Explain why.

Most professional athletes retire by age 40, though some like the pitcher Nolan Ryan stay on top of their game well past that age. John Glenn, well past retirement, could still make the grade as an astronaut. What happens in adulthood that causes motor functioning to decline, and why is this decline faster in some people than in others?

For one thing, the tissue that connects muscles to joints thickens, making the joints less flexible. Manual dexterity generally becomes less efficient after the mid-thirties (Vercruyssen, 1997)—though some pianists, such as Vladimir Horowitz, continued to perform brilliantly in their eighties. Arthritis (degeneration of the joints) can take its toll (see Chapter 4).

Muscle fibers become fewer and contain less protein, diminishing muscular power, speed, and (to a lesser extent) endurance. But individual differences are great and become greater with each passing decade (Spirduso & MacRae, 1990; Vercruyssen, 1997). "Use It or Lose It" is the motto of many middle-aged adults, who engage in jogging, racquetball, tennis, aerobic dancing, and other forms of exercise. Even some adults in their seventies still compete in marathons and triathlons. People who lead sedentary lives or have poor health tend to lose muscle tone and energy, while those who are active retain more strength, stamina, and resilience.

Eventually, though, if a person lives long enough, physiological changes do limit motor activity (Spirduso & MacRae, 1990). Generally, older adults can do most things that younger people can, but more slowly (Birren, Woods, & Williams, 1980; Salthouse, 1985). They are not as strong as they used to be and cannot carry as heavy loads. Age also brings changes in coordination and reaction time, which affect such abilities as driving. Let's look at some of these changes.

© Suzanne Haldane/Stock Boston

© Elizabeth Crews

© Spencer Grant/Stock Boston

Although motor functioning declines somewhat after young adulthood, middle-aged and older people who remain active can retain more manual dexterity, strength, and stamina than those who do not.

MUSCULAR STRENGTH AND ENDURANCE

Most adults are strongest during their twenties or thirties (Spirduso & MacRae, 1990). They gradually lose about 10 to 20 percent of their strength up to age 70; after that, the loss becomes greater. Some older adults have only half the strength they had at 30 (Spence, 1989). Muscles of the upper body keep their strength better than muscles of the lower body (Spirduso & MacRae, 1990). Most people notice a weakening first in the back muscles, by the early fifties, and then in the arm and shoulder—but not until well into the sixties (Katchadourian, 1987).

The reason for this loss of strength is a loss of muscle mass. Between ages 30 and 80, as much as 30 percent of muscle fiber can atrophy, depending on such factors as heredity, nutrition, and especially how much use a muscle gets. Lost fibers cannot replace themselves; instead, they are replaced by fat (Spence, 1989). By age 65, a man's body is typically 30 percent fat—the same as a woman's, but nearly three times the percentage he had at age 20, even if his weight does not change (Katchadourian, 1987).

A lifelong program of exercise may prevent or even reverse many physical changes formerly associated with "normal aging." Regular exercise prolongs life and can help prevent or reduce aging-related declines (Mazzeo et al., 1998; Rakowski & Mor, 1992). Exercise dramatically increases physical fitness, muscle size, and strength in older individuals. Besides rejuvenating muscles, resistance exercises ("pumping iron") also enhance bone strength, limiting the risk of osteoporosis and fractures of the hip, spine, and wrist. Exercise also improves balance, thereby decreasing the risk of falling, a common and life-threatening problem in older persons (Rowe & Kahn, 1998). In controlled studies with people in their sixties to nineties, weight training and resistance training programs lasting 8 weeks to 2 years increased muscle strength, size, and mobility and also improved speed and endurance (Ades, Ballor, Ashikaga, Utton, & Nair, 1996; Fiatarone et al., 1990; Fiatarone, O'Neill, & Ryan, 1994; McCartney, Hicks, Martin, & Webber, 1996). In another study, low-impact, moderate-intensity aerobic dance and exercise training led to gains in peak oxygen uptake, leg muscle strength, and vigor (Engels, Drouin, Zhu, & Kazmierski, 1998).

This finding of plasticity even among the oldest old—consistent with the lifespan developmental approach—is important because people whose muscles have atrophied are more likely to suffer falls and fractures and to need help with tasks of day-to-day living.

Endurance—how long a person can continue to exert maximum force before fatigue sets in—often holds up much better than strength. Probably, that is why many competitive runners, swimmers, and cyclists switch from short to longer races as they get older. Older athletes can do better in an endurance event, such as running a marathon, than in an event that depends on strength, such as the shotput (Spirduso & MacRae, 1990).

REACTION TIME AND COORDINATION

Older adults perform more slowly than younger adults on almost all kinds of tasks; in general, the more complex the task, the greater the age difference. Simple reaction time, which involves a single response to a single stimulus (such as pressing a button when a light flashes) slows by about 20 percent, on the average, between ages 20 and 60 (Birren et al., 1980), depending on the amount and kind of information to be processed and the kind of response required. When a vocal rather than a manual response is called for, age differences in simple reaction time are substantially reduced (Johnson & Rybash, 1993).

Tasks that involve a choice of responses (such as hitting one button when a light flashes and another button when a tone is heard) and complex motor skills involving many stimuli, responses, and decisions (as in playing a video game or driving a car) decline more; but the decline does not necessarily result in poorer performance. Typically, middle-aged adults are better drivers than younger people (Sterns, Barrett, & Alexander, 1985), and 60-year-old typists are as efficient as 20-year-olds (Spirduso & MacRae, 1990). In these and other activities, the improvement that comes with experience more than makes up for the decrements that come with age.

Driving becomes riskier for older adults, because of slower information processing, slower reaction time, and less efficient coordination. Drivers over age 65 have a high proportion of accidents, usually because of improper turns, failure to yield the right of way, and failure to obey traffic signs (Sterns, Barrett, & Alexander, 1985; AARP, 2006). In 1991, nearly 16 percent of people why died in traffic accidents were 75 or older, the most rapidly increasing group of drivers in the United States ("Elderly Driving Poses Challenges for Families," 1994). Automobile crashes are the leading cause of injury-related fatalities among 65- to 74-year-olds and the second leading cause (after falls) in the over 75 group. Case fatality ratios are nearly four times higher for the 75 and over group than for all ages combined (Sterns & Camp, 1998).

Training can help reaction time. In one study, for instance, older people who had never before played video games used "joy sticks" and "trigger buttons" for 11 weeks to play such games as Breakout, Kaboom, and Ms. Pacman. At the end of the study period, they showed quicker reaction times than a control group (Dustman, Emmerson, Steinhaus, Shearer, & Dustman, 1992).

For an older adult, driving can make the difference between active participation in society and enforced isolation. Older drivers' vision, coordination, and reaction time need to be retested regularly. They can compensate for any loss of ability by driving more slowly and for shorter distances, choosing easier routes, and driving only in daylight (Sterns et al., 1985). In many communities, courses in defensive driving help to keep older drivers behind the wheel as long as possible. Meanwhile, highway engineers explore ways to make signs easier to read and intersections safer (Schmidt, 1988).

SEXUAL AND REPRODUCTIVE FUNCTIONING

Many adults view sexuality as a hallmark of youth. Actually, despite changes in the male and female reproductive systems (summarized in Table 3.3), sexual activity and pleasure can continue throughout adult life.

CRITICAL THINKING

Based on your attitudes as a teenager or young adult, what do you predict your sexual desires will be like as a middle-aged and/or older adult?

The Female Reproductive System

The menstrual cycle is a powerful regulator of hormones that fluctuate in a woman's body for some 40 years of her life, from about age 12 until about age 50. To varying degrees, these hormones affect women's physiological, intellectual, and emotional states and even their sensory responses. For example, sight is keenest at the time of ovulation, hearing peaks at the beginning of a menstrual period and again at ovulation, smell is most sensitive at midcycle and is reduced during menstruation, and sensitivity to pain is lowest just before a period (Parlee, 1983). The cessation of menstruation in middle age is an important event with both physical and psychological effects.

TABLE 3.3

Age-Related Changes in Human Reproductive Systems

	Female	Male
Climacteric (approximate age)	45–55	55–60
Hormonal change	Drop in estrogen and progesterone	Drop in testosterone
Symptoms	Hot flashes, vaginal dryness, urinary dysfunction	Undetermined
Sexual changes	Takes longer to become aroused and to reach orgasm	Loss of psychological arousal, less frequent erections, slower orgasms, longer recovery between ejaculations, increased risk of impotence
Reproductive capacity	Ends	Continues; some decrease in fertility may occur

PREMENSTRUAL SYNDROME

Premenstrual syndrome (PMS) is a disorder involving physical discomfort and emotional tension during the 2 weeks before a menstrual period. Emotional or physical symptoms may include mood swings, anxiety, fatigue, irritability, headache, swelling and/or breast tenderness, swollen hands or feet, bloating, nausea, constipation, weight gain, depression, tearfulness, and difficulty concentrating or remembering (American Medical Association, 1998).

These symptoms are not distinctive in themselves; it is their timing that identifies PMS. Up to 70 percent of menstruating women may have some symptoms; about 3 to 5 percent have symptoms severe enough to interfere with normal functioning and to be considered a mental disorder, which is called *premenstrual dysphoric disorder* (PMDD) (American Psychiatric Association, 1994; "PMS: It's Real," 1994; Wurtman & Wurtman, 1989; NIMH, 2005).

The cause of PMS is not known. It may in part be related to biochemical changes of the menstrual cycle: the depletion of neurotransmitters in the brain that affect well-being or relaxation or stimulate the central nervous system. The most effective medications, such as Prozac and certain anti-anxiety medications, build up the levels of these chemicals or mimic their effects. One treatment for PMS is the birth control pill, because it provides a steady, daily dose of hormones that does not fluctuate (American Medical Association, 1998). Hormone treatments can be quite effective but can have undesirable side effects. For milder symptoms, some doctors recommend exercise and dietary changes, such as avoiding fat, sodium, caffeine, and alcohol ("PMS: It's Real," 1994). Treatment may target specific symptoms: for example, antidepressants for a woman who feels "blue" or diuretics for a woman who retains fluids. Since some women report relief after binge eating of carbohydrates, one research team suggests a high-carbohydrate diet (Wurtman & Wurtman, 1989).

PMS sometimes is confused with **dysmenorrhea**, menstrual cramps. Cramps tend to afflict adolescents and young women; PMS is more typical in women in their thirties or older. Dysmenorrhea is caused by contractions of the uterus, which are set in motion by prostaglandin, a hormone-like substance; it can be treated with prostaglandin inhibitors.

MENOPAUSE

CRITICAL THINKING
Do you perceive menopause as a distressing, neutral, or liberating experience?

Menopause takes place when a woman permanently stops ovulating and menstruating and can no longer conceive a child; it is generally considered to have occurred 1 year after the last menstrual period. The period of several years during which a woman experiences physiological changes that bring on menopause is called *perimenopause*, also known as the **climacteric**, or "change of life."

Beginning in her thirties, a woman's production of ova begins to decline imperceptibly. Then, as she nears her fiftieth birthday, the ovaries produce less of the female hormone estrogen. (Small amounts of estrogen continue to be secreted, even after menopause, by the adrenal and other glands.) Menstruation becomes irregular, with less flow than before and a longer time between menstrual periods. As the levels of estrogen and progesterone produced by the ovaries drop, menstruation stops completely.

Menopause occurs when the ovaries no longer produce enough estrogen to sustain full menstrual cycles (American Medical Association, 1998). In 4 out of 5 women this happens between ages 45 and 55—on average, at about age 51 (Avis, 1999; Merrill & Verbrugge, 1999; Planned Parenthood, 2003). Some women, however, experience menstrual changes in their thirties; others, not until their sixties. In women who have hysterectomies (surgical removal of the uterus resulting in the inability to become pregnant), menopause comes on abruptly, without preparation.

Physical Effects Three out of four women experience little or no physical discomfort due to menopause (NIA, 1993). Most common are "hot flashes" (sudden sensations of heat that flash through the body due to expansion and contraction of blood vessels); but many women never have them, while others have them continually (Avis, 1999). Administration of artificial estrogen, discussed later in this chapter, can alleviate hot flashes.

Other possible symptoms include vaginal dryness, burning, and itching; urinary problems; and vaginal infections. During menopause, the vagina becomes narrower and shorter, its walls become thinner and less

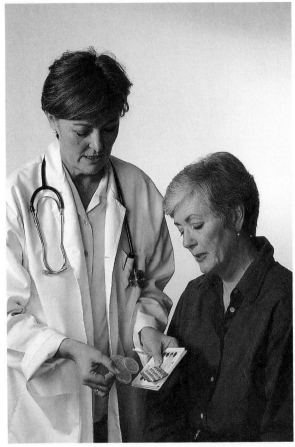

© Carolyn A. McKeone/Photo Researchers

Some postmenopausal women take estrogen in the form of a slow-release skin patch (worn on the thigh), a pill, or a vaginal cream to counteract hot flashes and vaginal dryness and to help prevent osteoporosis and heart disease. The advisability of estrogen therapy for an individual woman may depend on her medical history.

elastic, and lubrication diminishes, sometimes causing pain during intercourse or irritation of the bladder. Use of water-soluble gels can prevent or relieve such discomfort. Vaginal secretions also become less acidic, offering less protection against bacterial and yeast infections. The more sexually active a woman is, either with a partner or by masturbation, the less likely she is to experience such changes (Katchadourian, 1987; Spence, 1989). Other physical problems that are occasionally reported by menopausal women include joint or muscle pain, headache, insomnia, fatigue, dizziness, weight gain, and constipation; but such symptoms seem to be related to menopause only indirectly, if at all (Avis, 1999; te Velde & van Leusden, 1994).

The hormones most directly linked to sexual desire in both men and women are the androgens (such as testosterone). Declining estrogen levels in midlife do not seem to affect sexual desire for most women, as long as intercourse remains comfortable and there are no other health-related problems to interfere with a healthy sex life (American Medical Association, 1998). Still, women do go through sexual adjustments. Some do not become aroused as readily as before, and the sexual flush that accompanies arousal diminishes. Breast engorgement, nipple erection, and clitoral and labial engorgement may also diminish. Women can still reach orgasm, but it may take longer to reach and may be less intense.

Many of the troublesome physical effects of menopause—including higher risks of certain diseases (discussed in Chapter 4)—seem to be related to lower levels of estrogen. In the past, doctors have frequently prescribed **hormone replacement therapy (HRT)**: artificial estrogen, sometimes in combination with progestin, in the form of a pill, a slow-release skin patch or a vaginal cream. However, a recent study done by the Women's Health Initiative (WHI) found that estrogen taken in combination with progestin dramatically increased risks of breast cancer, coronary heart disease, blood clots and stroke, and gall bladder disease. This finding led researchers to stop the trial early, in 2002, instead of the planned 2005 date (NHLBI, 2002). Women taking estrogen and progestin were twice as likely to develop dementia, including Alzheimer's, as women not taking supplemental hormones (NIH, 2003a). In addition, WHI studied women taking estrogen only, and this study also was stopped early because estrogen did not reduce risk for heart disease and increased risk of stroke, endometrial cancer, and dementia (American Cancer Society, 2004). WHI also studied the effects of HRT on women who have had a hysterectomy. This study also ended early, as it increased risk for stroke and dementia, and did not reduce risk for heart disease (NIH, 2004). The FDA (2003) recommends that if hormone therapy is needed, it should be taken in the smallest dose possible for the shortest amount of time needed.

Psychological Effects In rural Ireland, not long ago, women who no longer menstruated would retire to their beds and stay there, often for years, until they died (U.S. Office of Technology Assessment, 1992). This traditional custom may seem extreme, but the attitude it expressed—that a woman's usefulness ends with her ability to reproduce—was typical in western societies until fairly recently (Avis, 1999; Crowley, 1994).

Women tend to view menopause with mixed emotions. Psychological problems in midlife are more likely to be caused by attitude than by anatomy—especially by negative societal views of aging (American Medical Association, 1998). In the United States today, most women who have gone through menopause view it positively, more so than younger women do (Avis, 1999). For many women, menopause is a sign of a transition into the second half of adult life, a time of role changes, greater independence, and personal growth.

In contrast, some cultures, such as that of the southwestern Papago Indians, appear to virtually ignore menopause. In other cultures, such as those found in India and South Asia, it is a welcome event; women's status and freedom of movement increase once they are free of taboos connected with menstruation and fertility (Avis, 1999; Lock 1994). See Box 3.3 on p. 104.

The Male Reproductive System

CRITICAL THINKING
Would you characterize male menopause as a biologically or psychologically based phenomenon?

Men do not undergo a sudden drop in hormone production at midlife, as women do. Instead, their testosterone levels decrease gradually from the late teens onward, adding up to a 30 to 40 percent reduction by age 70 (King, 1996).

The term **male climacteric** is sometimes used to refer to a period of physiological, emotional, and psychological change involving a man's reproductive system and other body systems. "Male menopause" is much more gradual than female menopause, and its severity varies widely from man to man (Rowe & Kahn, 1998). The prostate gland (the organ surrounding the neck of a man's bladder) may enlarge, causing urinary and sexual problems. Other symptoms supposedly associated with the male climacteric include depression, anxiety, irritability, insomnia, fatigue, weakness, lower sexual drive, erectile failure, memory loss, and reduced muscle and bone mass and body hair (Henker, 1981; Sternbach, 1998; Weg, 1989), but it is not clear that these often vaguely defined complaints are related to testosterone levels. Men's psychological adjustments, like women's, may stem from such events as illness, worries about work, children leaving home, or the death of parents, as well as from negative cultural attitudes toward aging (King, 1996).

Many men, as they grow older, greatly fear loss of sexual potency. Actually, the idea that this is a natural accompaniment of aging is a fallacy (Masters & Johnson, 1970). Very often, lessening of sexual activity is due to nonphysiological causes: monotony in a relationship, preoccupation with business or financial worries, mental or physical fatigue, depression, failure to make sex a high priority, or fear of inability to perform. Physical causes include chronic disease (such as diabetes), surgery, some medications, and too much food or alcohol (Weg, 1989; NIA, 2002b).

Men do show some changes in sexual functioning. Although a man can continue to reproduce until quite late in life, his sperm count begins to decline in the late forties or fifties, making it less likely that he will father a child (Merrill & Verbrugge, 1999). Erections tend to become slower and less firm, orgasms less frequent, and ejaculations less forceful; and it takes longer to recover and ejaculate again (Bremner, Vitiello, & Prinz, 1983; Katchadourian, 1987; King, 1996; Masters & Johnson, 1966; NIA, 2002b). Still, sexual excitation and sexual activity can remain a normal, vital part of life.

An estimated 20 percent of men ages 50–59 and 67 percent of 70-year-old men experience **erectile dysfunction** (popularly called **impotence**): persistent inability to achieve or maintain an erect enough penis for satisfactory sexual performance (Schneider, 2003). According to the Massachusetts Male Aging Study, about 5 percent of 40-year-old and 15 percent of 70-year-old men are completely impotent (Feldman et al., 1994). Diabetes, hypertension, high cholesterol, kidney failure, depression, neurological disorders, and many chronic diseases are associated with erectile dysfunction (Utiger, 1998). Alcohol, drugs, smoking, poor sexual techniques, lack of knowledge, unsatisfying relationships, anxiety, and stress can be contributing factors.

Some men suffering erectile dysfunction can be helped by treating the underlying causes or by adjusting medications ("Effective Solutions for Impotence,"

Japanese Women's Experience of Menopause

Many women accept hot flashes and night sweats as normal accompaniments of menopause. However, that apparently is not true everywhere.

Margaret Lock (1994) surveyed 1,316 Japanese women ages 45 to 55—factory workers, farm workers, and homemakers—and compared the results with information from 9,376 women in Massachusetts and Manitoba, Canada. Japanese women's experience of menopause turned out to be quite different from the experience of western women.

Fewer than 10 percent of Japanese women whose menstruation was becoming irregular reported having had hot flashes during the previous two weeks, compared with about 40 percent of the Canadian sample and 35 percent of the U.S. sample. In fact, fewer than 20 percent of Japanese women had *ever* experienced hot flashes, compared with 65 percent of Canadian women, and most of the Japanese women who had experienced hot flashes reported little or no physical or psychological discomfort. (Indeed, so little importance is given in Japan to what in western cultures is considered the chief symptom of menopause that there is no specific Japanese term for "hot flash," even though the Japanese language makes many subtle distinctions about body states.) Furthermore, only about 3 percent of the Japanese women said they experienced night sweats, and Japanese women were far less likely than western women to suffer from insomnia, depression, irritability, or lack of energy (Lock, 1994).

The Japanese women were more likely to report stiffness in the shoulders, headaches, lumbago, constipation, and other complaints that, in western eyes, do not appear directly related to the hormonal changes of menopause (Lock, 1994). Japanese physicians link such symptoms with the decline of the female reproductive cycle, which they believe is associated with changes in the autonomic nervous system (Lock, 1988).

The symptoms physicians noted were quite similar to those the women reported. Hot flashes were not at the top of the doctors' lists and in some cases did not appear at all. However, very few Japanese women consult doctors about menopause or its symptoms, and few physicians prescribe hormone therapy (Lock, 1994).

In Japan, menopause is regarded as a normal event in women's lives, not as a medical condition requiring treatment. The end of menstruation has far less significance than it does for western women; the closest term for it, *kônenki*, refers not specifically to what westerners call menopause, but to a considerably longer period comparable to the perimenopause or climacteric (Lock, 1994, 1998).

Traditional Japanese society focuses on a strict system of stages that each cohort experiences simultaneously, from birth to marriage to parenthood to death. Aging is a social process; individual biological changes are incidental. Even birthday celebrations are a recent innovation! *Kônenki* is just another process connected with aging (Lock, 1998).

Aging itself is less feared than in the west. Passage through most of adulthood is a matter of growing responsibility and status. Not until old age can women and men alike escape the daily round of duty and do as they please. Aging brings not only respect for wisdom, but newfound freedom—as does menopause. Today, Japanese culture is becoming somewhat westernized, and there is a growing tendency to medicalize *kônenki;* but so far, the traditional view prevails (Lock, 1998).

Cultural attitudes, then, may affect how women interpret their physical sensations, and these interpretations may be linked to their feelings about menopause. Hot flashes have been found to be rare or infrequent among Mayan women, North African women in Israel, Navajo women, and some Indonesian women (Beyene, 1986, 1989; Flint & Samil, 1990; Walfish, Antonovsky, & Maoz, 1984; Wright, 1983). For example, Mayan women, who are constantly pregnant or nursing babies, tend to regard childbearing as a burden and to look forward to its end (Beyene, 1986, 1989).

Nutritional practices also may influence the experience of menopause. Some plants, such as soybeans—a staple of Far Eastern diets—contain relatively high amounts of compounds known as *phytoestrogens*, which have a weak estrogen-like effect. A diet high in foods made with these plants, such as tofu and soy flour, may influence hormone levels in the blood. When natural estrogen levels fall during the climacteric, phytoestrogens may act like estrogen and inhibit symptoms of menopause. This, then, might help explain why middle-aged Japanese women do not experience the dramatic effects of a precipitous decline in estrogen levels, as many western women do (Margo N. Woods, M.D., Department of Family Medicine and Community Health, Tufts University School of Medicine, personal communication, November, 1996).

It also might explain Japanese women's low incidence of osteoporosis and of deaths from coronary heart disease (Margo N. Woods, M.D., Department of Family Medicine and Community Health, Tufts University School of Medicine, personal communication, November, 1996). In one small, prospective, randomized, controlled study, postmenopausal women who were not on hormone therapy experienced less severe hot flashes, night sweats, and vaginal dryness after six months of taking a placebo, but *not* after taking phytoestrogens (Balk, Whiteside, Naus, DeFerrari, & Roberts, 2002). On the other hand, in a placebo-controlled, double-blind study in Brazil, daily doses of soy isoflavene decreased hot flashes and other menopausal symptoms while decreasing total cholesterol and LDL, thus offering possible protection against heart disease (Han, Soares, Haidar, de Lima, & Baracat, 2002). The findings about Japanese women's experience of menopause show that even this universal biological event has major cultural variations, once again affirming the importance of cross-cultural research.

NOTE: Unless noted, the discussion in this section is based on Papalia, Olds, and Feldman (2004).

1994; NIH, 1992). Sildenafil (known as Viagra), taken in the form of pills, has been found safe and effective (Goldstein et al., 1998; Utiger, 1998). Other treatments, each of which has both benefits and drawbacks, include a wraparound vacuum constrictive device, which draws blood into the penis; injections of prostaglandin E1 (a drug found in semen, which widens the arteries); and penile implant surgery. Still being tested are a topical cream and a suppository, both based on prostaglandin E1 ("Effective Solutions for Impotence," 1994; National Institutes of Health [NIH], 1992; Bonder & Wagner, 2001); and another oral medication, Vasomax (Jordan & Schellhammer, 1998). If there is no apparent physical problem, psychotherapy or sex therapy with the support and involvement of the partner may help (NIH, 1992; Bonder & Wagner, 2001).

Sexuality and Aging

CRITICAL THINKING

Do you think that biological or cultural influence has the greater impact on sexuality during late adulthood?

Awareness of changes in the male and female reproductive systems can help couples enjoy more satisfying sexual relations throughout the adult life span.

In most young adults, sexual drive and capacity are high. People form relationships, whether heterosexual or homosexual. Today sexual lifestyles are more diverse than in the past. However, the fear of AIDS and other sexually transmitted diseases may be putting a damper on the widespread sexual freedom that has existed in the United States since the 1960s (see Chapter 9).

Most middle-aged adults take changes in reproductive and sexual capacities in stride, and some even experience a kind of sexual renaissance. Freed from worries about pregnancy, and having more time to spend with their partners, many people find their sexual relationship better than it has been in years. Because of men's slowed response, middle-aged lovers may enjoy longer, more leisurely periods of sexual activity. Women may find their partner's longer period of arousal helpful in reaching their own orgasm—often by means other than intercourse. In one study of 160 middle-aged women, most reported having a better sex life than before. They knew their own sexual needs and desires better, felt freer to take the initiative, and had more interest in sex (Rubin, 1982). Homosexual as well as heterosexual couples who hold and caress each other, both in and out of bed, without confining such touching to foreplay for genital sex, can experience heightened sexuality as part of a caring, close relationship (Weg, 1989).

The physical aspect of sex was not scientifically recognized as a normal element of the lives of older people until the 1960s, with the pioneering research of Masters and Johnson (see Box 2.1 in Chapter 2) and the findings of the Duke University Longitudinal Study that healthy older adults are both capable and desirous of sexual activity. More recent reports indicate a rich diversity of sexual experience well into late adulthood (Brecher & Editors of Consumer Reports Books, 1984; Starr & Weiner, 1981).

After interviewing men and women over age 60, Masters and Johnson (1966, 1981) concluded that people who have had active sexual lives during their younger years are likely to remain sexually active in later life. A healthy man who has been sexually active can usually continue some form of sexual expression into his seventies or eighties, and women are physiologically able to be sexually active as long as they live. The major barrier to a fulfilling sexual life for older women is lack of a partner.

Sex is, of course, different in late adulthood from what it was earlier. Older people feel less sexual tension, usually have less frequent sexual relations, and experience less intensity. They may express their sexuality by touching, holding, and other intimacies, with or without genital intercourse.

Sexual expression can be more pleasurable for older people if both young and old recognize it as normal and healthy—if older people accept their own sexuality without shame or embarrassment, and younger ones avoid ridiculing or patronizing older persons who show signs of healthy sexuality. Housing arrangements should give older men and women opportunities to socialize with ample privacy. Medical and social workers should consider the sexual needs of the elderly and of people with physical or mental disabilities. When possible, they should avoid prescribing drugs that interfere with sexual functioning, and when such a drug must be taken, the patient should be alerted about its effects. Professionals should discuss sexual activity matter-of-factly—for example, with a heart patient who may be embarrassed to ask about it.

© PhotoDisc

Older adults often express their sexuality by touching, holding, and hugging, with or without genital intercourse.

Human beings are sexual beings from birth until death. Sexual expression is part of a healthy lifestyle—a subject we explore in Chapter 4. But even when illness or frailty prevents older people from acting on sexual feelings, the feelings persist. People can express sexuality in many ways other than genital contact—in touching, in closeness, in affection, in intimacy (Kay & Neelley, 1982). Relationships at all ages have both physical and psychological aspects for expressing love and affection, which may be highly individual.

SUMMARY AND KEY TERMS

Life Span and the Aging Process

- Life expectancy has increased greatly as a result of medical advances and is expected to continue to rise. Race and gender are factors in life expectancy.

- Research on extension of the life span in several species, especially through caloric restriction, has yielded promising results. However, survival curves suggest that there may be a genetically determined limit to human life.

- Theories of biological aging fall into two categories: genetic-programming theories, which hold that the body is programmed to fail at a certain point; and variable-rate theories, which suggest that environment and lifestyle play an important role.

life expectancy (p. 73)
longevity (p. 73)
Hayflick limit (p. 75)
survival curves (p. 76)
senescence (p. 80)
genetic-programming
 theories (p. 80)

gene therapy (p. 80)
variable-rate theories (p. 81)
free radicals (p. 82)
primary aging (p. 83)
secondary aging (p. 83)
biomarkers (p. 83)

Physical Appearance

- Despite individual variations, certain changes in appearance commonly occur during the course of adulthood.
- Because physical attributes of young adults (such as smooth skin and a lean physique) are highly prized in American society, many middle-aged and older adults attempt to maintain a youthful appearance.

Sensorimotor Functioning

- As age advances, sensory and motor functioning vary widely among individuals. There often is a slowdown in various functions of the central nervous system.
- Aging generally brings a decline in visual acuity (especially for moving objects) and the development of presbyopia (loss of near vision). Corrective lenses and environmental modifications can compensate for most moderate visual problems.
- Visual disorders associated with aging, which may cause varying degrees of blindness, include cataracts, senile macular degeneration, glaucoma, and corneal disease.
- Presbycusis, a gradual hearing loss (at first for high-pitched sounds), begins before age 25 and increases thereafter. It is more pronounced in people frequently exposed to loud noise. Treatments include hearing aids and cochlear implants.
- Losses in taste and smell make food less flavorful to older adults. Older people also have less sensitivity to touch, but less tolerance for pain and temperature changes.
- Muscular strength diminishes gradually until age 70 and more significantly after that. Endurance holds up better. Muscle performance even in the very old can be improved by training and exercise.
- Reaction time slows with age, more so for complex tasks. But experience more than compensates in middle age. Driving becomes riskier for older adults, but training can improve reaction time.

visual acuity (p. 86)
dynamic visual acuity (p. 87)
presbyopia (p. 88)
cochlear implants (p. 89)
cataracts (p. 90)
age-related macular degeneration
 (p. 90)

glaucoma (p. 91)
corneal disease (p. 92)
sensorineural hearing loss (p. 93)
presbycusis (p. 94)
conductive hearing loss (p. 94)
mixed hearing loss (p. 94)
tinnitus (p. 94)

Sexual and Reproductive Functioning

- The menstrual cycle regulates hormones in women's bodies until menopause.

- Premenstrual syndrome (PMS) is most common among women in their thirties or older.

- Menopause, which usually occurs around age 50, brings a sharp decline in estrogen and progesterone levels; this can produce a number of physical symptoms. Psychologically, most women take menopause in stride.

- In males, testosterone levels decline gradually until age 60. Most men remain fertile until late in life. The male climacteric begins about 10 years later than the female climacteric.

- With advancing age, men experience more changes in sexual functioning than women do. Men's responses become slower and their need for sexual activity is less frequent. Impotence, or erectile dysfunction, becomes more common with age.

- Although forms of sexual expression may change with aging, people can have satisfying sexual relationships throughout adult life.

premenstrual syndrome
    (PMS) (p. 100)
dysmenorrhea (p. 100)
menopause (p. 100)
climacteric (p. 100)

hormone replacement therapy
    (HRT) (p. 102)
male climacteric (p. 103)
erectile dysfunction (or
    impotence) (p. 103)

Health and Body Systems

◆ FOCUS: STEPHEN HAWKING

Good health is a duty to yourself, to your contemporaries, to your inheritors, to the progress of the world.
—Gwendolyn Brooks, Report from Part One, *1972*

IN 1988, IN HIS best-selling book *A Brief History of Time,* the British astrophysicist Stephen Hawking—then in his mid forties—offered answers to such fundamental questions as: "Where did the universe come from? How and why did it begin? Will it come to an end, and if so, how?" (Hawking, 1988, p. vi). But even more fascinating than his explanations of the origins of black holes or the contradictions between quantum mechanics and Einstein's theory of relativity (which he and other theoretical physicists are trying to combine into a single, unified theory of the universe) is Hawking's own life story.

Hawking is the most famous living person with amyotrophic lateral sclerosis (ALS), commonly called *Lou Gehrig's disease* after a New York Yankees baseball star who died of it

© AP/Greg Gibson/Wide World Photos

in 1941 at age 38. ALS has also claimed the lives of the former U.S. Senator Jacob K. Javits of New York, actor David Niven, General Maxwell Taylor, and jazz bass player Charles Mingus, among others.

ALS is a degenerative disease of the neurological system: it afflicts some 30,000 Americans, with 5,000 new cases diagnosed yearly. In ALS, nerve cells in the brain and spinal cord that control motor activity die, and the unused muscles waste away. So far, there is no known cure. The disease progresses rapidly to paralysis; inability to swallow, speak, or (eventually) breathe; and finally death—usually within 2 to 5 years.

In this, as in his awesome mental abilities (which, fortunately, ALS does not affect), Stephen Hawking is an exception: He has survived for more than three decades. He first showed symptoms of the disease as a graduate student at Cambridge University (Angier, 1993), where he now holds the professorship once graced by Isaac Newton, the discoverer of the force of gravity (Sagan, 1988). Hawking was unusually young when diagnosed with ALS, which usually appears between ages 40 and 70 (ALS Association, undated).

Almost completely paralyzed and confined to a motorized wheelchair, Hawking lacks the physical ability to write or even to speak. He requires 24-hour nursing care. Able to move only the muscles of his face and two fingers of his left hand, he communicates by typing on a computer keyboard connected to a voice synthesizer. His terse remarks "are often laced with humor. . . . But he can be stubborn, abrasive and quick to anger, terminating a conversation by spinning around and rolling off, sometimes running one of his wheels over the toes of an offender" (Jaroff, 1992, p. 88).

Hawking and his former wife have three children. He socializes with students and colleagues. He goes to rock concerts and discos, where he wheels around the dance floor.

Hawking has been awarded 12 honorary degrees throughout his career and continues to publish books (the most recent, *The Universe in a Nutshell*, was published in 2001) and other scholarly works. He still travels the world giving lectures and attending conferences; in 2003 Hawking appeared on "Late Night with Conan O'Brien" with Jim Carrey (http://www.hawking.org.uk/home/hindex.html).

"Apart from being unlucky enough to get ALS . . . I have been fortunate in almost every other respect," Hawking (1988, p. vii) wrote in *A Brief History of Time*. "I was . . . fortunate in that I chose theoretical physics, because that is all in the mind. So my disability has not been a serious handicap."

AT FIRST GLANCE, IT MIGHT appear that Stephen Hawking's situation is highly unusual. His intelligence is extraordinary, his disease is relatively rare, and his incapacitation is extreme. And yet, this man and his circumstances reflect themes that run through this chapter.

First, ALS points up the delicate balance involved in the functioning of body systems essential to health. Health is an important aspect of adult development and aging because many of the physical processes that underlie changes in health are developmental. ALS is one of a number of diseases that are more likely to strike in middle or old age. As people age, their body systems tend to undergo structural and functional changes. In order to age successfully and healthfully, people must adapt to these changes. Furthermore, physical health can affect other aspects of development, such as work, retirement, intimate relationships, and mental health. Indeed, although we discuss physical health in this chapter and mental health in Chapter 12, we need to keep in mind that the two are interrelated.

Second, the effort to conquer ALS exemplifies the continual, painstaking quest for control over threats to physical well-being. Until very recently, scientists knew little about the cause of ALS, except that about 1 in 10 patients inherit it. Then, in 1993, researchers discovered a genetic defect that appears to be linked to those familial cases, though it is not clear how. More recent studies have turned up other possible causative factors (Angier, 1993; "Research Update," 1995; Rosen et al., 1993). Eventually, perhaps, one or more of these lines of research will lead to an effective treatment or a cure.

CRITICAL THINKING

How much choice should people have in deciding which genes to alter?

Because a number of other diseases, such as Alzheimer's disease, cancer, and heart disease, seem to have genetic forms, it is likely that genetic screening and therapy for a broad range of conditions will become increasingly common (see Box 4.1 on p. 114). But even when dealing with a hereditary disease, we need to recognize the importance of environmental and lifestyle factors that affect health. Every moment of every day, people make choices about how they live, what they eat, and how they handle stress. Stephen Hawking, for example, evidently spends his time thinking about black holes rather than about what his disease makes him unable to do.

In this chapter, you will learn about how body systems age across the adult life span and about direct and indirect influences on health. As you read, ask yourself: What am I doing now that will help me live to a healthy and happy old age? What should I change? Do I understand risk factors for diseases such as cancer, and do I know how to monitor my own health? How do I handle crises and the stresses of daily living? If I were told that I had ALS (or some other fatal disease), how would I react? What would I do with the rest of my life?

HEALTH AND AGING: A LIFESPAN DEVELOPMENTAL APPROACH

The peak of health for most people is in young adulthood, though most middle-aged and older adults continue to be healthy and able-bodied. Almost 95 percent of Americans age 15 to 44 consider their health excellent, very good, or good, as compared with 84 percent of middle-aged people, three-fourths of noninstitutionalized older adults age 65 to 74, and about two-thirds of those 75 and over (Older Americans, 2000).

Many young adults are never seriously ill or incapacitated; and fewer than 1 percent, as compared with close to 9 percent of middle-aged people, have chronic conditions or impairments that affect their mobility or activities (Rowe & Kahn, 1998). Although chronic ailments tend to increase with age, most older adults do not have to limit any major activities for health reasons before age 85, (Older Americans (2004); see Figure 4.1). Older people do need more medical care than younger ones. They go to the doctor more often, are

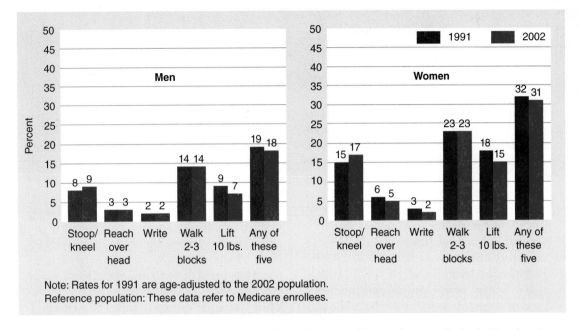

Note: Rates for 1991 are age-adjusted to the 2002 population.
Reference population: These data refer to Medicare enrollees.

FIGURE 4.1 *Percentage of Medicare enrollees age 65 and over who are unable to perform certain physical functions, by sex, 1991 and 2002.* SOURCE: Centers for Medicare and Medicaid Services, Medicare Current Beneficiary Survey in *Older Americans 2004: Key Indicators of Well-Being,* Federal Interagency Forum on Aging Related Statistics, p. 29.

hospitalized more frequently, stay longer, and spend more than 4 times as much on health care (Older Americans, 2000). They are also more likely to need home health care, including help with activities of daily living. This includes bathing, dressing, transfer from bed to wheelchair, using the toilet, and eating. Help may also be needed with instrumental activities of daily living including doing light housework, preparing meals, taking medications, shopping, using the telephone, and managing money.

Why does health often decline with age? A widely accepted explanation is that body systems and organs deteriorate, becoming more susceptible to problems. It is true that tissues and structures throughout the body tend to become less elastic and less efficient, and some normal changes may herald more serious dysfunctions or disorders. But such changes are not inevitable or universal. Individual differences—some of them related to socioeconomic, racial, and ethnic factors—cast doubt on the popular belief in a link between aging and disease.

As the "young old" become more numerous, it is becoming increasingly apparent that health is a matter not so much of age as of genes, lifestyle, and (to some extent) luck. The classic descriptions of age-related physical losses come mainly from cross-sectional studies. For example, cross-sectional observations of apparently healthy adults age 20 to 80 found a general drop in kidney functioning with age (Rowe et al., 1976). But such findings may be due to cohort differences. By contrast, the Baltimore Longitudinal Study of Aging, a long-term study of more than 1,000 adults of all ages, begun in 1958, measured

CRITICAL THINKING

How would you rate the health status of your grandparents, your parents, and yourself? Do you see a trend across generations or many individual differences?

Genetic Testing and Genetic Engineering

What are your chances of developing colon cancer or Alzheimer's disease, or another genetically influenced condition? Genetic testing is becoming more common as scientists find ways to identify people genetically at risk to develop a variety of diseases and disorders.

The Human Genome Project, a $3 billion research effort under the joint leadership of the National Institutes of Health and the U.S. Department of Energy, was designed to map the chromosomal locations of all the 10,000 to 25,000 human genes and identify those that cause or trigger particular disorders. The project was completed in April 2003, two years ahead of schedule. Since the completion of the project, goals have expanded to include identifying gene function, structure, and variation, and addressing critical societal issues arising from the increased availability of human genome data and related analytical technologies (Human Genome Project, 2004).

The genetic information gained from such research could save many lives and improve the quality of many others by increasing our ability to predict, control, treat, and cure disease. Already, genetic screening of newborns is saving lives and preventing mental retardation by permitting identification and treatment of infants

with sickle cell anemia or phenylketonuria (Holtzman, Murphy, Watson, & Barr, 1997). Genetic information can help people decide whether to have children and with whom. It also may allow more time to plan what to do in the event of illness or death (Post, 1994).

Gene therapy (repairing or replacing abnormal genes) is already an option for some rare genetic disorders and eventually will be possible *in utero* (Anderson, 1998). In utero gene therapy could head off a disorder and might prove more efficient than starting treatment after birth, when symptoms appear (Zanjani & Anderson, 1999). However, the prospect of human gene transfer experiments raises ethical concerns about safety, benefit to participants, and the difficulty of obtaining meaningful informed consent (Sugarman, 1999).

Genetic testing itself involves ethical issues. For one thing, predictions are imperfect. And what if a genetic condition is incurable? Is there any point in knowing you have the gene for a potentially debilitating condition if you cannot do anything about it (Holtzman et al., 1997)?

What about privacy? Although medical data are supposed to be confidential, it is almost impossible to keep such information private. And do parents, children, or siblings have a legitimate

---

kidney functioning repeatedly in the *same* subjects. Many showed only a slight decline with advancing age, and 35 percent showed no decline (Lindeman, Tobin, & Shock, 1985).

Physiological changes in late adulthood are highly variable; many of the declines commonly associated with aging could be the effects of disease rather than causes (T. F. Williams, 1992). Some body systems decline more rapidly than others (see Figure 4.2 on p. 116). The digestive system, including the liver and gallbladder, remains relatively efficient. Among the

claim to information about a patient that may affect them (Plomin & Rutter, 1998; Rennie, 1994)?

A major concern is *genetic determinism*: the misconception that a person with a gene for a disease is bound to get the disease. All that genetic testing can tell us is the likelihood that a person will get a disease. Most diseases involve a complex combination of genes or depend in part on lifestyle or other environmental factors (Plomin & Rutter, 1998). Is it fair to use a genetic profile to deny employment to a currently healthy person? Job and insurance discrimination on the basis of genetic information has already occurred—even though tests may be imprecise and unreliable and people deemed at risk of a disease may never develop it (Lapham, Kozma, & Weiss, 1996).

Some states have passed laws prohibiting job or insurance discrimination on the basis of genetic information and/or denying employers access to such information. The federal Equal Employment Opportunity Commission (EEOC) has stated that genetically based job discrimination violates the Americans with Disabilities Act (ADA), but an individual is covered by the act only if symptoms of a genetic disability are present. It does not protect against genetic conditions that have yet to develop (Centers for Medicare and Medicaid Services, 2002). The Health Insurance Portability and Accountability Act of 1996 prohibits group health insurance plans from using genetic information to establish eligibility or from treating such information as a preexisting condition, in the absence of a diagnosis. However, insurance companies can use genetic information to place limitations on coverage and to determine premiums (Human Genome Project, 2006). Current federal laws do not protect privacy or restrict access to genetic information (Rothenberg et al., 1997).

Within the next 15 years, genetic testing and gene therapy "will almost certainly revolutionize the practice of medicine" (Anderson, 1998, p. 30). It is not yet clear whether the benefits of these new biotechnologies will outweigh the risks.

The flood of data and related technologies generated by the Human Genome Project (HGP) and other genomic research presents a broad array of commercial opportunities. Seemingly limitless applications cross boundaries from medicine and food to energy and environmental resources, and predictions are that life sciences may become the largest sector in the U.S. economy (Human Genome Program, 2000).

most serious changes are those affecting the heart. Its rhythm tends to become slower and more irregular; deposits of fat may accumulate around the heart and interfere with functioning. Blood pressure often rises (Rowe & Kahn, 1998).

The lifespan developmental approach (Baltes, 1987) sheds new light on why adults age so differently. Why is one man's heart "fit as a fiddle" at age 70, while another needs a bypass operation? How can the same woman have a "young" heart but "old" eyes and "middle-aged" lungs? The concept of

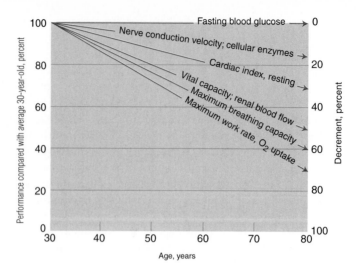

FIGURE 4.2 **Declines in organ functioning.** Differences in functional efficiency of various internal body systems are typically very slight in young adulthood but widen by old age. *SOURCE:* Katchadourian, 1987.

multidirectionality—change occurring in more than one direction or at more than one rate throughout the life span—may offer a clue to such differences among and within individuals.

As the lifespan approach suggests, gains in some areas can compensate for losses in others. For example, in adults free of heart disease, the Baltimore Longitudinal Study found that while the heart's ability to pump more rapidly during exercise tends to lessen with age, blood flow diminishes very little because the heart pumps more blood with each stroke (National Institutes of Health/National Institute of Aging [NIH/NIA], 1993; Rodehoffer et al., 1984). In Chapter 3, we cite examples of plasticity, another key concept of the lifespan developmental approach. In this chapter we note the brain's ability to rejuvenate itself by compensating for losses of threadlike *dendrites* that carry messages between nerve cells (NIH/NIA, 1993; Selkoe, 1992).

Finally, the lifespan perspective emphasizes history and context, reminding us that cultural factors such as diet and nutrition, sanitation, environmental pollutants, scientific knowledge, economic development, and even religious beliefs help determine patterns of health and disease, life and death (see Box 4.2 on p. 118). The newer longitudinal findings on organ functioning suggest that today's healthier lifestyles will allow more and more people to maintain a high level of physical functioning well into old age.

CHANGES IN BODY SYSTEMS

One important change that may affect health is a decline in **reserve capacity** (or *organ reserve*), a backup capacity that helps body systems function in times of stress. Reserve capacity is like money in the bank for a rainy day. Normally, people do not use their organs and body systems to the limit. Extra capacity is available for extraordinary circumstances, allowing each organ to put forth 4 to 10 times as much effort as usual. Reserve capacity helps to preserve **homeostasis,** the maintenance of vital functions within their optimum range (Fries & Crapo, 1981).

With age, reserve levels tend to drop. Although the decline is not usually noticeable in everyday life, older people generally cannot respond to the physical demands of stressful situations as quickly or efficiently as before. Someone who used to be able to shovel snow and then go skiing afterward may now exhaust the heart's capacity just by shoveling. Young people almost always can survive pneumonia; older people often succumb to it or, if not, are at high risk of dying within the next few years (Koivula, Sten, & Makela, 1999). For that reason, influenza vaccines and pneumonia vaccines are especially important for the elderly. Older pedestrians who cannot call on fast reflexes, vigorous heart action, and rapidly responding muscles to get out of harm's way are more likely to be victims of traffic accidents.

Most normal, healthy middle-aged adults—and even many older ones—barely notice changes in systemic functioning. Although no longer able to reach the peak performance levels of their youth, they retain enough reserve capacity to function well. If older adults pace themselves, they can do just about anything they need and want to do (Rowe & Kahn, 1998).

Let's "tour" five major body systems—skeletal, cardiovascular, respiratory, immunological, and neurological—and see what changes may occur with age.

> **CRITICAL THINKING**
> What approaches might aging adults take to maximize quality of life as reserve capacity declines?

Skeletal System

With aging, changes in bones and joints* can lead to two of the most common physical disorders in older adults: osteoporosis and arthritis.

STRUCTURAL AND FUNCTIONAL CHANGES

Aging often brings problems with the joints. The smooth, protective cushion of cartilage covering the ends of bonds tends to deteriorate, perhaps because of repeated stress or internal changes.

The bones themselves, especially in women, become less dense. Throughout life, the body constantly absorbs and replaces calcium in the bones. As people age, there is typically some net loss of bone as more calcium is absorbed than replaced. In women, bone loss usually begins at about age 30, speeds up at menopause, and then levels off. Men, whose bones contain more

---

*Unless otherwise noted, this discussion is based on Spence (1989) and Jaffe (1985).

How Traditional Beliefs Influence the Course of Disease

In traditional Chinese culture, medicine and astrology are intimately connected. Chinese healers teach that people born in years ending with certain numbers are ill-fated if they contract certain diseases. For example, heart disease is more likely to prove fatal to people born in a "fire year" (a year ending in 6 or 7, such as 1946 or 1967). People born in an "earth year: (ending in 8 or 9) are less likely than others to survive diabetes, peptic ulcers, or cancer. And those in "metal years" (ending in 0 or 1) do worse than average if they develop such respiratory diseases as bronchitis, emphysema, and asthma.

David P. Phillips (Phillips, Ruth, & Wagner, 1993), a sociologist at the University of California, San Diego, decided to test the effects of these traditional Chinese beliefs. Phillips and his colleagues looked at death certificates of 28,169 Chinese American adults, all of whom had died between 1969 and 1990. The investigators matched each deceased Chinese American with a randomly selected control group of 20 deceased white Americans of the

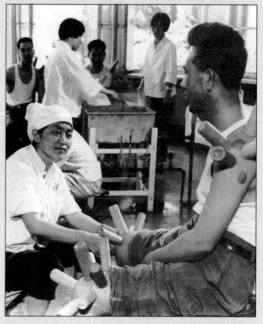

© AP/Wide World Photos

Traditional healers at a sanatorium in northeast China use methods such as cautery (burning off diseased tissue), along with western techniques. Studies suggest that cultural attitudes can influence the course of a disease.

calcium to begin with, typically do not have bone loss until after age 60 (American Medical Association, 1998).

Estrogen plays an important role in keeping blood calcium levels normal by aiding the absorption of calcium from food. It also promotes the absorption of calcium from the blood into the bone, assisting the renewal and repair activity of osteoblasts (the cells responsible for building up bone). When estrogen levels in the body fall, calcium absorption is less efficient and uptake of calcium into the bone slows down (Stoppard, 1999).

Excessive loss of calcium can cause bones to become thin and brittle, and, together with visual impairments, can lead to falls; 20 to 30 percent of falls among older persons lead to moderate to severe injuries (CDC, 2005). Fractures can be more damaging to older adults than to younger people—

same sex, born in the same year, who had also died in the same year and of the same cause. The researchers also tracked each person's health history to see when the fatal disease had begun.

As a group, Chinese Americans who had an "ill-fated" combination of birth year and disease died of the ailment more quickly than white controls, and about 1 to 5 years sooner than Chinese who had the same disease but were not born in an ill-fated year. Women with ill-fated combinations of disease and birth year died earlier than men. Chinese Americans with unlucky pairings who were presumed to be strongly committed to traditional beliefs—those who had been born in China, lived in large cities, and had not been autopsied (a traditionally disapproved procedure) also tended to have died sooner. For example, strongly traditional Chinese women born in metal years who had bronchitis, emphysema, or asthma died 8.3 years earlier than other Chinese who died of the same diseases.

The researchers interpreted their findings as showing a psychosomatic influence on the course of illness. People who expected to die early from a certain disease were more likely to do so. However, the study did not consider the possibility that some people with "ill-fated" diseases may have died of other causes. Also, it is possible that people who believe they are destined to die of a certain disease, such as lung cancer, may be less likely to take precautions against it (for example, avoiding smoking).

Still, this research—together with another study by the same group (described in Box 13.2 in Chapter 13), which found that Chinese and Jewish people are less likely to die during ethnic holidays—does suggest that culturally influenced attitudes can play an important role in the course of disease.

harder and slower to heal, and more likely to result in extended loss of mobility and independence.

Older people can minimize the risk of falling by having regular vision and hearing checkups; asking about side effects of medicines that may affect coordination and balance; avoiding alcohol, which can interfere with balance and reflexes; getting up slowly after eating or resting; keeping nighttime temperatures no lower than 65 degrees, since a drop in body temperature can cause dizziness; using a cane, walking stick, or walker on uneven or unfamiliar ground; walking cautiously on wet or icy pavements; wearing rubber-soled or low-heeled shoes (not socks only, or smooth-soled slippers); and exercising regularly. (See Table 3.2 in Chapter 3, a safety checklist for the home.)

CRITICAL THINKING

What activities and treatments can older people make use of that may reduce skeletal system decline?

OSTEOPOROSIS

Osteoporosis ("porous bones"), a disorder in which the bones become extremely thin and brittle as a result of rapid calcium depletion, is present in 1 in 4 women over age 60 and is a major cause of broken bones in old age. It is estimated that more than 1.5 million new fractures occur in the United States yearly as a result of osteoporosis (AMA, 2004; Barzel, 2001). Frequent signs of osteoporosis are loss in height and a "hunchbacked" posture due to compression and collapse of weakened bones in the spine. Osteoporosis is most prevalent in white women, those with fair skin or a small frame, those with a family history of the condition, and those whose ovaries were removed at an early age (NIA, 1993). African American women, who have greater bone density, have a lower risk of developing osteoporosis than white women (Stoppard, 1999). Although most common after menopause, osteoporosis may begin to develop before age 30 in young women who avoid milk products in order to lower their intake of fat, as many American women do. Studies have found value in calcium and vitamin D supplements beginning at the age of 40 for women (Dawson-Hughes, Harris, Krall, & Dallal, 1997; Eastell, 1998).

Proper nutrition, specifically a diet rich in calcium, and exercise begun in youth and maintained throughout life, along with avoidance of smoking, can slow the rate of bone loss and prevent osteoporosis (American Medical Association, 1998; NIA, 1993, 2002c). Women over age 40 should get 1,000 to 1,500 milligrams of calcium a day from low-fat milk, cheese, and yogurt or other foods, along with recommended daily amounts of vitamin D, which enables the body to absorb calcium (AMA, 2004; NIA, 1993). Affected women may lose up to 50 percent of their bone mass between ages 40 to 70 (American Medical Association, 1998). A predisposition to osteoporosis seems to have a genetic basis, so measurement of bone density is an especially wise precaution for women with affected family members (Rowe & Kahn, 1998). The best exercises for increasing bone density are weight-bearing activities, such as walking, jogging, aerobic dancing, and bicycling (NIA, 1993). Although the risk of developing osteoporosis is not as high for men as it is for women, men account for 2 million of the 10 million cases in the United States. Women, until their late sixties, lose bone density more rapidly than men. After that time, bone density loss occurs at the same rate in both (NIA, 2002c). Awareness of osteoporosis in men is a primary concern. By the time the condition is diagnosed, it is frequently too late for effective treatment because low bone density may have gone unnoticed for years (AMA, 2002).

Several factors increase the risk of developing osteoporosis. One very important factor is the postmenopausal loss of the hormone estrogen, which helps protect bone density. Besides relieving hot flashes and night sweats, HRT is the best-known treatment to prevent or stop bone loss after menopause, reducing the risk of osteoporosis and fractures. However, there are many issues to consider before undergoing estrogen replacement therapy (Davidson, 1995; Eastell, 1998; Levinson & Altkorn, 1998; Prestwood et al., 1994; see Table 4.1). In addition to HRT, several other options are available to treat and prevent osteoporosis. Bisphosphonates, such as

TABLE 4.1

Estrogen: Benefits and Risks

Estrogen's Benefits
- Relief from the classic symptoms of menopause: hot flashes, mood swings, vaginal dryness, thinning skin
- Proven reduced bone loss (osteoporosis) associated with menopause, including a probable reduction in hip fractures
- Possible lowered risk of colon cancer

Estrogen's Risks
- An increased risk of endometrial cancer, which may be countered by adding progesterone to a regimen of estrogen
- Symptoms similar to premenstrual ones (swelling, bloating, breast tenderness, mood swings, headaches)
- A menstrual discharge (when progesterone is taken with estrogen)
- Probable increased risk of breast cancer
- Stimulation of the growth of uterine fibroids and endometriosis
- Increased risk of blood clots, heart attack, and stroke
- Possible weight gain

SOURCE: Adapted from "Hormone Therapy," 1997, p. 2. Wasserthell-Smoller et al. 2003 Writing Group for the Women's Health Intiative Investigators, 2002.

Fosamax and Actonel, can be used to treat and prevent osteoporosis in women and to treat it in men. Bisphosphonates slow the breakdown of bone as well as increase bone density. Their drawbacks include the possibility of side effects such as nausea, heartburn or stomach; and muscle, joint, or bone pain; and they must be taken in a specific manner. Another option is a selective estrogen receptor modulator (SERM), such as Evista, which can be prescribed for postmenopausal women to treat osteoporosis. SERM reduces bone loss and increases bone density. It is beneficial because it works like HRT but does not have the risks that HRT does. However, a SERM does not treat the variety of symptoms that HRT does; it treats only osteoporosis and may have such side effects as hot flashes and risk of blood clots (NIA, 2002c).

ARTHRITIS

Arthritis is a general term for more than 100 disorders that cause pain and loss of movement, most often involving inflammation of the joints in the form of swelling, redness, warmth, and joint pain. These disorders affect 70 million people, or one in three adults. Arthritis occurs more frequently with advancing age and is the most common chronic health problem of older adults. However, arthritis commonly begins after age 40, which makes baby boomers the generation most at risk, as more than half of those affected are under the age of 65 (Arthritis Foundation, 2004). Arthritis can strike younger people, too; if so, they may have to live with the condition for the rest of their lives (AARP,

1999; Saxon & Etten, 2002). In Americans over the age of 15, arthritis is the leading cause of disability (Arthritis Foundation, 2004). Most forms of arthritis are chronic and endure for many years. Rheumatoid arthritis and osteoarthritis (often a noninflammatory condition) are the two most common forms seen in the aged (Tonna, 2001).

The most common form is *osteoarthritis*, or degenerative joint disease. This disease is often a milder condition than rheumatoid arthritis, exhibiting no symptoms initially; occasionally there is pain and joint stiffness, and sometimes considerable pain and disability occur (Tonna, 2001). Osteoarthritis occurs when a joint becomes chronically inflamed, perhaps because of wear and tear or repeated stress, and cartilage begins to break down. The rough, exposed ends of the bones rub together, causing the joint to swell and stiffen. Weight-bearing joints in the spinal column, hips, and legs, as well as the fingers and toes, are most commonly affected. Tennis players often develop osteoarthritis in the elbow and knees, and pianists and typists in the fingers.

Rheumatoid arthritis is a crippling disease that progressively destroys joint tissue. Rheumatoid arthritis is not considered a disease of old age, and in 70 percent of cases the disease makes its appearance between the ages of 25 and 54 years. It affects 75 percent more women than men (Tonna, 2001). Rheumatoid arthritis is most likely to affect the small joints in the hands, wrists, elbows, feet, and ankles. It starts with inflammation of the synovial membrane, which lubricates the joint and nourishes the cartilage. Without treatment, the cartilage may be damaged and the joint may become deformed. In severe cases, the bones may eventually fuse, immobilizing the joint.

The cause of either type of arthritis is unknown. One possibility is that rheumatoid arthritis may be a malfunction of the autoimmune system, which (as we'll discuss later) begins to attack the body's own cells.

Treatment usually involves a combination of medication, rest, physical therapy, application of heat or cold, and some method of protecting the joints from stress, such as canes or splints or just using a joint itself more carefully. Aspirin or other nonsteroidal anti-inflammatory drugs can relieve pain and control inflammation. Range-of-movement exercises can help, especially when done in a heated spa or pool. A radical treatment is replacing a joint, especially the hip. Withdrawal of fluid that may form in the joint cavity can relieve osteoarthritis. So can cortisone injections (especially in the knee). However, since cortisone itself can damage cartilage, this treatment cannot be repeated too often.

Cardiovascular System

Changes in the *cardiovascular system*—the heart and blood vessels, which circulate the blood that carries oxygen and other nutrients to the cells—may lead to life-threatening disease.*

---

*Unless otherwise noted, the discussion in this section is based on Bigger (1985) and Spence (1989).

STRUCTURAL AND FUNCTIONAL CHANGES

The heart is a muscle and, like other muscles, may become less flexible when healthy muscle tissue is replaced with fat or more rigid connective tissue. **Cardiac reserve**—the heart's ability to pump faster under stress—may decline substantially, and the remaining muscle tissue must work harder to compensate. In some older adults, the heart's output may be only half what it was at age 20. Both fat deposits and pumping capacity can be greatly influenced by diet and exercise.

Two interrelated changes in the blood vessels may be forerunners of disease. A gradual increase in **blood pressure** (the force of blood flow against the arterial walls) may begin as early as the twenties. Although a slight elevation of blood pressure is normal with aging, a significant rise may lead to severe health problems in middle or old age. High blood pressure tends to promote thickening and loss of elasticity of the arteries—**arteriosclerosis** ("hardening of the arteries"), which occurs as flexible tissue is gradually replaced by collagen fibers. Like a garden hose that becomes stiff, rigid arteries, in turn, offer greater resistance to blood flow, making the heart work harder and raising blood pressure.

CRITICAL THINKING

How do genetic predisposition and environmental variables influence functional changes in the cardiovascular system?

CARDIOVASCULAR DISEASES

Cardiovascular disease is the leading cause of death in the United States and other developed nations. Although the death rate from cardiovascular disease has dropped dramatically, these diseases still claimed 700,142 lives in the United States in 2001. This is 38.5 percent of all deaths or 1 of every 2.6 deaths (American Heart Association, 2004).

Hypertension (high blood pressure) is usually the first cardiovascular disease to develop, typically in midlife. Hypertension is a particularly widespread problem in older persons. Although blood pressure levels off after age 60, the degeneration of elastin in the walls of the arteries results in gradually increasing systolic blood pressure throughout later life. Elevated blood pressure increases the risk for stroke, heart disease, heart failure, kidney disease, and retinal damage with loss of vision (Sullivan, 2001). Thirty-two percent of noninstitutionalized older adults have hypertension (CDC, 2003). People who experience a great deal of stress, are obese, consume a large amount of alcohol or salt, or have a family history of hypertension are believed to be more at risk (Saxon & Elton, 2002). Women may incur additional risk factors, which include being on the Pill, being pregnant—especially during the last three months—and being postmenopausal (American Heart Association, 2004). African Americans in the United States have one of the highest prevalence rates of hypertension in the world. Just under 42 percent of African American men and nearly 45 percent of African American women have high blood pressure (American Heart Association, 2004). Hypertension accounts for 1 in 5 deaths among black people—twice as many as among whites (Older Americans, 2000).

Atherosclerosis, or *coronary artery disease*, is a buildup of *plaque*, fatty deposits on the inner walls of arteries. As the heart strains to force blood through the narrowed passages, pressure builds, increasing the risk of a swelling (*aneurism*) or rupture. A **myocardial infarction** (heart attack) happens when a blood clot or plaque buildup stops the flow of blood through a coronary artery that feeds the heart. Without oxygen, the affected heart muscle dies. **Congestive heart failure** can occur when a diseased heart can no longer pump an adequate supply of blood. Blood backs up into the lungs and other tissues, and fluid accumulates in the body.

In *cerebrovascular disease*, clogged blood vessels so restrict the flow of blood to the brain that nerve cells begin to die. If a blood vessel supplying the brain becomes completely choked off, or if a blood vessel in the brain bursts, a cerebrovascular accident—a **stroke**—will occur, causing brain damage, paralysis, or death. Blood pressure screening, low-salt diet, and education have prevented many deaths from heart disease and stroke (Rowe & Kahn, 1998).

PERSONALITY AND CARDIOVASCULAR DISEASE

In the late 1950s a secretary for two California cardiologists, Meyer Friedman and Ray Rosenman, observed that the chairs in their waiting rooms were tattered and worn, but only on the front edges.* The cardiologists had noticed the impatience of their cardiac patients, who often arrived exactly on time for an appointment and were in a great hurry to leave. Subsequently, they conducted a study of 3,000 healthy men between the ages of 35 and 59 over a period of eight years (Friedman & Rosenman, 1974). During the eight years, one group of men had twice as many heart attacks or other forms of heart disease as anyone else in the sample. Autopsies of the men who died revealed that this same group had coronary arteries that were more obstructed than those of other men. Friedman and Rosenman described the coronary disease group as characterized by **Type A behavior pattern**—cluster of characteristics (being excessively competitive, hard-driven, impatient, hostile) thought to be related to the incidence of heart disease. Rosenman and Friedman labeled the behavior of the other group, who were relaxed and easygoing, **Type B behavior pattern**.

However, further research on the link between Type A behavior and coronary disease indicates that the association is not as strong as Friedman and Rosenman believed (Suls & Swain, 1996; Williams, 1995, 2001). Researchers have examined the components of Type A behavior, such as hostility, competitiveness, a strong drive to accomplish goals, and impatience, to determine a more precise link with coronary risk. The Type A behavior component most consistently associated with coronary problems is hostility (Faber & Burns, 1996). People who are hostile outwardly or turn anger inward are more likely to develop heart disease than their less angry counterparts (Allan & Scheidt, 1996). Such people have been called "hot reactors" because of their intense physiological reactions to stress. Their hearts race, their breathing quickens, and their muscles tense up. Redford Williams (1995), a leading behavioral medicine researcher, believes that such people can develop the ability to control their anger and develop more trust in others, which he thinks can reduce their risk for heart disease.

---

*Unless otherwise indicated, discussion in this section is based on Papalia, Olds, & Feldman (2004).

Researchers examined the role of personality factors, including hostility, in health in one longitudinal study of more than 1,500 men from 28 to 80 years of age with an average age of 47 at the initial assessment (Aldwin et al., 2001). Men who had high, increasing symptoms of poor health were characterized by hostility and anxiety, were overweight, and smoked. Those with few symptoms of poor health were emotionally stable, educated, thin, nonsmokers.

Respiratory System

Because breathing is essential, physiological changes that restrict expansion of the lungs and other parts of the respiratory system can be life-threatening.*

STRUCTURAL AND FUNCTIONAL CHANGES

Beginning in the twenties, respiratory structures gradually tend to become more rigid. Cartilage in the walls of the *trachea* (the windpipe), and in the *bronchial tubes* that branch off from its lower end, begins to calcify, as does cartilage in the rib cage. The lungs lose elasticity because of changes in the chemical composition and structure of their fibers; and the bubble-like *alveoli*, the microscopic air sacs in the lungs, shrink. These changes, together with deterioration of the muscular and skeletal systems—which may cause the spine to curve forward, constricting the chest—can make breathing less efficient.

Vital capacity—the amount of air that can be drawn in with a deep breath and then expelled—diminishes beginning at about age 40 and may drop as much as 40 percent by age 70. In an ongoing longitudinal study of most of the population of the town of Framingham, Massachusetts, vital capacity has turned out to be the best single predictor of how much longer a person will live, regardless of level of activity (Walford, 1986), and thus may be an excellent biomarker of aging.

RESPIRATORY DISORDERS

It is normal for people to sleep less in their later years. Older people sleep more lightly, dream less, and have fewer periods of deep sleep (Webb, 1987; Woodruff, 1985).

Some "light sleepers" have a disturbance called **sleep apnea**, a halt in breathing for 10 seconds or more, which causes a person (especially an older male) to awaken frequently and then fall back to sleep, resuming normal breathing. An estimated 6 percent of the population (18 million people) experience as many as 20 to 60 episodes per hour every night. Sufferers may be aware only that they are sleepy in the daytime. Sleep apnea appears to be related to snoring, which also becomes more common, particularly among men, with advancing age (Prinz, 1987; Woodruff-Pak, 1987; National Sleep Foundation, 2005). It is more than twice as prevalent in elderly African Americans

---

*Unless otherwise noted, the discussion in this section is based on Spence (1989).

as in whites (American Lung Association, 2003a). People who use sleeping pills, drink alcohol, take daytime naps, sleep on their backs, or are overweight are more prone to sleep apnea. Because the condition is associated with a pronounced rise in blood pressure, adults who have it may be at increased risk of heart disease and strokes (Prinz, 1987; Roff & Atherton, 1989; "Sleep," 1995; Woodruff-Pak, 1987; American Sleep Apnea Association, 2004).

Emphysema is an irreversible disease in which chronic irritation from smoking, polluted air, or respiratory infections causes destruction of lung tissue and progressive difficulty in breathing. The lungs become inflexible, making exhaling difficult. Stale air gets trapped in the alveoli, so that they cannot take in fresh air. The walls of the alveoli are damaged, permitting less oxygen to enter the bloodstream. Symptoms include confusion, disorientation, and sometimes periods of unconsciousness as the brain literally suffocates. People suffering from emphysema often have to breathe pure oxygen on a regular basis. There is no cure. Death often results from heart failure: the disease places an extra load on the heart, whose pumping must become faster and harder to circulate more blood in a futile effort to get more oxygen from the lungs. Emphysema is usually avoidable through better health habits, such as quitting smoking.

Immune System

The *immune system* is the body's primary defense against invading foreign substances (*antigens*). The immune system attacks invaders by means of (1) *antibodies*, specialized proteins that counteract specific antigens; and (2) *T cells*, special white blood cells that attach themselves to antigens and destroy them. T cells originate in the bone marrow and mature in the thymus gland before entering the bloodstream (Ageworks, 2000; Braveman, 1987; Spence, 1989).

STRUCTURAL AND FUNCTIONAL CHANGES

After adolescence, the thymus begins to shrink; by the age of 60, it may shrink to 15 percent of its original size. This shrinkage results in a decrease in the level of hormones, produced by the thymus, which are necessary for the maturation of T cells (MedlinePlus Medical Encyclopedia, 2004). As a result, people tend to become more susceptible to infection and less able to recover from it. Because of the decline in the body's defensive capabilities, it is advisable for older adults to get flu shots.

Many scientists believe that heightened **autoimmunity**—a tendency for the body to mistake its own tissues for antigens—is responsible for aging (Saxon & Elton, 2002; Spence, 1989). According to this *autoimmune theory* of aging (a variation on the error theories discussed in Chapter 3), the immune system begins to release antibodies that destroy its own cells. The growing sensitivity of T cells to signals to self-destruct may help account for the weakening of the aging immune system (Aggarwal, Gollapudi, & Gupta, 1999).

DIABETES

Diabetes is a complex syndrome (or syndromes) of chronic hyperglycemia (high blood glucose levels) in association with vascular, hormonal, and metabolic abnormalities. Due to its high prevalence throughout the world and its association with vascular complications, diabetes gives rise to considerable morbidity, disability, and premature death (Sinclair, 2001). Autoimmune reactions may play a part in a number of diseases, including **Type II diabetes** (formerly called mature-onset diabetes). It typically develops in adults in their fifties and sixties. However, an increasing number of children and adolescents are also developing the disease, which is one reason the disease was renamed (Gorman, 2003).

In **Type I** (formerly called juvenile-onset, or insulin dependent) **diabetes,** the level of blood sugar rises because the body does not produce enough insulin to metabolize glucose. In Type II diabetes glucose levels rise because the cells lose their ability to *use* the insulin the body produces. Approximately 90–95 percent of the 18 million Americans with diabetes have Type II, or *non-insulin-dependent,* diabetes. People with Type II diabetes often do not realize it until they develop such serious complications as heart disease, stroke, blindness, kidney disease, or loss of limbs (American Diabetes Association, 1992). Mature-onset diabetes is a major health problem, with a prevalence of 6.8 percent in the United States and 18.3 percent of those aged 60 years and over. In the United States, annual costs of diabetes exceed $132 billion: $92 billion in direct medical costs, and $40 billion on disability, lost employment, and premature death (American Diabetes Association, 2006). Diabetes causes 300,000 deaths annually in the United States, but the toll may be much higher, as death certificates often list one of the other chronic conditions associated with the disease (Sinclair, 2001).

The definitive symptom of either type of diabetes is sugar in the urine. (Physicians also test the urine for *ketones*, poisons that may form in the blood if the body attempts to burn fats instead of sugar as a source of energy.) Other symptoms include abnormal thirst, frequent urination, rapid weight loss, tiredness, and wounds that will not heal, especially in the feet and hands. Mature-onset diabetes may be controlled by appropriate diet and exercise or may be treated with oral medications.

AIDS

The movie actor Rock Hudson died from it. The beloved basketball star Earvin "Magic" Johnson quit playing because he was infected with the virus that causes it. In 2002, an estimated 5 million people worldwide were infected with HIV, bringing the total to 42 million (CDC, 2003). AIDS has now become a worldwide epidemic.

Acquired immune deficiency syndrome (AIDS), a failure of the immune system that leaves affected persons vulnerable to a variety of fatal ailments, has been spreading rapidly since the early 1980s. AIDS results from a contagious disease, human immunodeficiency virus (HIV), which destroys the T cells that enable the immune system to fight off invasions. HIV is transmitted through bodily fluids (mainly blood and semen) and is believed to stay in the body for life. Symptoms of AIDS—which include extreme fatigue, fever, swollen lymph nodes, weight loss, diarrhea, and night sweats—may not appear until 6 months to 10 or more years after the initial HIV infection.

As of now, AIDS is not curable. However, researchers developed the "AIDS cocktail" drugs that slow that progression of the disease but do not eliminate it. A three-drug cocktail consisting of Efavirenz, Lamivudine, and Zidovudine, more commonly known as AZT, has proven the most effective combination. The death rate due to AIDS has dropped significantly since 1996, when the cocktail was introduced. To be most effective, treatment must begin early, before the immune system has become impaired (Douglas, 2004) and must be administered consistently (NIH, 1999). The drawbacks to the cocktail of drugs are numerous. Foremost is the cost. It costs $15,000 per year for one person to receive this combination of drugs (NIH, 1999). A second concern is the long-term health effects of the drugs, specifically on the heart. Those taking the cocktail have twice the rates of heart disease and suffer more heart attacks than non-HIV infected people (NIH, 2004a). The side effects include nausea, diarrhea, rashes, headaches, and higher triglyceride and cholesterol levels (NIH, 1999).

More than two-thirds of all the people living with HIV in the world (29.4 million) live in sub-Saharan Africa, accounting for 77 percent of the world's AIDS deaths (see Figure 4.3). An even higher proportion of the children living with HIV in the world are in Africa, an estimated 90 percent (WHO, 2002). There are a number of reasons for this. First, more women of childbearing age are HIV-infected in Africa than elsewhere. Second, African women have more children on average than those in other continents, so one infected woman may pass the virus on to a higher than average number of chil-

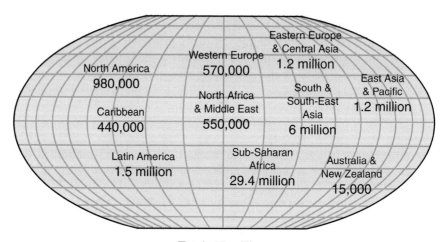

Total: 42 million

FIGURE 4.3   *Adults and children estimated to be living with HIV/AIDS as of end of 2002.*
SOURCE: World Health Organization, 2002.

dren. Third, nearly all children in Africa are breastfed. Breastfeeding is thought to account for between a third and a half of all HIV transmission from mother to child. Finally, new drugs which reduce transmission from mother to child before and around childbirth are far less readily available in developing countries, including those in Africa, than in the industrialized world (World Health Organization, 1999). A primary reason is cost. In African nations, an average of only $10 a year per person is spent on medical care.

Globally, most HIV-infected adults are heterosexual (Altman, 1992). Women presently account for approximately 50 percent of HIV and AIDS cases worldwide (CDC, 2003c). The number of new HIV infections in children worldwide was 800,000 in 2002, bringing the total number of HIV-infected children to 3.2 million (WHO, 2002). AIDS is the fourth leading cause of death worldwide (HST, 2004). In 2002, it claimed the lives of 3.1 million people, including 610,000 children (WHO, 2002), up from an estimated 2.5 million in 1998 (WHO, 2005).

In the United States, it is estimated that 980,000 people are living with HIV or AIDS (WHO, 2002). AIDS in the United States is most prevalent in men who have contracted the disease from having sex with other men and in intravenous drug users. However, the number of new infections each year from male homosexual contact began to decline in 1996 and has leveled off to 32 percent. Meanwhile, the prevalence of HIV from heterosexual contact has increased since 1998, accounting for 34 percent of new HIV infections in 2001 (CDC, 2001a). In children under the age of thirteen, the highest rates of new

Passport Foundation Chair Elizabeth Taylor, center, event chair, Earvin "Magic" Johnson, right, and co-chair Cindy Crawford pose for photographers during Macy's American Express Passport fashion show in Santa Monica, California, to raise funds for HIV/AIDS research and treatment. AIDS represents a significant risk to both young and old.

infections of HIV are in those that pass from mother to child (CDC, 2001b). HIV testing is now being done as part of the standard group of prenatal tests; however, the mother has the right to refuse the test. This will reduce the number of mothers transmitting the disease to her unborn child to 2 percent or less (CDC, 2005). Infection through a blood transfusion or tissue or organ transplant accounts for 1 percent of existing AIDS cases (CDC, 2001a).

AIDS does not attack only the young; people over age 50 now account for 11 percent of recorded cases in the United States (Ayya, 1994; WHO, 2002). About 17 percent of patients in this age group contracted it through contaminated blood transfusions before routine screening began in 1985. Now more older adults are contracting HIV through risky behaviors such as unprotected sex and intravenous drug use (CNN, 1998). Older women tend not to view unprotected sex as a risky behavior, and women past menopause do not need to worry about becoming pregnant and are therefore less likely to have their partner wear a condom (NIA, 2003). HIV and AIDS may go undiagnosed in older adults simply because of a lack of awareness and education about how the disease is spread or failure to communicate with doctors about sexual activity or drug use (NIA, 2003).

CRITICAL THINKING

Why is it important that older adults understand AIDS and that doctors acknowledge the sexual activity of older adults?

Neurological System

The *neurological*, or *nervous system* is a communication link among the cells and organs of the body and a key to the functioning of many other body systems, including sensory perception and muscular control.

The nervous system has two parts: the *central nervous system* and the *peripheral nervous system*. The central nervous system—brain and spinal cord—is responsible for higher-level functions such as memory, language, and intelligent behavior, as well as reflexes. The peripheral nervous system connects the central nervous system to the rest of the body.

STRUCTURAL AND FUNCTIONAL CHANGES

Although the brain does change with age, these changes vary considerably from one person to another. In normal, healthy older people, changes are generally modest and make little difference in functioning (Kemper, 1994). The brain increases in weight until about age 30; there is then a slight weight loss and later an increasingly rapid loss. By age 90, the brain may have lost up to 10 percent of its weight, probably because of a loss of nerve cells, or *neurons*. Nerve cells, like muscle cells, cannot replace themselves. Because some neurons die every day, the total number of cells in the nervous system declines throughout adulthood. Different parts of the brain lose varying numbers of neurons. The *cerebellum* may lose 25 percent of its cells, noticeably affecting balance and fine motor coordination, while other parts of the brain lose few cells and retain their functioning virtually intact (Spence, 1989).

A functional change that commonly accompanies loss of brain matter is a gradual slowing of responses, beginning in middle age. After age 70, many adults no longer show the knee jerk; by age 90 all such reflexes are typically gone (Spence, 1989). A slowdown of the central nervous system can affect not only physical coordination but also intellectual performance. It can worsen the performance of older adults on intelligence tests, especially timed tests, and can interfere with their ability to learn and to remember (Birren et al., 1980; Salthouse, 1985; Spence, 1989).

Not all brain changes are negative. Between middle age and early old age, nerve cells may sprout additional branches, or dendrites. This may compensate for the loss of neurons by increasing the number of *synapses*, or connections among remaining cells (NIH/NIA, 1993; Sapolsky, 1992; D. J. Selkoe, 1992).

The *autonomic nervous system*, a part of the peripheral nervous system, often declines in old age, making it more difficult to withstand extreme temperatures and lessening control over the anal and urethral sphincter muscles.

© Nina Winter/Image Works

Alzheimer's disease, a degenerative brain disorder with no known cure, is one of the most dreaded diseases associated with aging.

DEMENTIA

The confusion, forgetfulness, and personality changes sometimes associated with old age may or may not have physiological causes. The general term for physiologically based intellectual and behavioral deterioration is **dementia;** we discuss this further in Chapter 12. Contrary to stereotype, dementia is not an inevitable part of aging. Nor is moderate memory loss necessarily a sign of dementia. Although most dementias are irreversible, some can be reversed with proper diagnosis and treatment (American Psychiatric Association, 1994; NIA, 1993; Alzheimer's Association, 1998b). Many dementias formerly thought to be due to other causes are now being attributed to Alzheimer's disease.

"DREADED DISEASES" OF AGING

Alzheimer's Disease

Early in the 1990s, Ronald Reagan's longtime golf buddies began to realize something was wrong when the former U.S. president, a noted wit, would start to tell a joke and then be unable to finish it. Several years later, Reagan had to discontinue his weekly golf outings because he didn't know where he was. At the time of his death in 2004 at age 93, he hadn't recognized his children in years (Blood & Rogers, 2004).*

Alzheimer's disease (AD) is one of the most common and most feared terminal illnesses among aging persons; it affects at least 15 million people throughout the world (Reisberg et al., 2003) and is the sixth leading cause of death among older Americans (NCHS, 2004). It gradually robs patients of intelligence, awareness, and even the ability to control their bodily functions—and finally kills them. An estimated 4.5 million people in the Untied States have AD, and by 2050 the incidence is projected to be 13.2 million. The risk rises dramatically with age;

CRITICAL THINKING

What are the similarities and differences between dread diseases of the 21st century and those of previous centuries?

---

*Unless otherwise noted, the discussion in this section is based on Papalia, Olds, & Feldman (2004).

thus, increases in longevity mean that more people will survive to an age when the risk of AD is greatest (Herbert, Scherr, Bienias, Bennett, & Evans, 2003).

SYMPTOMS

The classic symptoms of Alzheimer's disease are memory impairment, deterioration of language, and deficits in visual and spatial processing (Cummings, 2004). The most prominent early symptom is inability to recall recent events or take in new information. A person may repeat questions that were just answered or leave an everyday task unfinished. These early signs may be overlooked because they look like ordinary forgetfulness or may be interpreted as signs of normal aging. (Table 4.2 compares early warning signs of Alzheimer's disease with normal mental lapses.)

Personality changes—most often, rigidity, apathy, egocentricity, and impaired emotional control—tend to occur early in the disease's development and may aid in early detection and diagnosis (Balsis, Carpenter, & Storandt, 2005). More symptoms follow: irritability, anxiety, depression, and, later, delusions, delirium, and wandering. Long-term memory, judgment, concentration, orientation, and speech all become impaired, and patients have trouble handling basic activities of daily life. By the end, the patient cannot understand or use language, does not recognize family members, cannot eat without help, cannot control the bowels and bladder, and loses the ability to walk, sit up, and swallow solid food. Death usually comes within eight to ten years after symptoms appear ("Alzheimer's Disease, Part I," 1998; Cummings, 2004; Hoyert & Rosenberg, 1990; Small et al., 1997).

CAUSES AND RISK FACTORS

Accumulation of an abnormal protein called *beta amyloid peptide* appears to be the main culprit contributing to the development of Alzheimer's disease (Bird, 2005; Cummings, 2004). The brain of a person with AD contains excessive amounts of **neurofibrillary tangles** (twisted masses of dead neurons) and large waxy clumps of **amyloid plaque** (nonfuctioning tissue formed by beta amyloid in the spaces between neurons). Because these plaques are insoluble, the brain cannot clear them away. They may become dense, spread, and destroy surrounding neurons (Harvard Medical School, 2003a).

Alzheimer's disease, or at least its age of onset, is strongly heritable (Bird, 2005; Harvard Medical School, 2003a). However, education and cognitively stimulating activities have consistently been associated with reduced risk of AD (Crowe, Andel, Pedersen, Johansson, & Gatz, 2003; Wilson & Bennett, 2003). A 4-year longitudinal study of older residents of a biracial community suggests that the protective effect is due, not to education itself, but to the fact that educated people tend to be cognitively active (Wilson & Bennett, 2003). In a study of 10,079 Swedish twins, complexity of work—especially of work with people—reduced the risk of AD (Andel et al., 2005).

How might cognitive activity protect against AD? One hypothesis is based on the concept of **cognitive reserve,** which—much like organ reserve—may enable a deteriorating brain to continue to function under stress, up to a point,

TABLE 4.2

Alzheimer's Disease Versus Normal Behavior: Warning Signs

Normal Behavior	Symptoms of Disease
Temporarily forgetting things	Permanently forgetting recent events; asking the same questions repeatedly
Inability to do some challenging tasks	Inability to do routine tasks, such as making and serving a meal
Forgetting unusual or complex words	Forgetting simple words
Getting lost in a strange city	Getting lost on one's own block
Becoming momentarily distracted and failing to watch a child	Forgetting that a child is in one's care and leaving the house
Inability to balance a checkbook	Forgetting what the numbers in a checkbook mean and what to do with them
Misplacing everyday items	Putting things in inappropriate places where one cannot usefully retrieve them; e.g., a wristwatch in a fishbowl
Occasional mood swings	Rapid, dramatic mood swings and personality changes; loss of initiative

SOURCE: Adapted from Alzheimer's Association (undated).

without showing signs of impairment. Ongoing cognitive activity may build cognitive reserve and thus delay the onset of dementia (Crowe et al., 2003).

Diet, exercise, and other lifestyle factors also may play a part. Foods rich in vitamin E, n-3 fatty acids, and unhydrogenated unsaturated fats—such as oil-based salad dressings, nuts, seeds, fish, mayonnaise, and eggs—may be protective against AD, whereas foods high in saturated and transunsaturated fats, such as red meats, butter, and ice cream, may be harmful (Morris, 2004). Smoking is associated with increased risk of AD (Launer et al., 1999; Ott et al., 1998). Other possible risk factors under investigation include sleep apnea and head injuries earlier in life ("Alzheimer's Disease, Part III," 2001).

DIAGNOSIS AND PREDICTION

AD can be diagnosed definitively only by postmortem examination of brain tissue, but scientists are rapidly developing tools to enable fairly reliable diagnosis in a living person. Neuroimaging is one such tool, particularly useful in excluding alternative causes of dementia (Cummings, 2004) and in allowing researchers to actually see brain lesions indicative of AD in a living patient (Shoghi-Jadid et al.,

CRITICAL THINKING

How is the person with Alzheimer's disease affected? How are family and friends affected by the person with Alzheimer's disease?

2002). A longitudinal study using brain scanning found that reduced metabolic activity in the hippocampus of healthy middle-aged and older adults can accurately predict who will get Alzheimer's or a related memory impairment within the next nine years (Mosconi et al., 2005). In what could lead to a definitive test of early AD, researchers at Northwestern University used a new bio-barcode amplification (BCA) technology to detect minuscule amounts of proteins called amyloid beta-derived ligands (ADDLs) in cerebrospinal fluid (Georganopoulou et al., 2005). Blood tests that measure levels of the amino acid homocysteine (Seshadri et al., 2002) and of amyloid precursor proteins (Padocani et al., 2002) may predict or diagnose AD or other forms of dementia in the early stages.

Neurocognitive screening tests can make initial distinctions between patients experiencing cognitive changes related to normal aging and those in early stages of dementia ("Early Detection," 2002; Solomon et al., 1998). In a study at the University of California in San Diego, performance on paper-and-pencil cognitive tests predicted which participants would develop AD within a year or two (Jacobson, Delis, Bondi, & Salmon, 20002). In the Seattle Longitudinal Study of Adult Intelligence (introduced in Chapter 15), results of psychometric tests were predictive of dementia as much as 14 years prior to diagnosis (Schaie, 2005).

Despite the identification of several genes associated with AD (Bertram et al., 2005; Bird, 2005) particularly an early-onset form that appears in middle age, genetic testing so far has a limited role in prediction and diagnosis. Still, it may be useful in combination with cognitive tests, brains cans, and clinical evidence of symptoms ("Alzheimer's Disease, Part I," 2001). Healthy, middle-aged people without apparent symptoms who have the APOE-e4 gene associated with early-onset AD have shown deficits in spatial attention and working memory (Parasuraman, Greenwood, & Sunderland, 2002) and in *prospective memory,* the ability to remember what to do at a future time, such as take medicine or keep an appointment (Driscoll, McDaniel, & Guynn, 2005). Such deficits may be indicative of early AD.

In the Nun Study, a longitudinal study of Alzheimer's disease and aging in 678 Roman Catholic nuns, a research team examined autobiographies the nuns had written in their early twenties. The women whose autobiographies were densely packed with ideas were least likely to become cognitively impaired or to develop Alzheimer's disease later in life (Riley Snowdon, Desrosiers, & Markesbery, 2005).

TREATMENT AND PREVENTION

Although no cure has yet been found, early diagnosis and treatment can slow the progress of Alzheimer's disease and improve quality of life. One medication approved by the U.S. Food and Drug Administration is memantine (commercially known as Namenda). Memantine inhibits the action of glutamate, a brain chemical that can overstimulate brain cells, resulting in cell damage or death. In a double-blind, placebo-controlled trial, daily doses of memantine taken for 28 weeks reduced deterioration in patients with moderate to severe AD without significant adverse effects (Reisberg et al., 2003).

Cholinesterase inhibitors, such as donepezil (commercially known as Aricept), have become standard treatment for slowing or stabilizing the progress of mild to moderate AD (Cummings, 2004). However, hopes for long-term effectiveness were shattered when a 5-year trial of Aricept found no significant difference after the first two years between patients taking Aricept and those given a placebo (AD2000 Collaborative Group, 2004). Similarly, in a 3-year double-blind study, donepezil therapy had no effect after the first year had none at all over the entire three-year period (Petersen et al., 2005).

Cholinesterase inhibitors are often given in combination with memantine and high-dose vitamin E. However, studies are mixed as to the effectiveness of vitamin E (Cummings, 2004); a recent three-year study found no benefit (Petersen et al., 2005). Also being tested are anti-inflammatory drugs and the herbal remedy gingko biloba, but there is insufficient evidence of their effectiveness (Cummings, 2004; Foley & White, 2002; Harvard Medical School, 2003a; Morris et al., 2002). A promising experimental approach is immunotherapy. In one study, Alzheimer's patients vaccinated with beta amyloid performed better on memory tests up to a year later than patients injected with a placebo (Fox et al., 2005; Gilman et al., 2005).

In the absence of a cure, management of the disease is critical (Cummings, 2004). In the early stages, memory training and memory aids may improve cognitive functioning (Camp et al., 1993; Camp & McKitrick, 1992; McKitrick, Camp, & Black, 1992). Behavioral therapies can slow deterioration, improve communication, and reduce disruptive behavior (Barinaga, 1998). Drugs can relieve agitation, lighten depression, and help patients sleep. Proper nourishment and fluid intake, together with exercise, physical therapy, and control of other medical conditions, are important, and cooperation between the physician and the caregiver is essential (Cummings, 2004).

Cancer: A Disorder of Many Systems

Cancer is a term for more than 100 different diseases involving uncontrolled growth of abnormal cells, which, if untreated, eventually invade healthy tissue. Unlike the other diseases discussed so far, cancer can arise in and spread to many body organs and systems.

Cancer is the second leading cause of death in older adults, after cardiovascular disease (American Cancer Society, 2004; NCHS, 2004; Older Americans, 2000). About 76 percent of the more than 1 million cancers diagnosed annually in the United States—and more than 60 percent of the roughly 500,000 annual cancer deaths—are in people over age 55 (American Cancer Society, 2004). One explanation is a weakened immune system. Another is that older people have had more time to develop cancers, which are often slow-growing.

Some cancers (such as basal cell carcinoma, a skin cancer) are far more curable than others. Although death rates have dropped dramatically for stomach, colorectal, ovarian, and cervical cancer, they have risen even more dramatically for lung cancer, the biggest killer—up 104 percent in men and 452 percent in women since 1960, largely because of smoking (American Cancer Society, 2000).

The discovery of two mutant genes responsible for many cases of cancer of the colon and rectum may someday enable doctors to identify and monitor people at risk of these types of cancer and possibly other types as well. The mutations apparently cause a failure to correct errors in DNA that arise during cell division, permitting cells to multiply uncontrolled (Fackelmann, 1993b; National Cancer Institute, 2004; G. Weiss, 1994).

CRITICAL THINKING

How must attitudes about cancer change in order to make further progress in its prevention and treatment?

Not all cancers appear to be genetic, however. Suspected or known environmental **carcinogens** (cancer-causing agents) include pollution, pesticides, plastics, and much else. Exposure to the sun can cause skin cancer. The best ways to prevent cancer or to stall its growth are to avoid smoking, drink alcohol only in moderation, exercise, and eat a healthy diet.

In the 1930s, 4 out of 5 cancer patients died within 5 years. Today—thanks to chemotherapy (anticancer drugs), radiation treatments, and surgery—the 5-year survival rate is near 63 percent (American Cancer Society, 2004). Many more people could be saved through periodic screening (especially of adults over 50 and those with a personal or family history of cancer), which would permit earlier diagnosis and treatment. The recent discovery of telomerase, an enzyme which is present in virtually all cancers and allows tumor cells to grow and proliferate indefinitely, has led to the testing of medications that could block its action. Such treatment might be less dangerous to healthy cells and more effective than present methods (Kim et al., 1994; Krishna, 2000).

Recently there has been an upsurge of concern about two gender-related cancers: breast cancer and prostate cancer.

BREAST CANCER

An estimated 215,990 women and 1,400 men were expected to be diagnosed with breast cancer in 2004 and approximately 40,510 people to die from it (American Cancer Society, 2003a). As with other cancers, the chance of developing breast cancer increases with age; 75 to 80 percent of breast cancers are found in women over 50 (NIH, 2003; American Cancer Society, 2003a).

Early detection is key in treating breast cancer. If the cancer is found and treated before it spreads beyond the breast, the chances of surviving at least 5 years are 97 percent (American Cancer Society, 2004). **Mammography,** a diagnostic X ray examination, is the best available tool for early detection. A mammogram can detect breast cancer an average of one to three years before a lump can be felt (CDC, 2002). The American Cancer Society recommends routine mammograms for women over the age of 40. Clinical breast examinations by a health care professional are also recommended, as some cancers cannot be detected by mammography (National Cancer Institute, 2004a), and clinical examinations can be more useful than mammography in detecting breast abnormalities in women in their twenties and thirties (American Cancer Society, 2004).

Scientists have located two genes that may be responsible for 5 to 10 percent of all breast cancer cases (National Cancer Institute, 2004b) as well as some cases of ovarian cancer. These discoveries have led to genetic screening of women with strong family histories of breast cancer, as these genes are responsible for approximately 25 percent of cases in women under 30 (National

Cancer Institute, 2004b). In addition to genetic screening, women with a high risk of breast cancer may benefit from taking Tamoxifen, which reduces the risk and is also used to prevent cancer from recurring.

Because the identified genes do not appear implicated in the vast majority of breast cancers, lifestyle factors may be important. The link between alcohol consumption and breast cancer is clear. Alcohol use increases the risk by 1 1/2 times for women who consume 2 to 5 drinks daily (American Cancer Society, 2003a). Long-term use of HRT increases the risk, but estrogen alone does not (American Cancer Society, 2003a). Using the Pill as a method of contraception increases risk, as does being overweight.

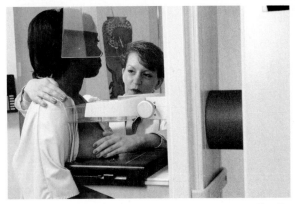

© PhotoDisc

Routine mammography (X-ray examination of the breasts) is recommended for all women age 40 and over to aid in early detection and treatment of breast cancer.

Treatment of breast cancer usually involves surgery, such as a **lumpectomy**, in which the tumor and a small amount of the surrounding tissue are removed; or a **mastectomy**, in which all or part of the breast is removed. Surgery may be combined with chemotherapy, radiation therapy, or hormone therapy. If chemotherapy is used before surgery, its purpose is to shrink the tumor. When used after surgery, it can help prevent recurrence. Radiation therapy uses high-energy rays to shrink or kill remaining cells. Hormone therapy uses estrogen-blocking drugs to help prevent cancer from coming back (American Cancer Society, 2003a).

PROSTATE CANCER

Cancer of the prostate gland at the base of a man's bladder has received extensive news coverage since 1993, when it claimed the lives of the rock musician Frank Zappa and the actors Don Ameche and Bill Bixby. Prostate cancer affects about as many men as breast cancer does women. About one-third of men over age 50 have latent prostate tumors, but many are unaware of the condition because these tumors grow so slowly. Prostate cancer was expected to kill 29,900 men in 2004 (American Cancer Society, 2003b), second only to lung cancer. While the chances of a man getting prostate cancer are 1 in 6, only 1 in 32 will die from it (American Cancer Society, 2004). The current survival rate for prostate cancer is 97 percent, up from 67 percent in 1983 (CDC, 2003d).

The cause of prostate cancer is unknown. Several risk factors have been identified, including age, family history, and race (National Cancer Institute, 2002; American Cancer Society, 2004; National Institutes of Health, 2003b). Seventy is the average age at the time of diagnosis, and men aged 65 and older account for 70 to 75 percent of cases (CDC, 2003d; NIH, 2003b). Prostate cancer rarely occurs in men under the age of 40. Men with a blood relative, in particular a father or brother, with prostate cancer have an elevated risk. African Americans have the highest rate of prostate cancer in the world, and they are twice as likely to die from it than white men (American Cancer Society, 2004). Some evidence suggests that men with diets high in red meat and high-fat dairy products have increased risk (National Cancer Institute, 2002; American Cancer Society, 2004; CDC, 2003d). Studies are ongoing to determine what relationship diet and exercise may have to do with prostate cancer.

Preliminary diagnosis of prostate cancer can be done with either a PSA (prostate-specific antigen) blood test or a DRE (digital rectal exam). Neither test can yield a diagnosis; these tests can only detect prostate abnormalities, which may come from a less serious condition, not cancer (National Cancer Institute, 2002). A PSA blood test is more effective then a DRE, but since neither test is completely accurate, the only way to be sure whether cancer exists is through a biopsy (American Cancer Society, 2004). The American Cancer Society recommends that men over the age of 50 (age 45 for high-risk men) should have a PSA blood test and DRE performed annually. However, because of the lack of evidence that screening and early treatment reduce mortality, the Centers for Disease Control and Prevention (CDC) and the National Cancer Institute do not recommend yearly screening tests (American Cancer Society, 2004; CDC, 2003d).

The treatments of prostate cancer are similar to those for breast cancer: surgery, radiation treatment, hormone therapy, and chemotherapy. Surgery is the most common treatment: a **radical prostatectomy**, in which the entire prostate gland and some of the tissue around it are removed; or **transurethral resection** of the prostate, which cuts out cancerous tissue. If the tumor is small and has not spread, radiation therapy can be used to treat it. Hormone therapy can be used to treat cancer that has spread, by preventing male hormones from reaching cancer cells, which stops the growth. This can be done through a surgery called **orchiectomy**, which removes the testicles, or through hormone reducing or blocking drugs (American Cancer Society 2004; National Cancer Institute, 2002). Some cases may call for watchful waiting, closely monitoring the health of the man, and seeking treatment only if symptoms appear or worsen (American Cancer Society, 2004; National Cancer Institute, 2002).

Indirect Influences on Health

How people take care of their bodies and how they respond to life's changes and challenges affect their health directly. But there are also indirect influences: age, gender, socioeconomic status, race or ethnicity, and relationships.

Age and Gender

How likely are young, middle-aged, and older men and women to develop specific diseases or disorders, and what are the chief causes of death at each period of adulthood? As we summarize health problems and risks by age and gender, keep in mind that not only do wide individual variations exist, but—as we'll show next—certain groups experience greater problems and risks at any age.

When young adults get sick, it is usually from a cold or other respiratory illness, which is easily shaken off. The most frequent chronic conditions, especially among those with low incomes, are back and spine problems, hearing impairments, arthritis, and hypertension (high blood pressure). Because most young adults are healthy, it is not surprising that accidents are the leading cause of death for Americans ages 25 to 44. Next come cancer, heart disease, suicide, and assault (Arias & Smith, 2003). Death rates for young adults have dropped, as have mortality rates for all other age groups except the oldest old, those above 85 (Hoyert et al., 1999). Cancer, heart disease, and strokes are down (Hoyert et al., 1999; USDHHS, 1999b; Wingo et al., 1999). While deaths from heart disease have declined since the 1960s, it remains by far the leading killer of people over 65, accounting for 40 percent of deaths. The next most common causes of death in this age group are cancer (21 percent) and stroke (8 percent) (Older Americans, 2000).

Most older adults have at least one chronic medical condition—most commonly, arthritis, hypertension, hearing impairment, heart disease, orthopedic impairments, cataracts, sinusitis, diabetes, tinnitus, or visual impairments, in that order (Older Americans, 2000). Chronic conditions become more frequent with age and may become disabling. Although people over 65 have fewer colds, flu infections, and acute digestive problems than younger adults, chronic conditions combined with loss of reserve capacity may cause a minor illness or injury to have serious repercussions.

Which sex is healthier: women or men?* One reason this question is hard to answer is that until recently women have been excluded from many important studies of health problems that affect both sexes (Healy, 1991; Rodin & Ickovics, 1990). As a result, much of what we know applies only to men.

We do know that women have a higher life expectancy than men and lower death rates throughout life (Anderson, 2001; Hoyert et al., 1999). Women's greater longevity has been attributed to genetic protection given by the second X chromosome (which men do not have) and, before menopause, to beneficial effects of the female hormone estrogen, particularly on cardiovascular health (Rodin & Ickovics, 1990; USDHHS, 1992). However, psychosocial and cultural factors, such as men's greater propensity for risk taking and their preference for meat and potatoes rather than fruits and vegetables, also may play a part (Liebman, 1995; Schardt, 1995).

Despite their longer life, women report being ill more than men, are more likely to seek treatment for minor illnesses, and report more unexplained symptoms. Men, by contrast, have longer hospital stays, and their health problems are more likely to be chronic and life-threatening (Kroenke & Spitzer, 1998; NCHS, 1998a; Rodin & Ickovics, 1990).

Women's greater tendency to seek medical care does not necessarily mean that women are in worse health than men, nor that they are imagining ailments or are preoccupied with illness (Kroenke & Spitzer, 1998). They may simply be more health-conscious. Women generally know more than men about health, think and do more about preventing illness, are more aware of symptoms and susceptibility, and are more likely to talk about their medical worries. Men may feel that illness is not "masculine" and thus may be less likely to admit that they do not feel well. It may be that the better care women take of themselves helps them live longer than men.

> **CRITICAL THINKING**
>
> What factors seem to be responsible for differences in illness reporting and treatment of illness between women and men?

*Unless otherwise noted, discussion in this section is based on Papalia, Olds, & Feldman (2004).

However, public awareness of men's health issues has increased. The availability of impotence treatment and of screening tests for prostate cancer is bringing more men into doctor's offices. Meanwhile, as women's lifestyles have become more like men's, so—in some ways—have their health patterns. Women now account for 39 percent of all smoking-related deaths in the United States. More women die of lung cancer than of any other type of cancer, including breast cancer (Satcher, 2001). The gap between men's and women's use of alcohol and illicit drugs also has narrowed (Center on Addiction and Substance Abuse [CASA], 1996), as has the gender gap in deaths from heart disease. Such trends help explain why the difference between women's and men's life expectancy shrank from 7.8 years in 1979 to 5.4 years in 2000 (Miniño et al., 2002).

Socioeconomic Status, Race, and Ethnicity

The connection between socioeconomic status and health has been widely documented (see Figure 4.4). Higher-income people rate their health as better and live longer than lower-income people. Education is important, too. The less schooling people have had, the greater the chance that they will develop and die from communicable diseases, injuries, or chronic ailments (such as heart disease), or that they will become victims of homicide or suicide (Pamuk, Makuc, Heck, Reuben, & Lochner, 1998).

This does not mean that income and education *cause* good health; instead, they are related to environmental and lifestyle factors that are likely to be causative. Poverty is associated with poor nutrition, substandard housing, exposure to pollutants and violent behavior, and limited access to health care (Adler & Newman, 2002; Otten, Teutsch, Williamson, & Marks, 1990; Pamuk et al., 1998). Indeed, the gap in health care access between rich and poor in the United States has widened (Kiefe et al., 2000). Better-educated and more affluent people have healthier diets and better preventive health care and medical treatment. They exercise more, are less likely to be overweight, and smoke less. They are more likely to use alcohol, but to use it in moderation (Pamuk et al., 1998; SAMHSA, 1998, 2001).

The associations between income, education, living conditions, and health help shed light on the relatively poor state of health in some minority populations (Kiefe et al., 2000). Young black adults are twenty times more likely to have high blood pressure than young white adults (Agoda, 1995). And African Americans are more than twice as likely as white people to die in young adulthood, in part because young black men are about seven times as likely to be victims of homicide (Hoyert et al., 1999). Hispanics are more likely than whites to be exposed to hazardous conditions in their living environments. Ninety percent of Hispanics live in urban areas, which puts them at greater risk for exposure to toxic waste, air pollution, crime, violence, older and poorly maintained buildings, lead paint, and other conditions associated with urban environments (Kaiser Permanente, 2001).

CRITICAL THINKING

What factors are poor people likely to experience that influence health problems and negatively affect their longevity?

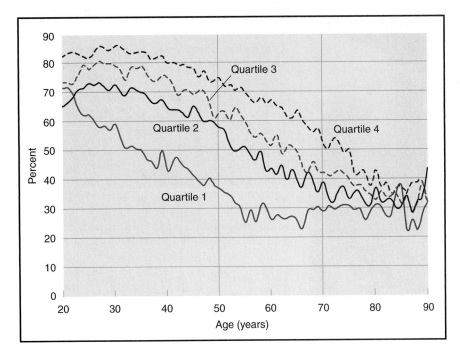

FIGURE 4.4 *Percent reporting excellent or very good health status by age-specific household income quartiles.* This figure shows that people in the highest income level, people in quartile 4, report the highest levels of health, followed by quartiles 3, 2, and 1. As people grow older they report having less excellent or very good health. *SOURCE:* Smith, 2005.

Ethnic differences in health are not wholly attributable to socioeconomic factors. For example, although African Americans smoke less than white Americans, they metabolize more nicotine in the blood, are more subject to lung cancer, and have more trouble breaking the habit. Possible reasons may be genetic, biological, or behavioral (Caraballo et al., 1998; Perez-Stable, Herrera, Jacob III, & Benowitz, 1998; Sellers, 1998). In a study of coronary risk factors among women ages 30 and under (Palaniappan et al., 2002), Caucasian American women were found to have lower cardiac risk factors than African American or Asian Indian American women and to engage in more physical activity. The African American women consumed more fat and cholesterol than the other two groups and had higher percentages of body fat and higher body mass indexes (BMIs).

Disparities in most indicators of health lessened during the 1990s for most racial and ethnic groups, though not for American Indians and Alaska Natives. However, racial and ethnic disparities in deaths from work-related injuries, motor vehicle crashes, and suicide widened (Keppel, Pearcy, & Wagener, 2002). A congressionally mandated research review of more than 100 studies found that racial and ethnic minorities tend to receive lower-quality health care than whites do, even when insurance status, income, age, and severity of conditions are similar (Smedley, Stith, & Nelson, 2002).

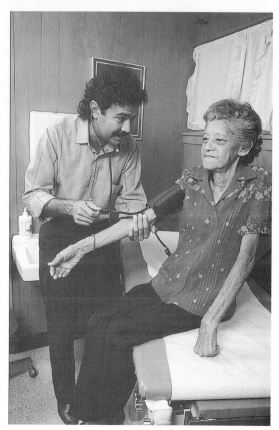
© Bob Daemmrich/Stock Boston

Hispanic Americans are especially prone to high blood pressure.

CRITICAL THINKING
What correlative factors do you believe are most influential in increasing the longevity of married people?

Relationships

Relationships have important effects on physical well-being. Adults without friends or loved ones are susceptible to a wide range of troubles, including traffic accidents, eating disorders, and suicide (Baumeister & Leary, 1995). The risk of death due to cardiovascular disease increases significantly in persons who are widowed, divorced or separated, or single (Johnson, Backlund, Sorlie, & Loveless, 2000).

Despite some evidence to the contrary (J. M. White, 1992), marriage seems to be associated with good health. Married people, especially men, tend to be healthier physically (and, in some research, psychologically) than those who are never-married, widowed, separated, or divorced (Horwitz, White, & Howell-White, 1996; Ross, Mirowsky, & Goldsteen, 1990; de Vaus, 2002). Married people have fewer disabilities or chronic conditions that limit their activities; and when they go to the hospital, their stays are generally short. Married people live longer, too, according to a study going back to 1940 in 16 industrial countries (Hu & Goldman, 1990; Johnson, et al., 2000). Those who have never married are the next-healthiest group, followed by widowed people and then by people who are divorced or separated.

Why should this be? Healthy people may attract mates more easily, may be more interested in getting married, and may be better marriage partners. Or married people may lead healthier, safer lives than single people. Because spouses can take care of each other, they may be less likely to need care in hospitals or institutions. Married people tend to be better off financially, a factor that seems to enhance physical and mental health (C. R. Ross et al., 1990). Then, even in less-than-ideal marriages, partners usually provide companionship, offer emotional support, and do many things that ease day-to-day life. The loss of these supports through death or separation may make widowed and divorced people more vulnerable to mental and physical disorders (Doherty & Jacobson, 1982). The quality of a marital relationship may make a difference.

The key to the correlation between marriage and health may be simply having another person to live with. A study of more than 25,000 women age 18 to 55 found that those who lived with another adult—whether married or not—were healthier than those who lived alone (Anson, 1989). Another large study with nearly 12,000 participants found that cohabiting couples also benefit from their relationship. Wu, Penning, Poland, and Hart (2003) found that cohabiting couples experience the same physical and psychological health benefits that married couples do.

Factors in Maintaining and Improving Health

Health is often directly linked to how adults live from day to day—whether and how much they drink, whether they smoke or abuse drugs, how they react to stress, what and how much they eat, how they take care of their teeth, and whether they get proper exercise. Healthful habits can modify a number of aspects of biological aging, such as cardiac and pulmonary (lung) reserve, glucose tolerance, bone loss, cholesterol levels, and blood pressure (Porterfield & St. Pierre, 1992). Since 1977, mortality has declined 30 percent for Americans age 25 to 64, largely because of changes in personal lifestyle (USDHHS, 1992). Although good health habits can't guarantee protection against disease, they can greatly reduce the risks, especially if started early in life (Porterfield & St. Pierre, 1992; see Table 4.3).

CRITICAL THINKING

What are the greatest deterrents to following recommendations for optimizing personal health outcomes?

Harmful Substances

Two of the most beneficial decisions a person can make are to stop smoking (or, better still, not to start) and to drink alcohol only in moderation.

TOBACCO

Smoking is the leading preventable cause of death in the United States (American Lung Association, 2003b; American Heart Association, 1995). It kills about 440,000 people yearly, disables millions and costs the United States an estimated $150 billion a year in direct health care costs and lost productivity. Smokers lose an average of 13.8 years of life from their habit (American Lung Association, 2005a).

Worldwide 4.2 million people die each year as a result of tobacco use and that number is projected to reach 10 million between 2025 and 2030, with more than twice as many tobacco-related deaths in developing, as in developed, countries. The United States is the second largest importer and exporter of tobacco leaves (Mackay & Eriksen, 2002).

Secondhand smoke, or **passive smoking,** is responsible for an estimated 3,000 lung cancer deaths and 35,000 to 40,000 heart disease deaths annually (American Cancer Society, 2004). A nonsmoking spouse who lives with a smoker has a 30 percent higher risk of lung cancer than he or she would otherwise. Nonsmokers are 25 percent more likely to have coronary heart disease from environmental smoke than those not exposed. Smoking in the workplace increases the risk of nonsmokers developing lung cancer by 17 percent (American Lung Association, 2003c).

The link between smoking and lung cancer is well established. Smoking is estimated to be responsible for 87 percent of lung cancer cases in the United States (American Lung Association, 2005b; Wingo et al., 1999). Smoking is also linked to cancer of the larynx, mouth, esophagus, bladder, kidney, pancreas, and cervix; to gastrointestinal problems, such as ulcers; to respiratory illnesses, such as

TABLE 4.3

Lifestyle Factors in Selected Diseases

Risk factor	Coronary Heart Disease	Stroke	Diabetes (non-insulin dependent)	Breast Cancer	Lung Cancer	Prostate Cancer	Colorectal Cancer	Melanoma (skin cancer)	Osteoporosis	Osteoarthritis
Cigarette smoking	X	X	X	X	X	X	X	X	X	X
Alcohol	?		?	?					X	
Dietary factors										
Cholesterol	X	X								
Calories			X							
Fat intake	X	X	?	?		X	?			
Salt intake		X								
Fiber			O							
Calcium									O	
Potassium	O									
Overweight	X	X	X						X	?
Physical activity	O	O	O						O	O
Exposure to toxins				X	X	X	X			
Exposure to ultraviolet rays								X		

NOTE: X = increases risk of disease; O = decreases risk of disease; ? = may increase risk of disease.
SOURCE: Adapted from Merrill & Verbrugge. 1999. Table IV, p.87; Papalia, Olds, & Feldman, 2004.

bronchitis and emphysema; to osteoporosis; and to heart disease (CDC, 2003; He et al., 1999; Hopper & Seeman, 1994; NIA, 1993; Slemanda, 1994; USD-HHS, 1987). A woman smoker's risk of heart disease, stroke, and certain types of cancer rises if she uses oral contraceptives. If a woman smokes during pregnancy the risk of low birthweight, premature birth, and infant death increases (American Lung Association, 2005a).

A smoker who has a heart attack is more likely than a nonsmoker to die from it (American Heart Association, 1992; 2004). Cigar and pipe smokers are in less danger of heart attack than cigarette smokers, but still at higher risk than nonsmokers; and they are more likely to get cancer of the lips, tongue, and mouth (Katchadourian, 1987; American Heart Association, 2004).

As these risks have become widely known, smoking in the United States has declined more than 37 percent since 1965 (American Heart Association, 1995). The trend among high school and college age persons has begun to reverse from the substantial increase in the early 1990s. Smoking in this age group has decreased from 37 percent to 24 percent in 2003 (Johnston, O'Malley, Bachman, and Schulenberg, 2003). Currently about 1 in 5 Americans age 18 and over is a smoker (American Cancer Society, 2005d; National Center for Health Statistics, 1998a). At least 90 percent of the people who stop smoking do so on their own (Fiore et al., 1990). Others turn to special programs, such as support groups. Nicotine chewing gum and nicotine patches, along with information on the drawbacks of smoking, have been quite successful (NIA, 1993; USDHHS, 1987).

However and whenever people stop smoking, their health is likely to improve immediately. After giving up smoking, the risk of heart attack drops within 24 hours (American Lung Association, 2005b). Ninety percent of the risk associated with tobacco use can be avoided if smokers quit before the age of 35, and quitting at any age substantially reduces risks (American Cancer Society, 2004).

CRITICAL THINKING

Given the combined effects of smoking and drinking alcohol on overall health, why do people continue to use these substances?

ALCOHOL

The United States is a drinking society. Advertising equates liquor, beer, and wine with the good life. About 69 percent of 18- to 44-year-olds report using alcohol, and the youngest adults tend to be the heaviest drinkers. Almost 39 percent of 18- to 25-year-olds, predominantly young men, are binge drinkers, downing five or more drinks at a session (SAMHSA, 2001).

Although moderate consumption of alcohol seems to reduce the risk of fatal heart disease, the definition of *moderate* is becoming more restricted. A recent large-scale study found that men who take more than one drink a day have much higher death rates. Apparently, increased risk of cancer of the throat, gastric system, urinary tract, and brain outweighs any benefits to the heart (Harvard Medical School, 2006). And other studies suggest that women can safely drink only about half as much as men.

Long-term heavy use of alcohol may lead to cirrhosis of the liver, other gastrointestinal disorders (including ulcers), certain cancers, heart failure, damage to the nervous system, psychoses, and other medical problems. Alcohol is also a major cause of deaths from automobile accidents; it is implicated in deaths from drowning, suicide, fire, and falls; and it is often a factor in family violence. We discuss alcohol abuse and alcoholism further in Chapter 12.

Stress

You've taken on a heavy course load and feel overwhelmed by deadlines. You're facing a major competitive challenge at work. You've just had an argument with your boyfriend or girlfriend. You can be under stress for an almost infinite number of reasons. Stress is an organism's physiological and psychological reaction to difficult demands made on it.

The more stressful the changes that take place in a person's life, the more likely the person is to become ill within the next year or two. That was the finding of a classic study in which two psychiatrists, on the basis of interviews with 5,000 hospital patients, ranked the stressfulness of life events that had preceded illness (Holmes & Rahe, 1976; see Table 4.4). Some of the events seemed positive—for example, marriage, a new home, or an outstanding personal achievement. Even happy events, though, call for adjustments. Change can be stressful, and some people react to stress by getting sick.

Stress—or rather, how people cope with stress—is coming under increasing scrutiny as a factor in causing or aggravating such diseases as hypertension, heart ailments, stroke, and ulcers. The most commonly reported physical symptoms of stress are headaches, stomachaches, muscle aches or muscle tension, and fatigue. The most common psychological symptoms are nervousness, anxiety, tenseness, anger, irritability, and depression. In one study of 227 middle-aged men, the 26 who had had heart attacks were more likely than the others to have worried and to have felt sad, anxious, tired, and lacking in sexual energy in the year before the attack (Crisp, Queenan, & D'Souza, 1984). Another study of 2,320 men who had had heart attacks found that men who were socially isolated and under stress were more likely to die within 3 years after an attack than more sociable men who were under less stress (Ruberman, Weinblatt, Goldberg, & Chaudhary, 1984). We discuss the psychology of coping with stress in Chapter 12. Here, our focus is on its physiological effects.

The body's ability to respond to stress tends to become impaired with age. Although body systems may function well under normal circumstances, when challenged by stressful events they do not respond as efficiently as in youth. An older person's body may both underreact and overreact to stress—not stepping up heart output enough during physical exertion, but releasing excessive amounts of adrenalin and other stress hormones well after the stress-provoking event is over (Lakatta, 1990).

Some theories (see Chapter 3) attribute biological aging itself to effects of a lifetime's accumulation of stress. Even adaptive responses can cause stress if repeated often enough. For example, a rise in blood pressure enables a person to flee an attacker; but a person whose blood pressure is consistently elevated for years—perhaps owing to stress on the job—is a prime candidate for a heart attack, ulcers, or colitis (Sapolsky, 1992). Long-term oversecretion of stress hormones may play a part in a number of age-related disorders, from

TABLE 4.4

Some Typical Life Events and Weighted Value for Stressfulness

Life Event	Value
Death of spouse	100
Divorce	73
Marital separation	65
Jail term	63
Death of close family member	63
Injury or illness	53
Marriage	50
Being fired at work	47
Marital reconciliation	45
Retirement	45
Change in health of family member	44
Pregnancy	40
Sex difficulties	39
Gain of new family member	39
Change in financial state	38

SOURCE: Adapted from Holmes & Rahe, 1976.

mature-onset diabetes to osteoporosis (Krieger, 1982; Munck, Guyre, & Holbrook, 1984).

There do seem to be limits to such degeneration, and some individuals seem to escape it entirely. By studying individual differences in reactions to stress—particularly to psychological stress, which has less uniform effects than physical stress—we may begin to find a key to prevention or treatment of stress-related disorders.

One reason the same event leads to illness in one person and not in another may have to do with a sense of mastery or control. When people feel that they can control stressful events, they are less likely to get sick. Research on human beings and animals has found links between stressful events perceived as uncontrollable and various illnesses, including cancer (American Cancer Society, 2000). One team of researchers suggested that belief in external, rather than personal, control suppresses the functioning of the immune system and creates health problems, including depression (Rodin et al., 1985). Stress management workshops teach people to control their reactions and to turn stress into an opportunity for constructive change. These workshops frequently incorporate such techniques as relaxation, meditation, and biofeedback.

Dramatic evidence of the power of stress comes from the reactions of New Yorkers to the September 11, 2001, terrorist attacks on the World Trade Center.*

---

*Unless otherwise noted, this discussion is based on Papalia, Olds, & Feldman (2004).

A survey of 1,008 adult Manhattan residents found a substantial amount of acute post-traumatic stress disorder (PTSD) and current depression five to eight weeks following the attacks, especially among those who lived near the site of the destruction and those who had suffered personal losses (Galea et al., 2002). One-third of the respondents—especially those who experienced PTSD or depression—reported using more alcohol, marijuana, or cigarettes since the attacks (Vlahov et al., 2002).

Diet

"You are what you eat" is not just a cliché. The cumulative effects of diet and nutrition become more apparent with age.

CRITICAL THINKING

Have you noticed how stress and poor diet interact to overload your body system? How might these combined factors influence older adults?

Obesity—defined as a body mass index (BMI) of 30 or more—is a serious health hazard that affects 1 in 5 adults. Being overweight affects the circulatory system, the kidneys, and sugar metabolism. It can raise blood pressure and cholesterol levels, and is considered a risk factor for many diseases, including diabetes, heart disease, and some cancers. Being overweight contributes to degenerative disorders and accounts for 300,000 premature deaths every year, making it the second leading preventable cause of death. The rate at which children and adolescents are becoming overweight and obese has more than doubled since the 1970s which is the fastest of any age group (CDC, 2004).

Current trends in weight loss techniques include fad diets such as the Atkins and South Beach diets, and surgery to shrink the stomach. The Atkins diet is based on the premise that the body first uses carbohydrates and then fat as fuel for energy. By reducing intake of carbohydrates, the body is forced to use stored fat for energy, resulting in weight loss. This approach is coming under question but has raised important issues about diet and nutrition. The South Beach diet is similar to the Atkins diet but allows "good" carbohydrates. Both diets were created by cardiologists. Both diets promise rapid and permanent weight loss, but the long-term health effects have yet to be established.

Gastrointestinal surgery is an option for persons whose BMI is 40 or more and who have been unsuccessful with other methods of weight loss. Two common types of gastrointestinal surgery are bariatric surgery and malabsorptive operations. Bariatric surgery limits the amount of food that the stomach can hold, thus limiting the amount of food intake. Malabsorptive operations restrict the amount of food intake as well as the amount of calories and nutrients that the body absorbs by not allowing food to pass through the first two segments of the small intestine. The risks of these surgeries include death (1% of those that undergo either surgery), need for another surgery due to complications (20%), and nutritional deficiencies (30%) (NIH, 2004). However, for the morbidly obese, the health benefits to be gained by losing massive amounts of weight may be of greater importance than the potential risks.

Reducing cholesterol levels in the bloodstream through diet and drugs can lower the risk of heart disease and death (Lipid Research Clinics Program, 1984a, 1984b; Scandinavian Simvastatin Survival Study Group, 1994). There are two kinds of cholesterol: low-density lipoprotein (LDL) cholesterol and high-density lipoprotein (HDL) cholesterol. Because HDL is protective, a key to preventing heart disease is the ratio between total cholesterol and HDL. Current guidelines recommend total cholesterol of 200 milligrams per deciliter or less and HDL of 35 milligrams or more. A more healthful goal, according to some cardiologists, is an HDL of at least 45 for men and 50 for women, with a 3.5 to 1 ratio of total cholesterol to HDL (American Heart Association, 2004). It is becoming more common for people to supplement diet changes with cholesterol-lowering medications over a period of time.

Nine major voluntary and government health agencies have proposed a "healthy American diet" for everyone from age 2 up (American Heart Association, 2000). It emphasizes a variety of nutritionally sound foods, with less fat, salt, and cholesterol and more fiber and complex carbohydrates found in fruits, vegetables, cereals, and grains. The "healthy American diet" takes the risk of cancer into account. Extensive worldwide research points strongly to a link between diet and certain cancers—particularly between a high-fat diet and colon cancer (Willett, Stampfer, Colditz, Rosner, & Speizer, 1990).

Dental Care

Few people keep all their teeth until very late in life. Loss of teeth, usually due to tooth decay or **periodontitis** (gum disease), can have serious implications for nutrition. Because people with poor or missing teeth find many foods hard to chew, they tend to eat less and to shift to softer, sometimes less nutritious foods (Lamy, Kalykakis, Legrand, Butz-Jorgensen, 1999; Wayler, Kapur, Feldman, & Chauncey, 1982). People with dentures tend to be less sensitive to dangerously hot foods and liquids and less able to detect bones and other harmful objects (NIA, 1993; 2002).

Dental health is related to inborn tooth structure and to lifelong eating and dental habits. Extensive loss of teeth—especially among the poor—may reflect inadequate dental care more than effects of aging. According to the Centers for Disease Control and Prevention (2001c), only 54 percent of adults over the age of 65 have been to the dentist in the past year.

Because the risk of tooth decay continues as long as a person has natural teeth, so does the need for regular checkups. In addition, gum disease becomes an increasingly common cause of tooth loss after age 35. Drinking fluoridated water, brushing daily with fluoride toothpaste, flossing, and using antibacterial or antiplaque mouth rinses can help prevent these conditions (NIA, 1993; ADA, 2004).

Exercise

Today's exercise boom is showing results. According to a recent survey, nearly 62 percent of American adults regularly engage in at least some leisure time physical activity, and 37 percent exercise strenuously at least three times a week (Schoenborn, Adams, Barnes, Vickerie, Schiller, 2004). Those who do reap many benefits. Aside from helping to maintain desirable body weight, physical activity builds muscles; strengthens heart, lungs; and bones; lowers blood pressure; protects against heart disease, stroke, diabetes, cancer, and osteoporosis; relieves anxiety, stress, and depression; improves sleep; and

Adults who exercise regularly—as close to 3 out of 4 American adults do—can cut their health risks dramatically.

lengthens life (American Heart Association, 1995, 2002; Lee & Paffenbarger, 1992; Lee, Franks, Thomas, & Paffenbarger, 1981; McCann & Holmes, 1984; Notelovitz & Ware, 1983; Pratt, 1999).

The benefits of exercise are not confined to marathon runners and aerobics fanatics. In one study, when more than 13,000 healthy men and women were tested on a treadmill, they fell into five categories of heart and respiratory fitness. The least fit led the most sedentary lives; the fittest exercised strenuously. Eight years later, the death rates of the least fit were more than three times the death rates of the most fit. But those who merely walked for 1/2 hour to 1 hour every day at a fast but comfortable pace also cut their health risks by half or more (Blair et al., 1989). Similarly, a 3-year study of 500 women between ages 42 and 50 found that moderate daily exercise—or even as little as three brisk 20-minute walks each week—can lower the risk of heart disease (Owens, Matthews, Wing, & Kuller, 1992).

Healthful aging is not merely a matter of chance. The message of the new research on biological aging, and the message of the lifespan developmental approach, is that individuals have some control over their physical destiny. The choices young and middle-aged adults make, day by day, may well help determine how they look and feel when they reach old age. We may or may not be able to extend the human life span, but we can make more of the life span vital and healthy. Good health habits can prevent, delay, or even reverse what used to be considered the inevitable ravages of aging. As we discuss in Chapters 5, 6, and 7, adults can also do much to maintain or improve their cognitive functioning, even into old age.

Health and Aging: A Lifespan Developmental Approach

- Although most adults remain fairly healthy into old age, the peak of health is generally in young adulthood.
- Many declines associated with aging may be effects of disease. Large variations between individuals and within the same person can be understood through a lifespan developmental approach.
- Healthier lifestyles can promote a high level of physical functioning well into old age.

Changes in Body Systems

- Despite a decline in reserve capacity, most aging adults can do necessary tasks and desired activities.
- A common change, especially in postmenopausal women, is thinning of the bones due to calcium depletion; excessive depletion can produce osteoporosis.
- Arthritis is the most common chronic health problem of older adults.
- The heart tends to lose elasticity as fat replaces muscular tissue, and the output of blood may diminish. Other age-related changes are a rise in blood pressure and arteriosclerosis.
- Cardiovascular disease is the leading cause of death in the United States and other developed nations, among both women and men. Women's risk rises after menopause.
- Respiratory structures tend to become less elastic with aging, and vital capacity diminishes, making breathing less efficient.
- Changes in the immune system can make older people more susceptible to infections and less able to recover. Heightened autoimmunity may cause or contribute to biological aging.
- Several diseases, including mature-onset diabetes, may result from autoimmune reactions. One is HIV infection, which causes AIDS, an eventually fatal failure of the immune system. AIDS is spreading rapidly throughout the world.
- Changes in the brain are usually minor, and new connections can compensate for loss of nerve cells. A slowing of the central nervous system can affect physical and intellectual functions, but dementia is not an inevitable part of aging.

reserve capacity (p. 117)
homeostasis (p. 117)
osteoporosis (p. 120)
arthritis (p. 121)
cardiac reserve (p. 123)
blood pressure (p. 123)
arteriosclerosis (p. 123)
hypertension (p. 123)
atherosclerosis (p. 123)
myocardial infarction (p. 123)
congestive heart failure (p. 124)
stroke (p. 124)
Type A behavior pattern (p. 124)

Type B behavior pattern (p. 124)
vital capacity (p. 125)
sleep apnea (p. 125)
emphysema (p. 126)
autoimmunity (p. 126)
Type II diabetes (formerly called mature-onset diabetes (p. 127)
Type I diabetes (formerly called juvenile-onset or insulin dependent) (p. 127)
acquired immune deficiency syndrome (AIDS) (p. 127)
dementia (p. 131)

"Dread Diseases" of Aging

- Both Alzheimer's disease and cancer are prolonged, progressively debilitating, and more prevalent with age.
- The causes of Alzheimer's disease have not been definitively established; but research points to genetic causes in some cases.
- Cancer is the second leading cause of death in older people. Genetic and environmental causes of certain cancers have been identified. Many cancers can be cured if treated early. Death rates have dropped for many cancers but have risen for lung cancer.

Alzheimer's disease (AD) (p. 131)   **mammography (p. 136)**
neurofibrillary tangles (p. 132)   **lumpectomy (p. 137)**
amyloid plaque (p. 132)   **mastectomy (p. 137)**
cognitive reserve (p. 132)   **radical prostatectomy (p. 138)**
cancer (p. 135)   **transurethral resection (p. 138)**
carcinogens (p. 136)   **orchiectomy (p. 138)**

Indirect Influences on Health

- Indirect influences on health include age, gender, socioeconomic status, race or ethnicity, and relationships.
- The prevalence of various chronic conditions and causes of death varies across the life span and between men and women.
- Although women report more frequent illness than men, they live longer and may be healthier because of their greater focus on health.
- In the United States, minority groups such as African Americans and Hispanic Americans are in significantly poorer health than white people, largely because of poverty, limited education, lack of access to treatment, and lifestyle factors.
- Supportive relationships, particularly marriage, are related to enhanced physical health.

Factors in Maintaining and Improving Health

- Smoking is the leading preventable cause of death in the United States, and passive smoking is third. Smokers who quit can dramatically improve their health.
- Although alcohol consumption has declined, heavy drinking still causes a number of medical problems, as well as accidental deaths.
- Stress seems to be a factor in illness. The body's ability to respond to stress tends to decline with age. There are also individual differences in ability to handle stress.
- Obesity is a life-threatening condition. The risk of being overweight is greatest in young adulthood.
- A high-fiber, low-fat, low-cholesterol diet can lessen the risk of heart disease and cancer.
- Dental health is related to inborn tooth structure and to lifelong eating and dental habits.
- Exercise improves health and protects against a number of major diseases.

passive smoking (p. 143)   **obesity (p. 148)**
stress (p. 146)   **periodontitis (p. 149)**

Memory

◆ FOCUS: LAURENCE OLIVIER

The memory . . . likes to paint pictures. Experience is not laid away in it like a snapshot . . . but is returned to us as a portrait painted in our own psychic colors, its form and pattern structured on that of our life.
—Lillian Smith, The Journey

© Bettmann/Corbis Images

IN HIS YOUTH, THE great British actor Laurence Olivier* had an exceptional memory. At age 20, while playing one part, he learned the leading role for another play in less than a week, letter-perfect. A noted colleague, Ralph Richardson, said of him, "In this respect [the ability to memorize rapidly] Larry was a genius—better than any of the rest of us" (Kiernan, 1981, p. 50).

At age 57, at the height of his career, Olivier began to experience attacks of paralyzing

---

*Sources of biographical information about Laurence Olivier are Amory (1987), Bragg (1984), Granger (1987), Holden (1988), Kiernan (1981), Miller (1987), and Spoto (1992).

stage fright. He would become breathless; his throat would tighten; the hall seemed to spin; his mind went blank; his face makeup beaded with perspiration; he had momentary blackouts. These anxiety attacks, which continued for almost 20 years, may have been related to fear of aging, of losing his memory. Indeed, he was having more and more trouble remembering lines (Bragg, 1984; J. Miller, 1987; Spoto, 1992). "I'm such a slow study these days," he complained at age 62. "A single scene takes me three weeks. . . . When I was young I learned [the role of] Romeo in two days." A fellow actor once found him in the wings, desperately going over his lines, when he was supposed to be making his entrance. Olivier looked up from the script and remarked, "This is no profession for an adult person" (Spoto, 1992, p. 351).

Throughout the rest of his long and distinguished career, Olivier was increasingly afflicted with memory lapses. In his late years, he limited himself to film and television work, in which short "takes" permit an actor to keep fewer lines in mind. At 73, in conversations with the theater critic Mark Amory (1987), he rattled off casts of plays in which he had appeared 50 or 60 years before and quoted passages from *Hamlet*, one of the roles that had made him famous on stage and screen. When retelling an incident, he made the scene come alive. Yet he couldn't seem to remember Amory's name. By 76, Olivier, "could no longer commit one line of dialogue accurately to memory"; but, on hearing of Richardson's death, he told "in vivid and colorful detail [a] cascade of anecdotes" about their six-decades-long association (Spoto, 1992, p. 403).

A few of Olivier's late-life characterizations—notably, King Lear, Lord Marchmain in *Brideshead Revisited*, and the blind Clifford Mortimer in *A Voyage Round My Father*—showed greater depth than ever (though it was generally agreed, when he retired on his eightieth birthday, that he had held on about 3 years too long). As he told a reporter, "Your mind expands as your body shrinks, and you adjust to it, giving in age what you couldn't give in youth" (Spoto, 1992, p. 398).

MEMORY IS THE RESIDUE OF experience. Without the ability to remember, the oldest adult would be like a newborn baby, greeting the world with ever-naive eyes. Reality would be like a picture that must continually be recreated—a series of fleeting images, no sooner perceived than lost.

Calling on stored experience is a key to thinking and to solving problems. Throughout the life span, memory enables human beings to learn from encounters with their environment and to put that knowledge to use. An apparent decline in this essential capacity troubles many middle-aged and older adults, even if their work is not so dependent on memorization as Laurence Olivier's. Small lapses in memory may arouse a fear—usually unfounded—that dementia is setting in.

Actually, as the lifespan developmental approach suggests—and as Olivier's example shows—problems with memory need not signal a general decline in mental abilities. Age may bring gains as well as losses. In fact, forgetting may have a positive side. Could there be a relationship between a tendency to forget detailed information (such as an actor's lines) and the growing depth of thought that often comes with maturity? Perhaps forgetting is not necessarily an enemy in old age but an ally, clearing away clutter so the mind can more readily recall important information and find meaningful connections.

In this chapter (which covers memory) and Chapters 6 and 7 (which deal with other aspects of cognition), we look at such changes—both positive and negative—and at how people of advancing age can maintain or enhance their intellectual powers. The information in this chapter may help you better understand your own memory. Do you remember certain kinds of things better than others? Does your memory fail you at times? Under what circumstances does it function best? Do you think your memory will get worse as you grow older? What strategies might help you make the most of your memory?

STUDYING MEMORY SYSTEMS

Changes in memory are a typical sign of aging. A man who always kept his schedule in his head now has to write it in a calendar. A woman who takes several medicines measures out each day's dosages and puts them where she is sure to see them. However, as with many other characteristics of aging, there are great differences in memory among older people (Rowe & Kahn, 1998; Hoyer & Verhaeghen, 2006). Jorge, age 58, can rattle off the batting average of every major league baseball player, but his mind is so occupied with his thoughts that he will come into a room and forget what he came for. Jorge's son Julio, age 35, also has trouble remembering what he was about to do, and he can't remember batting averages as well as his father does. And Jorge's mother Juanita, at 75, shows no obvious changes in memory at all.

CRITICAL THINKING

How does experience help aging people compensate for changes in memory?

What explains memory change and its variability during adulthood? Why, as in Laurence Olivier's case, do certain aspects of memory often seem to be more affected than others? A revolutionary new view of memory has developed since the 1950s, thanks to studies in a variety of disciplines, including psychology, biology, and medicine. Scientists now see memory, not as a single capacity, but as a complex, dynamic system of processes and "storehouses." Some, but not all, of these components may operate differently as people age.

Because computers can be programmed to "learn" and "remember," we may be able to understand how human memory works by comparing it with how a computer processes information. Human memory systems can be studied from two perspectives, each of which has produced an independent line of research. *Information-processing research* explores the mental operations involved in remembering: the software of memory. Using concepts from computer science, such as *encoding, storage, search,* and *retrieval,* information-processing researchers have produced elaborate theoretical models of the path a bit of information takes from the moment we perceive it to the moment—perhaps months or years later—when we call it up from memory. *Biological research* maps the physical structures, biochemical mechanisms, and "wiring" of the brain and nervous system: the hardware of memory. Through animal studies, through observations of people who have suffered brain damage, and by recording brain activity, neuroscientists have begun to pinpoint the actual physical locations where various memory functions and connections take place.

In the following three sections, we look at changes in the "software" and "hardware" of memory and at new directions for research. In the last section of the chapter, we examine how adults cope with changes in memory and how they use tools of memory and forgetting across the life span.

INFORMATION-PROCESSING APPROACH: SOFTWARE OF MEMORY

CRITICAL THINKING

What experiences influence cohort groups to demonstrate remarkably different performance on information-processing measures?

The goal of the information-processing approach is to discover what people do with information from the time they perceive it until they use it. Because this approach focuses on individual difference in intelligent behavior, it is particularly suited to describing changes that take place over the life span. It can distinguish between functions that change a great deal and those that change very little, either in the same person or in one person as compared with another (Lovelace, 1990). Most of the early information-processing research took the form of highly controlled laboratory studies in which people of various ages identified pictures, learned word lists, and repeated strings of numbers. During the 1980s and 1990s, some researchers have attempted direct study of how memory works in everyday life.

The information-processing approach assumes that:

- Human beings actively seek useful information about their world.
- Human beings can handle only a limited amount of information at a given time; information not currently being used must be stored in memory.
- Information that comes in through the senses is transformed by a series of mental processes into a form suitable for storage and later recall (Lovelace, 1990).

Let's look more closely at these processes and how they may be affected by aging. As we do, however, keep in mind that most information-processing studies are cross-sectional, and their findings may reflect cohort differences rather than age-related changes.

Processes: Encoding, Storage, and Retrieval

It is helpful to think of memory as a three-step filing system: **encoding, storage, and retrieval**. In order to file something in our memory, we first must decide what "folder" to put it in—for example, "people I know" or "places I've been." *Encoding* attaches a "code" or "label" to the information to prepare it for storage, so that it will be easier to find when needed. Next, we *store* the material (put the folder away in the filing cabinet). The last step is to *retrieve* the information when we need it (search for the file and take it out). The precise mechanisms involved in encoding, storage, and retrieval may vary with the situation, the type of information, and how the information is to be used (Lovelace, 1990); difficulties in any of these steps may impair memory (Zacks, Hasher, & Li, 2000).

Recognizing a familiar face may be easier for older adults than recalling the name of someone they have just met.

How information is encoded and stored can affect access (Lovelace, 1990; Wingfield & Stine, 1989). An item that is misfiled (inappropriately encoded or stored in the wrong place) will be hard to retrieve. For example, you would be unlikely to find information on Alaska if it had been filed under "tropical islands." Problems also can arise when an item fits in more than one category. For example, if you had filed the word *base* only under "terms used in baseball" and you wanted a synonym for *foundation*, you might not be able to retrieve it. Also, similar items, such as *principal* and *principle*, can cause confusion unless their encoding is distinctive.

How do these memory processes change with age? One finding is that the ability to retrieve newly encountered information seems to drop off. After several hours, days, or weeks, younger adults can remember word pairs or paragraphs, or recognize pictures, better than older people can (Craik, 1977; Park, Puglisi, & Smith, 1986; Park, Royal, Dudley, & Morrel, 1988; Poon, 1985). But when older people have trouble remembering, is this due to faulty retrieval or to actual loss of material from memory storage—or does it have more to do with the way they encoded the information in the first place? The answer may be any of the above.

- *Encoding problems.* In general, older adults seem to be less efficient than younger ones at encoding new information to make it easier to remember. For example, older people are less likely to spontaneously arrange material in alphabetical order or create mental associations.

Older adults can improve their encoding skills through training or instruction, but how much they benefit in comparison with younger adults depends on the task (Craik & Jennings, 1992). In addition, older people's encoding seems to be less precise (Craik & Byrd, 1982).

- *Storage problems.* One plausible explanation for forgetting is that stored material may deteriorate to the point where retrieval becomes difficult or impossible. Although most studies do not support the idea that older people forget more quickly than younger ones (Poon, 1985), recent research suggests that a small increase in "storage failure" may occur with age (Camp & McKitrick, 1989; Giambra & Arenberg, 1993). But if memories do decay, traces are likely to remain, and it may be possible to reconstruct them—or at least to relearn the material speedily (Camp & McKitrick, 1989; Chafetz, 1992).
- *Retrieval problems.* In retrieving learned information from memory, older adults may be able to answer a multiple-choice question but not an open-ended one. While they have more trouble *recalling* items than younger adults, they do about as well in *recognizing* items they know (Hultsch, 1971; Lovelace, 1990). Even then, it takes older people longer than younger ones to search their memories (Anders, Fozard, & Lillyquist, 1972; Lovelace, 1990). Recall of details of recent events can be enhanced by seeing photographs or reading descriptions of them (Koutstaal, Schacter, Johnson, Angell, & Gross, 1998). Age differences are minimized when older adults are familiar with the material, have an opportunity to practice, and can work at their own pace (Lovelace, 1990; Poon, 1985).

Why do certain memory processes seem to work less efficiently as people age? Where are breakdowns most likely to occur? To answer these questions, we need to look at the structure of memory—where information is kept and how it is handled during each stage of processing.

"Storehouses": Sensory, Short-Term, and Long-Term

CRITICAL THINKING

How do changes in body systems discussed in Chapter 4 influence sensory, short-term, and long-term memory? Do your observations agree with the research reported in the text?

How many sights do you see in a single day? How many sounds do you hear? If you tried to assimilate all the sensory inputs that flood your brain daily, you would suffer from information overload. How does your brain sort out the stimuli you need or want to remember, and where does this material go when you're not using it? Information-processing theorists visualize memory as consisting of at least three different but linked "storehouses": *sensory memory*, the system's initial entry point; *working memory* for short-term storage and manipulation of information; and *long-term memory* for virtually permanent storage.*

---

*Some researchers use the terms primary memory and secondary memory for short-term storage of information after it leaves sensory memory. In this system of classification, the term tertiary memory refers to long-term memory.

SENSORY MEMORY: INITIAL STORAGE

Sensory memory, the first of the mind's three "storehouses," temporarily registers incoming information: whatever you see, hear, smell, taste, or touch. This brief storage is called *echoic memory* for sounds and *iconic memory* for sights. But without some kind of processing, sensory memories fade quickly. The "echo" of the initial impression lasts only seconds, or fractions of a second (Lovelace, 1990).

Sensory memory shows little change with age; a 5-year-old's immediate recall is about as good as that of an adult (Siegler, 1998). Despite the visual losses that typically accompany aging, iconic memory (the part of sensory memory on which the most significant findings have been reported) seems to hold up fairly well. Differences in the ability of younger and older adults to identify a series of letters that flash on a screen are quite small. Any slight loss of sensory memory probably plays an insignificant role in problems older people have with learning and retrieval (Poon, 1985), though some researchers speculate that slight losses in sensory memory might lead to larger deficits in short-term and long-term memory (Craik & Jennings, 1992).

WORKING MEMORY: INTERMEDIATE, SHORT-TERM STORAGE

When you look up a telephone number and try to remember it before dialing, it goes from sensory memory into **working memory,** an intermediate, short-term "storehouse" or "workbench" for active files—the information your mind is currently encoding or retrieving.

Working memory can normally hold only about five to nine separate chunks of information (such as numbers, letters, or words) at a time (G. A. Miller, 1956). But it's possible to increase the amount of material held in working memory by grouping items into larger chunks. For example, you can more easily remember a telephone number like 2-9-7-5-3-8-4 by mentally combining the digits into 297-53-84, making three chunks instead of seven. Even then, a telephone number or any other item will remain in working memory only about 30 seconds unless you engage in **rehearsal**—conscious repetition—or some other purposeful effort. Rehearsal is a simple device to maintain information in working memory.

According to a widely used model (see Figure 5.1), a **central executive** controls the processing of information in working memory (Baddeley, 1981, 1986, 2002). The central executive can expand the capacity of working memory by moving information into subsidiary systems. When verbal information is to be remembered "as is," the central executive may send it to an **articulatory loop** (also known as the **phonological loop**) for rehearsal, or to the phonological loop for storage. (For example, you can repeat a telephone number over and over while thinking about what you want to discuss during the call.) A **visual, or spatial, scratch pad** serves a similar purpose, keeping visual images "on hold" while the central executive is occupied with other tasks. The **episodic buffer** serves as an interface between long-term memory and the subsidiary systems. Information is stored in episodes, which allows the buffer to simultaneously retrieve it from multiple sources (Baddeley, 2002). These subsidiary systems are part of **short-term memory,** meaning they store information only

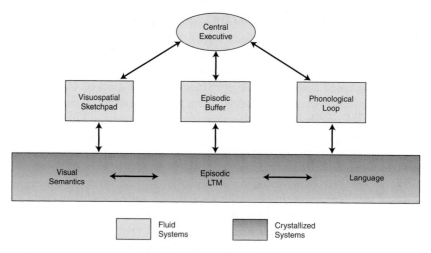

FIGURE 5.1 *Model of working memory with links to short-term and long-term memory systems.*
The central executive controls the processing of information in working memory. The episodic buffer
serves as an interface between long-term memory and the subsidary systems—visuospatial sketchpad
and phonological loop. *SOURCE:* Baddeley, 2002.

temporarily. Fluid systems represent transitory, ever-changing storage and
crystallized systems refers to in placed, stored long-term memory.

The central executive can order information prepared (encoded) for transfer
to **long-term memory**, a "storehouse" of virtually unlimited capacity that holds
information for very long periods of time. The central executive also retrieves
information, as needed, from long-term memory. Rehearsed information, if
repeated often enough, can be transferred to long-term memory. More sophisticated strategies to encode information for long-term storage are
(1) **organization**, categorizing the information or arranging it into some
sort of coherent pattern; and (2) **elaboration**, finding a relationship between items you are trying to remember, such as *tea* and *cup*, or *hot* and
cold; or making associations with something you already know.

The capacity of working memory to hold and process information is widely
believed to shrink with age. Some researchers assess age effects by asking people to repeat longer and longer sequences of digits (such as 4-9-7; 5-3-7-1-8-
2-9; 6-9-1-4-3-8-2-5-7-3-1). **Digit span**—the number of digits a person can
recall in the order presented—seems to be only slightly affected by age, though
it may take an older person a bit longer to respond (Craik & Jennings, 1992;
Poon, 1985; Wingfield & Stine, 1989). But when asked to repeat *backward*
several strings of numbers of increasing length, older adults generally do not
do as well as younger ones, though the difference is not dramatic (Craik &
Jennings, 1992; Lovelace, 1990).

A key factor seems to be the complexity of the task—how much effort it requires (Kausler, 1990); Wingfield & Stine, 1989). Tasks such as rehearsal, which
require only passive holding of information, show very little decline. Tasks that

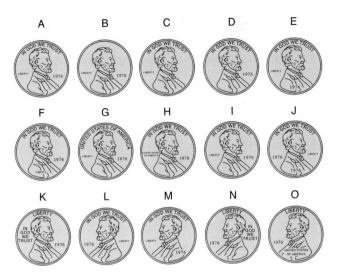

FIGURE 5.2 *Which is the real penny?* Most people can't tell, no matter how many times they have seen and held pennies, because they don't pay attention to minor details. Particularly as people age, they tend to conserve mental resources by reserving attention for things they consider important. *SOURCE:* Nickerson & Adams, 1979.

require reorganization, elaboration, or other mental manipulation show the greatest falloff (Craik & Jennings, 1992). For example, if you are asked to repeat a series of items (such as "Band-Aid, elephant, newspaper") in order of increasing size ("Band-Aid, newspaper, elephant"), you must call to mind your previous knowledge of Band-Aids, newspapers, and elephants (Cherry & Park, 1993). Similarly, if material needs to be reorganized, more mental effort is needed to keep it "in mind," using more of the limited capacity of working memory. Some researchers have suggested that as people get older they have less mental energy, or fewer **attentional resources**, to focus on a task (Craik, 1994; Craik & Byrd, 1982; Wingfield & Stine, 1989; Zacks et al., 2000). Perhaps for that reason, among others we'll discuss later, older adults tend not to use organization and elaboration, even though those are generally considered the most effective encoding strategies (Craik & Jennings, 1992; Salthouse, 1991).

Then, too, motivation may be a factor. Older people may be less attentive to certain kinds of material because they don't see any need to remember it and don't want to expend energy on the task (Craik & Byrd, 1982; see Figure 5.2). Albert Einstein, one of the fathers of nuclear physics, when asked how many feet are in a mile, reportedly said, "I don't know. Why should I fill my head with things like that when I could look them up in any reference book in 2 minutes?"

LONG-TERM MEMORY: INACTIVE STORAGE

Although long-term memory is believed to have nearly unlimited storage space, not all of its contents are equally accessible. Why is it easy to remember how to ride a bicycle, even after long periods of disuse, while names of

TABLE 5.1

Examples of Differing Contents of Declarative and Nondeclarative Memory

Declarative	Nondeclarative
Facts	*Habits*
What is bread made of?	Biting your nails
Language	*Motor skills*
What is the plural of *ox*?	Playing table tennis
Social customs	*Perceptual Skills*
How can you get money in a strange city?	Remembering the way to your home
Personal episodes	*Conditioned responses*
What dessert did you have at your last birthday party?	How do you react if you see a snake next to your foot?

people we haven't seen for years, or facts we rarely use, tend to escape us? One likely answer is that long-term memory is divided into "rooms" with different kinds of contents (see Table 5.1), and aging affects them differently. The two chief divisions are *declarative memory* and *nondeclarative memory*.

Names, dates, definitions of words, recollections of experiences, and many other kinds of information that can be brought to mind and "declared" belong to **declarative memory**. Declaration need not be verbal; it may consist of a mental image, such as a face, a place, or the scent of a rose. Either way, there is a feeling of familiarity, a sense that this is something you have seen, heard, touched, tasted, or smelled before (Squire, 1992, 1994). Declarative memory is often assessed by tests of recognition and recall.

Remembering how to ride a bicycle is an example of **nondeclarative memory** (sometimes called *procedural memory*). This part of long-term memory contains information generally pertaining to skills, habits, or ways of doing things. Much of this information apparently reaches long-term memory directly from sensory memory, largely or completely bypassing working memory and the control of the central executive. In simplest terms, declarative memory is knowing *that* . . . ; nondeclarative memory is knowing *how* (Lovelace, 1990; Schacter, 1992; Squire, 1992).

Recently, researchers have paid increasing attention to apparent differences in how these components of long-term memory are processed. **Explicit memory** is conscious or intentional recollection, usually of facts, names, events, or other things that people can state, or declare. **Implicit memory** refers to remembering that occurs without effort or even conscious awareness; it generally pertains to habits and skills, such as knowing how to throw a ball or ride a bicycle (Howard, 1996). Brain scans have provided direct physical evidence of the existence and location of these distinct memory systems (Squire, 1992; Vargha-Khadem et al., 1997). Declarative material, such as knowledge of facts, names, and events, usually requires explicit recall; by contrast, much nondeclarative (procedural) information seems to be processed implicitly. It may be encoded or retrieved without conscious effort—it is simply there when you need it.

Aging and Long-Term Memory: Stability or Decline?

If older adults have deficiencies in working memory, we might expect them to have more trouble remembering declarative information (facts, names, events) than nondeclarative information (skills and procedures), which may bypass working memory (Kausler, 1990; Lovelace, 1990). In general, that has been found to be true, but the picture is not entirely simple. Let's look more closely at some specific contents of declarative and nondeclarative memory. Then we'll discuss *priming*, an unconscious process that may be involved in remembering both kinds of information.

DECLARATIVE MEMORY: EPISODIC AND SEMANTIC

Do you remember what you had for breakfast this morning? Did you lock your car when you parked it? Did you feed the cat today? Personal experiences, activities, and events such as these—linked to specific times and places, or *episodes*—are stored in **episodic memory**, one of the two main subdivisions of declarative memory. The other main subdivision is **semantic memory**: general knowledge of historical facts, geographic locations, social customs, meanings of words, and the like. Episodic memory is what we generally mean when we say "I remember"; semantic memory is what we mean when we say "I know" (Backman, Small, & Wahlin, 2001; Lovelace, 1990). Semantic memory grows out of episodic memory. When you encounter information often enough, it becomes part of your general knowledge, or *knowledge base* (Camp, 1989).

Episodic memory is the one system in long-term memory most susceptible to age effects, with procedural memory and semantic memory often showing only negligible age effects (Hoyer & Verhaeghen, 2006; Smith & Earles, 1996). Even when older adults remember particular events as well as younger adults, they often do not remember as well the source in which the target event occurred—they have a *source memory* deficit (Chalfonte & Johnson, 1996). This deficit may be due to less encoding of the features of the source context, or to less adequate association or binding of contextual features to the target event (Naveh-Benjamin, 2000).

Older people have had so many similar experiences that individual ones may run together in their minds. A similar phenomenon may be behind older people's tendency to "recall" things that never occurred, or to be uncertain whether something occurred (Cohen & Faulkner, 1989). ("I'm sure I took my medicine today!" "Did I sign the check before mailing it?") Or they may tell the same story over and over to the same people without realizing that they've told it before. But when older people perceive an event as distinctive or novel, they can remember it as well as younger ones (Camp, 1989; Cavanaugh, Kramer, Sinnott, Camp, & Markley, 1985; Kausler, 1990).

CRITICAL THINKING

What do you believe differentiates episodic memory errors of younger and older adults?

© Addison Geary/Stock Boston

Games like Scrabble draw on world knowledge, a component of semantic memory. Although young adults may retrieve this knowledge more quickly, older adults tend to do well at such games because they have accumulated more general knowledge through the years.

Semantic memory, the other main component of declarative memory, takes several forms, none of which depends on remembering when and where something was learned. One is *world knowledge.* What is the capital of France? How many days does a leap year have? Is New York east or west of California? This is the sort of information featured in trivia games and television quiz shows. Older adults generally do well in games like Trivial Pursuit because they have accumulated a large quantity of factual knowledge during the course of a lifetime. And older adults seem to be able to retrieve this knowledge efficiently, even though younger adults may do it more quickly in some instances (Camp, 1989; Horn, 1982b; Lachman & Lachman, 1980; Backman, Small, & Wahlin, 2001).

Often, older adults are especially strong in a second type of world knowledge: *social knowledge,* or awareness of behavior appropriate to a situation. How long should a widow or widower remain in mourning? What should you do if a guest insults you at a dinner party? Older people are transmitters of such culturally sanctioned customs and values. In some cultures, they are explicitly recognized as keepers of social knowledge and preside over ceremonies that accompany life transitions, such as puberty and marriage (Mergler & Goldstein, 1983).

Language, too, is part of semantic memory. How many synonyms for *fat* can you list? What is the plural of *child*? What is the difference between *lying down* and *laying down*? Vocabulary and knowledge of linguistic rules, like world knowledge, generally do not decline and may even increase across adulthood (Camp, 1989; Horn, 1982b). However, older adults often have more trouble with some other aspects of linguistic memory. We've all had "tip-of-the-tongue" experiences, when we fumble for a word, or know something but can't quite express it, or (like Laurence Olivier in later life) can't recall someone's name—the last being the most troublesome memory problem for adults of all ages (Burke & Shafto, 2004; West, 1985). Older adults, even though their knowledge is greater, seem to have more of these experiences than younger ones, perhaps in part because of problems in working memory (Heller & Dobbs, 1993; Light, 1990; Schonfield, 1974; Schonfield & Robertson, 1960, as cited in Horn, 1982b).

NONDECLARATIVE MEMORY: MOTOR, PERCEPTUAL, AND CONDITIONED

If nondeclarative memory—the ability to *do* something rather than to recollect something—is the result of unconscious processing, it should be relatively unaffected by age-related problems in working memory. And in general, any deficiencies older people show in nondeclarative memory tend to be negligible or small (Hoyer & Verhaeghen, 2006; Kausler, 1990).

Researchers have learned much about unconscious learning by studying people with amnesia, Alzheimer's disease, and some types of brain damage,

CRITICAL THINKING

What explanations, other than those presented in the text, can you suggest that might influence adults to inaccurately recall events?

which severely impair memory. These patients often retain certain memory functions, which, by inference, must be independent of conscious control. Let's look more closely at several types of unconscious learning and how age affects them.

Motor Memory   Vladimir Horowitz, considered by many music lovers the greatest piano virtuoso of his time, gave sold-out, critically acclaimed performances up to his death at 85—4 days after he had completed his last recording and a month before two scheduled recitals in Germany (Schonberg, 1992). Another brilliant keyboard artist, Arthur Rubinstein, gave his farewell recital at 89, having put off his retirement for almost a year after he began to go blind (Rubinstein, 1980). These are but a few of many examples of the persistence of motor learning into very old age.

The fact that motor memory involves unconscious processing can be inferred from studies such as one in which amnesiacs and patients with Alzheimer's disease were successfully taught to hold a stylus to a rotating disk (Heindel, Butters, & Salmon, 1988). Such a feat would appear to be impossible if remembering how to perform a learned motor task required conscious recall. So would driving a car while talking to a passenger or listening to the radio. In fact, deliberately trying to remember how to do something can worsen performance. As Yogi Berra, a catcher for the New York Yankees baseball team, is said to have remarked, "How can you think and hit the ball at the same time?"

Unconscious processes involved in motor activity may also aid in recall of declarative information. In Liberia, Kpelle people had trouble recalling traditional epic songs—except when they were actually singing and dancing (Lancy, 1977). You may have experienced a similar effect: not being able to remember a familiar phone number except by tapping it out on a touch-tone phone. Your fingers "know" the number, even though your conscious mind draws a blank.

Motor memory seems to hold up well throughout adulthood, though older adults may need to compensate for the general slowing that occurs with age. Older people who are expert typists can copy a document as fast as younger ones; apparently they compensate by looking a few characters ahead to give them more time to process the material they haven't yet come to (Salthouse, 1985). And although young adults can write faster than older ones, practice and familiarity with the material can reduce the difference in speed (Dixon, Kurzman, & Friesen, 1993).

Perceptual Memory   Approximately how many times has the term *encoding* been used so far in this chapter? Is the answer closer to two or twelve? Which was mentioned first, *sensory memory* or *articulatory loop*?

Such questions call on *perceptual skills:* the ability to judge and reconstruct in your mind the physical features, frequency or order of occurrence, or location of something in relation to something else. With unconscious processing, you may be able to file such perceptual impressions in memory while focusing

© AP/Jeff Bradley/Wide World Photos

At age 92, Zhu Jingda of Canton had not forgotten his tennis form, which he had learned at age 10. Motor memory, which involves unconscious processing, seems to hold up well throughout adulthood.

on a conscious encoding task (such as trying to remember what you are reading). Later, you can consciously retrieve and assess your perceptions (Kausler, 1990; Lovelace, 1990).

If their encoding is indeed unconscious, we might expect perceptual skills to remain relatively constant with age. Estimation of frequency has been found to decline very little, and only after the middle years. However, memory of order and location fall off earlier and more sharply. In one study, which included large samples of young, middle-aged, and elderly adults, middle-aged people were as accurate in assessing word frequency as the younger ones, and elderly ones only slightly less so. By contrast, deficits in remembering order and location were fairly pronounced in middle-aged participants and even more so in older ones. In fact, the older people did just about as poorly in reconstructing the order of words and activities as they did in remembering word pairs, a declarative task (Salthouse, Kausler, & Saults, 1988, as cited in Kausler, 1990). Thus a distinction between conscious processing and unconscious processing may not fully account for whether or not age deficits appear in some forms of nondeclarative memory.

Conditioned Responses   Another form of unconscious learning that is generally believed to enter nondeclarative memory is **classical conditioning**. A *conditioned response* is one that a person has learned to make automatically to a certain stimulus by association with another stimulus that normally elicits the response. Perhaps the earliest and probably the most famous example of classical conditioning was an experiment in which the Russian physiologist Ivan Pavlov (1927) trained dogs to salivate at the sound of a bell by feeding them whenever the bell rang.

When rabbits and humans were conditioned to blink in response to a tone by blowing a puff of air into their eyes immediately after the tone was sounded, younger adults acquired the conditioned eyeblink much faster than older ones (Woodruff-Pak, 1990). A cross-sectional study of adults age 20 to 89 found that age differences in acquisition of conditioned responses are large. The age differences in eyeblink classical conditioning did not appear abruptly in the sixties and older. Rather, participants in their forties were already demonstrating a lower level of conditioning, but no significant declines were found (Woodruff-Pak & Jaeger, 1998). And in a longitudinal study in which older adults were followed for 2 or 3 years, cognitively normal participants—even among the oldest old—showed no significant change in ability to be classically conditioned. Those in the old-old group who did show declines in this ability were likely to be near death or to develop dementia (Ferrante & Woodruff-Pak, 1995). Thus earlier reports of large decrements in older adults' ability to be classically conditioned (Solomon, Pomerleau, Bennett, James, & Morse, 1989) may have been overstated or may have been related to illness rather than to normal aging.

PRIMING

Let's play "Wheel of Fortune." Can you guess the winning word by filling in the blanks?

P_A_U_

If you are playing alone at home, this might be hard to guess. But suppose, at the end of the show, the answer *peanut* flashes on your television screen. If you later see the same program again, in reruns, you may come up with the answer more easily. Much as priming a surface prepares it for the next coat of paint, the previous encounter has primed your memory to produce the information.

Priming is an increase in ability to do a previously encountered task or to remember previously encountered material. Both declarative and nondeclarative memory can show effects of priming. For example, you may be able to summon up factual knowledge to answer a test question more quickly if you've already seen the question and answer on a list for review. In one study of effects of priming on motor and perceptual memory (Benzing & Squire, 1989), amnesiacs who had lifted weights with one hand were better able to judge the weight of objects lifted with the other hand, even though they had extreme difficulty remembering that they had lifted the weights before.

Priming is an unconscious, automatic process. It can occur whether or not a person remembers where the information was first encountered, or even whether it was previously encountered at all (Ashcraft, 1994; Heindel, Salmon, & Butters, 1989, 1991; Squire, 1992). It's possible, of course, in our "Wheel of Fortune" example, that you would not only be able to give the answer *peanut* but might also remember having seen it on the first run. Similarly, you might remember having previously run across a test question. But whether or not you recall having seen information before will not affect priming. The amnesiacs in the weight-lifting experiment, who lacked episodic memory, showed what Roediger (1990) calls "retention without remembering": knowing something on the basis of prior experience, without remembering the experience itself (Lovelace, 1990). Likewise, during stem completion exercises (such as "Complete the word (S-T-R-_-_-_") amnesiacs tend to come up with words they were shown earlier, even though they have no recollection of having seen them (Camp & McKitrick, 1992; Schacter, 1992; Squire, 1992).

Speed is one indication that priming has occurred. Both normal adults and people with Alzheimer's disease can more rapidly identify pictures they have previously seen (Camp & McKitrick, 1992). For priming to be effective, earlier and later stimuli should be as close to identical as possible; showing a different picture of an object, or a name instead of a picture, reduces priming effects (Squire, 1992).

Priming seems to be equally efficient in younger and older adults; normal older people whose episodic memory has weakened can benefit as much from priming as younger ones (Backman, Small, & Wahlin, 2001; Lovelace, 1990). In one

> CRITICAL THINKING
>
> What functions seem to be dominated by unconscious learning and what purpose does it serve?

TABLE 5.2

Relationship Between Aging and Performance in Various Types of Memory

Memory	Increases with Age	No Change or Small Decline	Moderate to Large Decline
Sensory		X	
Working			
Digit span forward		X	
Digit span backward		X	
Organization			X
Elaboration			X
Long-term			
Declarative			
Episodic			
Memory for experiences and activities			X
Personal history			X
Semantic			
World knowledge	X		
Vocabulary	X		
Word finding			X
Nondeclarative			
Skills		X	
Perceptual abilities		X	
Motor learning		X	
Classical conditioning		X	

study, 48 young adults and 48 older adults were shown a group of pictures and then were asked to choose the same pictures from among others they hadn't yet seen. The tests were repeated 1 day, 1 week, and 3 weeks later. Approximately equal numbers of older and younger adults were better able to select the familiar pictures, and to do so more quickly, even though the older people were less able to say which pictures they had seen before (Mitchell, Brown, & Murphy, 1990).

Summing Up: Memory and Age

Information-processing theory and research suggest that memory is a highly complex set of processes and storage systems, and a number of questions remain to be answered. Still, we can draw several conclusions about effects of aging on memory (see Table 5.2).

Age seems to have little or no effect on sensory memory. Aging *does* negatively affect the capacity of working memory to successfully process certain kinds of declarative information and to access it in long-term memory. Older adults may have fewer attentional resources to focus on manipulating information and may not use the most effective strategies for encoding it. After years of living, recollection of specific episodes begins to fade and events tend to run together in memory. On the other hand, the ability to call on general knowledge *increases*, though the ability to express it verbally may not. Unconscious remembering, usually of skills or procedures, generally holds up well with age.

BIOLOGICAL APPROACH: HARDWARE OF MEMORY

If older adults have difficulty encoding information and retrieving certain kinds of memories, an explanation may lie in underlying changes in the "hardware," or "machinery," of memory: the brain. Like a machine, the brain has electrical circuits, "input" and "output" channels, and specific parts that seem to be involved in processing particular kinds of information. It may be that the reason people never forget how to ride a bicycle, for example, is that the muscular commands become "hard-wired" into brain cells or their connections, just as a computer's operating commands are permanently stored in its wiring. We need to keep in mind, however, that this analogy with computers is valid only up to a point. The brain is a living biological system. It needs adequate sleep and nutrition, as well as oxygen (see Box 5.1). If injured, it has some capacity to repair itself.

As we've already discussed, studies of brain-damaged people in whom certain memory functions remain intact point to the existence of more than one storehouse of memory. Now, recent research, some of it made possible by such high technology as *magnetic resonance imaging* (MRI) and *positron emission tomography* (PET), has directly confirmed that there are indeed multiple memory systems, which "are anatomically distinct, and . . . are involved in acquiring and storing fundamentally different kinds of information" (Squire, 1992, p. 214). Scientists today are getting an increasingly clear picture of which physical structures of the brain control which aspects of memory and how these brain structures change with age.

Structures Controlling Conscious Memory

Some of the most solid findings to date concern two areas of the brain that together play a major role in explicit, or conscious memory: the *hippocampus* and nearby structures, and the *frontal lobes* (see Figure 5.3 on page 172).

HIPPOCAMPUS

The **hippocampus,** a seahorse-shaped structure deep in the central portion of the brain (the medial temporal lobe), appears to be critical to memory for

CRITICAL THINKING

Do you think there is a relationship between the locations of the hippocampus and frontal lobes and their importance to memory and cognitive function?

The Best Memory Aid: A Healthy Lifestyle

Have you ever tried to take a test after cramming all night or eating a heavy meal? If so, you may have learned—the hard way—the connection between what you do with your body and what you can do with your mind. For example, cigarette smoking apparently has negative effects on complex problem solving that makes high demands on working memory and long-term memory (Spilich, June, & Renner, 1992). On the other hand, getting enough sleep and eating the right foods can make a positive difference in how well memory works across the adult life span.

Sleep

Burning the midnight oil can interfere with the transfer of information to long-term memory. Avi Karni (Karni, Tanne, Rubenstein, Askenasy, & Sagi, 1994), a neuropsychologist with the National Institutes of Health, made that discovery while studying how people acquire a specific visual skill: pinpointing the location of shapes on a computer screen. Noticing that participants did better the day *after* a training session, he and his colleagues reasoned that

something happens during sleep to strengthen neural connections in the brain and facilitate learning.

The researchers observed the participants during sleep and awakened them at various times during the night. Those who were awakened from light sleep (when the body is relaxed, the eyes move slowly, and brain waves are somewhat erratic) could remember the next morning what they had learned the previous day. But those who were awakened from *REM sleep*—the deeper stage when dreams occur, characterized by rapid eye movements and more regular brain waves—did not retain the new knowledge. Karni concluded that REM sleep is an important time for consolidation of new learning.

This finding has implications for young adults, who often put work, study, or social demands ahead of their need for sleep. It may also help explain some memory problems in older adults (especially men), who tend to sleep more lightly, wake more frequently, dream less, and have fewer periods of deep sleep than in their earlier years (Webb, 1987; Woodruff, 1985).

declarative information (Eichenbaum, Fortin, 2003).* Without the hippocampus, unconscious learning generally continues to function; conscious learning does not (Henke et al., 2003; Moscovitch & Winocur, 1992).

The hippocampus, together with related structures in the cortex, apparently acts like a switchboard, controlling the ability to remember many kinds of declarative information, from word pairs to life events. So long as you are

---

*Unless otherwise noted, this discussion is based on Squire (1992).

Nutrition

"You are what you eat" is as true of memory as of other mental and physical capacities. Specific foods can improve or impair memory.

The brain's chemical energy comes mainly from *glucose* extracted from starches in food. When you put unusual demands on your brain, it needs to draw extra glucose from the bloodstream. To test the effects of glucose on memory, one group of researchers (Manning, Hall, & Gold, 1990) on 2 successive days gave healthy older adults lemonade sweetened with glucose and then with an artificial sugar substitute. On the day they drank the glucose, the participants did better on declarative memory tasks, such as remembering a story and a list of words. Those who had poor glucose regulation—who tended to retain high levels of glucose in their blood—performed especially poorly after drinking the substitute, suggesting that (as with diabetics, who tend to show impaired memory) not enough glucose was getting to the brain. Glucose supplements might help in such cases.

Not all sugars are brain food. *Fructose*, used to sweeten many foods and drinks, can supply energy to bodily tissues but not to the brain. A better way to get a quick mental boost is to eat an apple or crackers. Both are rich in carbohydrates, which break down into sugars when digested.

Aspartame, a chemical used in diet drinks and artificial sweeteners, contains *phenylalanine*, the amino acid involved in *phenylketonuria (PKU)*, an enzyme disorder that can cause mental retardation. Even in normal people, too much diet soda can impair mental performance—especially when accompanied by cake or other sweets, which make it easier for phenylalanine to get into the brain. Eating protein-rich foods such as peanuts or cheese with diet drinks can offset the effects of phenylalanine.

Zinc is crucial to nerve cells in the cortex that control memory and high-level thinking. Classic signs of zinc deprivation are wounds that heal slowly, white spots on the fingernails, poor vision in dim light, and deadened taste or smell. Anyone with these symptoms should consult a doctor promptly. Zinc deficiency can be treated with diet supplements, but changing your own diet can be dangerous, as *too much* zinc can be toxic and may be associated with Pick's disease, a serious brain malfunction.

NOTE: Unless otherwise noted, material in the section on "Nutrition" is based on Chafetz, 1992.

looking at something (say, the information on this page) or keeping it in mind, your mental image of it remains intact. As soon as you shift your attention to something else (move on to another section of the text, for instance), your recall of that information depends on cortical connections activated by the hippocampal system. Without the hippocampus, these connections are not made and the memory cannot be stored. In terms of information processing, the hippocampus is vital to the encoding functions of working memory.

But the role of the hippocampus seems to be only temporary. It is involved in the creation and immediate retrieval of *new* memories, but eventually those

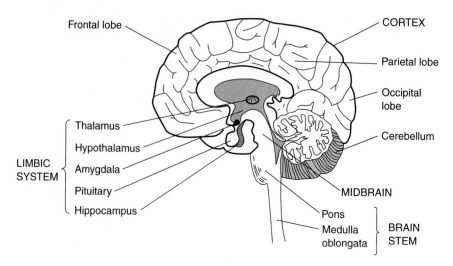

FIGURE 5.3 *Simplified side view of the human brain with some inner structures shown.* The hippocampus and frontal lobes of the cortex (the outer layer) appear to play key roles in the formation, initial storage, and retrieval of declarative memories. The frontal lobes seem to be involved in strategic aspects of memory. Various types of implicit (unconscious) memory are controlled by other structures. *SOURCE:* Adapted from Sagan, 1977.

are consolidated and permanently stored in another part of the brain, probably in the cortex, where they can be retrieved without the help of the hippocampus. (That's why amnesiacs who have suffered recent damage to the hippocampus may recall long-ago events but not recent ones.)

The hippocampus, which loses an estimated 20 percent of its nerve cells with advancing age (Ivy, MacLeod, Petit, & Markus, 1992), may be a key to understanding why many older adults have trouble assimilating new declarative information. The location and arrangement of arteries supplying the hippocampus make it particularly vulnerable to injury from changes in blood pressure that often occur during adulthood (Horn, 1982b). If older adults suffer hippocampal deterioration, the alertness, concentration, and organizational abilities needed to process new information efficiently may decline; but recall of *prior* learning, which is apparently independent of the hippocampus, may improve as a result of the growing complexity of neural connections in the cortex.

High levels of stress hormones in the bloodstream may play a part. In some older adults, the regulatory "switch" for production of stress hormones seems to be constantly "on": a continuous stream of hormones appears to affect the hippocampus, reducing performance on tests of attention and memory (Sapolsky, 1992). These, along with changes in other, related structures—particularly the frontal lobes—may make adults gradually less able to store new material in long-term memory.

FRONTAL LOBES

When a name or a fact escapes you, how can you jog your memory? The ability to think up strategies for encoding and retrieval seems to be one function of the brain's **frontal lobes**—the front portions of the *cerebral cortex*, the brain's outer layer, which controls higher-level thinking (Shimamura, Janowsky, & Squire, 1991). Current research suggests that the frontal lobes play a role in both normal and pathological memory changes.

© Corbis Images

Brain scans and other high-tech procedures, such as the MRI this physician is examining, have confirmed the existence of several anatomically distinct memory systems, used to acquire and store different kinds of material.

Since both the frontal lobes and the hippocampus appear to be involved in conscious memory, what is the relationship between them? According to one model (Moscovitch & Winocur, 1992), the actual encoding, storage, and retrieval of memories is the job of the hippocampus and its associated structures, under the supervision and control of the frontal lobes. The hippocampus encodes consciously perceived information rapidly, almost automatically, and without organization. It also can retrieve apparently associated information from long-term memory. But the hippocampus lacks "intelligent" discrimination. The information it comes up with (much like the data you may find when doing a key-word search by computer) may or may not be relevant. How, then, do you select the right "file drawer" for a piece of information, or come up with the right answer to a question?

According to this model, the frontal lobes give the hippocampus direction. They coordinate, interpret, and elaborate information to provide proper instructions for encoding and retrieval. It is the operations of this strategic frontal system, not the operations of the hippocampus or its associated structures, that you are aware of in searching your memory. The frontal lobes constantly evaluate the output of the hippocampal system: *Does this answer make sense? Which answer is the best one?* or *I need more information.* In other words, the frontal lobes seem to play a role similar to that of the central executive in working memory.

Growing evidence implicates the frontal lobes in selective declines in normal cognitive functioning (Parkin & Walter, 1992). The ability to remember when and where you learned something (episodic memory) seems to be related to the functioning of the frontal lobes (Craik, Morris, Morris, & Loewen, 1990). So does learning that requires organization and elaboration. But damage to the frontal lobes usually does *not* hamper learning of information that can be encoded without creating new categories or associations (Shimamura et al., 1991). Commonly observed deficits in working memory in older adults may be due to a large (as much as 50 percent) loss of nerve cells in the frontal lobes, which help focus attention and inhibit irrelevant responses (H. Brody, 1995, 1970; Shimamura et al., 1991). However, it is possible that the brain may compensate in part for this loss by adding new connections (see Chapter 4).

CRITICAL THINKING

After learning about changes in sensory systems and changes in neurological "hardware," do you feel more or less empowered to retain memory capacity?

Structures Controlling Unconscious Memory

Since nondeclarative memory for skills, habits, and procedures survives damage to the hippocampus, other brain structures must be responsible for them. A number of structures appear to control various kinds of implicit, or unconscious, learning (see Figure 5.3).

Perceptual and motor skills seem to depend on the *neostriatum*, a subcortical structure above the hippocampus, which controls motor activity (Squire, 1992). Patients with Huntington's disease, which involves destruction of the neostriatum, lose the ability to learn these skills; patients in the early stages of Alzheimer's disease, whose neostriatum is not yet affected, do not (Heindel et al., 1991).

Muscular conditioning—such as the eyeblink response described earlier, or changes in heart rate due to conditioned fear—appears to be linked to the *cerebellum*, the brain's coordinating center for muscular activity, which lies below the cortex near the back of the head. While simple conditioning can occur in both humans and other animals independently of the hippocampus, the hippocampus may contribute to more complex conditioning that is affected by surrounding sights, sounds, or smells (Penick & Solomon, 1991).

Emotional conditioning seems to be located in the *amygdala*, an almond-shaped structure near the hippocampus, adjoining the temporal lobe (Squire, 1992). An example of emotional conditioning can be seen when amnesiacs or persons with Alzheimer's disease learn to dislike a person who hurts or angers them, even if they don't recognize the person or remember the incident that provoked the emotional response (Camp et al., 1993).

Direct (repetition) priming—the simplest kind, in which the answer called for is identical with the stimulus initially presented—apparently results from changes in perceptual processing systems in the rear of the cortex. These changes occur in the early stages of processing, before any analysis of meaning or any involvement of the hippocampal system; thus amnesic and normal people benefit equally. Other priming functions seem to involve different cortical regions in either the right or the left hemisphere; for vision alone, as many as 30 specific areas that may contribute to priming have been identified (Squire, 1992).

New Directions for Research

In keeping with the lifespan developmental approach, it is becoming increasingly obvious that memory development cannot be properly studied from a single perspective. More and more, researchers studying "software" and "hardware" of memory are communicating and cooperating, either to confirm theories or to generate new ones (Hoyer & Verhaeghen, 2006). The discipline of *neuroscience* draws on biology, neuropsychology, cognitive psychology, neurology, and related disciplines. In the future, information-processing research on memory functioning and biological research on brain structures will be more closely linked. Recent technological advances allow researchers to peer into the brain while it is actively processing information, so that relationships between brain functions and brain structures can be tested directly.

The lifespan approach also suggests that cognitive abilities such as memory can be influenced by a variety of factors outside the brain: health, education, lifestyle, personality. In one series of studies (Moscovitch & Winocur, 1992), institutionalized older adults consistently did worse on neuropsychological measures than a carefully matched control group living in the community who were more active and felt more in control of their lives. Among the institutionalized group, those who were better adjusted tended to do better on tests of learning and memory; and changes in their activity level and perceived control correlated with changes in cognitive performance.

CRITICAL THINKING

How will longitudinal, cross-sectional, and cross-cultural research be instrumental in clarifying the influences of factors outside the brain?

Do gender and culture influence changes in memory? Although complaints of memory problems and inability to concentrate are frequently mentioned as associated with menopause, research so far is sparse on effects of lowered estrogen levels on memory. In one study comparing memory in 19 women immediately before and 2 months after surgical removal of the ovaries, women who received estrogen injections did as well as or better than before on a variety of memory tasks. Women who received a placebo (sesame oil) showed a decline in recall of word pairs but not in several other functions, such as digit span and recall of pictures. It is possible, then, that estrogen may affect rote verbal recall or the ability to learn new associations (Phillips & Sherwin, 1992).

A recent cross-cultural study of three cultures—mainland Chinese, mainstream American, and American Deaf—found a link between memory changes in older adults and cultural attitudes toward aging. Memory performance among young adults in the three cultures was identical. But among mainstream Americans, who held the most negative attitudes toward aging, older participants did worse than those in either of the other two cultural groups in the memory tasks, which involved explicit recall of new information. Older Chinese, whose culture seemed to promote the most positive view of aging, performed best, about as well as younger Chinese (Levy & Langer, 1994). These findings seem to confirm what the lifespan developmental approach would predict: social and psychological as well as biological forces influence how well memory holds up.

Future research needs to target a wide range of biological, functional, environmental, and psychosocial influences on memory development throughout adulthood. True lifespan studies may yield valuable knowledge, not only about why and how memory changes, but also about what adults can do to prevent, compensate for, and perhaps even reverse memory losses.

Aspects of Memory and Forgetting in Adulthood

Older adults often complain about memory failures. Memory failures can happen to anyone, regardless of age, but certain aspects of memory tend to be more problematic for older adults. After all, there are many negative effects of forgetting; for one thing, people who forget are viewed as less capable than others (Erber & Prager, 1999).

Why do older adults embellish stories? Why do they often have trouble remembering things they plan to do? Why do they tend not to use the most effective strategies for learning? Do younger adults have more understanding of how their memory works? What memory aids are most helpful to adults at various ages? Why do adults forget—and what would happen if they didn't? Although study of some of these aspects of memory is relatively new, some tentative conclusions have emerged.

Intrusion Errors: Remembering What Did Not Happen

How often have you heard someone relate an incident over and over, each time piling on additional (and often inaccurate) details? Such "tall tales" may be the unwitting result of **intrusion errors:** extraneous information coming into working memory through associations retrieved from long-term memory. These errors often show up on tests when people "remember" relevant or irrelevant information that wasn't originally presented. In one study (Pompi & Lachman, 1967), young adults read the following passage:

> Chief Resident Jones adjusted his face mask while anxiously surveying a pale figure secured to the long gleaming table before him. One swift stroke of his small sharp instrument and a thin red line appeared. Then an eager young assistant carefully extended the opening as another pushed aside glistening surface fat so that vital parts were laid bare. Everyone present stared in horror at ugly growth too large for removal. He now knew it was pointless to continue. (pp. 144–145; punctuation added)

After reading this paragraph, participants were shown a list of words and were asked to identify those that had appeared in the story. Many "remembered" words like *doctor, blood,* and *scalpel,* which were not in the text.

CRITICAL THINKING

Can you explain, from a psychosocial, information-processing, behavioral, or ecological perspective, why older adults embellish stories?

Older adults, with their extensive accumulation of experience, are particularly prone to intrusion errors, especially when retelling stories (Hasher, 1992). Their vast knowledge plays tricks on them, making them "recall" things that didn't happen. Some researchers believe that a tendency to be distracted by extraneous information may help explain difficulties with tasks involving working memory (Craik & Jennings, 1992; Hasher & Zacks, 1988). False recognition errors in older adults occur more frequently in response to common objects, possibly because common items are more easily retrieved from semantic memory. When abstract objects are presented, false memories are reduced to insignificant levels, compared to younger adults. Encouraging older adults to examine a stimulus carefully results in significantly fewer false recognition errors (Koutstaal, 1999, 2003).

On the other hand, older adults may be more interesting storytellers precisely *because* they embellish (Hasher, 1992). Oral transmission of stories about long-ago events or moral values is a role played by elders in many non-western cultures (Mergler & Goldstein, 1983). Contemporary South Ameri-

© Marc & Evelyne Bernheim/Woodfin Camp & Associates

An Aboure chief tells a legend to boys in the village of Yaou on the Ivory Coast of Africa. Older adults are often interesting storytellers because they add fresh details.

can Indians have a saying, "When an old man dies, a whole library burns" (Cole & Scribner, 1974). Older people can also be good at brainstorming, because they are less likely than younger ones to reject ideas that "come out of left field" (Hasher, 1992).

The reason for telling a story may affect its accuracy or embellishment, which then affects memory. One research team found that when older adults told a story for entertainment purposes, they told it in the present tense, and used more emotion words and words indicating certainty. When they told for the purpose of recounting information; they tended to use the past tense, fewer emotional words, and more "tentative" words such as possibly or maybe. When the same participants were asked to retell the story days later, the story told for entertainment had more intrusion errors, was less accurate, and had fewer details. The story told for information was recalled more accurately and had more details and fewer intrusion errors (Dudukovic, Marsh, Tversky, 2004).

Prospective Memory: Remembering to Do Something

Prospective memory—remembering to do something in the future—is like an alarm clock that the central executive sets as a reminder to perform a task at a certain time: make a telephone call, for instance, or keep an appointment, or study for a test. Does prospective memory decline with age, as it is commonly believed to do?

While some studies have found age-related deficits in certain kinds of tasks (Dobbs & Rule, 1987), in other studies prospective-memory *performance* of older adults—that is, whether they actually *did* what they wanted to remember to do—was equal to, or even better than, that of younger adults (Einstein & McDaniel, 1990; Hoyer & Verhaeghen, 2006; Sinnott, 1989). A reason for such contradictory results may lie in the conditions under which a task is presented. Einstein et al. (1997) found age-related differences when older adults had to remember to complete a task while performing a demanding activity. Age differences were minimal when the ongoing activity was not demanding. Other key factors are the significance and context of the task and the availability of external cues or aids to memory. If older adults feel a social obligation to carry out a real-world task and can refer to reminder notes, they perform as well as or better than younger ones (Sinnott, 1989). Age deficits show up when older people cannot rely on cues or external aids and must rely on an "internal clock" (Craik & Jennings, 1992; G. Einstein, 1992).

Planning and remembering to take medications are an important use of prospective memory for many older adults who may have to take several different medications at varying times throughout the day. Studies suggest that medication compliance for this population averages about 57 percent (van Eijken et al., 2003). Older adults may intend to take their medications but then may think that they have already done so, or may forget altogether. The more times medication must be taken each day, the less likely people over the age of 75 are to take it (Paes, Bakker, & Soe-Agnie, 1997).

To help older adults remember to take their medications, a number of strategies have been studied. Among the most common are pill boxes with an appropriate number of compartments to correspond with the amount of pills to be taken at specific times of the day or week. Cues can be used, such as taking medication at mealtimes or as part of another daily ritual (for example, after a shower). Linking an activity with the goal of taking prescribed medication enhances consistency. An alarm or flashing light set to the times medication is needed may also be used as a cue, but a person may not be able to hear or see it, or to remember what the alarm is signaling him or her to do (Cramer & Rosenheck, 1998). In one experiment electronic pill caps, which record the time and date a bottle is opened, when combined with cue-dose training (meeting with a trainer who provides feedback from the data obtained from the electronic pill cap) resulted in greater compliance than use of the pill cap without such feedback (Rosen et al., 2004). Electronic monitoring devices can send adherence information directly to a person's physician, who can be hooked up to a telephone line to call a person who has skipped a dose of medication.

Production Deficiencies in Strategies for Remembering

Older adults, as we've mentioned, are notably weak in elaboration and organization. They tend not to use these encoding strategies unless trained—or at least prompted or reminded—to do so (Craik & Jennings, 1992; Salthouse, 1991). This failure to spontaneously produce efficient strategies for memorization is called a **production deficiency**. It may help explain why older people often have trouble recalling new information.

Why do older people show production deficiencies? Cross-cultural studies may shed light on this question. Kpelle people of Liberia, for example, rarely use organization unless specifically told to do so, though they do spontaneously use rehearsal and other techniques. They *can* use organization—and can recall better—if given a structure for it, for example, if they are told a story in which items to be remembered are grouped by categories rather than presented haphazardly (Cole & Scribner, 1974).

Why don't the Kpelle normally think of using organization? Perhaps, lacking formal education, they have rarely needed to memorize. In a study in Yucatan, Mexico, only the most educated adults, who averaged 10 years of schooling, made extensive use of categories to aid recall (Sharp, Cole, & Lave, 1978). And, while production deficiencies can be overcome with schooling or training, people generally do best in the skills that are valued in their own culture (Dube, 1982; see Box 5.2).

Similarly, older adults in our culture may be less likely to use such strategies as organization and elaboration because they don't see much value in doing so. It may also be that production deficiencies are more related to cohort than to age, and that as the proportion of older adults with higher education increases, these deficiencies will lessen or disappear.

In any event, these cross-cultural studies suggest that production deficiencies are not biologically based (D. A. Wagner, 1981). Inability to benefit from training may be a sign of pathological, rather than normal, aging (Baltes, 1993), although there may be biological limits to *how much* individual adults can improve.

To test those limits, Baltes (1993; Baltes & Kliegl, 1992) trained healthy, well-educated older people to learn lists of 30 words using a complex memory strategy (the method of loci, described later in this chapter). Training and practice were extensive: 38 sessions in the course of 1 year, using a different word list each time. Then the investigators compared the performance of the older participants with that of young adults who had taken the same training. Baltes hypothesized that by pushing the participants as far as they could go, he would uncover age differences in the biological limits of plasticity, much as stress tests measure how hard the heart can work during vigorous exercise. And indeed, while the older adults in the study did benefit from learning the new strategy, the younger adults did even better and improved more rapidly, so that age differences were accentuated.

What might account for this apparent ceiling on trainability? Just as older people have less reserve capacity for physical functioning, Baltes suggests, they may have a smaller **developmental reserve**, or potential for memory enhancement. One factor is the complexity of the task. Just as older adults can often keep up with young people when walking but not when running, age differences are more likely to show up on more challenging memory tasks (Baltes, 1993). Also, older adults have more trouble giving up old ways of doing things and switching to new ones (Kliegl & Lindenberger, 1993).

CRITICAL THINKING

What circumstances may lead to different explanations for production deficiencies between members of the same cohort group within a culture?

Memory and Culture

Is memory influenced by culture? Research has highlighted intriguing differences in what kinds of material adults in various cultures remember and how they remember (D. A. Wagner, 1981).

What Adults Remember

One of the most famous memory prodigies of all time was a man born in Latvia, who at an early age had to memorize large amounts of information from the Talmud, a sacred Jewish book (Luria, 1968). But prodigious general memory, such as his, is rare. It's more common to see highly developed memory for specific types of information in which a person has intense interest or expertise. For example, students of the Koran, a sacred Muslim book—whom we might expect to have as well-trained memory as a student of the Talmud—did no better than unschooled rural Moroccans when tested on the ability to remember the position of animal cards. What's more, when asked to recognize pictures of oriental rugs, the scholars were bested by uneducated rug sellers as well as by the rural Moroccans, who presumably were more familiar with, and interested in, rug patterns (D. A. Wagner, 1978).

Familiar material would appear to be easier to encode than unfamiliar material; and people's

© Dave Bartruff/Corbis Images

People tend to remember what they are familiar with and interested in. When tested on recognition of oriental rug patterns, uneducated Moroccan rug sellers and peasants did better than scholars of the Koran, a sacred Muslim book.

knowledge base, which influences what they remember, varies from culture to culture (D. A. Wagner, 1978). While uneducated people do poorly on memory tasks unrelated to their cultural experience (Cole & Scribner, 1974), they

CRITICAL THINKING

How do you think older persons might answer if you asked them to explain the strategies they use to contend with everyday memory demands?

Of course, this research involved only one kind of memory task, and we cannot assume that its findings apply to other learning situations. How well older adults perform when instructed to use a strategy has been found to be highly dependent on the type of task and the strategy they are being taught (Craik, & Jennings, 1992). Older adults may be less likely to adopt an unfamiliar strategy or a strategy they feel requires too much effort (Anschutz, Camp, Markley, & Kramer, 1985, 1987; Brigham & Pressley, 1988). It has also been suggested that older adults may be less aware of a need to use strategies, or of which strategies work best. These are aspects of *metamemory*, the topic we turn to next.

can show excellent memory in areas their culture considers significant. In one classic study (Bartlett, 1932) a Swazi cowherder, 1 year after a series of cattle transactions, was able to recall precisely the price of each cow and its identifying markings. The Swazi remembered what was culturally important to him, much as an American baseball fan can rattle off scores, team standings, and batting averages (Cole & Scribner, 1974).

How Adults Remember

Adults "tend to excel in the skills which [their] culture encourages" (Dube, 1982, p. 275). Memory in traditional societies where songs and stories are passed on orally from generation to generation may utilize special techniques not needed in literate cultures. In the remote mountains of Yugoslavia before World War II, illiterate bards composed and sang, on the spot, epic poems several thousands of lines long. The performers knew a sort of script, or structural format, within which they could recreate an epic, incorporating familiar themes, words, and phrases. Because these words and phrases were formulas they had heard and repeated over and over ("When the dawn put forth its wings" or "When the sun had warmed the earth"), two versions of the same epic performed days or even years apart could be remarkably similar (Lord, 1982). Of course, the fact that the epics were *sung* undoubtedly helped the Yugoslav poets remember these themes and formulas, much as children in western cultures learn the alphabet more easily by singing the familiar alphabet song. Tune and rhythm are cues to remembering content.

On the other hand, some memory techniques common in western cultures, such as organizing items into categories, are less common in non-western cultures, such as that of the Kpelle in Liberia (Cole & Scribner, 1974). And, just as it may be misleading to measure adults in non-western cultures by the same yardstick as young adults in western societies who spontaneously use such strategies as organization, it may also be a mistake to judge the performance of older adults in western societies by what younger people do. Perhaps we need to think less in terms of deficiencies or deficits and more in terms of differences and change.

Metamemory: The View from Within

"I'm less efficient at remembering things now than I used to be."
"I have little control over my memory."
"I am just as good at remembering as I ever was."

When adults answer a questionnaire that asks them to agree or disagree with a list of statements like these, they are tapping **metamemory**—their beliefs or knowledge about how their memory works. These questions come from Metamemory in Adulthood (MIA), a questionnaire by Roger Dixon and David Hultsch which was one of the first tests specifically designed to measure metamemory in adults of all ages. The questions deal with several aspects of metamemory. Let's look at two aspects: beliefs about one's own memory, and selection and use of strategies.

BELIEFS ABOUT MEMORY

Older adults taking MIA report more perceived change in memory, less memory capacity, and less control over their memory than young adults do (Dixon, Hultsch, & Hertzog, 1988). Stereotyped expectations may lead older people to assume that minor lapses in memory are signs of age-related decline (Hertzog, Dixon, & Hultsch, 1990; Poon, 1985). Many older adults buy into this stereotype and report a greater decrement in their memory skills than actually exists (Hess & Pullen, 1996).

In a test of world knowledge, older and younger adults answered questions calling for either simple factual recall or recall plus inference (Camp & Pignatiello, 1988). Then the participants were asked how they thought their age influenced each of these abilities. Most older participants said they were not as good at remembering as before but had improved in making inferences—an answer consistent with conventional wisdom. In most cases, however, this belief did not correspond with the individual's actual performance. Yet when asked how confident they were about answers to particular questions, older adults were accurate in judging which of their answers were likely to be correct.

These findings reflect a general trend in the research literature. When asked for a blanket assessment of their own memory, older adults claim that it has declined; but when it comes to specific items or tasks, older adults are just about as accurate in judging their "feeling of knowing" as younger adults (Hertzog & Dixon, 1994; Salthouse, 1991).

Research also suggests that older adults' complaints about their memory are often unrelated to their objective performance. However, this conclusion does not consider individual differences. An older person who once had an outstanding memory may be well aware of a loss not detectable by comparison with the norm. A study that did take account of this factor found a modest link between memory complaints and objective performance (Levy-Cushman & Abeles, 1998).

METAMEMORY AND USE OF STRATEGIES

Most studies have found that older and younger adults are about equally knowledgeable as to what strategies are effective and what kinds of information are easiest to remember (Salthouse, 1991). Why, then, don't older adults use effective encoding strategies more often? One possibility is that they are less likely to be aware when strategies are needed and to monitor their use (Hertzog et al., 1990).

In one experiment designed to test monitoring of strategies (Brigham & Pressley, 1988), young adults were more than twice as likely as older ones to choose the more effective of two strategies for learning meanings of obscure words. Suppose, for instance, that the word to be learned was *handsel* (Old English), meaning "gift" or "payment." The superior "key word" strategy consisted of thinking of a sentence that included (1) a synonym for the word to be learned and (2) a word sounding like a key part of the word to be learned: in this case, say, "He held the *payment* in his *hand*." The inferior "context" strategy was to use the word itself in a sentence. When questioned after using both strategies, a greater percentage of young adults preferred the key-word strategy, which did yield better recall. Most older adults preferred the context method; they gave reasons like the following: "More direct method . . . easier than playing around and making things more complicated." "Because I've used it over the years." "That's how we learn the meaning of any word."

These older adults chose an easier and more familiar strategy that had worked for them in the past, rather than an unfamiliar strategy they may have found unwieldy. However, this seems questionable evidence for failure to monitor memory—especially since their gains from using the new strategy were relatively modest (Salthouse, 1991). It's also possible, as with other aspects of memory and aging, that the type of task makes a difference. Metamemory may function better for older adults in the real world than in an artificial laboratory situation.

When younger and older adults were briefly instructed in an effective memory strategy (visual imagery) for recalling associated word pairs, age differences in frequency of use of the strategy were fairly small. Thus, the use of the strategy did not adequately account for age differences in recall. This finding suggests that older adults might use the same strategy less effectively than younger adults (Dunlosky & Hertzog, 1998).

Mnemonics: Making the Most of Changing Memory

Suppose a friend recommends a restaurant you've never heard of, and you want to try it. Which would you be more likely to do to remember the name of the restaurant: (a) Repeat the name over and over? (b) Visualize the name in your mind? (c) Associate it with another name that rhymes or begins with the same letter? (d) Write it down?

If you're like most people, you probably chose (d). Paper and pencil are simple and effective memory aids. But other types of **mnemonics**—strategies to enhance encoding, storage, and recall—also may help adults make the most of changing memory.

The **E-I-E-I-O model** (Camp et al., 1993; see Table 5.3) is a convenient way to classify mnemonic techniques according to (1) type of remembering involved—explicit (E) or implicit (I); (2) where information is initially stored—external (E), that is, in the environment; or internal (I), inside the mind. "O" (for "Oh!") refers to a sudden realization that information originally stored externally or learned unconsciously has now been stored internally and is consciously available—as when you look up someone's phone number so often that you suddenly realize you know it by heart. The E-I-E-I-O model allows us to be precise about which storage sites and which memory processes are being tapped.*

---

*Unless otherwise indicated, the discussion in this section is based on Camp et al. (1993).

TABLE 5.3

E-I-E-I-O Model

Memory	External	Internal
	INITIAL STORAGE OF INFORMATION	
Explicit	Notes	Mental imaging
	Lists	Method of loci
	Calendars	Rehearsal
	Sensory or object cues	Organization
		Elaboration
		Rhymes
		First letter
		Stories
Implicit	Tactile-visual cues:	Spaced retrieval
	three-dimensional city maps	Conditioning

SOURCE: Adapted from Camp et al., 1993.

EXPLICIT EXTERNAL AIDS

Notes, lists, and calendars are explicit external aids—devices outside the person that assist with conscious learning or retrieval of facts, names, appointments, and so on. *Written reminders* are the most popular memory aids with adults of all ages—even, apparently, with memory researchers (Park, Smith, & Cavanaugh, 1990). But they are particularly helpful to older adults, to supplement limited or declining attention and storage space in working memory.

Sensory or object cues can compensate for the blurring of episodic memory. Many people leave a letter to be mailed in a place where they'll be sure to see it. Alarm clocks and timers are other cues to prospective memory. But the old custom of tying a string around a finger is generally not very effective; object cues work best when specifically linked to the information to be remembered (West, 1985). Among the Iatmul in New Guinea, learned men used leaves, shells, spears, and other objects to help them remember the thousands of names to which their clan laid claim as totems, or emblems (Bateson, 1982).

EXPLICIT INTERNAL AIDS

At age 31, the journalist Georgie Ann Geyer, then a foreign correspondent in Cuba, unexpectedly found herself face to face with Fidel Castro. Unfortunately, she had left her notebook at the hotel, but she couldn't let the opportunity to interview the revolutionary leader slip by. "So," she later wrote, "I began to work out a certain method I later perfected. I learned to focus—

virtually to set my mind on—certain important phrases as he uttered them. I had the conscious feeling of a hand coming out of my mind and grasping them and freezing them for a moment. I found that with this method I could keep quotes perfectly for at least three days" (Geyer, 1983, pp. 81–82).

The method Geyer evolved is a form of *mental imaging*. A more common use of visual images is in remembering names; for example, you might picture Mary Gates hopping merrily over a gate (West, 1985). Older adults are less likely than younger adults to use such imaging strategies spontaneously; when they do, the images tend to be relevant to their experience rather than arbitrary, "made-up" ones (Camp, Markley, & Kramer, 1983).

Have you ever found yourself able to remember who was at a meeting by picturing where each person sat? An ancient Greek named Simonedes is credited with originating this **method of loci**, another form of mental imaging. The idea is to identify a series of places associated with items you want to remember, and then mentally or physically revisit those places during recall. The method also works for prospective actions: you can associate things you want to remember to do with specific locations (such as rooms in your house), so that the desired actions will come to mind as you visualize or go to each place. Older adults have been trained to remember grocery lists this way (Camp, 1988; West, 1985).

Rehearsal, organization, and *elaboration* are verbal explicit internal aids. While elaboration and organization are more effective for encoding, information learned through elaborative techniques—such as rhyming, forming words or phrases from initial letters, and making up stories incorporating the information to be learned—will not be retained for any length of time without occasional rehearsal. Also, to use mnemonics effectively, the strategies themselves must be practiced frequently (West, 1985).

Because explicit internal strategies take conscious effort on the part of working memory, they tend to be more useful to younger adults than to older ones. Although both younger and older people can be trained to use these skills, older trainees show less improvement, especially for difficult tasks. Also, older adults, unless given periodic monitoring and support, tend to stop using the techniques, perhaps because the effort seems too great (Anschutz et al., 1987; Baltes, 1993; Camp, 1988; Camp et al., 1993; Scogin & Bienias, 1988; Verhaeghen, Marcoen, & Goossens, 1992).

IMPLICIT INTERNAL AIDS

Implicit memory aids can be effective for older adults—especially those with memory impairments, whose unconscious memory functioning is likely to be relatively intact (Howard, 1991).

Spaced retrieval, which may involve elements of priming or classical conditioning, is a training method to help normal or demented older adults recall information for longer and longer periods. If they miss, they are given the right answer and then retested after a shorter interval. People who ordinarily cannot associate a face with a name for more than 1 minute have been trained to remember such associations for as long as 5 weeks (Camp & Stevens, 1990). This technique has proved effective with Alzheimer's patients (Camp

& McKitrick, 1992; Riley, 1992), even in a prospective memory task (McKitrick, Camp, & Black, 1992).

Another technique utilizing *classical conditioning* was demonstrated at a day-care center for impaired older adults, where a group of demented women were constantly heaping verbal abuse on an African American man who triggered their remembered racial prejudice. Because of their dementia, they were unable to explicitly encode instructions from the staff to "be nice" to this man. But when he was given the task of handing out rewards and honors, they quickly became conditioned to associate him with positive feelings, and their verbal abuse diminished—though they couldn't explain why they liked him now, nor could they remember having abused him (Camp et al., 1993).

IMPLICIT EXTERNAL AIDS

Three-dimensional puzzle maps of foreign cities like Paris, sold in novelty shops, allow prospective travelers to internalize knowledge of the shapes and locations of major landmarks such as the Eiffel Tower and the Louvre. Putting these puzzles together gives people a cognitive map, which primes them to recognize landmarks. If and when they visit the city and see the actual structures, they may have an "O" experience: a flash of recognition that they already know this information (Camp et al., 1993). Such *tactile-visual cues* offer promise for improving implicit memory in older adults, especially those with memory impairments.

COMBINED AIDS

When Mark Twain found that his grandchildren were having trouble remembering the names and dates of reigns of English monarchs, he invented a painless method to make the information stick. Along the roadway on his farm, he pounded stakes in the ground at intervals proportional to the length of each monarch's reign. On each stake, he wrote the appropriate name and dates. As he and his grandchildren walked around the farm, the youngsters unconsciously absorbed a sense of the relative length of these reigns (implicit external aid). At the same time, the labels on the stakes served as explicit external aids. As a special motivator, Twain added a challenge to perceptual learning: he would throw an apple down the road, and the child who correctly estimated in whose "reign" the apple fell would get to eat it (Twain, 1963). In devising this highly creative mnemonic aid, Twain wisely recognized that (1) learning can and should be fun, and (2) the most powerful memory tools often combine more than one mnemonic strategy (West, 1985).

Memory intervention can extend to individuals with dementia. New intervention approaches are described in Box 5.3.

Forgetting and Its Surprising Benefits

A middle-aged man who, in his childhood, had been a highly successful quiz show contestant remarked, only partly in jest, "I am absolutely cursed with a good memory. I really do not know how to forget" (R. D. Feldman, 1982, p. 278).

Memory Interventions

Can people with dementia be helped to improve their memory? The answer is yes, according to psychologist Cameron Camp and his associates (Camp & Foss, 1997; Camp, Foss, Stevens, & O'Hanlon, 1996; Sterns & Camp, 1998). These researchers have refined a technique that enables persons with dementia to learn and retrieve pieces of new information over extended time periods. This procedure is called spaced retrieval. The idea is simple: persons with memory deficits practice first after a very short time, retrieving items of information, and then, when successful, after successively longer intervals. The technique seems to enable them to access relatively automatic (implicit) memory processing with little cognitive effort (Camp et al., 1996). Using this technique, persons with Alzheimer's disease and related dementias have learned to remember names of objects, face-name associations, and object-location associations, and to perform a prospective memory task (remembering to perform an action such as washing hands before meals). Persons trained in spaced retrieval have demonstrated the ability to remember new associations over periods of weeks when initially they could not remember new associations after only a few minutes.

To maximize the practical impact of the intervention in everyday life, researchers trained persons with Alzheimer's disease to remember a strategy, "Look at the calendar," which enabled them to use an external memory aid (Camp et al., 1996). At baseline testing, none of the participants were able to use the calendar without spaced retrieval training. Of the 23 community-dwelling persons taking part in the study, 87 percent learned the strategy, and 75 percent could put it into action by effectively using the calendar to perform daily activities. By changing the memos on the calendar each day, caregivers could enable persons with Alzheimer's disease to perform appropriate daily activities in spite of their extensive memory deficits—a sort of "cognitive prosthesis."

The next step was to train caregivers to do as the researchers had done; to deliver a spaced retrieval intervention to persons in their care (McKitrick & Camp, 1993). This important next step in intervention research is often overlooked in laboratory-based research.

Brush and Camp (1998) demonstrated that speech-language pathologists could be trained to use spaced retrieval for clients with dementia, most of whom were in long-term care, in regular speech therapy sessions. Recall that trials for spaced retrieval target behaviors (such as remembering to look at an appointment calendar to know what activities were scheduled for that day and for what hours of the day) were presented at natural breaks in the session, between other activities.

This series of studies demonstrates an important point about applied gerontological research: to have a large-scale impact, professionals who are to implement interventions must view them in practical terms. A finding that an intervention can elicit a desired effect is not enough; researchers also must show that the intervention can be applied within the setting and time frame in which the professional normally delivers service. In addition, because most professionals need to maintain a sufficient clinical caseload and to generate adequate income, the intervention must be one that can be viewed as a billable procedure.

It may seem strange to talk about forgetting as something a smart person would want to know how to do. From an information-processing perspective, forgetting is a breakdown of memory—either decay of stored material or inability to retrieve it. A computer, unless it's malfunctioning, does not delete information from its own memory. But the human mind can. An important difference between human beings and computers, then, is the ability to forget.

A novel way to think of memory is as a dynamic, ever-changing synthesis of remembering and forgetting, a unified system in which the two components must be in balance (Camp & McKitrick, 1989). Memory gives continuity and stability; forgetting clears the way for freshness, creativity, and innovation (Klass, 1986). Memory obviously has become dysfunctional when forgetting dominates remembering, as in Alzheimer's disease and other forms of dementia (Camp & McKitrick, 1989). But what if remembering dominates? Wouldn't it be nice never to forget a name, a face, a fact, or an appointment? Are there penalties to inability to forget?

Forgetting is the mind's overflow valve. In a cautionary tale by an Argentinian writer (Borges, 1964) a man who can't forget ends up drowning in his memories. A short-order cook who couldn't forget would be overwhelmed by orders he or she had already filled and wouldn't be able to remember the new ones (W. Epstein, 1977).

One clinical neuropsychologist called forgetting "an essential component of a memory system, preventing the mind from being cluttered by outdated and useless information" (Kihlstrom, 1983, p. 73). A mind that couldn't forget would contain an indiscriminate jumble of the important and unimportant, the relevant and irrelevant. A person with such a mind would very likely be a colossal bore, perpetually digressing into endless trivialities.

A person who couldn't forget details would have great difficulty generalizing (Camp, 1988; Camp & McKitrick, 1989). A famous memory whiz called "S.," who was studied by the noted Russian neuropsychologist Luria (1968), could recall a list of 50 words years after seeing them only once. But he had trouble recognizing a face! Why? He remembered each fleeting expression but couldn't form a composite mental image of the person. Perhaps the eminent philosopher and psychologist William James (1890) had such a phenomenon in mind when he observed a century ago, "if we remembered everything, we should on some occasions be as ill off as if we remembered nothing" (p. 680).

Can older adults forget more or less easily than younger ones? Two studies found no significant age differences in *intentional forgetting*—ability to forget when instructed to do so (Camp, Markley, & Spenser, 1987; Pavur, Comeaux, & Zeringue, 1984). But while younger and older adults seem equally able to forget in the laboratory, older people may be more likely to do it in everyday life. In fact, the idea of forgetting as an ability in its own right may put memory "losses" usually associated with aging in a different light.

Perhaps older people's reluctance to use certain strategies for remembering, even when taught, is a sign that those strategies are not suited to their needs. Older people may shift to a strategy of selective forgetting so they can use their mental energy and attention more efficiently for the tasks that matter at their time of life. Rather than trying to remember specific details, they may be more interested in discerning patterns and principles. By culling nonessential information, they may be better able to find meaning in things they consider worth remembering. From a lifespan perspective, forgetting may be the price for a developmental change that enables wisdom to emerge (Camp, 1988; Camp & McKitrick, 1989).

SUMMARY AND KEY TERMS

Studying Memory Systems

- Information-processing researchers study the processes involved in forming, retaining, and recovering memories, both in the laboratory and in everyday life.
- Biological researchers study the physical brain structures involved in memory.

Information-Processing Approach: Software of Memory

- Memories are processed by encoding, storage, and retrieval. Difficulties in any of these processes may impair memory.
- Recall of newly encountered information seems to drop off with age. Recall is more affected by age than recognition is.
- The information-processing model includes three interacting storage systems: sensory memory, short-term (working) memory, and long-term memory.
- Sensory memory seems virtually unaffected by age.
- Working memory handles effortful processing and retrieval.
- The capacity of working memory is limited and seems to decline with age, especially for complex tasks and strategies. Attention and motivation may affect its efficiency.
- Methods of encoding material for long-term storage include rehearsal, organization, and elaboration.
- Long-term memory contains both declarative and nondeclarative material. Most declarative information is processed effortfully (explicitly); nondeclarative information may be processed unconsciously (implicitly), bypassing working memory.
- Because individual memories become less distinctive with age, the episodic component of declarative memory is more affected than the semantic component.
- Most forms of unconscious learning—motor learning, some kinds of perceptual learning, classical conditioning, and priming—decline very little with age.

encoding (p. 156)
storage (p. 156)
retrieval (p. 156)
sensory memory (p. 159)
working memory (p. 159)
rehearsal (p. 159)

central executive (p. 159)
articulatory loop (phonological loop) (p. 159)
visual (spatial) scratch pad (p. 159)
episodic buffer (p. 159)
short-term memory (p. 159)

Biological Approach: Hardware of Memory

- The hippocampus, under direction by the frontal lobes of the cortex, initially encodes and retrieves declarative memories. Other brain structures appear to control various kinds of unconscious learning. Retrieval of long-term memories may be independent of the hippocampus.

New Directions for Research

- There is a trend toward interdisciplinary research involving the biological and information-processing approaches and incorporating environmental, lifestyle, and psychosocial factors.

Aspects of Memory and Forgetting in Adulthood

- Although older adults are subject to intrusion errors, some of these intrusions may be beneficial.
- The stability of prospective memory depends largely on the task and on availability of external cues or aids.
- Production deficiencies in encoding strategies may be remedied by training, but older adults seem to have more limited potential for improvement than younger adults.
- Older adults' overall assessment of their world knowledge may be affected by stereotypes about aging. It is not clear whether or to what extent metamemory is involved in production deficiencies.
- A variety of mnemonic devices—external or internal and explicit or implicit—can help enhance memory for adults of varying ages and circumstances.
- Lifestyle factors (sleep and nutrition) can affect memory.
- Memory may be viewed as a synthesis of remembering and forgetting; if either dominates, memory may become dysfunctional.
- Forgetting prunes out unneeded memories, prevents mental congestion, and permits generalization. The ability to forget seems unaffected by age, but older adults may be more likely to forget selectively in everyday life.

Intelligence and Creativity

◈ FOCUS: AKIRA KUROSAWA

Few of us make the most of our minds. The body ceases to grow in a few years; but the mind, if we will let it, may grow almost as long as life lasts.

—John Lubbock, The Pleasures of Life

THE JAPANESE FILMMAKER AKIRA Kurosawa,* who wrote and directed such classics as the Academy Award-winning *Rashomon* (1951) and *Seven Samurai* (1954), has been called a cinematographic genius. Kurosawa, who tried painting before going into filmmaking, uses the screen as his canvas. Artistic intelligence—an unerring sense of composition, form, color, and texture—pervades his scenes.

During his primary (elementary) school days, according to a schoolmate who later

© Roger Ressmeyer/Corbis Images

*Sources of biographical information about Akira Kurosawa are Goodwin (1994), Kurosawa (1981), and Richie (1965).

became his scriptwriting collaborator, he was "not the little-genius type who merely gets good grades" but a natural leader, a "commanding" figure (Richie, 1965, p. 10). He was president of his class as well as valedictorian. As a young adult, he continued to show leadership. As an assistant to the great film director Kajiro Yamamoto, he invariably brought Yamamoto and everyone else working on a production around to his way of thinking.

Kurosawa was in his midtwenties when he won an apprenticeship with Yamamoto at the studio later known as Toho. During the oral examination, he displayed unusual breadth and depth of knowledge and well-reasoned opinions. On the job, he was a quick study. Assigned to write scenarios, the talented novice polished off the first few and came up with idea after idea for more. He picked up editing with equal ease. He learned to look for visual solutions to dramatic problems, and he experimented with dubbing sound onto images. "He is completely creative," said Yamamoto (Richie, 1965, p. 12).

In his directorial debut, *Sanshiro Sugata* (1943), Kurosawa broke with Japanese tradition by borrowing tension-building techniques from western action movies. This film, adapted from a novel about the rise of judo as a martial art, portrayed the physical and spiritual development of a fighter. Kurosawa, a descendant of medieval warriors (*samurai*), wrote the screenplay at one sitting. Its "innovative exuberance, original imagery, and intuitive approach place *Sanshiro* in the company of inspired debut films" (Goodwin, 1994, p. 43).

"From the beginning," said Yamamoto, "Kurosawa was completely engrossed in separating what is real from what is false. He . . . holds out until everything is just the way that he sees it" (Richie, 1965, p. 13). For *The Most Beautiful* (1944), a story of women leaving home to work in a wartime factory, Kurosawa made the actors sleep in a real factory dormitory, trained them on the shop floor, and filmed the production line right there. In *Red Beard* (1965), his dedication to historical detail—which extended to creating "age stains" on teacups that would never be seen onscreen—dragged out the filming for 2 years.

By that time Kurosawa, who had left the Toho studio in protest following a labor dispute, had returned and formed his own production unit there. Now the arrangement fell apart. Kurosawa blamed the studio system for stifling social criticism and expressed regret that he had bowed to demands to limit his exposure of official corruption (*The Bad Sleep Well*, 1960). He had chafed under censorship; some of his films had been cut or never shown. *The Men Who Tread on the Tiger's Tail*, a commentary on a decaying feudal, militaristic society, filmed just as American occupation troops entered Japan after World War II, had not been released until 1952, 7 years later.

When dwindling movie audiences caused Japanese studios to stop financing his films, he hit a low point and, in 1971, became ill and attempted suicide. Since then, he has attracted support from foreigners, including the American producer-directors Steven Spielberg, George Lucas, and Francis Ford Coppola.

Always a keen social observer, Kurosawa has tackled such topics as the civil services bureaucracy (*Ikiru*, 1952) and, more recently, threats to the environment (*Dreams*, 1990) and atomic bomb survivors (*Rhapsody in August*, 1991). Before his death in 1998, he was working on *Not Ready Yet*, about the last phase of a writer's career. The title, a chant from the children's game of hide and seek, echoed his own refusal to retire. In the sixth decade of his career, he "remain[ed] passionately engaged in [its] creative challenges" (Goodwin, 1994, p. 56).

THE STORY OF AKIRA KUROSAWA touches on several themes of this chapter. One of these themes is the relationship between intelligence and creativity, and their influence on adult accomplishments. A second theme concerns various forms or aspects of intelligence—for example, artistic, verbal, practical, and interpersonal. A third theme is the role of personality, motivation, experience, and social context in intellectual achievement. A fourth theme is how age may affect productivity.

Do adults' minds continue to grow, though their bodies do not? Do some intellectual abilities, like some physical abilities, begin to falter and decline? Do adults develop new kinds of abilities as they get older? To answer such questions, we need to consider others. What are intelligence and creativity? How do they differ? How can they be measured? Are most highly creative people (like Kurosawa) highly intelligent, and vice versa? Can a person be creative but not intelligent, or intelligent but not creative? Does an ability to answer factual questions mean that a person is smarter than someone whose memory for facts is not as good? What about the ability to write a well-reasoned essay? To seize an opportunity? To get along with others? To cope with setbacks?

In this chapter, we discuss, in turn, intelligence and creativity throughout adulthood. In Chapter 7, we look at special features of mature thought, at wisdom, and at moral reasoning.

INTELLIGENCE AND ITS MEASUREMENT: THE PSYCHOMETRIC APPROACH

What Is Intelligence?

For years, psychologists argued about whether intellectual ability is inherited or acquired. Today there is general agreement that both factors play an important part, though their relative influence may be hard to determine. Still unresolved, however, are more basic questions about what intelligence is and how to measure it.

At a symposium in 1921 sponsored by the *Journal of Educational Psychology*, more than a dozen eminent psychologists tried to agree on a definition of intelligence but couldn't manage to do it (Sattler, 1988). A later attempt to pick up where the 1921 conference left off failed as well (Sternberg & Detterman, 1986).

While it's hard to define what intelligence *is*, there's a fair amount of agreement on what it *does*. **Intelligent behavior** is generally considered to be both *goal-oriented* (conscious and deliberate rather than automatic or accidental) and *adaptive* (aimed at identifying and solving problems). When more than a thousand experts in psychology, education, sociology, and genetics were asked to rate important elements of intelligent behavior, nearly all checked three of the thirteen choices: reasoning, capacity to acquire knowledge, and problem-solving ability (Snyderman & Rothman, 1987). But even this consensus may break down when we look at cross-cultural research, since some cultures have divergent views of intelligent behavior (see Box 6.1).

> **CRITICAL THINKING**
>
> What three elements of behavior do you believe are most important in defining intelligence? Why?

6.1 THE MULTICULTURAL CONTEXT

Is Intelligent Behavior the Same in All Cultures?

How would you answer the following test question?

> In the far north all bears are white. Novaya Zemlya is in the far north. What color are the bears there? (Luria, 1976)

Most educated western adults would say that bears in Novaya Zemlya are white. But the Russian psychologist Alexander Luria, who did research in rural areas of central Asia, found that unschooled peasants often failed to answer such questions correctly. Older adults in western cultures who have had less education than younger ones also tend to give wrong answers (Botwinick, 1978; Denney, 1974). Does this mean that the peasants and older adults are incapable of logical thought? Some researchers have made that inference.

But a closer look at Luria's findings reveals that many of the peasants simply *refused* to try to solve the problem about the bears in Novaya Zemlya. They said, for example, "You should ask the people who have been there and seen them" or "We don't talk about what we haven't seen." One investigator (Scribner, 1979), analyzing Luria's data, called such responses evidence of a "concrete bias," which would be corrected with formal education; and indeed Luria found that to

© PhotoDisc

If all bears in the far north are white, what color are the bears in a particular far northern province? Most educated western adults would answer, "White." Uneducated peasants of central Asia refused to answer, not because they couldn't think logically, but because they hadn't seen the bears.

be true. Moreover, even unschooled peasants occasionally took a more "theoretical" approach to the question and did get the right answer.

Why, then, did these peasants often perform differently from educated western adults on tasks involving formal logic?

We may find a clue in a study of the Kpelle (people from central Liberia in Africa). When Kpelle adults were asked to sort 20 objects, they

Intelligence Tests and Scores

Given the difficulty of defining intelligence, it's not surprising that the question of how to assess it is highly controversial. In everyday life, of course, people frequently make informal judgments about intelligence. Such remarks as "Juan is smarter than Philippe" and "Margaret is not very bright" imply that intelligence is something quantifiable, something individuals possess in greater or lesser amounts. And, indeed, this is the basic assumption of the **psychometric approach**, which has dominated the study of intelligence since

consistently did so on the basis of "functional" categories (that is, knife with orange or potato with hoe). Western psychologists associate functional sorting with a low level of thought, but the Kpelle kept saying that this was the way a "wise man" would do it. Finally, the experimenter asked, "How would a fool do it?" He then received the "higher-order" categories he had originally expected—four neat piles with food in one, tools in another, and so on (Glick, 1975, p. 636).

Gisela Labouvie-Vief (1985), a psychologist at Wayne State University, suggests that people in different cultures may define problems differently on the basis of their prior experience and knowledge, and their way of approaching a problem may be *correct* in that context. To illustrate, she cites another example from Luria's work. Three peasants in Uzbekistan were shown pictures of a saw, a hammer, and an ax. They then were shown a picture of a log and were asked whether it belonged in the same category with the other three (tools). They said it did—and proceeded to explain why.

> *Peasant 1:* . . . We make all sort of things out of logs—handles, doors, and the handles of tools.

> *Peasant 2:* We say a log is a tool because it works with tools to make things.
> *Experimenter:* But one man said a log isn't a tool since it can't saw or chop.
> *Peasant 3:* Yes you can—you can make handles out of it! . . .
> *Experimenter:* Name all the tools used to produce things . . .
> *Peasant 1:* We have a saying: take a look in the fields and you'll see tools. (Luria, 1976, pp. 94–95)

Luria saw this exchange as evidence that the peasants were unable to classify. But Labouvie-Vief suggests a different interpretation. What if the experimenter and the peasants were simply on different cultural wavelengths, with the experimenter rigidly trying to guide them toward the "correct" definition, *tools*, while the peasants banteringly argued for a more flexible definition?

Similarly, Labouvie-Vief observes, older western adults may have their own way of looking at a problem. And they are more likely than younger adults to question the validity of a task if they don't see the point of it. We need to be cautious, then, about making assumptions about intellectual "deficits" that may actually represent differences in outlook.

the late nineteenth century. *Psychometric* literally means "measuring the mind." Psychometric tests seek to measure intelligence through questions or tasks that serve as indicators or predictors of intellectual functioning in such areas as verbal comprehension, mathematical computation, and reasoning, as well as certain nonverbal performance skills. Psychometric tests are often evaluated by how well they predict intelligent behavior, such as performance in school. In this way, these tests have proven to be valuable indicators of intellectual abilities. However, they are sometimes criticized for attending primarily to cognitive products and being apparently unrelated to cognitive performance in everyday life (Dixon & Hultsch, 1999).

Intelligence test scores are based on comparisons with *standardized norms*, standards derived from scores of a large representative sample of people who took the same test. Because the early intelligence tests were designed for children, Alfred Binet—who, with his colleague Theodore Simon, introduced the first such test, the Binet-Simon Scale, in 1905—developed the concept of *mental age* to indicate a child's intellectual level (Binet & Simon, 1905, 1908). A child (regardless of chronological age) with a mental age of 9 is one who has scored about the same as the average 9-year-old.

But if, say, an 8-year-old and a 12-year-old both have a mental age of 9, are they equally intelligent? Plainly not. To more readily compare children of different ages, William Stern (1911), a German psychologist, came up with a "mental quotient," which, with further refinement, became the **intelligence quotient (IQ)**. IQ was obtained by dividing mental age by chronological age and then multiplying by 100 to eliminate the decimal point. An IQ of 100 would mean that a child's mental age and chronological age were the same. A 10-year-old with an IQ of 120 would have a mental age of 12. IQ was found to remain fairly constant throughout childhood.

Measuring adults' intelligence presented a special problem. As a rule, adults (unlike children) do not show steady, age-linked improvements on tested tasks. Thus, a method for calculating adults' intelligence needed scoring techniques divorced from mental age. The solution was the **deviation IQ**. Now used for children as well as for adults, deviation IQ is based on the distribution of raw scores and the *standard deviation from the mean* (see Figure 6.1). David Wechsler (1939), who developed the Wechsler-Bellevue Intelligence Scale, assigned an IQ of 100 to the mean, or average, score at each age level, with higher and lower IQs determined by their distance from the mean.

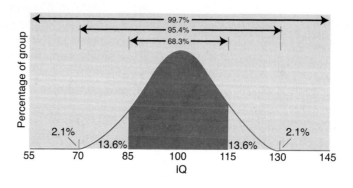

FIGURE 6.1 *"Deviation IQ" is based on a bell-shaped curve with the average IQ (100) at its center.* The farther a score deviates from this average, or mean, the fewer people make that score. More than two-thirds of test-takers score within 15 points on either side of 100—in other words, between 85 and 115. Fewer than 5 percent score below 70 or above 130. *SOURCE: R. S. Feldman, 1993.*

The **Wechsler Adult Intelligence Scale (WAIS)**—like the Wechsler tests for children—has subtests that yield separate scores. Items are not graduated by age. An emphasis on nonverbal performance (identifying the missing part of a picture, copying a design, or mastering a maze) gives the test less bias toward verbal abilities than some other psychometric tests. The eleven subtest scores are combined into a verbal IQ and a performance IQ, and, finally, a total IQ. (Figure 6.2 shows examples of items like those on WAIS.) The WAIS is now one of the major tests of intelligence, and the WAIS-III is especially relevant for testing adults (Wechsler, 1997). It is also used in assessment

CRITICAL THINKING

What purpose do intelligence tests serve for researchers and clinicians learning about aging persons? What value do intelligence tests have for the adult population in general?

VERBAL SCALE

Information   On what continent is the Taj Mahal?

Comprehension   Explain the meaning of this saying: "A journey of 1,000 miles begins with a single step."

Arithmetic   A pair of shoes that normally sells for $70 has been reduced 20 percent. How much do the shoes cost now?

Similarities   In what way are a radio and a television alike?

PERFORMANCE SCALE

1	2	3	4
<	)	:	~

1	4	2	3	4	3	1	2	3	1

Digit symbol (match symbols to numbers using the key).

Picture completion (identify what is missing).

Object assembly (put pieces together).

FIGURE 6.2 *Examples of items like those on the verbal and performance sections of the Wechsler Adult Intelligence Scale, revised version (WAIS-R).* SOURCE: Adapted from R. S. Feldman, 1993.

ANTHROPOMETRIC
LABORATORY

For the measurement in various ways of Human Form and Faculty.

Entered from the Science Collection of the S. Kensington Museum.

This laboratory is established by Mr. Francis Galton for the following purposes:—

1. For the use of those who desire to be accurately measured in many ways, either to obtain timely warning of remediable faults in development, or to learn their powers.

2. For keeping a methodical register of the principal measurements of each person, of which he may at any future time obtain a copy under reasonable restrictions. His initials and date of birth will be entered in the register, but not his name. The names are indexed in a separate book.

3. For supplying information on the methods, practice, and uses of human measurement.

4. For anthropometric experiment and research, and for obtaining data for statistical discussion.

Charges for making the principal measurements:
THREEPENCE each, to those who are already on the Register.
FOURPENCE each, to those who are not:— one page of the Register will thenceforward be assigned to them, and a few extra measurements will be made, chiefly for future identification.

The Superintendent is charged with the control of the laboratory and with determining in each case, which, if any, of the extra measurements may be made, and under what conditions.

PhotoScience Museum, London

A pioneer in psychometric testing was Francis Galton, a nineteenth-century English physician who established a laboratory to measure individual differences in such abilities as judging weights and hearing high-pitched sounds. Galton's measurements were forerunners of today's psychometric intelligence tests.

CRITICAL THINKING

Why is it almost impossible to separate intelligence from culture?

of intellectual functioning in special populations, such as those suffering from Alzheimer's disease (Dixon & Hultsch, 1999).

Many people think an IQ score represents a fixed, inborn quantity of intelligence. What it actually tells is how well a person does certain tasks at a particular time and place in comparison with other test takers. Thus, if intelligence tests measure aptitude, they do so only indirectly. Furthermore, performance on tested tasks almost inevitably reflects learned information and skills. It is, therefore, impossible to separate measured intelligence from achievement, which depends on memory, schooling, and other influences. For example, in one study of identical twins raised in different homes, differences in IQ were directly related to the number of years of education each twin had had (Bronfenbrenner, 1979). Furthermore, although scores of both school-age children and adults tend to be fairly stable, some individuals show marked change—further evidence that something beyond innate ability is being measured (Kopp & McCall, 1982). Of course, innate intelligence (even if it could be measured directly) is only one ingredient of competence, and not necessarily the most important one in a particular situation. Others include motivation or goals, education, and life experience.

Tests and Cultural Bias

While there are undoubtedly real differences in intellectual ability among individuals, there are serious questions about how accurately psychometric tests assess those differences. Members of certain ethnic groups do better than others on intelligence tests, for reasons that have been hotly debated. For example, there is a 15-point difference between average IQ scores of black and white Americans (E. B. Brody & Brody, 1976; Reynolds, 1988). Although it has been argued that the cause is largely genetic (Herrnstein & Murray, 1994; Jensen, 1969), this IQ gap is more commonly attributed to influences of income, education, and environmental stimulation, which can affect self-esteem and motivation as well as academic performance (Brooks-Gunn et al., 2003; Kamin, 1974, 1981). Indeed, the IQ and achievement test gaps between white and black Americans appear to be narrowing as the circumstances and educational opportunities for African Americans improve (Neisser et al., 1996).

Some critics attribute ethnic differences in IQ to **cultural bias:** * a tendency to include questions that use vocabulary or call for information or skills more familiar or meaningful to some cultural groups than to others (Sternberg, 1985a, 1987). These critics argue that intelligence tests are built around the dominant thinking style and language of white people of European ancestry, putting minority children at a disadvantage (Health, 1989; Helms, 1992). Cultural bias also may affect the testing situation. For example, a child from a culture that stresses sociability and cooperation may be handicapped taking a test alone (Kottak, 1994). Still, while cultural bias may play a part in some children's performance, controlled studies have failed to show that it contributes substantially to overall group differences in IQ (Neisser et al., 1996).

Test developers have tried to design **culture-free** tests—with no culture-linked content—by posing tasks that do not require language, such as tracing mazes, putting the right shapes in the right holes, and completing pictures. But they have been unable to eliminate all cultural influences. Test designers also have found it virtually impossible to produce **culture-fair** tests consisting only of experiences common to people in various cultures (Anastasi, 1988; Kottak, 1994; Miller-Jones, 1989; Sternberg, 1985a). Then, too, it is almost impossible to screen for culturally fostered values and attitudes. As we pointed out in Box 6.1, the Kpelle of Liberia customarily classify according to functional relationships; for example, *animal* with *eat*. In the United States, people who grow up in lower-class homes, where tasks and roles are less differentiated than in upper-class families, tend to classify more like the Kpelle than like upper-class Americans (Miller-Jones, 1989). Also, Americans in lower socioeconomic groups tend to value rote memory, while middle- and upper-class people value reasoning (Sternberg, 1985a, 1986; Sternberg, as quoted in Quinby, 1985). People from nonindustrial cultures, which place less emphasis on speed and competition than American culture, may be at a disadvantage on timed tests (Kottak, 1994). So, for different reasons, may older adults.

Influences on Older Adults' Test Performance

We've all had the experience of doing the same task better at one time than another. Health, comfort, energy, anxiety, motivation, study habits, and skill in taking tests can affect test scores. Some of these influences become accentuated as adults age. A number of physical and psychological factors that tend to lower older people's test scores can lead to underestimation of their intellectual ability. Their performance may be improved by attempting to control or alter some of these conditions:

> CRITICAL THINKING
>
> Judging from your own experiences with periods of stress or illness, what ongoing factors might influence older adults' test performance?

- *Physical health.* Higher mental ability is associated with higher levels of education, occupational status, and income. Adults with these advantages often also have access to better health care and have the financial resources to pay for it (Schaie & Willis, 1996). The Seattle and

---

*Unless otherwise noted, this discussion is based on Papalia, Olds, & Feldman (2004).

Education can affect results on intelligence tests. When army recruits were tested during World War I, southern white soldiers did better than southern black soldiers, who had gone to poor-quality segregated schools. But black soldiers who had attended integrated northern schools scored higher, on average, than white soldiers from some southern states. The longer the black soldiers had lived in northern cities, the higher their scores (Kottak, 1994).

Duke longitudinal studies, among others, found that adults who do best on intelligence tests are physically fit and well rested. They have few indicators of neurophysiological problems and a relatively low incidence of cardiovascular problems, which can restrict blood flow to the brain (Botwinick, 1984; Manton, Siegler, & Woodbury, 1986; Palmore, Burchett, Fillenbaum, George, & Wallman, 1985; Schaie, 1990; Schaie & Willis, 1996).

- *Vision and hearing.* Older adults may have trouble understanding test instructions and doing the tasks.
- *Speed, coordination, and mobility.* The time limits on most intelligence tests are particularly hard on older people. Because both physical and psychological processes, including perceptual abilities (Schaie, 1994), tend to slow with age, older adults do better when they are allowed as much time as they need (Hertzog, 1989; Horn & Cattell, 1966; Schaie & Hertzog, 1983). If, as some psychologists claim, it is misleading to

equate intelligence with speed (Sternberg, 1985a, 1987), then timing a test may inaccurately depict older people as less intelligent than younger ones. However, other psychologists argue that because speed is a function of the central nervous system, it is a true indicator of intellectual functioning. And some studies suggest that even when tests are not timed, older people do not do as well as younger ones (Botwinick, 1984).

- *Attitudes toward a testing situation.* Test anxiety is common among older adults, particularly if they are unfamiliar with the testing situation and have not taken tests for a long time. They may lack confidence in their ability to solve test problems, and the expectation that they will do poorly may become a self-fulfilling prophecy. Fear of failing memory may make them skip questions when they are not sure they know the answers (Cavanaugh & Morton, 1989). Or they may lack motivation: doing well may not mean much to them unless they are, for example, taking the test to qualify for a job or for some other important purpose.

Psychometric Testing: A Preliminary Evaluation

Psychometric testing has a long and useful history. Its critics, while many or all of their objectives may be well taken, have yet to come up with substitute methods that approach its sophistication. In addition, individual intelligence tests, the kind most often used with adults, can yield much useful information beyond simply a number that represents an ability. They are, in effect, clinical interviews that can reveal a great deal about how a person handles stress, failure, and success, as well as many other aspects of personality and personal history. Reports of IQ tests administered by psychologists generally include descriptions of physical appearance, level of anxiety, motivation, socioeconomic status, educational and occupational background, family history, reasons for having the test conducted, and other valuable data.

We do need to be conscious of the limitations of psychometric testing of adults. These tests have proved to be reasonably effective for the purpose for which they originally were designed: predicting academic success. They give reasonably accurate measurements of verbal and mathematical abilities, and they are fairly dependable predictors of performance in jobs that call for the specific skills they measure. But psychometric tests, as they are currently designed and used, may paint an unduly bleak picture of cognitive abilities in older adults. Furthermore, the picture may be incomplete; the tests may overlook certain abilities, particularly those abilities that may emerge or become more important in the adult years.

As we look now at basic issues concerning intellectual development in adulthood—and, in Chapter 7, as we focus on possible qualitative changes in intellectual functioning—we will continue to consider the appropriateness of psychometric tests of adults' intelligence.

CRITICAL THINKING

How satisfied are you that psychometric tests provide valuable descriptions of an older adult's ability? What future activities would you suggest in the development of standardized tests?

Intellectual Development
in Adulthood: Basic Issues

Four basic issues concerning the nature of intelligence are central to the study of intellectual development during adulthood (Dittman-Kohli & Baltes, 1990) and to the lifespan developmental approach (Baltes, 1987). Is intelligence one ability or many? Does it grow or decline, or both? Do these changes vary among individuals? Can intelligence be improved?

Is Intelligence One Ability or Many?

CRITICAL THINKING

If an older adult continues to live an independent and satisfying life, are declines in performance on intelligence tests important? Why?

Whether intelligence consists of a single ability or multiple abilities has been debated for more than a century. This question is not merely academic or semantic: the answer can affect what we seek to measure when we devise tests that may be used to decide who gets what educational and job opportunities (see Box 6.2 on p. 204). Tests that yield a single IQ reflect a unitary view of intelligence; tests that yield scores in several categories, such as abstract reasoning and practical problem solving, reflect a multidimensional view. There is also disagreement about how closely related various abilities are. Obviously, a single IQ of, say, 110, gives a very different picture from separate scores of, say, 90 for verbal abilities and 130 for nonverbal ones.

The issue is particularly important to a study of adult development and aging. A multidimensional view of intelligence allows for the possibility of simultaneous advances and declines; a unitary view does not. As both individual and group tests have been refined, their developers have turned from the original emphasis on general intelligence to more sophisticated distinctions among various kinds of abilities and have sought to adapt the tests to special needs (Anastasi & Urbina, 1997; Daniel, 1997).

FACTOR ANALYSIS: THE QUEST
FOR STATISTICAL CONFIRMATION

Beginning in the late 1920s with the work of Charles E. Spearman (1863–1945), psychometric researchers have used a method called **factor analysis** to try to determine statistically which of these two views is correct. Factor analysis seeks to identify underlying factors common to a group of tests on which the same people score similarly. For example, if adults with high scores on reading tests also have high scores on vocabulary tests, this correlation may suggest an underlying verbal ability. The trouble with factor analysis is that it can be quite subjective. The investigator's point of view may affect selection of data, statistical procedures, and designation of factors. As a result, factor analysis has furnished ammunition for both camps in the battle over whether intelligence is general or specialized.

Spearman (1927) proposed that a general factor *(g)* underlies the specific *(s)* factors measured by various kinds of tests that require complex mental effort (such as mathematical reasoning, verbal comprehension, and hypothesis testing). On the other hand, Louis L. Thurstone (1938), who developed the Primary Mental Abilities Test, maintained that intelligence comprises a group of eight "primary" abilities, each more or less independent of the others: for example, verbal comprehension, inductive and deductive reasoning, perceptual speed, and rote memory. However, later analysis showed that these factors were not as independent as Thurstone had first thought. Joy Guilford (1956, 1959, 1967, 1982) constructed a complex model of the "structure of intellect," with 150 separate though cross-linked factors.

The debate continues today (Box 6.2). One pair of analysts (Kranzler & Jensen, 1991a, 1991b) claim that *g* is the product of at least four independent underlying processes; another investigator (Carroll, 1991a, 1991b), applying a different method of analysis to the same data, claims that the results more appropriately support a unitary *g*. Because of its varied statistical procedures and rules, factor analysis can support a number of possible interpretations.

Two contemporary thinkers—Robert Sternberg, a psychologist at Yale University; and Howard Gardner, a neuropsychologist and educational researcher at Harvard University—are leaders in a growing trend toward viewing intelligence as multidimensional. Both claim that traditional psychometric tests fail to measure important mental abilities, and both have proposed theories and done research aimed at developing more comprehensive methods of assessment.

STERNBERG'S TRIARCHIC THEORY: THREE ASPECTS
OF INTELLIGENCE

Alix, Barbara, and Courtney applied to graduate programs at Yale. Alix had an almost straight-A college transcript, scored very high on the Graduate Record Examination (GRE), and had excellent recommendations. Barbara's grades were only fair, and her GRE scores were low by the university's high standards, but her letters of recommendation enthusiastically praised her exceptional research and creative ideas. Courtney's grades, GRE scores, and recommendations were good but not among the best.

Alix and Courtney were admitted to the graduate program. Barbara was not admitted but was hired as a research associate and took graduate classes on the side. Alix did very well for the first year or so, but less well after that. Barbara confounded the admissions committee by doing work as outstanding as her letters of recommendation had predicted. Courtney's performance in graduate school was only fair, but she had the easiest time getting a good job afterward (Trotter, 1986).

What explains these outcomes? Robert Sternberg (1997, 2003a) defines intelligence as a group of mental abilities necessary for people to adapt to any environmental context, as well as to select and shape the contexts in which they live and act. According to Sternberg (1985a, 1987, 1997), Barbara and Courtney were strong in two aspects of intelligence that psychometric tests miss: creative insight and practical intelligence. Unlike traditional psychometric researchers, Sternberg is less interested in the structure of the mind than in the processes that underlie intelligent behavior. His *triarchic* (three-part)

Are Intelligence Tests the Best Predictors of Job Performance?

Today, tests to screen prospective employees are common. But can the same kind of test accurately predict success in such varied kinds of work as bricklaying and data processing?

Two Texans—Malcolm James Ree, a psychologist at St. Mary's University; and James A. Earles, a mathematician in San Antonio—say yes. Ree and Earles (1992) touched off a controversy with their claim that tests of general intelligence (*g*, as researchers call it) are the best predictors of performance on any job, and that measures of specific aptitudes—verbal, quantitative, spatial, or mechanical—add little. The claim was based on a statistical review of a number of large-scale studies, many done in the armed services.

The article, published in *Current Directions in Psychological Science*, a journal of the American Psychological Society, provoked so much reaction that the journal devoted a special section to the subject. In a rebuttal entitled "The *g*-ocentric View of Intelligence and Job Performance Is Wrong," Robert Sternberg (whose multifactorial theory of intelligence we discuss in this chapter) and his colleague Richard K. Wagner compared the idea that all abilities revolve around general

intelligence to the discredited belief that the earth is the center of the universe. Sternberg and Wagner (1993) argued that intelligence tests predict job performance less reliably than school performance because real-life and academic problems require different kinds of intelligence. Academic problems, unlike those in real life, are well-defined, have one right answer and one method of obtaining it, and provide the solver with all needed information.

Other contenders weighed in on both sides. One (Jensen, 1993) argued that *g* is not limited to academic intelligence and that, although there *is* considerable variance between actual job performance and what the tests predict, such factors as personality, motivation, interests, and values are more likely than specific abilities to account for the difference. Another (McClelland, 1993) criticized the omission of such factors as gender, race, education, and social class: "Being white, male, better educated, and from an advantaged background often correlate with better job performance, particularly as measured by a supervisor's ratings. Any of these correlations . . . may predict job perfor-

theory of intelligence embraces three elements of information processing that are useful in different kinds of situations:

1. **Componential element**—*how efficiently people process information.* This is the *analytic* aspect of intelligence. It tells people how to solve problems, how to monitor solutions, and how to evaluate results. Alix was strong in this area; she was good at taking intelligence tests and finding holes in arguments.
2. **Experiential element**—*how people approach novel or familiar tasks.* This is the *insightful* aspect of intelligence. It allows people to compare new information with what they already know and to come up with new ways of putting facts and ideas together—in other words, to think

mance better than intelligence" (p. 6). The authors of the original article, replying to their critics (Ree & Earles, 1993), pointed to well-documented relationships between *g* and other job qualifications, such as motivation, leadership, and social skills. An applicant selected for general intelligence, they maintained, is likely to show these other characteristics as well.

The heated exchange skirted a troubling aspect of the modest relationship between test scores and job performance. White adults referred for jobs on the basis of a battery of tests used by state employment agencies tend to perform less well after being hired than their scores would predict, while African Americans do better on the job than on the tests. This situation led to the controversial practice—later outlawed—of "race-norming," ranking scores within racial categories to avoid screening out capable minority applicants. It also led to calls for revision of the tests to eliminate cultural bias, and pleas to employers to rely less on the tests in hiring. Ree and Earles (1992) gave passing recognition to this problem, suggesting the substitution of "content-free" tests designed to measure *g*

through such basic cognitive indicators as speed of information processing; but there is dispute over whether such tests could legitimately be related to job performance.

One question we should ask in weighing findings about job performance is just what they are measuring. If findings refer to occupational level—the difficulty or complexity of a job, which Ree and Earles (1992) used as one index of job performance—it is hardly surprising that an engineer has a higher IQ than a lumberjack; but is a mediocre engineer a better performer than a competent, industrious lumberjack? How does a finding that engineers have (and presumably need) higher measured intelligence than lumberjacks support the conclusion that intelligence tests can select the best performers in *any* field?

Much more thought and study need to go into the issue of how much weight should be given to intelligence (however measured) in employment decisions and what other factors, if any, should be taken into consideration to make predictions of performance more reliable for employers and fairer to applicants.

originally. Automatic performance of familiar operations (such as recognizing words) facilitates insight, because it leaves the mind free to tackle unfamiliar tasks (such as decoding new words). Barbara was strong in this area.

3. **Contextual element**—*how people deal with their environment.* This is the *practical* aspect of intelligence. It is the ability to size up a situation and decide what to do: adapt to it, change it, or find a new, more comfortable setting. Courtney was strong in this area.

Sternberg's theory is of special interest to students of adult development because it focuses on aspects of intelligence that may become increasingly valuable in adult life.

In our example, for instance, Alix's componential ability helped her sail through college examinations. But in graduate school, where original thinking is expected, it was Barbara's superior experiential intelligence—her fresh insights and innovative ideas—that began to shine. Courtney was strongest in practical, contextual intelligence—"street smarts." She knew her way around. She chose "hot" research topics, submitted papers to the "right" journals, and knew where and how to apply for jobs.

A major component of contextual, or practical, intelligence, is **tacit knowledge**—"inside influences" or "savvy," which is not formally taught or openly expressed. It is learned through experience and modified to fit the current environment. Getting ahead in a career, for instance, often depends on tacit knowledge (knowing how to win a promotion or cut through red tape). Sternberg's method of assessing tacit knowledge is to compare a person's chosen course of action in hypothetical, work-related situations with the choices of experts in the field and with accepted "rules of thumb." Tacit knowledge, measured in this way, seems to be unrelated to IQ and predicts job performance moderately well (Sternberg, 2003b; Sternberg & Wagner, 1993; Wagner & Sternberg, 1986). Further research is needed to determine how and when tacit knowledge is acquired, why some people acquire it more efficiently than others, and whether it can be taught directly or is best picked up by observing mentors.

GARDNER'S THEORY: MULTIPLE INTELLIGENCES

As a child, Brian was in an automobile collision that left him with severe damage to the left hemisphere of the brain. He cannot speak and does not seem to understand when spoken to. Yet he can draw, sing, and compose music. What explains a case like Brian's? And what about Loretta, a gifted lawyer who has trouble figuring out how to fit luggage into the trunk of a car?

Howard Gardner once believed that intelligence is a single quality measurable by written tests. But cases like these have convinced him that intelligence is plural (Gardner, 1983). He has identified seven autonomous "intelligences" or talents, which enable people to solve problems and do productive work in various fields: *linguistic* (writers, editors, translators), *logical-mathematical* (scientists, business people, doctors), *musical* (musicians, composers, conductors), *spatial* (architects, mechanics, city planners), *bodily-kinesthetic* (dancers athletes, surgeons), *interpersonal* (teachers, actors, politicians), and *intrapersonal* (counselors, psychiatrists, spiritual leaders). Gardner has added an eighth intelligence, *naturalist intelligence*, to his original list (Gardner, 1999).

High intelligence in one of these eight areas is not necessarily accompanied by high intelligence in any of the others. A person may be extremely gifted in art (a spatial ability), precision of movement (bodily-kinesthetic), social relations (interpersonal), or self-understanding (intrapersonal), but not have a high IQ. In fact, only a few of the "intelligences"—linguistic, logical-mathematical, and, to some extent, spatial—are tapped by conventional intelligence tests. But is someone who is good at analyzing paragraphs and making analogies necessarily more intelligent than someone who has perfect musical pitch, or someone who can organize a closet or a group project, or someone who can pitch a curve ball at the right time?

According to Gardner, brain research strongly supports the existence of multiple intelligences, since different parts of the brain seem to process different kinds of information. Thus the scientist Albert Einstein, the poet T. S. Eliot, and the cellist Pablo Casals may have been equally intelligent, each in a different area (Kirschenbaum, 1990).

Talents, says Gardner, develop into "competencies" through training and practice, often revealing themselves in a "crystallized moment" in which a person discovers an unsuspected ability. Environment plays an important part in this process. People tend to develop competencies that their families and culture value and encourage. A person who does not hear music, for example, is unlikely to develop competency in that field.

Gardner's ideas show how closely the issue of unitary versus multidimensional intelligence is tied to the other three issues we're about to discuss: growth versus decline, individual variability, and plasticity. According to Gardner, the various intelligences develop and change throughout the life span, often at different rates. For example, logical-mathematical ability tends to develop earlier and to decline more quickly than interpersonal ability. But these patterns vary from one person to another, and furthermore, they may be modifiable. Rather than try to measure inborn ability, Gardner would judge each intelligence by its products (competencies): how well a person can tell a story, remember a melody, or get around in an unfamiliar area. Assessments based on extended observation would be used to reveal an individual's strengths and weaknesses for purposes of guiding further development, rather than to compare individuals (Scherer, 1985; Gardner, 1999). Defenders of psychometric tests object to such unquantified assessments as too subjective and too prone to observer bias (Sattler, 1988).

© AP/Wide World Photos

The physicist Albert Einstein had a different kind of intelligence from that of an equally able poet or musician, according to Howard Gardner's theory of multiple intelligences.

Does Intelligence Grow or Decline During Adulthood?

Does intelligence (like physical strength) peak in early or middle adulthood and then diminish? During the 1970s, that question became a major issue among psychologists. In one camp were those who challenged the "myth" of general intellectual decline in late life (Baltes & Schaie, 1974, 1976; Schaie, 2001; Schaie & Baltes, 1977). In the other camp were those who dismissed this more positive view as too rosy (Horn & Donaldson, 1976, 1977; McArdle, Prescott, Hamagami, & Horn, 1998). However, the findings of these two groups of investigators were not truly contradictory. Their differences lay mainly in emphasis and interpretation, and their positions have drawn closer with time. It is becoming clearer and clearer, in examining the results of intelligence tests given to adults of various ages, that while some abilities may decline, others remain stable or even improve throughout most of adult life.

ADULT IQ: THE CLASSIC PATTERN

Older adults, as a group, do not perform as well as younger adults on the Wechsler Adult Intelligence Scale (WAIS). But when we look at scores on the component subtests of WAIS, it becomes plain that the decline is almost entirely in nonverbal performance. On the five subtests making up the performance scale, scores drop with age; however, on the six tests making up the verbal scale— particularly tests of vocabulary, information, and comprehension—scores fall only slightly and very gradually (see Figure 6.3). This is called the **classic aging pattern** (Botwinick, 1984).

What might account for this pattern? For one thing, the verbal items that hold up with age are based on straightforward knowledge; unlike the performance tests, they do not require the test taker to figure out or do anything new (Schonfield & Robertson, 1968, as cited in Botwinick, 1984). In addition to processing new information, the performance tasks involve speed and perceptual and motor skills. Part of the age difference in performance on this type of task is attributable to muscular and neurological slowing (Storandt, 1976).

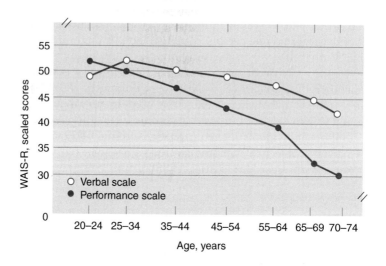

FIGURE 6.3 *Classic aging pattern of the Weschsler Adult Intelligence Scale (WAIS-R).*
Scores on the performance subtests decline far more rapidly with age than scores on the verbal subtests.
SOURCE: Botwinick, 1984.

FLUID AND CRYSTALLIZED INTELLIGENCE:
BIOLOGY VERSUS CULTURE

Another influential line of research that has found a divergence between two types of abilities is that of John L. Horn (1967, 1968, 1970, 1982a, 1982b) and Raymond B. Cattell (1965). On the basis of a variety of tests, these researchers proposed a distinction between *fluid intelligence* and *crystallized intelligence:* between forms of intelligence largely determined by genetic and physiological factors (primarily the state of the brain and nervous system), which decline with age, and forms of intelligence largely affected by cultural experience, which hold their own or even improve.

Fluid intelligence is the capacity to process novel information (for example, to follow diagrammed instructions for folding a paper square into a swan). It is the ability to apply mental powers to situations that require little or no previous knowledge (J. L. Horn, 1982a, 1982b). This kind of intelligence is based on perception of complex relationships, implications, and inferences. It is unique to an individual and largely uninfluenced by prior learning. Psychologists measure fluid intelligence by such tests as the Raven Progressive Matrices, which includes such tasks as selecting the pattern that best completes a larger one (see Figure 6.4).

Crystallized intelligence is the ability to apply learned information and experience—knowledge acquired over a lifetime. It depends on education and

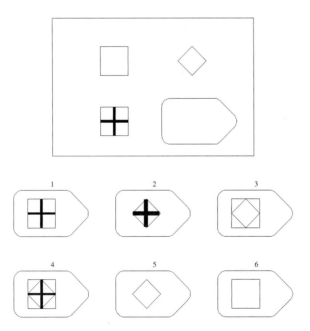

FIGURE 6.4 *Simulated item similar to those in the Raven's Progressive Matrices.* SOURCE: Copyright 1994 by Harcourt *Assessment,* Inc. Reproduced with permission. All rights reserved.

cultural background and, of course, on memory. Adults show crystallized intelligence in a wide range of situations that call for skills based on semantic memory (see Chapter 5), such as language comprehension, mathematical reasoning, and application of knowledge of facts, social customs, and values (J. L. Horn, 1982a, 1982b). Crystallized intelligence depends on well-learned, automatic information processing, especially in such complex tasks as reading, which call on many mental operations. Psychologists measure crystallized intelligence by tests of vocabulary, general information, analogies, word associations, and responses to social situations and dilemmas. In some tasks, both fluid and crystallized intelligence may be used.

Fluid and crystallized intelligence peak at different times (see Figure 6.5). Fluid intelligence begins to decline in young adulthood, perhaps because of changes in the brain. But crystallized intelligence typically improves through middle age and often until near the end of life. In fact, up to ages 55 to 65, the improvement in crystallized intelligence is about equal to the decline in fluid intelligence. Verbal abilities sharpen, especially when used regularly (J. L. Horn, 1982a, 1982b; J. L. Horn & Donaldson, 1980).

As in the classic aging pattern on WAIS, then, we see two kinds of intelligence that follow different paths. In the classic aging pattern, however, the trend in both verbal and performance scores is downward throughout most of adulthood; the difference, though substantial, is one of degree. Far more

CRITICAL THINKING

If you could stop the classic aging pattern, would you want to retain fluid intelligence capacity at the expense of increased crystallization intelligence? Why or why not?

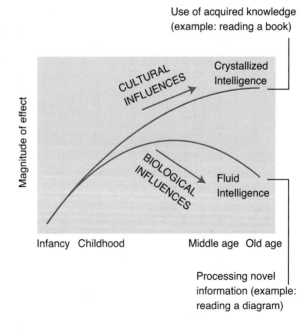

FIGURE 6.5 *Changes in fluid intelligence and crystallized intelligence over the life span*. Although fluid abilities (largely biologically determined) decline after young adulthood, crystallized abilities (largely culturally influenced) increase until late adulthood. *SOURCE: J. L. Horn & Donaldson, 1980.*

encouraging is the pattern of crystallized intelligence, which improves until fairly late in life, even though fluid intelligence declines.

THE DUAL-PROCESS MODEL: MECHANICS AND PRAGMATICS OF INTELLIGENCE

Age "adds as it takes away," the poet William Carlos Williams remarked in one of three books of verse written between his first stroke at age 68 and his death at age 79.

Baltes and his colleagues (1993; Baltes, Dittman-Kohli, & Dixon, 1984; Dixon & Baltes, 1986; Li et al., 2004) have proposed a **dual-process model** of adult intellectual functioning, which builds on Horn and Cattell's work on fluid and crystallized intelligence. The dual-process model includes aspects of intelligence that are subject to deterioration, and also aspects that may continue to advance. The model identifies and seeks to measure two kinds of intellectual processes: *mechanics* and *pragmatics*.

Mechanics of intelligence are the basic, physiologically determined functions of the brain. They include speed and accuracy of processing sensory input, visual and motor memory, and such abilities as comparing and categorizing, which operate in working memory. Like fluid intelligence, these processes often decline with age. One example is a deterioration in the ability to ignore extraneous information, a problem similar to intrusion errors in memory (see Chapter 5).

Pragmatics of intelligence build on the mechanics. These processes involve a wide range of accumulated, culture-based knowledge and skills, such as reading, writing, language comprehension, practical thinking, specialized expertise, and occupational abilities—all potential growth areas. This dimension is similar to crystallized intelligence and depends greatly on long-term memory.

Middle-aged and older adults are likely to improve in the use of information and know-how they have garnered from education, work, and other experience. In fact, says Baltes, these pragmatic abilities often outweigh the brain's mechanical condition. To take an obvious example, an older adult who has learned to read can intellectually outperform a younger person who is in better shape neurologically but has not developed that pragmatic skill (Baltes, 1993; Li et al., 2004).

SEQUENTIAL RESEARCH: THE SEATTLE LONGITUDINAL STUDY

Most of the studies of adult intelligence we've discussed so far have been cross-sectional and thus may confound cohort with age. Younger adults may do better than older adults not because of an advantage conferred by youth, but because they are healthier and better nourished, have had more or better schooling, have gained more information from television, have jobs that depend on thinking rather than on physical labor, or have had more—and more recent—experience taking tests. Older people's poorer average showing may also reflect **terminal drop**, a sudden decrease in intellectual performance shortly before death (Botwinick, 1984; K. F. Riegel & Riegel, 1972; see Chapter 13, Johansson et al., 2004).

In contrast with cross-sectional data, early longitudinal studies showed an increase in intelligence at least until the fifties (Bayley & Oden, 1955; W. A. Owens, 1966). But this research design may favor an older sample because of practice effects and *attrition*, a tendency of poorer scorers to drop out along the way (Botwinick, 1984; Schaie, 2000).

The Seattle Longitudinal Study of Intelligence, conducted by K. Warner Schaie and his colleagues over a span of more than four decades (Schaie, 1979, 1983, 1988a, 1988b, 1990, 1994; Schaie & Hertzog, 1983, 1986; Schaie & Strother, 1968; Willis & Schaie, 1999), sought to overcome drawbacks of both cross-sectional and longitudinal research. Although this ongoing study is called *longitudinal*, it uses *sequential testing* (see Chapter 2), a combination of cross-sectional, longitudinal, and time-lag methods (Baltes, 1985; Schaie, 1979, 1983; Schaie & Hertzog, 1983; Schaie & Strother, 1968).

The study began in 1956 with 500 randomly chosen participants—25 men and 25 women in each 5-year age bracket from 20 to 70. Participants took a battery of timed tests of five primary mental abilities (see Table 6.1) originally identified by Thurstone (1938). Additional measures of intellectual abilities were added as the study progressed. Every 7 years, the original participants were retested and new participants were added; by 1998, about 6,000 people, forming a broadly diverse socioeconomic sample, had been tested. The researchers also took personal and health histories and administered psychological tests.

What has the study found? Most fairly healthy adults apparently experience no significant impairment in most abilities until after age 60. If they live long enough, most people's intellectual functioning will show some decline at some point, but not in all or even most abilities. On the average, participants showed intellectual gains until the late thirties or early forties, stability until the mid fifties or early sixties, and then only small losses until the seventies. Even then, fewer than one-third at age 74, and fewer than half at age 81, had declined significantly during the previous 7 years. Although most people seem to lose some intellectual competence in their eighties and nineties, these losses show up mainly in unfamiliar, highly complex, challenging, or stressful circumstances (Schaie, 1990, 1994, 2000, 2005).

One of the major findings, which supports Baltes's lifespan developmental approach, is that change is multidimensional: there is "no uniform pattern of age-related changes . . . [for] all intellectual abilities" (Schaie, 1994, p. 306). Virtually none of the participants declined on all fronts, and many improved in specific areas. The study also found that fluid abilities decline earlier than crystallized abilities. However, the losses in fluid abilities such as inductive reasoning and spatial orientation did not begin until the mid sixties, and losses in crystallized abilities did not begin until the seventies or eighties (Willis & Schaie, 1999). These findings suggest that no single measure, such as IQ, can adequately describe either age changes in individuals or age differences among groups (Schaie, 1994).

Schaie (1990) suggests that adults might optimize overall cognitive functioning by maintaining some abilities and letting other abilities slide—a concept that Baltes (1993; Baltes & Baltes, 1980, 1990; Freund & Baltes, 2002), in his dual-process model, calls **selective optimization with compensation**. Through selec-

TABLE 6.1

Tests of Primary Mental Abilities Given in the Seattle Longitudinal Study of Adult Intelligence

Test	Ability Measured	Task	Type of Intelligence
Verbal meaning	Recognition and understanding of words	Find synonym by matching stimulus word with another word from multiple-choice list	Crystallized
Number	Applying numerical concepts	Check simple addition problems	Crystallized
Word fluency	Retrieving words from long-term memory	Think of as many words as possible beginning with a given letter, in a set time period	Part crystallized, part fluid
Spatial orientation	Rotating objects mentally in two-dimensional space	Select rotated examples of figure to match stimulus figure	Fluid
Inductive reasoning	Identifying regularities and inferring principles and rules	Complete a letter series	Fluid

SOURCE: Schaie, 1989.

tive optimization with compensation older people may use their pragmatic strengths to compensate for weakened mechanical abilities (Baltes, 1993; Baltes, Lindenbergh, & Staudinger, 1998; Baltes & Smith, 2004; Marsiske, Lange, Baltes, & Baltes, 1995). By using one or more forms of compensation, the gap between their ability and their expected level of performance can be closed. In this way, a satisfactory level of performance for a given skill can be attained, and an individual's potential can be increased (Dixon & Hultsch, 1999).

Concert pianist Arthur Rubinstein, who was still going strong in his eighties, once told a television interviewer how he managed to do it: he played fewer pieces, practiced each piece more often, and would slow down before a fast passage so that the audience would think he was playing it more rapidly than he actually was. As an octogenarian, the pianist Vladimir Horowitz also slowed his tempos and chose a less technically demanding repertoire, but his interpretations now showed extraordinary ripeness and finesse. A critic for the *New York Times* wrote of Horowitz: "Power does not necessarily diminish with age but simply changes its shape" (Schonberg, 1992, p. 288). Older adults—while they may take longer to do certain things and may no longer be as adept with unfamiliar material—can take advantage of mature judgment and insight developed from a lifetime of experience.

Do Changes in Intelligence Vary?

A striking feature of the Seattle Longitudinal Study is tremendous variation among individuals. For some people, intellectual abilities begin to decline during the thirties; for some, there is no decline until the seventies; and about one-third of people over age 70 score higher than the average young adult. Even in their eighties, more than half are maintaining their competence in at least four of the five primary areas. As a result, there is a wider range of ability among older adults than among younger ones. Some people remain relatively strong in one area, others in another (Schaie, 1990, 1994, 2000, 2005).

Some researchers, therefore, are shifting attention from overall age differences and age changes to individual patterns of change and to variables that might help explain them (Schaie, 1990, 1994, 2000). For example, people who have high scores in old age tend to be flexible and to have been satisfied with their accomplishments at midlife; not to have cardiovascular or other chronic diseases; to be relatively affluent and well-educated; to have stable marriages to intellectually keen spouses; to have done complex, nonroutine work and led active, stimulating lives; and to have maintained high perceptual processing speed (Dutta, Schulenberg, & Lair, 1986; Gribbin, Schaie, &

© Bettmann/Corbis Images

The pianist Vladimir Horowitz, who continued performing until his death at age 85, compensated for weakened mechanical abilities by choosing less technically demanding pieces, playing at slower tempos, and concentrating on interpretation.

Parham, 1980; Gruber & Schaie, 1986; Gruber-Baldini, 1991; Hertzog, Schaie, & Gribbin, 1978; Schaie, 1984, 1990, 1994, 2001). One important factor, which we'll discuss later, is how, and how much, individuals use their abilities. Other factors have to do with gender and culture.

CRITICAL THINKING

How would you describe the changes in intelligence that take place as people age?

GENDER DIFFERENCES

Do men and women differ in how their intellectual abilities change with age? The answer is yes, though the differences are generally small and may reflect the kinds of skills men and women have been encouraged to develop.

In the Seattle Longitudinal Study, men's overall functioning eroded faster than women's. Terminal drop may be a factor: at any age, more men than women are close to death. Women seem to decline earlier in fluid abilities and men in crystallized abilities (Schaie, 1994, 2001). For example, spatial abilities such as figuring out directions from a map or assembling a bookcase ebb about twice as much in women as in men, who start out ahead and often remain stable in this area well into the eighties. On the other hand, women tend to retain their initial advantage in inductive reasoning (for instance, figuring out how often buses run from looking at a schedule), which declines at about the same rate in both sexes. Women also keep their edge in verbal memory (recalling word lists, for example), word fluency (thinking of words that start with *b*), and verbal comprehension (recognizing words they know), though comprehension does decline in the eighties (Maitland et al., 2000). Men's spatial orientation, vocabulary, and verbal memory peak in the fifties; women's peak in the early sixties. However, women's perceptual speed declines faster than men's (Willis & Schaie, 1999).

Some research indicates a possible neurological basis for women's overall superiority. A study of the kinds of errors made by each sex suggests that men's frontal lobes, which control strategic planning and management of tasks, begin to show functional losses in the seventies, about 10 years earlier than women's frontal lobes (Hochanadel, 1991). A woman's brain has a thicker *corpus callosum*—the wide band of fibers connecting the two hemispheres. These denser interconnections may allow women to use their verbal strengths, concentrated in the left side of the brain, to compensate for spatial weaknesses in the right (Foreman, 1994; Innocenti, 1994).

CULTURAL AND COHORT EFFECTS

The Seattle Longitudinal Study found that health, work, and education influence intellectual performance across the adult years. If so, cultural factors such as availability and quality of health care and educational and job opportunities would seem to make a difference. Trends in health, education, and other lifestyle factors, as well as baby "booms" and "busts," technological advances, wars, plagues, famines, and other events, are part of the shared formative experience of different generations, or cohorts. And cohort differences can distort findings about effects of age.

In a factor analysis of WAIS scores done more than three decades ago, one team of investigators (Birren & Morrison, 1961) found that educational level played a much more significant role than age in *g* (general mental ability).

Since at that time older cohorts had less schooling than younger ones, cross-sectional comparisons could be misleading unless effects of education were eliminated (Botwinick, 1984; Kaufman, 2001; Schaie, 2000). If some of these early findings of apparently age-related declines actually reflected cohort differences, we would expect the differences to flatten out as young adults who have had the benefit of greater educational opportunity become older adults. Indeed, one study of 20 college students and 20 college-educated older adults found no significant age differences in formal reasoning (Blackburn, 1984).

Health is a trickier factor because of its closer connection with age. Studies show that healthy older people do better on intelligence tests than older people who are in poor health (Botwinick, 1984; Gottfredson & Deary, 2004). Does this mean that health, like education, should be factored out when studying effects of age? Or, since declining health often tends to accompany old age, would a study sample consisting only of healthy older people be artificially skewed? In any event, improvements in nutrition and medical care should, in time, diminish cohort differences due to health.

In the Seattle study, successive cohorts have—as we would expect—scored progressively higher at the same ages on inductive reasoning and verbal meaning. For example, the average 40-year-old in 1985 did better in both these areas than the average 40-year-old in 1971. But—again, as we would expect—this gain has leveled off. And performance in some other areas, particularly numerical skills, has actually declined among the most recent cohorts. Schaie (1990) concludes that we may be reaching a point where older adults no longer are at much of a competitive disadvantage and, at least in numerical skills, may even outperform younger ones. On the other hand, he suggests, American society may be approaching a limit on the improvement possible for successive older cohorts as a result of education and healthy lifestyles.

Does Intelligence Show Plasticity?

A key issue separating psychologists who have a relatively optimistic view of intellectual development in adulthood from those who have a less positive view is *plasticity*, or *modifiability:* whether or not intellectual performance can be improved during the middle to later years. Horn and Cattell, among others, stress the decline in fluid intelligence, which they view as biologically inevitable. Schaie, Baltes, and their colleagues stress the strong performance of crystallized or pragmatic abilities, along with the emergence of new abilities (discussed in Chapter 7); and they maintain that even fluid performance can be improved to some extent with training and practice.

Since plasticity is a key feature of Baltes's lifespan developmental approach, it is not surprising that he and his colleagues have been in the forefront of research on effects of training. Several of these studies have been based on the Adult Development and Enrichment Project (ADEPT), originated at Pennsylvania State University (Baltes & Willis, 1982; Blieszner, Willis, & Baltes, 1981; Plemons, Willis, & Baltes, 1978; Willis, Blieszner, & Baltes, 1981). A 7-year follow-up of ADEPT found that participants who received training declined significantly less than a control group (Willis, 1990; Willis & Nesselroade,

1990). In one study based on ADEPT, adults with an average age of 70 who received training in figural relations (rules for determining the next figure in a series), a measure of fluid intelligence, improved more than a control group who received no training. A third group who worked with the same training materials and problems, but without formal instruction, also did better than the control group, and this self-taught group maintained their gains better after 1 month (Blackburn, Papalia-Finlay, Foye, & Serlin, 1988). Apparently the opportunity to work out their own solutions fostered more lasting learning.

In *individual* training connected with the Seattle Longitudinal Study (Schaie, 1990, 1994; Schaie & Willis, 1986; Willis & Schaie, 1986), older people who had already shown declines in intelligence gained significantly in two other areas defined as fluid abilities: spatial orientation and, especially, inductive reasoning. In fact, about 4 out of 10 participants regained levels of proficiency they had shown 14 years earlier. Men improved more from training in inductive reasoning and women from training in spatial orientation, to the point of closing the gender gap in the latter. Also, trained participants retained an edge over an untrained control group, even after 7 years (Schaie, 1994). And gains measured with laboratory tasks showed substantial correlations with objective measures of everyday tasks (Willis, Jay, Diehl, & Marsiske, 1992; Schaie, 1994).

The fact that training can improve performance or even reverse losses associated with aging implies that some degree of normally observed decline may be due to disuse. Older adults decline partly because they no longer engage in activities, or lack the social and cultural support that would help them maintain certain intellectual abilities (Dixon & Hultsch, 1999). Adults may be able to maintain or expand this reserve capacity by engaging in a lifelong program of mental exercise. Taking up a musical instrument, learning to repair broken gadgets—almost any sort of mental challenge that involves new or unfamiliar tasks—can do the job (Golden, 1994). Old age need not be a time of intellectual decline if adults take steps to keep up or improve their mental powers throughout the life span (Dixon & Baltes, 1986).

> **CRITICAL THINKING**
> Since intellectual stimulation has an impact on cognitive performance and adaptive living skills, what level of effort should be made to promote continuing education for older adults?

Summing Up: Intelligence and Age

The four issues we've discussed—single versus multiple abilities, growth versus decline, variability, and plasticity—have generated intense controversy, and some dispute remains. However, most researchers and practitioners today believe that intelligence is made up of multiple abilities. Intelligence tests measure only some of these abilities.

Researchers tracking various intellectual abilities across adulthood have found that some—generally those that depend on the physical condition of the brain—decline with age (though at different rates); others, which depend on accumulated knowledge and skills, remain stable and may even increase. Differences—some of which are affected by gender and culture—exist among and within individuals. In fact, some older persons show no decline, or even improve, in abilities that typically diminish with age. Longitudinal findings on intellectual functioning, then, parallel results of recent research on internal biological systems (see Chapter 4), which, when measured longitudinally, range from marked decline to none.

Finally, research has demonstrated that it is possible for adults to improve their intellectual performance throughout the life span, even in tasks involving fluid intelligence. These findings parallel dramatic improvements in muscular strength and mobility achieved with weight-lifting programs for adults in their nineties (see Chapter 3). Still, research on memory (Chapter 5) suggests that, even for intellectual performance, biology may limit improvement in older adults more than in younger ones.

As Sternberg has noted, IQ tests tend to neglect the innovative and practical sides of intelligence. In the remainder of this chapter, we discuss creativity; in Chapter 7 we look at problem solving and other abilities that may emerge or deepen in mature adulthood.

CREATIVITY

What is creativity? Can it be measured? If so, how? What causes it to bloom? Does it increase or decrease with age?

What Is Creativity?

CRITICAL THINKING

What characteristics do you associate with creative people? Are you in agreement with the text?

At about age 40, Frank Lloyd Wright designed Robie House in Chicago, Agnes deMille choreographed the Broadway musical *Carousel*, and Louis Pasteur developed the germ theory of disease.* Charles Darwin was 50 when he presented his theory of evolution. Toni Morrison won the Pulitzer Prize for *Beloved*, a novel she wrote at about 55. But creativity is not limited to the Darwins and deMilles; we can see it in an inventor who comes up with a better mousetrap, or a promoter who finds an innovative way to sell it.

Creativity begins with talent, but talent is not enough. Children may show *creative potential*; but in adults, what counts is *creative performance*: what, and how much, a creative mind produces (Sternberg & Lubart, 1995). Creative performance is the product of a web of biological, personal, social, and cultural forces. It emerges from the dynamic interaction among the creator, the rules and techniques of the domain, and the colleagues who work in that domain (Gardner, 1986, 1988; Simonton 2000b).

Exceptional talents are less born than made—they require systematic training and practice (Simonton, 2000b). Extraordinary creative achievement, according to one analysis (Keegan, 1996), results from deep, highly organized knowledge of a subject; intrinsic motivation to work hard for the sake of the work, not for external rewards; and a strong emotional attachment to the work, which spurs the creator to persevere in the face of obstacles. What carries an Einstein "over the threshold from competent but ordinary thinker to

---

*Unless otherwise noted, the discussion in this section is based on Papalia, Olds, & Feldman (2004).

extraordinary and creative thinker," says Keegan (1996, p. 63), is the acquisition of expert knowledge. A person must first be thoroughly grounded in a field before she or he can see its limitations, envision radical departures, and develop a new and unique point of view.

However, the relationship between creativity and expertise is complex. In a study of the careers of 59 classical composers, creativity did not follow a straight upward course. Later compositions often were less aesthetically successful than earlier ones, and the amount of time spent in general musical training and composition was more predictive of aesthetic success in a particular genre, such as composing operas, than was the amount of time spent working in that genre. These findings suggest that overtraining in a particular genre may hamper creativity, and that versatility, not just expertise, may count (Simonton, 2000a).

Highly creative people are self-starters (Torrance, 1998) and risk takers; they tend to be independent, nonconformist, unconventional, and flexible, and they are open to new ideas and experiences (Simonton, 200b). Their thinking processes are often unconscious, leading to sudden moments of illumination (Torrance, 1988). Like Gandhi, they look at a problem more deeply than other people do and come up with solutions that do not occur to others (Sternberg & Horvath, 1998).

Creativity develops over a lifetime in a social context, and not necessarily in nurturing environments. Instead, it seems to emerge from diverse experiences that weaken conventional constraints and from challenging experiences that strengthen the ability to persevere and overcome obstacles. The political and cultural environment can affect the flowering or inhibiting of creativity—as occurred, for example, in the former Soviet Union (Simonton, 2000b).

Creativity and Intelligence

The three *aspects* of intelligence identified by Sternberg (see Chapters 9 and 13) may play a role in the relationship between intelligence and creativity (Sternberg & Lubart, 1995).

The *insightful* component helps to define a problem or to see it in a new light. Creative people show special insight in three ways: (1) they pick out information relevant to the problem—often information that no one else thought to consider; (2) they "put two and two together," seeing relationships between apparently unrelated pieces of information; and (3) they see analogies between a new problem and one they have already encountered. Again, these abilities become more efficient with experience and knowledge (Sternberg & Horvath, 1998).

The *analytic* component of intelligence can evaluate an idea and decide whether it is worth pursuing. James D. Watson, a molecular biologist who won the Nobel Prize for the discovery of the structure of DNA, was described by one of his graduate students at Harvard University as having "an uncanny instinct for the important problem, the thing that leads to big-time results. He seems to . . . pluck it out of thin air" (Edson, 1968, pp. 29—31).

The *practical* aspect of intelligence comes into play in "selling" an idea—getting it accepted. Thomas Edison held more than 1,000 patents for his inventions, created several companies to market them, and had a knack for getting his name and picture in the newspapers. This practical aspect may well be strongest in middle age.

Studying and Measuring Creativity

CRITICAL THINKING

What type of creativity do you find most interesting? What approach would you use to study it?

How can we compare the creativity of a distinguished artist, scientist, or film-maker with the creative activities and abilities of ordinary people? One way to do this is to think of creativity as having five levels: (1) spontaneous expression, as in a child's scribblings; (2) producing artistic or scientific works; (3) inventing a new and useful object, method, or technique; (4) modifying a concept; and (5) originating a revolutionary new principle or movement (Taylor, 1959). Of course, the fifth level is rarely attained, and psychometric studies of creative behavior have therefore focused on the other four (Torrance, 1988). Much as intelligence tests attempt to measure abilities that predict success in school, psychometric tests of creativity attempt to measure abilities that predict creative productivity. Other investigators use biographical methods, case studies, or self-reports to identify sources and aspects of creativity in the lives and work of acknowledged innovators. Still other researchers use laboratory-based methods to identify elements of the creative process. Let's look at these three approaches.

THE PSYCHOMETRIC APPROACH: DIVERGENT THINKING

Some of the earliest psychometric research on creativity focused on its relationship to IQ. Indeed, general intelligence, as measured by standard IQ tests, has little relationship to creative performance (Simonton, 2000b). Although creative people tend to be fairly intelligent, the *most* academically gifted children or adults did not prove to be the most original thinkers (Getzels, 1964, 1984; Getzels & Jackson, 1962; MacKinnon, 1962). More recent research suggests that the optimal IQ for creative development is only about 19 points above average for a particular field (Simonton, 1985).

If highly intelligent people are not the most creative, then creative thinking and scholastic success may require different abilities. Guilford (1956, 1959, 1960, 1986) distinguished between convergent and divergent thinking: **convergent thinking** seeks a single right answer (usually the conventional one); **divergent thinking** comes up with a wide array of fresh possibilities. Divergent thinking is not only fluent (able to generate many answers), but also flexible, original, and elaborative.

Unlike intelligence tests, which call for convergent thinking, tests of creativity call for divergent thinking (see Figure 6.6). The **Torrance Tests of Creative Thinking** (Torrance, 1966, 1974; Torrance & Ball, 1984), probably the most widely used psychometric tests of creativity, include such tasks as listing unusual uses for a common object (like a paper clip), completing a figure, and writing down what a sound brings to mind. Using these tests, Torrance has

QUESTIONS	COMMON ANSWER	CREATIVE ANSWER
How many things could these drawings be?		
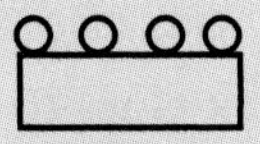 (drawing)	Table with things on top.	Foot and toes.
 (drawing)	Three people sitting around a table.	Three mice eating a piece of cheese.
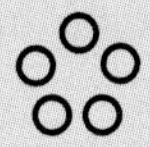 (drawing)	Flower.	Lollipop bursting into pieces.
 (drawing)	Two igloos.	Two haystacks on a flying carpet.
What do meat and milk have in common?	Both come from animals.	Both are government-inspected.
How many ways could you use a newspaper?	Make paper hats.	Rip it up if you're angry.

FIGURE 6.6   *Tests of creativity seek to identify divergent thinking.*   SOURCE: Adapted from Wallach & Kogan, 1967.

tried to learn what kind of person typically engages in creativity. He found that creative people tend to be courageous, independent, honest, tenacious, curious, and willing to take risks. Above all, like Akira Kurosawa, they have a passion for what they do.

Although tests such as Torrance's are fairly reliable (they yield consistent results), there is dispute over whether they have *construct validity*—that is, whether they identify people who are creative in real life (Anastasi, 1988; Mansfield & Busse, 1981; Simonton, 1990). Torrance's (1988) claim of validity rests on longitudinal studies of elementary and high school students, begun when the tests were in preparation (Torrance, 1972a, 1972b, 1981). Follow-up studies after intervals ranging from 7 to 22 years found that the tests had successfully predicted which youngsters would become creative achievers as adults. However, because these tests are given to adults less frequently than to children, we know very little about their predictive value across the adult life span. And, as Guilford recognized, divergent thinking is not the only factor in creativity; also important are sensitivity to problems and the ability to redefine or reinterpret them so as to obtain unique solutions. Highly creative people look at problems more thoroughly than other people do and come up with solutions that do not occur to others (Sternberg & Horvath, 1998).

THE BIOGRAPHICAL APPROACH: STUDYING CREATIVE ACHIEVERS

The difficulty of defining and measuring creativity has led some investigators to turn to an earlier approach: studies of people, living or dead, who have been recognized as creative. Such investigators seek clues to the nature and workings of creativity by studying biographies and autobiographical writings or self-reports such as diaries and letters.

One current advocate of this approach is Howard Gardner, whose theory of multiple intelligences we've already discussed. Whereas psychometric researchers assume that creativity is the same for scientists, artists, and others, Gardner suggests that it is *multifactorial* and may operate differently in different fields. According to Gardner, creativity starts with a high degree of talent in one or more cognitive areas, but talent is not the whole story. Creativity is a web of biological, personal, social, and cultural forces.

Because creativity is so complex and because we know so little about it, Gardner (1986, 1988) has called for comprehensive interdisciplinary research enlisting the expertise of psychologists, cognitive scientists, historians, anthropologists, and neurobiologists to study the lives and work of acknowledged creative giants. Gardner has sketched preliminary outlines for such a study of the life of Sigmund Freud, based chiefly on the classic biography by Ernest Jones (1961).

Freud was highly talented in several of Gardner's realms of intelligence: linguistic, logical, intrapersonal (since he built his psychoanalytic theory on insights into his own psyche), and interpersonal (though he could repel as well as attract followers). But Jones believes that what raised Freud to the pinnacle of creative achievement was his ability to see in an isolated fact (such as his discovery of his previously submerged feelings toward his parents) a key to the forces motivating human behavior.

Freud himself attributed his success more to his personality than to his intellectual abilities. He depreciated his intellect and complained that he had no talent for science or mathematics. He felt that his strengths were compulsive curiosity, a bold adventurous nature, and a passion to conquer, combined with strong self-discipline, tenacity, perseverance, and an ability to withstand hostile criticism. He was a workaholic, often seeing patients until late at night and then writing into the early morning hours—a schedule he maintained almost until his death.

Creativity does not develop in a vacuum. Besides *cognitive gifts* and *personality traits*, a biographical study such as Gardner proposes would examine two environmental dimensions: the person's *field* of work and his or her *society*. Freud, of course, did not merely contribute to a field of knowledge; he created a new one. One avenue for biographical research would be to examine the state of knowledge at the time he began his work and then trace how his ideas changed at each step of the way, as the psychologist Howard Gruber (1981) did in his pioneering study of Charles Darwin's notebooks (see Box 6.3). It might then be possible to design computer simulations of Freud's mental processes. But such a study would still be incomplete without a historical analysis of conditions in Vienna at the turn of the century—a repressive society, but at the same time an unparalleled center of learning. Since the ultimate purpose would be to illuminate not merely the creative life of one individual but sources of creativity and conditions under which it develops, many such case studies would be needed to provide sufficient raw material for generalization.

© Mary Evans Picture Library/
Sigmund Freud Copyrights

Sigmund Freud, the founder of psychoanalysis, (shown here with his daughter Anna) maintained that creativity is a result of sublimated sexual tension.

Gardner (1988) suspects that tension serves as a springboard for creativity. The source of such tension may be a poor fit between two or more elements of a person's life: biological constitution, intellectual strengths and weaknesses, intellectual and personality styles, and chosen field. This tension motivates the individual "to strike out in a new direction and, ultimately, to fashion a creative product" (p. 320). In Freud's case, the problem of fit showed up in his search for a field in which he could make his mark. Not until his late thirties did he begin to focus on the areas of investigation that would bear fruit in his life's work. In the case of Kurosawa, exposure to both eastern and western cultures produced a creative tension that enabled him to brilliantly reinterpret the themes of Shakespearean tragedies such as King Lear *(Ran)* and Macbeth *(Throne of Blood)* in the context of a breakup of the tightly ordered structure of traditional Japanese society.

According to Freud, it is sexual tension that is at the root of creative endeavor; if a child's sexual curiosity is *sublimated*, or directed into socially acceptable channels, highly creative work may result. In one of his own biographical studies, Freud (1910/1957, 1947) suggested that the most famous painting by the Renaissance master Leonardo da Vinci—the *Mona Lisa*—was an expression of long-buried desire for the unwed mother from whom Leonardo had been torn in early childhood.

For Freud (1949), the act of creation arises from childlike dreams and fantasies tamed by the conscious, rational mind. Whether or not these processes originate in sublimated sexual drives, as Freud believed, alternation of spontaneous insights with conscious, rational effort is a recurrent theme in self-reports by noted artists and scientists. Jonas Salk, who developed the Salk polio vaccine, recalls that he used to try to picture what it would feel like to be a virus or a cancer cell. Jacob W. Getzels (1964), a pioneer in the study of creativity, observed that insights often flash into a creator's mind after such a period of idle daydreaming or seemingly fruitless struggle.

Extraordinary creative achievement, according to one analysis (Keegan, 1996), results from deep, highly organized knowledge of a subject; **intrinsic motivation** to work hard for the sake of the work, not for external rewards; and a strong emotional attachment to the work, which spurs

Creativity Takes Hard Work at Any Age

At 48, the jazz singer Ella Fitzgerald began to record a 19-album series of nearly 250 popular classics; at 59, she finished it. Leonard Bernstein was 53 when he composed his *Mass* in memory of President John F. Kennedy. The British author William Golding produced 11 novels after *Lord of the Flies*, which came out when he was 43; he won Britain's prestigious Booker Prize for *Rights of Passage*, published when he was 69. The artist Marc Chagall designed the monumental mosaic *The Four Seasons* when he was in his late eighties and the stained glass *America Windows* when he was 90. These are but a few examples of creative achievements in middle and old age.

What goes on in the minds of highly creative people? What enables some of them to remain productive beyond the usual peak years for their fields? We may find some clues in an intensive study the psychologist Howard Gruber did of the mental processes of Charles Darwin, who published his controversial theory of evolution at 50, well beyond the age when most scientists make their most important breakthroughs (Gardner, 1981).

Darwin's theory was based on his meticulously recorded observations of fossils, plants, animals, and rocks he had seen along the coast of South America and in the Pacific islands during a 5-year voyage of exploration two decades earlier. Gruber pored over Darwin's notebooks to map the path of his thinking during the 18 months after his return from that voyage.

© Bettmann/Corbis Images

Many creative accomplishments occur in middle age or later. In her forties, the jazz singer Ella Fitzgerald began recording a 19-album series of popular classics; she took 11 years to finish it.

Gruber was struck by how long it took Darwin, then in his late twenties, to think through a new idea. Darwin had gone down at least one blind alley before he came upon an essay by the English economist Thomas Malthus, which de-

the creator to persevere in the face of obstacles. One recent study, which confirmed the importance of intrinsic motivation, mapped thoughts and feelings of twelve internationally known scientists during various phases of the creative process. The study also found that *affect tolerance*—ability to tolerate negative feelings—is required for creative work (Runco &

scribed how natural disasters and wars keep human population increases under control. After reading Malthus's description of the struggle for survival, it occurred to Darwin that species whose characteristics were best adapted to their environment would tend to survive, and others would not. Even then, it took Darwin several months after reading Malthus's essay to develop his principle of natural selection, which explains how adaptive traits are passed on through reproduction. And it was not until more than 2 decades later that he finally published his theory and the supporting evidence.

Although each mind works somewhat differently, Gruber found some commonalities between Darwin's thought processes and those of other highly creative achievers in the arts and sciences:

- They work *painstakingly and slowly* to master the knowledge and skills they need to solve a problem. Darwin studied barnacles for 8 years, until he probably knew more about them than anyone else in the world.
- They constantly *visualize* ideas. Darwin drew one particular image—a branching tree—over and over, refining his theory of how more complex species evolve on the "tree" of nature.
- They are *goal-directed*; they have a strong sense of purpose and know where they want to go.

- They have *networks of enterprises*, often juggling several seemingly unrelated projects or activities.
- They are *able to set aside problems* they have too little information to solve and go on to something else, or adopt temporary working assumptions. Darwin did this when he got stuck on questions about heredity for which he had no reliable answers.
- They are *daring*. It took courage for Darwin to publish a theory that shattered the entrenched ideas of his day.
- Rather than work in isolation (as they are often thought to do), they *collaborate* or discuss their ideas with others, by choosing peers and designing environments that nurture their work.
- They *enjoy turning over ideas* in their minds. Darwin was reading Malthus's essay for amusement.
- Through hard work, they *transform themselves*, until what would be difficult for someone else seems easy for them.

In Gruber's view, creative growth in adults may be a developmental process that spans a period of years, much like children's cognitive growth. If that is true, then we need to study why this development seems to stop or slow down for some people in young adulthood, while in others it continues throughout the life span.

Albert, 1990; Shaw, 1992a, 1992b). Because the scientists understood that such feelings as anger, fear, sadness, shame, depression, anxiety, self-depreciation, and sensitivity to rejection are a necessary part of the process, they were able to cope with and surmount them (Shaw, 1989, 1992a, 1992b).

LABORATORY RESEARCH: "PROBLEM FINDING"

> The formulation of a problem is often more essential than its solution, which may be merely a matter of mathematical or experimental skill. To raise new questions, new possibilities, to regard old questions from a new angle, requires imagination and marks real advance in science. (Einstein & Infeld, 1938, p. 92)

Einstein's comment foreshadowed an observation about the molecular biologist James D. Watson. Watson and Francis Crick won a Nobel prize for their discovery of the structure of DNA, the genetic substance that directs the functioning of all body cells. One of Watson's graduate students at Harvard University later remarked: "His greatest talent is an uncanny instinct for the important problem, the thing that leads to big-time results. He seems to . . . pluck it out of thin air" (Edson, 1968, pp. 29–31).

Still, widespread recognition of **problem finding**—the ability to identify and formulate novel and important problems—as a hallmark of creative thought awaited the completion of a classic longitudinal study of young adult art students, one of the first attempts to investigate creativity in the laboratory. Getzels and Mihaly Csikszentmihalyi (1968, 1975, 1976), another pioneer in the study of creativity, asked these art students to select and arrange objects for a still life. In doing so, the students set up their own artistic problems, which they then proceeded to solve. The students whose works were judged by art experts as best and most original, and who later proved to be most successful, were those whose "problems" had been most unusual and complex. The study was later replicated by another investigator, with similar results (Arlin, 1975, 1984).

This research supports Sternberg's suggestion that creativity may be linked to the development of mature thought. A shift in emphasis from problem solving to problem finding is sometimes described as characteristic of *postformal thought*, a mature way of thinking that we explore in Chapter 7.

Creativity and Age

Is there a relationship between creative performance and age? On psychometric tests of divergent thinking, age differences consistently appear. Whether data are cross-sectional or longitudinal, scores peak, on average, around the late thirties. A similar age curve emerges when creativity is measured by variations in output (number of publications, paintings, or compositions). A person in the last decade of a creative career typically produces only about half as much as during the late thirties or early forties, though somewhat more than in the twenties (Simonton 1990).

There are three ways to achieve a large lifetime output: (1) start early, (2) keep going, and (3) be unusually prolific. Not only are all three factors associated with high total production, the three factors are linked. Creative people who start producing early and maintain a large output generally continue to be highly productive in later life (Feist & Barron, 2003). Pablo Picasso, considered by many to be the greatest artist of the twentieth century, began painting in childhood and, up to his death in 1973 at the age of 91, produced more than 200 paintings and sculptures a year.

However, the age curve varies depending on the field. Poets, mathematicians, and theoretical physicists tend to be most prolific in their late twenties or early thirties. Research psychologists reach a peak around age 40, followed by a moderate decline. Novelists, historians, and philosophers become increasingly productive through their late forties or fifties and then level off. These patterns hold true across cultures and historical periods (Dixon & Hultsch, 1999; Simonton, 1990).

CRITICAL THINKING
Based on the age at which professionals in various fields experience career peaks, what career choice would you make?

Of course, not everything a creator produces is equally notable; even a Picasso is bound to produce some minor material. The *quality ratio*—the proportion of major works to total output—bears no relationship to age. The periods in which a person creates the largest number of memorable works also tend to be the ones in which that same person produces the largest number of forgettable ones (Simonton, 1998). Thus, the likelihood that a *particular* work will be a masterpiece has nothing to do with age. Some of the composer Irving Berlin's top song hits were written in his fifties, sixties, seventies, and eighties, and they were no more or less likely to prove immortal than songs he wrote in his early twenties.

Sometimes losses in productivity are offset by gains in quality. Age-related analyses of themes of ancient Greek and Shakespearean plays show a shift from youthful preoccupation with love and romance to more spiritual concerns (Simonton, 1983, 1986). And a study of the "swan songs" of 172 composers found that their last works—usually fairly short and melodically simple—were among their richest, most important, and most successful (Simonton, 1989).*

A classic theory (Beard, 1874) offers a simple explanation for this phenomenon—and for why even *quantity* of production in such fields as philosophy and history often holds up until late in life. According to this theory, there are two factors in creativity: enthusiasm and experience. Enthusiasm peaks early, and thereafter production wanes. But experience continues to build, infusing later works—especially those requiring seasoned reflection—with mature insight and wisdom missing from the products of youth.

The German poet Rainer Maria Rilke (1984) wrote, "Ah! but verses amount to so little when one writes them young. One ought to wait and gather sense and sweetness a whole life long, and a long life if possible, and then, quite at the end, one might perhaps be able to write ten lines that were good." This growth of mature thought and wisdom—along with a parallel growth in moral reasoning—is the focus of Chapter 7, the third of our trilogy on intellectual development in adulthood.

---

*Unless otherwise noted, the discussion in this section is based on Papalia, Olds, & Feldman (2004).

Intelligence and Its Measurement: The Psychometric Approach

- Most psychologists agree that intelligent behavior is goal-oriented and adaptive and involves reasoning, acquiring knowledge, and solving problems.
- The psychometric approach assumes that individuals possess varying, measurable quantities of intelligence. Psychometric tests assess verbal comprehension, mathematical computation, reasoning, and nonverbal performance.
- Intelligence tests for adults are scored by comparison with standardized norms using the deviation IQ.
- Intelligence tests infer ability from performance and may be subject to cultural bias. Their appropriateness for mature adults has been questioned.

intelligent behavior (p. 193)　　　　**cultural bias (p. 199)**
psychometric approach (p. 194)　　　**culture-free (p. 199)**
intelligence quotient (IQ) (p. 196)　**cultur-fair (p. 199)**
deviation IQ (p. 196)
**Wechsler Adult Intelligence Scale
　(WAIS) (p. 197)**

Intellectual Development in Adulthood: Basic Issues

- A multifactorial view of intelligence can accommodate simultaneous advances and declines; a unitary view cannot.
- Sternberg has proposed three elements of intelligence: componential, experiential, and contextual. The experiential and contextual elements (including tacit knowledge) may become more important in adulthood.
- Gardner has proposed seven independent "intelligences": linguistic, logical-mathematical, spatial, musical, bodily-kinesthetic, intrapersonal, and interpersonal.
- The classic aging pattern on WAIS shows a much larger and sharper decline in performance (nonverbal) tasks than in verbal tasks. Fluid intelligence has been found to decline with age, while crystallized intelligence remains constant or improves.
- According to Baltes's dual-process model, gains in the pragmatics of intelligence (crystallized) may compensate for losses in the mechanics of intelligence (fluid).
- The Seattle Longitudinal Study of Adult Intelligence, using a sequential design, found that intellectual development is multidirectional and shows great individual variability, small gender differences, and significant cohort effects.
- Training and practice can improve performance even of fluid tasks; declines may be largely related to lack of mental exercise.

factor analysis (p. 202)　　　　　**crystallized intelligence (p. 209)**
componential element (p. 204)　　**dual-process model (p. 211)**
experiential element (p. 204)　　 **mechanics of intelligence (p. 211)**
contextual element (p. 205)　　　 **pragmatics of intelligence (p. 211)**
tacit knowledge (p. 206)　　　　　**terminal drop (p. 211)**
classic aging pattern (p. 208)　　 **selective optimization with
fluid intelligence (p. 209)　　　　　　**compensation (p. 212)**

Creativity

- Creativity has been defined in terms of products, attitudes, projects, abilities, or processes. It is often considered a form of problem solving. Creativity has been studied by psychometric testing, by biographical studies, and by laboratory research.
- Biographical case studies may examine cognitive and personality factors, field of work, and cultural environment.
- Suggested sources and conditions of creativity include tension, intrinsic motivation, affect tolerance, problem finding, and an interplay of conscious and unconscious, rational and irrational thought.
- An age-related decline in creativity shows up in both psychometric tests and actual output. Peak ages and rates of decline vary by occupation.
- Individuals tend to produce the greatest number, though not necessarily the greatest proportion, of major works at peak periods of productivity (midlife or earlier, depending on the field).

convergent thinking (p. 220)
divergent thinking (p. 220)
Torrance Tests of Creative Thinking (p. 220)

intrinsic motivation (p. 223)
problem finding (p. 226)

Mature Thought, Wisdom, and Moral Intelligence

◈ FOCUS: NELSON MANDELA

To accept all experience as raw material out of which the human spirit distills meanings and values is a part of the meaning of maturity.

—Howard Thurman, Meditations of the Heart, 1953

NELSON MANDELA'S* FIRST name, Rolihlahla, means "stirring up trouble"—something he did throughout his long struggle to topple *apartheid*, South Africa's rigid system of racial separation and subjugation. But whereas the young Mandela has been described as passionate, hotheaded, and quick to anger, the 71-year-old man who in 1990 emerged from 26 years of imprisonment was coolly reasonable and highly controlled. "I came out mature," he says (Stengel, 1994).

The historic accord that resulted in Mandela's election 4 years later as his country's first black president was the realization of a childhood dream—

© Reuters/Juda Ngwenya/Corbis Images

---

*Sources of biographical information about Nelson Mandela are Benson (1986), Goodrich (1995), Hargrove (1989), Mandela (1994), Meer (1988), Nelan (1994), Stengel (1994), P. Taylor (1994), and Watson (1994).

formed as young Mandela, born into a royal family, listened to elders recall a bygone era of peace, freedom, and equality. Later, suspended from college for participating in a student protest, Mandela in 1941 became one of thousands of young men from rural communities who headed for industrial Johannesburg looking for jobs. There he saw firsthand the effects of the color bar: squalid, crime-ridden shantytowns on the fringes of a prosperous city. He managed to find work, finish college by correspondence, and become a lawyer. Every day his office overflowed with people charged with violating unjust laws.

Meanwhile, Mandela had joined the African National Congress (ANC). He helped organize nonviolent demonstrations, which only brought violent repression, increasingly harsh laws, and police harassment. In 1952, after becoming a deputy president of ANC, he, like many other militant blacks, was banned from attending meetings or traveling outside Johannesburg.

In December 1956, in a nighttime raid, he and 155 other ANC leaders were arrested and charged with conspiracy to overthrow the government. After a 4-year trial, during which police at one point opened fire on peaceful spectators, the defendants were acquitted. But ANC was banned, and so, as before, was Mandela. He went into hiding and organized a national 3-day work stoppage. The government, in an unsuccessful attempt to abort it, imprisoned more than 10,000 Africans, most without trial.

Mandela reluctantly concluded that the movement would have to meet force with force—but aimed at property, not people. He masterminded a bombing raid of 23 targets in major cities. "I did not plan it in a spirit of recklessness, nor because I have any love of violence," he said at his trial. "I planned it as a result of a calm and sober assessment of the po-

litical situation that had arisen after many years of tyranny, exploitation, and oppression of my people" (Benson, 1986, pp. 146–147).

Handed a life sentence in 1964 at age 45, Mandela continued to direct his people's struggle from his island prison. When he wasn't chopping rocks, he was educating himself and his jailmates in history, economics, and Afrikaans, the language of their white adversaries. He began a long dialogue with government officials, first by letter and then in secret meetings.

Supremely patient, confident, and resolute, Mandela planned to wear down the opposition. The longer he remained in prison—a man of justice caught in an unjust system—the more his moral authority grew. In 1985, he rejected an offer of release in exchange for a promise to refrain from violent or illegal action. Mandela—by then an international symbol of resistance—explained, in a statement to the African people, that his freedom was inseparable from theirs. Five years later, seeing the handwriting on the wall, South Africa's new president, F. W. de Klerk, released him, legalized ANC and other black political organizations, lifted discriminatory laws, and promised a nonracial constitution. ANC, in turn, gave up armed struggle. Despite the distrust between them, Mandela and de Klerk managed to reach agreement on a new constitution, set up free elections, and avoid all-out civil war. For these accomplishments, they received a Nobel Peace prize in 1993.

After defeating de Klerk for president, Mandela at 75 had the daunting task of reforming South Africa's political and economic system. He approached it with the same cautious determination and moral courage he had shown during his long imprisonment. Despite the hardships he and his people had suffered, he knew that bitterness would not help achieve his goals. In the name of cultural inclusiveness, he urged black

South Africans to learn Afrikaans and to sing the old national anthem along with the new one. "We are starting a new era," he said, "of hope, of reconciliation, of national building" (Nelan, 1994, p. 28). Nelson Mandela retired from public life in June 1999. He currently resides in his birth place, Qunu, Transkei, and he remains active on a selective basis.

NELSON MANDELA IS A GIFTED LEADER, a man of great intelligence and drive. In his youth, he was a man of action. In his middle and old age, he has also shown himself to be a man of disciplined thought and measured words. Did Mandela's experiences (as he suggests) shape a wiser, more mature way of thinking that helped him move South Africa from authoritarian white rule to a multiracial democracy? Do mature adults whose experience may be less unusual or dramatic than Mandela's develop new ways of thinking as well? Have you noticed any apparent changes in how your parents or grandparents think as they get older? And if mature cognition does show distinctive characteristics, what processes are involved?

Rather than focusing on *quantitative* changes in intellectual abilities (as we do, for the most part, in Chapter 6), a growing body of theory and research—arising chiefly from organismic and contextual perspectives—looks for *qualitative* changes, whether universal or individual, and their implications for the assessment of intelligence across the adult life span. In the first section of this chapter, we describe thought processes that capitalize on experience: expert and everyday problem solving and integrative thought. Next, we look at mature thought as a stage of cognitive development. Then we examine several meanings of *wisdom*. We go on to discuss moral development: how adults resolve moral dilemmas, from the purely personal to epochal issues such as those that confronted Nelson Mandela.

THE ROLE OF EXPERIENCE

According to Jean Piaget, cognitive development from infancy through adolescence culminates for many people in a last stage of formal operations. This progression results from a combination of biologically programmed maturation and experience. What happens then as an adult? A number of researchers have focused on the accumulation of experiences through intensive learning and practice, which can lead to the development of specialized expertise (Sinnott, 1994, 1996). Others have gone further and have identified an additional stage of logical complexity called *postformal thought* (discussed later in this chapter), which can be seen in mature adults.

Applying Expertise

Two young resident physicians in a hospital radiology laboratory examine a chest X ray. They study an unusual white blotch on the left side. "Looks like a large tumor," one of them says finally. The other nods.

Just then, a longtime staff radiologist walks by and looks over their shoulders at the X ray. "That patient has a collapsed lung and needs immediate surgery," he declares (Lesgold, 1983).

According to many studies, in mature adults the ability to solve novel problems (fluid intelligence) may gradually diminish, yet they show increasing competence in solving problems in their chosen fields. Why? The answer, according to William Hoyer and his colleagues (Hoyer & Rybash, 1994; Rybash, Hoyer, & Roodin, 1986), lies in specialized knowledge—a form of crystallized or pragmatic intelligence—which depends on accumulating and organizing a great deal of very specific information about concepts and procedures, and on efficiently accessing this knowledge in memory. This expertise seems to be relatively independent of any declines in general intelligence and in the brain's information-processing machinery.

In one study (Ceci & Liker, 1986), researchers identified 30 middle-aged and older men who were avid spectators and bettors at a horse racing track. On the basis of skill in picking winners, the investigators divided the men into two groups: "expert" and "nonexpert." An IQ test found no significant difference in intelligence. But the "experts" were found to use a sophisticated method of reasoning, incorporating interpretations of much interrelated information about each horse; "nonexperts," by contrast, tended to use simpler, less successful methods. Again, this difference was not related to IQ—"experts" with low IQs used more complex reasoning than "nonexperts" with higher IQs.

The Hoyer group's explanation for this seeming paradox is that, with experience, information processing and fluid thinking become dedicated to specific knowledge systems. This process of **encapsulation** makes knowledge within the field of expertise easier to add to, access, and use. Indeed, there is a good deal of evidence that efficiency of information processing depends on the kind of material being processed (Hoyer & Rybash, 1994). Encapsulation is largely unidirectional and irreversible; adults, as long as they remain healthy and vigorous, continue to gain expertise. On the other hand, encapsulated abilities become less available for general use—for solving problems outside the specific field. Thus, despite a general loss in fluid intelligence, encapsulation "captures" or salvages fluid abilities for expert problem solving.

According to this model, encapsulation results in distinctively adult ways of thinking and knowing. Children and adolescents are better able to assimilate a wide variety of *new* knowledge; adults, however, concentrate on refining and broadening *existing* knowledge in a flexible, open-ended way that allows for application to ill-defined, multifaceted real-life situations, such as picking stocks or picking winners at the racetrack.

CRITICAL THINKING

How has your formal education, combined with other life experiences, influenced the sophistication of your reasoning ability?

© Tim Davis/Photo Researchers

Expertise in interpreting X rays, as in many other fields, depends on accumulated, specialized knowledge, which continues to increase with age. Experts often appear to be guided by intuition and cannot explain how they arrive at conclusions.

"Expert thinking" often seems automatic and intuitive. Because experts generally are not aware of the thought processes that lie behind their decisions (Dreyfus, 1993–1994; Rybash et al., 1986), they can't readily explain how they arrive at a conclusion or where a nonexpert has gone wrong. In our earlier example, the experienced radiologist might not see why the residents would even consider diagnosing a collapsed lung as a tumor; similarly, a chess master might not even consider moves a novice would mentally debate about. Nor do experts rely on rules; instead, they intuitively apply their accumulated experience—or what Sternberg calls *tacit knowledge* (see Chapter 6)—to particular cases (Dreyfus, 1993–1994). In one study, for example, novice nurses stuck to rules they had learned for taking care of babies; experienced nurses used intuition to guide them in deciding when it was better *not* to be bound by rules (Benner, 1984).

In a study (Hoyer & Ingolfsdottir, 2003) of medical laboratory technologists, two age groups, 24 and 49 years, were tested on the identification of different types of bacteria. Age-matched novices also were given the same task. Target-detection performance of middle-aged medical technologists was equal to that of young adult medical technologists when location cues and contextual cues were present. This finding suggests that knowledge of regularities based on past experience with similar tasks allowed middle-aged experts to shortcut some operations and steps. Medical technologists who did not have location cues and a congruent context showed age-related deficits on one of the tasks. This study supports the idea that acquired knowledge about the regularities in certain tasks enables continued efficient performance with no age-related differences for experienced persons.

The encapsulation model is consistent with Baltes's lifespan developmental approach as a way of explaining increased competence in some areas despite measured losses in others. According to the encapsulation model, advances in expertise continue at least through middle age, before physiologically based deterioration may limit them.

Solving Everyday Problems

The ability to carry out activities considered essential for living independently is one aspect of what we mean by everyday intelligence. Aids to everyday cognition include designing labels that make it easier to take medications correctly and providing clear instructions on how to use an appliance (Stine-Morrow & Miller, 1999). Another aspect of everyday intelligence is the application of cognitive abilities and skills to everyday problems that are complex and multidimensional (Schaie & Willis, 1996).

If expertise allows adults to become better problem solvers in specialized fields, what about practical problems of daily living? Does experience make adults "experts" in everyday problem solving?

In one study (Denney & Palmer, 1981), 84 adults between ages 20 and 79 were given two kinds of problems. One kind was like the game "twenty questions." Participants were shown 42 pictures of common objects and were told to figure out which one the examiner was thinking of, by asking questions that could be answered yes or no. Scoring was based on how many questions it took to get the answer and what percentage of questions eliminated more than one item at a time ("Is it an animal?" rather than only one item ("Is it a cow?"). The older the participants were, the worse they did on this part of the test.

The second kind of problem involved situations like the following: *Your basement is flooding; You are stranded in a car during a blizzard. Your 8-year-old child is 1 1/2 hours late coming home from school.* Higher scores were given for responses that showed self-reliance and recognition of a number of possible causes and solutions. In this part of the test, the best practical problem solvers were people in their forties and fifties who based their answers on experiences of everyday living. There was a follow-up study, which tried to give the elderly an advantage by posing problems with which they would be most familiar (retirement, widowhood, and ill health); but people in their forties still came up with better solutions than either younger or older adults (Denney & Pearce, 1989). The implication was that the benefits of experience in dealing with problems reach a limit at some point during adulthood—perhaps in middle age.

CRITICAL THINKING

What everyday problems characterize lives of young, middle-aged, and older adults? What are the resultant demands on cognitive ability?

Other researchers who studied everyday problem solving obtained different results though (Cornelius & Caspi, 1987). These investigators constructed an inventory consisting of sample problems that younger, middle-aged, or older adults were likely to experience as consumers; in managing a home; in resolving conflicts with family members, friends, and co-workers; and in dealing with technical information. For each situation, four possible responses were presented. For example: You find out that you have been passed over for a better job. Would you: (a) try to find out why you didn't get it? (b) try to see the positive side of the situation? (c) accept the decision? (d) complain to a friend about the unfairness of the decision? A group of judges of various ages, most of whom had no formal training in psychology, rated the effectiveness of the responses. This time, everyday problem-solving capability (as defined by the judges) did *not* drop off after middle age. Rather, like crystallized intelligence, performance on the inventory improved into late adulthood.

In an attempt to resolve the discrepancies in previous research, Camp, Doherty, Moody-Thomas, and Denney (1989) devised a study based in part on problems used in Denney's earlier studies and in part on real problems the participants had faced, such as marital quarrels, disputes with neighbors, health emergencies, loss of a job, and street violence. This time, the participants themselves generated the solutions, which were rated on *quality* rather than quantity. As in Cornelius and Caspi's study, older adults showed no age deficits. They did no worse than younger adults in solving their own problems and were more satisfied with their solutions.

Thinking Integratively

The ability of mature adults to solve the kinds of problems they are familiar with may hinge on thinking *integratively*—integrating new experience with what they already know. Mature adults interpret what they read, see, or hear in terms of its meaning for them. Instead of accepting something at face value, they filter it through their own life experience and learning. This integrative characteristic of adult thought has implications for many aspects of life.

In one series of studies, college students and older adults were asked to recall and to summarize stories (Labouvie-Vief & Hakim-Larson, 1989). One (Labouvie-Vief, Schell, & Weaverdyck, 1982) was a fable about a wolf who promises to reward a crane for removing a bone stuck in the wolf's throat. The crane dislodges the bone with its beak—a maneuver that involves putting its head into the wolf's jaws—and then asks for the promised reward. The wolf replies that the crane's reward is to get away alive!

Both age groups could recall the story in detail, but they gave very different summaries. The students' summaries were longer and more detailed and were confined to material in the text. The summaries produced by older adults (whose average age was 74) tended to be shorter and more to the point. The older adults integrated the "moral" of the story with observations based on experience and real-world learning. For example, one older participant drew the moral that good deeds should be their own reward, but also noted "a certain shrewdness" on the part of the wolf, "who sought help in time of need, but was unwilling to give of himself even in a small way to show any appreciation" (Labouvie-Vief & Hakim-Larson, 1989, p. 13). The thinking of the older adults was more flexible than that of the younger ones, whose attempts at summarizing were limited to step-by-step recall of the story.

Integrative thinking has emotional and social implications. The ability to interpret events in a mature way enables many adults to come to terms with childhood episodes that once disturbed them (Schafer, 1980). Research has shown, for example, that women's adjustment in adulthood is related not to what actually happened between them and their mother but to how they view their mother's behavior toward them (Main, 1987).

Society benefits from this integrative feature of adult thought. It is often mature adults who create inspirational myths and legends, who translate truths about the human condition into symbols to which younger generations can turn for guidance (Gutmann, 1977). People may have to be capable of integrative thought before they can become moral and spiritual leaders.

Intuition, integrative thinking, and subjective interpretation are important features of what some investigators have begun to see as a special, mature stage of intellectual development: postformal thought. We turn to this topic next.

BEYOND PIAGET: NEW WAYS OF THINKING IN ADULTHOOD

According to Piaget, thinking begins in early childhood with manipulation of sensory information. It then progresses to concrete problem solving, for example, judging whether the amount of water in a flask changes when it is poured into a flask of a different shape. Many adolescents reach Piaget's highest stage, formal operations: they can think abstractly, systematically, and logically; they can make and test hypotheses about reality. Although Piaget described the stage of formal operations as the pinnacle of cognitive achievement, some developmental scientists maintain that changes in cognition extend beyond that stage. One line of Neo-Piagetian theory and research concerns higher levels of abstract reasoning, or *reflective thinking*. Another line of investigation deals with *postformal thought*, which combines logic with emotion and practical experience in the resolution of ambiguous problems.

Reflective Thinking

Reflective thinking is a complex form of cognition, first defined by the American philosopher and educator John Dewey (1910/1991) as "active, persistent, and careful consideration" of information or beliefs in the light of the evidence that supports them and the conclusions to which they lead. Reflective thinkers continually question supposed facts, draw inferences, and make connections. Building on Piaget's state of formal operations, reflective thinkers can create complex intellectual systems that reconcile apparently conflicting ideas or considerations—for example, by putting together various theories of modern physics or of human development into a single overarching theory that explains many different kinds of behavior (Fischer & Pruyne, 2003).

The capacity for reflective thinking is thought to emerge between ages 20 and 25. Not until then are the cortical regions of the brain that handle higher-level thinking myelinated. At the same time, the brain is forming new neurons and synapses and dendritic connections. Environmental support can stimulate the development of thicker, denser cortical connections. Thus, though almost all adults develop the *capacity* for becoming reflective thinkers, few attain optimal proficiency in this skill, and even fewer can apply it consistently to various kinds of problems. For example, a young adult may understand the concept of justice but may have difficulty weighing it in relation to other concepts such as social welfare, law, ethics, and responsibility. This may help explain why, as we discuss later in this chapter, few adults—not to speak of adolescents—reach Kohlberg's highest levels of moral reasoning. For many adults, college education stimulates progress toward reflective thinking (Fischer & Pruyne, 2003).

Postformal Thought

CRITICAL THINKING

What evidence do we have to support the concept of postformal thought?

Researchers during the late 1960s and early 1970s wanted to see how young, middle-aged, and older adults would do on the kinds of tasks Piaget used to measure cognitive development in children (Papalia, 1972; Papalia & Bielby, 1974; K. H. Rubin, 1973; Rubin, Attewell, Tierney, & Tumulo, 1973; Sanders, Laurendeau, & Bergeron, 1966; Tomlinson-Keasey, 1982). When some older adults gave answers similar to those of young children—saying, for example, that water poured from a thin flask into a wide one weighed more "because it's larger"—the researchers interpreted this as possible evidence of regression to an earlier stage of thought (Papalia, 1972). But later studies suggested that some older adults gave "wrong" answers because their thinking took more factors into account. For example, when asked whether there was the same amount of space in differently shaped houses made with the same number of blocks, one elderly woman said: "When you start getting fancy, you always lose some space because [you] have to have a hallway upstairs as well as downstairs, which takes away space" (Roberts, Papalia-Finlay, David, Blackburn, & Dellman, 1982, p. 191). Investigators thus began to wonder whether such "preformal" responses might actually represent an *advance* in cognitive development, a stage beyond formal operations.

Since the late 1970s, a number of researchers have suggested that mature thinking may be far richer and more complex than the abstract intellectual manipulations Piaget described. Thought in adulthood often appears to be flexible, open, adaptive, and individualistic. It relies on intuition as well as logic. It applies the fruits of personal experience to ambiguous situations that adults face every day. It can transcend a particular social system or system of thought. It is sometimes called **postformal thought**, and it is generally characterized by the ability to deal with uncertainty, inconsistency, contradiction, imperfection, and compromise (Arlin, 1984; Labouvie-Vief, 1985, 1986, 1990; Labouvie-Vief & Hakim-Larson, 1989; Sinnott, 1984, 1994, 1996, 1989a, 1989b, 1991, 1998, 2003).

HOW POSTFORMAL THOUGHT DEVELOPS

CRITICAL THINKING

Under what circumstances do you expect thought processes to remain stable or to demonstrate advancement?

According to postformal theorists, people at the stage of formal operations are in the grip of polarized thinking. They do not see that there may be truth, logic, or validity in more than one point of view. When there is conflict, one side must be right and the other wrong. Polarized thinking often shows up in emotional clashes. Immature thinkers, when angered, blame the other person rather than accepting part of the responsibility (Blanchard-Fields, 1986; Labouvie-Vief, 1990a, 1990b; Labouvie-Vief, Hakim-Larson, DeVoe, & Schoeberlein, 1989). Polarized thinkers excel at structured problems with definite answers. They view any ambiguity as a result of muddled thinking. They see everything as black or white. Postformal thinkers see shades of gray (Labouvie-Vief, 1990a, 1990b).

Postformal thought is relativistic. Like reflective thinking, it enables adults to transcend a single logical system (such as geometry or a particular theory of human development or an established political system) and reconcile or choose among conflicting ideas or demands (such as those of the Israelis and Palestinians or those of two romantic partners), each of which, from its own perspective, may have a valid claim to truth (Labouvie-Vief, 1990a, 1990b; Sinnot, 1996, 1998, 2003).

Postformal thought may develop through experiences that open up a possibility of looking at things in unaccustomed ways. For many students of traditional college age, the academic and social challenges of college offer a chance to question childhood assumptions. The college experience undermines belief in absolute, eternal, objectively verifiable truths. Many students do a 180-degree swing and come to believe that "everything is relative"—all reality is subjective, all meaning tied to context. Eventually, though, they generally move beyond a totally relativist position and search for some means of assessing competing claims (Labouvie-Vief, 1990a, 1990b).

In a study that inspired much of the research on postformal thought, William Perry (1970) interviewed 67 Harvard and Radcliffe students throughout the undergraduate years. He found that their thinking progressed from rigidity to flexibility and ultimately to freely chosen commitments. First, said Perry, as students encounter a wide variety of ideas, they recognize the existence of several different points of view. They also accept their own uncertainty. They consider this stage temporary, however, and expect to learn the "one right answer" eventually. Next, they come to see all knowledge and values as relative. They recognize that different societies and different individuals have their own value systems. They now realize that their opinions on many issues are as valid as anyone else's, even those of a parent or teacher. But they feel abandoned and lost; they cannot find solid meaning or value in this maze of systems and beliefs. Order has been replaced by chaos. Finally, they achieve **commitment within relativism**. They make their own judgments and choose their own beliefs, values, and commitments despite uncertainty and the recognition of other valid possibilities.

Building on Perry's work, Gisela Labouvie-Vief (1982, 1990a, 1990b, 1997), a psychologist at Wayne State University, has proposed three levels of adult cognitive development:

1. **Intrasystemic level.** People at this level, which corresponds to Piaget's stage of formal operations, can reason within a single system of thought—for example, Euclidean or non-Euclidean geometry, capitalism or socialism, Christianity or Buddhism—but they cannot move outside it to reflect on it. Adolescents and entering college students are able to deal with only one logical system as "correct." While they may acknowledge that other people hold different opinions, it is hard for them to see that an alternative argument or system may be as valid as their own.

2. **Intersystemic level.** People become more aware of multiple, contradictory systems of thought. Although they can discuss and elaborate on these systems and are increasingly able to tolerate conflict, they still see the systems as distinct and irreconcilable.

3. **Integrated level.** This level is characterized by openness, flexibility, and responsible, autonomous reflection. People see change and diversity as positive, and they can draw on differing perspectives and value systems. Like Nelson Mandela, they choose their own principles and act on them—not haphazardly or arbitrarily, but by integrating subjectivity with a new, more mature form of objectivity. Truth is no longer seen either as absolute or as totally relative but is judged on the basis of rational, disciplined reflection and collective thought and discussion.

There is no set age for reaching any of these levels. While people generally do not achieve postformal thought until late adolescence or early adulthood, adults in their forties do not necessarily think more maturely than those in their twenties (Labouvie-Vief, Adams, Hakim-Larons, Hayden, & DeVoe, 1987).

SOCIAL REASONING AND POSTFORMAL THOUGHT

Postformal thinking often operates in a social and emotional context. Unlike the problems Piaget studied, which involve physical phenomena and require dispassionate, objective observation and analysis, social dilemmas are less clearly structured and often fraught with emotion. It is in these kinds of situations that mature adults tend to call on postformal thought (Berg & Klaczynski, 1996; Sinnot, 1996, 1998, 2003). Social problems involve **necessary subjectivity.** They arise out of interactions in which each person's view of a situation inevitably affects the other and colors the situation as a whole—in which reality is partly a creation of the person's experience (Sinnott, 1984).

In an intimate union, a couple must deal with three different logical realities: those of each partner and of the relationship itself, which comes to take on a life of its own. Instead of allowing one partner's way of thinking to dominate and expecting the other partner to capitulate, postformal thought may permit a synthesis, a win-win situation for both partners, leading to cognitive and emotional growth. For example, if a dual-career couple disagree about who should do what around the house, postformal thought can help them get beyond attitudes and beliefs about gender roles that have been shaped by family history and societal dictates (Sinnott, 2003).

Some research has found a progression toward postformal thought throughout young and middle adulthood, especially when emotions are involved. In one study, participants were asked to judge what caused the outcomes of a series of hypothetical situations, such as a marital conflict. Adolescents and young adults tended to blame individuals, whereas middle-aged people were more likely to attribute behavior to the interplay among persons and environment. The more ambiguous the situation, the greater were the age differences in interpretation (Blanchard-Fields & Norris, 1994).

Empirical evidence of the value of postformal thought emerged from a longitudinal study of 130 freshman medical students. Their degree of tolerance for ambiguity, together with their empathy as juniors and seniors (a combination of emotion and cognition), predicted their clinical performance as rated by patients (Morton et al., 2000).

CULTURAL CHANGE AND POSTFORMAL THOUGHT

Does postformal thought occur in cultures where higher education is not common? Can cross-cultural contact facilitate postformal thought?

A study of women pig farmers in Honduras (described in Box 7.1) found that a shift to postformal thinking seems to occur when people's ideas, perceptions, or interpretations of reality "can no longer adequately make sense of the world" (L. Johnson, 1991, p. 62). The resulting tension may force them to open their minds to other ideas, perceptions, or interpretations that may work better in a changed situation (Sinnott, 1989). One way to identify the potential for development of postformal thought, then, is to look at groups undergoing highly stressful experiences while isolated from normal social contact.

An account of 45 Uruguayan travelers whose airplane crashed in the snow-covered Andes mountains in winter provides an example of how such a new social reality may develop (Read, 1974). Search parties had given everyone up for dead, but 10 weeks later two survivors managed to find their way down the mountain and get help for 14 others. An analysis of diaries kept by some of these survivors during the first month (Sinnott, 1984) reveals the levels of thinking on which various people operated.

Immediately after the crash, panic had reigned. After the first few moments, some survivors managed to calm the others down, but those who were operating at concrete or formal levels did not recognize that normal roles and behaviors would not work in this crisis situation. Attempts to "talk down" to those who were still hysterical only ended up with everyone upset. A month later, the diaries showed, the group had restructured itself. Relationships and roles had been drastically revised. Many people had raised their predominant level of thinking. Those who took a flexible, postformal approach had emerged as leaders. They could talk to anyone in the group on an intellectual

CRITICAL THINKING

What worldwide shifts in culture do you anticipate? How might these shifts influence changes in thought processes in the global society?

Postformal Thinking and Cultural Change

In 1984, the Agency for International Development (AID) launched a program to "empower" women living on subsistence farms in Honduras: these women would be trained to start and run a cooperative business raising and marketing pigs. The project fundamentally challenged established customs in these rural communities; thus its success would depend on a major shift in cultural attitudes toward women's roles.

In the existing social system, women were subservient to men and had little or no experience with independent decisions or self-directed action. They often tended pigs tethered near their homes, but when a pig was ready for market, a man would take it and keep the money. In the new AID program, the women would be raising a different breed of pigs, imported from the United States, which were larger and leaner than those usually raised in the area and required more care. Rather than raise a few pigs at home, the women were to be taught to operate pig farms, and they were to handle all phases of the operation, including marketing, themselves.

The administrators of the program realized that, to have any chance of success, the women would need a supportive environment. Before the program was introduced in a village, staff members met with village leaders and the husbands of the women who were to participate. They described how the project would operate and discussed the new behaviors that would be introduced into the social system. A village would not become part of the program unless the husbands and the village leaders accepted the women's new roles.

To give them role models for decision making, the women met regularly in small groups with a facilitator who was to guide them in dealing with problems that arose during the first year. The facilitators were to act as moderators, mentors, and agents of change. Each facilitator led two groups. Nine months after the project began, the two groups led by one of the facilitators were managing to keep pigs successfully; the other two were not.

What explains this result? According to a trained observer who regularly sat in on the groups (L. Johnson, 1991), the two facilitators showed markedly different levels of thinking. The facilitator of the two successful groups ap-

level and could deal with people both in terms of their former social roles and in terms of their roles in this new society.

CRITERIA FOR POSTFORMAL THOUGHT

One prominent researcher, Jan Sinnott (1984,1998, 2003), has proposed several criteria of postformal thought:

- *Shifting gears.* Ability to think within at least two different logical systems and to shift back and forth between abstract reasoning and practical, real-world considerations. ("This might work on paper but not in real life.")

peared to operate at a postformal level in her interactions with the rural women, and the women in her groups appeared better able to define and solve problems connected with the enterprise.

The unsuccessful facilitator, who appeared to be at the level of formal operations, dominated group discussions. She was rigidly moralistic, depreciated local customs, and tried to impose her own ideas. Because she seemed unable to move beyond her own way of thinking, she gave the women in her groups no model for moving beyond theirs and no assistance in bridging differing viewpoints. The successful facilitator acted on the assumption that local customs were different from, but not necessarily inferior to, the way she was trying to teach. Using two-way, back-and-forth communication, she helped the women and the other villagers see that their old ways were not as well adapted to the new situation (raising the imported pigs). As a result, the women's own thinking expanded; they were able to think and behave in a new way.

The postformal facilitator encouraged cooperative problem solving and decision making. She enabled the women she worked with to learn how to solve problems in new ways, and, perhaps most important, to believe that they *could* acquire new knowledge, skills, and outlooks. When one of the groups began to argue about how money was being spent and accused the treasurer of appropriating funds for her own use, this facilitator explored possible causes of the problem from several viewpoints. She suggested more than one possible solution and ultimately focused on the one that seemed best suited to the situation: having the treasurer prepare a list of what had been spent for what purposes, with attached receipts, and in the future provide monthly financial reports—practices that were unfamiliar to these women. What would the other facilitator have done in such a situation? The observer's discussions with her suggest that she would have decided whether or not the treasurer was guilty and, if so, would have replaced her. By acting unilaterally and moving immediately to what she deemed the right solution, she would have deprived the women in her groups of experience with cooperative decision making and a chance to develop the confidence to function on their own.

- *Problem definition.* Ability to define a problem as falling within a class or category of logical problems and to define its parameters. ("This is an ethical problem, not a legal one, so judicial precedents don't really help solve it.")
- *Process-product shift.* Ability to see that a problem can be solved either through a *process* with general application to similar problems or through a *product*, a concrete solution to the particular problem. ("I've come up against this type of problem before and this is how I solved it" or "In this case, the best available solution would be . . . ")

- *Pragmatism.* Ability to choose the best of several possible logical solutions and to recognize criteria for choosing. ("If you want the cheapest solution, do this; if you want the quickest solution, do that.")
- *Multiple solutions.* Awareness that most problems have more than one cause, that people may have differing goals, and that a variety of methods can be used to arrive at more than one solution. ("Let's try it your way; if that doesn't work, we can try my way.")
- *Awareness of paradox.* Recognition that a problem or solution involves inherent conflict ("Doing this will give him what he wants, but it will only make him unhappy in the end.")
- *Self-referential thought.* A person's awareness that he or she must be judge of which logic to use; in other words, that he or she is using postformal thought.

A LIFESPAN MODEL OF COGNITIVE DEVELOPMENT

CRITICAL THINKING

How is Schaie's model of cognitive development similar to and different from Piaget's model?

One of the few investigators to propose a full lifespan model of stages of cognitive development from childhood through old age is Schaie (1977–1978; Schaie & Willis, 2000), whose work on the Seattle Longitudinal Study is discussed in Chapter 6. Schaie describes intellectual development as proceeding according to changes in what is important to people and how they interpret and respond to their experiences. The stages in his model (see Figure 7.1) represent transitions from acquisition of information and skills (*what* I need to know) through practical integration of knowledge and skills (*how* to use what I know) to a search for meaning and purpose (*why* I should know). The seven stages are as follows:

1. **Acquisitive stage** (childhood and adolescence). Children and adolescents acquire information and skills mainly for their own sake or as preparation for participation in society.
2. **Achieving stage** (late teens or early twenties to early thirties). Young adults no longer acquire knowledge merely for its own sake; they use what they know to pursue goals, such as career and family.
3. **Responsible stage** (late thirties to early sixties). Middle-aged people use their minds to solve practical problems associated with responsibilities to others, such as family members or employees.
4. **Executive stage** (thirties or forties through middle age). People in the executive stage, which may overlap with the achieving and responsible stages, are responsible for societal systems (such as governmental or business organizations) or social movements. They deal with complex relationships on multiple levels.
5. **Reorganizational stage** (end of middle age, beginning of late adulthood). People who enter retirement reorganize their lives and intellectual energies around meaningful pursuits that take the place of paid work.
6. **Reintegrative stage** (late adulthood.) Older adults, who may have let go of some social involvement and whose cognitive functioning may be

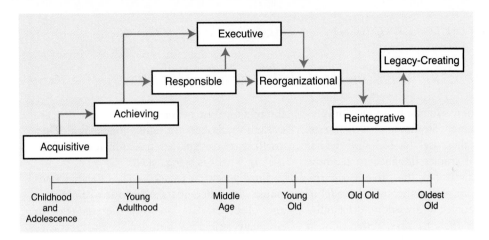

FIGURE 6.1   *Stages of cognitive development in adults.*   SOURCE: Based on Schaie & Willis, 2000.

limited by biological changes, are often more selective about what tasks they expend effort on. They focus on the purpose of what they do and concentrate on tasks that have the most meaning for them.

7. **Legacy-creating stage** (advanced old age). Near the end of life, once reintegration has been completed (or along with it), older people may create instructions for the disposition of prized possessions, make funeral arrangements, provide oral histories, or write their life stories as a legacy for their loved ones. All of these tasks involve the exercise of cognitive competencies within a social and emotional context.

Again, if adults do go through stages such as these, then traditional psychometric tests, which use the same kinds of tasks to measure intelligence at all periods of life, may be inappropriate for them. Tests developed to measure knowledge and skills in children may not be suitable for measuring intellectual competence in young and middle-aged adults, who use knowledge and skills to solve practical problems and achieve goals they set for themselves. If conventional tests fail to tap abilities central to adult intelligence, we may need measures that have what Schaie (1978) calls **ecological validity**—tests that show competence in dealing with real-life challenges, such as balancing a checkbook, reading a railroad timetable, or making informed decisions about medical problems.

Schaie's model also calls attention to an important cognitive development of late adulthood: a focus on tasks that have personal meaning. This may fit in with what is sometimes meant by *wisdom*—our next topic.

WISDOM

Wisdom (like *intelligence* or *creativity*) has many meanings but no precise definition; yet most people seem to think they know it when they see it (see Box 7.2 and Table 7.1). How can we describe wisdom? Is it intellectual,

CRITICAL THINKING

What aspects of behavior do you believe are most important in characterizing wisdom? Why?

Comparing Wisdom with Intelligence and Creativity

"The processes of wisdom, intelligence, and creativity are the same," Sternberg (1990) asserts. "What differs is their use" (p. 153). On the basis of a series of studies designed to see how adults distinguish among the three attributes, Sternberg came up with a theoretical model of intelligence, creativity, and wisdom: three intellectual processes that, he says, differ only in their applications (see Table 7.1).

What do intelligent, wise, and creative people do with knowledge? Intelligent people recall, analyze, and use it effectively. Wise people excel in **metacognition**, or knowledge about knowledge. They probe inside knowledge to find its deeper meaning. They understand what they do and don't know, the limits of what can be known, and how knowledge affects their thinking. Creative people go beyond what is already known to create something new. Thus, "if we view existing knowledge as setting constraints, much like a prison, we might view the wise person as seeking to understand the prison and just what its boundaries are, the intelligent person as seeking to make the best of life in prison, and the creative person as seeking to escape from the prison" (Sternberg, 1990, p. 153).

A second difference has to do with how information is processed. An intelligent person uses automatic thought processes to deal efficiently with routine or familiar tasks. A creative person resists automatization, preferring to deal with what is novel and nonroutine. A wise person tries to understand how and why automatization works.

Intellectual style is the way people direct or govern their own mental functioning. Intelligent people are like executives; they apply rules and solve problems. Creative people are like legislators; they decide what to do and make up new ways of doing things. They are likely to answer test questions with answers the testmaker never thought of. Wise people are like judges; they are evaluative, though not rigidly judgmental. They are likely to size up a test question and try to figure out why it is being asked.

Intelligence, creativity, and wisdom are associated with different attitudes toward ambiguity and obstacles. An intelligent person tries to eliminate ambiguity and get around obstacles within the problem as defined. A creative person sees ambiguity as a necessary evil and looks for a way to redefine the problem to avoid obstacles. A wise person is comfortable with ambiguity and simply wants to understand the obstacles and why they exist.

What are the goals of intelligent, wise, and creative behavior? The intelligent person is motivated to know and understand more and more things. The wise person seeks to understand deeply—to get at underlying meaning. The creative person "wants to see things in a way different from the way others see them" (Sternberg, 1990, p. 156).

Finally, each attribute is more likely to be valued in certain kinds of environments. A person who is considered intelligent in school may be viewed as naive or pretentious in some real-world settings. A person who is seen as creative in one environment may be considered an oddball in another. A person who is viewed as wise in one context may be called a fool or a dreamer in another.

Other research suggests that some of these distinctions may blur with age—that wisdom and creativity, for example, may become more integrated (Simonton, 1990). Problem finding has been identified as a characteristic of both creativity and postformal thought, or mature intelligence (Arlin, 1984). Perhaps, then, as people age, the connections among intelligence, wisdom, and creativity may become more complex and the differences less clear-cut (Sternberg & Lubart, 2001).

TABLE 7.1

Comparison of Six Aspects of Wisdom, Intelligence, and Creativity

Aspect	Wisdom	Intelligence	Creativity
Knowledge	Understanding of its presuppositions and meaning as well as its limitations	Recall, analysis, and use	Going beyond what is available
Processes	Understanding of what is automatic and why	Automatization of procedures	Preference for novel tasks
Primary intellectual style	Judicial	Executive	Legislative
Personality	Understanding of ambiguity and obstacles	Eliminating ambiguity and overcoming obstacles within conventional framework	Tolerance of ambiguity and redefinition of obstacles
Motivation	To understand what is known and what it means	To know and to use what is known	To go beyond what is known
Environmental	Appreciation in environment of depth of understanding	Appreciation in environment of extent and breadth of understanding	Appreciation in environment of going beyond what is currently understood

SOURCE: Sternberg (1990).

emotional, or spiritual, or all three? Do people become wiser as they get older, as is commonly believed, or is wisdom independent of age?

Wisdom in Folklore, Myth, and Philosophy

Although the concept of wisdom is at least as old as civilization, only recently has it begun to be investigated systematically. In their investigations, modern psychologists have drawn on earlier concepts found in folklore, myth, and philosophy.

Folk wisdom is a collection of parables, proverbs, and stories reflecting special pragmatic knowledge or mastery of life. It has three major functions: practical, moral, and spiritual. It is a guide to living and a source or manifestation of spiritual growth. These sayings and tales often revolve around a person, such as King Solomon in the Bible, whose words and actions are seen as embodying seasoned judgment (Holliday & Chandler, 1986).

In ancient times, these tales were orally transmitted, often by elders, for the instruction and entertainment of listeners, both adults and children. (Nelson Mandela, in South Africa, absorbed such lore as a child while sitting in on communal councils.) When writing was invented, many of these stories were recorded by scribes. Ancient wisdom found in books such as the Bible and the Koran includes moral pronouncements and principles that form the basis of religious teachings.

Mythical writings in all cultures depict young heroes exploring and mastering the outer world. By contrast, tales about mature adults center on a search for wisdom (Chinen, 1985). The young warrior setting out on a hero's quest and the mature seeker of self-knowledge are examples of what the Swiss psychiatrist Carl Jung (1933) called **archetypes**. They represent recurrent ideas important in a culture's mythic tradition, which survives in its "collective unconscious." One such archetype, which appears in the Russian Tale "Vasilisa the Wise," is about a girl's initiation into the use of her intuitive powers (Estés, 1992). Another is that of a wise elder who appears when a young hero needs help or advice. This archetypical image harks back to such ancient sources as the Greek tale of Mentor, the tutor who advised Odysseus's son Telemachus, to keep him out of danger. The word *mentor* came to mean a person who uses accumulated experience and wisdom to guide a young protégé.

A modern throwback can be seen in the movie *Star Wars*. Young Luke Skywalker is attempting to destroy the evil empire's monstrous Death Star spaceship. At first, he plans to aim his weapons by using the computer on his small fighter craft. Then he hears the voice of Obi-Wan Kenobi, his counselor and teacher, telling him to turn off the computer and trust the "force." Luke does so, and the life force of the universe helps direct his fire to destroy the Death Star.

CRITICAL THINKING

What symbols and recurring themes from literature, plays, and films are suggestive of wisdom?

For the classical Greek philosophers, wisdom was a guide to right conduct. But rather than pithy sayings or allegorical legends, its source was reasoned reflection. For Socrates, wisdom lay in enlightened self-examination and moral behavior. For Plato, virtuous action was the product of rational thought. Aristotle distinguished between two sorts of wisdom: practical ethics and a quest for the nature and origins of the universe and human life. Thus wisdom began to be related to knowledge and learning (Holliday & Chandler, 1986).

While views of wisdom in western philosophy have focused largely on judgments about the external world and human behavior, some of the older eastern philosophical traditions look inward to the development of "higher," spiritual states of consciousness. According to the Vedas, sacred Hindu writings, wisdom lies in being fully attuned to the inner nature of the self and to the universal, underlying laws of nature (Alexander, 1982; Alexander, Kurth, Travis, Warner, & Alexander, 1991; Alexander, Swanson, Rainforth, Carlisle, & Todd, 1991). Spiritual development begins with detachment from both body and mind and their relationships with the outer world, "slowing down the flow of thought," and "going with the flow of life." Ultimately, one may experience "existence without thought"—a state of "nonpersonal consciousness" that rises above the narrow emotions, limited understanding, and self-centered consciousness of everyday life (Atchley, 1991, pp. 3, 4). In some forms of Buddhism, too, wisdom is attained by "transcending the boundaries" of the self (Dittman-Kohli & Baltes, 1990, p. 68). The key elements of these and other eastern definitions of wisdom are rejection of logic as the basis of higher thought and ability to achieve a perspective beyond the self.

Psychological Concepts and Assessments

Today, with the graying of the planet, wisdom—regarded in many cultural traditions as largely the province of old age—has become an important topic of psychological research. Interest in wisdom has grown out of several lines of investigation, each of which reflects different aspects of its traditional meanings. The classical approach was to see wisdom as an aspect of late-life personality development. Today, some theorists, taking a more contextual perspective, describe wisdom as a cognitive ability. Others see wisdom as an integration of intellect and emotion. Another approach, which has roots in eastern philosophy, focuses on the spiritual domain. Let's look at each of these approaches.

CRITICAL THINKING

How do developmental psychologists characterize wisdom?

© Alex Webb/Magnum Photos

In contrast with western philosophy, eastern concepts of wisdom are based on higher, spiritual states of consciousness and harmony with the universe. Jainism stresses physical self-denial, reverence for all life, and good deeds as a path to nirvana, or extinction of the conscious self. This Jain pilgrim in India bows to a figure of Lord Bahūbali, revered as a saint, who is said to have stood, unmoving, in a yoga position for a full year while vines climbed up his arms.

ERIKSON: WISDOM AND LATE-LIFE PERSONALITY DEVELOPMENT

For Erikson, wisdom is a "virtue" that results from successful resolution of the last of eight conflicts in personality development, that of *integrity versus despair* (see Chapter 11). Wisdom is the insight into life's meaning that can come to people contemplating the approach of death, an "informed and detached concern with life itself in the face of death itself" (Erikson, 1985, p. 61). Wisdom means accepting the life one has lived without major regrets. It involves accepting one's parents as people who did the best they could. It implies accepting death as the inevitable end of a life lived as well as one knew how to live it. In sum, it means a realistic acceptance of imperfection in oneself, in one's parents, and in life itself.

CLAYTON AND MEACHAM: COGNITIVE DEFINITIONS

One of the first cognitive researchers to give an operational definition of wisdom was Vivian Clayton (1975, 1982), then at the University of Southern California. In contrast with *intelligence* (which she defined as an ability to think logically and abstractly), Clayton defined *wisdom* as an ability to grasp paradoxes, reconcile contradictions, and make and accept compromises. Because wise people weigh the effects of their acts on themselves and others, wisdom is particularly well suited to practical decision making in a social context. Whereas intelligence can figure out how to do something, wisdom asks whether it *should* be done. Wise people, then, are better than other people at solving social problems involving values—problems like easing racial tensions or deciding which divorcing spouse should have custody of the children.

Who is more likely to be wise: a child or an older person? John A. Meacham (1990), a psychologist at the State University of New York at Buffalo, gives a surprising answer. He claims that wisdom is more likely to be an attribute of youth because older people know too much and are too sure of their knowledge.

The idea that humility is an important ingredient of wisdom goes back to Socrates, who was considered wisest of all the Greeks because he knew how much he did not know. According to Meacham (1982, 1990), wise people balance their acquisition of knowledge with a recognition of its inherent fallibility. Wise people don't know more than unwise people—they just use their information differently. They excel at asking questions and applying facts to real situations. Experience, rather than producing wisdom, "presents the greatest threat to our wisdom, particularly when it leads merely to the accumulation of information, to success, and to power" (Meacham, 1990, p. 209). Instead, wisdom comes from knowing less or becoming less positive about what one knows. It can be lost in old age unless a person is surrounded by supportive companions to allow the expression of doubts and challenge certainties.

BALTES: TOWARD AN EMPIRICAL DEFINITION

In contrast to Meacham, Baltes (1993) and his associates see wisdom as a special kind of expert knowledge. Since the late 1980s, they have been working out a definition that is empirically testable and consistent with the meanings ordinary people have historically attached to the term. And they have done extensive research to verify their definition.

Wisdom, for Baltes, is expert knowledge of the **fundamental pragmatics of life**, "permitting excellent judgment and advice about important and uncertain matters" (Baltes, 1993, p. 586). The fundamental pragmatics of life consist of knowledge and skills that go to the heart of the human condition—the conduct, interpretation, and meaning of life. This factual and procedural knowledge of the fundamentals of living constitutes two basic criteria of wisdom.

Three other criteria are awareness of life's uncertainties; knowledge of the relativism of values, goals, and priorities; and understanding of the importance of context and societal change (Baltes, 1993; Staudinger, Smith, & Baltes, 1992; see Figure 7.2).

Wisdom, in Baltes's dual-process model (see Chapter 6), is part of the *pragmatics of intelligence*, a cognitive domain that remains stable and may even continue to improve into late adulthood (Baltes, 1993; Dittmann-Kohli & Baltes, 1990). Thus, whereas Clayton sees wisdom as distinct from intelligence, Baltes sees it as a component of intelligence (Blanchard-Fields, Brannan, & Camp, 1987). In effect, wisdom becomes the functional equivalent of expertise in a specialized field: knowledge of how to live well (Rybash et al., 1986).

Not everyone, of course, becomes wise, just as not everyone becomes an expert in chess or computers. In fact, Baltes suggests, wisdom can be expected to be fairly rare. Although wisdom may develop at any period of life, aging would seem to provide fertile soil for its growth. A longer life means more time for the development of favorable conditions such as general mental ability; education or training; practice in using the requisite skills; guidance from mentors; leadership experiences; and professional specialization. Eventually, however, losses in the physiologically based mechanics of cognition may limit further refinement of wisdom.

To test the relationship between age and wisdom, Baltes's team did a series of studies comparing the responses of adults of various ages and professional backgrounds to hypothetical dilemmas. Responses were evaluated according

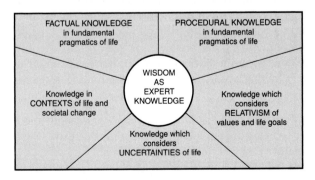

FIGURE 7.2 *Five criteria of wisdom.* SOURCE: Baltes, 1993.

to criteria similar to those in Figure 7.2; to be considered "wise," an answer had to score high in all five areas.

In one study (Smith & Baltes, 1990), 60 well-educated German professionals age 25 to 81 were asked to respond to four hypothetical dilemmas: (1) A 33-year-old professional woman is trying to decide whether to accept a major promotion or start a family. (2) A 63-year-old man whose company is closing the branch office where he works has been offered a choice between early retirement and a move to the main office for 2 or 3 years. (3) A laid-off mechanic can either move to another city to look for work or stay home with his preschool children while his wife continues the nursing career she has just gone back to. (4) A 60-year-old widow who has just finished a business course and opened her own firm now learns that her son has been left with two young children and wants her to help care for them. A panel of experienced human-services professionals rated the responses according to the five criteria. Of 240 solutions, only 5 percent were rated "wise." Older participants showed no more and no less wisdom than younger ones; the 11 "wise" responses were distributed nearly evenly among young, middle-aged, and older adults. Both younger and older participants showed more wisdom about decisions applying to their own stage of life; for example, the oldest group gave its best answers to the problem of the 60-year-old widow.

To see whether certain kinds of life experience lend themselves to the development of wisdom, the researchers set up a similar study of a group of distinguished middle-aged and older adults (their average age was 67) who had been identified by others as wise (Baltes, Staudinger, Maercker, & Smith, 1993). Nearly 60 percent of these people had published autobiographies, and more than 40 percent of them had been in the German resistance movement against the Nazis. When presented with two dilemmas—the one described above about the 60-year-old widow and another about a phone call from a friend who intends to commit suicide—these participants outdid older clinical psychologists (who had previously performed best on such tasks) as well as control groups of older and younger adults with similar education and professional standing.

Perhaps the most significant contribution of Baltes and his associates to the study of wisdom is their attempt to study it systematically and scientifically. Their key finding is that wisdom, though not exclusively the province of old age, is one area in which older people, especially those who have had certain kinds of experiences, can hold their own—or better. A similar insight may be found in the following observation, made by a man in his sixties shortly before his death:

> Many people never reach any kind of maturity or wisdom at any age. Life experiences to many are not additive but simply repetitive. For others wisdom and maturity may occur early in life. There is, however, the unique quality some older and mature and hopefully wise people have, and that is the perspective of looking back over the years and seeing themselves in a way that younger, mature and wise people cannot do. (Shier, 1992)

LABOUVIE-VIEF: INTEGRATING INTELLECT AND AFFECT

If the problems wise people solve best are value-centered, is intellect all that is needed to solve them? According to some theorists, solving value-laden problems requires a synthesis of intellect and affect (emotion). Labouvie-Vief (1990a, 1990b), one of the most prominent of these theorists, defines *wisdom* as an integration of two basic modes of knowing: *logos* (objective, analytic, and rational) and *mythos* (subjective, experiential, and emotional). She sees this integration as the major developmental task of a healthy adulthood. Full, mature mental functioning consists of a continuous dialogue between *mythos* and *logos*, in which "one mode [*mythos*] provides experiential richness and fluidity, the other [*logos*] logical cohesion and stability" (1990b, p. 53).

This wisdom does not necessarily come with advanced age; in fact, it appears to peak in middle age. Nor is it simply expertise. What makes people wise is not merely specialized knowledge, "but rather knowledge of issues that are part of the human condition . . . . Wisdom consists . . . in one's ability to see through and beyond individual uniqueness and specialization into those structures that relate us in our common humanity." If wisdom does have its own domain, says Labouvie-Vief, it must be broad enough to encompass morals and ethics, "understanding one's own emotions and inner life and differentiating them from those of others," and using that understanding rationally and reflectively (1990b, pp. 77–78). On this point, Baltes (1993) would presumably agree; indeed, he cites Labouvie-Vief's work as complementary to his own. In later stages of cognitive development, emotions enhance cognitive processing (Isaacowitz, Charles, & Carstensen, 2000).

WISDOM AND SPIRITUAL DEVELOPMENT

Many eastern cultures, rather than focusing on rationality and knowledge, seek detachment from the conscious mind as a path to inner spiritual growth (Atchley, 1991). Some investigators, influenced by eastern philosophy, believe that wisdom is based on spiritual development and is likely to develop late in life.

According to one such definition (Achenbaum & Orwoll, 1991), wisdom has three interrelated facets: **intrapersonal wisdom** (self-examination, self-knowledge, and integrity); **interpersonal wisdom** (empathy, understanding, and maturity in human relationships); and **transpersonal wisdom** (capacity to transcend the self and strive for spiritual growth). Transpersonal wisdom—similar to the "nonpersonal consciousness" of the vedantic philosophy of Hindu India—is the key to the other two, since it provides a vantage point beyond the narrow concerns of self from which to observe oneself and one's relationships. Contemplation can foster all three facets of wisdom (Atchley, 1991).

If wisdom is traditionally associated with age, then, it may be because contemplation and spiritual development are more likely to occur in later life. *Interiority*, a tendency toward introspection and concern with the inner life, which has been associated with aging (Jung, 1966; Neugarten, 1977), may serve as a stimulus. In one experiment, when 92 retired adults carried electronic pagers for 1 week, they reported that they voluntarily spent nearly half their waking time in solitude—often absorbed in challenging, focused thought (Larson, Zuzanek, & Mannell, 1985). An older person, freed from youthful preoccupation with worldly goals and concerns, may be more open to "self-realization . . . the flowering of a world within that has hitherto been obscured by the drama of everyday life" (Atchley, 1991, p. 5).

Summing Up: Wisdom and Age

So far, research findings on wisdom and age are not clear-cut. Baltes surmises that age may be conducive to wisdom but has not found confirming data—though certain kinds of "wisdom-producing" experience may give older people an edge. Labouvie-Vief's work suggests that wisdom is at its height in middle age. Why, then, do classic western literary traditions and eastern spiritual traditions describe wisdom as the province of old age?

One possible reason, which would be consistent with Labouvie-Vief's finding, is increased longevity. Ancient peoples may well have pictured the "wise elders" of myth and legend as being in their forties or even younger. Then again, the discrepancy may be a matter of definition. Research using other definitions of wisdom, or focusing on other features of it, might yield different results. If, for example, wisdom requires transcendence of the self, it may indeed take a very long time to acquire. Such a definition, however, would be difficult to test in the laboratory.

Self-transcendence may provide a way to view—and ameliorate—narrow, selfish thinking (Csikszentmihalyi & Rathunde, 1990). G. Stanley Hall (1922), a pioneer in the study of aging, saw such a role as especially suited to older adults, who, freed from anxiety about careers and capable of impartiality and breadth of vision, can take a fresh look at their society and its ills, offering a wisdom "which learning cannot give . . . a kind of higher criticism of life" (pp. 410–411). Here we see one of the oldest functions of wisdom: moral guidance. But how does such moral development occur?

MORAL DEVELOPMENT

A woman is near death from cancer. A druggist has discovered a drug that doctors believe might save her. The druggist is charging $2,000 for a small dose—10 times what the drug costs him to make. The sick woman's husband, Heinz, borrows from everyone he knows but can scrape together only $1,000. He begs the druggist to sell him the drug for $1,000 or let him pay the rest later. The druggist refuses, saying "I discovered the drug and I'm going to make money from it." Heinz, desperate, breaks into the man's store and steals the drug. Should Heinz have done that? Why or why not? (Kohlberg, 1969)

Kohlberg's Theory: Moral Reasoning

"Heinz's" problem is the most famous example of Lawrence Kohlberg's approach to moral development. For more than 30 years, Kohlberg studied 75 young men, starting in the 1950s, when they were age 10 to 16. He told them stories, posing hypothetical dilemmas like Heinz's; at the heart of each was the concept of justice. By asking his respondents how they would resolve the problems, Kohlberg concluded that many people arrive at moral judgments independently; they do not simply adopt standards of parents, teachers, or peers.

Kohlberg was less interested in the answers people gave to his dilemmas than in the reasoning behind the answers. Two people who gave opposite answers to Heinz's dilemma could be at the same moral level if their reasoning was based on similar factors. On the basis of the thought processes shown by the responses, Kohlberg (1969) described three levels of moral reasoning that, in theory, roughly follow Piaget's cognitive stages of preoperational, concrete operational, and formal operational thought:

- *Level I:* **Preconventional morality.** People, under external controls, obey rules to avoid punishment or damage to people or property; or they act in their own self-interest, recognizing that others will do the same. This level is typical of children age 4 to 10.
- *Level II:* **Morality of conventional role conformity.** People have internalized the standards of authority figures. They are concerned about being "good," pleasing and caring for others, and maintaining the social order. This level is typically reached after age 10; many people never move beyond it, even in adulthood.
- *Level III:* **Morality of autonomous moral principles.** Morality is fully internal. People now recognize conflicts between moral standards and make their own moral judgments on the basis of principles of right, fairness, and justice. People generally do not reach this level of moral reasoning until at least age 13, or more commonly in young adulthood, if ever.

> CRITICAL THINKING
>
> Which vocations or professions require each of Kohlberg's stages of moral reasoning?

Each of the three levels is divided into two stages; Kohlberg later added a transitional level and a seventh stage. Table 7.2 gives descriptions of the levels and stages typically seen in adults.

"LIVE AND LEARN": EXPERIENCE AND MORALITY

Experience leads adults to reevaluate their criteria for what is right and fair. Some adults spontaneously offer personal experiences as reasons for their answers to moral dilemmas like Heinz's. People who have had cancer, or whose relatives or friends have had cancer, are more likely to condone a man's stealing an expensive drug to save his dying wife, and to explain this view in terms of their own experience (Bielby & Papalia, 1975). Such experiences, strongly colored by emotion, trigger rethinking in a way that hypothetical, impersonal discussions cannot, and are more likely to help people see other points of view.

TABLE 7.2

Kohlberg's Levels and Stages of Moral Reasoning Typically Seen in Adults*

Levels	Stages of Reasoning
Level II: Conventional morality. Parental and social standards are internalized in the form of a desire to be seen as "good" or to follow accepted rules.	*Stage 3: Maintaining mutual relations and expectations.* Empathic viewpoint: it is right to fulfill one's expected role (i.e., daughter, brother, friend) and show mutual care and concern so as to appear "good" in the eyes of oneself and others. People evaluate an act by its motive or by putting themselves in another person's place (golden rule).
	Stage 4: Maintaining social system and conscience. "Social contract" viewpoint: it is right to fulfill societal obligations, obey laws, and contribute to society in order to keep society going and to have a clear conscience. ("What if everyone did it?") An act is wrong if it violates a rule, except in extreme cases of conflict with other established duties or rights.
Level II–III: Postconventional but not yet principled morality. At this transitional level, people recognize conflicting moral standards. They have moved beyond their society's moral system but have not yet developed their own system of moral principles.	*Stage 4½: Subjective emotional choice.* Arbitrary, relativist viewpoint: it is right to pick and choose among moral ideas or obligations on the basis of personal feelings, rather than being bound by societal standards.

*Level I, Preconventional Morality, is typically seen in children under age 10.
SOURCES: Adapted from Kohlberg (1969), Kohlberg & Ryncarz (1990), Lickona (1976).

Although cognitive awareness of higher moral principles develops in adolescence, most people do not commit themselves to these principles until adulthood, when turning points of identity often have to do with moral issues (Kohlberg, 1973). Two experiences that advance moral development in young adulthood are encountering conflicting values away from home (as happens in college or the armed services or sometimes in foreign travel) and being responsible for the welfare of other people (as in parenthood).

With regard to moral judgments, then, cognitive stages do not tell the whole story. Of course, someone whose thinking is still at Piaget's level of concrete operations is unlikely to make moral decisions at a postconventional level. But even someone who is at the stage of formal operations may not reach the highest level of moral thinking unless experience catches up

Levels

Level III: Morality of autonomous moral principles.
Moral decisions are based on internal, rationally
derived principles that embrace fundamental
values of justice and human welfare.

Stages of Reasoning

Stage 5: Utilitarianism and fundamental rights. "Prior
to society" viewpoint: it is right to judge a social
system by standards that exist prior to the
establishment of a particular society. Laws should be
based on rational calculation of the greatest good
for the greatest number. Generally, laws should be
obeyed, so as to treat people impartially and to fulfill
the obligations of the social "contract." However,
protection of certain fundamental values and rights
outweighs majority rule.

Stage 6: Universal ethical principles. Absolutist viewpoint:
it is right to be committed to universal, rationally valid
principles, such as equality of human rights and respect
for human dignity, whether or not these principles
conflict with the laws of a particular society.

Stage 7: Cosmic perspective. Transcendental viewpoint:
it is right to see oneself and one's conduct, not only
as part of humanity, but as part of the universe. All
parts of the universe are integrally connected, and an
individual's actions impinge on the welfare of the
whole. Human rights and ethical principles are based
on the laws of nature (natural law).

with cognition. Many adults who are capable of logical reasoning do not
break out of a conventional mold to make their own moral judgments unless, as in the case of Nelson Mandela, their experiences have prepared them
for the shift.

In this and other respects, Kohlberg's work intersects the literature on
postformal thought. Although Kohlberg himself equated postconventional morality with formal reasoning, its parallels with postformal
thinking are striking—particularly the roles of experience, emotion, and
individually chosen principles in resolving ambiguity and conflict. A
connection between postformal thought and postconventional morality
would also explain why many people do not fully achieve the postconventional level until adulthood, if at all.

A SEVENTH STAGE: THE COSMIC PERSPECTIVE

CRITICAL THINKING

What universal moral principles, if any, transcend cultures and religions?

At one point Kohlberg questioned his sixth stage, citing the difficulty of finding people at such a high level of moral development (Muuss, 1988). Yet shortly before his death Kohlberg was working on a seventh stage, which moves beyond considerations of justice and has much in common with self-transcendence in eastern tradition. In this seventh stage, adults reflect on the question, "*Why* be moral? Why be just in a universe that appears unjust?" (Kohlberg & Ryncarz, 1990, p. 192; emphasis added).

The answer, Kohlberg suggested, lies in achieving a **cosmic perspective:** "a sense of unity with the cosmos, nature, or God." This perspective enables a person to see moral issues "from the standpoint of the universe as a whole" (Kohlberg & Ryncarz, 1990, pp. 191, 207). It may or may not involve religious belief, but it parallels the most mature stage of faith the theologian James Fowler (1981) identified in interviews with about 400 people age 4 to 80. In that most developed stage of faith, "one experiences a oneness with the ultimate conditions of one's life and being" (Kohlberg & Ryncarz, 1990, p. 202).

In stage 7, ethics are grounded in *natural law*—principles based on human nature and embedded in the natural order of things. In experiencing oneness with the cosmos, a person comes to recognize that everything is connected. This means that one person's actions affect everything and everyone else, and the consequences reflect back on the doer.

In the mid nineteenth century, the Native American chief Seattle eloquently expressed similar thoughts about people's intimate connections with one another and with all of nature. This is how he responded when the United States government tried to buy his tribe's lands:

> We are part of the earth and it is part of us. . . . What befalls the earth befalls all the sons of the earth. . . . All things are connected. . . . Man did not weave the web of life, he is merely a strand in it. Whatever he does to the web, he does to himself. . . . So, if we sell you our land, love it as we have loved it. Care for it as we have cared for it. . . . As we are part of the land, you too are part of the land. We *are* brothers after all. (Campbell & Moyers, 1988, pp. 34–35)

CROSS-CULTURAL RESEARCH ON KOHLBERG'S THEORY

The American boys that Kohlberg and his colleagues followed into adulthood progressed through Kohlberg's stages in sequence, and none skipped a stage. Their moral judgments correlated positively with age, education, IQ, and socioeconomic status (Colby, Kohlberg, Gibbs, & Lieberman, 1983). Cross-cultural studies confirm this sequence—up to a point. Older people from countries other than the United States do tend to score at higher stages than younger people. But people from nonwestern cultures rarely score above stage 4 (C. P. Edwards, 1977; Nisan & Kohlberg, 1982; Snarey, 1985). It is possible that these cultures do not foster higher moral development, but it seems more likely that some aspects of Kohlberg's moral hierarchy may not fit the cultural values of some societies. Let's look more closely at three cultures in which Kohlberg's dilemmas have been studied: China, Israeli kibbutzim, and India.

China The dilemma of Heinz, who could not afford a drug for his sick wife, was revised for use in Taiwan. In the revision, a shopkeeper will not give a man food for his sick wife.

This version would seem unbelievable to Chinese villagers, who in real life are more accustomed to hearing a shopkeeper in such a situation say, "You have to let people have things whether they have money or not" (Wolf, 1968, p. 21). Other cultural differences are involved as well (Dien, 1982). In Kohlberg's format, respondents make an either-or decision based on their own value systems. In Chinese society, people faced with such a dilemma discuss it openly, are guided by community standards, and try to find a way of resolving the problem to please as many parties as possible. The Chinese view is that human beings are born with moral tendencies whose development has to do with intuitive, spontaneous feelings supported by society, rather than with analytical thinking, individual choice, or personal responsibility. In the west, even good people may be harshly punished if, under the force of circumstances, they break a law. The Chinese are unaccustomed to universally applied laws; they prefer to abide by the sound decisions of a wise judge. Whereas Kohlberg's philosophy is based on justice, the Chinese ethos leans toward conciliation and harmony.

© Thelma Shumsky/Image Works

The Native American chief Seattle exemplified Kohlberg's highest stage of ethical thinking in his response to the United States government's request to buy his tribe's lands.

How, then, can Kohlberg's theory, rooted in western values and reflecting western ideals, be applied to moral development in an eastern society that works along very different lines? Some say that an alternative view is required, which measures morality by the ability to make judgments based on norms of reciprocity, rules of exchange, available resources, and complex relationships (Dien, 1982).

However, we need to be careful to avoid making broad-brush generalizations about cultural attitudes. Concepts of rights, welfare, and justice exist in all cultures, though they may be differently applied. To say that western cultures are individualistic and eastern cultures are collectivist ignores individual differences and even diametrically opposed attitudes within each culture, and the specific contextual situations in which moral judgments are applied (Turiel, 1998). For example, the outpouring of relief funds from the United States for victims of the tsunami in Southeast Asia showed that compassion may be as strong a part of the American ethos as competition.

Gibbs's Theory: Moral Judgment Development

A recent alternative approach is that of John Gibbs, a long-time colleague of Kohlberg's whose "neo-Kohlbergian" theory builds on Kohlberg's theory but also departs from it. Kohlberg's theory makes certain basic claims about morality and moral development. Gibbs and other neo-Kohlbergians agree with these basic points:

- An important aspect of morality is how people reason morally. Thus it is important to study the development of moral judgment or reasoning.
- The development of moral judgment is a lifelong process that is more than just internalizing the moral norms of society. Children "construct" basic notions of fairness or reciprocity through the give-and-take of peer interaction and other perspective-taking opportunities. Moral judgment further develops in adolescence and adulthood through the expansion of social perspectives in settings such as that of a college or university or diverse work environments.
- Such social perspective taking, along with general cognitive development, brings about a standard sequence of stage of moral judgment. The sequence should be evident in all cultures, western and eastern.

As we have seen, however, Kohlberg's stage hierarchy has not fared well in studies conducted in nonwestern cultures, and his postconventional stages 5 and 6 are uncommon even in the United States; these stages seem to represent elite western philosophies rather than stages of general moral maturity. In fact, stages 5 and 6 are not particularly evident even among moral leaders in middle and late adulthood (see Box 7.3 on p. 262). Kohlberg himself questioned his sixth stage because it is so rare.

The problem according to Gibbs, lies in some part in Kohlberg's dilemma approach. Instead, Gibbs and his colleagues (Gibbs, Basinger, & Fuller, 1992) developed a structured questionnaire. Gibbs points out that Kohlberg derived this three-level hierarchy not directly from data but instead from the speculative writings of the philosopher and educator John Dewey (Dewey & Tufts, 1908). However, as Kohlberg's longitudinal study progressed, the data increasingly suggested that Dewey's hierarchy was not a good fit. The notion that some moral judgment at the "conventional" level is the result of internalization does not square well with Kohlberg's idea that moral judgment is constructed. And examples of truly "postconventional" thinking continued to be rare even as his participants reached their adult years. In Gibbs's view, removing the Dewey scheme from Kohlberg's theory results in a more valid picture of moral development.

In his *Moral Development and Reality* (2003), Gibbs pictures moral judgment as a lifelong, ongoing process of achieving clearer and deeper moral understanding. His theory entails two overlapping phases within lifespan moral development: standard and existential. Whereas standard development involves universally identifiable stages, existential development does not. Gibbs's theory of lifespan moral development is depicted in Table 7.3.

Gibbs's Neo-Kohlbergian Theory of Lifespan Moral Judgment Development

The lifespan development of moral judgment consists of overlapping phases, standard and existential.

I. Standard Development (age norms are from Gibbs et al., 1992 and Basinger, et al., 1995) encompasses immature and mature levels of stages.

   A. The immature or superficial stages. (Constructed in early childhood; typically, by adolescence, usage of Stage 1 thinking is negligible, and Stage 2 thinking has appreciably declined.) This level is superficial in that the moral is confused with the physical or momentary (Stage 1) or with the pragmatic (Stage 2). Morality is also confused with egocentric biases and motives (blatantly at Stage 1, more subtly at Stage 2).

      1. *Stage 1: Centrations.* Morality tends to be confused with physical size or power ("Daddy's the boss because he's big and strong") or with the momentary egocentric desires of one's mental life ("It's fair because I want it"). Adult might-makes-right philosophies derive from this stage.

      2. *Stage 2: Pragmatic Exchanges.* Gains in psychological understanding lead to more developed perspective taking; however, morality is still based on how one treats others or how others treat you and is self-centered (e.g., the Golden Rule is misinterpreted as "do for others if they did or will do for you").

   B. The mature or profound stages. (Typically constructed and socialized during late childhood and adolescence, with elaborations in later years; construction of the Mature Level may take place during adulthood for developmentally delayed adults.) Moral judgment is mature insofar as it appeals to the intangible, ideal bases (mutual trust, caring, respect) and moral point of view (Golden Rule, How would you wish to be treated?) of adult social life. Mature normative morality applies mainly to interpersonal relationships or homogenous communities (Stage 3) but may expand in scope to social systems (Stage 4). These stages presuppose the hypothetical and deductive abilities Piaget referred to as formal operations.

      1. *Stage 3: Mutualities.* Do-as-one-would-be-done-by or Golden Rule morality, based on third-person perspective. Ideal reciprocity, mutual trust, or intimate sharing is the basis for interpersonal relationships. A relativized version of Stage 3 (a truly sincere person's morals are right for him or her) is termed Transition ¾ Type R (Gibbs et al., 1992) or 3 ½ (Colby, 1978).

      2. *Stage 4: Systems.* The social contexts for mutualities expand beyond the one-to-one to address the need for commonly accepted values and standards in a complex social system.

II. Existential Development (qualitative changes no longer characterizable as a standard stage sequence. Although associated with adulthood, this phase of life can begin as early as adolescence for formal and postformal operational thinkers; throughout the lives of others, however, this phase may remain absent). Existential development transcends the standard moral judgment stages. The existential phase involves hypothetical contemplation, meta-ethical reflection, the formulation of moral principles or philosophies, and spiritual awakening or ontological inspiration. Existentially deep inspiration can diminish cognitive distortions in one's morality and revitalize dedication to the moral life.

Moral Leadership in Middle and Late Adulthood

What makes a single mother of four young children, with no money and a tenth-grade education, dedicate her life to religious missionary work on behalf of her equally poor neighbors? What leads a pediatrician to devote much of his practice to poor children instead of to patients whose parents could provide him with a lucrative income?

In the mid 1980s, two psychologists, Anne Colby and William Damon, sought answers to questions like these. They embarked on a two-year search for people who showed unusual moral excellence in their day-to-day lives. The researchers eventually identified 23 "moral exemplars," interviewed them in depth, and studied how they had become moral leaders (Colby & Damon, 1992).

To find moral exemplars, Colby and Damon worked with a panel of 22 "expert nominators," people who in their professional lives regularly think about moral ideas—philosophers, historians, religious thinkers, and so forth. The researchers drew up five criteria: sustained commitment to principles that show respect for humanity; behavior consistent with one's ideals; willingness to risk self-interest; inspiring others to moral action; and humility, or lack of concern for one's ego.

The chosen exemplars varied widely in age, education, occupation, and ethnicity. There were 10 men and 13 women, age 35 to 86 of white, African American, and Hispanic backgrounds. Education ranged from eighth grade up through M.D.s, Ph.D.s, and law degrees; and occupations included religious callings, business, teaching, and social leadership. Areas of concern included poverty, civil rights, education, ethics, environment, peace, and religious freedom.

The research yielded a number of surprises, not least of which was this group's showing on Kohlberg's classic measure of moral judgment. Each exemplar was asked about "Heinz's dilemma," and about a follow-up dilemma: how the man should be punished if he does steal the drug. Of 22 exemplars (one response was not scorable), only half scored at the postconventional level; the other half scored at the conventional level. The major difference between the two groups was level of education: those with college and advanced degrees were much more likely to score at the higher level, and no one who had only a high school diploma scored above the conventional level. Clearly, it is not

The standard phase occurs mainly during childhood and adolescence. Gibbs's stages in the standard phase look something like Kohlberg's stages, but Gibbs maintains they must be characterized differently: Stages 1 and 2 are at an immature level, whereas Stages 3 and 4 are not merely "conventional" but instead are already at a mature level. The immature stages are superficial; people at these stages confuse morality with impressive appearances or physical power (Stage 1) or with concrete you-scratch-my-back-I'll-scratch-yours reciprocity (Stage 2). The mature stages are profound; they penetrate through the superficial to infer the intangible and ideal bases of interpersonal relationships (stage 3) necessary to score at Kohlberg's highest stages to live an exemplary moral life.

How does a person become morally committed? The 23 moral exemplars did not develop in isolation, but responded to social influences. Some of these influences, such as those of parents, were important from childhood on. But many other influences became significant in later years, helping these people evaluate their capacities, form moral goals, and develop strategies to achieve them.

These moral exemplars had a lifelong commitment to change: they focused their energy on changing society and people's lives for the better. But they remained stable in their moral commitments, in what they felt was important in determining their actions. At the same time, they kept growing throughout life, remained open to new ideas, and continued to learn from others.

The processes responsible for stability in moral commitments were gradual, taking many years to build up. They were also collaborative: leaders took advice from supporters, and people noted for independent judgment drew heavily on feedback from those close to them—both those people who shared their goals and those who had different perspectives.

Along with their enduring moral commitments, certain personality characteristics seemed to remain with the moral exemplars throughout middle and late adulthood: enjoyment of life, ability to make the best of a bad situation, solidarity with others, absorption in work, a sense of humor, and humility. They tended to believe that change was possible, and this optimism helped them battle what often seemed like overwhelming odds and to persist in the face of defeat.

While their actions often meant risk and hardship, these people did not see themselves as courageous. Nor did they agonize over decisions. Since their personal and moral goals coincided, they went ahead and did what they believed needed to be done, not calculating personal consequences to themselves or their families, and not feeling that they were sacrificing or martyring themselves.

Of course, there is no "blueprint" for creating a moral giant, just as it does not seem possible to write directions to produce a genius in any other field. What studying the lives of such people can bring is the knowledge that ordinary people can rise to greatness and that openness to change and new ideas can persist throughout adulthood.

or, more broadly, social systems (stage 4). This age trend in moral judgment, according to Gibbs, is broadly found across western and nonwestern cultures.

Insight into deeper moral understanding during standard development owes much to Piaget's formal operational stage of detached reflection, according to Gibbs. The process of achieving deeper moral understanding does not stop with the stages of the standard phase. Citing other researchers, Gibbs points out that the reflection can bring about not only a deeper understanding of moral reciprocity, it can also bring about a deeper understanding and appreciation of the moral life in general.

Gilligan's Theory: Gender and Postformal Morality

Because Kohlberg's original studies were done on boys and men, Carol Gilligan (1982, 1987a, 1987b) argued that his system gives a higher place to "masculine" values of justice and fairness than to "feminine" values of compassion, responsibility, and caring. Gilligan suggested that a woman's central moral dilemma is the conflict between her own needs and those of others. While most societies typically expect assertiveness and independent judgment from men, they expect from women self-sacrifice and concern for others.

To find out how women make moral choices, Gilligan (1982) interviewed 29 pregnant women about their decisions to continue or end their pregnancies. These women saw morality in terms of selfishness versus responsibility, defined as an obligation to exercise care and to avoid hurting others. Gilligan concluded that women think less about abstract justice and fairness than men do and more about their responsibilities to specific people. (Table 7.4 lists Gilligan's proposed levels of moral development in women.)

However, other research has not, on the whole, found significant gender differences in moral reasoning (Brabeck & Shore, 2003). One large-scale analysis comparing results from 66 studies found no significant differences in men's and women's responses to Kohlberg's dilemmas across the life span (L.J. Walker, 1984). In the few studies in which men scored slightly higher, the findings were not clearly gender-related, since the men generally were better educated and had better jobs than the women. A more recent analysis of 113 studies reached a slightly more nuanced conclusion. Although women were more likely to think in terms of care, and men were more oriented to justice, these differences were small, especially among university students. Ages of respondents and the types of dilemmas or questions presented were more significant factors than gender (Jaffee & Hyde, 2000). Thus the weight of evidence does not appear to back up either of Gilligan's original contentions: a male bias in Kohlberg's theory or a distinct female perspective on morality (L. Walker, 1995).

In her own later research, Gilligan has described moral development in *both* men and women as evolving beyond abstract reasoning. In studies using real-life moral dilemmas (such as whether a woman's lover should confess their affair to her husband), rather than hypothetical dilemmas like the ones Kohlberg used, Gilligan and her colleagues found that many people in their twenties become dissatisfied with a narrow moral logic and become more able to live with moral contradictions (Gilligan, Murphy, & Tappan, 1990). It seems then, that if Gilligan's earlier research reflected an alternative values system, it was not gender-based. At the same time, with the inclusion of his seventh stage, Kohlberg's thinking evolved to a point of greater agreement with Gilligan's. Both theories now place responsibility to others at the highest level of moral thought. Both recognize the importance for both sexes of connections with other people and of compassion and care.

TABLE 7.4

Gilligan's Levels of Moral Development in Women

Stage	Description
Level 1: Orientation of individual survival	The woman concentrates on herself—on what is practical and what is best for her.
Transition 1: From selfishness to responsibility	The woman realizes her connection to others and thinks about what would be the responsible choice in terms of other people (such as the unborn baby), as well as herself.
Level 2: Goodness as self-sacrifice	This conventional feminine wisdom dictates sacrificing the woman's own wishes to what other people want—and will think of her. She considers herself responsible for the actions of others, while holding others responsible for her own choices. She is in a dependent position, one in which her indirect efforts to exert control often turn into manipulation, sometimes through the use of guilt.
Transition 2: From goodness to truth	The woman assesses her decisions not on the basis of how others will react to them but on her intentions and the consequences of her actions. She develops a new judgment that takes into account her own needs, along with those of others. She wants to be "good" by being responsible to others, but also wants to be "honest" by being responsible to herself. Survival returns as a major concern.
Level 3: Morality of nonviolence	By elevating the injunction against hurting anyone (including herself) to a principle that governs all moral judgment and action, the woman establishes a "moral equality" between herself and others and is then able to assume the responsibility for choice in moral dilemmas.

SOURCE: Adapted from Gilligan, 1982.

INTELLIGENCE, CREATIVITY, WISDOM, AND MORAL DEVELOPMENT: A LAST WORD

© Hulton-Deutsch Collection/Corbis Images

Mahatma Gandhi's philosophy of non-violence was a formidable moral weapon in India's struggle for independence from Britain.

CRITICAL THINKING

Why do you think acts of nonviolent self-sacrifice elicit passionate violent responses?

There is a limit to . . . progress in intelligence; but the development of the qualities of the heart knows no bounds. (M. K. Gandhi, as quoted in Kumar & Puri, 1983)

Caring was at the core of life for Mohandas Karamchaud Gandhi, known as Mahatma, or "great soul." Gandhi struggled for decades to achieve an independent India free of British domination, in which Hindus, Muslims, and all other peoples could live in harmony. He believed that violence is never justified, even in the noblest causes. Although often imprisoned for his activities, he did not waver in his beliefs or goals. When India finally attained independence in 1947, and a separate Muslim state of Pakistan was created, Gandhi—then in his late seventies—went on a hunger strike in an effort to stop the ensuing violence. This moral weapon accomplished what, according to the *London Times*, "several divisions [of troops] could not have done." Moved by Gandhi's act of self-sacrifice, both Hindus and Muslims laid down their arms. Another hunger strike, in Delhi in January 1948, led to cooperative efforts to secure protections for the Muslim minority. But 12 days after breaking his fast, Gandhi—then 78—was shot and killed on his way to a prayer meeting. The assassin was a fellow Hindu who could not accept Gandhi's vision of brotherhood.

Gandhi's philosophy of nonviolence profoundly influenced other great leaders, among them Nelson Mandela and Martin Luther King, Jr. Gandhi himself exemplifies the ability to deal with almost intractable problems through a creative fusion of intellect and emotion, spirituality and moral suasion. In his efforts to defuse conflicts and inspire cooperation, he showed great wisdom—wisdom grounded in a transcendent moral vision.

Few of us reach the heights of intelligence, creativity, and wisdom or achieve the moral and spiritual leadership Gandhi did, and few of us have such influential careers. But caring and concern for others are important qualities in any adult, as is the work to which one chooses to devote one's life. We turn to these aspects of the social world of adulthood in subsequent chapters.

SUMMARY AND KEY TERMS

- A growing body of theory and research focuses on qualitative changes in mature thought, rather than on quantitative changes that can be measured psychometrically.

The Role of Experience

- According to Hoyer's model, adults maximize their intellectual functioning through encapsulation of fluid abilities within specialized fields of expert knowledge.

- Everyday problem solving improves in middle age and may remain stable or continue to improve in old age.
- Mature adults integrate new experience with existing personal knowledge and interpret information or events in terms of their own life experience.
  encapsulation (p. 233)

Beyond Piaget: New Ways of Thinking in Adulthood

- Several investigators have proposed a postformal stage of adult thinking—beyond Piaget's highest stage, formal operations.
- A shift to postformal thought is said to occur in college, when students are exposed to ambiguities and opposing viewpoints, and their thinking typically progresses from rigidity to flexibility to freely chosen commitments.
- Labouvie-Vief has proposed three levels of adult cognitive development: intrasystemic, intersystemic, and integrated.
- Criteria for postformal thought include shifting gears, awareness of multiple causes and solutions, pragmatism, awareness of paradox, and contractions and expansions of formal thinking.

reflective thinking (p. 237)   **intrasystemic level (p. 240)**
postformal thought (p. 238)   **intersystemic level (p. 240)**
commitment within relativism   **integrated level (p. 240)**
    (p. 239)   **necessary subjectivity (p. 240)**

A Lifespan Model of Cognitive Development

- Schaie has proposed five stages of age-related cognitive development: acquisitive (childhood and adolescence), achieving (young adulthood), responsible and executive (middle adulthood), and reintegrative (late adulthood).
- This model suggests a need to develop new kinds of intelligence tests that are ecologically valid for adults.

acquisitive stage (p. 244)   **reorganizational stage (p. 244)**
achieving stage (p. 244)   **reintegrative stage (p. 244)**
responsible stage (p. 244)   **legacy-creating stage (p. 245)**
executive stage (p. 244)   **ecological validity (p. 245)**

Wisdom

- Sternberg, on the basis of studies of adults' views of creativity, intelligence, and wisdom, distinguishes the three concepts on the basis of automaticity of information processing, approach to knowledge, styles of mental regulation, personality factors, fundamental motivations, and supportive environments.
- Modern psychologists who investigate wisdom have drawn on folk, mythic, and philosophical traditions.
- According to Erikson, wisdom is a virtue emerging from the final crisis of human personality development, *integrity versus despair*. It permits acceptance of one's life and approaching death.
- Among cognitive definitions of wisdom, that of Baltes has been empirically tested. Baltes sees wisdom as expertise in "fundamental pragmatics of life."

- For Labouvie-Vief, wisdom is a synthesis of reason with emotion, or subjective experience, and appears to peak in middle age.
- Some investigators, influenced by eastern philosophy, see wisdom as a product of spiritual development or self-transcendence.

metacognition (p. 246)

archetypes (p. 248)

fundamental pragmatics of life (p. 251)

intrapersonal wisdom (p. 253)

interpersonal wisdom (p. 253)

transpersonal wisdom (p. 253)

Moral Development

- Kohlberg's theory of moral reasoning holds that people reason out moral principles; thus moral development is related to cognitive development.
- Many adults remain at Kohlberg's conventional level of morality; some advance to a postconventional level of autonomous moral principles.
- Gibbs's theory of moral thinking takes a lifespan approach; development occurs in stages.
- Gilligan has criticized Kohlberg's emphasis on justice as a predominantly male value and has proposed a theory of women's moral development centered on caring and responsibility.
- Gilligan's recent work suggests that many adults, both men and women, reach a stage of relativist morality that reflects postformal thought.

preconventional morality (p. 255)

morality of conventional role conformity (p. 255)

morality of autonomous moral principles (p. 255)

cosmic perspective (p. 258)

Education, Work, Leisure, and Retirement

◈ FOCUS: JIMMY CARTER

© AP/Wide World Photos

*What am I
But an unfinished poem
I am constantly working on?*
      —Rita Duskin "My Portrait,"
         in *The Frugal Chariot,*1970

JAMES EARL ("JIMMY") CARTER, Jr.,* was one of the most unpopular presidents of the United States in the twentieth century. Yet a little more than a decade after having been turned out of office, he is one of the most active and most admired ex-presidents in modern American history, "pursuing lost and neglected causes with a missionary's zeal"—and an amazing degree of success (Nelson, 1994).

As a boy in tiny, rural Plains, Georgia, Carter helped

*Sources of biographical information on Jimmy Carter are Bird (1990), Carter (1975), Carter Center (1995), J. Nelson (1994), *World Book Yearbook 1977*, Wooten (1995), and various newspaper articles.

with chores on the family farm, sold peanuts and cotton, and absorbed his parents' traditional values: education, hard work, religious faith, and public service. His career choice, influenced by an uncle who was a radioman in the Pacific fleet, was to be a naval officer. He won an appointment to the U.S. Naval Academy and served as engineering officer of the first nuclear-powered submarine under Captain Hyman G. Rickover. Rickover "had a profound influence on my life," Carter later wrote. ". . . He expected the maximum from us, but he always contributed more" (*World Book Yearbook*, 1977, p. 53).

Carter's career took a new turn after his father's death. He resigned from the Navy and returned to Plains to run the family farm and peanut warehouse. An outspoken foe of racial segregation, he was narrowly elected to the Georgia Senate in 1962 and to the governorship in 1970. As governor, he streamlined the state government and pushed through legislation to equalize state aid to rich and poor school districts, establish community centers for retarded children, and protect the environment. He initiated merit selection of judges and state officials and greatly increased the number of black appointees and employees.

In 1976, in the wake of the Watergate scandal that toppled President Richard M. Nixon, Carter, previously little known outside Georgia, won the Democratic nomination on the first ballot after sweeping 18 primary elections. He went on to become the first southerner in the twentieth century to be elected president. His appeal was as an outsider who would clean up government and restore a moral tone. But despite such historic achievements as peace between Israel and Egypt and a treaty relinquishing control of the Panama Canal, he became bogged down in the interminable Iranian hostage crisis and took the blame for high fuel prices, gasoline lines, and a sagging economy. After a devastating defeat by Ronald Reagan in the 1980 election, he retired from political life.

Or so it seemed. Just look at what Carter has done since then:

He is a professor at Emory University and serves as a deacon as well as teaching Sunday school for a Baptist church. He helps build houses for low-income families through Habitat for Humanity. He established the Carter Center, which sponsors international programs in human rights, education, preventive health care, agricultural techniques, and conflict resolution and has secured the release of hundreds of political prisoners. As a roving peacemaker and guardian of freedom, Carter oversaw the Nicaraguan elections that ousted the Sandinistas. He brokered a cease-fire between Bosnian Muslims and Serbs. He pressed China to release political prisoners. He has helped set up or observed fair elections in Indonesia, China, Nigeria, Mozambique, and several other developing countries. He was the first former U.S. president to visit Cuba. For these acts of courage, idealism, and service, he received the Presidential Medal of Freedom and the first United Nations Human Rights Prize. In 2002, at 78, he won the Nobel Peace Prize.

It has been said that Carter "used his presidency as a stepping stone to higher things" (Bird, 1990, p. 564). Freed from the pressures of politics, he has risen to the role of elder statesman.

Carter has written more than 15 books, one of the most recent being *The Virtues of Aging*. What does Carter see as the virtues of aging? "We have an unprecedented degree of freedom to choose what we want to do . . . We have a chance to heal wounds . . . We have an opportunity to expand the ties of understanding with the people we love most." And there are still new worlds to conquer. "Our primary purpose," says Carter, "is not just to stay alive . . . but to savor every opportunity for pleasure, excitement, adventure, and fulfillment" (Beyette, 1998, pp. 6A–7A).

JIMMY CARTER'S "FORCED RETIREMENT" WAS more publicized than most, and few adults have the resources and opportunities of an ex-president. But Carter is far from unique in using his retirement years productively. He is one of many older adults whose late-life activism is leading to a new view of how life can be structured throughout adulthood.

The typical life structure in industrialized societies is **age-differentiated:** roles are based on age (as in the left side of Figure 8.1). Young people's primary role is that of students. Young and middle-aged adults are predominately workers. Older adults organize their lives around retirement and leisure. Yet, as Matilda Riley (1994), a senior social scientist at the National Institute on Aging, observed:

> . . . these structures fail to accommodate many of the changes in people's lives. After all, does it make sense to spend nearly one-third of adult lifetime in retirement? Or to crowd most work into the harried middle years? Or to label as "too old" those as young as 55 who want to work? Does it make sense to assume that . . . physically capable older people—an estimated 40 million of them in the next century—should expect greater support *from* society than they contribute *to* society? . . .Surely, something will have to change! (p. 445)

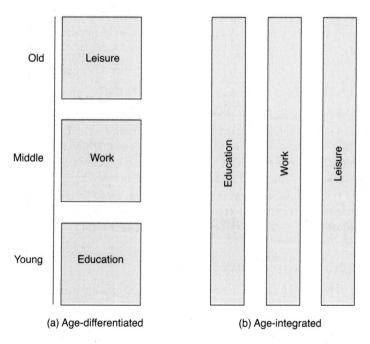

(a) Age-differentiated   (b) Age-integrated

FIGURE 8.1 *Contrasting social structures.* (a) Traditional age-differentiated structure, typical of industrialized societies. Education, work, and leisure roles are largely "assigned" to different phases of life. (b) Age-integrated structure which would spread all three kinds of roles throughout the adult life span and help break down social barriers between generations.   *SOURCE:* M. W. Riley, 1994, p. 445.

CRITICAL THINKING

How do distinctions between work and leisure pursuits change through the adult years?

Age-differentiated roles are a holdover from an earlier era, when life was shorter and social institutions were less diverse. The result is a *structural lag*: increasing numbers of older adults are able to contribute to society, but opportunities to use and reward their abilities are inadequate. Also, by devoting themselves to one aspect of life at a time, people do not enjoy each period of life as much as they might and may not prepare themselves adequately for the next phase. For example, by concentrating on work, adults may forget how to play; then, when they retire, they may not know what to do with a sudden abundance of leisure time.

In an **age-integrated** society (as in the right side of Figure 8.1), all kinds of roles—learning, working, and playing—would be open to adults of all ages (Bolles, 1979; Riley, 1994). They could intersperse periods of education, work, and leisure throughout the life span. Things seem to be moving in that direction. College students may take work-study programs or "stop out" for a while before resuming their education. Middle-aged and older adults may go back to school or take, say, a year off work to pursue a special interest. A person may have several careers in succession, each requiring additional education or training. People may retire earlier or later than in the past, or not at all. Retirees may devote time to study or or a new line of work.

As we discuss education, work, leisure, and retirement, keep in mind that much of the research reflects the older, age-differentiated model of social roles, and the cohorts whose lives it describes. With "age integration" emerging in many societies, future cohorts may have very different experiences and attitudes.

EDUCATION

CRITICAL THINKING

When do you expect to stop working on your education formally? What are your plans for lifelong educational pursuits?

One of the last drawings by the Spanish artist Francisco de Goya—made in his eighties—is a sketch of an old man hobbling on a crutch and cane. On it, Goya wrote *Aún aprendo:* "I keep learning" (Lewis, 1968). Although formal education traditionally ends in young adulthood, people continue to learn from the school of life. And today more and more adults of all ages are enrolling in educational programs to gain degrees, learn new skills, pursue interests, improve literacy, or keep up with the challenges and opportunities of the world of work—or simply because they enjoy learning.

College and University Studies

The face of higher education in the United States is changing. More people than ever are receiving degrees. More people than ever, especially more women, are receiving degrees. Of young adults ages 25 to 29 in 2003, 28 percent had completed bachelor's degrees, 1 percent less than the record high set in 2002 (U.S. Bureau of the Census, 2004). College completion rates for women in that age group exceeded rates for young men (32 percent and 27 percent, respectively). Approximately 58 percent of all degrees granted for the 2001 to 2002 school year were awarded to women. Women earned more associate's, bachelor's, and master's degrees than men. Although men still earned more doctoral (53 percent) and professional (52 percent) degrees, the percentage of women earning such degrees was greater than in previous years (NCES, 2005a).

Undergraduate enrollment reached 14.3 million in 2002, nearly double that in 1970 (NCES, 2005). This increase has been accompanied by a decrease in the proportion of "traditional" students (those who enroll full time immediately after high school, work part time or not at all, and are financially dependent on parents). Such students now account for only 27 percent of undergraduates. Forty-four percent of undergraduates are enrolled in two-year colleges, and 39 percent are enrolled part time (NCES, 2002).

"Nontraditional" students, by contrast, represent a growing proportion of the student body in postsecondary education. Among undergraduates, 43 percent are 24 and older, and 56 percent are women. In addition, 27 percent have dependents, 13 percent are single parents, and 80 percent are employed, 39 percent full time (NCES, 2002). Nontraditional students include married or divorced women who need to increase their income, "empty nesters" seeking midlife careers, and women who are striving to be independent and self-supporting.

Many colleges make it easy for students to take leaves of absence or to earn credit for independent study or work done at other institutions, and some actively seek mature students who may have dropped out years before. Most colleges give credit for life experience and previous learning. They also attempt to accommodate the practical needs of students of nontraditional age through part-time matriculation, Saturday and night classes, independent study, on-campus child care, financial aid, free or reduced-tuition courses, and "distance learning" via computers or closed-circuit broadcasts. Adults who choose to go back to school are highly motivated. They bring individuality and life experience to the classroom.

The number of minority students in higher education has nearly doubled since 1980. Minorities made up 25 percent of undergraduate enrollment in four year institutions and 36 percent in public two year institutions (NCES, 2005b) during 2002. The number of African Americans with four or more years of college increased more from 1990 to 2004 (6.3 percent) than in the previous 20 years (4.8 percent). In comparison, the number of white Americans with equivalent educational attainment grew 10.3 percent from 1970 to 1990 but 6.2 percent from 1990 to 2004. Participation rates for minority women have grown more rapidly since 1990 than rates for black, white, and Hispanic men. However, the percentage of the minority population with degrees still lags behind that of whites. In 2004, 26.4 percent of white women and 30.0 percent of white men ages 25 and over had completed 4 or more years of college. Comparable figures are 18.5 and 16.6 percent for black women and men and 12.3 and 11.8 percent for Hispanic women and men, respectively (U.S. Bureau of the Census, 2005).

These statistics are important because education is a key to employment, especially in today's rapidly changing workplace. Persons with lower levels of education are more likely to be unemployed than those with higher levels of educational attainment. Based on 1999 earnings averages, lifetime earnings

CRITICAL THINKING

How does your motivation to attend classes and complete coursework compare to that of your peers and to that of younger and older adults you have observed?

are estimated to be approximately $0.5 million for high school graduates and $1 million—twice as much—for holders of bachelor's degrees. However, men continue to earn more than women at each level of education. Men with professional degrees, such as doctors or lawyers, will earn approximately $2 million more than women with equivalent degrees over their lifetimes. (U.S. Bureau of the Census, 2002).

Lifelong Learning

CRITICAL THINKING

What changes can we expect in higher education to promote lifelong learning?

Qian Likun, a star student who walks to his classes on health care and ancient Chinese poetry, took part in a 2.3-mile foot race. This might not seem unusual, until you learn that Qian is 102 years old, one of thousands of students in China's network of "universities for the aged." More than 800 of these schools have been founded since the 1980s, showing China's commitment to its elderly population—and older people's willingness and ability to learn everything from basic reading and writing to esoteric subjects (Kristof, 1990). China's program exemplifies a trend toward **lifelong learning**—organized, sustained study by adults of all ages.

Educational programs specifically designed for mature adults are booming in many parts of the world. Elderhostel, for example, is an international network of approximately 1,600 educational and cultural institutions in more than 90 countries, offering nearly 10,000 lower-cost, noncredit travel and education programs each year. These programs combine learning and leisure activities for adults age 55 and over and are designed to foster learning as a lifelong pursuit. Programs vary considerably; they may include traditional opportunities to study arts and culture, outdoor activities such as hiking or kayaking, or opportunities to combine volunteer service with learning. Research on Elderhostel has found that satisfaction with the learning experience has no relationship to age (Abraham, 1998). This finding supports the purpose of the organization: to provide innovative approaches to lifelong learning, under the assumption that "sharing new ideas, challenges, and experiences is rewarding in every season of life."

Since establishment of the Act for Lifelong Learning in 1949, the government of Japan has officially supported learning as a lifelong process. *Kouminkans* (adult community educational centers) were established and government financial subsidies provided to encourage lifelong education and learning. Programs include a variety of educational, hobby, and sports activities. Japanese companies, to encourage updating of workplace skills, commonly subsidize courses and offer money to employees obtaining certificates or diplomas in a wide range of subjects (Kobayashi, 1996). However, "mature" students (22 years and older) make up less than one percent of undergraduate and ten percent of graduate enrollment in universities (Fuwa, 2001).

In the United States, today's older adults are better educated than their predecessors, and this trend will continue as younger cohorts age (Federal Interagency Forum on Aging-Related Statistics, 2004). Ninety percent of the employed civilian labor force have high school diplomas (U.S. Bureau of the

Census, 2000). The National Center for Education Statistics (NCES) lists a variety of available formal lifelong learning activities, including basic training skills, apprenticeships, work-related training, courses of personal interest, and English as a Second Language (ESL) courses. Excluding traditional-age college students ages 16 to 24, participation in adult education programs increased from 34 percent of U.S. adults in 1991 to 47 percent 2001. More than half of the participants engaged in learning utilizing some form of technology, such as computers, computer conferencing, and Web-based instruction. The highest rates of participation in adult education were among women, whites, Asian and Pacific Islanders, and those with higher levels of educational attainment (NCES, 2002). Three out of four participants in part-time educational activities are between 25 and 34 years old (Kopka, Schantz, & Korb, 1998).

Work-related courses are reported to be the most prevalent form of lifelong learning among nontraditional-age students (30 percent), followed by personal interest courses (21 percent). Much of the work-related education is employer supported (Kopka et al., 1998). More than 40 percent of the workforce and more than 50 percent of high school graduates lack basic skills needed in their jobs, according to a government-assisted survey of more than 40 public and private employers in a variety of fields. Employers see benefits of workplace education in improved morale, increased quality of work, better teamwork and problem solving, and greater ability to cope with new technology and other changes in the workplace. Employees also gain in such basic skills as reading, math, and critical thinking (Conference Board, 1999).

Why do mature adults go to school? A review of the literature (Willis, 1985) identified five common goals:

1. *To gain adaptive knowledge and skills,* often to keep up with new developments in their fields, move up the career ladder, or prepare to go into business for themselves. In the United States, almost two-thirds of adults who take part-time classes do so for job-related reasons (U.S. Department of Education, 1986).
2. *To train for new occupations* when their old ones become obsolete or when their needs and interests change. Some middle-aged women who have devoted their young adult years to homemaking and parenthood are taking the first steps toward reentering the job market.
3. *To understand and cope with technological and cultural change,* such as the use of computers (see Box 8.1). Older adults often want to talk with children and grandchildren who are computer literate, to send and receive e-mail, or to explore the Internet.
4. *To understand their own aging processes,* particularly changes in memory and other aspects of cognition, and to learn strategies for making the most of their abilities.
5. *To develop new and satisfying retirement and leisure roles;* for example, studying a foreign language to prepare for travel abroad. People who are close to retirement often want to explore interests they didn't have time to pursue earlier in life.

Computer Training: Teaching Older Adults New Tricks

At a college in New Orleans that offers free mini-courses for people age 65 or older, by far the most popular offering is computer training. Each semester more than 100 students enroll, and the waiting list is equally long. Work training programs of the American Association of Retired Persons (AARP) cannot begin to accommodate all the requests for introductory or advanced courses in using computers and word processing.

Why do so many older adults want to learn to use computers? Some are just curious. Some need to acquire new job skills or update old ones. Some want to keep up with the latest technology: to communicate with children and grandchildren who are computer-literate, or to emulate friends who are on the information highway.

Initially, there were indications that some older adults had less positive attitudes toward computers than younger ones—that they considered computers dehumanizing (Brickfield, 1984; Nickerson, 1981). A randomized telephone survey in 1981 found that use of computers decreased with age (from 40 percent among 45- to 54-year-olds down to 19 percent among people 65 and older) but was also related to socioeconomic status and educational level. The survey found similar patterns for other technological innovations: electronic calculators, video recorders, video games, and electronic teller machines (Brickfield, 1984).

Today, as computers have become more affordable and easier to use, computer usage has become more evenly distributed across age groups. Approximately 70 percent of the population ages 25 to 50 use computers. After age 50 computer usage tapers off, but even among those age 70 and above computer usage increased from approximately 5 percent in 1991 to greater than 25 percent in 2001 (U.S. Department of Commerce, 2002). A portion of these increases is likely due to cohort effects, as those who responded to surveys in 1991 are not the same group of people responding in 2001. Other contributing factors are the increase in income and education level of the older population as the baby boom generation ages.

Research consistently shows that older adults can be trained to become computer-literate (Garfein, Schaie, & Willis, 1988; Hartley, Hartley, & Johnson, 1984; Rogers & Fisk, 2000). Older people's performance on computer tasks improves with time and experience (Czaja & Sharit, 1998, 1999; Czaja 2001), but they may take longer than younger people to master skills,

With the increase in longevity, there will be a growing interest in educational programs that can make retirement more meaningful and enjoyable. And with the disparity in life expectancy between men and women, there is a growing need for educational programs for widows, focusing on independent living, management of personal finances, and development of new relationships.

It seems clear that in today's complex society, education is never finished. Getting a college degree in one's early twenties will not be enough for most adults in the future. Expanding technology and shifting job markets will re-

and they may need more help (Charness, Schumann, & Boritz, 1992; Elias, Elias, Robbins, & Gage, 1987; Zandri & Charness, 1989). Well-educated older adults who went through 2 weeks of training in desktop publishing ended up more comfortable and more confident about their abilities (Jay & Willis, 1992). A recent study in Ontario, Canada, found that, for both younger and older adults, anxiety before training in word processing did not affect final performance. The researchers observed, "If older adults can be persuaded to seek retraining, despite any initial negative attitudes, their success in training will be more a function of their training program than their attitudes" (Charness et al., 1992, pp. 103–104). One caution: The participants in this research were volunteers, who wanted to learn word processing and presumably believed they could do it. The findings may not apply to people who are required to undergo computer training in job situations.

Do older people need special training techniques? In general, the answer is no: the most effective methods for younger adults are also best for older adults (Charness et al., 1992). For example, modeling the use of a computer along with a tutorial program is more effective than a tutorial alone (Gist, Rosen, & Schwoerer, 1988); and having an instructor and a manual is better than totally computer-based training. In the Canadian study, a self-paced method worked better than fixed pacing for both age groups. However, the pace of training can be more critical for older learners than for younger ones (Charness et al., 1992).

The following suggestions, which reflect a need to be sensitive to biological and cognitive changes that commonly occur with advancing age (Charness et al., 1992, 2001; Rogers & Fisk, 2000; Zandri & Charness, 1989), can facilitate computer instruction for older adults:

- Offer slower or self-paced instruction, and expect older learners to take longer than younger ones.
- Do hands-on training, perhaps in pairs or in small groups.
- Have an instructor available to answer questions about unfamiliar concepts and terms.
- Give older learners more help with novel problems.
- Monitor progress to forestall any problems that might sap confidence.
- Use a menu- rather than command-based interface.

quire a lifespan approach to education. Individuals must be prepared to have several careers, each perhaps quite different from the others. And as some occupations become obsolete and others emerge or require new skills, retraining will become more and more essential.

Lifelong learning experiences that hold the most appeal for mature adults deal with subjects that are personally meaningful, taught in environments that provide direct learning experiences, allow adults control over all aspects of the learning process, and are not too expensive. Older adults are most interested in learning about things that enrich their lives, that help them stay healthy, and that bring them enjoyment (AARP, 2000). One special need of many adults of all ages is literacy training.

Adult Illiteracy

Ed is a 29-year-old silkscreen printer, a trade he learned in high school. Because he's quick-witted, personable, and determined, his employers and co-workers do not realize, at first, that he cannot read beyond a fourth- or fifth-grade level. "I've lost lots of jobs because of my reading problem," he says (Feldman, 1985).

According to national and international literacy surveys conducted during the 1990s, nearly half of U.S. adults cannot understand written material, manipulate numbers, and use documents well enough to succeed in today's economy (Sum, Kirsch, & Taggart, 2002). In 2003, U.S. adults performed worse on an international literacy test than adults in Bermuda, Norway, and Switzerland but better than those in Italy (Lemke, et al. 2003). People at the lowest literacy levels were more likely to be unemployed. For U.S. test takers, the single most important factor in literacy continues to be level of educational attainment. Nearly half of adults in the United States received scores representing the lowest levels of literacy in a nationwide survey. Surprisingly, these adults represent all levels of education and occupations. Although years and level of education are important factors, quality of education and socioeconomic status also make a difference (U.S. Department of Education, 2001).

Nearly 800 million adults in the world were illiterate in 2002. Illiteracy is especially common among women in developing countries, where education typically is considered unimportant for females. The widest-ranging evaluation ever carried out in basic education has shown that, although significant progress has been achieved in some countries, illiteracy is still a fact of the twenty-first century—in both developing and developed countries—despite the universality of primary schooling (UNESCO, 2004). Unfortunately, in many developing countries more than half their youth and adult populations are illiterate—and two-thirds of these are girls and women.

Illiteracy creates its own vicious cycle, decreasing opportunities for many adults and contributing to a social stigma that keeps many who need basic skills training from seeking it. Because literacy is a fundamental requisite for participation in a modern, information-driven economy, expansion of literacy programs—the most basic form of adult education—is a pressing need.

CRITICAL THINKING

What explanations do you have for the large discrepancy in educational attainment across the life span by people in various nations?

WORK AND LEISURE

"What do you do?" is often the first question one adult asks when meeting another. What work adults do is central to who they are. Work is entwined with all aspects of development. Intellectual, physical, social, and emotional factors affect our work; and our work can affect every other area of our lives.

First, let's define some terms that are used, sometimes interchangeably, to describe work. A *job* can be any activity performed for pay, but this term typically refers to employment by someone or some organization other than oneself. A job may be temporary or transient. The term *occupation,* by contrast, refers to a regular, relatively permanent field of work or means of livelihood. The term *vocation* usually refers to a chosen field. A *profession* is an occupation or vocation that generally requires college or postgraduate training and involves a good deal of independent judgment and control. The word *career* has a dynamic quality; it is a developmental path of achievement, which, if followed to its natural conclusion, may represent a life's work.

Leisure is discretionary use of time. Leisure time is free time, when people are not gainfully employed and can do whatever they wish. The line between work and leisure is not always easy to draw. The same type of activity—say, photography—may be work for one person and a leisure pursuit for another, and both may enjoy it equally. Leisure activities normally have no monetary reward; but what about a Sunday painter who occasionally sells a canvas at an art fair, or a homeowner who picks up pocket money by having a garage sale?

Only in modern, developed societies is leisure a significant aspect of adult life, and not until after retirement does it become a central focus. The United States in the 1930s adopted an 8-hour, 5-day work week for most of the population; paid vacations also became standard. Still, many workers who are starting or running businesses or trying to get ahead in their careers have little leisure time.

In this section, let's look at how people choose vocations and develop careers. Then we'll describe changing occupational patterns. We'll consider how age affects work performance. We'll discuss stress and burnout. Finally, we'll examine the interaction of work, leisure, and intellectual growth. In the next section, we'll discuss how adults use leisure time in retirement.

Vocational Choice and Career Development

What influences decisions about vocation? How do adults progress along their chosen career paths? Why do some people have stable careers, while others go through one or more changes?

PARSONS: TRAITS, ABILITIES, AND INTERESTS

In an early study of career selection, Frank Parsons (1909) developed a method for matching individuals to appropriate careers based on their traits and abilities. An initial assessment deals with past achievements, current skills and abilities, and aptitudes (the potential for developing new skills). Work and general interests are also examined. This information can then be used to identify specific types of tasks for which a person is suited. One well-known instrument for vocational guidance, the Strong Interest Inventory, relates interests to occupational success (Sharf, 1992). Its developers collected information about the interests of a group of people who did well in and were happy about their jobs or careers. Thus test takers can see how their interests match up with those of successful people in various occupations.

HOLLAND: PERSONALITY TYPES AND VOCATION

John Holland (1985) matched six personality types—investigative, social, realistic, artistic, conventional, and enterprising—with corresponding occupations or work environments. According to Holland's theory, people with predominantly *investigative* personalities are likely to become scientists or detectives; *social* types may choose mental health or teaching; *realistic* people may be mechanics or electricians; *artistic* people become writers, artists, or musicians; *conventional* people go into accounting or banking; and *enterprising* people enter sales or management. Women tend to show artistic, social, and conventional traits and to go into corresponding occupations. Job satisfaction is highest when a personality type matches the work environment, and the worker is most likely to stay in that position. Of course, neither people nor work environments can be described in terms of a single "pure" trait; the question is which type is predominant.

Holland's theory has been influential, particularly in the development of personality inventories used in vocational guidance. But it has several important limitations. First, some jobs require a mix of traits and skills, and some people are happiest in such jobs. Second, Holland's theory does not deal with environmental or cultural forces that limit or influence career choices. What jobs are available at a given time and place will depend in part on the physical environment and its exploitation. A person living in a coal-mining area is more likely to become a miner than is a person growing up in a major urban

© Tim Barnwell/Stock Boston

Does personality determine occupational choice? One theory says yes. Gender makes a difference, even after four decades of the women's movement; for instance, the vast majority of nurses are women.

center. Socioeconomic differences, including educational opportunities, often limit vocational choice.

Gender, too, makes a difference. A poll of teen career interests suggests that male and female students still tend to gravitate to stereotypical careers and job roles. College-educated women still choose "pink collar" jobs such as nursing and teaching, neither of which are often chosen by college-educated men (Gallup, 2003).

Finally, Holland's theory fails to explain *how* the choice of a career—the vital match-up between personality and work environment—occurs, or how careers develop across the adult life span. The work environment itself can be an agent of change; for example, an electrician hired to help with lighting in a theater might discover an artistic bent and begin to specialize in theatrical lighting. The interaction between person and environment is dynamic.

Research has raised additional questions about the validity of the theory. For example, people's expectations seem to have more effect on their job satisfaction than does the match between personality type and job. Holland (1996) has recently revised his theory to include interactive effects between the individual and the work environment, the role of *vocational identity* in job satisfaction, and the role of personality in career stability and job satisfaction. **Vocational identity** is the level of clarity and stability of one's goals, interests, personality, and talents and how these factors influence decision making in an ambiguous environment (Carson & Mowsesian, 1993).

SUPER: STAGES IN CAREER PLANNING AND DEVELOPMENT

Some theorists who take an organismic perspective have proposed that vocational choice and career development occur in stages.

Donald Super's (1957, 1985) influential theory encompasses eight stages of career exploration and development from puberty through adulthood, which evolve along with a person's maturing self-concept. These stages are (1) crystallization, (2) specification, (3) implementation, (4) establishment, (5) consolidation, (6) maintenance, (7) deceleration, and (8) retirement. (George Vaillant and Daniel Levinson, whose theories of personality development we discuss in Chapter 11, describe somewhat similar stages of career development.)

During the **crystallization stage,** in early adolescence, a person has only vague, general ideas about a career. According to Erikson's theory of personality development (see Table 2.2 in Chapter 2), identity confusion is typical of the teenage years. As young people begin to develop a firm sense of self, they develop a concept of occupation as a defining feature of the self.

In the **specification stage,** from late adolescence into the college years, young people learn more about various occupations and about what goes on in the workplace. They begin to focus on specific career tracks and recognize that choosing one vocation requires abandoning other possibilities.

The **implementation stage** begins in the early twenties. Young adults try out one or more entry-level jobs or start professional training. Coming face to face with the actual world of work may lead to changes of mind before making a final career choice.

In the **establishment stage,** which starts in the mid twenties, young adults have made a commitment to a career goal—advancement along a chosen path. They now see their work as an intrinsic part of their self-concept.

On the basis of expertise developed during the establishment stage, adults in the mid thirties move into the **consolidation stage.** They strive to move up in their fields as fast and as far as possible, continually consolidating their gains as a firm footing for the next step up the ladder.

By middle age, career goals either have been met or are now seen as out of reach, and the urge to advance slackens. During the **maintenance stage,** which generally begins in the mid forties, middle-aged people focus on maintaining, rather than acquiring, prestige, authority, and responsibility.

People may reduce their workload as they gradually shift into the **deceleration stage** in the late fifties, when they face the need to retire in the not-too-distant future and gradually begin to distance themselves from their work, both physically and emotionally. Those whose self-concept is too deeply enmeshed in work may have difficulty letting go.

Finally, the **retirement stage,** which traditionally begins at age 65, brings formal separation from the job and requires adjustment to lack of a career as a defining feature of the self.

Super's theory, then, sees career decisions as based on a rational, realistic understanding of the self and the world of work. However, critics question the idea that a clear self-concept guides career development and point out that career paths often do not proceed in such an orderly, reasoned manner; they are often more a result of luck or emotional factors. Nor does the theory take account of constraints on the freedom to make career decisions (Neff, 1985).

Super's theory was developed at a time when fewer women worked outside the home, and decisions made in the late teens or twenties often shaped a man's entire working life. Today many people start second, third, or even fourth or fifth careers at some point during adulthood, and retirement at 65 no longer is as typical as it was during the 1950s. A universal set of stages does not seem to adequately explain the many ways careers develop.

Changing Occupational Patterns

CRITICAL THINKING

In what ways will changing patterns in the workplace affect the life quality of older adults?

The structure of the American workforce is changing profoundly. For the first time, there are more people in executive, professional, and technical jobs (nearly 1 out of 3 workers) than in manufacture or transport of goods (1 in 5). The number of white-collar jobs jumped 38 percent from 1980 to 1990, while the number of skilled blue-collar jobs declined. Only 4 percent of the work force have unskilled jobs (U.S. Bureau of the Census, 2000). One result has been a sharp decline in job opportunities and wages for less educated workers (Eisenberg, 1995).

Current workplace changes include loss of manufacturing jobs; a shift to service and knowledge work; downsizing of organizations; trends toward flatter hierarchies with fewer managers or supervisors, which put more responsibility on more workers; and increasing focus on the need for higher, more efficient productivity (NIOSH, 2002). More than 28 percent of U.S. employees were on flexible work schedules in 1998 (BLS, 1999, 2001); white men in managerial or professional occupations were the most likely to work a flexible schedule. As organizations transition from pyramidal to flatter, more streamlined configurations through downsizing and restructuring, middle-aged and older employees may experience job loss, job plateauing, and skills obsolescence (Farr, Telsuk, & Klein, 1998; Sterns & Miklos, 1995). Older workers may be singled out in downsizing on the basis of such stereotypes as being considered unsuitable for retraining or for fast-paced work environments (Hall & Mirvis, 1995a; Hall & Mirvis, 1995b; Mirvis & Hall, 1996). Furthermore, depending on age of career entry, middle-aged and older workers may be more likely to occupy the midlevel managerial positions that are often the focus of downsizing and restructuring strategies. Additionally, slow company growth may lead to less opportunity for advancement (Farr, Tesluk, & Klein, 1998). These changes suggest that older workers may need to take increased responsibility for their career management (Sterns & Gray, 1999; Sterns & Kaplan, 2003).

Organizational changes are altering the nature of the relationship between organizations and employees (Hall & Mirvis, 1996). Employers' commitment to employees may last only as long as there is need for their skills and performance. Similarly, employees' commitment to the employer may last only as long as their expectations are met. These changes place greater emphasis on employees' adaptability and their abilities in learning to learn (Hall & Mirvis, 1996).

GENDER IN THE WORKPLACE

Women made up 47 percent of the total labor force in 2003 (Dept. of Labor, 2003). The increase in women's employment is a global phenomenon (see Figure 8.2). A longer life span means that women no longer spend most or all of their adult lives raising children (Rowe & Kahn, 1998). Trends toward later marriage, later childbearing, and smaller families, as well as flexible schedules and job sharing, have made it easier for women in some countries to pursue occupational goals. Still, women throughout much of the world tend to have clerical, sales, and service jobs, especially during the child-rearing years (UNESCO, 2000).

In the United States, gender has far less to do with vocational choice than before. But while there are more American women in business, government, and the professions than in the past, the top ranks are still male-dominated. U.S. women have far more varied occupational choices than in the past, and their relative earnings have improved as more women have moved into traditionally male fields. In 2002, half of all managerial and professional specialty positions were held by women, up from 41 percent in 1983 (BLS, 2004). Still the largest occupational group of female professionals is the 4.2 million female teachers, who in 2002 constituted 35 percent of professional women (BLS, 2004). Women constitute 98 percent of preschool and kindergarten teachers, as well as 96 percent of administrative assistants and secretaries, 80 percent of elementary school teachers, and 90 percent of registered nurses, but only 15 percent of chemical engineers (BLS, 2004).

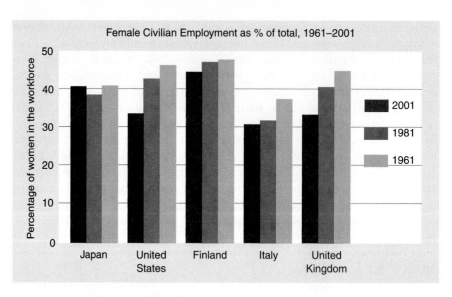

FIGURE 8.2 *Women and work.* Internationally, women still account for less than half of the overall workforce. However, in 2003, nearly 60 percent of the U.S. female population held a job outside of the home (U.S. Department of Labor, 2004), up from slightly less than 50 percent in 2001. *SOURCE:* OECD Labor Force Statistics.

Laws mandating equal opportunity in employment are designed to give both sexes equal rights in hiring, pay, and promotion. But reality still falls far short of this ideal. On average, women's earnings are approximately 78 percent of men's (BLS, 2004), and the picture is no brighter for women in managerial and professional positions. Although college graduates in 2002 overall earned 76 percent more than those with only a high school diploma, female college graduates had median earnings of $809 per week, compared with $1,089 for male college graduates (BLS, 2003). Still, college-educated women's earnings (adjusted for inflation) have risen nearly 27 percent since 1979, while men's real earnings increased only 1 percent (BLS, 2004).

MINORITIES IN THE WORKPLACE

Employment rates and wages of African Americans have fallen in comparison with those of white people, despite the strides made by blacks since 1940 in education. About 80 percent of young adults of both races now finish high school, and differences in standardized test scores have narrowed. But more white people still go to college and qualify for better-paying jobs. Unemployment rates for African Americans (10.2 percent) and Hispanic Americans (7.6 percent) are nearly twice as high as for white people (5.1 percent). (BLS, 2002).

Overall, black men working full-time earn only 75 percent as much as white men, and black women make 86 percent as much as white women. In 2002, median earnings of Hispanics ($423 a week) were lower than those of either black ($498 a week) or white ($624 a week) workers (BLS, 2002). Even at the highest professional levels, income disparities are great. Black men earn only 79 percent of what white men in similar positions earn, and black women only 57 percent (BLS, 2004).

Age and Job Performance

Does age affect performance on the job? In view of the increasing number of age-discrimination cases, the elimination of mandatory retirement for most occupations, and the increasing number of older workers, there has been a growing need for an understanding of the relationship between age and work performance. Researchers' inability to find a consistent linear relationship between age and work performance may suggest that such a relationship does not exist (Sterns, Junkins, & Bayer, 2001).

CRITICAL THINKING
Why is it necessary to enact laws to ensure that competent older workers have opportunities to work and earn wages to support themselves?

Studies on absenteeism give conflicting results. Apparently that is because younger workers have more avoidable absences than older workers (possibly owing to a lower level of commitment), while older workers have more unavoidable absences (probably owing to poorer health and slower recovery from accidents).

When we look at how well adults do their work, the picture again is not clear-cut. Experience has been found to be a better predictor of performance than age is (Sterns & Gray, 1999). When older people perform better, it may be because they have been on a job longer; and people in older cohorts may have changed jobs less than younger people. In general, age differences seem to depend largely on how performance is measured and on the demands of a specific kind of work.

In a study of inexperienced persons asked to learn and perform an information search and retrieval task utilizing a computer database, differences in quantitative output were mediated by speed. Any differences between younger and older workers in the number of searches completed were due to decline in physical speed associated with aging. No differences were found in efficacy of navigation; and although there was a difference in how accurately each task was documented, that difference decreased over three days of testing. After the first day of testing (following completion of training), middle-aged adults improved the most on days 3 and 4, but the oldest improved the most from days 4 to 5 (Czaja, Sharit, et al., 2001). Thus, while older workers may learn more slowly, differences in performance decrease and may disappear over time. Another examination of computer skills, this time among experienced computer programmers, found no differences among age groups in specialized skills (Perry et al., 2003). This suggests that the older workers are keeping up with younger workers by updating their skills to remain marketable. These findings contrast with stereotypes of the older worker as unwilling to change or learn new skills.

Attitudes toward work can affect performance. Young adults tend to be less satisfied with their work than older adults are (Salthouse & Maurer, 1996). A job requiring quick reflexes is likely to be done better by a young person; a job that depends on mature judgment may be better handled by an

Age Discrimination and Public Safety

Should the police, firefighters, prison guards, and others doing dangerous work essential to public safety be required to retire at age 65?

When the United States Congress amended the Age Discrimination in Employment Act (ADEA) in 1986 to outlaw mandatory retirement, it left an exception for public safety officers, pending study of whether older workers could be counted on to protect the public.

An interdisciplinary task force commissioned by Congress spent almost 2 years reviewing more than 5,000 research articles and collecting data from more than 500 cities. The chair was Frank Landy (1992, 1994), professor of psychology and director of the Center for Applied Behavioral Sciences at Pennsylvania State University. The task force examined effects of age on critical abilities, as well as the probability that a disabling medical emergency, such as a heart attack or stroke, would occur on the job, endangering the public.

The research team uncovered some interesting facts. The age at which public safety officers were required to retire in various places ranged from 55 to 72. Only 30 percent of an officer's time was spent on tasks that directly involved public safety; the rest of the time, a firefighter, for example, might be cleaning equipment, cooking meals, inspecting dwellings for smoke detectors, or giving tours of the firehouse to schoolchildren.

The study, echoing lifespan psychologists, found that physical fitness and mental abilities varied increasingly with age and differed more within age groups than between age groups. In fact, 60- to 65-year-old public safety officers were more fit overall than 45- to 55-year-olds, probably because those who are not fit leave such jobs early. Any decline in abilities critical to performing public safety tasks was slight, on average, and was not uniform; some people declined faster than others, some not at all, and some improved with age, depending largely on lifestyle, nutrition, exercise, and health.

The conclusion? Tests of specific psychological, physical, and perceptual-motor abilities can predict job performance far better than a person's age. Furthermore, the likelihood is

older person. Older workers are often more productive than younger workers. Although they might work slower than younger people, they tend to be more accurate (Czaja & Sharit, 1998; Salthouse & Maurer, 1996; Treas, 1995). The most appropriate conclusion is that each individual, regardless of age, should be evaluated based on her or his own merits, skills, abilities, and motivation, and not based on the stereotypic characteristics of a particular age group with which she or he happens to be associated (Sterns & Gray, 1999).

A comprehensive study commissioned by the United States Congress found that, even in such highly demanding, responsible work as policing and firefighting, age in and of itself does not appear to be an accurate predictor of job performance (see Box 8.2). Many older workers are not only experienced and skilled but also dependable, loyal, and respectful of authority (AARP, 1999).

very small that a disabling medical emergency such as a heart attack or stroke will jeopardize performance of a critical task. In a 500-member police department, such an episode might occur only once in 25 years. And because many tasks directly involving public safety are done in teams, a partner could take over in such a rare event. The task force noted that older officers often move into safe desk jobs, where they can share their knowledge with younger workers. The researchers recommended replacing the mandatory retirement age with tests (which already exist) to assess the ability of particular individuals to perform on the job. The bottom line? There are no grounds for the idea that older workers *as a group* endanger public safety.

However, that is not the end of the story. During the Congressional debates, unions representing public safety officers attacked the methods, procedures, results, and even the goals and motives of the study. They opposed forcing older workers to undergo periodic fitness tests, a proposal they had consistently fought in con-

tract negotiations. The unions also feared that the report, in downplaying the risks and stress of public safety work, would call into question their members' large pension benefits (Landy, 1994). The mandatory retirement exemption for public safety officers was allowed to expire at the end of 1993, but Congress in 1996 reinstated the exception and repealed the expiration date. Early in 2000, the U.S. Supreme Court held that state employees challenging age bias in employment have protection only from their state statute and no longer from federal law (Sterns, Doverspike, & Lax, 2005). Thus, mandatory retirement cases involving public safety workers will have to be tested at the state court level.

Political fallout aside, the task force established a benchmark that will have an influence beyond this specific legislation. Its findings and recommendations have already begun to be cited in court cases. Landy (1994) concludes that there is "a clear recognition now of the scientific foundation for eliminating this last vestige of age discrimination" (p. 20).

Yet managers often assume that older workers are less energetic, less efficient, less flexible, and unwilling or unable to adapt to change; therefore, companies are less likely to invest in their training. In hard times older workers have tended to be first to be laid off or pushed into retirement ("Negative Stereotypes," 1995; "Older Workers," 1993). However, Labor Department statistics indicate that older workers did well compared to younger workers in the 2003 recession (*New York Times,* 9/8/03). Although such positive signs for older workers are due in part to demographic changes as the baby boomers inch toward retirement age, the positive numbers remain even when this demographic shift is accounted for.

When discussing stereotypes of workers, it is important to recognize both stereotypes of older adults and stereotypes of older workers. Although the content of these stereotypes undoubtedly overlaps, there are also differences. Stereotypes of older adults seem to encompass older ages and include a wider range of contexts. Stereotypes of older workers encompass relatively younger ages and relate specifically to the work context (Sterns & Gray, 1999).

Although psychologists have made substantial progress in dispelling age stereotypes, it is abundantly clear that there is work left to do. This is especially true in the workplace," writes Frank J. Landy (1994, p. 10), then director of the Center for Applied Behavioral Sciences at Pennsylvania State University. The Age Discrimination in Employment Act (ADEA), as amended in 1986, protects most workers age 40 and older from being denied a job, fired, paid lower wages, or forced to retire because of age. The law applies to firms with 20 or more employees. ADEA has eliminated some blatant practices, such as help-wanted ads that specify "age 25 to 35." But, as Landy (1994, p. 10) observes, "many employers have been reluctant to recognize" the protections against age discrimination built into ADEA. Complaints of unfair terminations and pay and promotional policies and unequal availability of training are increasing; and, with a growing backlog of cases, the Equal Employment Opportunity Commission is averaging nearly 1 year to investigate each. Furthermore, age discrimination can often be very difficult to prove. A worker has to establish that it was age, not some other reason the employer may come up with, which actually motivated an action. A review of almost 700 cases filed between 1970 and the mid 1980s (Snyder & Barrett, 1988) found that the employer had won about two-thirds of the time.

Occupational Stress

The Japanese have a word for it: *karoshi,* "death from overwork." One survey found that 40 percent of Japanese workers are afraid of literally working themselves to death.

Occupational stress—stress that is job-related—has become a worldwide epidemic, and not only in the executive suite. It affects waitresses in Sweden and bus drivers in continental Europe. It strikes in developing countries, where assembly-line workers must cope with the unfamiliar strains of industrialization (U.N. International Labor Organization [UNILO], 1993). In the United States, estimated costs of stress-related injuries and diseases have reached $400 billion a year, in soaring workers' compensation claims, medical expenses, health insurance, absenteeism, and loss of productivity (NIOSH, 2002). Occupational stress results from an interaction between the individual worker and the work environment. Therefore, characteristics of both the individual and the workplace need to be considered. However, certain work situations are stressful to many people and therefore should receive greater attention (NIOSH, 1999). These conditions include work overload, conflicting demands, and environmental conditions that include noise and crowding. Other workplace stressors include role conflict, where demands of work and/or home roles may be in opposition; role ambiguity, or uncertainty about what a role requires one to do; high workload; low control in the job; interpersonal conflict; and sense of wasted time or effort (Nelson & Burke, 2000).

Today many U.S. workers are working harder and longer to maintain their standard of living. Some middle-income workers hold two jobs to make ends meet (McGuire, 1999). Employees who feel overworked, or who believe that their skills are not adequately recognized, or who do not have clear goals, tend to show high stress and low morale and productivity (Veninga, 1998). Another cause of stress on the job is conflict with supervisors, subordinates, and co-workers. Violence in the workplace, as a response to fear, uncertainty, or a perception of unfairness, is an increasing problem (Clay, 1995; Freiberg, 1998).

High levels of stress have been linked to such varied health problems as cardiovascular disease, arthritis, back and upper extremity musculoskeletal disorders, psychological disorders, and workplace injuries (Huang et al., 2003; Johnston et al., 2003; Spector et al., 2002). Stress is also linked to negative work outcomes including absenteeism, turnover, and intentions to quit. Such interventions as recognition of employee contributions, addressing problems in job design, and stress prevention programs can benefit both employers and employees (NIOSH, 1999).

As the nature of work changes, organizations need to change as well. These changes can have both positive and negative effects on worker's stress. Higher productivity demands and adjustment to new types of jobs can contribute to stress; but increased flexibility and additional learning opportunities may have more positive outcomes. Increased responsibility however, is a double-edged sword; it may have positive effects on workers looking for greater challenge and negative effects on those who prefer not to make decisions.

Many women are under special pressure in the workplace. The stress of balancing work and family demands is greater for women than for men. Women report heavier demands from family members and more interference of work with family life (Cinamon & Rich, 2002; Heymann, 2000). Both women and men agree that the burdens of household chores and caregiving remain mostly on the woman (Heymann, 2000). Additional stressors for women include tokenism in traditionally male roles or workplace; organizational politics that deny access to information, resources, and/or opportunities; and social sexual behavior including sexual harassment and gender harassment (actions insulting, degrading, and/or hostile to women) (Nelson & Burke, 2000).

Some women complain that an invisible but inflexible "glass ceiling" inhibits their advancement to the highest ranks (Federal Glass Ceiling Commission, 1995). Many companies have programs to help women develop positive ways to cope with occupational stress. Another approach is to train female workers to become more assertive and task-oriented, behave more impersonally, and think more analytically. A third suggested approach, based on qualities commonly thought to be women's strengths, is to offer workshops for both male and female employees on how people can work together more effectively (I. Stiver, personal communication, 1993).

The law defines two types of sexual harassment: (1) sexual favors demanded under threat of employment consequences, such as getting fired; and (2) creation of a "hostile environment," within which severe, repeated abuse based on gender interferes with job performance (Gutman, 2000). The harasser may be male or female, and the victim does not need to be of the opposite sex (Equal Employment Opportunity Commission, 2004). Although most sexual harassment charges are filed by women, 15 percent of charges filed with the Equal Employment Opportunity Commission (EEOC) in 2002 were filed by men, up from 9 percent in 1992 (EEOC, 2004). Sexual harassment is a violation of Title VII of the federal Civil Rights Act; complaints can be filed with the EEOC.

The psychological pressure created by unwelcome sexual overtures, particularly from a superior, can be extremely distressing. But distinguishing between harassment and normal behavior between the sexes has been a vexing problem. The United States Supreme Court has held that to constitute *sexual harassment,* behavior must be so "severe and pervasive" as to create a working environment that "a reasonable person would find hostile or abusive," whether or not the victim suffers actual psychological harm. A hostile or abusive environment is not merely offensive; it is one that may interfere with performance, impede advancement, or affect psychological well-being—for example, a workplace "permeated with 'discriminatory intimidation, ridicule, and insult'" (Equal Employment Opportunity Commission, 1994, p. 7166).

Workplace violence that ends in death is often a subject of intense media coverage. However, some types of workplace violence occur much more frequently but receive far less attention. These include verbal threats, gossip intended to harm others, insults, and bullying. Female workers are particularly at risk for workplace assault due to the types of jobs they often hold. Women are the victims in approximately two-thirds of such assaults, and 70 percent of these women work in service occupations such as health care and social work (NIOSH, 2001).

Burnout can be a result of work-related stress; it involves emotional exhaustion, a feeling of being unable to accomplish anything on the job, and a sense of helplessness and loss of control. It is especially common among people in the helping professions (such as teaching, medicine, therapy, social work, and police work) who feel frustrated by their inability to help people as much as they would like to. Burnout is usually a response to long-term stress rather than a reaction to an immediate crisis. Its symptoms include fatigue, insomnia, headaches, persistent colds, stomach disorders, abuse of alcohol or drugs, and trouble getting along with people. A burned-out worker may quit a job suddenly, may pull away from family and friends, and may sink into depression (Briley, 1980; Maslach & Jackson, 1985).

Unemployment

Perhaps the greatest work-related stressor is sudden, unexpected loss of a job. The unemployment rate in the United States was 6 percent in 2003 (BLS, 2004).

Research on unemployment since the 1930s (concentrating almost entirely on men) has linked it to physical and mental illness (such as heart attack, stroke, depression, and anxiety); to marital and family problems; to health, psychological, and behavior problems in children; and to suicide, homicide, and other crimes (Brenner, 1991; Merva & Fowles, 1992; Voydanoff, 1990). Stress comes not only from loss of income and the resulting financial hardships, but also from the effect of this loss on the unemployed person's self-concept. Workers who derive their identity from their work, men who define manhood as supporting a family, and people who define their worth in terms of the dollar value of their work lose more than their paychecks when they lose their jobs. They lose a piece of themselves and their self-esteem (Voydanoff, 1987, 1990).

Women are as likely as men to feel upset over loss of a job. In a study of former employees of a plant in Indiana that closed in 1982, the unemployed of both sexes reported headaches, stomach trouble, and high blood pressure, and felt less in control of their lives (Perrucci, Perrucci, & Targ, 1988).

A sense of control has been identified as crucial to coping with unemployment. A study of 190 unemployed workers found that those who believed they had some influence on their circumstances were less anxious and depressed, had fewer physical symptoms, and had higher self-esteem and life satisfaction than those who believed external forces were in control (Cvetanovski & Jex, 1994).

Those who cope best with unemployment have some financial resources to draw on, often savings or earnings of other family members. Rather than blaming themselves for losing their jobs, or seeing themselves as failures, they assess their situation more objectively. They have the support of understanding, adaptable families and friends (Voydanoff, 1990). People who can look at loss of a job as a challenge for growth may develop emotionally and professionally. They may change not only jobs but the entire direction of their careers.

Work, Leisure, and Intellectual Growth

Do people change as a result of what kind of work they do and how they use their leisure time? Some research says yes.

A combination of cross-sectional and longitudinal studies (Kohn, 1980) revealed a reciprocal relationship between the **substantive complexity** of work—the degree of thought and independent judgment it requires—and a person's flexibility in coping with intellectual demands. People with more complex work tend to become more flexible thinkers; and flexible thinkers are likely to continue doing more complex work. Why is the complexity of work tied so closely to intellectual growth? One reason may be that, in a society in which work plays a central role in people's lives, mastery of complex tasks gives people confidence in their ability to handle problems. It also may open their minds to new experience and stimulate them to become more self-directed.

Nor does growth stop at the end of the work day; what kind of work people do affects and is affected by what they do in other areas of life. People with substantively complex work "come to engage in more intellectually demanding

> **CRITICAL THINKING**
>
> How would an age-integrated structure influence one's ability to productively engage in work, leisure, and intellectual growth?

leisure-time activities. In short, the lessons of work are directly carried over to nonoccupational realms" (Kohn, 1980, p. 204).

This idea of a link between work and leisure—because learning is carried over from one to the other (the **spillover hypothesis**) or because of personality factors that affect both—is one of several ways of looking at the two domains. Three other hypotheses are these:

1. **Compensation hypothesis**—Leisure activities make up for what is missing in work (Wilensky, 1960). People who do dull work look for stimulating leisure activities; people who do challenging work let down and relax during their time off.
2. **Resource provision-depletion hypothesis**—Work promotes or constrains certain kinds of leisure activities by providing or depleting resources of time, energy, and money (Staines, 1980).
3. **Segmentation hypothesis**—Work and leisure are independent; choices in one area have no relationship to the other (Dubin, 1956; Kabanoff, 1980).

A follow-up to the initial research on substantive complexity of work explored more deeply the relationship between work and intellectual aspects of leisure (Miller & Kohn, 1983). The key finding, supporting the spillover hypothesis, was that the substantive complexity of work—more than any other aspect of a job situation—strongly influences the intellectual level of leisure activities for both men and women, regardless of income and educational level.

For many adults, it seems, work and leisure are two sides of the same coin; choices in one facet of life affect the other. If so, then the kind of work people do should make a difference in how they spend their time after retirement. And, in a society in which work is increasingly complex and leisure options are more sophisticated, we can expect to see continuing intellectual gains in late life.

RETIREMENT AND OTHER LATE-LIFE OPTIONS

Retirement is a relatively new idea. It took hold in many industrialized countries during the late nineteenth and early twentieth centuries; but in less developed countries, most people still work until they are no longer physically able.

How Retirement Has Changed

A brief history of retirement in the United States illustrates the continual evolution of this life transition (Sterns & Kaplan, 2003). Through the 1700s and the mid-1800s, retirement was uncommon. Older adults were valued for wisdom and experience, and forced retirement would have been contrary to the social ideology of the time.

The emergence of retirement in the late 19th century was influenced by the rise of labor unions, which sought worker privileges based on seniority. Management's response was that older workers were less able and more expensive. Prevailing theories of older adults as worn out and useless reinforced policies that assumed older adults were incompetent to work (Richardson, 1993).

Mandatory retirement became a mechanism for removing older workers so as to provide job opportunities for younger workers. Workers who were mandatorily retired had little hope of finding another job and often had insufficient financial resources to support themselves. Retirement was seen in a negative light, associated with poverty and uselessness.

The economic depression of the 1930s was the impetus for the Social Security system, which, together with company-sponsored pension plans negotiated by labor unions, opened the door to almost universal retirement at age 65. The Social Security Act of 1935 was passed in response to the growing number of older adults in poverty (Richardson, 1993).

But retirement, like many other aspects of adult development, has become far more complicated than it once was. The Age Discrimination in Employment Acts (1967, 1978, 1986) have, for the most part, eliminated mandatory retirement in the United States. The ADEA legislation in 1967 created a protected class of people ages 40 and over, but maintained mandatory retirement at age 65. In the revisions of 1978, mandatory retirement age was raised to age 70 and was removed entirely for federal workers. Eight years later, in the 1986 revisions, all mandatory retirement was eliminated with specific exceptions for commercial airline pilots, air traffic controllers, safety officers (firefighters and law enforcement officers), age authenticity in actors, the military, certain elected and appointed officials, and individuals in key leadership positions with pensions greater than $44,000 per year (Sterns, Doverspike, & Lax, 2005). (Refer back to Box 8.2.)

With mandatory retirement virtually outlawed as a form of age discrimination, adults have far more choices, among them early retirement, retiring from one career to start another, working part-time to keep busy or supplement income, going back to school, doing volunteer work, pursing other interests, or not retiring at all. The elimination of mandatory retirement ages for almost all occupations has increased individual autonomy and responsibility for choosing when and how to leave the workforce (Sterns & Gray, 1999).

In response to changing social and organizational environments, self-management has emerged as a major theme. With workers changing employers, occupations, or jobs within their current company, individual responsibility is required for maintaining and updating knowledge, skills, and abilities (Farr, Tesluk, & Klein, 1998; Sterns & Sterns, 1995). Similarly, retirement has become a matter of self-management. The individual has become the focal point of decision making concerning whether, when, and how to retire. The transition from work to retirement can take many forms, including bridge jobs, part-time work, and new careers (Sterns & Gray, 1999; Sterns & Kaplan, 2003).

Multiple pathways from work to retirement highlight retirement as a process. Changing economic environments have had a dramatic effect on individual financial well-being and retirement planning. Some people may have to work longer than they had planned or may have to accept an early buyout

> **CRITICAL THINKING**
>
> How are changes in social policy such as manditory retirement at a particular age and the Age Discrimination in Employment Act (ADEA) influenced by job markets and economic conditions?

package rather than risk being laid off or fired at a later date. Individual characteristics, as well as work-related and nonwork-related factors, impact work and retirement choices and influence anticipatory retirement planning and decision making (Sterns & Kaplan, 2003).

To Retire or Not to Retire

CRITICAL THINKING

What will influence your decisions to work and retire? How long do you anticipate that you will continue to work?

"I get shivers thinking about not working. I'd hate to sit in a park. . . . Retirement is death."

"I can't wait. . . . It should be as delightful as the rest of my life has been, just a different way of investing my activity."

These contrasting comments exemplify the wide range of feelings adults in the latter part of middle age have about the prospect of retirement.

Nowadays there are plenty of role models for continuing to work in old age. "I—will—never—retire!" wrote the comedian George Burns (1983, p. 138) at age 87. "I firmly believe that you should keep working as long as you can." Burns, who was still performing in his late nineties, is one of a considerable number of late-life achievers who keep their minds and bodies active doing the work they love. The actress Jessica Tandy, at 81, won an Academy Award for her starring role in the film *Driving Miss Daisy* and went on to another Oscar nomination for *Fried Green Tomatoes*. When she died at 85 in 1994, she was up for an Emmy award. At 91, Armand Hammer headed Occidental Petroleum (Wallechinsky & Wallace, 1993). Julia Child was still writing cookbooks and hosting television shows in her 90s. During the 10 years before his death at 80, Jonas Salk was working on an AIDS vaccine (Bronte, 1993; Schmeck, 1995). Many other people without famous names quietly go to work each day as typists, lawyers, nurses, or cashiers.

How older workers evaluate their employment situation is based, in part, on how they believe they are viewed by supervisors, outcomes of appraisals, perceived growth opportunities within the organization, salary increases, involvement in organization planning and policy, and observations of treatment received by other employees. Also essential is an understanding of one's own strengths and weaknesses, such as the ability to meet assignments and deadlines. New work opportunities may be an important incentive to continue to work full time, or bridge opportunities may provide a gradual change in responsibilities to part time. A major dimension in continued employment is maintaining professional competence. Remaining competitive with up-to-date skills may make an employee more valuable to an organization (Sterns & Kaplan, 2003). Perceived organizational culture provides important messages to current employees. Middle-aged and older employees are usually very aware of a changing climate in the treatment of long-service employees.

How people feel about their work situation may be highly influenced by relationships with co-workers. Middle-aged and older workers tend to value relationships on the job. A negative relationship with co-workers may lead a valuable older worker to decide to retire. On the other hand, an older employee who, for financial reasons, feels the need to work longer than he or she wanted to may present a challenge for co-workers and supervisors (Sterns & Kaplan, 2003).

Marriage and other significant relationships can have a major influence on decisions regarding work and retirement. Formal retirement education enables couples to engage in planning exercises that often may create new awareness of each other's needs and wishes. Caregiving responsibilities for parents may be a concern; an employee may choose, or feel forced, to retire in order to provide care to loved ones (Sterns & Kaplan, 2003). Choosing to be near children, grandchildren, or other important family members may be a reason to retire from one's current job, move, and reestablish one's household in a new location. New part-time or full-time employment may be a choice after such a move. However, 80 percent of older adults choose to stay in their home communities to be near family and friends (Sterns & Kaplan, 2003).

Even without mandatory retirement, most adults who can retire do retire; (see Figure 8.3) and with increasing longevity, they spend more time in retirement than in the past (Kinsella & Gist, 1995). For men, average time spent in retirement has increased from little more than a year in the 1960s to 12 years by 1995; for women, the average increased from 9 to 21 years over the same period (U.S. Census Bureau, 2001). In the United States, only about 16 percent of older men and 8 percent of older women stayed in the workforce past age 65, a trend that has held steady for the past 10 years (AARP, 2003).

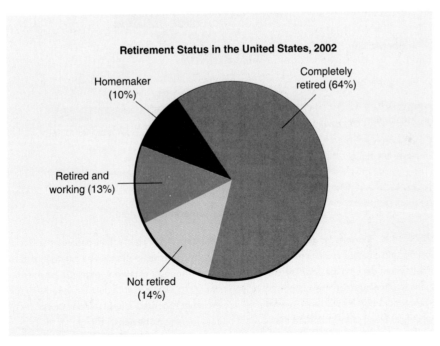

FIGURE 8.3   *Retirement and work: Self-declared retirement status (ages 65+).*   SOURCE: NCOA, 2002.

In most of the developing world, by contrast, large numbers of older adults continue to work for income (Ferraro & Lu, 1999; Kaiser, 1993; U.S. Census Bureau, 2001): more than 40 percent in Peru and South Korea, and over 50 percent in Mexico (U.S. Census Bureau, 2001). Older adults in many underdeveloped and developing countries remain economically and socially useful, engaging in household tasks and family and community functions such as teaching, counseling, negotiating marriages, and leading religious rituals; still, more than 90 percent cannot or can barely meet their basic needs. Although the great majority say they are satisfied with their lives, it is questionable how much real choice they have, in comparison with older adults in developed nations such as the United States.

Financing Retirement

Why do people retire? (see Figure 8.4) Poor health is a factor in some decisions (Sammartino, 1987), but usually not the most important factor (Parnes & Sommers, 1994; NCOA, 2002). More important is financial security, which usually depends on some sort of public or private retirement plan. Only

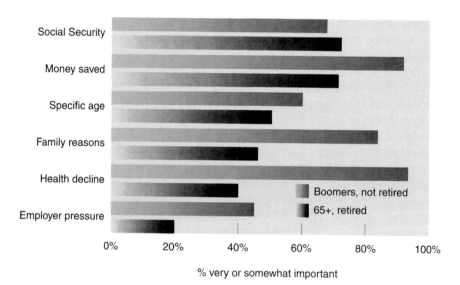

% very or somewhat important

FIGURE 8.4 *Reasons for decision to retire.* In the context of early retirement, debates over Social Security, and changes in the pension system, will the baby boom generation have a different pattern of retirement decision making? The chart compares the responses of current retirees to boomer responses to the question "How important do you think _____ will be in your decision to retire?" (The 6 percent of boomers who are already retired are excluded.) Boomers rate all reasons except Social Security as being more important than current retirees rate them. The gaps are larger for the factors current retirees rated as not so important: family reasons, health decline, and employer pressure. *SOURCE:* NCOA, 2002.

about one-third of the world's older adults (age 60+) are believed to be covered by public old age security programs (U.S. Census Bureau, 2001). The bulk of social support in old age comes from family systems.

Government-sponsored old age protection usually takes one of four forms. Workers in most industrialized countries, including the United States, get *social insurance*. Lifetime benefits, based on prior contributions by employers, employees, or both, depend on how long a person worked and how much he or she earned. A few developed countries have *universal pensions* for all citizens as a matter of right, independent of prior earnings; and a few have a combination of the two systems (see Box 8.3). Some, such as the United Kingdom and the United States, also have *voluntary pension plans* encouraged by tax deferrals or other devices. Some developing countries have government-run *provident funds*, compulsory savings plans funded by employer and employee. At retirement, a worker gets the money in a lump sum. Often certain groups, such as agricultural workers, are not covered, and the funds are frequently inadequate for long-term protection (O'Grady-LeShane, 1993; Schulz, 1993b; U.S. Census Bureau, 2001).

In most developing countries, social insurance programs have had a spotty record. Often a majority of the population, especially workers in the "informal sector" and in rural areas, are left out, and mismanagement is common (Schulz, 1993c, p. 70). A new system in Chile—a variation on the provident fund, combined with public regulation and financial guarantees—may represent a meaningful alternative. While preliminary results are promising, there are questions about whether the plan can survive downturns in investment markets and provide enough income for future retirees (Schulz, 1993c; U.S. Census Bureau, 2001).

In the United States, many workers can retire and live relatively comfortably. (See Figure 8.5 on p. 300 for a breakdown of retirees' sources of income.) However, in the recent economic downturn of 2003, many people lost considerable amounts of their retirement savings due to significant drops in the stock market. These losses will affect the retirement plans of many Americans over the coming years (*New York Times*, 09/08/03). Social security and other government programs, such as Medicare, which covers basic health insurance for people 65 and over, have enabled today's older adults, as a group, to be about as well off financially as younger and middle-aged adults, and their median net worth is well above the national average (AARP, 2001).

However, with a growing elderly population and proportionately fewer workers contributing to the social security system, it seems likely that benefits—in real dollars—will not continue to rise and may even decline. For people born after 1937, the age of eligibility for full social security benefits is scheduled to rise gradually from 65 to 67 in 2010. This change was predicated on the rise in life expectancy, decreases in mortality, and improvements in health among older adults (Crimmins, Reynolds, & Saito, 1999). As for private pensions, a shift from defined benefit plans that guarantee a fixed retirement income to riskier defined contribution plans, in which benefits depend on

CRITICAL THINKING

How important is social insurance in financing retirement in the United States? What purpose does social insurance usually serve?

Work and Retirement in Japan

In contrast to the United States, where downsizing, early retirement incentives, and economic dislocations are pushing older adults out of the workforce, Japan offers an alternative approach: an official goal, targeted at the year 2010, of keeping all healthy persons in the workforce until age 65.

Japan, which has the longest life expectancy and one of the lowest birthrates in the world, is the only industrialized country with a history of policies to encourage the employment of older adults (Raymo et al., 2004). These policies aim not only to enhance the well-being of older persons, but also to help employers meet workforce needs in the face of an expected shortage of younger workers and to reduce pressure on an insufficiently funded pension system. The expected worker shortage is similar in nature to that anticipated in the United States due to "birth dearth" that followed the WWII baby boom. A network of governmental and organizational policies and programs is designed to encourage older workers to stay on the job while enabling the career development of younger workers. Government support for employment of older adults takes the form of three pillars: grants for employers who continue to employ older workers, policies to improve government employment services and to promote re-employment, and placement assistance for workers seeking employment as well as companies seeking older workers (Geneva Association, 2003).

Support for employment of older people befits a culture that has traditionally promoted respect for elders and collectivist policies for the benefit of all. During times of economic hardship, before considering employee layoffs a Japanese company is expected to seek other ways to achieve cost savings: reducing payments to shareholders, cutting managers' benefits, or even eliminating management positions (Usui, 1998). Thus, during the economic recessions between 1970 and 1985, Japanese workers experienced fewer layoffs than U.S. workers, and cuts that occurred, rather than targeting the lowest-paid, least skilled workers, were more equally distributed among white collar and blue collar jobs.

An aging workforce and recent investment losses have placed severe pressure on Japan's public pension system. Trust in the system is so low that 37 percent of those who are eligible do not contribute (*Economist*, 12/20/03). The system has two tiers: an earnings-related Employee Pension System and a basic, flat-rate pension. To support a process of gradual retirement, 1994 amendments provide for partial disbursement of the Employee Pension between ages 60 to 65 (Usui, 1998) and a phased increase to age 65 for eligibility for the full pension (Geneva Association, 2003). The basic pension would be available at age 65 or, at a reduced rate, at age 60.

The practices of *teinen* (mandatory retirement) and *shukko* (employee transfer) coordi-

returns from invested funds, is making the financial future less certain for many workers (Rix, 1994).

Many companies are downsizing and are therefore offering strong incentives to encourage early retirement. Often private pension plans penalize employees who continue to work past the early sixties (Quinn, 1993; Burtless &

nate with the public pension system to help companies retain older workers at lower cost. Larger and medium size firms enforce *teinen*, a type of forced partial retirement (Geneva Association, 2003; Usui, 1998). At age 60, an employee receives a lump sum payment, terminating the lifetime work contract. The employee then may move into a second-level position, often with the same company but with lower wages and lower status. The employee also may receive a partial government pension to offset the loss of income, while the employer may receive government money to support continued employment of that worker.

Under *shukko*, middle-aged and older workers may be transferred to smaller subsidiaries of the parent company (Geneva Association, 2003). The worker is offered continued employment and potential career development opportunities, while the smaller company gains a worker with valuable experience. The larger organization saves money by removing the older employee from its age-related wage and promotion system, opening the way for promotion of younger workers. *Shukko* helps explain the high percentage of older workers at smaller firms in Japan.

As a result of these policies, the employment rate for men ages 60 to 64 is very high in Japan: 75 percent, as compared with 55 percent in the United States and Britain and only 20 to 40 percent in continental Europe. Approximately half of all workers reaching *teinen* age are reemployed by the same organization, and many others move to jobs in the service sector (*Economist*, 03/27/04).

Still, in the face of governmental policies that favor employment of older adults, contrary pressures exist. Economic change requires companies to remain competitive in the global marketplace. As competition increases, so do early retirement schemes, and reemployment is difficult. Some companies are closing factories and moving them to China, where an engineer can be hired for one-fourth of the pay of an engineer in Japan (*New York Times*, 2004). Despite the culture of respect for elders, age discrimination is pervasive. According to one report, 80 percent of the "help wanted" ads list an upper age limit averaging around 41 (*Economist*, 3/27/04; Geneva Association, 2003). Women are generally not covered by promises of lifetime employment. Many are forced to quit upon marriage or childbirth and they remain unprotected when they reenter the workforce after their child-rearing years (Geneva Association, 2003; Raymo et al., 2004).

Although problems exist, the Japanese model provides an interesting perspective on the treatment of older workers and how societal organizations can collaborate to support their employment.

Quinn, 2002) but the shift away from such plans helps alleviate this pressure. However, for those who live long enough, social security can have the opposite effect, penalizing early retirement. The trend toward early retirement among men appears to have leveled off. Among women, it has been offset by a rise in midlife careers (Quinn, 1993; Burtless & Quinn, 2002).

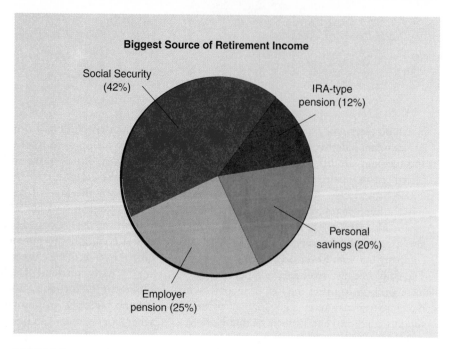

Biggest Source of Retirement Income

Social Security (42%)

IRA-type pension (12%)

Personal savings (20%)

Employer pension (25%)

FIGURE 8.5 *Sources of retirement income, United States, 2000.* SOURCE: NCOA, 2002.

Preparing for Retirement

"Being useful is essential to my sense of who I am," says a librarian who "slid" into retirement and has mixed feelings about the decision. "My job gave my life structure. It was the thing around which everything else revolved."

Retirement is an important transition. Preparation can be a key to making that transition successful and rewarding. Ideally, retirement planning should begin by middle age.

How well are today's middle-aged adults planning for retirement? In an earlier survey of 45- to 59-year-olds, 4 in 10 respondents said they had saved too little or nothing at all for retirement, and 2 out of 3 expected to have serious problems living on their retirement incomes (Rix, 1994). The "baby boom" generation, who will begin retiring soon, as a group are better educated and have higher incomes than their parents; and many couples will have social security and pension benefits from two wage-earners rather than one. But if social security and pension benefits do not keep pace with the cost of living, many "boomers" may suffer real hardships (Farrell et al., 1994; Rix, 1994). The early boomers are expected to do as well as current retirees, but late boomers are estimated to be less likely to maintain their pre-retirement standard of living (Butrica & Uccello, 2004). Never-married women, divorced women, and blacks are expected to be especially vulnerable.

Planning for retirement should include not only providing for financial needs, but also structuring life to make it enjoyable and productive after retirement, anticipating physical or emotional problems, and discussing how retirement will affect a spouse. Assistance can come from preretirement workshops, self-help books, and company-sponsored programs.

How Do Retired People Use Their Time?

"Most people I know who are retired are so busy that they don't know how they found time to work," says a retired speech therapist.

Someone who retires does not become a new person overnight; lifelong habits and attitudes generally continue to influence behavior (Kelly, 1994). The work ethic by which many people have lived throughout their adult lives may translate into what has been called a *busy ethic*—a need to keep busy and active so as not to appear or feel lazy or useless (Ekerdt, 1986). Thus one study found that the most satisfied retirees are physically fit people who are using their skills in part-time paid or volunteer work (Schick, 1986). Let's look at three ways of using time after retirement: paid work, volunteerism, and leisure activities.

CRITICAL THINKING

What specific characteristics and factors do you believe influence the activity choices retired people make?

PAID WORK AFTER RETIREMENT

Some people are not happy unless they are gainfully employed. Some retirees find part-time or new full-time jobs; some (who may call themselves "semi-retired") keep doing what they were doing before but cut down on their hours and responsibilities. Self-employed men are less likely to make an abrupt switch from full-time work to complete retirement (Burkhauser & Quinn, 1989). A longitudinal study of men originally identified as gifted in childhood found that those who had been self-employed at any time before retirement were more likely to do some type of part-time work after retirement (Elder & Pavalko, 1993).

VOLUNTEERISM

One-third to one-half of U.S. adults ages 45 and over (dependent on how survey questions are worded), report participating in traditional forms of community service such as volunteering at hospitals and schools. When less traditional forms of service are included in such survey questions, 87 percent of this age group report participating. African Americans are the most active in efforts targeting the homeless, minority rights, neighborhood issues, and tutoring (AARP, 2003). In a 2003 survey by the U.S. Department of Labor, about 24 percent of those ages 65 and over report volunteering compared to 35 percent of those ages 35 to 44, 33 percent of those 45 to 54, and 24 percent of those ages 16 to 24 (BLS, 2003).

Most older volunteers work alongside adults of all ages, more than half in churches or synagogues (Chambre, 1993). Countless community-based programs are built specifically around older volunteers. Government-sponsored services include retired executives who advise small businesses, retired accountants who help fill out tax returns, senior companions who visit frail elderly people in their homes, and foster grandparents who for a small stipend provide social and emotional support to neglected or autistic children, teenage parents, and substance abusers.

What accounts for the high rates of volunteerism? One reason is a changing public image of older adults and their capabilities—a recognition that older people can be active, healthy, contributing members of a community. Then, volunteer work itself has taken on higher status. Finally, today's better-educated older population has more to contribute and more interest in contributing (Chambre, 1993).

In less developed nations, such as India, Cameroon, and Malta, older adults regularly make useful, informal, unpaid contributions, such as looking after children, working with local officials and civic organizations to solve community problems, and checking on elderly neighbors who may be ill or in need of help (S. C. Taylor, 1993). Finding ways to use older volunteers most effectively will be a worldwide challenge in coming years.

LEISURE DURING RETIREMENT

For many retirees, life in some ways is not much different from before. There is simply more time for the same kinds of leisure activities they always enjoyed.

Interviews with 25 "unexceptional" men and women of modest means, who had retired from routine jobs at a midwestern food-processing plant, revealed more continuity than change in lifestyles. These people, none of whom were college-educated, were "aging in place" in the homes they had lived in before. Most had made only vague plans for what they wanted to do. After taking one or two car trips and perhaps doing a few projects around the house, they had settled into new yet familiar routines. The important difference was a new sense of freedom ("I can do what I want to do when I want to do it") and relief from pressure, fatigue, and ringing alarm clocks (Kelly, 1994, p. 490). Their activities were generally accessible and low-cost and revolved around family, home, and companions: conversation, watching television, visiting with family and friends, informal entertaining, going to inexpensive restaurants, playing cards, or just doing "what comes along" (Kelly, 1994, p. 491).

Interestingly, none of these retirees participated in activities for senior citizens. One explanation for this often-observed phenomenon is the concept of the *ageless self*—the idea that people tend to see themselves as the same person regardless of how old they get (Kaufman, 1986). Because many older adults do not think of themselves as fundamentally different from before, they may avoid activities that redefine them as "old."

Additional research using longitudinal data found continuity in the activity level of adults, as well as in choice of activities (Atchley, 1999; Verbrugge, Gruber-Baldini, & Fozard, 1996). However, the number of activities narrows with age, and the most physically demanding activities are discontinued or given less time (Verbrugge, Gruber-Baldini, & Fozard, 1996).

The **family-focused lifestyle** of the former factory workers was one of two common patterns of retirement activity identified in an earlier study by the same researcher (Kelly, 1987). The other pattern—**balanced investment**—was typical of more educated people who allocated their time more equally among family, work, and leisure. These patterns may change with age. Younger retirees who were most satisfied with their quality of life were those who traveled regularly and went to cultural events; after 75, family- and home-based activity yielded the most satisfaction (Kelly, Steinkamp, & Kelly, 1986). A Canadian study (Mannell, 1993) found that retirees who were extraordinarily satisfied with their lives engaged in **serious leisure**—activity that "demands skill, attention, and commitment" (Kelly, 1994, p. 502). Sunday painters, amateur carpenters, and others who have made an effort to become good at something they love often use their expanded leisure time during retirement to make this interest the central focus of their lives.

An ethnic perspective on leisure comes from a nationwide survey of nearly 1,700 older Americans. Fewer than 1 in 4 older African Americans engage in outdoor sports—such as boating, bird watching, golf, or tennis—compared with 85 percent or more of older whites, Hispanics, and Native Americans. Most older African Americans do things that produce something useful, such as sewing, gardening, and fishing. Perhaps because poverty and racial discrimination have shut them out of many leisure activities throughout their lives, they may not think of doing things just for fun. Or they may continue to lack the resources to do so (Brown & Tedrick, 1993).

There are many paths to enjoying retirement, but they have two things in common: doing satisfying things and having satisfying relationships. For most older people, both "are an extension of histories that have developed throughout the life course" (Kelly, 1994, p. 501).

How Does Retirement Affect Well-Being?

A familiar saying, "It's better to be rich and healthy than poor and sick," sums up many people's feelings about retirement. Not surprisingly, retirees who are financially secure and feel well are happier in retirement than those who miss their income and do not feel well enough to enjoy their leisure (Barfield & Morgan, 1974, 1978; Bossé, Aldwin, Levenson, & Workman-Daniels, 1991; Kim & Moen, 2001). A common fear is that retirement may erode financial security and health, as well as supportive social contacts.

BECOMING POOR IN RETIREMENT

Between 1959 and 1999, the proportion of older Americans living in poverty dropped from 35 percent to less than 10 percent. Older women are more likely than older men to live in poverty, and older African Americans are three times and Hispanic Americans are nearly two times as likely as older white Americans to have incomes below the poverty line (AOA, 2004). Married couples rarely become poor after retirement, especially if they have pension benefits. When a husband dies, however, his widow is 4 times as likely as a married person to fall below the poverty line (Burkhauser, Holden, & Feaster, 1988). Older people who live alone or with nonrelatives are over 3 times as likely to be poor as older persons who live with family members (AOA, 2004).

Because many jobs typically held by minority-group workers are not covered by social security, these workers are more likely than others to end up on Old Age Assistance. More than 23 percent of older African American adults and more than 19 percent of elderly Hispanics are poor, compared with only 11 percent of older white adults (AOA, 2004).

Money and health are the main worries of retired people, and the cost of long-term health care is one of the most significant worries of all. To allay the risk of poverty resulting from long-term illness, many people believe there is need for a government-sponsored, self-supporting insurance program. This has been a continuing issue for over a decade.

PHYSICAL AND MENTAL HEALTH

Retirement itself generally has little effect on physical health (Herzog, House, & Morgan, 1991; Palmore, Fillenbaum, & George, 1984), but does it affect mental health? The answer may depend on when and why people retire. An analysis of data from six longitudinal studies—three national and three local—found that although retirement generally has little effect on morale, early retirement, which is often a result of poor health, tends to lead to greater declines in health and in satisfaction (Palmore et al., 1984). Among 1,516 older men surveyed in the cross-sectional Boston Veterans Administration Normative Aging Study, retirees were more likely than workers to report depression, obsessive-compulsive behavior, and physical symptoms with no organic cause. Those who had retired early (before age 62) or late (after age 65) reported the most symptoms (Bossé, Aldwin, Levenson, & Ekerdt, 1987). It's possible, then, that retirement did not bring on their mental problems, but rather that they retired when they did because they were having problems. A study of 200 men in the same sample who had retired in the previous year suggested that "those who are forced to retire unexpectedly or involuntarily, for reasons of health, plant closings, etc., or who experience health or financial declines after retirement may experience greater retirement stress than those whose retirement is voluntary, on schedule, and not financially burdensome" (Bossé et al., 1991, p. P13).

© Preuss/Image Works

During retirement, leisure-time friends may replace co-workers as sources of social support.

A study that looked directly at the effects of voluntary versus involuntary retirement found that, at least for people age 65 and older, those who had control over the decision were more satisfied with their lives and had less cognitive impairment than those who did not (Herzog et al., 1991). These findings are consistent with earlier research that found negative effects of unexpected or involuntary retirement (Beck, 1982).

Unexpected or involuntary retirement may affect women especially severely (Matthews & Brown, 1988). Interviews with 124 women and 176 men who had been retired about 8 years and were living in an urban area of Ontario, Canada, found that although retirement was not traumatic in general, the strongest predictor of its effect on morale was whether or not people retired at a time of their own choosing. Women were more likely than men to have to retire for reasons having to do with other people—for example, the retirement or infirmity of a spouse or some other family member.

SOCIAL SUPPORT

For most adults, work is a convenient source of social contact; and social contact can be an important source of support, especially as people age. Does the loss of these extensive, regular contacts with co-workers (who may also be friends and confidants) affect people's well-being after retirement?

Cross-sectional comparisons have found that older adults who have been retired for a long time have fewer social contacts than more recent retirees or those who continue to work at least part-time. But, although the extent of the social network and the frequency of contacts decline, the quality of support—having people to rely on in times of crisis—apparently does not. A 3-year longitudinal study of 1,311 relatively healthy older men in the Boston Normative Aging Study confirmed this finding (Bossé, Aldwin, Levenson, Spiro, & Mroczek, 1993). Two lifespan developmental explanations for this phenomenon are *convoy theory* and *selectivity theory.*

Convoy theory, proposed by Robert Kahn and Toni Antonucci (1980), distinguishes relationships in terms of their relative intimacy. Only a person's outer circles of social contact are significantly affected by retirement. Co-workers in these circles tend to drop away, to be replaced by new leisure friends or by more time spent with other friends and acquaintances. But, regardless of what happens to these relatively casual friendships, retirees still have a stable inner circle of close friends and family members and thus do not feel a loss of social support or well-being.

Family and friendship networks, as well as group affiliations, promote adjustment to retirement. The retirement transition is easier if retirees have friends and family to support them in their new role (Kim & Moen, 2001). In a study of 753 late midlife retirees and workers (ages 58–64), marital status had a significant effect on positive attitudes toward retirement, indicating that being married may provide social support that buffers the uncertainty of retirement (Mutran et al., 1997). In a longitudinal study of recent retirees marital quality was positively related to retirement adjustment. Decreased marital satisfaction after retirement was related to declining morale among late midlife women (but not among midlife men) (Kim & Moen, 2001).

Laura Carstensen's (1991, 1995, 1998) **selectivity theory** focuses on changes in how social contacts function in adult life. According to this theory, social interaction has three functions: (1) it is a source of information; (2) it helps people develop and maintain a sense of self; and (3) it is a source of pleasure or emotional well-being. The first two functions—information and identity—decline, because they are needed less as time goes on; but the emotional function, which depends on the quality of social support, becomes central. Retired people become more selective about their social interactions so as to maintain a high quality of dependable social support—people they truly enjoy and can count on in time of need. Thus, far from diminishing well-being, limitations on an aging person's social support network can be positive and adaptive.

SELF-CONCEPT IN RETIREMENT

A person's self-concept in retirement is influenced by many factors. One factor influencing self-concept is the understanding of change and an awareness of the passage of time. How we view change in others and ourselves and how we see and understand the implications of future time are major aspects of personal cognitive integration leading to increased self-understanding. First there is the understanding of one's past self and what values, preferences, and desires are based in the past. Retirement offers opportunities to return to where family used to live, maintain close contact with old friends, or make use of a family summer home. This enriched understanding of one's past may be complemented by a new perspective on one's future self. New lifestyles, new living environments, new friends, and new activities become realistic options. A person may choose to carry out a new set of life activities in a familiar community environment (Sterns & Kaplan, 2003).

A second factor influencing self-concept is the perception of control over one's life. A person in the world of work may feel in control because of financial resources, position held, or seniority, or may feel extremely vulnerable based on the current financial situation and business climate. Many people in retirement have had to change lifestyle or return to work for pay in order to maintain a desired standard of living.

A third factor is personal insight: how well one understands oneself—one's motivations, desires, approach to work, and relations with family, friends, and organizations. Self-study, education, and counseling may aid this process.

The orchestration of all of these influences on self-concept and the needed interpretation, planning, sophistication, and wisdom are all part of how well people are able to manage their retirement.

How Does Retirement Affect Society?

Whether and when people retire affects not only themselves and their immediate families but society as a whole. Almost all industrialized countries are concerned about the cost of supporting their growing older populations. In the

United States, massive federal deficits have raised doubts about the ability to continue to fund social security entitlements. One response has been to encourage older adults to keep working, by eliminating mandatory retirement and raising the age for collecting full social security benefits. On the other hand, unemployment and high labor costs for experienced workers create pressures for policies to nudge (or push) older people out of the work force, as is done in France, Germany, and the Netherlands. However, these policies are now being reexamined (Kinsella & Velkoff, 2001).

The social impact of retirement is closely linked to the **dependency ratio:** the comparative size of the productive and dependent parts of a population. With older adults living longer and growing in numbers, the portion of the population in the productive years (age 18 to 64) will diminish relative to the portion presumed to be dependent (age 65 or older). In the United States this ratio is expected to drop from 5.5 in 1980 to 2.5 in 2040 (Adamchak & Friedmann, 1983), suggesting that in the future there may not be enough workers to support the aging population. But older people are not the only "dependent" group. As the number of older Americans increases, the number of children and teenagers will decline, keeping *total* dependency below what it was in 1960, when the "baby boomers" were growing up (Adamchak, 1993). An important question, then, is how willing working adults will be to assume more of a burden for supporting the older generation instead of the younger generation.

In actuality, of course, some older adults and some people under 18 work, while many people of "working age" do not. Thus a more realistic (though more difficult) way to calculate a dependency ratio is to look at who actually is and is not in the labor force. Studies that attempted to do this have concluded that the total burden on the working segment of the population is likely to *decrease* because there will be more workers, including more women and minorities, to share the load (Adamchak & Friedmann, 1983; Crown, 1993). This will be especially true if a large proportion of older adults in future cohorts remain in the workforce.

Dependency calculations are only as good as the assumptions on which they are based—assumptions about birth, immigration, and unemployment rates, who participates in the labor force, when people retire, social policies and programs, patterns of aging, cultural attitudes, and other factors that are subject to change and hard to anticipate. Since all these factors vary considerably from one country to another, so will the costs and challenges of supporting a graying population. Above all, Crown (1993) argues, "the affordability of an aging population will be dictated largely by future economic growth" (p. 36). If workers' incomes in industrialized countries rise faster than tax rates to fund programs for the elderly, the dependency burden will be lighter.

We also need to recognize that adults, particularly women, who are not "working" often spend a considerable amount of time caring for their children, their grandchildren, their parents, and each other—a significant economic contribution that is not figured into dependency calculations or, usually, into pensions (O'Grady-LeShane, 1993). A United Nations (1991) report observed that if housework and family care were included in calculations

CRITICAL THINKING

Why is it important to identify and monitor conditions that influence future dependency ratios?

of national productivity, the total world output would rise by 25 to 30 percent. Women's advocates argue that we need to redefine work to include caregiving functions that are still the central tasks of many women the world over, and that we need to find ways to compensate women for that work during their productive years and beyond (O'Grady-LeShane, 1993).

For both economic and psychological reasons, some experts, pointing to examples of productive aging in less developed cultures as well as in our own, are predicting an "end of retirement as we know it" (S. C. Taylor, 1993, p. 32). They do not mean a return to the harsh system of yesteryear—"work until you drop"—but a proliferation of options for productive activity that can benefit older adults and society as a whole. As M. W. Riley (1994) suggested, the later years could be made more satisfying by restructuring the course of life. Today, young adults generally plunge into education and careers, middle-aged people use most of their energy earning money, and some older people have trouble filling their time. If people at all ages wove more balanced proportions of study, work, and leisure into their lives, young adults would feel less pressure to establish themselves early, middle-aged people would feel less burdened, and older people who want to and are able to continue doing productive work would be more stimulated and would feel—and be—more useful.

SUMMARY AND KEY TERMS

- Increased longevity and changing social institutions may herald a change from age-differentiated to age-integrated roles.

Education

- A large proportion of today's college students are of nontraditional age; a majority are women. Many dropped out and have returned to complete their education.
- Lifelong learning is an important trend. Adult education takes a wide variety of forms, from college-level courses to programs that are practically or socially oriented.
- Goals of older learners are to gain adaptive knowledge and skills, to train for new occupations, to understand and cope with technological and cultural change, to understand their own aging processes, and to develop new and satisfying retirement and leisure roles.
- Adult illiteracy is a worldwide problem. In complex societies, functional literacy requires an increasing level of skill.

age-differentiated (p. 271) **lifelong learning (p. 274)**
age-integrated (p. 272)

Work and Leisure

- According to Holland's theory, vocational choice is based on a match between personality type and work environment.

- Super's theory traces eight stages of career development tied to the maturing self-concept.
- Significant changes in the American workforce include a shift from manufacturing and transport to service and information, from blue-collar to white-collar work, from full-time salaried positions to independent contracting and part-time or temporary jobs, and from a preponderance of white males to an increasing number of women and minorities.
- An increase in women's employment is occurring worldwide. Women tend to have part-time, low-status jobs and to earn less than men; but that pattern is changing in the United States, where gender discrimination in the workplace is illegal.
- In the United States, African Americans have the highest rates of unemployment. Among professionals, African Americans have the lowest earnings.
- Apparent age differences in job performance seem to depend on experience, on how performance is measured, and on the demands of the job.
- Causes of occupational stress include a combination of high pressure and low autonomy; interpersonal conflict; work overload; and tensions affecting women and minorities.
- Unemployment has both physical and psychological effects for men and for women.
- People who do more complex work tend to engage in more intellectually demanding leisure activities.

vocational identity (p. 281)
crystallization stage (p. 281)
specification stage (p. 281)
implementation stage (p. 281)
establishment stage (p. 282)
consolidation stage (p. 282)
maintenance stage (p. 282)
deceleration stage (p. 282)

retirement stage (p. 282)
burnout (p. 290)
substantive complexity (p. 291)
spillover hypothesis (p. 292)
compensation hypothesis (p. 292)
resource provision-depletion
hypothesis (p. 292)
segmentation hypothesis (p. 292)

Retirement and Other Late-Life Options

- Most adults in industrialized countries retire. Many older adults in less developed countries work but cannot meet their basic needs.
- Finances rather than health will usually determine the decision to retire.
- Most American workers retire before age 65, but the trend toward early retirement has leveled off.
- Options for use of time after retirement include paid work, volunteerism, and leisure activities. Lifestyle after retirement tends to be related to the things a person enjoyed doing before.
- Widows, minorities, and people with long-term illnesses are most likely to become impoverished after retirement.
- Although the quantity of social contacts diminishes after retirement, the quality of social support networks generally does not.

- Self-concept influences how well a person manages his or her retirement, and is affected by understanding of the past, perception of control, and personal insight.
- The societal impact of retirement has to do with the dependency ratio. Studies suggest that the total burden of dependency is not likely to increase, but economic growth will be a key factor in keeping the burden bearable.
- With increased longevity, a shift from retirement to "productive aging" may be under way.

family-focused lifestyle (p. 303)	**convoy theory (p. 305)**
balanced investment (p. 303)	**selectivity theory (p. 306)**
serious leisure (p. 303)	**dependency ratio (p. 307)**

Intimate Relationships and Lifestyles

◆ FOCUS: INGRID BERGMAN, "NOTORIOUS" ACTRESS

Relationship is life, and this relationship is a constant movement, a constant change.
—J. Krishnamurti, *You Are the World*, 1989

© Bettmann/Corbis Images

INGRID BERGMAN* (1915–1982) was one of the world's most distinguished stage and screen actresses. Perhaps best remembered for her starring role in *Casablanca*, she won Academy Awards for *Gaslight*, *Anastasia*, and *Murder on the Orient Express*; the New York Film Critics' Award for *Autumn Sonata*; and an Emmy for *The Turn of the Screw*. In 1981, a year before her death, she came out of retirement to play the Israel prime minister Golda Meir in the Emmy-winning *A Woman Called Golda*.

*Sources of biographical information about Ingrid Bergman were Bergman & Burgess (1980) and Spoto (1997).

Bergman's personal life was as dramatic as any movie plot. One of her film titles, *Notorious*, sums up the abrupt change in her public image in 1949, when Bergman—known as a paragon of wholesomeness and purity—shocked the world by leaving her husband and 10-year-old daughter for the Italian film director Roberto Rossellini. Compounding the scandal was the news that Bergman was pregnant by Rossellini, a married man.

Bergman had been obsessed with acting since she had seen her first play at the age of 11 in her native Sweden. Tall, awkward, and shy, she came alive onstage. Plucked out of Stockholm's Royal Dramatic School at 18 to make her first film, she braved the wrath of the school's director, who warned that movies would destroy her talent.

At 22, she married Dr. Petter Lindstrom, a handsome, successful dentist 8 years her senior, who later became a prominent brain surgeon. It was he who urged her to accept the producer David Selznick's invitation to go to Hollywood to make *Intermezzo*. At 23, she arrived, to be joined later by her husband and infant daughter, Pia.

Her filmmaking was punctuated by periodic spells of domesticity. "I have plenty to do as usual, and having a home, husband and child ought to be enough for any women's life," she wrote during one such interlude. "But still I think every day is a lost day. As if only half of me is alive" (Bergman & Burgess, 1980, p. 110).

Bergman began to see her husband—whom she had always leaned on for help and decision making—as overprotective, controlling, jealous, and critical. The couple spent long hours, days, and weeks apart—she at the studio or on tour, he at the hospital.

Meanwhile, Bergman was becoming dissatisfied with filming on studio lots. When she saw Rossellini's award-winning *Open City*, she was stunned by its power and realism and by Rossellini's artistic freedom and courage. She wrote to him, offering to come to Italy and work with him. The result was *Stromboli*—and the end of what she now saw as a constrictive, unfulfilling marriage. "It was not my intention to fall in love and go to Italy forever," she wrote to Lindstrom apologetically. "But how can I help it or change it?"

At 33, Bergman, who had been number one at the box office, became a Hollywood outcast. Her affair made headlines worldwide. So did the illegitimate birth of Robertino in 1950, Bergman's hurried Mexican divorce and proxy marriage there to Rossellini (who had had his own marriage annulled), the birth of twin daughters in 1952, and the struggle over visitation rights with Pia, who took her father's side and did not see her guilt-ridden mother for 6 years.

The tempestuous Bergman-Rossellini love match did not last. Every picture they made together failed, and finally, so did the marriage. But their mutual bond with their children, to whom Bergman gave Rossellini custody to avoid another bitter battle, made these ex-spouses a continuing part of each other's lives. In 1958, at the age of 43, Ingrid Bergman—her career, by this time, rehabilitated and peace made with her eldest daughter—began her third marriage, to Lars Schmidt, a Swedish-born theatrical producer. It lasted 16 years, despite constant work-related separations, and ended in an amicable divorce. Schmidt and Bergman remained close friends for the rest of her life.

THE STORY OF INGRID BERGMAN touches on several topics we will cover in this chapter: friendship, love, marriage, and parenthood.* Of course, no one story can encompass today's wide range of intimate relationships and lifestyles. In many societies, people are no longer simply expected to get married, stay married, have children, and maintain distinct roles for men and women (Eisenberg, 1995; O'Grady-LeShane, 1993; Thornton, 1989). Adults can decide whether and when to marry, divorce, or remarry and whether, when, and how to become parents. Some choose an unwed partnership with someone of the same or the other sex. Some remain single and live alone or in group settings. Some couples decide to remain childless; some delay parenthood until their thirties, middle age or later. An increasing number become single parents—either by choice or through divorce or widowhood. In this chapter, as we discuss intimate relationships and lifestyle patterns, you may gain insights into your own relationships and find useful information about an important and perplexing aspect of adult development: dealing with people who are as complicated as yourself.

FOUNDATIONS OF INTIMATE RELATIONSHIPS

Young adulthood is the time when people establish relationships that may continue for much of their adult lives—relationships based on friendship, love, and sexuality. But in many societies, chronological age is no longer as important as social age. In a highly mobile society, friendships may come and go. In a freer society, so may marital and sexual partners. And in a society that is taking a more realistic look at older people and their needs and desires, it's virtually never too late for romance and sexual satisfaction.

> **CRITICAL THINKING**
>
> What sequence do you believe is most healthy in developing an intimate relationship? What are the difficulties in following a desirable pathway?

The Internet has brought a new dimension to relationships. Online relationships tend to be weaker than face-to-face ones. In a longitudinal study of 93 Pittsburgh families from diverse neighborhoods, Internet users tended to become less socially involved, to communicate less within the family, and to have fewer friends. Internet use also was associated with increases in loneliness and depression (Kraut et al., 1998). However, a follow-up study suggests that these negative effects may have been related to initial use of a new technology and may diminish with accustomed use (Kraut et al., 2002).

What can research tell us about how intimate relationships develop and change throughout adult life?

Relationships: A Developmental Perspective

Erikson saw the development of intimate relationships as the crucial task of young adulthood. *Intimacy* may or may not include sexual contact. An important element of intimacy is *self-disclosure*: "revealing important information

---

*Some of the discussion in this chapter is based on Papalia, Olds, & Feldman (2004).

about oneself to another" (Collins & Miller, 1994, p. 457). People become intimate—and remain intimate—through shared disclosures, responsiveness to one another's needs, and mutual acceptance and respect (Harvey & Omarzu, 1997; Reis & Patrick, 1996).

Intimacy includes a sense of belonging. The need to form strong, stable, close, caring relationships is a powerful motivator of human behavior. The strongest emotions—both positive and negative—are evoked by intimate attachments. People tend to be healthier, physically and mentally, and to live longer, if they have satisfying close relationships (Baumeister & Leary, 1995; Myers & Diener, 1995).

As young adults enter college or the workplace—as they take responsibility for themselves and make their own decisions—they must complete the negotiation of autonomy begun in adolescence and redefine their relationships with their parents (Lambeth & Hallett, 2002; Mitchell, Wister, & Burch, 1989). Unless young adults can resolve conflicts with parents in a wholesome way, they may find themselves reenacting similar conflicts in the new relationships they develop with friends, colleagues, and partners. They may also—perhaps for the first time—encounter peers of diverse ethnic groups; and they need to become aware of how intercultural differences shape perceptions and attitudes (Lambeth & Hallett, 2002).

As they become their own persons, young adults seek emotional and physical intimacy in relationships with peers and romantic partners. These relationships require such skills as self-awareness, empathy, the ability to communicate emotions, sexual decision making, conflict resolution, and the ability to sustain commitments. Such skills are pivotal as young adults decide to marry, form unwed or homosexual partnerships, or live alone, and to have or not to have children (Lambeth & Hallett, 2002).

As people age, they tend to spend less time with others (Carstensen, 1996). Work is often a convenient source of social contact; thus, longtime retirees have fewer social contacts than more recent retirees or those who continue to work. For some older adults, infirmities make it harder to get out and see people. Studies also show that older people often bypass opportunities for increased social contact and are more likely than younger adults to be satisfied with smaller social networks. Yet the social contacts older adults *do* have are more important to their well-being than ever (Lansford, Sherman, & Antonucci, 1998).

Why is this? According to *social convoy theory*, introduced in Chapter 8, changes in social contact typically affect only a person's outer, less intimate social circles. After retirement, as co-workers and other casual friends drop away, most older adults retain a stable inner circle of social convoys: close friends and family members on whom they can rely for continued social support and who strongly affect their well-being for better or worse (Antonucci & Akiyama, 1995; Kahn & Antonucci, 1980).

According to *socioemotional selectivity theory* (Carstensen, 1991, 1995, 1996), older adults become increasingly selective about the people with whom they spend their time. When people perceive their remaining time as short, immediate emotional needs take precedence over long-range goals. A college student may be willing to put up with a disliked teacher for the sake of gaining knowledge to get into graduate school; an older adult may be less willing to spend precious time with a friend who gets on her nerves. Young adults with a free half hour and no urgent commitments may choose to spend the time with someone they would like to get to know better; older adults tend to choose someone they know well.

Even though older people may have fewer close relationships than younger people do, they tend to be more satisfied with those they have (Antonucci & Akiyama, 1995). While the size of the social network and the frequency of contacts decline, the quality of social support apparently does not (Bosse, Aldwin, Levenson, Spiro, & Mroczek, 1993).

Most older people's lives are enriched by the presence of longtime friends and family members. Although older adults may see people less often, personal relationships continue to be important—perhaps even more so than before (Antonucci & Akiyama, 1995; Carstensen, 1995; C. L. Johnson & Troll, 1992).

Friendship

Friendships are an important part of life at every age. Friends provide companionship, someone to share activities with, emotional support through difficult times, and a sense of identity and history. Friendships are usually based on mutual interests and values and usually develop among people of the same generation or at the same stage of family life, who validate each other's beliefs and behavior (Dykstra, 1995). Young adults who are building careers and perhaps caring for babies have limited time to spend with friends. Still, friendships are important to them. People with friends tend to have a sense of well-being; either having friends makes people feel good about themselves, or people who feel good about themselves have an easier time making friends (Hartup & Stevens, 1999; Myers, 2000).

Women typically have more intimate friendships than men and find friendships with other women more satisfying than those with men. Men are more likely to share information and activities, not confidences, with friends (Rosenbluth & Steil, 1995).

Social networks tend to become smaller and more intimate at midlife. As compared with younger people, many middle-aged people have little time and energy to devote to friends; they are too busy with family and work and with building up security for retirement. Still, friendships do persist and are a strong source of emotional support and well-being, especially for women (Adams & Allan, 1998; Antonucci et al., 2001). Friendships often revolve around work and parenting; others are based on neighborhood contacts or on association in volunteer organizations (Antonucci et al., 2001; Hartup & Stevens, 1999). A woman who has delayed parenthood until her late thirties or her forties may become friendly with other mothers who are several years younger than she is, as well as with professional colleagues who are several years older.

The quality of midlife friendships often makes up for what they lack in quantity of time spent. Especially during a crisis, such as a divorce or a problem with an aging parent, adults turn to friends for emotional support, practical guidance, comfort, companionship, and talk (Antonucci & Akiyama, 1997; Hartup & Stevens, 1999; Suitor & Pillemer, 1993). The meaning of friendship changes little over the life span, but its context and content may change.

Among older adults, friendships are typically no longer linked to work and parenting, as in earlier periods of adulthood. Instead, they are focused on companionship and support (Hartup & Stevens, 1999).

The fact that people *choose* their friends may be especially important to older people, who often feel control over their lives slipping away (Adams, 1986). This element of choice may help explain why most older people have close friends, and why those who have an active circle of friends are happier and healthier (Babchuk, 1978–1979; Lemon, Bengtson, & Peterson, 1972; Steinbach, 1992).

Intimacy is important to older adults, who need to know that they are still valued and wanted despite physical and other losses. This is especially true for formerly married women (Essex & Nam, 1987). Well into old age, women continue to see their friends at least as often as in the past. Older men see friends less, see them more in groups rather than one to one, and consider friendship less important (Field & Minkler, 1988).

Older people spend more active leisure time with friends, and the lightheartedness and spontaneity of friendships help them rise above daily concerns. The relative brevity and infrequency of time spent with friends may add to its special savor. Older people enjoy time spent with their friends more than time spent with their families (Antonucci & Akiyama, 1995). Friends and neighbors often take the place of family members who are far away. And although friends cannot replace a spouse or a partner, they can help compensate for the lack of one (Hartup & Stevens, 1999).

Adults older than 85 maintain friendships, often calling a someone friend who formerly would have been considered merely an acquaintance. Because disabilities may hamper face-to-face contact, friendships may be maintained by telephone or mail and tend to be less intimate than in earlier years (Johnson & Troll, 1994).

CRITICAL THINKING

What importance do friends, significant others, and family members have in your life? Is one more important than the others?

Love

For most adults, a loving relationship with a partner, of the same or the other sex, is a pivotal element of their lives. According to Robert J. Sternberg's **triangular theory of love** (1985b; Sternberg & Barnes, 1985; Sternberg & Grajek, 1984), love has three faces, or elements: intimacy, passion, and commitment. *Intimacy*, the emotional element, involves self-disclosure, which leads to connection, warmth, and trust. *Passion*, the motivational element, is based on inner drives that translate physiological arousal into sexual desire. *Commitment*, the cognitive element, is the decision to love and to stay with the beloved. The degree to which these three elements are present determines what kind of love people feel (see Table 9.1), and mismatches can lead to problems

Patterns of Loving

Type	Description
Nonlove	All three components of love—intimacy, passion, and commitment—are absent. This describes most of our personal relationships, which are simply casual interactions.
Liking	Intimacy is the only component present. This is what we feel in true friendship and in many loving relationships. There is closeness, understanding, emotional support, affection, bondedness, and warmth. Neither passion nor commitment is present.
Infatuation	Passion is the only component present. This is "love at first sight," a strong physical attraction and sexual arousal, without intimacy or commitment. This can flare up suddenly and die just as fast—or, given certain circumstances, can sometimes last for a long time.
Empty love	Commitment is the only component present. This is often found in long-term relationships that have lost both intimacy and passion, or in arranged marriages.
Romantic love	Intimacy and passion are both present. Romantic lovers are drawn to each other physically and bonded emotionally. They are not, however, committed to each other.
Companionate love	Intimacy and commitment are both present. This is a long-term, committed friendship, often occurring in marriages in which physical attraction has died down but in which the partners feel close to each other and have made the decision to stay together.
Fatuous love	Passion and commitment are present, without intimacy. This is the kind of love that leads to a whirlwind courtship, in which a couple make a commitment on the basis of passion without allowing themselves the time to develop intimacy. This kind of love usually does not last, despite the initial intent to commit.
Consummate love	All three components are present in this "complete" love, which many of us strive for, especially in romantic relationships. It is easier to reach it than to hold onto it. Either partner may change what he or she wants from the relationship. If the other partner changes, too, the relationship may endure in a different form. If the other partner does not change, the relationship may dissolve.

SOURCE: Sternberg, 1985b.

in relationships. Some research suggests that trust, which is essential to intimacy with a lover, depends on the security of earlier attachments—attachments to parents or caregivers in infancy and childhood (DeAngelis, 1994).

Do opposites attract? Not as a rule. Research has found a tendency toward **assortative mating:** just as people choose friends with whom they have something in common, they tend to fall in love with and marry someone much like themselves (Epstein & Gutmann, 1984). According to the matching hypothesis, dating partners who are about equally attractive are the most likely to develop close relationships (Harvey & Pauwels, 1999). Lovers often resemble each other in physical appearance and attractiveness, mental and physical health, intelligence, popularity, and warmth. They are likely to be similar in the degree to which their parents are happy as individuals and as couples, and in such factors as socioeconomic status, race, religion, education, and income (Murstein, 1980). Husband and wife often have similar temperaments, too; risk takers tend to marry other risk takers—though they may be risking early divorce (Zuckerman, 1994)!

Of course, love doesn't always last. Among college students who were asked to recall how or why they fell in and out of love with a previous partner, the students who could explain why their earlier relationships ended were more satisfied with their current partners than those whose earlier relationships appeared to be unresolved (Clark & Collins, 1993).

Sexuality

Sexual development has a physical side (see Chapter 3), but also has a social side. In the United States today there is far more openness in discussing and expressing sexuality than there was in the past, and greater acceptance of sexual activity as normal, healthy, and pleasurable. One major change is greater acceptance of premarital or nonmarital sex, particularly in a loving, monogamous relationship. A related change is a decline in the *double standard*, the code that traditionally gave males more sexual freedom than females. A third change is more openness about, and acceptance of, homosexuality.

SEXUAL ORIENTATION

CRITICAL THINKING

Do you think that cultural pressure, learned behavior patterns, or inherited characteristics play a greater role in sexual orientation?

Three **sexual orientations** are commonly recognized: **homosexual,** attraction to individuals of one's own gender; **heterosexual,** attraction to individuals of the other gender; and **bisexual,** attraction to members of either gender. Persons with a homosexual orientation are sometimes referred to as "gay" (both men and women) or "lesbian" (women only). Sexual orientation is different from sexual behavior in that it refers to feelings and self-concept. A person's sexual orientation might or might not be expressed in behavior (American Psychological Association, 2001).

Homosexuality has been accepted as normal in many societies (Evans-Pritchard, 1970; Ford & Beach, 1951; Herdt, 1981, 1987; Schieffelin, 1976), or even as preferable to heterosexuality (Kelly, 1976; van Baal, 1966); and its incidence seems to be similar in a number of cultures (Hyde, 1986). In the

United States, although homosexuality has become more visible in recent years, only 2.8 percent of men and 1.4 percent of women in a major, nationally representative survey identified themselves as homosexual or bisexual. However, 5 percent of men and 4 percent of women reported at least one homosexual encounter as adults. Homosexual identification was more prevalent (9 percent for men and 3 percent for women) in the largest cities (Michael, Gagnon, Laumann, & Kolata, 1994).

Homosexual orientation is not limited to a particular type of person. Gay men and lesbians are of all ages, cultural backgrounds, races, religions, and nationalities. They work in all occupations and live in all parts of the country (American Psychological Association, 2001). Sexual orientation emerges for most people in early adolescence without any prior sexual experience. Furthermore, some people report trying very hard over many years to change their sexual orientation from homosexual to heterosexual, with no success. For these reasons, psychologists do not consider sexual orientation to be a conscious choice that can be voluntarily changed (American Psychological Association, 2001).

What causes sexual orientation? Freud believed that it is determined by parenting styles; learning theorists claim that (like any other behavior) it is learned through imitation and reinforcement. So far, neither of these perspectives is strongly supported by research.

A review of a large number of studies indicates that biology may play an important role in sexual orientation (Gladue, 1994). A man or woman who is the identical twin of a homosexual has about a 50 percent probability of being homosexual himself or herself; by comparison, the figure for a fraternal twin is only about 20 percent, and the figure for an adopted sibling is 10 percent or less. Although one series of studies linked male homosexuality to a small region of the X chromosome inherited from the mother (Hamer, Hu, Magnuson, Hu, & Pattatucci, 1993; Hu et al., 1995), later research failed to replicate this finding (Rice, Anderson, Risch, & Ebers, 1999). How hormonal activity affects brain development and how differences in brain structure may lead to a difference in sexual orientation have not been established (Golombok & Tasker, 1996). However, an anatomical difference between homosexual and heterosexual men in an area of the brain that governs sexual behavior has been reported (LeVay, 1991).

We can't, of course, be sure that a correlation between sexual orientation and brain structure or functioning indicates a causal relationship. Still, while not all men and women may achieve their sexual orientation in the same way, it appears increasingly likely that the process is a complex one in which genes may interact with certain critical hormonal and environmental events.

Negative attitudes toward homosexuality are slowly diminishing in the United States, but nearly three out of four men and more than two out of three women still disapprove (Gardiner et al., 1998). According to a *Newsweek* poll (2000), nearly half of the population surveyed consider homosexuality a sin, and one-third of the respondents in another survey (*Americans on Values*, 1999) believe that it is an illness—contrary to the stated position of the American Psychiatric Association (APA, 2000).

The social stigma against homosexuality, and the discrimination that reflects it, may have significant effects on gays' and lesbians' mental health. Studies have found a higher risk of anxiety, depression, and other psychiatric disorders among gays and lesbians than among heterosexuals (Cochran, 2001).

SEXUAL ATTITUDES AND BEHAVIOR

Views about sexual activity fall into three main categories, according to a major national survey of sexual attitudes and behavior. About 30 percent of Americans have traditional, or *reproductive* attitudes about sex—that sex is permissible only for reproductive purposes within marriage. Another 25 percent (more men than women) have a *recreational* view of sex: that whatever feels good and doesn't hurt anyone is fine. Roughly 45 percent take a *relational* view: that sex should be accompanied by love or affection, but not necessarily marriage (Laumann & Michael, 2000). These three views structure the national debate about what is right and wrong when it comes to sexual behavior.

According to one report, 61 percent of men but only 12 percent of women born before 1910 admit to premarital sex. By the 1980s, women had nearly as much sexual experience before marriage as men did (T. W. Smith, 1994).

The change in attitudes toward premarital sex among young adults in the United States since the 1960s is striking. Between 1965 and 1994, disapproval of sex before marriage fell from 63 percent to 30 percent among men and from 80 percent to 44 percent among women (Scott, 1998).

In some other respects, however, the change in sexual attitudes and behavior is not so dramatic. Neither men nor women appear to be as promiscuous as is sometimes thought. The median number of sex partners after age 18 is two for women and six for men. Most people meet their partners through mutual acquaintances and thus tend to be similar in age, educational level, and racial, ethnic, and religious background (see Figure 9.1).

Disapproval of extramarital sex today is even greater in U.S. society than disapproval of homosexuality—94 percent—though perhaps not as intense or as publicly expressed as in Ingrid Bergman's time. The pattern of strong disapproval of extramarital sex and far weaker disapproval of premarital sex also holds true in European countries such as Britain, Ireland, Germany, Sweden, and Poland, though degrees of disapproval differ from one country to another. The United States has more restrictive attitudes than any of these countries except Ireland, where the influence of the Catholic Church is strong. For example, in Germany and Sweden only 3 to 7 percent of adults disapprove of premarital sex (Scott, 1998). In China, sexual attitudes and premarital and extramarital sexual activity have liberalized dramatically despite official prohibition of sex outside marriage (Gardiner et al., 1998). Surveys taken at five-year intervals in the Netherlands found that, much as in the United States, attitudes toward extramarital sex liberalized between 1965 and 1975 and then became more restrictive. Younger, more educated, and less re-

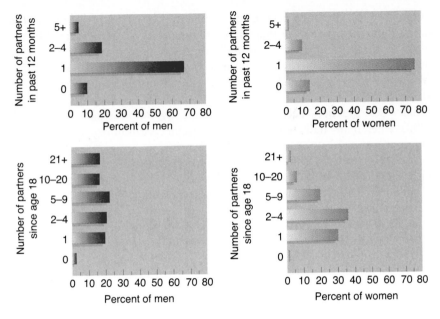

FIGURE 9.1 *Number of sex partners in past 12 months and since age 18.* SOURCE: Data from Michael, Gagnon, Laumann, & Kolata, 1994.

ligious people tend to have more liberal attitudes about sex, and men are still more liberal than women (Kraaykamp, 2002).

Although a good sexual relationship is viewed as important to quality of life for a majority of older adults, the quality of interpersonal relationships is even more important. Reported sexual activity declines for both men and women with age. This can be due to medical conditions and the loss of a partner (AARP, 1999).

The generation gap in sexual attitudes between those who came of age in the 1960s and their parents may foreshadow a more active sex life for the younger generation as it ages. Women 45 through 59 are much more likely to approve of sex between unmarried partners and less likely to believe that "sex is only for younger people"—than are women 60 and older. Older men also espouse more conservative values than younger men, but the gap is much narrower. A generation gap in attitudes toward sexuality suggests that future generations of older adults may not be as accepting of abstinence as the current older generation (AARP, 1999).

AIDS AND SEXUAL BEHAVIOR

About 30 percent of adults, because of the threat of AIDS, say they have modified their sexual behavior by having fewer partners, choosing them more carefully, using condoms, or abstaining from sex (Feinleib & Michael, 2000; Laumann, Gagnon, Michael, & Michaels, 1994; Michael, Gagnon, Laumann, &

Kolata, 1994). In fact, according to a major, nationally representative study, about 11 percent say they are abstaining from sex altogether (Michael et al., 1994). Similarly, in a nationally representative sample of 15- to 44-year-old unmarried, sexually experienced women, one-third had changed their behavior, most often by limiting the number of partners (McNally & Mosher, 1991).

Safer sex practices became prevalent among homosexuals in the early 1990s, when many had come to view promiscuity without regard for possible consequences as irresponsible.

According to the Centers for Disease Control, the number of Americans with AIDS is 816,149 (CDC, 2001). Worldwide the number is estimated at 42 million (CDC, 2001), and 21.8 million have died, including 3.1 million in the year 2002. Each year 5 million people are newly infected, 15,000 a day (CDC, 2001). More than 448,000 U.S. citizens are known to have died from AIDS. New drugs, in part, helped the number of deaths per year decline from 50,610 in 1995 to 16,371 in 2002. (CDC, 2003; Pear, 2001). Availability of affordable drug treatment in Africa is a current concern.

NONMARITAL AND MARITAL LIFESTYLES

CRITICAL THINKING

What factors influence people to choose lifestyles other than traditional marriage?

Today's rules for acceptable behavior are more elastic than they were during the first half of the twentieth century. Current norms no longer dictate that people must get married, stay married, or have children, and at what ages. People may stay single, live with a partner of either sex, divorce, remarry, be single parents, or remain childless; and a person's choices may change during the course of adulthood.

The proportion of U.S. households consisting of married couples with their own children dropped from 40 percent in 1970 to 24 percent in 2000. Meanwhile, the proportion of households in which one person lives alone increased from 17 percent to 26 percent (Fields & Casper, 2001; U.S. Bureau of the Census, 2002). People marry later nowadays, if at all; more have children outside of marriage, if at all; and more break up their marriages (Fields & Casper, 2001; T. Smith, 1999). Still, an overwhelming 95 percent of men and women have been married at some time before age 65, "indicating that marriage is still very much a part of American life" (Fields & Casper, 2001; Fields 2004, p. 10).

In this section, we look at marriage and its alternatives. In the next major section we examine parenthood.

Single Life

The number of young adults who have not yet married has increased dramatically. In 2000, about 45 percent of 25- to 29-year-olds had never married, a threefold increase since 1970. Even among 35- to 44-year-olds, 15.5 percent still had never married (Fields & Casper, 2001). The trend is particularly pronounced among African American women, 35 percent of whom remain unmarried in their late thirties (Teachman, Tedrow, & Crowder, 2000).

In a study of 300 black, white, and Latina single women in the Los Angeles area (Tucker & Mitchell-Kernan, 1998), members of all three groups had difficulty finding eligible men with similar educational and social backgrounds; but unlike the other two groups, African American women, whose average age was 40, seemed relatively untroubled by the situation.

While some young adults stay single because they have not found the right mates, others are single by choice. More women today are self-supporting, and there is less social pressure to marry. Some people want to be free to take risks, experiment, and make changes—move across the country or across the world, pursue careers, further their education, or do creative work without worrying about how their quest for self-fulfillment affects another person. Some enjoy sexual freedom. Some find the lifestyle exciting. Some just like being alone. And some postpone or avoid marriage because of fear that it will end in divorce. Postponement makes sense, since, as we'll see, the younger people are when they first marry, the likelier they are to split up. By and large, singles like their status (Austrom & Hanel, 1985). Most are not lonely (Cargan, 1981; Spurlock, 1990); they are busy and active and feel secure about themselves.

In more than half of the world, 5 percent or less of elderly men and 10 percent or less of elderly women have never married. In Europe, this gender difference may reflect the toll on marriageable men taken by World War II, when the current elderly cohort were of marrying age. In some Latin American and Caribbean countries, proportions of never-marrieds are higher, probably due to the prevalence of consensual unions (Kinsella & Velkoff, 2001). In the United States, only 4 percent of men and women 65 years and older have never married (Administration on Aging, 2001). This percentage is likely to increase as today's middle-aged adults grow old, since larger proportions of that cohort, especially African Americans, have remained single (U.S. Bureau of the Census, 1991a, 1991b, 1992, 1993).

Older never-married people are more likely than older divorced or widowed people to prefer single life and less likely to be lonely (Dykstra, 1995). Never-married, childless women in one study rated three kinds of roles or relationships as important: bonds with blood relatives, such as siblings and aunts; parent-surrogate ties with younger people; and same-generation, same-sex friendships (Rubinstein, Alexander, Goodman, & Luborsky, 1991).

Previously married older men are much more likely to date than older women, probably because of the greater availability of women in this age group. Most elderly daters are sexually active but do not expect to marry. Among both whites and African Americans, men are more interested in romantic involvement than women, who may fear getting "locked into" traditional gender roles (K. Bulcroft & O'Conner, 1986; R. A. Bulcroft & Bulcroft, 1991; Tucker, Taylor, & Mitchell-Kernan, 1993).

As black women age, they are increasingly less likely than black men to be married, romantically involved, or interested in a romantic relationship—perhaps for practical reasons, as unmarried black women tend to be better off financially than married ones (Tucker et al., 1993). Yet a single state entails risk: a black woman living alone in late life is three times as likely to be poor as a white woman in that situation (U.S. Bureau of the Census, 1991b).

Gay and Lesbian Relationships

CRITICAL THINKING

Should people with homosexual orientation be allowed to marry? Adopt children? Be covered by a partner's health care plan?

Adults are more likely than adolescents to identify themselves as homosexual. Because of strong societal disapproval of homosexuality, **coming out**—the process of openly disclosing a homosexual orientation—is often slow and painful. Coming out generally occurs in four stages, which may never be fully achieved (King, 1996):

1. *Recognition of being homosexual.* This may take place early in childhood or not until adolescence or later. It can be a lonely, painful, confusing experience.
2. *Getting to know other homosexuals* and establishing sexual and romantic relationships. This may not happen until adulthood. Contact with other homosexuals can diminish feelings of isolation and improve self-image.
3. *Telling family and friends.* Many homosexuals cannot bring themselves to do this for a long time—if ever. The revelation can bring disapproval, conflict, and rejection; or it may deepen family solidarity and support (Mays, Chatters, Cochran, & Mackness, 1998).
4. *Complete openness.* This includes telling colleagues, employers, and others. Homosexuals who reach this stage have achieved healthy acceptance of their sexuality as part of who they are.

Because of the secrecy and stigma that have surrounded homosexuality, studies of gays and lesbians tend to have sampling problems. What little research exists on gay men has focused mostly on urban white men with above-average income and education. Lesbians studied so far also tend to be mostly white, professional, and middle or upper class.

This research suggests that gay and lesbian relationships take many forms, but most homosexuals (like most heterosexuals) seek love, companionship, and sexual fulfillment through a relationship with one person. Such relationships are more common in societies that tolerate, accept, or support them (Gardiner et al., 1998). The ingredients of long-term satisfaction are very similar in homosexual and heterosexual relationships (Patterson, 1995b).

Lesbians are more likely to have stable, monogamous relationships than gay men. Since the AIDS epidemic, however, gay men have become more interested in long-term relationships. Gay and lesbian partners who live together tend to be as committed as married couples (Kurdek, 1995).

Gay and lesbian relationships tend to be stronger if known as such to family and friends, and if the couple seek out supportive gay and lesbian environments (Haas & Stafford, 1998). Coming out to parents is often difficult but need not necessarily have an adverse impact on the couple's relationship (LaSala, 1998). When family and friends are supportive and validate the relationship, its quality tends to be higher (R. B. Smith & Brown, 1997).

Gay and lesbian couples tend to be more egalitarian than heterosexual couples, but, as with many heterosexual couples, balancing commitment to careers and relationship can be difficult. Gay couples in which one partner is less career-oriented than the other have an easier time, but couples in which both partners are relationship-centered tend to be happiest.

Gays and lesbians now in middle age grew up at a time when homosexuality was considered a mental illness, and homosexuals tended to be isolated not only from the larger community but from each other. Today this pioneer generation is just beginning to explore the opportunities inherent in the growing acceptance of homosexuality.

Since many homosexuals still do not come out until well into adulthood, the timing of this crucial event can affect other aspects of development. Middle-aged gays and lesbians may be associating openly for the first time and establishing relationships. Many are still working out conflicts with parents and other family members (sometimes including spouses) or hiding their homosexuality from them.

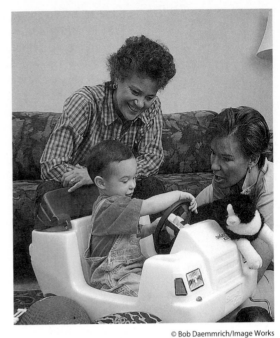

© Bob Daemmrich/Image Works

Lesbians tend to have stable, monogamous relationships. An estimated 8 to 10 million American children are living with homosexual parents.

In one study, more than 25 percent of middle-aged lesbians lived alone, even if they were in intimate relationships (Bradford & Ryan, 1991). This may in part be a cohort effect; lesbians who grew up in the 1950s may be uncomfortable about living openly with a partner, as many younger lesbians do now.

Gay men who do not come out until midlife often go through a prolonged search for identity, marked by guilt, secrecy, heterosexual marriage, and conflicted relationships with both sexes. By contrast, those who recognize and accept their sexual orientation early in life often cross racial, socioeconomic, and age barriers within the gay community. Some move to cities with large gay populations, where they can more easily seek out and form relationships.

There is little research on homosexual relationships in old age. This is largely because the current cohort of older adults grew up at a time when living openly as a homosexual was rare (Huyck, 1995). An important distinction is between elderly homosexuals who recognized themselves as gay or lesbian before the rise of the gay liberation movement in the late 1960s and those who did not do so until that movement (and the shift in public discourse it brought about) was in full swing. Whereas the self-concept of the first group was shaped by the prevailing stigma against homosexuality, the second group tend to view their homosexuality simply as a *status:* a characteristic of the self, like any other (Rosenfeld, 1999).

Older homosexual adults, like older heterosexual adults, have strong needs for intimacy, social contact, and generativity. Gays' and lesbians' relationships in late life tend to be strong, supportive, and diverse. Many homosexuals have children from earlier marriages; others have adopted children. Friendship networks or support groups may substitute for the traditional family (Reid, 1995).

Many gays and lesbians, especially those who have maintained close relationships and strong involvement in the homosexual community, adapt to aging with relative ease. Coming out—whenever it occurs—is an important developmental transition, which can enhance mental health, life satisfaction, self-acceptance, and self-respect and smooth the adjustment to aging (Friend, 1991; Reid, 1995).

The main problems of many older gays and lesbians grow out of societal attitudes: strained relationships with the family of origin, discrimination, lack of medical or social services and social support, insensitive policies of social agencies, and dealing with health care providers or bereavement and inheritance issues when a partner falls ill or dies (Berger & Kelly, 1986; Kimmel, 1990; Reid, 1995).

Today, gays and lesbians in the United States and Europe are struggling to obtain legal recognition of their unions, as in the Netherlands and the state of Vermont, and the right to adopt children or raise their own. Many homosexuals who have been married and had children before coming out have been unable to gain or keep custody. Others are adopting children or conceiving via assisted reproduction techniques. To give these children the benefit of two parents, the American Academy of Pediatrics Committee on Psychosocial Aspects of Child and Family Health (2002) supports laws permitting adoption by the parent's same-sex partner.

Gays and lesbians also are pressing for an end to discrimination in employment and housing. A current issue is whether unmarried domestic partners—homosexual or heterosexual—should be entitled to coverage under each other's health insurance and pension plans, should be able to file joint tax returns, and should receive bereavement leave and other customary benefits of marriage. Such provisions already are in effect in France, Sweden, Norway, Denmark, and the Netherlands (Trueheart, 1999).

Cohabitation

Cohabitation is a lifestyle in which an unmarried couple involved in a sexual relationship live together in what is sometimes called a *consensual* or *informal union.* Such unions have become the norm in many European countries, such as Sweden and Denmark, where cohabiting couples have practically the same legal rights as married ones, and are becoming increasingly common in the United States and Canada (Popenoe & Whitehead, 1999; Seltzer, 2000). In

CRITICAL THINKING

From your experience, is it a good idea to live with a lover before marriage? Why or why not? Does it make a difference whether children are involved?

Britain, 70 percent of first partnerships are cohabitations, and 60 percent of cohabiting couples eventually marry (Ford, 2002). In Canada, 12 percent of couples were cohabiting in 1996, twice as many as in 1981 (Wu, 1999).

Cohabitation can be either a substitute for marriage or a "trial marriage." Consensual unions have long been accepted as an alternative to marriage in many Latin American countries; this may explain why, for example, Puerto Ricans have higher rates of cohabitation and are less likely than non-Hispanic white Americans to marry their live-in partners. Although family law in the United States gives cohabitors few of the rights and benefits of marriage, this is changing, particularly with regard to protections for children of cohabiting couples. And, as cohabitation becomes increasingly common, cohabiting couples are under less social pressure to marry (Seltzer, 2000).

Premarital cohabitation has accompanied the trend toward delayed marriage, discussed in the next section (Seltzer, 2000). More than half of all U.S. couples who marry have lived together first, as did Ingrid Bergman and Roberto Rossellini (Popenoe & Whitehead, 1999; Seltzer, 2000). Looking at the data another way, more than half (58 percent) of first cohabitations that last three years, and 70 percent of those that last five years, result in marriage (Bramlett & Mosher, 2002). However, cohabiting unions tend to be less stable than marriages (Bramlett & Mosher, 2002; Popenoe & Whitehead, 1999; Seltzer, 2000). Thirty-nine percent break up within three years and 49 percent within five years (Bramlett & Mosher, 2002). Many adults have two or more live-in partners before marriage (Michael et al., 1994; Popenoe & Whitehead, 1999). Couples who have a child together are less likely to break up, whether or not they marry (Seltzer, 2000).

According to national surveys, most young adults think cohabitation before marriage is a good idea. Yet, according to some research, couples who live together before marriage tend to have unhappier marriages and greater likelihood of divorce (Bramlett & Mosher, 2002; Popenoe & Whitehead, 1999; Seltzer, 2000). In part, the higher divorce rates of couples who cohabit before marriage may reflect the kinds of people who choose cohabitation, and not the effects of cohabitation itself. Cohabitants tend to have unconventional attitudes about family life, and they are less likely than most other people to select partners like themselves in age, race or ethnicity, and previous martial status. They are more likely to have divorced parents and stepchildren and to have liberal attitudes toward divorce. All these factors tend to predict unstable marriages (Cohan & Kleinbaum, 2002; Fields & Casper, 2001; D. R. Hall & Zhao, 1995; Popenoe & Whitehead, 1999; Seltzer, 2000). However, Teachman (2003) found that cohabitation does not increase the risk of divorce for women, if cohabitation is limited to the future husband.

CRITICAL THINKING

Should one enter into marriage with the idea that it will be a permanent relationship? Why or why not?

Marriage

Marriage doesn't have the same meaning everywhere. In Tibet, a man and his father have the same wife. In Zaire, a woman shares her husband with her mother (World Features Syndicate, 1996). But the universality of some form

CRITICAL THINKING

How has culture influenced your decision about whether or not to marry? Are cultural influences conflicting? If so, how was the conflict resolved?

of marriage throughout history and around the world (Kottak, 1994) shows that it meets a variety of fundamental needs. Marriage is usually considered the best way to ensure orderly raising of children. It provides for division of labor within a consuming and working unit. Ideally, it offers intimacy, friendship, affection, sexual fulfillment, and companionship.

The typical "marrying age" varies greatly across cultures (Bianchi & Spain, 1986). In eastern Europe, people tend to marry early; in Hungary, for example, 70 percent of women and 33 percent of men age 20 to 24 have already married. Industrialized nations are seeing a trend toward later marriage as young adults take time to pursue educational and career goals or to explore relationships. In Scandinavia, 85 percent of women and 95 percent of men age 20 to 24 have not yet married (though most eventually will marry), and cohabitation is common among young adults. Japan, too, has a high proportion of unmarried young adults, but rather than cohabiting they tend to live with their parents. In France, the average bridegroom is 30 and his bride, 28, five years older than their counterparts a quarter-century ago (Ford, 2002). In Canada, the average age of first marriage for women has risen from about 23 to 27, and for men from about 26 to 29, since 1961 (Wu, 1999). In the United States the median age of first-time brides is 25, and of first-time bridegrooms, nearly 27—a rise of more than 3 years since 1975 (U.S. Bureau of the Census, 2002).

In 1998 in the United States, 110.6 million adults (56.0 percent of the adult population) were married and living with their spouse (see Fig. 9.2). Among people ages 25 to 34 years old, 13.6 million had never been married, representing 34.7 percent of all people in the age group. Among African Americans in this age group, 53.4 percent had never been married (U.S. Bureau of the Census, 1998). The dramatically lower marriage rate among African Americans today may be due in part to high unemployment among black men and greater economic independence among black working women. Also, the lower life expectancy of black men, and their tendency to marry much younger women, reduces marital prospects for older black single women (U.S. Bureau of the Census, 2000). In 2003, older men (71 percent) were more likely to be married than older women (41 percent) (AOA, 2004).

MARRIAGE AND HAPPINESS

National surveys have shown that marriage is the most important factor in happiness—more important than work, friendships, or anything else. However, some benefits of marriage are no longer confined to wedlock. Single people can get both sex and companionship outside of marriage, and marriage no longer is the sole (or even the most reliable) source of security for women. Since most married women now continue to work, and most husbands do not share the burdens of homemaking and child care equally (see Box 9.1), marriage may increase rather than decrease women's stress.

The two sexes often have different expectations about marriage. To women, marital intimacy entails sharing of feelings and confidences. Men tend to ex-

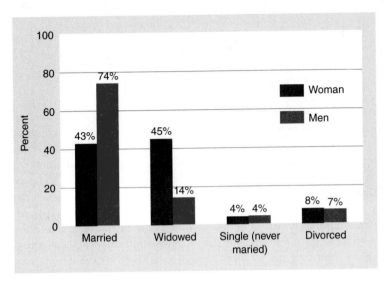

FIGURE 9.2 *Marital status of persons age 65 and over, 2000.* *Source:* Administration on Aging, 2001; based on data from U.S. Bureau of Census; Papalia, Olds, & Feldman, 2004.

press intimacy through sex, practical help, companionship, and doing things together (Thompson & Walker, 1989). Many men are uncomfortable talking about feelings, or even listening to their wives talk about theirs. Since women are more likely to do things that matter to men, men often get more of what is important to them, while wives are left feeling dissatisfied. Perhaps that helps explain why the association between marriage and psychological well-being is more pronounced for men (Ross, Mirowsky, & Goldsteen, 1990).

MARITAL AND EXTRAMARITAL SEXUAL ACTIVITY

Americans apparently have sex less often than images in the media suggest, but married people have it more often than singles who are not cohabiting. Comprehensive face-to-face interviews with a random sample of 3,432 men and women age 18 to 59 found that about one-third have intercourse two or more times a week: 40 percent of married couples, more than 50 percent of cohabiting couples, and fewer than 25 percent of those who do not live with a sex partner (Michael et al., 1994). However, married couples report more emotional satisfaction from sex than single or cohabiting couples (Waite & Joyner, 2000).

Most couples have sexual relations more frequently during the first year of marriage than ever again. Frequency of sexual activity tends to be related to a couple's satisfaction with the marriage (Call, Sprecher, & Schwartz, 1995). Because of physical changes in sexual capacity (see Chapter 3), most older married couples have sex less frequently but still may find it intensely pleasurable.

How Dual-Earner Couples Cope

The growing number of marriages in which both husband and wife are gainfully employed represents a major change from traditional family patterns. In 1940 women made up one-quarter of the labor force; by 1997 they constituted nearly half of it (Smith & Bachu, 1999).

Nearly two out of three U.S. families consisting of a married couple with children under 18 are dual-earner families (Bureau of Labor Statistics, 1999). Fewer women than ever are taking time out for motherhood. Two out of three prospective first-time mothers work during pregnancy, and three-fourths of them return to work within a year after giving birth.

Why do so many women work? Many factors may play a part—the rising cost of living; changes in the divorce, social security, and tax laws; changing attitudes about gender roles; availability of labor-saving household appliances; and the reduced income gap between male and female workers. Some women simply want to be gainfully employed (Jones, McGrattan, & Manuelli, 2002).

It is important in studying dual-earner couples to recognize the diversity of these families (Barnett & Hyde, 2001). Besides the more traditional pattern of a main provider (usually the man) and a secondary provider (usually the woman), there are families in which both earners have high-powered careers and high earnings (like Petter Lindstrom and Ingrid Bergman). There also are many middle-class families in which one or both partners "scale back": cut back on working hours or refuse overtime or turn down jobs that require excessive travel, so as to increase family time and reduce stress (Becker & Moen, 1999; Crouter & Manke,

1994). Or a couple may make trade-offs: trading a career for a job, or trading off whose work takes precedence, depending on shifts in career opportunities and family responsibilities.

Dual-earner marriages present both opportunities and challenges. On the positive side, a second income raises some families from poverty to middle-income status and makes others affluent. It makes women more independent and gives them a greater share of economic power, and it reduces the pressure on men to be providers; 47 percent of working wives contribute half or more of family income (Louis Harris & Associates, 1995). Less tangible benefits may include a more equal relationship between husband and wife, better health for both, greater self-esteem for the woman, and a closer relationship between a father and his children (Gilbert, 1994).

On the downside, working couples face extra demands on time and energy, conflicts between work and family, possible rivalry between spouses, and anxiety and guilt about meeting children's needs. The family is most demanding, especially for women who are employed full time, when there are young children (Milkie & Peltola, 1999; Warren & Johnson, 1995). Careers are especially demanding when a worker is getting established or being promoted. Both kinds of demands frequently occur in young adulthood.

Working men and women seem equally affected by physical and psychological stress, whether due to work interfering with family life or the other way around (Frone, Russell, & Barnes, 1996). However, men and women may be stressed by different aspects of the work-family situation. Among 314 spouses with relatively high income and education, husbands were more likely to suffer from overload (perhaps because they had not been socialized to deal with domestic as well as occupational responsibilities). Women were more likely to feel the strain of conflicting role expectations—the need to be aggressive and competitive at work but compassionate and nurturing at home (Paden & Buehler, 1995).

Overall, two researchers in women's studies suggest, combining work and family roles is generally beneficial to both men and women in terms of mental and physical health and the strength of their relationship (Barnett & Hyde, 2001). That conclusion is based on a large body of empirical research, including findings that most psychological gender differences are not large or immutable enough to require highly differentiated roles. Besides added income, factors that contribute to the beneficial effects of multiple roles include increased opportunities for social support; opportunities to experience success in more than one arena; balancing of failure or stress in one role by success and satisfaction in another role; broader perspective or frame of reference; increased complexity of the self-concept, which may buffer swings in mood and self-esteem; and similarity of experiences, which can enhance communication and marital quality. However, the benefits of multiple roles depend on how many roles each partner carries, the time demands of each role, and—most important—the success or satisfaction the partners derive from their roles. The benefits also can be moderated by the extent to which couples hold traditional or nontraditional attitudes about gender roles.

Research suggests that "the inevitability of a 'second shift' for wives is overstated" (Gilbert, 1994). Dual-career families fall into three patterns: conventional, modern, and role-sharing. In a *conventional* marriage, both partners consider household chores and child care "women's work." The husband may "help," but his career takes precedence; he is usually more ambitious, earns more than his wife, and sees it as "her choice" to add a career to her primary domestic role. In the *modern* pattern, husband and wife share parenting, but the wife does more housework. The man's active fathering may stem not from egalitarian principles but from wanting to be involved with his children. The *role-sharing* pattern, the most egalitarian, occurs in at least one-third of heterosexual dual-career families. Both husband and wife are actively involved in household and family responsibilities as well as careers (Gilbert, 1994). Even among couples highly committed to dual-career lifestyles, tasks tend to be gender-typed: wives buy groceries and husbands mow the lawn (Apostol et al., 1993).

Nevertheless, the burdens of the dual-earner lifestyle generally fall most heavily on the woman. In 1997, employed married men spent nearly one hour more on household chores and one-half hour more with their children on workdays than in 1977; yet the husbands still did only about two-thirds as much domestic work and child care as employed married women (Bond & Galinsky, 1998).

The effects of a dual-earner lifestyle on a marriage may depend largely on how husband and wife view their roles. Unequal roles are not necessarily seen as inequitable, and it may be a *perception* of unfairness that contributes most to marital instability. A national longitudinal survey of 3,284 women in two-income families found greater likelihood of divorce the more hours the woman worked—*if* she had a nontraditional view of marital roles. Given that men generally do less household work than women, an employed woman who believes in an equal division of labor is likely to perceive as unfair the greater burden she carries in comparison with her husband; and this perception of unfairness will probably be magnified the more hours she puts in on the job (Greenstein, 1995).

What spouses perceive as fair may depend on the size of the wife's financial contribution, whether she thinks of herself as a coprovider or merely as supplementing her husband's income, and the meaning and importance she and her husband place on her work (Gilbert, 1994). In nearly one in four dual-earner households, the wife earns more than the husband. In such households, women may have a greater say in family financial and career decisions. When the woman is regarded as the primary breadwinner, there may be a reversal of traditional gender roles (Winkler, 1998). Whatever the actual division of labor, couples who agree on their assessment of it and who enjoy a harmonious, caring, involved family life are more satisfied than those who do not (Gilbert, 1994).

Some married people seek sex outside of marriage, especially after the first few years, when the excitement and novelty of sex with the spouse wear off or problems in the relationship surface. According to recent surveys, extramarital sex is much less common than is generally thought. Only about 21 percent of men and 11.5 percent of women who have ever been married report having had extramarital relations. Young adults are more likely to engage in extramarital activity than those born before 1940 (T. W. Smith, 1994).

Divorce and Remarriage

CRITICAL THINKING

What issues do you believe must be resolved to reduce the percentage of divorce in the United States?

Divorce rates reflect differences among cultures. Divorce has increased dramatically in such countries as the United Kingdom, Sweden, France, and the former Soviet Union. This increase has accompanied the passage in most western countries, mainly in the 1960s and 1970s, of more liberal divorce laws, which eliminate the need to find one partner at fault. Japan, a more traditional society, had a lower, more stable divorce rate than any of these countries between 1948 and 1988 (Burns, 1992). Countries such as Italy (see Figure 9.3) and Ireland, where religious opposition to divorce is strong, have not experienced appreciably higher rates. This may change in Ireland, where a November, 1995, referendum ended a constitutional ban on divorce.

The United States has had one of the highest divorce rates in the world (Bruce, Lloyd, & Leonard, 1995; Burns, 1992; U.S. Bureau of the Census, 1992; again, see Figure 9.3). The rate seems to have diminished somewhat since 1980, after having risen for two decades. In 2000, there were 19.8 million currently divorced Americans, representing 9.8 percent of the U.S. population (U.S. Bureau of the Census, 2001).

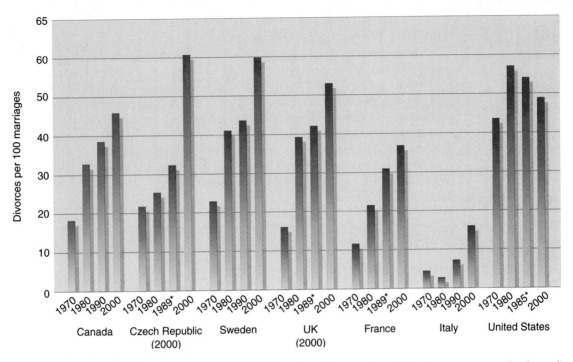

FIGURE 9.3 Divorce rates have risen since 1970 in many developed countries; but rates remain relatively low in Italy, where religious opposition remains strong. The U.S. divorce rate is slightly decreasing. *SOURCE: Bruce, Lloyd, & Leonard, 1995, p. 20; based on data from Monnier & Guibert-Lamone, 1993, United Nations Economic Commission for Europe, 2003, and Divorce Magazine.com, 2003.*

Decreasing marriage rates and increasing divorce rates are especially striking among African Americans. Since 1950, the percentage of African American women who are married declined from 62 percent to 36.1 percent, while divorce rose from 3 percent to 11.7 percent. The decline in percentage of married white women is less stark, from 66 percent to 57.4 percent, while the rise in divorce is comparable: from 2 percent to 10.2 percent (U.S. Census Bureau, 2000 from JointCenter.org 2003). One-third of divorces occur during the first 10 years of marriage (Bramlett & Mosher, 2001).

Divorce rates among aging baby boomers now in their fifties, many of whom married later and had fewer children than in previous generations, are projected to continue to rise (Hiedermann et al., 1998; Uhlenberg, Cooney, & Boyd, 1990). Even in long marriages, the increasing number of years that people can expect to live in good health after child rearing ends can make the dissolution of a marginal marriage and the prospect of possible remarriage a more practical and attractive option (Hiedermann et al., 1998). Contrary to common belief, research suggests that no-fault laws, at least in most parts of the United States, are *not* significantly responsible for the rise in divorce. It appears that changes in the old, stiffer laws (which were widely evaded) were more a response to a greater demand for divorce than a cause of the demand (Marvell, 1989; Wright & Stetson, 1978).

Several societal developments underlie the overall increase in divorce in the past. Women who are more financially independent of their husbands were less likely to stay in bad marriages. Instead of staying together "for the sake of the children," spouses may be more likely to conclude that staying in an unhappy, conflict-filled marriage may do greater psychological damage. Of course, for the increasing number of childless couples, it's easier to return to a single state (Berscheid & Campbell, 1981; Eisenberg, 1995). Perhaps most important, while most people *hope* their marriage will endure, fewer *expect* this. Table 9.2 summarizes other factors in divorce.

TABLE 9.2

Personal Factors Associated with Probability of Divorce

Factor	Remarks
Premarital cohabitation	This factor has been explained as a result of the fact that people who live together are less conventional. As this lifestyle becomes more common, it should exert less influence. And in fact, for recent cohorts the effect is weaker. If cohabitation is with a future husband, cohabitation does not increase risk of divorce.
Young age at marriage	This is the strongest predictor of divorce in the first 5 years of marriage.
Bearing a child before marriage	Premarital pregnancy of itself does not seem to increase the risk of divorce.
Having no children	Having at least one child reduces the risk of divorce, especially if that child is a boy. Fathers tend to be more involved with sons than with daughters, and greater involvement of the father in child care reduces risk of divorce.
Stepchildren in the home	The presence of children from a previous marriage brings additional stresses and divided loyalties.
Divorce of own parents	This is still an important risk factor, even now that it is more common to have divorced parents.
Being African American	This difference still exists when socioeconomic status, fertility, sex ratios, and age at marriage are controlled.

SOURCES: Schoen, 1992; L. K. White, 1990; Teachman, 2003.

Economic Consequences of Divorce

Despite highly publicized celebrity settlements—for example, the $100 million the Hollywood producer Steven Spielberg paid his ex-wife, Amy Irving, in 1989—most women are financially worse off after divorce (Kreider & Fields, 2002). Changes such as the sharp curtailing of spousal maintenance, or alimony, were intended to treat both spouses as equals. But in most marriages, husbands and wives do not have equal economic resources or equal bargaining power (Seltzer & Garfinkel, 1990).

Alimony is now awarded to either spouse in only about 1 out of 7 cases, and then for only 2 to 5 years. Expecting a middle-aged woman who has not worked for pay or whose income is significantly less than her ex-husband's to rapidly become self-supporting can create obvious hardships. Women's power is further reduced by the fact that most states now allow one spouse to obtain a divorce without the other's consent (Sitarz, 1990). A requirement of mutual consent would give a dependent wife leverage to press for better terms (Becker, 1992).

Because the woman usually has custody of the children, and child support—if awarded at all—is generally inadequate and often evaded, many women and their families have to make a major financial adjustment after divorce. Including earnings from employment, the average divorced woman receives only 70 percent of her former income in the year following the divorce; 5 years afterward, her economic position has not appreciably improved. More than 40 percent of

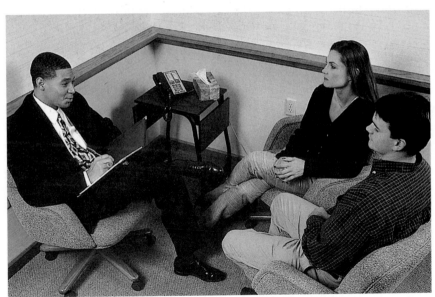

© Aaron Haupt/Stock Boston

A divorce mediator tries to help a couple reach an agreement acceptable to both. For some couples, mediation can be more amicable, quicker, and less expensive than negotiating through attorneys and can result in better compliance with the terms of the decree.

divorced women have their incomes cut by more than half. Meanwhile, the man's standard of living tends to rise because he is allocating a smaller proportion of his income to support of his family. The result is a dramatic increase in poverty rates for women and children involved in divorce or separation (Duncan & Hoffman, 1985; Seltzer & Garfinkel, 1990). More than half of poor families in the United States are headed by single mothers, 4 out of 5 of whom were once married (Weitzman, 1985). Worldwide, female-headed households, which are increasing in number, tend to be poorer than households headed by men (Brocas, Cailloux, & Oget, 1990; United Nations, 1991).

Wives who have the least income of their own tend to obtain the least favorable property settlements (Seltzer & Garfinkel, 1990). In states that require equal division of property after divorce, the court may order the house (frequently the main asset) to be sold and the proceeds divided between the ex-spouses, leaving the woman and children unable to find comparable housing (Weitzman, 1985). If a woman does get the home, it is often encumbered with a mortgage, while the man typically gets the liquid assets (Illinois Task Force, 1990). On the other hand, in most states the unpaid contributions a homemaker made to the marriage are now considered in the property settlement (Sitarz, 1990).

In many countries, such as Canada, Australia, New Zealand, and the United States, no-fault divorce has been accompanied by increased use of mediation to resolve issues regarding the divorce settlement (Davidson, 1985; Foy, 1987). Rather than having the parties negotiate through their attorneys, a neutral third party—the mediator—guides them in sorting out their rights and responsibilities. The goal is to reach a fair agreement acceptable to both sides. Full and frank disclosure of all assets is essential, as is confidentiality (Ferstenberg, 1992; Payne & Overend, 1990).

Mediation can be more amicable, less time-consuming, and less expensive than adversarial negotiations, and because the agreement is voluntary, mediation can result in better compliance. It also may help a couple to cooperate in dealing with the needs of the children (Ferstenberg, 1992; Lemmon, 1983). Couples who are not under severe financial pressure and are coping well with the breakup of their marriage are most likely to reach a mediated settlement and to be satisfied with the process (Irving & Benjamin, 1988).

EMOTIONAL ADJUSTMENT TO DIVORCE

Divorce is not a single event. It is a *process*—"a sequence of potentially stressful experiences that begin before physical separation and continue after it" (Morrison & Cherlin, 1995, p. 801). Ending even an unhappy marriage can be extremely painful, especially when there are children.

Reactions to stress may show up in poor health. Separated and divorced people have elevated rates of illness and death (Kitson & Morgan, 1990). Another common reaction is difficulty in performing ordinary social activities—

a problem that, according to some research, affects divorced women more than widows (Kitson & Roach, 1989).

Even though some people may seem to adjust rather quickly, divorce tends to reduce long-term well-being, especially for the partner who did not initiate the divorce or does not remarry. Reasons may include disruption of parent-child relationships, discord with a former spouse, economic hardship, loss of emotional support, and having to move out of the family home (Amato, 2000). Divorce can bring feelings of failure, blame, hostility, and self-recrimination, as well as high rates of depression, illness, and death (Kitson & Morgan, 1990; Thabes, 1997). On the other hand, when a marriage was highly conflicted, its ending can improve well-being (Amato, 2000).

Women are more negatively affected by divorce at any age than men are (Marks & Lambert, 1998). Among 272 divorced women surveyed an average of fourteen years after divorce, about half had initiated the breakup, but about 80 percent of the whole sample said it had taken them three years or more to feel comfortable being unattached. Older women, those without young children, those who had not been abused during their marriage, those with higher incomes, and those who had had good legal representation during the divorce tended to adjust better (Thabes, 1997). Women are more likely than men to live in poverty after separation or divorce (Kreider & Fields, 2002). Many have to deal with continued struggles with an ex-spouse who may default on child support (Kitson & Morgan, 1990).

An important factor in adjustment is emotional detachment from the former spouse. People who argue with their ex-mates or have not found a new lover or spouse experience more distress. An active social life, both at the time of divorce and afterward, helps (Amato, 2000; Thabes, 1997; Tschann, Johnston, & Wallerstein, 1989).

Divorce can be especially traumatic for middle-aged and older people, who expect their lives to be relatively settled. People who divorce after age 50, particularly women, tend to have more trouble adjusting and less hope for the future (Chiriboga, 1982). Older divorced and separated men are less satisfied with friendships and leisure activities than married men. For both sexes, rates of mental illness and death are higher, perhaps because social support networks for older divorced people are inadequate (Uhlenberg & Myers, 1981).

REMARRIAGE AFTER DIVORCE

Remarriage, said Samuel Johnson—an eighteenth-century scholar, essayist, and poet—"is the triumph of hope over experience." An estimated three-quarters of divorced women in the United States remarry within ten years. Young women (under age 25) are more likely to remarry than older ones, but also more likely to redivorce (Bramlett & Mosher, 2001, 2002). Men are even likelier to remarry than women (U.S. Bureau of the Census, 1998). Thus only

8 percent of men and 10 percent of women are currently divorced. Half of those who remarry after divorce from a first marriage do so within about three years (Kreider & Fields, 2002). Remarriage rates are somewhat lower in Canada and Europe (Coleman et al., 2000).

Remarriages are more likely than first marriages to end in divorce. The likelihood of redivorce is greatest during the first five years, especially when there are stepchildren (Parke & Buriel, 1998). Remarried partners may be less likely than partners in first marriages to have similar interests and values. And, having once divorced, they may be more likely to see divorce as a solution to marital problems (Booth & Edwards, 1992).

Remarriage in late life may have a special character. Among 125 well-educated, fairly affluent men and women, those in late-life remarriages seemed more trusting and accepting, and less in need of deep sharing of personal feelings. Men, but not women, tended to be more satisfied in late-life remarriages than in midlife ones (Bograd & Spilka, 1996).

Remarriage has societal benefits, since older married people are less likely than those living alone to need help from the community. Remarriage could be encouraged by letting people keep pension and social security benefits derived from a previous marriage and by greater availability of shared living quarters, such as group housing.

What Makes Marriages Succeed?

Divorce has become so common that social scientists are studying why some marriages do *not* break up. One of the most important factors in marital success is a sense of commitment. Among a national sample of 2,331 married people, the partners' dependence on each other played a part in commitment to marriage, but the strongest factor was a feeling of obligation to the spouse (Nock, 1995). Similarly, in an in-depth study of 15 couples who had been married more than 30 years, the factors that emerged most consistently were enjoyable relationships and commitment—both to the idea of marriage and to the partner. Another key factor was intimacy balanced with autonomy, which in turn either affected or was affected by good communication, similar perceptions of the relationship, and religious orientation (Robinson & Blanton, 1993).

Other studies have found that success in marriage is closely associated with how partners communicate, make decisions, and deal with conflict. In long-lived marriages, spouses tend to work out problems together rather than letting them fester (Brubaker, 1983, 1993). How couples handle disagreements and fights may predict the course of a marriage. Whining, defensiveness, stubbornness, and withdrawal (walking away or not talking to the spouse) are signs of trouble. But arguing and showing anger (as a form of communication) seem to be good for a marriage (Gottman & Krokoff, 1989). In one study that followed 150 couples through the first 13 years of marriage, those who learned to "fight fair" were 50 percent less likely to divorce (Markman, Renick, Floyd, Stanley, & Clements, 1993; Clements, Stanley, & Markman, 2004).

Age at marriage is a major predictor of whether a union will last. Teenagers have high divorce rates; people who wait until their twenties to marry have a better chance of success. College graduates and couples with high family income are less likely to end their marriages than those with less education and income (Bramlett & Mosher, 2001, 2002). Cohabitation before marriage and having divorced parents are predictive of divorce; so are becoming pregnant or bearing a child before marriage, having no children, and having stepchildren in the home (Bramlett & Mosher, 2002; Schoen, 1992; White, 1990). People who attach high importance to religion are less likely to experience marital dissolution (Bramlett & Mosher, 2002).

Economic hardship can put severe emotional stress on a marriage. In a four-year longitudinal study of more than 400 married couples, those who were most resilient when faced with economic pressures were those who showed mutual supportiveness—who listened to each other's concerns, tried to help, were sensitive to each other's point of view, and expressed approval of each other's qualities (Conger, Rueter, & Elder, 1999).

FAMILY LIFE

What is often called the *traditional family*—a husband, a wife, and their biological children—is far from universal. Family life throughout the world is highly diverse and rapidly changing (O'Grady-LeShane, 1993).

Particularly in the United States and western Europe, dramatic changes have occurred in families' size, composition, structure, and living arrangements (Eisenberg, 1995; Gilliand, 1989). What do today's families look like? Why, when, and how do adults become parents, and how does parenthood influence their development? Why do some people choose not to become parents? As we look at what has happened to the American family, keep in mind that similar trends are taking place elsewhere.

Changing Family Structures

The structure, or makeup, of families in the United States has changed dramatically. In earlier generations, the vast majority of children grew up in traditional families with two married, heterosexual biological or adoptive parents. Today, although most children under 18 live with two parents, the proportion has declined drastically (see Figure 9.4). In addition, many two-parent families are cohabiting families or stepfamilies, resulting from divorce and remarriage. There also are a growing number of other family types, including single-parent families, gay and lesbian families, and grandparent-headed families. The proportion of all households in which a married couple live with their biological, adopted, or stepchildren fell from about 40 percent in 1970 to only 24 percent in 2000 (Fields & Casper, 2001).

Other things being equal, children tend to do better in a traditional two-parent family than in a divorced, single-parent, or stepfamily (Bramlett & Mosher, 2001; Bray & Hetherington, 1993; Bronstein, Clauson, Stoll, &

> CRITICAL THINKING
>
> What explanations can you offer for worldwide changes in family size and structure?

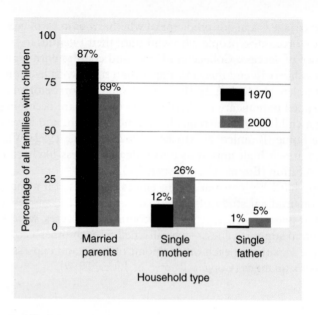

FIGURE 9.4 *Families with children younger than 18, 1970 and 2000.* Most children under 18 in the United States live with two married parents, but this proportion has dropped during the past three decades. Many of these two-parent families are stepfamilies. *SOURCE:* Data from Fields & Casper, 2001 in Papalia, Olds, & Feldman, 2004.

Abrams, 1993; D. A. Dawson, 1991; Hetherington, Bridges, & Insabella, 1998). However, structure in itself is not the key; the parents' relationship with each other and their ability to create a favorable atmosphere affect children's adjustment more than does marital status (Bray & Hetherington, 1993; Bronstein et al., 1993; D. A. Dawson, 1991; Emery, 1988; Hetherington, 1989).

Parenthood Today

At one time, a blessing offered to newlyweds in the Asian country of Nepal was, "May you have enough sons to cover the hillsides!" Today, Nepali couples are wished, "May you have a very bright son" (B. P. Arjyal, personal communication, February 12, 1993). While sons still are preferred over daughters, even boys are not wished for in such numbers as in the past.

In preindustrial societies, large families were a necessity: Children helped with the family's work and would eventually care for aging parents. The death rate in childhood was high, and having many children made it more likely that some of them would reach maturity. Today, because of technological progress, fewer workers are needed; because of modern medical care, more children survive; and because of government programs, some care of the aged is provided. Now overpopulation and hunger are major problems in some parts of the world, and children have become an expense rather than an economic asset.

One response to these changes in developing countries such as Nepal, as well as among more educated adults in industrial countries like the United States, is greater interest in limiting family size and in spacing children farther apart.

Still, the desire for children is almost universal. This urge is not limited to married people—which may be one reason that a growing number of single women have children.

CRITICAL THINKING
Why do couples choose to have children in spite of increased educational costs and marginal community support?

LIVING IN A ONE-PARENT FAMILY

One-parent families result from divorce or separation, unwed parenthood, or death. The number of single-parent families in the United States has more than doubled since 1970 (Fields & Casper, 2001) with rising rates of divorce and of parenthood outside of marriage. Today one child in four lives with only one parent (Children's Defense Fund, 2001), and a child has at least a 50 percent chance of living with only one parent at some point (Bianchi, 1995; Hines, 1997; NCES, 1998).

Although the growth of one-parent families is slowing, in 2000 they comprised almost one-third (about 31 percent) of U.S. families with children under 18, as compared with 13 percent of all families in 1970 (Fields & Casper, 2001). In Canada, the proportion of such families in 1996 (the most recent date for which such data are available) was 15 percent, less than half the current U.S. rate (Statistics Canada, 1996).

About one in six single-parent U.S. families is headed by the father (Fields & Casper, 2001). The number of father-only families has more than quadrupled since 1974, apparently due largely to an increase in the number of fathers having custody after divorce (Garasky & Meyer, 1996; U.S. Bureau of the Census, 1998).

In 2000 about one in three births—up from fewer than one in twenty-five in 1940—was to an unwed mother (Martin, Hamilton, Ventura, Menacker, & Park, 2002; National Center for Health Statistics [NCHS], 1993, 1994). Births to single mothers have increased dramatically in many other industrialized countries as well (Bruce, Lloyd, & Leonard, 1995; WuDunn, 1996). However, these data can be misleading because many of these women are in cohabiting unions, some of them with the child's biological father (Seltzer, 2000). In the early 1990s, 39 percent of U.S. nonmarital births were to cohabiting couples (Bumpass & Lu, 2000).

STEPFAMILIES

With today's high rate of divorce and remarriage, families made up of "yours, mine, and ours" are becoming more common. In 1987 there were 4.3 million such families and about 6 million stepchildren in the United States (Glick, 1989). These families face special challenges.

A **stepfamily** (also called a *reconstituted family* or *combined family*) results from the marriage or cohabitation of adults who already have children. It is different from a "natural" family. First, it usually has a larger supporting cast, including former spouses, former in-laws, and absent parents, as well as aunts, uncles, and cousins on both sides. It is, in short, burdened by much baggage not carried by an "original" family, and it cannot be expected to function in the same way. A welter of family histories can complicate present relationships. Previous bonds between children and their biological parents or loyalty to an absent or dead parent may interfere with forming ties to the stepparent—especially when children move back and forth between two households. The adjustment to living in a stepfamily can be stressful for both adults and children.

Stepfamilies have to deal with stress from losses (due to death or divorce) undergone by both children and adults, which can make them afraid to trust or love. Stepparents need to have realistic expectations and to allow time for loving relationships to develop. Stepfamilies need to see what is positive about their differences: to welcome diversity instead of resisting it.

Because the increase in stepfamilies is fairly recent, social expectations for such families have not caught up. In combining two family units, each with its own web of customs and relationships, remarried families must invent their own ways of doing things (Hines, 1997).

LIVING WITH GAY OR LESBIAN PARENTS

It is estimated that between 1 and 9 million U.S. children have at least one gay or lesbian parent. Some gays and lesbians are raising children born of previous heterosexual relationships. Others conceive by artificial means, employ surrogate mothers, or adopt children (Perrin and AAP Committee on Psychosocial Aspects of Child and Family Health, 2002).

Several studies have focused on the personal development of children of gays and lesbians, including physical and emotional health, intelligence, adjustment, sense of self, moral judgment, and social and sexual functioning. A considerable body of research has indicated no concerns (AAP Committee on Psychosocial Aspects of Child and Family Health, 2002; Mooney-Somers & Golombok, 2000; C. J. Patterson, 1992, 1995a, 1995b, 1997; Perrin and AAP Committee on Psychosocial Aspects of Child and Family Health, 2002). There is no consistent difference between homosexual and heterosexual parents in terms of emotional health or parenting skills and attitudes (Perrin and AAP Committee on Psychosocial Aspects of Child and Family Health, 2002). Openly gay or lesbian parents usually have positive relationships with their children, and the children are no more likely than children raised by heterosexual parents to have social or psychological problems (Chan, Raboy, & Patterson, 1998; C. J. Patterson, 1992, 1995a, 1997).

Children of gays and lesbians are no more likely to be homosexual themselves, or to be confused about their gender, than are children of heterosexuals (Anderssen, Amlie, & Ytteroy, 2002; B. M. King, 1996; C. J. Patterson, 1997). In one study, the vast majority of adult sons of gay fathers were heterosexual (Bailey, Bobrow, Wolfe, & Mikach, 1995). Likewise, in a longitudinal study of adult children of lesbians, a large majority identified themselves as heterosexual (Golombok & Tasker, 1996).

Such findings have social policy implications for legal decisions on custody and visitation disputes, foster care, and adoptions. The American Academy of

Pediatrics supports legislative and legal efforts to permit a partner in a same-sex couple to adopt the other partner's child, so that the child may enjoy the benefits of two parents (AAP Committee on Psychosocial Aspects of Child and Family Health, 2002).

DELAYED PARENTHOOD

By and large, adults in industrialized countries today have children later in life than before. Between 1970 and 1987, the percentage of American women who had a first child after age 30 quadrupled, though most births were still to women in their twenties (National Center for Health Statistics, 1990; see Figure 11.4 in Chapter 11). In England and Wales, the birthrate among women age 35 to 39 increased by 44 percent in the 1980s, while births to women in their twenties declined by 19 percent (P. Brown, 1993). More educated women have babies later; educational level is the most important predictor of the age at which a woman will bear her first child (Rindfuss, Morgan, & Swicegood, 1988; Rindfuss & St. John, 1983).

Today the median age of first-time mothers in the United States is 24.6, having risen consistently for three decades. Since the mid-1970s the percentage of women who give birth in their thirties and even after 40 has increased steadily, often thanks to fertility treatments. Meanwhile, birthrates for women in their late twenties, which had declined after 1990, are again on the rise. Women ages 25–29 had the highest birthrate in 2001 (National Center for Health Statistics, 2003; see Figure 9.5).

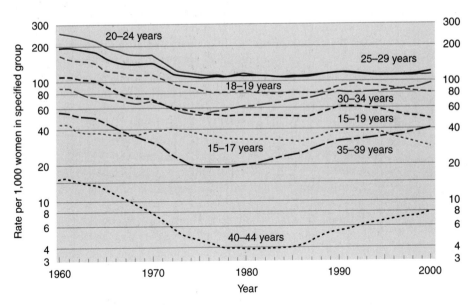

FIGURE 9.5 *Birthrates by age of mother, 1960 to 2000.* SOURCE: Martin et al., 2002, Figure 2 in Papalia, Olds, & Feldman, 2004.

Economically, delaying childbirth may pay off for women who intend to work later on. Among women born between 1944 and 1954, the first cohort to combine child raising and employment on a large scale, those who gave birth between ages 20 and 27 tend to earn less than women who gave birth at later ages (Taniguchi, 1999). Further research may show whether this holds true in later cohorts.

The risks of delayed childbearing appear to be less than previously believed. There is a greater chance of miscarriage after age 35, and more likelihood of chromosomal abnormalities or birth-related complications. But most risks to the baby's health are only slightly greater (Berkowitz, Skovron, Lapinski, & Berkowitz, 1990; P. Brown, 1993).

INFERTILITY AND NEW WAYS TO PARENTHOOD

An estimated 7 percent of U.S. couples experience **infertility:** inability to conceive a baby after twelve months of trying (CDC, 2001c). Women's fertility begins to decline in the late twenties, with substantial decreases during the thirties. Men's fertility is less affected by age but declines significantly by the late thirties (Dunson, Colombo, & Baird, 2002).

The most common cause of infertility in men is production of too few sperm. Although only one sperm is needed to fertilize an ovum, a sperm count lower than 60 to 200 million per ejaculation makes conception unlikely. Sometimes an ejaculatory duct is blocked, preventing the exit of sperm; or sperm may be unable to "swim" well enough to reach the cervix. Some cases of male infertility seem to have a genetic basis (King, 1996; Phillips, 1998; Reijo, Alagappan, Patrizio, & Page, 1996).

If the problem is with the woman, she may not be producing ova; the ova may be abnormal; mucus in the cervix may prevent sperm from penetrating it; or a disease of the uterine lining may prevent implantation of the fertilized ovum. A major cause of declining fertility in women after age 30 is deterioration in the quality of their ova (van Noord-Zaadstra et al., 1991). However, the most common female cause is blockage of the fallopian tubes, preventing ova from reaching the uterus. In about half of these cases, the tubes are blocked by scar tissue from STDs (King, 1996).

Infertility burdens a marriage emotionally. Partners may become frustrated and angry with themselves and each other and may feel empty, worthless, and depressed (Abbey, Andrews, & Halman, 1992; H. W. Jones & Toner, 1993). Such couples may benefit from professional counseling or support from other infertile couples.

Hormone treatment may raise a man's sperm count or increase a woman's ovulation. Sometimes drug therapy or surgery can correct the problem. However, fertility drugs increase the likelihood of multiple, and often premature, births (King, 1996). Also, men undergoing fertility treatment are at increased risk of producing sperm with chromosomal abnormalities (Levron et al., 1998).

New research suggests that couples who have been unable to bear children after one year should not necessarily rush into fertility treatments. Unless there is a known cause for failure to conceive, the chances of success after eighteen months to two years are high. Among 782 women in six European countries, 9 out of 10 even of those in their late thirties were able to conceive by the end of the second year of trying, unless the male partner was over 40 (Dunson, 2002).

For couples who give up on the natural way, science today offers several alternative ways to parenthood.

In 2000, more than 25,000 U.S. women delivered with technological help, giving birth to more than 35,000 babies (Wright, Schieve, Reynolds, & Jeng, 2003), nearly 1 percent of all babies born in the United States in that year (Martin, Hamilton et al., 2002).

In **in vitro fertilization** (IVF), the most common procedure, fertility drugs are given to increase production of ova. Then one or more mature ova are surgically removed, fertilized in a laboratory dish, and implanted in the woman's uterus. Usually 50,000 to 100,000 sperm are used to increase the chances of fertilization, and several embryos are transferred to the uterus to increase the chances of pregnancy. This also increases the likelihood of multiple births. A newer technique, **in vitro maturation (IVM)** is performed earlier in the monthly cycle, when as many as 30 to 50 egg follicles are developing. Normally, only one of these will mature. Harvesting a large number of follicles before ovulation is complete and then allowing them to mature in the laboratory can make hormone injections unnecessary and diminish the likelihood of multiple births.

A technique called **intracytoplasmic sperm insection (ICSI)** involves a single sperm injected into the ovum. This method can address severe male infertility, as well as women whose fallopian tubes are blocked or scarred beyond surgical repair.

Artificial insemination—injection of sperm into a woman's vagina, cervix, or uterus—can be done when a man has a low sperm count. Sperm from several ejaculations can be combined for one injection. Thus, with help, a couple can produce their own biological offspring.

A woman who is producing poor-quality ova or who has had her ovaries removed may try **ovum transfer.** In this procedure, an ovum, or *donor egg*—provided, usually anonymously, by a fertile young woman—is fertilized in the laboratory and implanted in the prospective mother's uterus. In **blastocyst transfer,** the fertilized ovum is kept in the culture until it grows to the blastocyst stage; but this method has been linked to an increase in identical twin births. Alternatively, the ovum can be fertilized in the donor's body by artificial insemination. The donor's uterus is flushed out a few days later, and the embryo is retrieved and inserted into the recipient's uterus.

Although success rates have improved since 1978 (Duenwald, 2003), only 30.8 percent of the 99,629 U.S. women who attempted assisted reproduction in 2000 had live births, and 53 percent of these were multiple births. Two newer techniques with higher success rates are **gamete intrafallopian transfer (GIFT)** and **zygote intrafallopian transfer (ZIFT),** in which either the egg and sperm or the fertilized egg is inserted in the fallopian tube (CDC, 2002b; Schieve et al., 2002; Society for Assisted Reproductive Technology, 1993, 2002).

Some couples turn to **surrogate motherhood:** impregnation of a fertile woman with the prospective father's sperm. She then bears the baby and surrenders it to the man and his wife.

New and unorthodox means of conception raise a number of ethical questions. Must people who use them be infertile, or should people be free to make such arrangements simply for convenience? Should single people and homosexual couples have access to these methods? What about women past menopause (see Box 9.2)? Should the children know about their parentage? Should chromosome tests be performed on prospective donors and surrogates? What happens if a couple who have contracted with a surrogate divorce before the birth?

Surrogate motherhood is in legal limbo, partly as a result of the "Baby M" case, in which a surrogate mother changed her mind and wanted to keep the baby (Hanley, 1988a, 1988b; Shipp, 1988). She was not granted custody of the child, but she did receive visiting rights. The American Academy of Pediatrics (AAP, 1992) recommends that surrogate parenting be considered a tentative, preconception adoption agreement in which, before birth, the surrogate mother is the sole decision maker. AAP also recommends a prebirth agreement on a period of time in which the surrogate may assert her parental rights. Perhaps the most objectionable aspect of surrogacy, aside from the possibility of forcing the surrogate to relinquish the baby, is the payment of money (up to $30,000, including fees to a "matchmaker"). The idea of a "breeder class" of poor and disadvantaged women who carry the babies of the well-to-do strikes many people as wrong. Still, one thing seems certain: as long as there are people who want children and who are unable to conceive or bear them, human ingenuity will come up with ways to satisfy the need.

ADOPTION

Since 1970, more Americans—including single people, older people, working-class families, and homosexual couples—have become adoptive parents. Adults adopt children for various reasons. Overall, about 60 percent of legal adoptions are by relatives, usually stepparents or grandparents (Goodman, Emery, & Haugaard, 1998; Haugaard, 1998). Because advances in contraception and legalization of abortion have reduced the number of adoptable healthy white American babies, many children available for adoption are disabled, are beyond infancy, or are of foreign birth. The percentage of babies born to never-married white women who were placed for adoption dropped from 19.3 percent in the early 1970s to only 1.7 percent in the early 1990s (Chandra, Abma, Maza, & Bachrach, 1999), and black women have consistently been far less likely to put up their babies for adoption (Brodzinsky, 1997).

Although adoption is accepted in the United States, there are still prejudices and mistaken ideas about it. One mistaken belief is that adopted children are bound to have problems because they have been deprived of their biological parents. Actually, a recent federally funded study of 715 families with

Motherhood After Menopause

While many women in their fifties and sixties are enjoying their grandchildren, some women in this age group still want to bear their own children. A woman past menopause may be able to bear a child by "borrowing" ova from a younger woman.

This procedure already has been used widely with women in their thirties and forties, past what is usually considered childbearing age. A donated ovum is fertilized with sperm from the woman's husband. The resulting embryo, grown in the laboratory, is implanted in the mother-to-be, who has been given hormones to prepare her uterus for pregnancy (Lutjen et al., 1984). A research team led by Mark V. Sauer, an obstetrician and gynecologist at the University of Southern California in Los Angeles, has found this procedure as effective with women 40 to 44 years old as with women under 35 (Sauer, Paulson, & Lobo, 1990).

Now, Sauer and his colleagues have shown that women over age 50 also can have babies this way. Eight of 14 postmenopausal women treated with the technique became pregnant; one had a miscarriage, four gave birth to healthy infants, and three were still pregnant when the report was published (Sauer, Paulson, & Lobo, 1993). According to Sauer, these rates are as good as those normally obtained with 30-year-olds ("Brave New Biology," 1993). One caution, based on experience in Britain, is that *in vitro* mothers have a greater chance of multiple births (P. Brown, 1993).

Why would a woman past 50 want to have a baby? Some of the women in Sauer's study were already mothers (and even grandmothers) but had remarried and wanted to start a second family with the new spouse. Some had been too busy with their careers to have children earlier. Some couples who had already raised children simply wanted more. All were screened psychologically before being allowed to participate.

The number of older women who take advantage of this new technology is likely to remain small, in part because of the need to find donors. But what if young women could ensure their future fertility by freezing and storing their *own* ova, or sections of productive ovarian tissue, for later use? Already, four babies have been born from ova that were frozen and then thawed. Scientists in London, Melbourne, and Edinburgh are refining preservation techniques through research on mice and other animals and are also experimenting with mice as incubators for transplanted ova (P. Brown, 1993).

Such research holds out a promise of giving women greater control over their reproduction. As the editors of the British journal *New Scientist* observed: "Removing the pressure to become a mother before middle age is potentially as revolutionary a step for women as the right to vote or equal pay" ("Mind and Body," 1993).

But the prospect of postmenopausal births troubles some observers. Is there any upper limit to the age at which a woman can have a baby with the aid of science? And, just because older women *can* have babies, *should* they? Is it fair to give birth to a child knowing that there's a strong chance of not being able to see the job of parenting through?

teenagers who had been adopted in infancy found that nearly 3 out of 4 saw their adoption as playing only a minor role in their identity. However, adoption did contribute to identity problems in some cases (Bemon & Sharma, 1994). In another study of 85 adopted children, most of them viewed adoption positively—though teenagers saw it less positively than younger children (Smith & Brodzinsky, 1994).

Adopting a child does carry special risks and challenges. Besides the usual issues of parenthood, adoptive parents need to deal with acceptance of their infertility (if this is why they adopted), awareness that they are not repeating their own parents' experience, the need to explain the adoption to their children, and possible discomfort about their children's interest in the biological parents.

Parenthood as a Developmental Experience

Whether or not a child is a biological offspring, and whether or not the parents are married, parenthood is a developmental experience. As children develop, parents do too.

The coming of a child marks a major transition in parents' lives. Both women and men often feel ambivalent about the emotional and financial responsibilities and the necessary commitment of time and energy. About one-third of mothers find parenting both enjoyable and meaningful, one-third find it neither, and one-third have mixed feelings (Thompson & Walker, 1989). Husbands consider having children more important and are more apt to want them than wives do (Secombe, 1991); but once the children come, fathers enjoy looking after them less than mothers do.

Fathers today are more involved in their children's lives, and even in child care and housework, than ever before. Still, most are not nearly as involved as mothers are (Coley, 2001). A recent study of parents of 4-year-olds in 10 European, Asian, and African countries and the United States found that fathers think they are contributing more than they actually are. Internationally, fathers average less than 1 hour a day in sole charge of their children during the work week. When men do supervise their children, it is usually with the mother. American fathers spend only 1 hour a day in such shared child care, as compared with 3 hours for Belgian and Thai fathers. American mothers, on the other hand, spend an average of nearly 11 hours each weekday caring for preschoolers—more than mothers in any of the other 10 countries (Olmsted & Weikart, 1994). However, the time fathers spend with children becomes more nearly equal to mothers' on weekends, and increases as children get older. Fathers spend considerably *more* time with children than mothers in television or video viewing, outdoor play, and coaching or teaching sports (Yeung, Sandberg, Davis-Kean, & Hofferth, 2001).

Ultimately, parenthood is a process of letting go. From the moment of birth, children's normal course of development leads toward independence. This process reaches its climax as children move through adolescence.

It is ironic that people at the two times of life most popularly linked with emotional crises—adolescence and midlife—often live in the same household. It is usually middle-aged adults who are the parents of adolescent children. While dealing with their own special concerns, parents have to deal daily with young people who are undergoing great physical, emotional, and social changes. Sometimes parents' own long-buried adolescent fantasies resurface as they watch their children turning into sexual beings. Seeing their children at the brink of adulthood makes some parents realize even more sharply how much of their own life is behind them. They may become resentful and jealous and may overidentify with the child's fantasies (Meyers, 1989).

Although recent research contradicts the stereotype of adolescence as a time of inevitable turmoil and rejection of parental values, some rebellion against parental authority is necessary for the maturing youngster to achieve independence (Offer, 1982, 1987; Offer & Schonert-Reichl, 1992). An important task for parents is to accept children as they are, not as what the parents had hoped they would be. Parents must realize that they cannot make children into carbon copies or improved models of themselves. Children may choose directions very different from those the parents want them to follow.

When Children Leave: The Empty Nest

Research is also challenging popular ideas about the empty nest, a supposedly difficult transition, especially for women. Although some women, heavily invested in mothering, do have problems at this time, they are far outnumbered by those who find the departure liberating (Antonucci et al., 2001; Antonucci & Akiyama, 1997; Barnett, 1985; Chiriboga, 1997; Helson, 1997; Mitchell & Helson, 1990). Today, the refilling of the nest by grown children returning home (discussed in an upcoming section) is far more stressful (Thomas, 1997).

The **empty nest** does not signal the end of parenthood. It is a transition to a new stage: the relationship between parents and adult children. For many women, this transition brings relief from what Gutmann called the "chronic emergency of parenthood" (Cooper & Gutmann, 1987, p. 347). They can now pursue their own interests as they bask in their grown children's accomplishments. The empty nest may be harder on couples whose identity is dependent on the parental role, or who now must face marital problems they had previously pushed aside under the press of parental responsibilities (Antonucci et al., 2001).

In a longitudinal study of employed married women with multiple roles, the empty nest had *no* effect on psychological health, but cutting back on employment *increased* distress, whereas going to work full-time *decreased* it (Wethington & Kessler, 1989). On the other hand, in a comparison of stress at various stages of life, men in the empty nest stage were most likely to report health-related stress (Chiriboga, 1997).

CRITICAL THINKING

Would you be surprised or upset to learn that your parents experienced a sense of relief when you left for college?

Parenthood, Role Changes, and Marital Satisfaction

A couple's joint responsibilities as parents inevitably affect their own relationship. Today, with the rise in both life expectancy and divorce, about 1 marriage in 5 lasts 50 years (Brubaker, 1983, 1993). What happens to the quality of longtime marriages as the partners deal with changing roles and patterns of childrearing, work, and retirement?

In general, marital satisfaction seems to follow a U-shaped curve. From an early high point, it declines until late middle age and then rises again through the first part of late adulthood (Anderson, Russell, & Schumm, 1983; Gilford, 1984; Glenn, 1991; Gruber & Schaie, 1986). The least happy time is the period when most couples are heavily involved in child rearing and careers. Positive aspects of marriage (such as cooperation, discussion, and shared laughter) follow the U-shaped pattern. Negative aspects (such as sarcasm, anger, and disagreement over important issues) decline from young adulthood through age 69 (Gilford, 1984; Gilford & Bengtson, 1979)—perhaps because many conflict-ridden marriages end along the way.

An analysis of data from two surveys of individuals in first marriages, conducted in 1986 and 1987–1988 (Orbuch et al., 1996), sought to ascertain just when the dip and rise in satisfaction occur, and why. The samples were, of necessity, cross-sectional (there are no comparable longitudinal data covering the entire span of adulthood); but they were large (a total of 8,929), and one was nationally representative. Both women and men were included and marital satisfaction was measured against the duration of a marriage. To control for any skewing of data due to termination of unsatisfactory marriages, statistical techniques simulated the inclusion of such couples, attributing to them low marital quality.

The picture that emerged is a clear affirmation of the U-shaped pattern. During the first twenty to twenty-four years of marriage, the longer a couple have been married, the less satisfied they tend to be. Then the association between marital satisfaction and length of marriage begins to turn positive. At thirty-five to forty-four years of marriage, a couple tend to be even more satisfied than during the first four years.

Let's look more closely at three sections of the curve: the early years (when parenthood usually begins), the middle years, and the later years.

THE EARLY YEARS

For most couples, when children come the honeymoon is over. In a 10-year longitudinal study of predominantly white couples who married in their late twenties, both husbands and wives reported a sharp decline in satisfaction during the first 4 years, followed by a plateau and then another decline. Spouses who had children, especially those who became parents early in their marriages and those who had many children, showed a steeper decline.

What distinguishes marriages that deteriorate after parenthood from those that improve? In deteriorating marriages, according to one study, the partners are likely to be younger and less educated, to have less income, and to have been married for a shorter time. One or both partners tend to have low self-esteem, and husbands are likely to be less sensitive. The mothers who have the hardest time are those whose babies have difficult temperaments. Surprisingly, couples who were most romantic "pre-baby" tend to have more problems "post-baby," perhaps because they had unrealistic expectations. Also, women who planned their pregnancies tend to be unhappier, possibly because they expected life with a baby to be better than it turned out to be (Belsky & Rovine, 1990).

One often-violated expectation involves division of chores. If a couple share such chores fairly equally before the baby is born and then, after the baby's birth, the burden shifts to the wife, marital happiness tends to decline, especially for nontraditional wives (Belsky, Lang, & Huston, 1986).

THE MIDDLE YEARS

The U-shaped curve hits bottom during the first part of the middle years, when many couples have teenage children. Identity issues of midlife appear to affect wives' (though not husbands') feelings about their marriages; women become less satisfied with the marriage as childrearing makes fewer demands and their feelings of personal power and autonomy increase (Steinberg & Silverberg, 1987).

Communication between partners can often mitigate the stress caused by physical signs of aging, loss of sex drive, changes in work status or satisfaction, and the death of parents, siblings, or close friends. Many couples report that hard times have brought them closer (Robinson & Blanton, 1993).

In a good marriage, the departure of grown children may usher in a "second honeymoon." In a shaky marriage, though, the "empty nest" may pose a personal and marital crisis. With the children gone, a couple may realize that they no longer have much in common and may ask themselves whether they want to spend the rest of their lives together.

THE LATER YEARS

Couples in their sixties are more likely than middle-aged couples to call their marriage satisfying. Many say that their marriage has improved over the years (Gilford, 1986). Spouses who are still together late in life are likely to have worked out their differences and to have arrived at mutually satisfactory accommodations. However, people may say that their marriage is happy as a conscious or unconscious justification for having stayed in it so long.

The ability of married people to handle the ups and downs of late adulthood with relative serenity may well result from mutual supportiveness, which reflects three important benefits of marriage: intimacy (sexual and emotional), interdependence (sharing of tasks and resources), and the partners' sense of belonging to each other (Atchley, 1985; Gilford, 1986). Marital satisfaction may also depend on a couple's ability to adjust to the freedom that results from shedding the roles of breadwinner and childrearer (Zube, 1982). The couple may find more interest in each other and more enjoyment in each other's company. On the other hand, as the husband becomes less involved with work and more interested in intimacy, the wife may be more interested in personal growth and self-expression. In changing roles, couples may argue over who does what. Retirement-age husbands spend less than 8 hours a week, on average, on household chores, while their wives spend nearly 20 hours a week more and do more than three-fourths of the housework (Rexroat & Shehan, 1987).

People over 70 consider themselves less happily married than those age 63 to 69. Women, who generally expect more warmth and intimacy from relationships than men do, tend to be less satisfied with marriage at this age. Advancing age and physical ills may aggravate strains on a marriage. People who have to care for disabled partners may feel isolated, angry, and frustrated, especially when they are in poor health themselves (Gilford, 1986). Caring for a spouse with dementia is especially demanding (as we discuss in Chapters 10 and 12). Caregiving spouses who are optimistic and well-adjusted to begin with, and who stay in touch with friends, do best (Hooker, Monahan, Shifren, & Hutchinson, 1992; Skaff & Pearlin, 1992).

Remaining Childless

An increasing number of couples remain childless by choice (Seccombe, 1991). Some of these couples want to concentrate on careers or social causes. Some feel more comfortable with adults or think they would not make good parents. Some want to retain the intimacy of the honeymoon. Some enjoy an adult lifestyle, with freedom to travel or to make spur-of-the-moment decisions. Some women worry that pregnancy will make them less attractive and that parenthood will change their relationship with their spouse (Callan, 1986).

Some people may be discouraged by the financial burdens of parenthood and the difficulty of combining parenthood with employment. In 2000 the estimated expenditures to raise a child to age 18 in a middle-income two-parent, two-child family were $165,630 (Lino, 2001). Better child care and other support services might help couples make truly voluntary decisions.

What about the increasing number of older adults without living children? In 1998, one out of five women in the United States had no children (Kinsella & Velkoff, 2001). How will childlessness affect them as they age? Early studies suggested that childless people are no lonelier, no more negative about their lives, and no more afraid of death than those with children (C. L. Johnson & Catalano, 1981; Keith, 1983; Rempel, 1985). However, some older women who never had children expressed regret, and that feeling became more intense the older they got (Alexander, Rubinstein, Goodman, & Luborsky, 1992).

Widows without grown children may lack an important source of solace (O'Bryant, 1988; Suitor et al., 1995). Childless people also may lack a ready source of care and support if they become infirm. In Canada, where 5 to 10 percent of older adults are unmarried and childless, three-fourths of this group report a lack of support, especially emotional support (Wu & Pollard, 1998).

Whether an adult remains single, forms homosexual relationships, cohabits, marries, divorces, remarries, has children or not—all are choices that involve the establishment (or nonestablishment) of intimate relationships. Ties with parents, with grandchildren, and with siblings are different. People do not form these bonds; they are simply part of their lives. But these relationships, too, evolve and change during adulthood, as we discuss in Chapter 10.

SUMMARY AND KEY TERMS

Foundations of Intimate Relationships

- Intimate relationships based on friendship, love, and sexuality develop and change throughout adulthood; they may be affected more by social age than by chronological age.
- Across the adult life span, friends can be an important source of emotional support. Older people may enjoy being with friends more than with family members. Very old people maintain friends and make new ones, but they may define friendship more broadly than before.
- According to Sternberg's triangular theory of love, the relative presence or absence of intimacy, passion, and commitment determines the nature and quality of love.
- Major changes in attitudes toward sexuality in the United States include a decline in the double standard and greater acceptance of premarital and nonmarital sex and of homosexuality.
- Research on causes of sexual orientation has found little support for environmental theories. Recent evidence points to a genetic cause or predisposition. Interaction among genetic, hormonal, and environmental events may be crucial.

triangular theory of love (p. 316) **homosexual (p. 318)**
assortative mating (p. 318) **heterosexual (p. 318)**
sexual orientation (p. 318) **bisexual (p. 318)**

Nonmarital and Marital Lifestyles

- The percentage of adults who remain single has increased dramatically.
- Lesbians are more likely than male homosexuals to have stable, monogamous relationships. Homosexuals today are seeking societal recognition of their unions, as well as other rights.
- Cohabitation is increasingly accepted, in part because of the increased span between sexual and social maturity.
- The "marrying age" varies across cultures. In the United States, it tends to be later than in the past.
- Married people tend to be happier than singles, but the gap has narrowed dramatically and is less evident in women than in men.
- Divorce rates have risen sharply in many western countries. The rate in the United States is one of the highest in the world but has now leveled off.
- Societal developments contributing to the increase in divorce include greater financial independence of women, less willingness to put up with an unhappy marriage, and decreased expectations about the permanence of marriage. The economic impact of divorce is most likely to be negative for women and children.

- Most divorced people remarry. Men are more likely to remarry than women.
- Spouses in long-time marriages attribute their success to such factors as enjoyment and commitment.

coming out (p. 324)   **cohabitation (p. 326)**

Family Life

- Families have undergone dramatic changes: single-parent households; working mothers; children raised by stepparents in blended families, by homosexual parents, or by grandparents.
- Out-of-wedlock births are increasing, especially among educated and professional women.
- Adults today in industrialized countries have fewer children and have them later.
- Infertility has new solutions: some infertile couples still adopt, but others use technologically assisted methods to conceive and bear children.
- Children raised by homosexual parents show no greater tendency toward homosexuality than other children.
- Blended families are becoming more common because of high rates of divorce and remarriage.
- Parenthood is a developmental experience: the coming of a child marks a major transition in parents' lives.
- Once grown children leave, the "empty nest" is liberating to many mothers; it may be harder on fathers who now regret not having spent more time with their children.
- Marital satisfaction generally declines during the childrearing years, then rises until age 69, then undergoes another dip.
- Remaining childless has become more socially accepted. Research has found few important drawbacks to childlessness in late life.

stepfamily (p. 341)   **blastocyst transfer (p. 345)**

infertility (p. 344)   **gamete intrafallopian transfer**

in vitro fertilization (IVF) (p. 345)   **(GIFT) (p. 346)**

in vitro maturation (IVM) (p. 345)   **zygote intrafallopian transfer**

intracytoplasmic sperm injection   **(ZIFT) (p. 346)**

    (ICSI) (p. 345)   **surrogate motherhood (p. 346)**

artificial insemination (p. 345)   **empty nest (p. 349)**

ovum transfer (p. 345)

Mature Kinship Ties and Living Arrangements

◈ FOCUS: MARIAN ANDERSON

Time necessarily brings changes in any relation, and one must be prepared to recognize these changes and to grow and to change with time.
—Helen Merrell Lynd, *On Shame and the Search for Identity*, 1958

©UPI/Corbis Images

THE AFRICAN AMERICAN CONTRALTO Marian Anderson,* had—in the words of the great Italian conductor Arturo Toscanini—a voice heard "once in a hundred years." She was also a pioneer in breaking racial barriers. Turned away by a music school in her home town of Philadelphia, she studied voice privately and in 1925 won a national competition to sing with the New York Philharmonic. She performed in European capitals throughout the 1930s but was often forced to put up with second-class

*The chief source of biographical information about Marian Anderson and her family is Anderson (1956, 1992). Some details come from Kernan (1993) and from obituaries published in *Time* (April 19, 1993), *People Weekly*, *The New Yorker*, and *Jet* (April 26, 1993).

treatment at home. When she was refused the use of a concert hall in Washington, D.C., Eleanor Roosevelt—who was then First Lady—arranged for her to sing on the steps of the Lincoln Memorial. The unprecedented performance on Easter Sunday, 1939, drew 75,000 people and was broadcast to millions. Several weeks later, Marian Anderson was the first black singer to perform at the White House. But not until 1955, a year after the Supreme Court outlawed segregated public schools, did Anderson, at age 57, become the first person of her race to sing with New York's Metropolitan Opera.

A remarkable story lies behind this woman's "journey from a single rented room in South Philadelphia" (McKay, 1992, p. xxx). It is a story of nurturing kinship ties—bonds of mutual support that extended from generation to generation.

Marian Anderson was the eldest child of John and Annie Anderson. Two years after her birth, the family left their one-room apartment to move in with her father's parents and then, after two more baby girls came along, into a small rented house nearby. John Anderson peddled coal and ice, and Annie Anderson took in laundry.

The family maintained close contact with their relatives. When 6-year-old Marian showed interest in music and joined the junior choir at church, her father brought home a piano that had been sitting unused in her uncle's house. Her aunt sang duets with her and arranged for her to do a benefit concert.

When John Anderson died, the family again moved in with his parents, his sister, and her two daughters. Marian Anderson's grandfather had a steady job. Her grandmother took care of all the children, her aunt ran the house, and her mother worked as a cleaning woman to contribute to household expenses. Years later, the singer had vivid memories of her grandmother:

"What she said was law. Everyone knew she was the boss, and if she wanted any of us at any time we came flying. . . . There was an old-fashioned organ in Grandmother's parlor, and I remember that she occasionally played it, her body swaying to the rhythmic pressure of her feet on the pedals. We would sit and listen quietly, knowing better than to disturb her. . . . Grandmother loved children and always had scads of them living in her house. . . . Grandmother saw to it that we each had our little jobs to do. . . . And there were useful things for us to learn, . . . how to share a home with others, how to understand their ways and respect their rights and privileges" (Anderson, 1992, pp. 17–18).

But the most important influence in Marian Anderson's life, even during her adult years, was the counsel, example, and spiritual guidance of her hardworking, unfailingly supportive mother. When her first major recital in New York's Town Hall was a financial and critical failure, her mother advised her: "Whatever you do in this world, no matter how good it is, you will never be able to please everybody. All you can strive for is to do the best it is humanly possible for you to do" (Anderson, 1992, p. 76).

Anderson and her mother had bought a small house across the street from her grandmother's, using a modest inheritance and the singer's savings from her early tours. Anderson's mother, who lived to be 89, insisted on remaining in that house even when her daughter—by then a world-renowned concert star—offered to buy her a bigger one. Annie Anderson shared the house with one of her other two grown daughters; the third daughter lived next door with her son, James DePriest.

"It is the pleasantest thing in the world to go into that home and feel its happiness. . . ." Marian Anderson wrote in 1956. "They are all comfortable, and they cherish and protect one another. . . . I know that it warms [Mother] to have her grandson near her as he grows up, just as I think that when he gets to be a man, making his own life, he will have pleasant memories of his home and family" (1992, p. 93).

The singer and her husband, an architect, never had a child of their own. During the summer, their nephews would come to stay with them on their Connecticut country estate. In 1992, Marian Anderson—widowed and frail at age 95—went to live with her nephew, De-Priest, then music director of the Oregon Symphony. She died of a stroke at his home the following year.

MARIAN ANDERSON "LIVED THROUGH MOMENTOUS changes in America and the world" and in African American life (McKay, 1992, p. xxiv). But one thing that never changed was the strong, supportive network of intergenerational and intragenerational relationships that sustained her and her family.

Relationships with family members continue to be important into very old age (Johnson & Troll, 1992). Among these important relationships are ties to the family in which one grew up—to parents, brothers, and sisters—and to new families created by one's grown children. This complex interweaving of kinship ties, extending to distant relatives, is what is meant by an **extended family**.

In less developed countries, people customarily live in multigenerational extended-family households (see Box 10.1). But that pattern is changing (Gorman, 1993). In Ghana, for example, where old age was traditionally regarded as a blessing and older adults were venerated, young adults willingly undertook their care. Now modernization, industrialization, migration to urban centers, and the coming of western religions are undermining extended family life and respect for the elderly (N. M. Brown, 1990).

In the United States and other industrialized countries, the **nuclear family**— a two-generation family made up of parents and their growing children—is the usual household unit. Adult children and parents generally want to be independent of each other. Many elderly Americans prefer to live independently and resist dependency on their children for as long as possible (Luborsky & McMullen, 1999). But at times—especially among minority families like Marian Anderson's—adults do live with adult relatives. This most often happens when a son or daughter has trouble getting established financially, needs a place to live after the loss of a spouse, or has other problems; or when a parent is too frail, infirm, or poor to live alone.

In this chapter, we look at ties between adults and their families of origin— their parents and siblings—and at how these roles and relationships develop and change throughout life.* We discuss grandparenthood and great-grandparenthood, including special issues that may arise after adult children divorce and when grandparents are confronted with the challenge of raising

---

*Some of the discussion in this chapter is based on Papalia, Olds, & Feldman (2004).

The Extended-Family Household in Hispanic Cultures

In the colorful novels of Latin American authors such as Isabel Allende, Gabriel García Márquez, and Mario Vargas Llosa, households throb with the lively doings of grandparents, parents, and children, as well as uncles and aunts. Although these novelists infuse their stories with brilliant imaginative elements, their picture of multigenerational life in one household is rooted in fact.

Most elderly Latin Americans live in extended-family households. In Colombia, Costa Rica, the Dominican Republic, Mexico, Panama, and Peru, the proportion of extended-family households ranges from just over half (52 percent) in Mexico to almost two-thirds (64 percent) in the Dominican Republic (de Vos, 1990). In all six countries, unmarried people are more likely than married people to live in extended-family households. Overall, two-thirds of unmarried people live in extended-family households, compared with about one-half of married people. As in the United States, two married couples rarely live together, unless one couple is very old or very young. But in the United States, unlike Latin American, unmarried older people tend to live alone rather than with family.

Since gender is even more important in Latin America than in North America in determining social roles, it is not surprising that women are more likely than men to live in extended-family households. This finding may reflect women's greater life expectancy, their closeness to their children, or their greater financial need. On the other hand, neither the age of an older person nor residence in a rural or urban setting affects the likelihood of living with relatives (de Vos, 1990).

The importance of the extended family in these cultures is reflected in Hispanic communities in the United States. Among Hispanic families, older people have traditionally received a great deal of respect. In these families (as in African American families), grandparents have played an important role in childrearing and have exerted considerable influence over family decisions. In recent years, this pattern has been breaking down, so that relations between the generations are becoming more like those in the population as a whole. Still, Hispanic people show a strong extended-family pattern, with active helping networks, and the position of the elderly remains relatively high.

© Bob Daemmrich/Stock Boston

Extended-family households are prevalent in Latin America. There is extensive family support and helping networks, and the position of the elderly remains important.

their grandchildren. We also look at a variety of living arrangements, particularly in late life; at problems that arise when adults become caregivers for aging parents or other relatives; and at community support programs, both in the United States and in other societies.

THE ADULT FAMILY: CHANGING ROLES AND RELATIONSHIPS

Elliott Roosevelt, a son of President Franklin Delano Roosevelt, used to tell this story: At a state dinner, Elliott's mother, Eleanor Roosevelt, who was seated next to him, leaned over and whispered in his ear. A friend later asked Elliott, then in his forties, what she had said. "She told me to eat my peas," he answered.

Even after the years of active parenting are over and the children have left home, parents are still parents. Yet the parent-child relationship does change with advancing age. So, too, do relationships with adult sisters and brothers.

CRITICAL THINKING
What defines the relationship an individual has with his/her family?

Young Adult Children and Middle-Aged Parents

The midlife role of parent to young adults raises new issues and calls for new attitudes and behaviors on the part of both generations (see Box 10.2). In middle-class families, at least, middle-aged parents generally give their children more support than they get from them as the young adults establish careers and families (Antonucci et al., 2001). Some parents have difficulty treating their offspring as adults, and many young adults have difficulty accepting their parents' continuing concern about them. In a warm, supportive family environment, such conflicts can be managed by an open airing of feelings (Putney & Bengtson, 2001).

Still, young adults and their parents generally enjoy each other's company and get along well. Most parents of children age 16 or over express satisfaction with their parenting role—85 percent in one nationwide survey of more than 3,000 people. Four out of 5 parents are happy with how their children turn out, though more than 3 out of 4 are bothered or upset about them at times (Umberson, 1992). Sore points may include conflicts in values and parents' desire for their children to be like them.

Young newlyweds (especially women) tend to maintain close ties with their middle-aged parents, who often help them financially, with baby-sitting, and with setting up their first homes. Parents and adult children visit frequently, and young couples spend a great deal of time talking with and about their parents (Aldous, 1987; Troll, 1986, 1989; Troll, Miller, & Atchley, 1979).

CRITICAL THINKING
Based on your observations, why do some young adults get along well with their parents while others experience continued conflict?

Establishing Mature Relationships with Parents

When does a person become an adult? According to one study, this transition usually occurs in the late twenties—at least for white middle-class high school graduates. A dramatic shift in psychological maturity typically occurs between ages 24 and 28; it can be tracked by measuring a young adult's relationship with his or her parents. Men and women mature differently, but whether a person is married or unmarried does not seem to matter.

These conclusions emerged from interviews with 150 high school graduates from a midwestern suburb: 78 women and 72 men between ages 22 and 32 (Frank, Avery, & Laman, 1988). Participants were assessed according to 11 aspects of maturity. Five of the measures evaluated autonomy, including how well the young adults could make decisions and take responsibility for their own lives. Another five measures evaluated relationships between the generations—how close they were, how they communicated, and how the young people felt about their parents.

The researchers found six major patterns:

1. *Individuated.* Young adult (YA) feels respected by parents, freely seeks their advice and help, acknowledges their strengths, enjoys being with them, and has few conflicts with them. Yet YA feels separate from parents and is aware of (and untroubled by) a lack of intensity and depth in the relationship.

2. *Competent-connected.* YA is strongly independent, with life views that differ radically from parents' beliefs, but feels more empathic toward parents than individuated YA and often helps parents resolve their own problems of health, drinking, or relationships. The mother may be seen as demanding and critical, but YA understands her limitations, keeps conflicts within limits, and stays close to her.

3. *Pseudoautonomous.* YA pretends not to care about conflicts with parents and disengages rather than confronting parents openly. Fathers are often seen as uninterested and mothers as intrusive; both are seen as unable to accept YA for himself or herself.

4. *Identified.* In this unusually open and intimate relationship, YA accepts parents' values and outlook on life, seeks advice on most major decisions, and feels secure in the parents' availability. There is little tension, and parents are seen as nonjudgmental and supportive.

Middle-Aged Children and Elderly Parents

"My mother is my best friend," says a 45-year-old woman. "I can tell her anything." A 50-year-old man visits his retired father every evening, bringing him news and asking his opinions about problems in the family business. A 40-year-old divorced mother sees her parents more often now than she did during her 15 years of marriage and needs their help more now than at any

5. *Dependent*. YA cannot cope with ordinary life situations without parents' help, feels troubled by this but unable to change, and sees parents as overbearing and judgmental or emotionally detached and preoccupied with themselves. YA either goes along with parents' wishes or gets into childish power struggles.

6. *Conflicted*. This pattern emerged only with fathers. YA sees the father as hot-tempered and incapable of a close relationship, feels constantly under attack, is ashamed of the father's inadequacies, and longs to be closer to him.

Young women were most likely to be "competent-connected" with their mothers and "identified" or "conflicted" with their fathers. Men were most often "individuated" with both parents or "pseudoautonomous" with their fathers. And women were somewhat more likely than men to be "dependent" on their mothers. For both sexes, age was important. About half of those over 28 felt that they could cope with most aspects of life without asking their parents for help, and only 1 in 5 had serious doubts that they could manage on their own. For people under 24, however, these propor-

tions were reversed: only 1 in 5 felt that they could cope with most aspects of life independently, and half had serious doubts that they could manage on their own.

Recent research indicates that more than half of present twenty-one year olds live at home. This group is the leading edge of the Generation Y baby boom, 72 million individuals, born between 1974 and 1997. They want to connect with their parents and feel comfortable about living at home or returning home after college graduation. They feel emotionally close to their parents and admire them (Weiss, 2003).

If findings like these are borne out of broader research, developmental scientists will need to take a new look at the timetable for the end of adolescence and the beginning of adulthood, and what this means for education, career planning, and relationships between the generations. However, we need to look closely at the populations involved. This new schedule for achieving adulthood probably reflects the fact that middle-class young people remain dependent on their parents for support longer today than they did in the past. Adulthood may come sooner for less affluent young people, who become economically independent at earlier ages.

time since her teens. A couple in their early sixties find that the time they had hoped to spend traveling and playing with their grandchildren is being spent instead caring for their widowed mothers.

The bond between middle-aged children and their elderly parents is strong, growing out of earlier attachment and continuing through the rest of their lives (Cicirelli, 1980, 1989b; Rossi & Rossi, 1990). Most middle-aged adults and their parents have close relationships based on frequent contact and mutual help (Antonucci & Akiyama, 1997). According to a study done in 1984, 4 out of 5 older adults have living children, and 2 out of 3 live within 30 minutes of at least one child. Six out of 10 see their children at least once a week, and 3 out of 4 talk on the phone that often (AARP, 1994). Older people in better health have more contact with their families than those in poorer health and report feeling closer to family members (Field, Minkler, Falk, & Leino, 1993).

CRITICAL THINKING

Why do some relationships between parents and children show limited change across the adult years while others become increasingly mature?

Mothers and daughters are more likely to stay in close contact than any other combination of family members (Lee, Dwyer, & Coward, 1993; Troll, 1986). Daughters who have a good relationship with their parents are more likely than those with a poor relationship to report a sense of well-being and less likely to suffer anxiety or depression (Barnett, Kibria, Baruch, & Pleck, 1991). Among African Americans, adult children are more likely to visit their mothers than their fathers, and the mother-daughter relationship is especially strong (Spitze & Miner, 1992).

Many middle-aged people look at their parents more objectively than before, seeing them as individuals with both strengths and weaknesses. Something else happens during these years: One day a son or daughter looks at a mother or father and sees an old person, and that realization may be distressing (Troll & Fingerman, 1996). Older adults, for their part, may look at a middle-aged child who is at a peak of achievement with new, more respectful eyes.

The balance of mutual aid that flows between parents and their adult children tends to shift as parents age, with children providing a greater share of support (Bengtson, Rosenthal, & Burton, 1990; 1996). This is especially true in developing countries. Even there, however, older adults make important contributions to family well-being—for example, through housekeeping and child care (Kinsella & Velkoff, 2001).

In the United States and other developed countries, institutional supports such as social security and Medicare have lifted some responsibilities for the elderly from family members; but many adult children do provide significant assistance and care to aged parents. Still, elderly parents in North America are more likely to provide financial support than to receive it (Kinsella & Velkoff, 2001). An exception is immigrants who arrive as older adults; they are more likely to live with adult children and to be dependent on them (Glick & Van Hook, 2002.)

Of course, many parents continue to show concern about their children. Elderly parents whose children have serious problems are more likely to be depressed themselves (Pillemer & Suitor, 1991). In one study (Greenberg & Becker, 1988) more than half of the elderly mothers and one-third of the fathers experienced significant stress because of their children's problems—in the fathers' case, more because of their wives' reactions than because of the problems themselves. For mothers, the most stressful relationships were those in which a daughter had broken off contact with the family; for fathers, the most stressful relationships were with sons who continued to depend on their parents emotionally and financially.

Older adults help their children in various ways, and when they need help their children are the first people they turn to and the ones likely to do the most (Field & Minkler, 1988). Middle-class parents generally "give more services and money to their children throughout their life, and children give more emotional support, household help, and care during illness" (Troll, 1986, p. 23). Among working-class families, money is more likely to flow from child to parent (Troll et al., 1979).

Many older adults resume a more active parenting role when their children need help. Single adult children receive more financial assistance from elderly parents than married ones do; divorced children are more likely to get emotional support and help with child care and housework. Unhappily married, divorced, and widowed adults often get from parents the emotional support they do not get from spouses. Parents of divorced children see them more often than before and may take them into their homes. Many parents of alcoholics and drug abusers support their children financially as well as emotionally. Parents of mentally ill, moderately retarded, or physically disabled children often maintain their protective roles as long as they live (Aldous, 1987; Greenberg & Becker, 1988; Ryff & Seltzer, 1995). Today many parents serve as caregivers for adult children with AIDS (Brabant, 1994).

Help goes the other way, as well. Although most older adults are physically fit, vigorous, and independent, some seek their children's assistance in making decisions and may even depend on them for daily tasks and financial support. If older people become ill or infirm, their children may be faced with managing their lives.

Older adults are likely to be depressed if they need help from their children. In a society in which both generations value their independence, the prospect of dependency can be demoralizing. Parents do not want to be a burden on their children or to deplete their children's resources. Yet parents also may be depressed if they fear that their children will *not* take care of them (G. R. Lee, Netzer, & Coward, 1995).

People in American society do not fall naturally into a pattern common in many other societies, in which older people expect to live and be cared for in their children's homes, just as the parents once cared for the children. Still, most are conscious of their obligations to their parents and often expect more of themselves than the parents do of them. However, parental care is not equally shared by daughters and sons. Research findings indicate that daughters are usually the primary caregivers to ill or disabled parents (Stephens & Franks, 1999). In a study of 144 parent-child pairs, both generations gave top ranking to the same three filial responsibilities: helping parents understand their resources, giving emotional support, and talking over matters of importance (see Table 10.1). Both generations gave less weight to adjusting work or family schedules to help parents. The children felt that they should give money to their parents, but most of the parents did not. More children than parents considered it important to make room for a parent in their homes in an emergency, to care for parents when they were sick, and to sacrifice personal freedom (Hamon & Blieszner, 1990). (Caregiving of elderly parents by adult children is discussed later in this chapter.)

TABLE 10.1

Expectations of Adult Children and Their Parents Regarding Filial Responsibility

Item	___ ADULT CHILDREN ___		_____ PARENTS _____	
	Percent	Rank	Percent	Rank
Help understand resources	99.3	1	97.2	2
Give emotional support	97.2	2	95.7	3
Talk over matters of importance	96.5	3	98.6	1
Make room in home in emergency*	94.4	4	73.0	7
Sacrifice personal freedom*	93.7	5	81.0	6
Give care when sick*	92.4	6	64.3	9
Be together on special occasions	86.0	7	86.7	5
Give financial help*	84.6	8	41.1	13
Give parent advice	84.0	9	88.7	4
Adjust family schedule to help*	80.6	10	57.4	10
Feel responsible for parent*	78.2	11	66.4	8
Adjust work schedule to help*	63.2	12	42.1	12
Parent should live with child*	60.8	13	36.7	15
Visit once a week	51.4	14	55.6	11
Live close to parent	32.2	15	25.7	16
Write once a week	30.8	16	39.4	14

NOTES: (1) Ranking reflects percentage of respondents who "strongly agreed" or "agreed" with each item on the Hamon Filial Responsibility Scale. (2) Asterisk indicates significant differences in proportion of endorsement for children and parents.
SOURCE: Adapted from Hamon & Blieszner, 1990, p. P111.

CRITICAL THINKING

If you have at least one sibling, have you noticed a consistent or changing pattern in your relationship(s) since childhood? If you noticed change, what influenced it?

Siblings

For most people, relationships with brothers and sisters are the longest-lasting. In some cross-sectional research, sibling relationships over the life span appear to take the form of an hourglass, with the most contact at the two ends— childhood and middle to late adulthood—and the least contact during the childraising years. Other studies indicate a decline in frequency of contact throughout adulthood. Sibling conflict tends to diminish with age—perhaps because siblings who do *not* get along see each other less (Putney & Bengtson, 2001).

Sibling relationships seem to serve somewhat different purposes for men and women. For women, positive feelings toward siblings are linked with a favorable self-concept; for men, with high morale. The more contact both men and women have with their siblings, the less likely they are to show symptoms of psychological problems (Paul, 1997).

Sisters, especially, stay in touch and stand ready to help each other (Cicirelli, 1980, 1995; H. G. Ross, Dalton, & Milgram, 1980; Scott & Roberto, 1981). Step- and half-siblings are also likely to maintain contact, depending on how long they lived together during childhood, but they do not see each other as often as full siblings do, and they may provide less help. These differences may diminish as stepfamilies become more common (Antonucci et al., 2001).

SIBLING RELATIONSHIPS IN MIDDLE AGE

After establishing their own identities through career and family, middle-aged siblings often make special efforts to renew ties, and earlier rivalry tends to be replaced by intimacy and affection (Cicirelli, 1980; Ross, Dalton, & Milgram, 1980; Scott & Roberto, 1981) (Bedford, 1995; Cicirelli, 1995, Putney & Bengtson, 2001). More than two-thirds of people with living siblings—some 85 percent of middle-aged Americans—feel close or very close to their brothers and sisters and have good relationships with them; more than three-fourths say that they get along well or very well (Cicirelli, 1980). Closeness—both emotional and geographic—and a sense of responsibility for each other's welfare are the most important influences on how often brothers and sisters see each other (Lee, Mancinni, & Maxwell, 1990). Siblings usually get together at least several times a year—in many cases, once a month or more. It is unusual for them to lose touch completely (Cicirelli, 1980).

Dealing with the care of aging parents brings some siblings closer together but causes resentment and conflict among others (Antonucci et al., 2001; Bedford, 1995; Bengtson et al., 1996). The quality of a sibling relationship

© Jacques Chenet

Bessie and Sadie Delany, daughters of a freed slave, were best friends all their lives (more than 100 years) and wrote two books together about the values they grew up with and the story of their long, active lives. Elderly siblings are an important part of each other's support network, and sisters are especially vital in maintaining family relationships.

during the early years—cooperative or conflictual—may affect the way adult siblings handle such issues (Bedford, 1995). Disagreements may arise over the division of care (Lerner, Somers, Reid, Chiriboga, & Tierney, 1991; Strawbridge & Wallhagen, 1991) or over an inheritance, especially if the sibling relationship has not been good. Among 95 married daughters caring for parents with dementia, siblings were a strong source of support, but also the most important source of interpersonal stress (Suitor & Pillemer, 1993).

SIBLING RELATIONSHIPS IN LATE LIFE

When Elizabeth ("Bessie") Delany was 102 and her sister Sarah ("Sadie") was 104, they published a best-selling book, *Having Our Say: The Delany Sisters' First 100 Years* (Delany, Delany, & Hearth, 1993). The daughters of a freed slave, Bessie overcame racial and gender discrimination to become a dentist, and Sadie became a high school teacher. The sisters never married. Determined to be independent, for three decades they lived together in Mount Vernon, New York. Although their personalities were as different as sugar and spice—and had been since childhood—the two women were best friends, sharing a sense of fun and the values their parents instilled in them (Delany, Delany, & Hearth, 1993).

For people who have only one or two children, or none, relationships with siblings in late life may be increasingly important as a source of emotional support and practical help (Cicirelli, 1980; Rubinstein, Alexander, Goodman, & Luborsky, 1991; Scott & Roberto, 1981). Both brothers and sisters and their children provide such support to never-married women (Rubinstein et al., 1991).

Sisters are especially vital in maintaining family relationships and well-being, perhaps because of women's emotional expressiveness and traditional role as nurturers (Bedford, 1995; Cicirelli, 1989a, 1995). Older people who are close to their sisters feel better about life and worry less about aging than those without sisters, or without close ties to them (Cicirelli, 1977, 1989a). Among a national sample of bereaved adults in the Netherlands, those coping with the death of a sister experienced more difficulty than those who had lost a spouse or a parent (Cleiren, Diekstra, Kerkhof, & van der Wal, 1994).

Looking back, older people who feel close to their brothers or sisters express a sense of peace with life and with themselves, whereas those who are estranged from their siblings often feel upset, as if they had failed to live up to expectations. Siblings who have reestablished ties generally feel that they have accomplished something important (Ross et al., 1980).

Multigenerational Late-Life Families

The late-life family today has special characteristics (Brubaker, 1983, 1990; C. L. Jonhson, 1995). Historically, even when and where the multigenerational family was prevalent, the years people spent in such a family were few, and the family rarely spanned more than three generations. Today, many families in developed countries include four or even five generations (with fewer members in each successive generation), making it possible for a person to be both a grandparent and a grandchild at the same time (Kinsella & Velkoff, 2001).

The presence of so many family members can be enriching but can also create special pressures. As we'll see in the next section, the role of grandparent is not as clear as it used to be. Divorce and remarriage can interfere with grandparent-grandchild relationships. On the other hand, despite sagging energy, some grandparents and even great-grandparents step in and raise grandchildren.

In addition, more "young-old" people have at least one parent who has lived long enough to have several chronic illnesses and whose care may be physically and emotionally draining. Many women today spend more of their lives caring for parents than for children (Abel, 1991). Now that the fastest-growing group in the population is age 85 and over, many people in their late sixties or beyond—whose own health and energy may be faltering—find themselves in this position. The *parent-support ratio*—the number of people 85 and over for every 100 people age 50 to 64—tripled (from 3 to 10) between 1950 and 1993; it may triple again by 2053 (U.S. Bureau of the Census, 1995).

GRANDPARENTHOOD AND GREAT-GRANDPARENTHOOD

In some African communities, grandparents are called "noble." In Japan, grandmothers wear red as a sign of their status (Kornhaber, 1986). Although most western societies have no badges or titles of honor, becoming a grandparent can be an extremely important event in a person's life.

CRITICAL THINKING

What do you believe causes families or a society to value older members?

Often grandparenthood begins before the end of active parenting. Adults in the United States become grandparents at an average age of 48, according to a telephone survey of 1,500 grandparents belonging to the American Association of Retired Persons (AARP) (Davies & Williams, 2002). With today's lengthening life spans, many adults spend several decades as grandparents. Since women tend to live longer than men, grandmothers typically live to see at least the oldest grandchild become an adult and to become great-grandmothers (Szinovacz, 1998). More than 75 percent of older Americans are grandparents, and more than 40 percent are great-grandparents (Menninger Foundation, 1994).

Men and women whose adult children have postponed or decided against parenthood often feel disappointed and somehow cheated. Some become foster grandparents or volunteer in schools or hospitals (Porcino, 1983, 1991).

The Grandparent's Role

Today's grandparents are likely to be designing rocking chairs rather than sitting in them, marketing cookies rather than baking them, and wearing jogging suits instead of aprons. The changes grandparents have lived through have resulted in lifestyles and roles very different from those of previous generations.

In families like Marian Anderson's, grandparents were an essential part of the family's economic and emotional health. In some cultures, they still are. In many developing societies, such as those in Latin America and Asia, extended-family households predominate, and grandparents play an integral role in child raising and family decisions. In such Asian countries as Thailand and Taiwan, about 40 percent of the population ages 50 and over live in the same household with a minor grandchild, and half of those with grandchildren ages 10 or younger—usually grandmothers—provide care for the child (Kinsella & Velkoff, 2001).

In the United States, the extended-family household is common in some minority communities, but the dominant household pattern is the nuclear family. When children grow up, they typically leave home and establish new, autonomous nuclear families wherever their inclinations, aspirations, and job hunts take them. Although 68 percent of the grandparents in the AARP survey see at least one grandchild every one to two weeks, 45 percent live too far away to see their grandchildren regularly (Davies & Williams, 2002). However, distance does not necessarily affect the quality of relationships with grandchildren (Kivett, 1991, 1993, 1996).

Grandparenthood, especially when families were large, used to be seen as a natural extension of parenthood; the youngest child was barely launched, or still at home, when the eldest began having babies. Today, there may be a gap between the emptying of one generation's nest and the filling of the next, and this is a time when many middle-aged parents spread their own wings and make important life changes. Like young adults, they may move wherever their inclinations or aspirations take them. And rising living standards, together with social security, have made the generations less financially dependent on each other (Cherlin & Furstenberg, 1986b; Kornhaber & Woodward, 1981).

Grandparenthood today is different in other ways from grandparenthood in the past. The average U.S. grandparent has six grandchildren (Davies & Williams, 2002), compared with twelve to fifteen around the turn of the century (Szinovacz, 1998; Uhlenberg, 1988). With the rising incidence of midlife divorce, about one in five grandparents is divorced, widowed, or separated (Davies & Williams, 2002), and many children have stepgrandparents. Grandmothers of younger children are more likely to be in the workforce (and thus less available to help out). On the other hand, trends toward early retirement free more grandparents to spend time with older grandchildren. Many grandparents still have living parents, whose care they must balance with grandchildren's needs. And many grandparents in both developed and developing countries provide part-time or primary care for grandchildren (Kinsella & Velkoff, 2001; Szinovacz, 1998). And some grandparents, as we will see, raise a grandchild when the parents cannot or will not do it.

Today's busy, lively grandparents face a conflict between personal and family needs (Cherlin & Furstenberg, 1986b, Kornhaber & Forsyth, 1994). Many feel that they have raised their children and now are entitled to pursue their own interests. Yet they may have an uneasy feeling that they are missing out on something important: intimacy with their grandchildren (Kornhaber, 1986; Kornhaber & Woodward, 1981).

Active grandparents like Marian Anderson's grandmother can still be an important influence on their grandchildren's development. They are a link to the extended family. Grandparent and grandchild know each other intimately, on many levels. The grandparent serves as teacher, caretaker, role model, and sometimes negotiator between child and parent.

While grandparenthood has changed, the role can still be positive and significant. A major study of a three-generational, nationally representative sample found that "grandparents play a limited but important role in family dynamics" and that many have strong emotional ties to their grandchildren (Cherlin & Furstenberg, 1986a, p. 26). The researchers found three styles of grandparenting: remote, companionate (the predominant style), and involved. *Remote* grandparents (29 percent) see their grandchildren so infrequently that the relationship is more symbolic than real. *Companionate* grandparents (55 percent) do not intervene directly in the children's upbringing but enjoy frequent, casual companionship. Only 16 percent of grandparents are *involved* to the extent of disciplining or correcting their grandchildren, giving advice, discussing the child's problems, being consulted on important decisions concerning the child, and exchanging help with errands, chores, and projects. (Figure 10.1 shows the most frequent grandparent-grandchild activities.) Younger grandparents, those who see

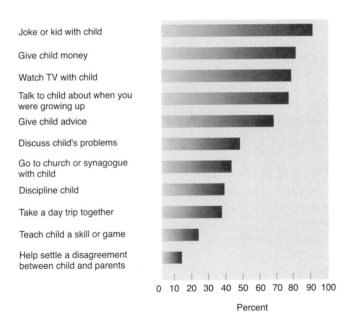

FIGURE 10.1 What grandparents do with their grandchildren: proportions of grandparents in a nationally representative sample who had engaged in various activities with their grandchildren in the previous 12 months. *SOURCE:* Cherlin & Furstenberg, 1986b, p. 74.

their grandchildren almost every day, and those who have a close relationship with the child's mother are more likely to be involved.

Grandparenting styles may differ with different grandchildren, and at different times in a child's life. Grandparents are likely to be more involved during a child's preadolescent years (Cherlin & Furstenberg, 1986b). As grandchildren grow older, contact tends to diminish, but affection grows. The decline in contact is more rapid among younger cohorts of grandparents, who tend to have better health, more money, and busier lives (Silverstein & Long, 1998). However, satisfaction with grandchildren stays high into very old age, even though the generations see each other less often as children grow up (Field & Minkler, 1988).

The most frequent activities grandparents in the AARP sample do with their grandchildren are having dinner together, watching television, going shopping, and reading to them; more than half exercise or play sports with their grandchildren. More than half spend money on their grandchildren's educational needs, and about 45 percent say they help pay grandchildren's living expenses. About 15 percent of these grandparents provide child care while the parents work (Davies & Williams, 2002). Indeed, grandparents are now the nation's number one child care providers; 21 percent of all preschoolers and 15 percent of grade-school-age children stay with grandparents while their mothers work (Smith, 2002). A similar trend exists in some other developed countries (Kinsella & Velkoff, 2001).

Grandparents frequently walk a tightrope between reluctance to interfere in adult children's family lives and obligation to provide help and support, and their level of involvement is often up to the parents (Silverstein, Giarrusso, & Bengtson, 1998). One prominent researcher (Troll, 1980, 1983) sees grandparents as family "watchdogs." They stay on the fringes of their children's and grandchildren's lives, watching to be sure that things are going well, but rarely play a strong role unless they need to. In a crisis—after a divorce, for example, or during illness or money troubles—they may step in and become more active (Cherlin & Furstenberg, 1986a, 1986b).

GENDER AND RACIAL/ETHNIC DIFFERENCES

Grandmothers tend to be kinkeepers; they are the ones who keep in touch with the grandchildren. In general, grandmothers have closer, warmer, more affectionate relationships with their grandchildren (especially granddaughters) than grandfathers do, and see them more (Putney & Bengtson, 2001). The mother's parents are likely to be closer to the children than the father's parents and are more likely to become involved during a crisis (Cherlin & Furstenberg, 1986a, 1986b; Hagestad, 1978, 1982; B. Kahana & Kahana, 1970). Grandmothers tend to be more satisfied with grandparenting than grandfathers are (Thomas, 1986). However, grandfathers may be more nurturing and more physically demonstrative with their grandchildren than they were with their own children; they may regard grandparenthood as a "second chance" to make up for their failings as parents

(Kivnick, 1982). Grandfatherhood may be more central for African American men than for white men (Kivett, 1991). African American grandparents are more likely to become involved in raising their grandchildren, even when there is no crisis (Cherlin & Furstenberg, 1986a, 1986b; Goodman & Silverstein, 2002).

GRANDPARENTING AFTER DIVORCE AND REMARRIAGE

One result of the rise in divorce and remarriage is a growing number of grandparents and grandchildren whose relationships are endangered or severed. Another result is the creation of large numbers of stepgrandparents.

After a divorce, since the mother usually has custody, her parents tend to have more contact and stronger relationships with their grandchildren, and the paternal grandparents tend to have less (Cherlin & Furstenberg, 1986b; Myers & Perrin, 1993). A divorced mother's remarriage typically reduces her need for support from her parents, but not their contact with their grandchildren. For paternal grandparents, however, the new marriage increases the likelihood that they will be displaced or that the family will move away, making contact more difficult (Cherlin & Furstenberg, 1986b).

Because ties with grandparents are important to children's development, every state in the Union has given grandparents (and in some states, great-grandparents, siblings, and others) the right to visitation after a divorce or the death of a parent, if a judge finds it in the best interests of the child. However, a few state courts have struck down such laws, and some legislatures have restricted grandparents' visitation rights. The Supreme Court in June 2000 invalidated Washington State's "grandparents' rights" law as too broad an intrusion on parental rights (Greenhouse, 2000a).

The remarriage of either parent often brings a new set of grandparents into the picture, and often stepgrandchildren as well. Stepgrandparents may find it hard to become close to their new stepgrandchildren, especially older children and those who do not live with the grandparent's adult child (Cherlin & Furstenberg, 1986b; Longino & Earle, 1996; Myers & Perrin, 1993). Such issues as birthday and Christmas presents for a "real" grandchild's half- or stepsiblings, or which grandparents are visited or included at holidays, can generate tension. Creating new family traditions; including *all* the grandchildren, step and otherwise, in trips, outings, and other activities; offering a safe haven for the children when they are unhappy or upset; and being understanding and supportive of all members of the new stepfamily are ways in which stepgrandparents can build bridges, not walls (T. S. Kaufman, 1993; Visher & Visher, 1991).

The Great-Grandparent's Role

When Dorothy Bernstein died at age 86, six great-grandchildren under age 6 were at her funeral. Her three adult grandchildren spoke of how proud she had been of becoming a great-grandmother, and how—even during her final illness—her eyes had lit up when the little ones came to visit her (R. D. Feldman, personal observation, March 6, 1994).

When grandchildren grow up and become parents, grandparents move into a new role: great-grandparenthood. Because of age, declining health, and the scattering of families, great-grandparents tend to be less involved than grandparents in a child's life. And because four- or five-generation families are relatively new, there are few generally accepted guidelines for what great-grandparents are supposed to do (Cherlin & Furstenberg, 1986b).

Still, most great-grandparents find the role emotionally fulfilling. When 40 great-grandfathers and great-grandmothers, age 71 to 90, were interviewed, 93 percent were enthusiastic. More than one-third (mostly women) were close to their great-grandchildren; the others had less contact. The ones who were close to the children were likely to live nearby and to be close to the children's parents and grandparents. They often helped out with loans, gifts, and baby-sitting (Doka & Mertz, 1988).

Both grandparents and great-grandparents can be important to their families. They are sources of wisdom, companions in play, links to the past, and symbols of the continuity of family life. As Erikson has observed (see Chapter 11), they express a natural longing to transcend mortality by investing themselves in the lives of future generations.

Raising Grandchildren and Great-Grandchildren

"We hadn't had children in our home for years; suddenly they were there almost 24 hours a day," said Mary Etta Johnson (Larsen, 1990–1991, p. 32). Johnson and her husband, Albert, took their two preschool-age grandchildren into their home after their daughter and son-in-law became involved with drugs and divorced. About 1 year later, the Johnsons obtained permanent custody.

An increasing number of American grandparents and great-grandparents from their late thirties to their late seventies are serving as "parents by default" for children whose parents are addicted to drugs or alcohol, divorced, dead, physically or mentally ill, unwed, underage, unemployed, abusive, neglectful, or in jail, or who have simply abandoned them (Allen et al., 2000; Chalfie, 1994; Hayslip & Goldberg-Glen, 2000). In 2000, more than 4.5 million children lived in 2.4 million grandparent-headed households—a 30 percent increase since 1990 (AARP, 2002). In the AARP survey mentioned earlier, 6 percent of grandparents had grandchildren living with them, and in more than 43 percent of those homes, no parent was present (Davies & Williams, 2001). Many of these grandparents are their grandchildren's sole or primary caregivers.

This phenomenon is occurring elsewhere as well. One reason, in developing countries, is the migration of rural parents to urban areas to find work. These "skip-generation" families exist in all regions of the world, particularly in Afro-Caribbean countries. In sub-Saharan Africa, the AIDS epidemic has left many orphans whose grandparents step into the parents' place (Kinsella & Velkoff, 2001). In many parts of Africa, the older generation are giving double care—first for adult children with AIDS and then for *their* orphaned children.

CRITICAL THINKING

What are the advantages and disadvantages of grandparents raising their children's children? Do current social policies recognize the roles grandparents play?

Unplanned surrogate parenthood can be a physical, emotional, and financial drain on middle-aged or older adults. Many of these caregiver-grandparents are divorced or widowed and live on fixed incomes (Hudnall, 2001), and many are in dire financial straits (Casper & Bryson, 1998). They may have to quit their jobs, shelve their retirement plans, drastically reduce their leisure pursuits and social life, and endanger their health (Burton, 1992; Chalfie, 1994; Minkler & Roe, 1992, 1996). Most grandparents do not have as much energy, patience, or stamina as they once had and may not be up on current educational and social trends (Hudnall, 2001).

Most grandparents who take on this responsibility do it because they love the children and do not want them placed in foster homes with strangers. Two-thirds of custodial grandparents, according to one study, report a greater sense of purpose in life (Jendrek, 1994). But many are ambivalent. The age difference between grandparent and grandchild can become a barrier; and both generations may feel cheated out of their traditional roles. At the same time, grandparents often have to deal with grief, anger, and pain; with a sense of guilt and failure because the adult children they raised have failed their own children; and with rancor between themselves and their adult child. For some caregiver couples, the strains may produce tension in their own relationship (Crowley, 1993; Larsen, 1990–1991). If parents later resume their normal role, the grandparent may find it emotionally wrenching to return the child (Crowley, 1993).

Grandparents who do not become foster parents or gain custody have no legal status and no more rights than unpaid baby-sitters; they face many practical problems, from getting medical insurance for the child to enrolling the child in school or qualifying for public housing. Obtaining legal custody can be difficult, time-consuming, and expensive, and custody can be taken away if a parent later challenges it. Custody laws vary from state to state. Grandparents' rights activists are urging national custody standards, as well as other legal remedies such as allowing a primary caregiver's insurance to cover a child. Some family advocates propose a new legal category called *kinship adoption*, which would allow the birth parent to retain a limited role, with the right, for example, to visit the child and to see school records (Crowley, 1993; Landers, 1992).

LIVING ARRANGEMENTS, CAREGIVING, AND COMMUNITY SUPPORT

Living independently is a hallmark of adulthood in the United States. Sometimes, however, circumstances limit choices. Let's look at what happens when adult children do not leave their parents' household, or when they return to it. Then we'll examine where older adults live and with whom, the role of community support, and what happens when aging adults need long-term care.

Adult Children at Home: The Not-So-Empty Nest

Since the 1980s, in most western nations, more and more adult children have delayed leaving home. Furthermore, the **revolving door syndrome** (sometimes called the *boomerang phenomenon*) has become more common, as increasing

> CRITICAL THINKING
>
> Historically, what appears to influence whether or not single adult children or older family members live in a home with other family members?

numbers of young adults, especially men, return to their parents' home, sometimes more than once, and sometimes with their own families. The family home can be a convenient, supportive, and affordable haven while young adults are getting on their feet or regaining their balance in times of financial, marital, or other trouble (Aquilino, 1996; Putney & Bengtson, 2001).

In the United States, in the year 2000—a time of economic decline—10.5 percent of 25- to 34-year-olds were living in the family home (Grieder, 2001). This "nonnormative" experience is becoming less so, especially for parents with more than one child. Rather than an abrupt leave-taking, the empty nest transition may be seen as a more prolonged process of separation, often lasting several years. Most likely to come home are single, divorced, or separated children and those who end a cohabiting relationship (Aquilino, 1996; Putney & Bengtson, 2001).

Prolonged parenting contradicts traditional expectations (Putney & Bengtson, 2001). As children move from adolescence to young adulthood, parents normally expect them to become independent, and they themselves normally expect to do so. An adult child's autonomy is a sign of parental success. A grown child's delaying departure from the nest, or returning to it, may lead to tension. Serious conflicts or open hostility may arise when a young adult child is unemployed and financially dependent or has returned after the failure of a marriage. Relations are smoother when the parents see the adult child moving toward autonomy, for example by enrolling in college (Antonucci et al., 2001; Aquilino, 1996).

Adult children tend to be less satisfied with having to live in their parents' home than the parents are with having them there (Putney & Bengtson, 2001). Disagreements may center on household responsibilities and the adult child's lifestyle. The young adult is likely to feel isolated from peers, while the parents may feel hampered in renewing their intimacy, exploring personal interests, and resolving marital issues (Aquilino & Supple, 1991). The return of an adult child works best when parents and child negotiate roles and responsibilities, acknowledging the child's adult status and the parents' right to privacy (Aquilino, 1996).

Living Arrangements for Older Adults

Many factors affect older people's living arrangements: marital status, finances, health, and family size. Decisions about where and with whom to live also are affected by broader societal influences: cultural traditions and values, availability of social services, and the types of housing available (Kinsella & Velkoff, 2001).

In developing countries, both elderly men and women typically live with adult children and grandchildren in multigenerational households. In developed countries, such as the United States, Canada, and most European nations, the minority of older adults living alone has increased greatly since the 1960s. Also, with increases in survival, the main person many older people in both developed and developing countries depend on for care and support is their spouse (Kinsella & Velkoff, 2001).

In 2000, 95.5 percent of Americans age 65 and older lived in the community, about one-third of them alone and almost all the rest with a spouse (55 percent) or other family members (Administration on Aging, 2001; Kramarow et al., 1999; see Figure 10.2). Elderly men are more likely than women, and white people are more likely than black people, to live with a spouse (U.S. Bureau of the Census, 2000). About 30 percent live alone—41 percent of the women, though only 16 percent of the men. The likelihood of living alone increases with age.

Most older people want to live in the community. Those who do feel better than those in institutions, even when their health is about the same (Chappell & Penning, 1979). About eight out of ten elderly heads of households own their homes, and most prefer to stay there; many, even after being widowed (Administration on Aging, 2001; Treas, 1995).

"Aging in place" may make sense for those who can manage on their own or with minimal help, have an adequate income or a paid-up mortgage, can handle the up-keep, are happy in the neighborhood, and want to be independent, to have privacy, and to be near friends, adult children, or grandchildren (Gonyea, Hudson, & Seltzer, 1990; Lawton, 2001). But living arrangements can become a major problem as people age. A person may no longer to able to manage three flights of stairs. A neighborhood may deteriorate, and helpless-looking older people may become prey to young thugs. Because of the flight

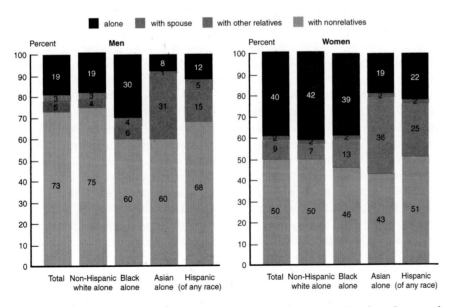

FIGURE 10.2 *Living arrangements of noninstitutionalized persons age 65 and over by sex and race and Hispanic origin, 2003.* Older men were more likely to live with their spouse than were older women. Living with other relatives indicates no spouse present. Living with non relatives indicates no spouse or other relatives present. *SOURCE:* Older Americans, 2004.

from the cities after World War II, there are now many aging suburbanites who may find it more and more difficult to live in homes built for young families and in communities designed around the automobile. Mental or physical disability may make living alone impractical.

Older adults who cannot or do not want to maintain a house, do not have family nearby, prefer a different locale or climate, or want to travel may move into low-maintenance or maintenance-free townhouses, condominiums, cooperative or rental apartments, or mobile homes.

Most older people do not need much help; those who do need help can usually remain in the community if they have at least one person to depend on. The single most important factor keeping people out of institutions is being married (Health Care Finance Administration, 1981; Johnson & Catalano, 1981). As long as a couple are in relatively good health, they can usually live fairly independently and care for each other. The issue of living arrangements becomes more pressing when one or both become frail, infirm, or disabled, or when one spouse dies.

An emerging array of housing options and community support programs are making it easier for older people to live with some degree of independence (see Box 10.3 and Table 10.2).

LIVING ALONE

CRITICAL THINKING

Which living arrangements do you think are most desirable for older adults in general? Which arrangement will you choose for yourself?

Because women live longer than men and are more likely to be widowed, older women in the United States are more than twice as likely as older men to live alone, and the likelihood increases with age. Among women 75 and over, almost 50 percent live alone (Administration on Aging, 2001). The picture is similar in most developed countries: older women are more likely to live alone than older men, who usually live with spouses or other family members. In the Scandinavian countries, where home help services are especially common, as many as one-fourth of elderly men and one-half of elderly women live alone. The growth of elderly single-person households may be due in part to governmental policies: increased old age benefits, "reverse mortgage" programs that enable people to live off their homes' equity, construction of elder-friendly housing, and long-term care policies that discourage institutional living (Kinsella & Velkoff, 2001).

About four out of five older Americans who live alone are widowed, and almost half have no children or none living nearby. They are older and poorer on the average than elderly people who live with someone else. However, they are generally in better health than older people without spouses who have other living arrangements. The overwhelming majority value their independence and prefer to be on their own (Commonwealth Fund, 1986; Kramarow et al., 1999; U.S. Bureau of the Census, 1992).

It may seem that older people who live alone, particularly the oldest old, would be lonely. However, other factors, such as personality, cognitive abilities, physical health, and a depleted social network may play a more significant role in vulnerability to loneliness. (P. Martin, Hagberg, & Poon, 1997). Social activities,

TABLE 10.2

Options for Living Arrangements

	Financing			Amenities										Restrictions				
	Own	Rent	Extra fees/dues	Home health care	Housekeeping services	Laundry services	Meals provided	Nursing care	Property maintenance	Recreational facilities	Resident governance	Social activities	Transportation	Age	Waiting list	Rules/regulations	Children allowed	Pets allowed
Accessory apartment	■	■												▲				
Apartment		•	▲		▲	▲			•	■	■	■		▲	■	■	■	■
Assisted-living facility/board-and-care home		•		•	•	•	•	■	•	■		■	•	■	■	•		■
Congregate housing		•	•	■	•	•	•	▲	•	•	■	•	•	■		■	▲	■
Continuing-care retirement community	■	■	•	•	•	•	•	•	•	•	•	•	•	■		■	▲	■
Cooperative housing			•	▲	▲	▲	▲	▲	•	■	•	■	▲	■	■	■	•	■
ECHO housing	■	•												■				
Foster-care home		•		•	•	•	•	▲	•	■	▲	■	•	■	■	•	■	■
Manufactured (mobile) home	•	■	•	▲	▲	▲	▲	▲	•	■	■	■	▲	■	■	■	■	■
Retirement community	■	■	•	■	■	■	■	■	■	•	•	•	■	•	■	•		■
Retirement hotel		•	■	▲	•	■	•	▲	■	■	▲	■	▲	■	•	■	▲	▲
Shared housing	■	■	■	▲	■	■	■	▲	■	▲	•	■		■	■	■	•	■
Single-family residence	•	■																
Townhouse/condominium	•	■	•	▲	▲	▲	▲	▲	■	■	•	■		▲	▲	•	■	■

Key: • = usually; ■ = sometimes; ▲ = rarely.
SOURCE: "Which Living Arrangement Is Right for You?" 1993, pp. 32–33.

Choosing Living Arrangements

Three friends in their late sixties bought a big old house and turned it into a "geriatric commune" with shared kitchen and dining room. "It takes a lot of the stress out of aging to know you have a place that's yours and people who will care," they say (Porcino, 1993, pp. 28, 30).

This is but one of an almost bewildering range of choices in living arrangements available to older adults today (see Table 10.2). Let's see how various options match up with specific lifestyles and needs.

Those who want or need a higher level of amenities, services, or care without sacrificing independence or dignity may want to consider the following options:

• *Retirement hotel.* Hotel or apartment building remodeled to meet the needs of independent older adults. Typical hotel services (switchboard, maid service, message center) are provided.

• *Retirement community.* Large, self-contained development with owned or rental units or both. Support services and recreational facilities are often available.

• *Shared housing.* Housing can be shared informally by adult parents and children or by friends. Sometimes social agencies match people who need a place to live with people who have houses or apartments with extra rooms. The older person usually has a private room but shares living, eating, and cooking areas and may exchange services such as light housekeeping for rent.

• *Accessory apartment or ECHO (elder cottage housing opportunity) housing.* An independent unit created so that an older person can live in a remodeled single-family home or in a portable unit on the grounds of a single-family home—often, but not necessarily,

such as going to church or temple or a senior center, or doing volunteer work, can help an older person stay connected to the community (Steinbach, 1992).

LIVING SEMI-INDEPENDENTLY

When Wilma Bingham could no longer manage to live in her home, she wanted a place where she could have help with housekeeping chores—and keep her cat. Her daughter found a solution: a one-bedroom apartment in an assisted-living facility, where she could keep her independence and dignity (and her pet) while getting the services she needed (Glasheen, 1993).

In recent years, creative social planning has enabled more and more older Americans in Wilma Bingham's position to remain in the community. Box 10.3 describes a number of options—some traditional and some innovative—for older people who can and want to be partially self-sufficient. Besides assisted living, these alternatives include retirement communities, housing shared by friends or relatives, group homes run by social agencies,

that of an adult child. These units offer privacy, proximity to caregivers, and security.

- *Congregate housing.* Private or government-subsidized rental apartment complexes or mobile home parks designed for older adults. They provide meals, housekeeping, transportation, social and recreational activities, and sometimes health care. One type of congregate housing is called a *group home.* A social agency that owns or rents a house brings together a small number of elderly residents and hires helpers to shop, cook, do heavy cleaning, drive, and give counseling. Residents take care of their own personal needs and take some responsibility for day-to-day tasks.
- *Assisted-living facility.* Semi-independent living in one's own room or apartment. Similar to congregate housing, but residents receive personal care (bathing, dressing, and grooming) and protective supervision according to their needs and desires. *Board-and-care homes* are similar but smaller and offer more personal care and supervision.
- *Foster-care home.* Owners of a single-family residence take in an unrelated older adult and provide meals, housekeeping, and personal care.
- *Continuing care retirement community.* Long-term housing planned to provide a full range of accommodations and services for affluent elderly people as their needs change. A resident may start out in an independent apartment; then move into congregate housing with such services as cleaning, laundry, and meals; then into an assisted-living facility; and finally into a nursing home. *Life-care communities* are similar but guarantee housing and medical or nursing care for a specified period or for life; they require a substantial entry fee in addition to monthly payments.

accessory housing in or on the grounds of a private residence, and congregate housing—apartments clustered around a central dining room, with housekeeping, recreation, and transportation services. One promising trend is the development of continuing-care or life-care communities, where an aging person can stay as needs change (Gonyea et al., 1990; Hare & Haske, 1983–1984; Lawton, 1981, 2001; Porcino, 1983, 1991, 1993; Steinbach, 1992).

LIVING WITH ADULT CHILDREN

Older people in many African, Asian, and Latin American societies can expect to live and be cared for in their children's or grandchildren's homes; in Singapore, for example, about nine out of ten elders live with their children (Kinsella & Velkoff, 2001). Most older people in the United States, even those in difficult circumstances, do not wish to do so. They are reluctant to burden their families and to give up their own freedom. It can be inconvenient to absorb an extra person into a household, and everyone's privacy—and relationships—may suffer. The elderly parent may feel useless, bored, and isolated from friends. If the adult child is married and parent and spouse do not get along well, or caregiving duties become too burdensome, the marriage may be threatened (Lund, 1993a; Shapiro, 1994).

Despite these concerns, many older Americans, with advancing age, do live with adult children. The success of such an arrangement depends largely on the quality of the relationship that has existed in the past and on the ability of both generations to communicate fully and frankly. The decision to move a parent into an adult child's home should be mutual and needs to be thought through carefully and thoroughly. Parents and children need to respect each other's dignity and autonomy and accept their differences (Shapiro, 1994).

LIVING IN INSTITUTIONS

The use of nonfamily institutions for care of the frail elderly varies greatly around the world. Institutionalization is very rare in developing regions but is becoming less rare in Southeast Asia, where declines in fertility have resulted in a rapidly aging population and a shortage of family caregivers. In developed countries the percentage of elderly people in residential care in the 1990s ranged from 2 percent in Portugal to nearly 9 percent in the Netherlands and Sweden (Kinsella & Velkoff, 2001). Comprehensive geriatric home visitation programs in some countries, such as the United Kingdom, Denmark, and Australia have been effective in preventing functional decline and holding down nursing home admissions (Stuck, Egger, Hammer, Minder, & Beck, 2002).

In the United States in 2000, 4.5 percent of older adults were in institutions, as compared with 5.1 percent in 1990 (U.S. Census Bureau, 2001). But the lifetime probability of spending time in a nursing home is higher, especially for women, who live longer than men. About half of the women and one-third of the men who were 60 years old in 1990 will eventually stay in a nursing home at least once (AARP, 1999; Center on Elderly People Living Alone, 1995; Treas, 1995). In all countries, the likelihood of living in a nursing home increases with age (Kinsella & Velkoff, 2001)—in the United States, from about 1 percent at ages 65 to 74 to 18 percent at ages 85 and over (Administration on Aging, 2001).

At highest risk of institutionalization are those living alone, those who do not take part in social activities, those whose daily activities are limited by poor health or disability, and those whose caregivers are overburdened (McFall & Miller, 1992; Steinbach, 1992). Three-fourths of nursing home residents are women (Kinsella & Velkoff, 2001), mostly white widows in their eighties. A large minority of residents are incontinent. Many have visual and hearing problems. A little over half are cognitively impaired. On average, they need help with four to five of six basic activities of daily living: bathing, eating, dressing, getting into a chair, toileting, and walking (Sahyoun, Pratt, Lentzner, Dey, & Robinson, 2001).

A good nursing home has an experienced professional staff, an adequate government insurance program, and a coordinated structure that can provide various levels of care. It offers stimulating activities and opportunities to spend time with people of both sexes and all ages. It provides privacy—among other reasons, so that residents can be sexually active and so they can visit undisturbed with family members. A good nursing home also offers a full range of social, therapeutic, and rehabilitative services.

An essential element of good care is the opportunity for residents to make decisions and exert some control over their lives. Among 129 intermediate-care nursing home residents, those who had higher self-esteem, less depression, and a greater sense of satisfaction and meaning in life were less likely to die within four years—perhaps because their psychological adjustment motivated them to want to live and to take better care of themselves (O'Connor & Vallerand, 1998).

Federal law (the Omnibus Budget Reconciliation Act of 1987 and 1990) sets tough requirements for nursing homes and gives residents the right to choose their own doctors, to be fully informed about their care and treatment, and to be free from physical or mental abuse, corporal punishment, involuntary seclusion, and physical or chemical restraints. Some states train volunteer ombudsmen to act as advocates for nursing home residents, to explain their rights, and

© Ursula Markus/Photo Researchers

Only 5 percent of older adults in the United States live in institutions at any one time, but the probability of spending time in a nursing home increases dramatically with age. A good nursing home offers stimulating activities and companionship, as well as a full range of social, therapeutic, and rehabilitative services.

to resolve their complaints about such matters as privacy, treatment, food, and financial issues.

As the baby-boom generation born after World War II ages, and if current nursing home usage rates continue, it is projected that the number of residents will double by 2030 (Sahyoun, Pratt, et al., 2001). However, with liberalization of Medicare coverage and the emergence of widespread private long-term care insurance, there is a shift toward less expensive home heath care services and group housing alternatives. Home health services are most prevalent in Scandinavia and the United Kingdom (Kinsella & Velkoff, 2001).

Family Caregiving

CRITICAL THINKING

What impact does family caregiving have on the immediate caregiver(s) and on other peripheral family members?

Caregiving is informal, unpaid care of a person whose independence is physically, mentally, emotionally, or economically limited (Lund, 1993a). It may include errands, chauffeuring, help with finances or housework, or complete physical care. The work is confining, often distressing, and usually continuous.

Approximately 1,293,000 older adults in the United States were home health patients in 1998. This represents a decrease of 26 percent from 1996 (Vierck & Hodges, 2003).

Most long-term care is provided by informal caregivers. Almost one in three individuals, totaling 52 million people, provide informal care to ill or disabled people of all ages. Approximately 67 percent of older adult long-term care recipients rely solely on informal caregiving.

More than seven million individuals, mostly family members, give 120 millions hours of unpaid care for older adults with functional disabilities living in the community. Fifty percent of older adults in long-term care who do not have family members to provide care live in nursing homes. Only seven percent of those who have family members to provide care live in nursing homes (Vierck & Hodges, 2003).

Sixty-eight percent of primary caregivers to older adults live in the same household with the disabled person for whom they provide care. The majority of primary caregivers are spouses (40 percent) or adult children (Vierck & Hodges, 2003).

Women are most likely both to give and to receive care. When an adult child provides care for a parent, the arrangement most commonly involves a daughter and mother. Often the need arises when a husband dies, leaving a widow who cannot manage on her own. Because women tend to marry older men and to outlive them, they are more likely to end up in need of care and to have to rely on a child (Lee et al., 1993). Daughters are the ones who generally take on the responsibility for aging, ailing mothers (Troll, 1986), though many grandchildren serve as caregivers as well (Barnhart, 1992). While daughters are more likely than sons to provide care for either parent, the likelihood is far greater when the recipient is the mother. Perhaps because of the intimate nature of the contact and the strength of the mother-daughter bond, mothers may prefer a daughter's care (Lee et al., 1993).

BURDENS AND STRAINS OF CAREGIVING

Adult children and parents get along best while the parents are healthy and vigorous. When older people become infirm, especially if they suffer from mental deterioration or personality changes, the burden of caring for them may strain the relationship (Stephens & Franks, 1999). See Table 10.3.

Caregiver burnout is physical, mental, and emotional exhaustion that affects many adults who care for aged relatives (Barnhart, 1992). The strains created by incessant, heavy demands can be great—sometimes so great as to lead to abuse, neglect, or even abandonment of the dependent elderly person (see Chapter 12). Even the most patient, loving caregiver may become frustrated, anxious, or resentful under the constant strain of meeting an older person's seemingly endless needs—especially if there is no one else to turn to. Table 10.3 lists the most common stressors encountered in caring for elderly parents.

Some studies show that adults who care for patients with Alzheimer's disease or some other form of dementia are under more stress than the patients (Barnhart, 1992). The uncertainty of a diagnosis of Alzheimer's may produce even more stress than the disease itself (Garwick et al., 1994). Strains tend to affect the whole family, including the caregiver's adult children and their spouses (Fisher & Lieberman, 1994). Often, related emotional issues—such as conflicts with siblings who do not provide their expected share of help—aggravate the strain (Strawbridge & Wallhagen, 1991).

TABLE 10.3

Stressors Identified in the Parent-Care Role

Stressor	Percentage Endorsing
Parent criticized or complained	71.6%
Parent was unresponsive	67.4
Parent was uncooperative or demanding	67.4
Helped parent with personal care needs	67.3
Parent asked repetitive questions	67.3
Parent was agitated	66.4
Managed legal/financial affairs of parent	66.4
Parent's health declined	66.3
Supervised parent	63.1
Did not receive help with caregiving from friends or family	61.1
Had extra expenses due to caregiving	54.7
Parent was forgetful	53.6

SOURCE: From Stephens, Franks, & Townsend, 1994.

A caregiver for a family member with Alzheimer's disease may experience more stress than the person receiving care. Caregiving also can provide great satisfaction. Extended, demanding care can lead to physical, mental, and emotional exhaustion and result in caregiver burnout.

Not all caregivers experience significant stress, however; it depends on their age, circumstances, relationship to the patient, and available resources (Harper & Lund, 1990; Stephens & Franks, 1999). In one study, more than half of the adult children surveyed felt some strain, and one-third reported substantial strain, in connection with helping their parents. The strain most often showed up as physical or emotional exhaustion and a feeling that the parent was impossible to satisfy (Cicirelli, 1980).

How a person reacts to the demands of caregiving is likely to be affected by other responsibilities and stresses. Caregivers who feel their burden most keenly are those who work full time, are raising young children, lack support and assistance, and have limited financial resources. Burdens are exacerbated if the caregiver does not feel close to the person who is receiving the care, and if that person is aggressive or violent (Lund, 1993a). African American daughters report less strain than white daughters, but for both, conflict between caregiving and personal and social life leads to emotional strain. In one group of black caregivers, women in poor health with other conflicts in their lives and no respite from caregiving were most likely to feel strain (Mui, 1992). White caregivers but not African Americans feel more strain when their relationship with their parents is not good and when they are having conflicts at work (Mui, 1992; Walker, Martin, & Jones, 1992).

The unavoidable demands and strains of caregiving are often complicated by deep feelings about the parent-child relationship and other aspects of the caregiver's life. Adult children who care for aging parents may be torn between love and resentment, between their duty to their parents and their duty to their spouses and children, between wanting to do the right thing and not wanting to change their lives.

The needs of aging parents seem to fall into the category of nonnormative, unanticipated demands. New parents expect to assume the full physical, financial, and emotional care of their babies, with the assumption that such care will gradually diminish as children grow up. Most people do *not* expect to have to care for their parents; they ignore the possibility of their parents' infirmity and rarely plan ahead for it. When their elderly parents' dependency becomes undeniable, many adult children are shocked, grief-stricken, and angry. They have trouble coping with the changes they see taking place (Barnhart, 1992), and they may perceive the need to deal with these changes as interfering with other obligations and plans (Vierck & Hodges, 2003).

The need to care for elderly parents often arises at a time when middle-aged adults are trying to launch their own adolescent or young adult children. This "generation in the middle," sometimes called the **sandwich generation,** must allocate time, money, and energy to both. Caregivers who have full-time jobs may have to quit or cut back to part-time work in order to devote a large portion of their time to caring for parents, sometimes for years on end. The caregiver's marriage may suffer, and sometimes even end in divorce (Lund, 1993a). Adults who have been looking forward to the end of responsibility for their children—and who now sense keenly that their own remaining years are limited—may feel that caring for their parents will deprive them of any chance to fulfill their dreams. Perhaps the greatest loss involved in caregiving is loss of a sense of control over one's life (Evans, 1994). The feeling of being tied down, of not being able to take a vacation or make other plans, is, for some adult children, the hardest thing about caring for elderly parents (Robinson & Thurnher, 1981).

A common source of negative feelings is the disappointment, anger, or guilt many adults feel when they realize that they, rather than their parents, now have to be the strong ones. Anxiety over the anticipated end of their parents' lives may be tinged with worry about their own mortality (Cicirelli, 1980; Troll, 1986). When caregiving ends because of a parent's death, adult children must come to terms with feelings that are often ambivalent.

Recent research has challenged the prevalence of the sandwich generation (Kinsella & Velkoff, 2001; Putney & Bengtson, 2001; Staudinger & Bluck, 2001). Studies in the United States, Europe, and Canada have found relatively few middle-aged adults sandwiched between caregiving, work, and dependent children (Hagestad, 2000; Marks, 1998; Penning, 1998; Rosenthal, Martin-Andrews, & Matthews, 1996), as children generally have left the nest before the need for caregiving arises. Furthermore, while role conflicts undeniably can bring severe stress, that is not necessarily the case. Some caregivers flourish in multiple roles. Particular circumstances and contexts make a difference, as do the attitudes individuals bring to the task (Bengtson, 2001). Caregiving can be an opportunity for growth if a caregiver feels deeply about a parent and about family solidarity, looks at caregiving as a challenge, and has adequate personal, family, and community resources to meet the challenge (Bengtson, 2001; Bengtson, Rosenthal, & Burton, 1996; Biegel, 1995; Lund, 1993a). Table 10.4 lists some of the most commonly reported rewards of parental caregiving.

REDUCING THE STRAINS: COMMUNITY SUPPORT

> He or she grows weaker, you take over, nobody sees. Whatever he can no longer do, you do. . . . The loss of control over his body frustrates him and he tries to exert control over yours. His wish is your command. . . . Most everybody identifies with him. "How is he doing?" At first, that's all you cared about, too. Now you sometimes wonder why no one asks about you. . . . You start to feel that you don't exist. (Strong, 1988, p. 75)

Caregivers need care, too. Often families and friends fail to recognize that caregivers have a right to feel discouraged, frustrated, and put upon. Caregivers need to give themselves permission to care for *themselves* by taking some time for activities that give them a life outside of the loved one's disease (Evans, 1994).

In addition, there is an urgent need for more community support to reduce the strains of caregiving and prevent burnout. Expanded support programs

TABLE 10.4

Rewards Identified in the Parent-Care Role

Reward	Percentage Endorsing
Knew parent was well cared for	100.0
Fulfilled family obligation	93.7
Spent time in the company of parent	92.6
Gave care because wanted to not because had to	89.5
Saw parent enjoy small things	84.2
Parent showed affection or appreciation	81.1
Helped parent with personal care	81.0
Parent was cooperative or not demanding	77.8
Parent's good side came through despite the illness	73.7
Parent was calm or content	70.5
Relationship with parent became closer	64.2
Parent's health improved	47.3

SOURCE: From Stephens, Franks, & Townsend, 1994.

for caregivers could reduce or postpone the need for institutionalization. Such support services may include free or low-cost daytime activity programs; transportation and escort services; in-home services providing meals, housekeeping, and home health aides; and, most important, respite care—letting caregivers get away for a day, a weekend, or a week.

Flexible work schedules and leave provisions can benefit working adults with dependents who need care. The Family and Medical Leave Act, adopted in 1993, guarantees workers a period of unpaid leave to care for a spouse, parent, or child. Some large corporations are already providing time off for caregiving.

Adult day care centers, which provide stimulating activities and care while caregivers are at work, are a growing trend; about 3,000 such centers have opened across the country. Researchers at the University of Utah have developed a series of videotapes for use by caregivers, as well as in adult day care centers and nursing homes. The tapes are designed to engage the attention of patients with Alzheimer's disease, giving the caregiver or professional staff an uninterrupted respite of 20 to 60 minutes (D. Lund, personal communication, November 1994).

Counseling, support, and self-help groups enable caregivers to share problems, gain information about community resources, and improve caregiving skills. One such program helped daughters recognize the limits of their ability to meet their mothers' needs and the value of encouraging their mothers' self-reliance. This understanding lightened the daughters' burden and improved their relationship with their mothers, with the result that the mothers became less lonely (Scharlach, 1987). In one longitudinal study, caregivers who had adequate community support reported many dimensions of personal growth. Some had become more empathic, caring, understanding, patient, and compassionate, closer to the person they were caring for, and more appreciative of their own good health. Others felt good about having fulfilled their responsibilities. Some had "learned to value life more and to take one day at a time," and a few had learned to "laugh at situations and events" (Lund, 1993a; Stephens & Franks, 1999).

LEGAL INTERVENTION

When parents can no longer handle their own financial and practical affairs, a son or daughter may have to step in (Porcino, 1983). Parents who are mentally competent (that is, capable of making decisions and understanding the consequences) may agree to put money into a bank account held jointly with an adult child, a living trust, or a trust account with automatic inheritance by surviving adult children. A power of attorney, which can be withdrawn at any time, can give an adult child the power to make financial decisions for the parent.

A much more serious step is to have an older adult declared legally incompetent. In that case, the older adult becomes the ward of a guardian or conservator (usually an adult child or other relative, a friend, or a financial institution). A person placed under guardianship loses, permanently, the right to conduct business, to sign contracts, to vote, or even to decide where to live. The guardian controls not only the ward's property but also his or her *person* and can place the ward in an institution or make any other decisions on her or his behalf. To make sure that the guardian acts in the best interest of the older person, some courts appoint a second type of guardian, called a guardian *ad litem*. Because of the potential for abuse, it is a good idea for all adults to specify in advance (usually in a will) the person they want to act as guardian in case they become mentally incompetent (Moye, 1999).

Care of Frail Elderly: An International Perspective

CRITICAL THINKING

What are the advantages and disadvantages of deinstitutionalization? Why do you believe that changes to community-based care have taken place slowly in some countries?

Other industrialized nations are struggling with issues similar to those that have emerged in the United States regarding care of the frail elderly. In several European countries, notably England and the Netherlands, there was a shift to less restrictive residential facilities and to home and day care in the 1980s (Davies, 1993). A stated goal of government policy in Great Britain is "to enable persons as far as possible to live in their own homes or in a homelike environment in the local community" (Cm. 849, 1989, paragraph 1.8). Neighborhood volunteers are used extensively as home helpers (Nishio, 1994). However, aging in place is not seen as a panacea; English policy encourages the most suitable and cost-effective solution for each individual (Davies, 1993).

Although the goal of moving away from institutionalization is not new, changes in the balance of spending between residential and community-based care have been slow to come. Concern over cost containment and efficient use of public funds is widespread, even in countries such as the Netherlands, Sweden, and Australia, which are strongly committed to a welfare state (Davies, 1993). A trend toward diversification of care has been particularly marked in Australia. Between 1986 and 1991, along with a 25 percent increase in funding, government financial incentives induced a partial shift from nursing home care toward hostels, a semi-independent living arrangement operated either privately or not for profit. Hostels typically offer a single room with private or shared bath; staff members are available 24 hours a day for nonmedical care (Borkowski & Ozanne, 1993).

Efforts are growing to relieve the burdens of family and other nonprofessional caregivers, without whom agencies and institutions would be badly understaffed. There is more official recognition of the value of informal caregivers' contributions and of their right to be consulted in assessments and decisions (Davies, 1993). Finland, Denmark, Norway, Sweden, and the United Kingdom have the highest levels of people receiving home services to ease burdens of family caregivers. The proportion of older adults receiving home help in these five countries ranges from 15 percent to 24 percent.

In the developing nations of Asia, Africa, and Latin America, institutions for the elderly are rare. Family care is still the norm, even though migration to cities and the consequent breakup of the extended family make it less feasible. Any residential care tends to be funded by religious groups and other nonprofit organizations with limited resources (Gorman, 1993). Many developing nations are adopting new policies aimed at meeting current and future long-term care needs. Long-term care services and/or homes for the aged are becoming more accepted in countries found in Southeast Asia, where there are fewer children to serve as family caregivers (Kinsella & Velkoff, 2001).

In Japan, where the aged population is growing faster than in many other industrialized nations, reliance on family care remains strong. The number of extended family households in Japan has been declining and the number of elderly living alone or with a spouse has been increasing (see Figure 10.3). These trends suggest that the culture of Japan regarding care of the elderly is moving toward greater dependence on the nuclear family. Also, the financial and health status of some older adults is making it possible for them to afford to live alone and to choose to live in independent households. There is still close familial contact and support (Kinsella & Velkoff, 2001).

Japan's exploding older population overstrains family-based care. Accordingly, the number of nursing homes, infirmaries, and other institutions is rapidly increasing; since 1990 there has been a tenfold rise in facilities serving remote areas (see Figure 10.3). However, the official strategy is to limit the need for hospitalization and institutionalization by broadening and professionalizing home care, promoting preventive programs, and enhancing the general quality of life. Social work and care specialties have been recognized as official positions, with qualifying examinations.

In China, government policies reinforce traditional customs. The family and the local community are expected to provide medical and long-term care; the role of the central government is minimal (Olson, 1994). In rural areas, most care is in the home; only limited supplementary medical services are available. County-operated hospitals are for acute or short-term illnesses only. Families can hire semiskilled nursemaids to care for bedridden patients in the hospital as well as at home; otherwise, family members are expected to stay at the bedside. For people with no children to care for them, village committees in some rural communities make agreements with neighbors, schools, or other entities to

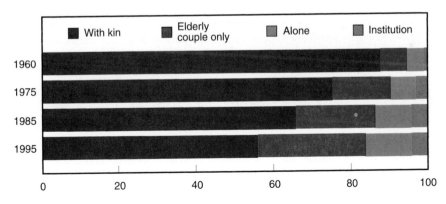

FIGURE 10.3 *Living arrangements of Japanese elderly: 1960 to 1995.* SOURCE: Japan Management and Coordination Agency, cited in Atoh, 1998; Kinsella & Velkoff, 2001. NOTE: "With kin" includes very small numbers of elderly cohabiting with nonkin.

deliver groceries, medicine, and coal. The Chinese government has begun to prod rural townships to establish homes for the aged—independent living facilities with communal baths and a common dining and recreation room. A town committee decides when it is time for a childless elderly person to enter such a home.

In urban areas, too, primary responsibility rests with the family, community, and work unit, not the central government. For most urban workers, health insurance continues into retirement but normally does not cover long-term care. Local committees identify older people who need in-home care and assign a trained person to visit them, run errands, prepare meals, and contact doctors when needed. Those not ill enough to need hospitalization receive drug therapy, physical therapy, medical examinations, and traditional Chinese treatments in their homes. Childless people may be able to live in one of the few government-operated social welfare institutes, which provide both assisted living facilities and complete, continuous care for the bedridden.

Policies regarding long-term care are still evolving. Policymakers in developed and developing nations may be able to learn from each other's experience as they seek ways to care for dependent older people with dignity—to avoid warehousing on the one hand and exploitation of family caregivers on the other.

Despite the challenging needs of frail older adults and their families, the vast majority of older people lead active, fulfilling lives. It's sometimes tempting, even for professionals who deal with problems and issues of aging, to focus on numbers and categories, to lose sight of the fact that the journey through adulthood is highly personal. Now that we've explored the social contexts of adult life, let's move on to the world of personality and mental health, including ways of coping with losses that occur throughout the adult life span.

Summary and Key Terms

- Extended-family households are common in Asia and Latin America. In the United States, where independence is a primary value, parents and adult children generally live together only when one or the other is in need of help.
  extended family (p. 357)   **nuclear family (p. 357)**

The Adult Family: Changing Roles and Relationships

- Young adults need to establish their own identity and a mature relationship with their parents; this need calls for new attitudes and behaviors on the part of both generations.
- Contact between middle-aged children and older parents (especially daughters and mothers) remains high, and mutual help continues. Parents may resume an active parenting role for a child who needs special help.
- Sibling relationships are the longest-lasting in most people's lives. Sibling contact throughout the life span follows an hourglass pattern; middle-aged siblings often renew or strengthen ties after their children leave home.

Grandparenthood and Great-Grandparenthood

- Although most American grandparents today are less intimately involved in grandchildren's lives than in the past, they often play a more active role when problems arise.
- Women tend to be closer to their grandchildren than men are, but men may be more attentive to their grandchildren than they were to their children.
- African American grandparents tend to be more involved in their grandchildren's lives, and are perceived as more successful grandparents overall, than white grandparents.
- Divorce and remarriage of an adult child often affect grandparent-grandchild relationships and create new stepgrandparenting roles.
- The great-grandparent's role is less clear and less involved than that of grandparents, but most great-grandparents find it emotionally fulfilling.
- An increasing number of children are being raised by grandparents and great-grandparents. This unplanned role can create physical, emotional, and financial strains.

Living Arrangements, Caregiving, and Community Support

- Recently, more young adults are returning to live in the parents' homes for such reasons as financial need and divorce.
- Most older adults want to—and do—live in the community, not in nursing homes; and alone or with a spouse, not with adult children.
- Most older adults who live alone are widowed women, who tend to be older, poorer, and more vulnerable than other older adults, and are more likely to end up in institutions.
- A wide range of alternatives now exists for older adults who can live semi-independently: these include assisted living, retirement communities, shared housing, group homes, accessory housing, congregate housing, and continuing-care or life-care communities.
- When older adults live with adult children, the success of the arrangement depends on their relationship and on their ability to communicate.
- Although only about 4 percent of older adults live in nursing homes, people are much more likely to spend time in an institution as they get older.
- For many infirm older adults, family care is an alternative to institutionalization. Women are more likely than men to need care and to become caregivers. Adult day care centers, in-home services, and support groups are among community programs that can help ease caregivers' burdens.
- When older adults cannot manage their affairs, legal intervention may be necessary. Such measures may range from a power of attorney to court appointment of a guardian.
- There is a trend toward less institutional care and more home- or community-based care in many industrialized countries. In addition, some of these countries are instituting policies to help caregivers.

revolving door syndrome (p. 373)
aging in place (p. 375)
caregiving (p. 382)

caregiver burnout (p. 383)
sandwich generation (p. 385)

Personality Development

◈ FOCUS: EVA PERÓN

*In most of us, by the age of thirty, the character
has set like plaster, and will never soften again.*
—William James, ***The Principles of Psychology,*** 1890

*Human beings are not born
once and for all on the day
their mothers give birth to
them. . . . Life obliges them
over and over again to give
birth to themselves.*
—Gabriel García Márquez, ***Love
in the Time of Cholera,*** 1988

© Corbis Images

MARÍA EVA DUARTE DE
Perón* was a contro-
versial figure, a woman of
myth and mystery who (as
would later be dramatized in
Andrew Lloyd Webber's mu-
sical *Evita*) rose from tawdry
origins to become first lady of
Argentina. During her 6-year
"reign," she was both adored

*Sources for biographical information on Eva Perón are Barager (1968), Blanksten
(1953), Flores (1952), Perón (1951), and Taylor (1979).

and hated. Her followers saw her as a selfless friend of the downtrodden and a champion of women's rights. Her enemies saw her as power-hungry, manipulative, and ruthless. On one point all agree: she was a beautiful woman. And she knew how to use her beauty to advantage.

Eva (affectionately known as Evita) began life in 1919 in the small, dusty village of Los Toldos. She was the fifth illegitimate child of a poor uneducated peasant woman and a married man from a nearby town. Eva and her brother and sisters were shunned by respectable people; when their father died, his wife's family tried to bar them from the funeral. Eva's destitute mother moved in with a man who had a modest restaurant; they also took in lodgers, but the family remained very poor. It was these early experiences, common among the Argentinean underclass, that Eva Perón had in mind when, later, she called herself a "woman of the people."

Eva was an intense, frail child, given to tantrums and driven by dreams of glory. She attended school only through the primary grades. Her real schooling was in her mother's tempestuous household, where, one journalist observed, the little girl learned "that life was a struggle for survival in which the prizes went to the toughest and the most unscrupulous" and men were to be used for a woman's ends (Flores, 1952, p. 22).

At age 15, during the Great Depression, Eva migrated to the capital, Buenos Aires, where she pursued an acting career. She was not very talented, but by 1943 she was starring in a radio series and had begun to develop a popular following. At that time, a new military government seized power, and Eva became the mistress of Colonel Juan Domingo Perón, a widower twice her age. Perón quickly advanced from undersecretary of war to secretary of labor, minister of war, and vice-president. He made Eva head of the officially recognized union of radio workers,

gave her an office near his, and appointed her friends to government posts.

Perón's growing support from labor, and Eva's influence, disturbed his military colleagues. In October 1945, he was arrested and imprisoned. At one point, an angry mob dragged Eva from a car and beat her. On October 17, however, in a "spontaneous" demonstration that Eva (as she later claimed) had actually helped organize, thousands of workers marched on the government house and successfully demanded Perón's restoration.

Perón and Eva were married immediately, and the following year he became president of the "new Argentina." Eva, by now a political force in her own right, worked tirelessly, putting in 18-hour days and receiving as many as 26 delegations daily. She toured Europe, met with heads of state, and signed treaties—though her trip was marred in Rome, where she was the object of a bomb threat, and in Switzerland, where demonstrators opposed to Perón's fascist regime threw tomatoes at her.

By 1948, she owned three newspapers in Buenos Aires and had a daily bylined column. She persuaded her husband to push through a women's suffrage law, and she herself organized a women's branch of the Peronist party. She also established the multimillion-dollar Eva Perón Foundation, funded by mandatory contributions from workers and by donations that her opponents claimed were extorted. The foundation built hospitals, clinics, and schools, distributed toys, dispatched emergency aid, and bought arms for a workers' militia. As Eva Perón became an international figure, she combed her hair back and put away her flamboyant clothes; she wore sober suits or sweaters and slacks, saving her resplendent gowns and jewels for formal occasions.

Juan Perón always insisted he had made Eva what she was, but many observers thought otherwise: "She lacked formal training, but not political intuition; she was impetuous, domineering, and spectacular. . . . She accepted ideas [from Perón], but she added passion and courage. . . . She was a fiery little thing—indomitable, aggressive, spontaneous, at times barely feminine" (Barager, 1968, pp. 230–231). Humorless and unforgiving, she often demanded the resignations of those who crossed her.

Eva made a bid for the vice presidency in 1951 but retreated under pressure from military leaders. When she developed cancer, she kept up her frantic pace; during her husband's second inaugural parade in June 1952, she stood at his side in an open car, supported by a contraption of wire and plaster. When she died the following month at age 33, the line of mourners stretched for 35 blocks. For a time, she was worshipped as a saint, and the dates of her birth and death became national observances. Three years later, however, when Perón was overthrown, mobs tore down her statues and burned items bearing her name.

EVA PERÓN WAS AN ENIGMA. Who, really, was she? In a few years, she transformed herself from an illegitimate, outcast waif to one of the most powerful women of all time. But even the basic facts of her life are open to question, for she destroyed whatever records she could and intimidated interviewers into silence or flattery; and even less clear are the motives and attitudes that shaped her behavior. Was she a "Lady Bountiful dedicating her life to humble folk" (Flores, 1952, p. 14)? A loyal, devoted wife? A vicious, conniving shrew? The real power behind her husband's "throne"? Or—as some claim—a naive girl whose husband used the common people's devotion to her to bind them closer to him?

To what extent was she a product of family background and societal conditions? Her early experiences may well have fueled her hatred for the establishment, her will to be heard, her fight for women's rights, her disregard for normal channels of authority, her need for control, and her hunger for her people's love—themes that run consistently through her short life. But did success change her, or did her character remain essentially the same throughout her meteoric rise? Of course, she did not live long enough to experience midlife and the challenges of aging. She did not witness the fall of Perón in 1955, his brief return to power in 1972, or his death in 1974. How might Eva Perón—and history—have been affected had she lived through those times? What if she, rather than Perón's third wife, Isabel, had succeeded him as president?

Not many personalities are as paradoxical as Eva Perón's, but her story raises fundamental questions we can ask about every adult. Is an adult's personality a product more of inborn tendencies or of experience? How, and how much, does personality change during adult life? How much is it influenced by culture? By gender? In this chapter, we discuss important issues in the study of adult personality and describe several lines of theory and research that attempt to explain it.

DEFINING AND STUDYING PERSONALITY

How often have you heard comments such as "She has a lot of personality," or, "He has as much personality as a wet dishrag"? In everyday conversation, *personality* often seems to refer to something that a person has more or less of. In reality, personalities differ not so much in quantity as in quality. When we speak of your personality, we are talking about your basic nature—what kind of person you are: brave or fearful, stingy or generous, cheerful or gloomy. But even this may not be quite accurate. You may be brave at one time and fearful at another, or perhaps both fearful and brave at once.

Personality, like intelligence, is complex—hard to define and measure. Indeed, according to some psychologists the influences on personality are so haphazard and so idiosyncratic that we cannot make any general statements at all about it. What is personality? How does somebody get one? How can something so intangible be measured? Let's begin with the problem of definition.

CRITICAL THINKING

What characteristics in others lead you to make categorizations of their personality?

What Is Personality?

There are almost as many definitions of *personality* as there are investigators in the field. But one concept seems to underlie virtually all of them: that personality is the essence of a *person*—a unique, recognizable individual.

Personality is hard to define because we can't see, hear, or touch it; we have to infer it from behavior. Behaviorists, such as B. F. Skinner, see no point in making such inferences; they simply define personality as observable behavior. However, most psychologists think of personality as including not just overt behavior, but also some sort of inner structure of mind and emotions that lies behind what people say and do (Hjelle & Ziegler, 1992). Although this structure is constantly developing, it is generally assumed to be responsible for attitudes and behavior patterns that are fairly consistent. Suppose a friend suddenly begins to act "different." One day he or she is shy, the next day gregarious; one moment passive, the next moment aggressive. You'd probably find such shifts strange and unsettling. You might say your friend "isn't himself" or "isn't herself."

CRITICAL THINKING

What assessment approaches should be followed to draw valid conclusions about personality?

Adaptation—adjustment to the events, circumstances, and conditions of life—is an important function of personality. People may adapt by changing something about themselves, their surroundings, or both. But the ways in which a person adapts show continuity. One prominent researcher has suggested that people develop "generalizations" which they apply consistently to different situations (Block, 1993). For example, one student who fails a test may complain that it was unfair; another may blame himself or herself for not studying harder. If these two students were involved in an automobile accident, each would be likely to react in the same characteristic way. To sum up, then, **personality** is a set of "distinctive patterns of behavior, . . . thoughts and emotions . . . that characterize each individual's adaptation to the situations of his or her life" (Mischel, 1986, p. 4)—that is, a person's unique and relatively consistent way of feeling, thinking, and behaving.

Does Personality Predict Health and Longevity?

In the Terman study of gifted children, childhood personality characteristics and family environment played an important part in adult success. Now it appears that such factors may influence how long people live.

Most of the approximately 1,500 California schoolchildren chosen for the study at about age 11 on the basis of high IQ have been followed periodically since 1921. Between 1986 and 1991, when the survivors were approaching age 80, a group of researchers (Friedman et al., 1993; Friedman, Tucker, Schwartz, Martin et al., 1995; Friedman, Tucker, Schwartz, Tomlinson-Keasey et al., 1995; Tucker & Friedman, 1996)* decided to find out how many had died and at what ages, so as to spot predictors of longevity. Because the "Termites" as a group were bright and well educated, the results were not likely to be confounded by poor nutrition, poverty, or inadequate medical care. Although these highly intelligent people, on the whole, have lived longer than average, their individual

*Unless otherwise referenced, the aforementioned studies are the sources for this box.

longevity was affected by such factors as health-related behaviors, psychological adjustment, personality, and social relationships, which influence mortality risk of people in general (Friedman & Markey, 2003).

Surprisingly, neither childhood self-confidence, energy, nor sociability turned out to be related to longevity. Nor was optimism in childhood associated with long life. In fact, the reverse was true: Cheerful children were more likely to die young. What *did* strongly predict longevity was the personality dimension called *conscientiousness*, or dependability—sometimes described as orderliness, prudence, or self-control.

This research suggests that cheerful children may grow up to be more careless about their health than conscientious children. Although a carefree, optimistic approach to life may be helpful in coping with short-term situations, such as recovery from illness, in the long run it may be unhealthy if it leads a person to ignore warnings and engage in risky behaviors (Martin et al., 2002). On the other hand, an analysis of many studies found that conscientious people tend to engage in behaviors beneficial to health. They are unlikely to smoke, to drink ex-

Measuring Personality

Longstanding research confirms the essential continuity of personality. For the most part, bubbly junior high schoolers grow up to be cheerful 40-year-olds, complaining adolescents turn into querulous adults, assertive 20-year-olds become outspoken 30-year-olds, and people who cope well with problems of youth are equally able to handle problems of later life (Block, 1981; Costa & McCrae, 1980; Eichorn, Clausen, Haan, Honzik, & Mussen, 1981; Haan & Day, 1974; Livson, 1976; Noberini & Neugarten, 1975; Vaillant, 2002). Attitudes shown in young adulthood even seem to affect physical health in middle age (see Box 11.1). However, some aspects of personality do soften with maturity. Although impul-

cessively, to use drugs, to adopt sedentary lifestyles, and to choose unhealthful diets. They are also unlikely to engage in violence, risky sexual behavior, risky driving, and suicide (Bogg & Roberts, 2004).

Similarly, in a longitudinal study of 883 aging members of Catholic clergy, highly conscientious people had half the risk of death during a 5-year period as people low in conscientiousness. People high in neuroticism, by contrast, had nearly double the risk compared with those low in neuroticism (Wilson, Mendes de Leon, Bienias, Evans, & Bennett, 2004).

In the Terman study, conscientiousness was related to a variety of variables that have positive influences on longevity. By midlife, conscientious children tended to have finished more years of education than less conscientious children and were less likely to have shown mental problems. They also were less likely to have been divorced or to have experienced parental divorce in their childhood.

Apparently it is not marriage itself but marital *stability* that can lead to long life. Termites who, at age 40, were in their first marriages tended to live significantly longer than those who had been divorced, whether or not the latter had remarried. By contrast, Termites who had *never* married had only slightly increased risk of early death.

Marital instability in the childhood home also was a threat to longevity. People who, before the age of 21, had experienced the divorce of their parents—13 percent of the sample—lived, on average, four years less than those whose parents had stayed together. Early death of a parent, on the other hand, made little difference.

The findings about marital stability and personality are interrelated. Children rated as impulsive were more likely to grow into adults with unstable marital histories and were more likely to die young. Also, children of divorce were more likely to go through divorce themselves—explaining part of the influence of parental divorce on longevity.

It seems, then, that people who are dependable, trustworthy, and diligent both in taking good care of themselves and in preserving their marriages—and who are fortunate enough to have had parents who stayed married—may be rewarded with more years of life.

sive children usually grow up to be restless impatient adults, as adults they are less impulsive than they were earlier (Stewart & Olds, 1973).

How do researchers make such determinations, and how valid are they? To study personality scientifically, psychologists need some way to measure it. One common method is a **personality inventory**—a psychometric test that asks people to rate themselves or others on traits such as thoroughness, confidence, and irritability; to report on activities they do or don't enjoy; or to give opinions on a variety of topics. By comparing ratings taken from adults of different ages—either the same people or different people—researchers attempt to gauge how much personality changes over time.

Another basic technique is the **Q-sort**. A person is given a deck of cards. On each card is a statement or an adjective referring to a personality characteristic. A card may say "I am often lonely" or "I solve problems easily," or simply "energetic," "anxious," or "friendly." The person is asked to sort the cards into categories, depending on how closely they describe him or her. A variation, which can be used to measure results of therapy, is to have a person do Q-sorts for both the **real self** (who he or she actually is) and the **ideal self** (who he or she would like to be), and then to compare the results on successive occasions.

A number of other techniques have been devised. For example, Ravenna Helson and her associates, whose longitudinal studies of Mills College alumnae we discuss later in this chapter, have asked women to graph their involvement in the roles of mother, partner, and worker at various times in their lives.

Each of these methods can be affected by observer bias (see Chapter 2) or subjectivity. Other methods, such as interviews and self-reports, are not only subjective but often open-ended, and thus somewhat harder to reliably quantify and compare. Indeed, it has been argued that any data based on fallible human judgment and intuition cannot be accurate or reliable (Ross, 1977; Ross & Nisbett, 1991).

Still, considerable research has demonstrated that human judgment, while imperfect, can provide information as useful as other kinds of data psychologists collect. Numerous studies show strong correlations between different people's judgments of someone's personality (Kenrick & Funder, 1988). Judgments of personality also stand up well against observations, predictions, and experimental findings about behavior. Today, most psychologists acknowledge not only that personality is coherent enough to merit study, but that human judgments can describe it reasonably well (Block, 1993; Funder, 1993).

Origins of Personality: Inheritance and Experience

Despite its essential continuity, personality is not fixed at birth: it is an "evolving process subject to a variety of internal and external influences" (Hjelle & Ziegler, 1992). Changes in environment and maturation in personal development affect how one's character is expressed over time while the underlying traits remain stable (Vaillant, 2002).

From infancy on, some people seem to be constitutionally able to adapt more easily than others. **Temperament**, or disposition—an important shaper of personality—is a person's characteristic, biologically based emotional style of approaching and reacting to people and situations. Whether a person is, for example, flexible and easygoing, resistant to new experiences, or slow to warm up appears to be largely determined by heredity (Braungart, Plomin, DeFries, & Fulker, 1992; Emde et al., 1992; McCrae et al., 2000; Thomas & Chess, 1984). Researchers have found evidence for varying degrees of genetic influence on a wide range of personality characteristics (McGue, Bacon, & Lykken, 1993), from shyness (Daniels & Plomin, 1985; Kagan, 1989) to leadership (Tellegren et al., 1988).

But genes do not tell the whole story. One group of investigators (Eaves, Eysenck, & Martin, 1989) reviewed a large amount of research involving identical twins (who have exactly the same heredity), fraternal twins (who, like any other siblings, share many, but not all, hereditary traits), and other family members in Great Britain, Australia, Sweden, and the United States at various periods of life. Environmental influences accounted for fully half the measured variations in personality. Such influential experiences are unique even for people who grow up in the same household at the same time. This may help explain why Eva Perón, and not one of her sisters, became the first lady of Argentina.

The uniqueness of early experience may reflect temperamental differences. Children's behavior may evoke responses, such as a parent's smiling back at a smiling baby, which reinforce the inborn disposition that produced the behavior (Caspi, 1993; Lytton, 1990). In one study, the temperament of three- to six-year-old children affected the way their parents interacted with them three years later, and temperament and parenting style together helped to explain differences among the same children in optimism or pessimism 21 years later (Heinonen, Raikkonen, & Keltikangas-Jarvinen, 2005). In antoher study, children's temperament and their parents' parenting style each affected the other over the course of a year (Lengua & Kovacs, 2005). As children grow up, they often seek out environments that strengthen their genetic tendencies, for example, by selecting friends and eventually mates who are like themselves (Caspi, 1993). Some genetically influenced differences between fraternal twins seem to increase during adulthood, perhaps because of such new, reinforcing experiences (Eaves et al., 1989). Thus an interaction of inheritance and experience affects personality at all ages (Bates & Wachs, 1994).

Sorting out the sources of personality and their complex interrelationships is a formidable task. Much research remains to be done before we can fully understand how personality develops. Further study of how heredity and environment interact throughout life could make an important contribution.

MODELS OF ADULT PERSONALITY: STABILITY OR CHANGE

The two quotations at the beginning of this chapter represent the extremes of a debate over stability versus change in adult personality. Is personality "set like plaster" in early adulthood, or can adults keep "giving birth" to themselves? Different investigators—representing conflicting metatheoretical perspectives and often using different definitions, assumptions, and measuring tools—have come up with differing answers.

- *Trait models* focus on mental, emotional, temperamental, and behavioral traits, or attributes. Trait models are somewhat mechanistic: they attempt to reduce personality and behavior to basic elements, and they assume that traits fairly predictably influence behavior. Studies based on these models find that adult personality changes very little.

- *Self-concept models* are concerned with how people view themselves. These models describe people as actively regulating their own personality development by means of processes similar to those in organismic theories such as that of Piaget. Such models incorporate both stability and change.
- *Stage models*, which are more clearly organismic, portray a typical sequence of age-related development that continues throughout the life span. Studies framed in this way find significant, predictable changes in adult personality.
- The *timing-of-events model* is contextual. Researchers who take this approach find that change is related not so much to age as to the varied circumstances and events of life.

CRITICAL THINKING

How do the theories of development presented in Chapter 1 fit with models of personality discussed here?

Not surprisingly, researchers representing these differing perspectives often come out with results that are difficult to reconcile or even to compare. One leading team of trait researchers (Costa & McCrae, 1994a, 1994b) has attempted to make sense of this diversity by mapping six interrelated elements that "make up the raw material of most personality theories" (1994a, 1994b, p. 23). These elements are (1) *basic tendencies*, (2) *external influences*, (3) *characteristic adaptations*, (4) *self-concept*, (5) *objective biography*, and (6) *dynamic processes*.

Basic tendencies include not only personality traits, but also physical health, appearance, gender, sexual orientation, intelligence, and artistic abilities. These tendencies, which may be either inherited or acquired, interact with external (environmental) influences to produce certain characteristic adaptations: social roles, attitudes, interests, skills, activities, habits, and beliefs. For example, it takes a combination of musical inclination (a basic tendency) and exposure to an instrument (an external influence) to produce musical skill (a characteristic adaptation). Basic tendencies and characteristic adaptations, in turn, help shape the **self-concept**, or sense of self, which bears only a partial resemblance to the objective biography, the actual events of a person's life. Thus a woman may think of herself as having more musical ability than she has objectively demonstrated, and her behavior may be influenced by that self-image. *Dynamic processes* link the other five elements; one such process is learning, which enables people to adapt to external influences (for example, to become accomplished in playing a musical instrument).

Various theorists emphasize one or another of these elements. Trait models focus on basic tendencies, which are the least likely to change. Self-concept models deal with the sense of self. Stage models and the timing-of-events model highlight universal or particular aspects of the objective biography. Let's look more closely at each of these approaches.

Trait Models

Are you cheerful? Are you generally persistent? Are you easily irritated? Cheerfulness, persistence, and irritability are three examples of personality traits. Some researchers have grouped related traits into categories called

personality dimensions. They seek to identify constellations of attributes that define an individual and to determine how much or how little these dimensions change. According to one influential trait model, the answer is: not much after age 30.

COSTA AND MCCRAE: THE FIVE-FACTOR MODEL

A trait model that has substantially influenced the study of personality across the adult life span is that of Paul T. Costa and Robert R. McCrae (1994a; 1994b), gerontology researchers with the National Institute on Aging. Their **five-factor model** (as the term implies) has five dimensions, or domains: (1) *neuroticism*, (2) *extraversion*, (3) *openness to experience*, (4) *conscientiousness*, and (5) *agreeableness*. Each comprises several associated traits (see Figure 11.1).

Neuroticism is a cluster of six negative traits: anxiety, hostility, depression, self-consciousness, impulsiveness, and vulnerability. Highly neurotic people are nervous, fearful, irritable, easily angered, and sensitive to criticism. They may feel sad, hopeless, lonely, guilty, and worthless. We can speculate that Eva Perón would have had high scores on some facets of this dimension.

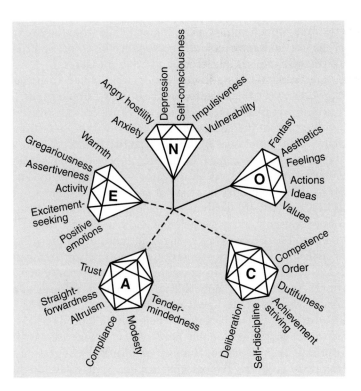

FIGURE 11.1 *Costa and McCrae's five-factor model.* Each factor, or domain of personality, represents a cluster of related traits or facets. N = neuroticism, E = extraversion, O = openness to experience, A = agreeableness, C = conscientiousness. *SOURCE:* Adapted from Costa & McCrae, 1980.

Extraversion also has six facets: warmth, gregariousness, assertiveness, activity, excitement-seeking, and positive emotions. Extraverts are sociable, take-charge types who have close, compassionate relationships and like attention. They keep busy and active; they are constantly looking for excitement, and they enjoy life. Extraversion, too, seems to describe Eva Perón's personality.

People who are *open to experience* are willing to try new things and embrace new ideas. They have a vivid imagination and strong feelings. They appreciate beauty and the arts and question traditional values. Eva Perón would probably have scored high on this dimension.

Conscientious people are achievers: They are competent, orderly, dutiful, deliberate, and disciplined. Most of these characteristics could be identified with Eva Perón.

Agreeable people are trusting, straightforward, altruistic, compliant, modest, and easily swayed. Eva Perón would have had a low score on this dimension.

By analyzing a combination of cross-sectional, longitudinal, and sequential data from several large samples, including their own Baltimore Longitudinal Study of Aging, Costa and McCrae (1980, 1988, 1994a, 1994b; Costa et al., 1986; McCrae & Costa, 1984; McCrae, Costa, & Busch, 1986; McCrae et al., 2000) have found a remarkable degree of stability in all five dimensions. Their samples consisted of men and women ranging in age from the twenties to the nineties. Their methodology included personality inventories, structured interviews, ratings by spouses and peers, and other measures.

Because the Baltimore Longitudinal Study was limited to predominantly white, college-educated volunteers, it could be open to sampling bias. Costa and McCrae therefore compared their findings on neuroticism, extraversion, and openness with ratings of the same traits in a nationwide cross-sectional sample of more than 10,000 people age 32 to 88. The differences were quite small and confirmed the stability, on average, of all three dimensions. This was true even for the midlife period, which some investigators—as well as many writers in the popular press—have described as a time of psychological upheaval. However, Costa and McCrae (1994b) did find age-related differences in cross-sectional comparisons of college students with young and middle-aged adults.

Based on studies that cross age, race, and cultural differences, McCrae, Costa and colleagues suggest that on average, neuroticism, extraversion, and openness to experience decline from eighteen to thirty years of age, declining more slowly thereafter, while agreeableness and conscientiousness appear to increase slowly with age (McCrae, Costa, Martin et al., 2004; McCrae and Costa, 1997; McCrae, Costa, Ostendorf et al., 2000). Indeed these researchers have found consistency in personality development across five vastly different cultures (British, Czech, German, Spanish, and Turkish), suggesting that personality traits may be largely biological in origin and may develop through intrinsic maturation, independent of environmental influences (McCrae et al., 2000; see Figure 11.2). Results for each culture remained consistent across cohorts. The rate of change appears to slow similarly after about age thirty across cultures (McCrae et al., 2004; McCrae et al., 2000). Changes in these di-

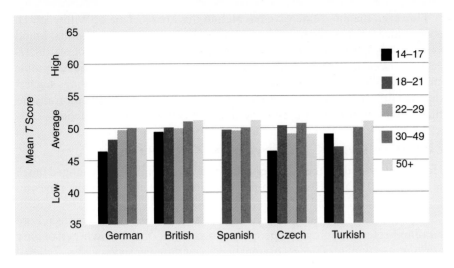

FIGURE 11.2 *Mean levels of agreeableness at various ages in five cultures.* *SOURCE:* McCrae et al., 2000.

mensions over time are small and people tend to maintain their general pattern of characteristics. This research suggests that although culture may affect the ways that personality is expressed, patterns of traits remain similar across cultures (Hofstede & McCrae, 2004).

Some psychologists—for example, Helson (1993)—have criticized trait research in general, and Costa and McCrae's work in particular, as too limited, because it does not appear to account for aspects of personality that have been found by other research to change. Costa and McCrae (1994a) argue that even what may seem to be drastic changes actually reflect stable tendencies. For example, people who make dramatic career changes in midlife are likely to have a basic tendency to be open to experience. Another view is that while the Big Five personality traits may represent the major dimensions of personality, they do not necessarily account for all variations in personality (O'Connor, 2002).

PERSONALITY DIMENSIONS IN LATE LIFE

Research on personality development in late life has had mixed results. In a longitudinal study of 74 Californians between ages 69 and 93, which used a trait model somewhat different from Costa and McCrae's, some dimensions of personality did show change. Over 14-year periods, *agreeableness* increased, especially in the oldest old, while *extraversion* (including talkativeness, frankness, and excitability) and *activity, energy, and health* decreased. The most stable dimension was *satisfaction*, including self-esteem, cheerfulness, satisfaction with oneself and one's circumstances, and little tendency to worry or be restless. Another highly stable dimension was *intellect*, comprising cognitive functioning and openmindedness (Field & Millsap, 1991).

CRITICAL THINKING

What changes in personality can you identify in older family members? What change might you expect in yourself?

However, the most extensive research in this area (Schaie & Willis, 1991), a sophisticated cross-sequential study of more than 3,000 older adults, found very little longitudinal change over 7 years. Instead, it found cohort differences. As a group, older people today seem to be more flexible and adaptable and less socially responsible than previous generations. These findings suggest that age differences found in cross-sectional studies may reflect culturally influenced differences among cohorts more than change within individuals.

LAYPEOPLE'S VIEWS ABOUT PERSONALITY CHANGE

How would you describe your personality? Do you think it has changed much in the past 10 years? How much do you think it will change by the time you are, say, 10 years older?

CRITICAL THINKING

In assessing your own personality, has your viewpoint changed after reading about the models proposed by various theorists?

Much of the trait research we have described is based on self-ratings. Longitudinal research compares people's assessments of their own personality attributes—say, agreeableness or impatience—at different times. Cross-sectional research, which is more common, compares self-assessments of people of different ages at the same time. From these comparisons, researchers make inferences about stability or change.

However, trait researchers rarely ask people how stable or changeable they *believe* personality to be. Several studies have asked people to rate their beliefs about their personalities in the past, present, and future (Fleeson & Heckhausen, 1997; see Lachman & Bertrand, 2001 for review). Researchers were then able to compare what adults think they were like in the past (retrospected) to what they think they are like now (present)—participants were in middle adulthood ranging from 26 to 64—and how they expect themselves to be in the future (anticipated) (see Figure 11.3). These studies found that people perceive themselves as changing over time, and that they see that change as both positive and negative. For example, middle-aged persons see themselves as being the most confident, best able to handle stress, and most self-reliant they ever will be (Lachman & Bertrand, 2001). They perceive their well-being as better now than in the past and expect to continue to improve in relationships and self-acceptance. However, purpose in life, personal growth, and environmental mastery are areas of expected decline (Fleeson & Heckhausen, 1997). Another study of personality change over a 6- to 9-year period suggests that people may be biased in a self-serving manner in their beliefs about their personality change, and are more likely to report that they have increased in desirable traits (agreeableness) than in undesirable traits (neuroticism) (Herbst, McCrae, Costa, Feaganes, & Siegler, 2000). On the other hand, prior longitudinal research found in comparing actual personality scores taken twenty years earlier to what people remembered about themselves at that time, that people reported more change in their personalities than the test score comparisons actually showed (Birren & Woodruff, 1972 in Lachman & Bertrand, 2001).

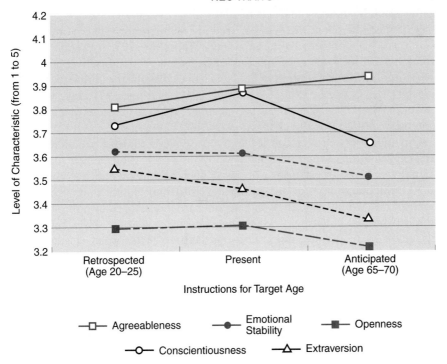

FIGURE 11.3 Self-perception of one's own personality traits at three target ages anticipated late adulthood personality contained more losses than gains. *SOURCE:* Fleeson & Heckhausen, 1997.

Self-Concept Models

"Who in the world am I? Ah, *that's* the great puzzle," said Alice in Wonderland, after her size had abruptly changed—again. Solving Alice's "puzzle" is a lifelong process of getting to know our developing selves.

According to self-concept models, our view of ourselves is the core of personality. Although the sense of self might seem the most personal thing imaginable, many psychologists see it as a *social* phenomenon, which grows out of interaction with others. People peer into a mirror created by their social world and blend the image they see reflected there with the picture they already have of themselves.

Self-concept theorists are concerned with the cognitive side of personality: what people think about who they are. The self-concept, they say, is made up of **schemas**—working models, or constructs, of reality around which behavior is organized. (For instance, a person's self-concept may include a schema for musicianship.) The self-concept includes knowledge of what a person has been and done, and it guides that person in deciding what to be and do in the future (Markus & Cross, 1990; Markus & Nurius, 1986). Thus it includes both self-understanding and self-regulation.

Schemas, like scientific theories, are only tentative; people continually revise them to conform with experience (Bowlby, 1973; Epstein, 1990; Tomkins, 1986). But interpretations of experience are subjective; a schema may filter out information that challenges one's beliefs about oneself (Caspi, 1993; Darley & Fazio, 1980; Greenwald, 1980; Markus, 1977; Snyder, 1987; Swann, 1983, 1987). Thus the self-concept is caught in constant dynamic tension between stability and change.

One model of self-concept development suggests that people make a subjective evaluation of their personal development in relation to their social surroundings. These evaluations are based on what they could become, what they would like to become, and what they are afraid of becoming. Feelings of hope and fear about who they may become are internalized into the structure of self (Markus & Nurius, 1986). This concept of possible selves helps people adapt to new roles and transitions across the life span (Lachman & Bertrand, 2001).

Another current self-concept model is that of Susan Krauss Whitbourne (1987; Whitbourne & Connolly, 1999; Whitbourne & Primus, 1996). It focuses on the development of **identity styles:** characteristic ways of confronting, interpreting, and responding to experience. According to Whitbourne, identity is made up of accumulated images of the self, both conscious and unconscious. Perceived personality traits, such as sensitivity and stubbornness, form part of that identity. These self-images normally remain stable unless contradicted by changes in life circumstances or roles. Even then, such changes do not shatter the personality's fundamental continuity but are incorporated into a modified, restabilized image of the self.

In Whitbourne's model, self-perceptions are confirmed or revised through two continuing processes of interaction with the social environment (similar to those Piaget described for children's cognitive development): *identity assimilation* and *identity accommodation*. **Identity assimilation** is an attempt to fit new experience into an existing self-concept. Most people will go to great lengths to confirm a favorable view of the self. A woman who thinks of herself as a proud and loving mother will see her interactions with her children in a positive light. If her relationship with one of the children begins to sour, she is likely to dismiss the problem as a temporary "phase" or to find a specific reason for an upsetting encounter. However, if something happens that she cannot satisfactorily explain to herself (for example, if her child is constantly stealing from her), she will be forced to adjust her self-image and her view of the relationship. This **identity accommodation**, though painful, is necessary for effective adaptation.

Overuse of either assimilation or accommodation is unhealthy. People who constantly assimilate are blind to reality; they see only what they are looking for. People who constantly accommodate are weak and easily swayed. A balance between the two processes is vital. Where a person generally strikes that balance determines his or her identity style.

Whitbourne's model, then, incorporates into an essentially stable concept of personality a mechanism for dealing flexibly with new experience in a way unique to the individual. However, this model does not as yet have a strong research base.

Stage Models

Stage models attempt to describe **normative personality change:** age-related patterns of personality development common to most members of a population. These changes emerge in successive periods, often marked by emotional "crises." Stage models do not suggest that everyone's life follows exactly the same course; but they do portray a common core of "life tasks" that occur in a certain sequence at approximately the same ages (Levinson, 1980, 1986). If these tasks are not accomplished, development in the next stage may be weakened.

A classic normative-crisis model is that of Erik Erikson, who broke with Freud in part because of his conviction that personality is not frozen at puberty—that people grow and change throughout adult life. Let's look at Erikson's stage model and at two others that were influenced by it: those of George Vaillant and Daniel Levinson. All three models are summarized in Table 11.1, along with another model (Helson's) that we discuss later in this chapter.

CRITICAL THINKING
How are stage models of personality similar to and different from trait models of personality?

ERIKSON: BALANCING POSITIVE AND NEGATIVE TENDENCIES

For Erikson (1950, 1985; Erikson, Erikson, & Kivnick, 1986), personality develops through a balancing of positive and negative tendencies at eight critical stages across the life span (see Table 2.2 in Chapter 2). Successful resolution of a crisis results in the emergence of a particular "virtue."

The sixth crisis, *intimacy versus isolation*, is the major issue of young adulthood. Young adults who have developed a strong sense of self are ready to fuse their identity with that of another person. Not until a person is ready for intimacy can "true genitality" occur—mutual orgasm in a loving, male-female relationship. Young adults who cannot, or are afraid to, make deep commitments to others may become isolated and self-absorbed. However, adults do need a certain amount of isolation to think about their lives. Resolution of the conflicting demands of intimacy and isolation results in the "virtue" of love: devotion between partners who have chosen to share their lives, to have children, and to help those children achieve their own healthy development. Critics object that people may acquire the virtue of love in a wide variety of lifestyles other than heterosexual marriage that produces children.

Erikson's seventh crisis, *generativity versus stagnation*, occurs in middle age. Although Erikson did not invent the term *midlife crisis* (see Box 11.2 on page 410), he did see the years around age 40 as a critical time, when adults develop **generativity:** a concern for establishing and guiding the next generation. Looking ahead to the waning of their own lives, mature adults need to participate in life's continuation. The generative impulse is not necessarily limited to a person's own children and grandchildren; although Erikson (1985) believed that people who have not been parents cannot easily fulfill it, his view

TABLE 11.1

Four Stage Models of Adult Personality Development

Approximate Age	Erikson	Vaillant	Levinson	Helson
Twenties	Crisis 6: Intimacy versus isolation	Intimacy	Novice phase of early adulthood (entry life structure)	Bad self, bad partner
Thirties		Career Consolidation	Age 30 transition	Struggle for independent identity
			Culminating phase of early adulthood (culminating life structure)	
Forties	Crisis 7: Generativity versus stagnation	Generativity	Midlife transition	Unpleasant consequences of independence
			Entry life structure for middle adulthood	Troubling relationships; overload
Fifties		Keeper of the meaning	Age 50 transition Culminating life structure for middle adulthood	Prime of life
Sixties	Crisis 8: Integrity versus despair	Integrity	Late adult transition	

is considered narrow by many psychologists today. Erikson did say that generativity can be expressed through teaching or mentorship, through productivity or creativity, and through "self-generation," or self-development. The "virtue" of this period is care: "a widening commitment to *take care of* the persons, the products, and the ideas one has learned *to care for*" (1985, p. 67). People who do not find a satisfying outlet for generativity become self-absorbed, self-indulgent, and stagnant. As in all of Erikson's stages, it is the balance that is important; even the most generative person goes through fallow periods.

In Erikson's final crisis, *integrity versus despair*, older adults need to accept the way they have lived in order to accept their approaching death. They struggle to achieve a sense of integrity, a sense of the coherence and wholeness of their lives, rather than give way to despair over the impossibility of going back and doing things differently (Erikson et al., 1986). People who succeed in this final task gain a sense of order and meaning in life. The "virtue" that develops during this stage is wisdom (see Chapter 7). People who do not achieve wisdom—acceptance—are overwhelmed by despair when they realize that time is too short to follow other paths. Some despair is inevitable, Erikson maintained; people need to mourn, not only for their own misfortunes and lost chances but for the vulnerability and transience of the human condition. Yet he also believed that late life is a time to play, to recapture a childlike quality. Although the time for procreation is over, creation can take place. Even as physical functions weaken, people can enjoy enriched experiences of body and mind.

© PhotoDisc

Erickson's sixth "crisis," intimacy versus isolation (the major issue of young adulthood) is successfully resolved by a commitment to share one's life with a beloved. According to Erikson, young adults who do not make such a commitment may become isolated and self-absorbed.

VAILLANT: RELATIONSHIPS AND LIFE ADJUSTMENT

An important longitudinal study that supported a progression of normative stages was the Grant Study of Harvard University graduates. The 268 men selected for the study, which began in 1938 when they were still in college, were self-reliant and emotionally and physically healthy. Retesting them in middle age, Vaillant (1977; Vaillant & Vaillant, 1990) concluded that people's lives are shaped by important sustained relationships. Of the men who at age 47 were considered best adjusted, 93 percent had established stable marriages before age 30 and were still married at 50.

With some variations, Vaillant (1977) saw a typical pattern. At age 20, many of the men were still dominated by their parents—a finding that has appeared again in later research (Frank, Avery, & Laman, 1988). During their twenties, and sometimes their thirties, they established themselves: achieved autonomy, married, had children, and deepened friendships. Somewhere between the twenties and the forties, these men entered a stage of *career consolidation*. They worked hard at strengthening their careers and devoted themselves to their families (Vaillant, 1977, p. 217).

The stage of career consolidation ends, according to Vaillant, when "at age 40—give or take as much as a decade—men leave the compulsive, unreflective

Navigating the Midlife Crossing

Changes in personality and lifestyle during the early to middle forties are often attributed to a **midlife crisis,** a stressful period triggered by review and reevaluation of one's life, which may herald the onset of middle age. The term was coined by the psychoanalyst Elliott Jacques (1967) and burst into public consciousness in the 1970s, with the popularization of the normative stage theories of Erik Erikson and Daniel Levinson. It has become a trendy catchphrase, which may pop up as an explanation for an episode of depression, an extramarital affair, or a career change.

According to Jacques, what brings on the midlife crisis is awareness of mortality. The first part of adulthood is over; its tasks are largely done. Time has become shorter, and many people now realize that they will not be able to fulfill all the dreams of their youth, or they realize that fulfillment of their dreams has not brought them satisfaction.

According to the Swiss psychologist Carl Jung (1966), the need to acknowledge eventual mortality and to give up youthful self-images are two necessary tasks of middle age. These tasks require a gradual shift from an outward orientation, a concern with finding a place in society, to an introspective preoccupation with the inner life (Jung, 1966), which the gerontologist Bernice Neugarten (1977) calls **interiority.** Because the tasks of midlife and the inner dialogue they call for involve threatening ideas, this can be a stressful period. Questioning their goals, people may temporarily lose their sense of direction.

Today the idea of a universal, psychologically necessary midlife crisis is in doubt. Although Ravenna Helson (1992) found evidence of it in her studies of Mills College alumnae, other research has failed to support it (Costa & McCrae, 1980; Costa et al., 1986; Lacy & Hendricks, 1980; Vaillant, 1977). Instead, many psychologists now talk about a *midlife transition,* which, although sometimes stressful, does not necessarily amount to a crisis (Brim, 1977; Chiriboga, 1989; Haan, 1990; Rossi, 1980).

busywork of their occupational apprenticeships, and once more become explorers of the world within" (Vaillant, 1977, p. 220). The midlife transition may be stressful because of new demands, such as changing the parenting role to meet the needs of teenage children. Many men reassess their past, come to terms with long-suppressed feelings about their parents, and reorder their attitudes toward sexuality.

Still, as troubling as these middle years sometimes were for the men in the Grant Study, the transition rarely amounted to a crisis. They were no more likely at midlife than at any other time during the life span to get divorced, to become disenchanted with their jobs, or to become depressed. By their fifties, the best-adjusted men in the group saw the years from 35 to 49 as the happiest in their lives. The best-adjusted men also were the most generative, as measured by their responsibility for other people at work, their gifts to charity,

How a man handles the midlife transition may reflect his place in society (Farrell & Rosenberg, 1981). In one study, only 12 percent of 300 middle-aged men in a socioeconomically diverse sample experienced a full-blown midlife crisis, though about two-thirds had some adjustment problems. Unskilled laborers were much more likely to show stress than professional men or middle-class executives, but the lower-class men were more likely to deny or avoid their problems or to express them through authoritarian attitudes.

Studies of nearly 300 women between ages 35 and 55 with diverse incomes and lifestyles (Barnett, 1985; Baruch, Barnett, & Rivers, 1983) found no evidence of midlife crisis. The two key factors in healthy adjustment, regardless of age, were a sense of mastery over one's life and the amount of pleasure derived from living. Paid work was the single best predictor of mastery; a positive experience with husband and children, including a good sex life, was the best predictor of pleasure; and the single best key to general well-being was a challenging job that paid well and offered opportunities to use skills and make decisions. The women who scored highest overall on both mastery and pleasure were employed married women with children; the lowest scorers were unemployed, childless married women.

For many people, then, entering middle age may be just one more of life's many transitions. Whether a transition turns into a crisis may depend on particular circumstances and how a particular person deals with them: "One person may go from crisis to crisis while another . . . experience[s] relatively few strains" (Schlossberg, 1987, p. 74). And timing of life events may play a part. In a study by Taguiri and Davis (Baruch et al., 1983), men in their thirties who had achieved success quite young were struggling with questions usually thought to be characteristic of midlife: "Was it worth it?" "What next?" and "What shall I do with the rest of my life?"

and their children, whose academic achievements equaled those of the fathers (Vaillant, 1989).

The fifties were a generally mellower and more tranquil time of life than the forties. Vaillant noted tendencies that also have been observed by others: a lessening of sexual differentiation with advancing age and a tendency for men to become more nurturant and expressive.

The researchers again examined the physical and mental health of 173 of the men at age 65 (Vaillant & Vaillant, 1990). The best adjusted 65-year-olds had been rated in college as well organized, steady, stable, and dependable; and they continued to show these traits. But some other characteristics linked with good adjustment in young adulthood, such as spontaneity and making friends easily, no longer influenced adjustment. Similarly, in a longitudinal study of 306 inner-city men, those who at age 47 used mature coping techniques, such as projection (attributing one's own negative thoughts and feelings

© Joel Gordon

According to Erikson, middle-aged adults like this volunteer tutor may express "generativity" (a concern for guiding the next generation) by teaching or being mentors to young people, as well as through relationships with their own children and grandchildren. People who do not find a satisfying outlet for generativity may become self-absorbed, self-indulgent, and stagnant.

to others) and fantasy, were the worst adjusted (Soldz & Vaillant, 1998).

The most recent summary of this work is in Vaillant's (2002) book, *Aging Well*. Here he identifies a series of developmental tasks, which are similar to Erikson's stages of development. The tasks are usually completed sequentially, but completion of one task is not a necessary prerequisite to moving on to the next.

The first task is to establish an identity separate from one's parents; this is usually completed by the end of adolescence. At this stage a person strives to develop a sense of self, which includes values, politics, and passions that are his (or her) own. The second task, *intimacy*, involves "expanding the self to include another person" (Vaillant, 2002, p. 46). This development usually occurs in the twenties. It entails the building of a reciprocal relationship that involves commitment, contentment, and interdependence. The third task, *career consolidation*, occurs in the thirties. It requires the development of a work identity in addition to the personal identity. According to Vaillant, four developmental criteria transform a job into a career: commitment, competence, compensation, and contentment. One needs to have a strong sense of self as a worker with a focus on one's career.

The fourth task, *generativity*, as in Erikson's theory, is unselfishly giving of oneself to the next generation through mentoring, guiding, leading or teaching. Self-development, the objective of the first three tasks should now give way to the "sensitive responsibility for other adults" (p. 48). The final task is divided into two parts: *keeper of meaning* and *integrity*. The keeper of meaning takes on the responsibility for preserving culture, traditions, and institutions. One is now taking care of the past rather than developing the future as they did in generativity. Integrity is the last of the life's tasks. Again, following Erikson, one needs to make sense of one's life and accept what has happened. Wisdom about life is a key aspect of integrity.

LEVINSON: BUILDING AND CHANGING LIFE STRUCTURES

Levinson (1978, 1980, 1986) and his colleagues at Yale University conducted in-depth interviews and personality tests with 40 men age 35 to 45, equally divided among four occupations: industrial workers, business executives, biologists, and novelists. From this study, as well as from biographical sources and from other research, Levinson formed a theory of personality development in adulthood.

In a companion study of 45 women, Levinson & Levinson (1996) found that women go through similar eras, phases and transitions; but because of traditional cultural divisions between masculine and feminine roles, women may face different psychological and environmental constraints in forming their life structures, and their transitions tend to take longer.

At the heart of Levinson's theory is an evolving **life structure**—"the underlying pattern or design of a person's life at a given time" (1986, p. 6), which is built around whatever a person finds most important. Most people build a life structure around work and family. Levinson's stages, which he called *phases* (see Table 11.1), are linked by transitional periods when people reappraise their life structure. Indeed, Levinson said, people spend nearly half their adult lives in transitions, which may involve crises. Each phase has its own tasks, whose accomplishment becomes the foundation for the next life structure.

In the *novice* phase of early adulthood (ages 17–33),* a man† needs to leave his parents' home and become financially and emotionally independent. He forms relationships, usually leading to marriage and parenthood, and chooses an occupation. Two important tasks are forming a dream and finding a mentor. A **dream** usually has to do with a career: a vision of, say, winning a Nobel Prize. A **mentor** is a slightly older man who offers guidance and inspiration and passes on wisdom, moral support, and practical help in both career and personal matters.

In the *culminating phase* (ages 33–45), after the age-30 transition, a man settles down. He sets goals (a professorship, for instance, or a certain level of income) and a time for achieving them (say, by age 40). He anchors his life in family, occupation, and community. At the same time, he chafes under authority; he wants to speak with his own voice. He may discard his mentor and be at odds with his wife, children, lover, boss, friends, or co-workers.

Life structures change appreciably at midlife. The realization that a cherished dream will not come true may bring on an emotional crisis. Four out of 5 of the men in the study often felt upset and acted irrationally between ages 40 and 45. Levinson maintained that such turmoil is inevitable as people question their previously held values. Reevaluation helps people come to terms with their youthful dreams, to emerge with a more realistic self-image, and to substitute more attainable goals.

Between ages 45 and 50, men carve out new life structures, possibly by taking a new job or a new wife. Those who make no changes may lead a constricted life in middle age. Others make a recommitment to what they have been doing (Sterns & Huyck, 2001). They may be busy and well-organized but unexcited. Often those who do change their life structures find middle age the most fulfilling and creative time of life. Although Levinson and his colleagues did not follow their sample into the fifties and sixties, they made projections for those years (see Table 11.1).

EVALUATING STAGE MODELS

The participants in the classic normative studies were, for the most part, fairly small samples of privileged white men born in the 1920s or 1930s. The resulting models cannot readily be generalized to people of other races or socioeconomic levels.

---

*All ages are approximate in Levinson's model.
†Levinson (1986) claimed that his conclusions also applied to women, with some variations, and this claim has been followed up in Levinson & Levinson (1996).

Furthermore, these models have been criticized for taking male development as the norm. In Erikson's model, intimacy follows achievement of a stable identity, which is supposed to take place in late adolescence. But according to Erikson, a woman achieves identity and intimacy at the same time, defining herself by the man she will marry. In one study, which tested the relationship between identity and intimacy (Kahn, Zimmerman, Csikszentmihalyi, & Getzels, 1985), researchers measured the "identity strength" of sophomore and junior art students. Eighteen years later, 60 percent of the sample responded to a questionnaire about their marital status, as an indication of how successfully they had achieved intimacy in young adulthood. The results showed dramatic gender differences. The men who had shown strong identity in their student days were much more likely than other men to be married, but no more or less likely to have stable marriages. With women, it was just the opposite: those who had a strong identity in their youth were no more or less likely to have married; but if they had married, they were far more likely to have stayed married. Findings like these, which suggest differences in the meaning and development of intimacy for men and women, have led some researchers to insist on models that focus specifically on women's development (Gilligan, 1982). Later in this chapter we'll report on one such model.

Another problem with classic normative models is that cohorts with different experiences may develop differently. These studies were done before, and thus do not reflect, the dramatic increase in career changes, dual-earner marriages, and openly heterosexual and homosexual cohabitation. Nor have these theories been tested in other cultures, some of which have very different concepts of life's stages.

In traditional Hinduism—the religion that dominates much of the culture of India—men go through four stages of development (Zimmer, 1956). These resemble the stages of western models in some ways but are quite different in other ways. (Again, studies of personality development in other cultures have often focused on male development.) Unlike normative models in western culture, which attempt to describe actual stages in personality development, the Hindu stages represent a spiritual ideal that few people will ever fully achieve. The stages, which apply to all but the lowest caste, correspond roughly to youth, young adulthood, middle adulthood, and late adulthood. There are no transitional periods and, presumably, no crises; each stage is viewed as preparation for the next.

The first stage is that of the *obedient pupil* receiving knowledge from his spiritual teacher, or guru. This mentor-like relationship is exclusive and all-encompassing. Sexual relations are forbidden and severely punished.

When the student stage is over, the young man is suddenly thrust into married life. His parents having chosen a wife for him, he becomes a *householder*—the second stage—and supports his family by taking over his father's craft, business, or profession.

The third stage, *departure to the forest*, which begins in the latter part of middle age, is another abrupt change. Up to now, the man has dutifully played socially imposed roles. Now he throws off his social "mask," withdraws from family life and material concerns, and lets his sons take over the "joys and burdens of the world" as he retreats from everyday life "to enter upon the path of the quest for the Self" (Zimmer, 1956, p. 157). This period of meditation and self-discovery prepares him for the fourth and final stage.

The fourth stage is that of the *wandering holy beggar*. The man casts off everything that defines and limits him—his clothing, memories, emotions, habits, likes, and dislikes. He thinks neither of the present nor of the future, neither of his mind nor of his body. His goal now is to strip away the personal self, to identify with all existence and enter a state of perfect harmony and bliss.

The Gusii, a polygamous society in western Kenya (Levine, 1980), have a "life plan" with well-defined expectations, which is very different from either the Hindu life path or the classic western normative models. The Gusii have no words meaning "adolescent," "young adult," or "middle-aged." People continue to reproduce as long as they are biologically able. A man is circumcised sometime between ages 9 and 11 and will become an "elder" when his first child marries. Between these two events, he goes through only one recognized stage of life—*omomura*, or "warrior." The *omomura* phase may last anywhere from 25 to 40 years, or even longer. Women have an additional middle stage—*omosubaati*, or "married woman"—because of the greater importance of marriage in a woman's life.

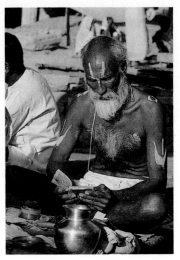

© Paolo Koch/Photo Researchers

The final stage of the Hindu life path is that of a wandering holy beggar, who strips himself of everything that defines his past identity and seeks to enter a state of perfect bliss and harmony with all existence.

In Gusii society, then, transitions depend not on age but on life events. Status is linked to circumcision, marriage (for women), having children, and becoming a parent of a married child and thus a prospective grandparent. The Gusii do have a **social clock**, a set of norms or expectations for when these events should occur. People who marry late or do not marry at all, and people who have their first child late or have no children, are ridiculed and ostracized.

Although the Gusii have no recognized midlife transition, some of them do reassess their lives around the time they are old enough to be grandparents. Awareness of mortality and of waning physical powers can bring on something resembling a midlife crisis, from which a man or woman may emerge as a ritual healer. The quest for spiritual powers has a generative purpose, too: elders are responsible for ritually protecting their children and grandchildren from death or illness.

Stage models have captured both the professional and the public imagination, largely because of their main message: that adults continue to change, develop, and grow. Whether or not people grow in the particular ways suggested by these models, they have challenged the notion that hardly anything important happens to personality after adolescence.

The Timing-of-Events Model

In childhood, internal maturational events signal transitions from one developmental stage to another. A baby says the first word, takes the first step, loses the first tooth. The body changes at the onset of puberty. But although age

© PhotoDisc

In the timing-of-events model, the impact of an event such as parenthood depends on whether it is "on time" or "off time" according to the social clock. According to this model, having a baby in the forties is more likely to cause stress than having children in the twenties. But with more American women delaying parenthood, one study found that age was not a factor in adjustment.

may be fairly indicative of children's development, individual circumstances or life events may be more significant for adults.

The **timing-of-events model**, supported by Bernice Neugarten and others (Neugarten, Moore, & Lowe, 1965; Neugarten & Neugarten, 1987), views major life events as markers of development. According to this model, people develop in response to the times in their lives when key events do or do not occur. Life events are of two types. Events people expect because they happen to most adults are called **normative life events;** examples are parenthood and retirement. Unusual events that cannot be expected are called **nonnormative life events;** examples are a traumatic accident, an unanticipated promotion, or a lottery prize.

Whether or not an event is normative—and therefore expected—often depends on its timing. Events that are normative when they are "on time" (according to the social clock) become nonnormative when they are "off time"—that is, early or late. Marrying at 14 or 41 or retiring at 41 or 91 would be a nonnormative event. People are usually keenly aware of their own timing and describe themselves as "early," "late," or "on time" in marrying, having children, settling on careers, or retiring. Normative events that come "on time" are generally taken in stride; "it is the events that upset the expected sequence and rhythm of the life cycle that cause problems" (Neugarten & Neugarten, 1987, p. 33).

Crises are caused, then, not by reaching a certain age, but by the expected or unexpected occurrence and timing of life events. If events occur as expected, development proceeds smoothly. If not, stress can result. Stress may occur in response to an unexpected event (such as losing a job), an event that happens earlier or later than expected (being widowed at age 35, having a first child at 45, being forced to retire at 55), or the failure of an expected event to occur at all (never being married, or being unable to have a child).

The typical timing of some events, such as marriage, varies from culture to culture (Bianchi & Spain, 1986) and from one generation to the next. One example is the rise in average age at first marriage in the United States from 20 in 1960 to 25 for women and 23 to 27 for men in 2002. Another is the rise in average age of first-time mothers in the United States from 21 in 1970 to 25 in 2000 (CDC, 2002). Since the midtwentieth century, American society has become less age-conscious; the feeling that there is a "right time" to do certain things is less widespread (Neugarten & Hagestad, 1976; Neugarten & Neugarten, 1987). Today people are more accepting of 40-year-old first-time parents and 40-year-old grandparents, 50-year-old retirees and 75-year-old workers, 60-year-olds in blue jeans and 30-year-old college presidents—as well as a president of the United States in his mid forties. Major events that once characterized a certain time of life, such as marriage, the first job, and the birth of children and grandchildren, are now less predictable. According to the timing-of-events model, we should expect this uncertainty to produce stress (Neugarten & Neugarten, 1987).

However, rapid social change tends to undermine the predictability which the timing-of-events model assumes. Today, for example, American couples who delay becoming parents until ages 28 to 37 seem to adjust no better and no worse than younger parents with similar demographic characteristics (Roosa, 1988). Does this finding suggest that the timing-of-events model is wrong about the effects of not being "on time," or does it merely reflect a current "blurring of traditional life periods" (Neugarten & Neugarten, 1987, p. 32)?

The timing-of-events model has made an important contribution to our understanding of adult personality by emphasizing the importance of the individual life course and challenging the idea of universal, age-related change. Yet ultimately its usefulness, like that of the classic stage theories, may well be limited to cultures and historical periods in which norms of behavior are stable and widespread.

GENDER AND PERSONALITY

Do women's personalities develop differently from men's across the adult life span? Theorists and researchers who have explored that topic have come up with almost as many questions as answers.

Gender Stereotypes, Gender Roles, and Gender Identity

Are women the "weaker sex"? Are men "strong and silent"? **Gender stereotypes**—exaggerated generalizations about differences between men and women—pervade many cultures (Williams & Best, 1982). Although not all individuals conform to them, these stereotypes often form a part of a society's **gender roles:** cultural norms or expectations for appropriate male or female behavior, interests, attitudes, abilities, and personality traits.

In most cultures women have been expected to care for the household and children and to make sure that the family functions smoothly, while men are protectors and providers. Such gender roles, transmitted through socialization in early childhood, are incorporated into an individual's **gender identity:** awareness of what it means to be male or female (Huyck, 1990). As part of their socially sanctioned gender roles, men are generally expected to be active, aggressive, autonomous, and achievement-oriented; women are regarded as more nurturing, deferential, dependent, empathic, and concerned with relationships. Both in everyday speech and in psychological measurement, the first group of characteristics traditionally have been called *masculine* and the second group *feminine*.

Differences between men and women have been found in several areas of social interaction (Yoder, 1999). Women tend to be more influenced by others and may be more likely to conform to the behaviors of someone perceived to have more status or power. Men tend to behave more aggressively, whereas women seem more concerned with the consequences of such behavior. In situations in which inhibitions are decreased, such as when drinking alcohol, women act more aggressively than they otherwise would. In some studies, men show more helping behaviors than women, though these studies often measure "rescuing" behaviors, such as stopping to help change a flat tire. In situations less likely to raise concerns of safety or discomfort, this gender difference does not seem to hold. Women tend to engage in more self-disclosure in interpersonal relationships, to show better social skills, and to enjoy more closeness, but this is also affected by perceptions of status in interactions and the gender of those involved. Overall, although research seems to show some gender differences, the reasons for such differences are difficult to determine and may involve a mixture of biology, socialization, and the social context of the interactions being studied. Often these differences are greater within a gender than between genders. Still, although measurable differences between the sexes are generally small, men and women tend to believe they are more different then they actually are (Matlin, 1987).

Another way of looking at gender is to look separately at a person's attitudes, attributes, interests, roles, and behaviors (Spence, 1993). The same person may show different patterns of masculinity/femininity in different aspects of personality (Koestner & Aube, 1995). Thus, a person who has very masculine attitudes and interests may play some roles that are culturally considered feminine, or vice versa. For example, someone may be a football player on the weekends but may be responsible for laundry in the household or may be a stay-at-home parent during the week. A woman may be a cut-throat corporate lawyer during the day but may go home and watch a ball game or work in her flower garden. Each of these individuals may view certain aspects of their attitudes and behaviors as more or less feminine or masculine but may focus on other characteristics when defining their gender identity.

CRITICAL THINKING

What examples from your life experiences demonstrate the influence of gender stereotypes?

Gender identity is an integral part of the sense of self; and, like other aspects of the self-concept, it may represent a filtered view of reality. Men and women who absorb gender stereotypes into their self-concept may deny their natural inclinations and force themselves into ill-fitting academic, vocational, or social molds. Stereotypes can affect the simplest everyday tasks as well as far-reaching life decisions. A man may be "all thumbs" when it comes to preparing a baby's bottle or mending a button; a woman "can't" nail boards together or bait a fishhook (Bem, 1976).

Many psychologists today recognize that "masculinity" and "femininity" are not polar opposites. People of both sexes have a mixture of "masculine" and "feminine" personality characteristics. Some people are **androgynous**— that is, they are high in both "masculine" and "feminine" characteristics. Some people are **undifferentiated**—low in both. Some people are high in one or the other. Sandra Bem (1974, 1976), a leader in the study of gender roles, maintains that the androgynous personality is the healthiest. An androgynous person may be assertive, self-reliant, and dominant, as well as compassionate, sympathetic, and understanding.

Bem's Sex Role Inventory (Bem, 1974) places people in one of four categories—masculine, feminine, androgynous, or undifferentiated—by asking them to rate themselves according to a list of adjectives or phrases. This and similar instruments can be used to study whether men and women become more or less "masculine" or "feminine" across the adult life span. Before we turn to such research, let's look at some theories of how gender identity develops and whether and how it can change.

HOW DO GENDER ROLES AND GENDER IDENTITY DEVELOP?

There are a number of theories—many of them conflicting—about how gender roles and gender identity develop in childhood, and each has specific consequences for later life.

In classical Freudian psychoanalytic theory, boys and girls achieve permanent gender identity by identifying with the parent of the same sex and repressing or giving up the idea of possessing the parent of the other sex.

According to **self-in-relation theory**, proposed by Jean Baker-Miller (1976), a feminist psychotherapist, men and women develop gender identity differently, and this difference explains much about adult personality development. While masculine identity requires a distancing from the mother, feminine identity does not; a girl's tie with her mother widens to include nurturant relationships with others as well. Self-in-relation theory holds that men, too, have a primary desire for connection with other people. When that desire is frustrated by a culturally induced pursuit of autonomy and avoidance of close attachments, the result may be a sense of emptiness, loneliness, and depression in midlife (Bergman, 1991; Miller, 1991). In this view, a woman's "weaknesses"—vulnerability, dependence, and emotionality—are actually strengths: "valuable attributes that foster connection, intimacy, and growth" (R. Weiss, 1994, p. 3).

According to **social-learning theory**, of which Albert Bandura is the most prominent advocate, young children learn to identify with and act like the parent of the same sex. They learn gender roles the same way they learn other kinds of socially approved behavior: through observation, imitation, and reinforcement from parents and society. ("Don't be a sissy!" "Girls don't climb trees!") Since gender identity and gender roles are learned, they can later be modified through selection and imitation of new models, or through reinforcement of different kinds of behavior.

Other psychologists, such as Kohlberg (1966), have proposed **cognitive-developmental theories**. Rather than depending on adults as models or dispensers of reinforcement, these theorists hold, children learn about gender (and other aspects of their world) by actively thinking about their experience. They organize their behavior around these perceptions, adopting behaviors they see as consistent with their identity as male or female. One cognitive-developmental model (Pleck, 1975; Rebecca, Hefner, & Oleshansky, 1976) proposes that people learn about gender roles in four stages. In childhood, they move from vague notions (stage 1) to rigid ideas (stage 2) of what males and females are and do. In adulthood, their self-concept becomes more flexible and androgynous (stage 3). In stage 4, *gender-role transcendence*, gender roles become irrelevant and people do whatever is most adaptive in a situation.

Bem's (1981, 1983, 1985) **gender-schema theory** combines elements of the social-learning and cognitive-developmental approaches. According to Bem, people develop *gender schemas*, patterns of behavior organized around gender, which help them sort out their observations of what it means to be male or female. They pick up these schemas in childhood as they see how society classifies people and behavior. As in social-learning theory, learned schemas can be modified; but modification may require altering culturally ingrained attitudes, which are highly resistant to change.

As early as 1910, for instance, the founders of kibbutzim (communal settlements) in Israel tried to do away with special roles for men and women by changing family structure and assigning chores without regard to sex. Later, however, people on kibbutzim reverted to traditional gender roles, with men doing agricultural and mechanical work and women cooking, laundering, and caring for children (Tiger & Shepher, 1975). In the United States, although the past several decades have brought major changes in how men and women think, feel, and act with regard to gender, many people still view certain activities as unmasculine or unfeminine.

DO GENDER ROLES CHANGE DURING ADULTHOOD?

There is considerable evidence that people may become more androgynous in midlife. Costa and McCrae (1980), in keeping with their findings of stability in other areas of personality, have questioned the significance of such data. However, a number of studies have found that middle-aged men tend to be more open about feelings, more interested in intimate relationships, and more nurturing than younger men; while middle-aged women are more assertive, active, self-confident, and achievement-oriented (Chiriboga & Thurnher, 1975; Cooper & Gutmann, 1987; Cytrynbaum et al., 1980; Helson & Moane, 1987; Huyck, 1990; Neugarten, 1968). Some social scientists attribute these apparent developments to the hormonal changes of menopause and the male climacteric (Rossi, 1980); others offer psychological and cultural explanations.

One of the earliest and most influential theorists to describe normative changes in gender roles across the adult life span was the Swiss psychologist Carl Jung, whose work, like that of Erikson, departed from Freudian theory. Jung (1953, 1969) held that healthy development calls for a balance or integration of conflicting parts of the personality. Until about age 40, adults concentrate on obligations to family and society and develop those aspects of personality that will help them reach these external goals. According to Jung, women emphasize expressiveness and nurturance; men are primarily oriented toward achievement. Men suppress their feminine aspects; women suppress their masculine aspects. At midlife, when careers are established and children are grown, men and women seek a "union of opposites" by expressing their previously "disowned" aspects.

The psychologist David Gutmann (1975, 1977, 1985), who reviewed a large number of cross-cultural studies, suggests that traditional gender roles evolved to ensure the security of the young and the well-being of the growing family After child raising is over, says Gutmann, there is not just a balancing of roles but often a reversal of roles. Men are now free to explore their previously repressed "feminine" side and thus become more passive (see Box 11.3); women become more dominant and independent.

Such changes may be most characteristic of societies or cohorts with relatively conventional gender roles. For example, in American society many middle-aged men have become more interested in intimacy at a time when women have been entering the workplace or exploring other facets of their personalities. This mismatch between men's and women's needs may help explain why midlife has been found to be the low point in marital satisfaction, and why many men seem to regret the "empty nest" while many women welcome it (see Chapter 9). Now that most younger women combine paid work with parenthood, and some younger men are more active in child rearing, we may no longer see such dramatic switches in gender roles at midlife. Indeed, a recent time-sequential comparison (Hyde, Krajnik, & Skuldt-Niederberger, 1991), which used a modified version of Bern's Sex Role Inventory, found more "masculine" women age 21 to 40 and more androgynous men at all ages than in a similar sample 10 years before.

With regard to late life, the current sample, like the earlier one, had more androgynous men and more "feminine" women in the oldest group (61 to 86) than in younger groups. This finding suggests that both older men and older women may become more "feminine," reflecting increased dependency (Hyde et al., 1991). Such comparisons do not, of course, establish whether individuals actually change. For that, we need longitudinal research.

Could such changes be related more to life events than to chronological age? One research team (Abrahams, Feldman, & Nash, 1978; Feldman, Biringen, & Nash, 1981; Nash & Feldman, 1981) examined people at successive stages in the family life cycle and found that the prospect and advent of parenthood intensified "masculinity" and "femininity." A number of studies have found that both women's and men's concepts of gender identity are affected by their life situation, social context, and social roles (Blanchard-Fields & Abeles, 1996). For example, a recent finding that older people are more sensitive than younger people (Blanchard-Fields, Suhrer-Roussel, & Hertzog, 1994) may reflect not an age-related increase in androgyny but an increase in emotional expressiveness related to grandparenthood or other role changes (Blanchard-Fields & Abeles, 1996).

Women's Personality Development: The Mills Studies

The issue of how similarly or differently men and women develop takes us back to a major criticism of classic stage models: their use of male samples and norms, which may not be generalizable to women. Let's look at some longitudinal research that has sought to correct this imbalance and to track changes in women's roles.

Druze Men: New Roles in Late Middle Age

The Druze are an Islamic sect in the middle east; they live in isolated highland farming villages. Although similar to other Muslim peoples in language and most other aspects of lifestyle, in one respect they are unique. The Druze broke with the rest of Islam on doctrinal grounds more than 800 years ago, and since then they have lived as an often oppressed, highly self-sufficient minority. They will fight to the death any threat to their beliefs and traditions.

To protect their religion and their identity, the Druze operate as a secret society within the Islamic world and even within their own villages. Their sacred texts, which control their culture, are open only to men; and even men are generally given access to this hidden knowledge only in late middle age and only after living an exemplary life. Younger men "are not instructed in the religion or even told that they are Druze until they reach the age of discretion" (Gutmann, 1974, p. 235).

Once accepted into the inner circle of *Aqil* ("those who know"), Druze men radically change their lifestyle. They shave their heads, put on special clothing, stop smoking and drinking, and spend much of their time in prayer. The initiate "is expected to devote himself to good and pious thoughts and to forget the errors and stupidities of his life before he was introduced to true knowledge" (p. 235).

Despite these highly specific features of Druze life, psychologist David Gutmann (1974, 1977), who studied the Druze of Israel and the Golan Heights, found parallels with changing gender roles of aging men in other cultures. When Druze men were given a projective personality test, their responses were similar to those of Navajo and Mayan men, as well as to an urban sample from Kansas City. In all four cultures, older men's interpretations of pictures were less aggressive and competitive than those of younger men. For example, when shown a picture of a man climbing (or perhaps descend-

One of the most comprehensive longitudinal studies of women's personality development is that of Ravenna Helson and her associates, who for more than three decades have followed 140 women from the classes of 1958 and 1960 at Mills College in Oakland, California. Using a combination of psychological ratings and open-ended questions, Helson and her colleagues found three types of systematic personality change that correspond roughly to stage, life events, and trait approaches: *normative change*, which applied to the sample as a whole; change associated with *role patterns and paths;* and change associated with particular *personality patterns.*

NORMATIVE CHANGES

The Mills studies suggest a progression of stages different from those of the men in Vaillant's and Levinson's studies (refer back to Table 11.1). But, like the

ing) a rope, a younger man would describe the man in the picture as demonstrating strength and boldness, competing against other climbers, training for competition, or perhaps escaping from prison. An older man was more likely to see him as playing, resting, or diving into water; as fleeing from danger; as struggling against his own weakness; or as exhausted and clinging desperately to the rope. Older men were also likely to give magical or imaginative interpretations, perhaps seeing the man on the rope as impaled by a spear, or the rope as a snake.

According to Gutmann, such reactions reveal an age-related shift from *active mastery* to *passive mastery*. In many agrarian, preliterate societies, "young men are expected, through their *own* energies, to wrest resource and power from physical nature, from enem[ies] or from both; older men are expected . . . to coax power from the [gods]" (1977, p. 305). Older Druze men show passive or "feminine" leanings not in outward behavior, but in their spiritual life.

While they retain positions of prestige and involvement in society, often "laying down the law" to their grown sons and other younger relatives, in their relationship to God they are humble, docile, and unquestioningly subservient. They believe that this passivity enables them to tap into the power of the supernatural world to safeguard and increase the production of children, flocks, and crops. The *Aqil*, then, "relinquishes his own productivity" to become "the bridge between the community and the productive, life-sustaining potencies of Allah, . . . carr[ying] forward the moral rather than the material work of the community" (Gutmann, 1974, p. 244).

Thus, says Gutmann, the Druze religion seems to provide a useful role for older men undergoing personality changes common to their age, which have no comparable, constructive outlet in modern secular societies—a role suited to a stage of life when the tasks of parenthood and physical productivity are over.

men in those studies, these women do appear to have gone through periods of reorganizing their perceptions to bring new meaning to their "life stories."

Helson (1992) asked 88 Mills alumnae in their early fifties to identify the "most unstable, confusing, troubled, or discouraged time in your life since college—the one with the most impact on your values, self-concept, and the way you look at the world" (p. 336). The early forties turned out to be the time of greatest turmoil for the largest number of women, supporting the notion of a female midlife crisis. The outcome of this struggle was a "revision of the life story," giving "the plot of their lives a self-chosen new direction" (p. 343).

Crises also appeared at other times of life. Many of them could be categorized by themes which were often age-related, though motherhood tended to delay these critical times. Typical themes among women in their early to mid twenties were *bad self* and *bad partner*. The "bad self" theme was characterized by feeling lonely, isolated, unattractive, inferior, and often passive. The "bad partner" theme often revolved around a husband who was a substance abuser, suicidal, or exploitive.

A theme common enough to be considered a stage in women's development was a struggle for *independent identity*, status, and power, and the desire to achieve control over one's life. This theme, which often arose around age 30 to 40, might involve graduate training, a career, or a love affair (heterosexual or lesbian).

As the participants moved into middle age, between ages 36 and 46, these women's stories involved themes of *unpleasant consequences of independence and assertiveness:* rebuffs at work, for instance, or abandonment by their husbands. Later midlife themes, between ages 47 to 53, often focused on *troubling relationships* with partners, parents, or children; or on *overload*, sometimes caused by the demands of other people, sometimes by economic strain or heavy responsibilities at work.

When is the prime of life? Among nearly 700 Mills alumnae age 26 to 80 who were studied in 1983, women in their early fifties most often described their lives as "first-rate." In 1989, women in the original Mills longitudinal sample, then in their early fifties, also rated their quality of life as high (Mitchell & Helson, 1990). Generally, these women were young enough to be in good health and old enough to have launched all their children and to be well off financially. Life at home was simpler; the energy that had gone into childrearing was redirected to partners, work, community, or themselves. They had developed greater confidence, involvement, security, and breadth of personality. The women with the most positive outlook were optimistic; they had good relationships, a favorable self-concept, a feeling of control over their lives, and active interests; and they were managing their lives sensibly. They were likely to be caring for others—the generativity described by Erikson.

The normative changes these women experienced seem to bear out the idea proposed by Jung, Gutmann, and others "that young adult roles increase women's femininity but that women become more confident and assertive around midlife" (Helson, 1993, pp. 101–102). The highest quality of life was associated, not with a reversal of gender roles, but with an androgynous balance of "masculine" autonomy and "feminine" involvement in an intimate relationship.

Further evidence for change in gender roles is provided by self-reports and personality ratings. On a standard measure of gender-related characteristics, the California Psychological Inventory (CPI), traits associated with femininity—sympathy and compassion combined with a sense of vulnerability, self-criticism, and lack of confidence and initiative—increased during the twenties and then declined across middle age (see Figure 11.4). Between ages 21 and 43, the women developed more self-discipline and commitment, independence, confidence, and coping skills (Helson & Moane, 1987); from ages 43 to 52, they continued to grow in independence and self-confidence. They became more decisive, dominant, and self-affirming and less self-critical

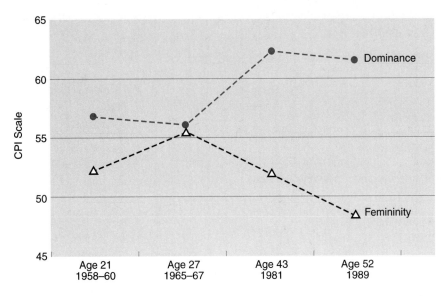

FIGURE 11.4 *Changes in femininity and dominance resulting from shifting gender roles from age 21 to age 52.* SOURCE: Roberts, Helson, & Klohnen, 2002.

(Roberts, Helson, & Klohnen, 2002; see Table 11.2). This normative personality change was unrelated to such typical midlife events as the empty nest, menopause, or caring for aging parents (Helson & Wink, 1992).

As with the classic normative studies of male samples, of course, the experience of these Mills graduates has to be considered in terms of their socioeconomic status, cohort, and culture. They are a group of educated, predominantly white, upper-middle-class American women who lived through a time of great change in women's roles brought about in part by the women's movement, by economic changes, by changing patterns of family life, and by new patterns in the workplace. The Mills women were undoubtedly influenced by these factors.

Thus the normative changes found in the Mills research are not necessarily the same as maturational changes, which would occur regardless of class, cohort, and culture. For example, on a measure designed to show women's psychological dependence on their husbands, the Mills women at age 52 scored significantly lower (that is, showed less dependence) than their mothers had at the same age (Wink & Helson, 1993). Today's young women, in turn, may be developing differently from the women in the Mills sample. As Helson and Moane (1987) observe, "If a substantial number of women continue to launch careers in their 20s and have children in their 30s, the pattern of normative change may take a different form" (p. 185).

TABLE 11.2

Selected Feelings About Life by Women in Their Early Fifties

	More True Now	Less True Now
Identity questioning and turmoil		
Excitement, turmoil about my impulses and potential	21	56
Searching for a sense of who I am	28	47
Anxious that I won't live up to my potential	25	47
Coming near the end of one road and not finding another	27	45
Assurance of status		
Feeling established	78	11
Influence in my community or field of interest	63	24
A new level of productivity	70	11
Feeling selective in what I do	91	2
A sense of being my own person	90	3
Cognitive breadth and complexity		
Bringing both feeling and rationality into decisions	76	1
Realizing larger patterns of meaning and relationship	72	7
Appreciating my complexity	69	10
Discovering new parts of myself	72	11
Present rather than future orientation		
Focus on reality—meeting the needs of the day and not being too emotional about them	76	6
More satisfied with what I have; less worried about what I won't get	76	11
Feeling the importance of time's passing	76	10
Adjustment and relational smoothness		
Feeling secure and committed	71	12
Feeling my life is moving well	74	15
Feeling optimistic about the future	58	20
A new level of intimacy	53	30
Doing things for others and then feeling exploited	14	56
Feeling very much alone	26	45
Feelings of competition with other women	7	63
Feeling angry at men and masculinity	14	52
Awareness of aging and reduced vitality		
Looking old	70	15
Being treated as an older person	64	14
Reducing the intensity of my achievement efforts	44	26
Liking an active social life	27	52
Being very interested in sex	19	64

NOTE: The women judged whether each item was more applicable to them now in their early forties, less applicable now than then, or about the same.
SOURCE: Helson & Wink, 1992.

CHANGE ASSOCIATED WITH ROLE PATTERNS AND PATHS

Certain aspects of personality development in the Mills women seemed to be related to life events. Some women, for example, followed the expected pattern for their generation—marrying and starting families in young adulthood—and by age 43 continued to maintain their traditional roles. These women did not exhibit the gains in dominance and independence that the rest of the sample showed. They also became increasingly "overcontrolled," a pattern some theorists have noted in women who place others' needs before their own (Helson & Picano, 1990).

Still, more than one kind of lifestyle seemed to foster positive development. Women who committed themselves during their twenties to career, family, or both developed more fully than women who had no children and who chose work beneath their capabilities. Between age 27 and the early forties, women who had faced the challenges of career or parenthood became more disciplined, independent, hard-working, and confident and improved their "people skills." Compared with women who had made neither commitment, they were more dominant, more motivated to achieve, more emotionally stable, more goal-oriented, and more interested in what was going on in the world (Helson & Moane, 1987). Of course, this was not a controlled experiment, and so these correlations can only suggest—not establish—causal relationships.

CHANGES ASSOCIATED WITH PERSONALITY PATTERNS

The Mills researchers found certain changes related to specific personality patterns. For example, by means of a prototype of the Q-sort technique some women were identified as *willful*—a form of what Freud called a *narcissistic*, or excessively self-absorbed, personality. These women became more effective, happier, more sociable, and more confident between ages 21 and 27. But, as Freudian theory would predict, they became more maladjusted by midlife. They tended to have problems with drugs, relationships, and careers (Wink, 1991, 1992).

The Mills studies are notable for their eclectic combination of research tools and their attempt to combine several approaches to the study of adult personality development. This research avoids a simplistic, either-or approach and points toward further synthesis that needs to be done.

SYNTHESIZING APPROACHES TO ADULT PERSONALITY DEVELOPMENT

Advocates of stability and advocates of change often defend their positions zealously. Still, it seems plain, as the historian C. Vann Woodward (1989) has observed, that "there would be no history at all without some of both." The same is true of adult personality. As we noted at the beginning of this chapter, the search for evidence of stability began in response to claims "that personality is largely an illusion, that behavioral outcomes depend on particularities of situations" (Helson, 1993, p. 94). In the 1970s, theories of

CRITICAL THINKING

How would you organize the approaches to adult personality development in relation to Baltes' lifespan developmental theory?

normative change took center stage, only to yield to the timing-of-events model. Since then, Costa and McCrae have redirected attention to the essential stability of personality.

Recently, there have been efforts to pull these diverse approaches together. One, mentioned earlier in this chapter, is the broad conceptual framework developed by Costa and McCrae (1994a, 1994b) to embrace interactions among basic tendencies, external influences, self-concept, and life events. Perhaps even more promising, and more fully developed, is Helson's use of techniques for exploring personality from several theoretical perspectives, acknowledging the roles of gender, class, cohort, and culture. The Mills College studies found that "personality does change from youth to middle age in consistent and often predictable ways" (Helson & Moane, 1987, p. 185). But there were important areas of stability as well. For example, certain persistent traits, such as optimism, affected quality of life at various ages (Mitchell & Helson, 1990).

Recognizing that Costa and McCrae have made a strong case for the stability of basic traits, Helson (1993) emphasizes the importance of longitudinal research to discover how adults do and do not change. More sophisticated instruments will be required to permit comparisons among longitudinal studies that have used different methods and often small, disparate samples. Such methods might uncover specific processes that promote continuity or change. Of course, we need to remember that continuity and change often go hand in hand. A personality dimension that is basically stable may manifest itself differently at different times (Costa & McCrae, 1994a). For example, an extraverted 25-year-old shoe salesman may, at 70, be lobbying against cuts in social security.

The study of adult personality embodies several features of the lifespan developmental perspective. The entire life span contributes to the shaping of personality. We can see the multidirectionality of development in, for example, men's greater need for intimacy in middle age, when women show increased independence. History and context—that is, cohort and culture—are essential in considering normative versus nonnormative change. Indeed, it may be impossible to develop any theory of personality development that is entirely culture-free. And the interdisciplinary nature of the field can be seen in the efforts of geneticists, anthropologists, sociologists, psychologists, and others who are involved in the study of personality.

An important function of personality, as we mentioned at the beginning of this chapter, is adaptation. In Chapter 12, we look more closely at how people cope with difficult circumstances and particularly at how they adapt to the challenge of aging.

Summary and Key Terms

Defining and Studying Personality

- Common themes in definitions of personality include uniqueness or individuality, attitudinal and behavioral continuity, and characteristic adaptive patterns.

- Commonly used instruments for measuring personality include the personality inventory, the Q-sort, and interviews or self-reports.
- Interacting genetic and experiential influences contribute to personality development throughout life.

adaptation (p. 395)
personality (p. 395)
personality inventory (p. 397)
Q-sort (p. 398)

real self (p. 398)
ideal self (p. 398)
temperament (p. 398)

Models of Adult Personality: Stability or Change

- A major issue in the study of adult personality is stability versus change. In general, trait theories find stability, stage and life-events theories describe change, and self-concept theories seek to account for both.
- In Costa and McCrae's five-factor model, all dimensions of personality appear to remain stable after about age 30. According to other trait research, differences in late life seem to reflect cohort effects. Cultural change can influence personality.
- Self-concept models focus on the self-image and its cognitive interaction with the social environment. In Whitbourne's model, identity styles represent a balance between identity assimilation (stability) and identity accommodation (change).
- Stage models, such as the classic models of Erikson, Vaillant, and Levinson, portray normative personality changes as a series of stages across the adult life span, with critical transitions. Levinson maintains that midlife turmoil is inevitable, but Vaillant and a number of other researchers have found little evidence of it. Normative personality development may be influenced by socioeconomic status, gender, cohort, and culture.
- The timing-of-events model, supported by Neugarten and others, focuses on the impact of the timing of important life events.

self-concept (p. 400)
personality dimensions (p. 401)
five-factor model (p. 401)
schemas (p. 405)
identity styles (p. 406)
identity assimilation (p. 406)
identity accommodation (p. 406)
normative personality change (p. 407)
generativity (p. 407)

midlife crisis (p. 410)
interiority (p. 410)
life structure (p. 413)
dream (p. 413)
mentor (p. 413)
social clock (p. 415)
timing-of-events model (p. 416)
normative life events (p. 416)
nonnormative life events (p. 416)

Gender and Personality

- Gender roles, often stereotyped, are incorporated into men's and women's gender identity and may influence their attitudes and behavior as adults.
- The Bem Sex Role Inventory has identified four categories of gender roles: masculine, feminine, androgynous, and undifferentiated.

- Theories of how gender identity develops, such as Freudian theory, self-in-relation theory, social-learning theory, cognitive-developmental theories, and gender-schema theory, have different implications for personality development in adulthood.
- Several prominent theorists and researchers have noted a balancing or reversal of gender roles in middle age.
- The Mills College studies of women have found normative changes that differ from those previously identified for men. This research has also found changes associated with particular role paths and personality patterns.

gender stereotypes (p. 417)

gender roles (p. 417)

gender identity (p. 417)

androgynous (p. 418)

undifferentiated (p. 418)

self-in-relation theory (p. 418)

social-learning theory (p. 419)

cognitive-developmental theory (p. 419)

gender-schema theory (p. 420)

Synthesizing Approaches to Adult Personality Development

- Recently there have been attempts to synthesize various approaches to adult personality development.

Mental Health, Coping, and Adjustment to Aging

◈ **FOCUS: ARTHUR ASHE**

The health of the mind is of far more consequence to our happiness than the health of the body, although both are deserving of much more attention than either of them receives.
—Charles Caleb Colton, *Lacon*, 1855

THE TENNIS CHAMPION Arthur Ashe* was one of the most respected athletes of all time. He was known for his quiet, dignified manner on and off the court; he did not dispute calls, indulge in temper tantrums, or disparage his opponents.

On April 8, 1992, Ashe called a press conference and announced to the world that he had AIDS. It was the latest and worst in a series of what to many people would have been crushing blows, beginning at age 6 with the loss of his mother.

© Hulton-Deutsch Collection/Corbis Images

———
*Sources of biographical information on Arthur Ashe are Ashe and Rampersad (1993), Finn (1993), and Witteman (1993).

Ashe, an African American, was born in segregated Richmond, Virginia. Tennis—the game he loved to play—was almost the exclusive province of white people, and so he became a special target for bigotry. His father taught him always to maintain his composure, to behave better than his oppressors, and to channel his aggressive impulses into the game itself.

For Ashe, tennis became a means of combating racial prejudice. Though he was twice refused a visa to play in the South African Open, he was finally allowed to compete in 1973, and again in 1974 and 1975. Despite South Africa's rigid apartheid system, he insisted that there be no segregated seating at his matches. During one tournament, a young black boy kept following him around. Ashe asked him why. The child replied that Ashe was the first free black man he had ever seen.

Ashe continued to work against apartheid, for the most part quietly, behind the scenes. Once, he was accused of being an "Uncle Tom" by angry militants who shouted him down while he was giving a speech. He politely rebuked them: "What do you expect to achieve when you give in to passion and invective and surrender the high moral ground that alone can bring you to victory?" (Ashe & Rampersad, 1993, pp. 117, 118). Years later, he felt tremendous pride when he saw Nelson Mandela, the symbol of opposition to apartheid, freed from prison and riding in a ticker-tape parade in New York City. But Ashe would not live to see Mandela become president of South Africa.

In 1979, at age 36, while still engaged in a brilliant career that had included winning the United States Open, the Australian Open, and Wimbledon, Ashe suffered the first of several heart attacks and had quadruple bypass surgery. Forced to retire from tennis, he had to figure out how to move on with his life. A book by Daniel Levinson, which his wife gave him, prompted

him to try a brief period of psychotherapy to gain insight into his troubled feelings.

Ashe now embarked on a new phase of his career, serving for 5 years as captain of the United States Davis Cup tennis team. Before one crucial match, he told John McEnroe—an uninhibited and rambunctious player—that another outburst would cause Ashe to forfeit the match. McEnroe listened in silence and went on to win a grueling 5-set match—quietly. Yet Ashe also learned to admire McEnroe, whose flare-ups represented a different way of dealing with powerful emotions.

After two consecutive Davis Cup victories, Ashe in 1983 watched his team lose in the first round, underwent a double bypass operation, and returned to lead the team into the finals, only to lose to Sweden. When he was criticized for not being a forceful enough leader, he began to realize that there are times when bold action is required—and not only on the tennis court. In 1984, the same year in which he was replaced as captain of the team, he was arrested in a protest outside the South African embassy in Washington, D.C.

One summer morning in 1988, Ashe woke up and could not move his right arm. He was given two options: immediate brain surgery, or wait and see. He opted for action. Preparatory blood tests showed that he was HIV-positive, probably from a blood transfusion during his heart surgery 5 years earlier. The surgery revealed a parasitic infection linked to AIDS, and the virus had progressed to AIDS itself. Like an athlete who is outscored but still in the game, Ashe refused to panic or to give up. Relying on the best medical knowledge, he chose to do all he could to fight his illness. He also chose to keep quiet about it.

In 1992, Ashe learned that *USA Today* planned to reveal that he had AIDS. Reluctantly, he went public first—but he then used the opportunity to become a leader in the movement for AIDS research. He established a foundation, launched a $5 million fund-raising campaign, and worked tirelessly for the cause until his death.

Arthur Ashe died of AIDS-related pneumonia in 1993, at age 49. Shortly before, he had summed up his situation in his usual style: "I am a fortunate, blessed man. Aside from AIDS and heart disease, I have no problems" (Ashe & Rampersad, 1993, p. 328).

ARTHUR ASHE'S CHARACTERISTIC WAY OF coping with trouble was to meet it as he did an opponent on the tennis court: with grace, determination, and coolness under fire. He managed to keep his head to the end, under conditions that might have driven some people to drink, depression, or worse. Again and again, he turned adversity into opportunity.

Mental health has been defined as an "attempt to live meaningfully, in a particular set of social and environmental circumstances, relying on a particular collection of resources and supports"—in other words, trying "to do the best we can with what we have" (Kivnick, 1993, p. 15). It involves developing inner strengths and using external resources to compensate for weaknesses and deficits. Efforts toward self-development—thriving rather than merely surviving—are signs of a healthy personality (Butler, Lewis, & Sunderland, 1991; Sherman, 1993). Mental health may include how people see themselves, how they integrate various roles and aspects of the self (see Box 12.1), and whether or not they strive for growth. It may also include identification with, and commitment to, something beyond the self—family, community, nation, culture, religion, or a cause, such as the fight against racial prejudice or AIDS (Jahoda, 1958; Sherman, 1993). A correlate of mental health is *life satisfaction,* which is sometimes defined as *morale,* or as how a person judges the quality of his or her life (Schulz, 1985). A favorable self-image and high self-esteem enhance morale. So do autonomy and a sense of mastery (Sherman, 1993). On all these counts, Arthur Ashe, even as his physical health deteriorated, was in extremely good mental health.

Many people, of course, have dealt with threats to mental health, with varying degrees of success. Some succumb to mental disorders that interfere with normal cognitive functioning or social roles. Almost half of all American adults have experienced a mental disorder, mild or severe, at some time in their lives. Most common is major depression, followed by alcohol dependence and phobias (Blazer, Kessler, McGonagle, & Swartz, 1994; Kessler et al., 1994). Poorly educated, low-income urban dwellers are most susceptible to mental illness. Men are more likely to abuse drugs or to have antisocial behavioral disturbances; women are more prone to anxiety and depression (Robins et al., 1984; Wykle & Musil, 1993).

Both Job and Family Roles Affect
Men's Psychological Well-Being

Traditionally, women's mental health has been assessed in terms of family, and men's in terms of work. In recent years, however, researchers have paid more attention to the neglected aspects of both men's and women's lives. A number of studies have emphasized the importance of work in women's lives (see Box 11.2 in Chapter 11), and recent research has shown the importance of family connections to men's well-being.

In one study (Barnett, Marshall, & Pleck, 1992), researchers asked 300 employed husbands, age 25 to 40, who were part of two-earner couples, to evaluate their work, marital, and parental roles, noting both rewards and concerns. For example, in terms of work, the men were asked how rewarding it was "to have a variety of tasks" and how much of a concern "lack of job security" was. For the marital role, they rated such rewards as "enjoying the same activities" and such concerns as "your partner's being critical of you." For the parental role, rewards included "seeing your children mature and change," and concerns included "having

too many arguments and conflicts with them." Each man received a "quality" score for each role (his "reward score" minus his "concern score"). The men also were assessed for anxiety and depression.

The study's main finding was surprising: the widely held view that work is the main determinant of mental health for men turned out not to be so. Apparently, men's family roles are just as important, and their various roles are related. Good relationships with wife and children can make up for a poor experience on the job. When both job and family roles are unsatisfactory, the result is often psychological distress. One difference between men and women is that for working women merely being a parent often offsets job concerns; whereas for men what is important is not parenthood itself, but how rewarding the parental role is. Being a father may be less central to a man's sense of self than motherhood is to a woman, but rewards from parenthood are just as important to fathers as to mothers.

Younger adults tend to be subject to emotional problems, anxiety, and substance abuse; older adults, especially men, are more likely to have severe cognitive impairment (Regier et al., 1988; Wykle & Musil, 1993). Perhaps because mental illness has traditionally been stigmatized, fewer than 40 percent of all victims seek treatment; but many adults manage to overcome their conditions without professional help (Blazer et al., 1994; Kessler et al., 1994).

In this chapter, we discuss both positive and negative aspects of mental health throughout the adult life span, and its biological, psychological, and social roots. Let's begin by looking at how adults cope with stress, including the challenge of aging—one match Arthur Ashe never got to finish.

MODELS OF COPING

Stress is an inevitable part of life. As a leading researcher has said, "Complete freedom from stress is death" (Selye, 1980, p. 128). The question is how—and how well—someone copes with it.

Coping is adaptive thinking or behavior aimed at reducing or relieving stress that arises from harmful, threatening, or challenging conditions. Psychologists and laypeople alike recognize coping as an important aspect of mental health. Let's look briefly at three traditional approaches to the study of coping: *environmental, behavioral,* and *coping-style* models. Then we'll take a closer look at the *cognitive-appraisal* model.

CRITICAL THINKING

How do you cope with stress? Does your approach promote successful adaptation to the situation, or does it interfere with your ability to respond appropriately?

Environmental Models

One of the earliest approaches to the study of coping was quantitative. Researchers asked 5,000 hospital patients about important life events that had preceded their illness—both negative events (such as the death of a spouse) and positive events (such as the birth of a child)—and how much adjustment each required (Holmes & Rahe, 1976). On the basis of these reports, the investigators assigned numerical values called "life change units" (LCUs) to each type of event (see Table 4.3 in Chapter 4). About half the people with 150 to 300 LCUs in a year, and about 70 percent of those with 300 or more LCUs, had become ill within the next 1 or 2 years. In other words, the more major changes a person faced within a given time, the harder it was to cope with them.

Such an approach represents an *environmental model* of coping, and it is essentially mechanistic. Human beings are considered *react*ors rather than *act*ors; size and frequency of environmental demands determine how well a person can cope. Too many stressors (sources of stress), or a single major stressor (such as the death of a spouse), can overwhelm a person's ability to cope—much as putting too much stress on machinery can cause overload and can damage the operating parts.

An environmental model has several shortcomings. First, it does not consider how an individual interprets an event. Second (as we discuss in Chapter 11), the timing of an event may make a difference. Third, stress also may result from *lack* of change—boredom, inability to advance at work, or unrewarding personal relationships. Fourth, several studies suggest that both physical and mental health are more likely to be affected by ongoing irritations and strains of everyday life than by major, isolated events (George, 1980; Lazarus, 1981; Pearlin, 1980; Pearlin, Lieberman, Menaghan, & Mullan, 1981). Fifth, the model ignores individual differences. Why does one person break down under the stress of a deadline or emergency, while another rises to the occasion?

CRITICAL THINKING

What types of stress have you experienced that you would characterize as resulting from positive or negative life events?

Two environmental models attempt to solve one or more of these problems. The **congruence model** (Kahana, 1982; Kahana, E., Lovegreen, Kahana, B., & Kahana, M., 2003) recognizes that people's needs differ, and environments differ in how they meet those needs. Levels of life satisfaction or stress

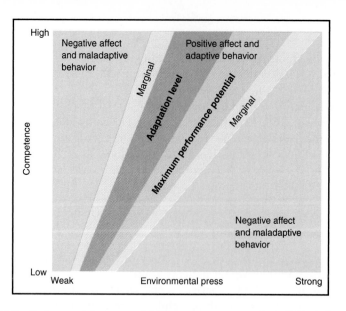

FIGURE 12.1 *Environmental-press model.* The more competent the individual, the wider the range of environmental situations in which a sense of comfort will be experienced and behavior will be adaptive (top of figure). Less competent individuals (bottom of figure) are more likely to feel stress as a result of environmental demands. *SOURCE:* Lawton & Nahemow, 1973, p. 661.

depend on congruence—the match—between person and environment. For example, placing an older adult who has a strong need for independence in a nursing home is likely to increase stress.

The **environmental-press model** (Lawton, 1982; Lawton & Nahemow, 1973) emphasizes differences in demands that environments make (*environmental press*) and in individuals' *competence*—their ability to meet those demands. As shown in Figure 12.1, when both press and competence are relatively high or relatively low, people are comfortable in their environment and tend to take it for granted—they are at their normal *adaptation level.* When moderately pressed by the environment, they reach their maximum potential. But when environmental press is too low or too high, people become uncomfortably aware of the environment, perceiving it as boring or overwhelming.

The environmental-press model has implications for aging. If environmental press increases (for example, when an older person's city neighborhood becomes unsafe) or competence diminishes (for example, when an older adult living in a suburb can no longer drive), that person will fall below the adaptation level and feel stress. To restore an adaptive fit, ways must be found either to reduce environmental demands or to increase the individual's competence.

These two models, then, offer reasons why different situations may be more or less stressful for different people. But, like other environmental models, they do not tell us *how* people cope.

Behavioral Models

Behavioral models of coping give the individual a somewhat more active role. These models, based on animal studies, seek to explain behavior in terms of classical or operant conditioning, or both. From a behavioral perspective, coping involves learned adaptations to environmental stressors, leading to a reduction of perceived stress. An animal confronted by an enemy, or a person confronted by a stressor, generally has three options: flee to a safer place, fight and attempt to master the situation, or stay put and try to endure it. When escape or avoidance is impossible and attempts at mastery fail or are punished, organisms adapt through **learned helplessness.** Over a period of time they learn to live with what originally was an extremely stressful situation and give up trying to change it (Evans & Stecker, 2004; Ursin, 1980). We can see learned helplessness in battered spouses who stay with their mates, or in citizens who stay home on election day because they do not believe their vote means anything.

Coping-Style Models

A third, more complex, approach to coping is based on the psychoanalytic tradition. It focuses more on thoughts and attitudes than on outward behavior. From this perspective, coping is a form of problem solving, and individual *coping strategies* or *styles*, like personality traits, tend to be fairly stable.

Some researchers attempt to rank coping styles according to effectiveness. One such model came out of the longitudinal Grant Study of Harvard University men, described in Chapter 11. Vaillant (1977) identified four kinds of **adaptive mechanisms**—characteristic ways of coping or interacting with the environment: (1) *mature* (such as using humor or helping others); (2) *neurotic* (such as repressing anxiety, or saying the opposite of what one feels); (3) *immature* (such as fantasizing, or experiencing imaginary aches and pains); and (4) *psychotic* (distorting or denying reality). Men who used mature adaptive mechanisms were happier and mentally and physically healthier than others; they got more satisfaction from work, enjoyed richer friendships, made more money, and seemed better adjusted. In midlife the best-adjusted men were four times more likely to cope with life events in "mature" rather than "immature" ways (Vaillant, 1989). Likewise, at age 65, those who used "mature defense mechanisms"—who handled problems without blame, bitterness, or passivity—showed the healthiest adjustment (Vaillant & Vaillant, 1990).

Richard Lazarus and his colleagues, proponents of the cognitive-appraisal model (to be discussed next), make several criticisms of coping-style models (Lazarus, 2003; Lazarus & Folkman, 1984). First, coping styles may fail to capture the multidimensionality of human behavior. A middle-aged man who must deal simultaneously with, for example, (a) a threatened layoff, (b) a wife who has breast cancer, (c) a homosexual son who has just come out of the closet, and (d) the care of an aging mother may not cope in the same way with all four situations. And a particular coping style may not work equally well for all adults. Second, these models do not distinguish between coping and other forms of adaptive behavior that do not involve effort. When you are driving a car, you do many things that enable you to get to your destination in one piece: stopping at a red light, yielding the right-of-way, and so on. These learned responses are so automatic that you hardly have to think about them. However, you must call on your coping skills if you suddenly find your car sliding on a patch of ice or about to collide with another vehicle. Third, models that evaluate coping styles in terms of outcomes tend to confuse the process with the product. Coping is struggle, not success; management, not mastery.

Cognitive-Appraisal Model

In the **cognitive-appraisal model** (Lazarus, 2003; Lazarus & Folkman, 1984), coping is an evolving process, which occurs only in situations that a person sees as taxing or exceeding his or her resources and thus demanding unusual effort. According to this contextual model, people choose coping strategies on the basis of their cognitive appraisal of a situation. Coping includes anything an individual thinks or does in trying to adapt to stress, regardless of how well it works. Because the situation is constantly changing, coping is dynamic, not static; choosing the most appropriate strategy requires constant reappraisal of the relationship between person and environment (see Figure 12.2). Arthur Ashe, for instance, made significant reappraisals and changed his coping strategies at several points in his adult life.

The choice and effectiveness of a coping strategy are influenced by personal resources and by personal and environmental constraints, as well as by how great the threat appears to be. *Personal resources* include health, energy, beliefs about personal control or supernatural control, commitments and moti-

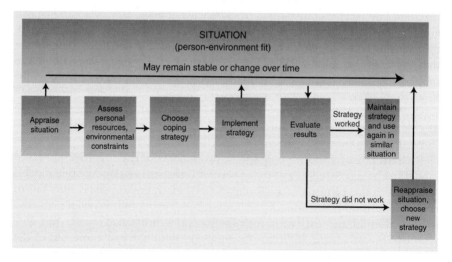

FIGURE 12.2 *Cognitive-appraisal model of coping.*   SOURCE: Based on Lazarus & Folkman, 1984.

vations, social skills and problem-solving skills, social support, and material resources (money, goods, and services). Use of personal resources may be limited by *personal constraints:* psychological problems, such as fear of failure, or attitudes reflecting societal norms, such as gender roles. *Environmental constraints* might be, for example, competing demands for the same resources, or institutions that thwart coping.

To identify characteristic coping strategies, cognitive-appraisal researchers try to get people to recall what they actually felt and did in stressful situations. Most of the time, people strike a balance between two modes of coping: *problem-focused* and *emotion-focused*. Which one predominates depends on the situation, the person, and the available options (Lazarus, 2003; Monat & Lazarus, 1985).

Problem-focused coping is directed toward eliminating, managing, or improving a stress condition. It generally predominates when a person sees a realistic chance of effecting change. **Emotion-focused coping,** sometimes called *palliative coping,* is directed toward "feeling better"—managing the emotional response to a stressful situation to relieve its physical or psychological impact. This form of coping is likely to predominate when a person concludes that little or nothing can be done about the situation itself. Some emotion-focused strategies divert attention from a problem; others consciously or unconsciously reinterpret the situation—for example, by giving in to it or pretending it doesn't exist. Box 12.2 describes an emotion-focused strategy used by factory workers in Malaysia to cope with stress caused by economic and social change.

Emotion-focused strategies generally rank low on coping-style hierarchies; denying a problem, for example, is seen as merely putting off something that may become harder to deal with. The cognitive-appraisal model, however, does not view any strategy as inherently good or bad. Effectiveness depends on the context. As Arthur Ashe observed, denial may be harmful if it keeps a person with chest pains from seeing a doctor; but "good denial—refusal to dwell on the idea of death," or to accept the idea that death is imminent, can allow a person who is terminally ill to "go calmly on with . . . life" for the time that remains (Ashe & Rampersad, 1993, pp. 328, 327). People must cope—if nothing else, by managing their emotions in the face of the inevitable.

In general, older adults do more emotion-focused coping than younger ones (Folkman, Lazarus, Pimley, & Novacek, 1987; Prohaska, Leventhal, Leventhal, & Keller, 1985). Is that because older people are less able to focus on problems or because they are more selective about when to focus? In a study by Blanchard-Fields, Jahnke, & Camp, (1995), 70 adolescents, 69 young adults, 74 middle-aged adults, and 74 older adults wrote essays on how to solve each of 15 problems. Regardless of age, participants most often recommended problem-focused strategies, especially in situations that were not highly emotional, such as returning defective merchandise. But age differences showed up in problems that were more emotional, such as moving to a new town or taking care of an older parent. In such situations, older adults chose more emotion-regulating strategies than younger adults did.

Coping with Economic Change in Rural Malaysia

In the former British crown colony of Malaysia in the south Pacific Ocean, industrialization is transforming rural life. Since 1970, Japanese, western European, and American corporations seeking to cut labor costs have moved hundreds of factories producing food, clothing, and electronics to Malaysia, where poverty has forced thousands of farm families off the land.

How do rural Malays cope with this radical change of lifestyle? One study (Ong, 1987) focused on a newly industrialized area, where young, poor, unmarried peasant women from neighboring villages assemble components for transistors and capacitors. The electronics factories have a hierarchy based on ethnicity and gender. Top management positions are filled by Japanese men. Production supervisors are Chinese or Malay men. At the bottom are the female Malay workers, wearing overalls and rubber gloves instead of their traditional tunics and sarongs.

Malay communities cooperate in providing this workforce. The Japanese management makes concerted efforts to stay on good terms with the villagers, donating money for village events and assuring parents that their daughters are well cared for. Village schools train future workers by insisting on order, obedience, and hard work.

Assembling electronics is grueling work; it requires constant, close concentration and frequent overtime. Lives that were formerly based on seasonal cycles of planting and harvesting are now regulated by factory shifts and schedules. Women who were once in charge of their own work now must deal with rigid shop routines, production quotas, and constant supervision. The male bosses, said one woman, "exhaust us very much, as if they do not think that we too are human beings" (Ong, 1987, p. 202). The women work for low wages, which they are often expected to turn over to their families. Without unions, there is no job security. Many workers last only a few years.

A common response to these exploitative, dehumanizing conditions is "possession by spirits." First one worker, then another, then another will see "spirits," which are believed to have come for vengeance because a factory has been built on a traditional burying ground. These "displaced spirits" are said to throng onto the shop floor and enter the women, who begin to sob, laugh hysterically, scream, and curse. A hundred or more workers may be affected at one time. The bosses may call in ritual healers to keep the spirits away by sacrificing chickens and goats, but still the "possession" continues.

How does "possession" help these Malay women cope? It can be seen as an unconscious or symbolic protest against factory discipline and male control—a form of rebellion that the bosses cannot easily stop because it is considered acceptable in Malay society. Since this behavior does nothing to improve working conditions, it is an *emotion-focused* rather than *problem-focused* strategy. In fact, it may help maintain the status quo by providing a socially acceptable outlet for the tensions of factory life (Ong, 1987).

These findings, along with several other studies, suggest that with age, people may be more able to control their emotions when a situation calls for it (Blanchard-Fields & Irion, 1987; Folkman & Lazarus, 1980; Labouvie-Vief, Hakim-Larson, & Hobart, 1987), and this style of coping can be quite adaptive. For many people, especially older ones, religious behavior seems to be an effective coping strategy (see Box 12.3 and Table 12.1).

Of course, one unavoidable condition adults must cope with is aging itself. How do they do it? Some theories and studies have dealt specifically with that question.

TABLE 12.1

Spontaneously Reported Emotion-Regulating Coping Strategies Used by Older Adults

Rank Order	FREQUENCY OF MENTION	
	Number	**(%)**
Religious	97	(17.4)
Kept busy	84	(15.1)
Accepted it	63	(11.3)
Support from family or friends	62	(11.1)
Help from professional	34	(6.1)
Positive attitude	31	(5.6)
Took one day at a time	29	(5.2)
Became involved in social activities	19	(3.4)
Planning and preparing beforehand	15	(2.7)
Optimized communication	13	(2.3)
Limited activities, didn't overcommit	11	(2.0)
Sought information	8	(1.4)
Exercised	8	(1.4)
Helped others more needy	7	(1.3)
Realized that time heals all wounds	7	(1.3)
Avoided situation	6	(1.1)
Experience of prior hardships	5	(.9)
Carried on for others' sake	5	(.9)
Ingested alcohol, tranquilizers	5	(.9)
Carried on as usual	4	(.7)
Took a vacation	3	(.5)
Realized others in same situation or worse	3	(.5)
Released emotion (cried or cursed)	3	(.5)
Lowered expectations or devalued	3	(.5)
Miscellaneous	31	(5.6)
Totals	556	(100.6)

NOTES: 100 older adults reported 556 coping behaviors for 289 stressful experiences. Percentages add up to more than 100 because of rounding.
SOURCE: Koenig et al., 1988, p. 306.

Religion and Emotional Well-Being in Late Life

Religion seems to play a supportive role for many elderly people.* Some possible explanations include social support, encouragement of healthy lifestyles, the perception of a measure of control over life through prayer, fostering of positive emotional states, reduction of stress, and faith in God as a way of interpreting misfortunes (Seybold & Hill, 2001). But does religion actually improve health and well-being?

Substantial evidence points to a positive link between religion or spirituality and health, but much of this research is not methodologically sound (Miller & Thoresen, 2003; Seeman, Dubin, & Seeman, 2003; Sloan & Bagiella, 2002), and definitions of these terms are often imprecise (Hill & Pargament, 2003; Miller & Thoresen, 2003; Wink & Dillon, 2003). A review of studies with relatively sound methodology found a 25 percent reduction in risk of mortality among healthy adults who attended religious services weekly. Religion or spirituality tended to protect against cardiovascular disease, mainly through the healthy lifestyle it encourages, but there was no evidence that either slows the progression of cancer, improves recovery from acute illness, or protects against disability (Powell, Shahabi, & Thoresen, 2003).

Another research review found positive associations between religiosity or spirituality and

measures of health, well-being, marital satisfaction, and psychological functioning and negative associations with suicide, delinquency, criminality, and drug and alcohol use (Seybold & Hill, 2001). Still another review found evidence supporting the physiological benefits of meditation (Seeman et al., 2003). In a study of 223 British older adults, spiritual or religious beliefs significantly predicted well-being and moderated the negative impact of frailty on well-being (Kirby, Coleman, & Daley, 2004).

In one study, interviewers asked 100 well-educated white men and women—age 55 to 80, about evenly divided between working class and upper middle class, and 90 percent Protestant—to describe the worst events in their lives and how they had dealt with them (Koenig, George, & Siegler, 1988). The respondents described 289 stressful events and 556 coping strategies.

Heading the list of strategies (see Table 12.1) were behaviors associated with religion, cited by 58 percent of the women and 32 percent of the men. Almost three-fourths of these religious strategies consisted of placing trust and faith in God, praying, and getting help and strength from God. Other religious sources of help included friends from church, church activities, the minister, and the Bible.

The next most common strategy was taking one's mind off a problem by keeping busy—for example, in work-related, social, recreational, and family activities; by reading or watching television; or by working at hobbies.

*Unless noted, discussion in this section is based on Papalia, Olds, & Feldman (2007).

The third and fourth strategies involved acceptance—and other people. Many respondents were helped by the philosophy expressed in the "serenity prayer": "God grant me the serenity to accept things I cannot change, the courage to change those I can, and the wisdom to know the difference." These people would think about a problem and do everything they could to resolve it—but then would accept the situation, if necessary, and get on with their lives. Support and encouragement from family and friends also helped; when asked, most people said that others had helped them through bad times. Relatively few respondents had turned to a health worker; when they did, that person was 4 times more likely to be a personal physician than a mental health professional.

In a study of 836 older adults from two secular and three religiously oriented groups, morale was positively associated with three kinds of religious activity: *organized* (going to church or temple and taking part in the activities), *informal* (praying, reading the Bible), and *spiritual* (personal cognitive commitment to religious beliefs). The more religious people had higher morale and a better attitude toward aging and were more satisfied and less lonely. Women and people over 75 showed the strongest correlations between religion and well-being (Koenig, Kvale, & Ferrel, 1988).

Relatively little of the research on religion and spirituality has been done with racial/ethnic minorities. Among 3,050 older Mexican Americans, those who attended church once a week had 32 percent lower mortality risk than those who never attended. This was true even when sociodemographic characteristics, cardiovascular health, activities of daily living, cognitive functioning, physical functioning, social support, health behaviors, mental health, and perceived health were controlled (Hill, Angel, Ellison, & Angel, 2005).

Older African Americans tend to be more involved in religious activity than elderly white people, and black women tend to be more involved than black men (Coke & Twaite, 1995; Levin & Taylor, 1993; Levin, Taylor, & Chatters, 1994). For elderly black people, religion is closely related to life satisfaction and well-being (Coke, 1992; Coke & Twaite, 1995; Krause, 2004a; Walls & Zarit, 1991). A special factor is the belief held by many black people that the church helps sustain them in confronting racial injustice (Krause, 2004a). Elderly black people who feel supported by their church tend to report high levels of well-being; and the more religious older black people are, the more satisfaction they report with life (Coke, 1992; Walls & Zarit, 1991). For all ages and both sexes, the most common religious activity among black adults is personal prayer (Chatters & Taylor, 1989).

Since almost all research on religion in the lives of older Americans has been cross-sectional, it is possible that turning toward religion in old age is a cohort effect rather than a result of aging. It is also likely, however, that as people think about the meaning of their lives and about death as the inevitable end, they may focus more on spiritual matters.

"SUCCESSFUL AGING"

> "Successful aging"—what the heck does that mean? . . . Is our society so achievement-oriented that it is now possible to fail at growing old? By encouraging the definition of a right and a wrong way to age, you are discouraging attempts to treat ourselves with kindness. (King, 1993, p. 14)

CRITICAL THINKING

What areas would you include in your definition of "Successful aging"?

This letter to a magazine from an indignant reader challenges a concept that gerontologists have been studying and arguing about for nearly half a century. Are some adaptations to aging more successful—psychologically healthier—than others? Is "successful aging" the same for everyone? Or is the only relevant definition a personal one?

The concept of *successful*, or *optimal aging*—in contrast to the older idea that aging results from inevitable, intrinsic processes of loss and decline—represents a major change in focus in gerontology in response to the growing number of active, healthy older adults.* Given that modifiable factors play a part in rates of aging, it follows, according to the "new" gerontology, that some people may age more successfully than others (Rowe & Kahn, 1998).

A considerable body of work supported by the MacArthur Foundation Research Network on Successful Aging (Rowe & Kahn, 1998) has identified three main components of successful aging: (1) avoidance of disease or disease-related disability, (2) maintenance of high physical and cognitive functioning, and (3) sustained, active engagement in social and productive activities (activities, paid or unpaid, that create social value). Successful agers tend to have social support, both emotional and material, which aids mental health; and as long as they remain active and productive, they do not think of themselves as old.

Another approach is to examine subjective experience: to what degree individuals attain their goals and how satisfied they are with their lives. One model, for example, emphasizes the amount of control people retain over various aspects of their lives (Schulz & Heckhausen, 1996). In one study, people reported greater feelings of control over their work, finances, and marriages as they aged, but less control over their sex lives and relationships with children (Lachman & Weaver, 1998). Another study found that people tend to live longer if they have a sense of control over the role (such as spouse, parent, provider, or friend) that is most important to them (Krause & Shaw, 2000).

All definitions of *successful*, or *optimal, aging* are value-laden—unavoidably so. These terms, critics say, may burden, rather than liberate, older people by putting pressure on them to meet standards they cannot or do not wish to meet (Holstein & Minkler, 2003). The concept of successful aging, according to these critics, does not pay enough attention to the constraints that may limit lifestyle choices. Not all adults have the good genes, education, and favorable circumstances to "construct the kind of life they choose" (p. 792),

---

*Unless otherwise noted, this discussion is based on Papalia, Olds, & Feldman (2007).

and the "already marginalized" are most likely to "come up on the wrong side of . . . the either-or divide" (p. 791). An unintended result of labeling older adults as successful or unsuccessful may be to "blame the victims" and drive them to self-defeating "anti-aging" strategies. It also tends to demean old age itself and to deny the importance of accepting, or adapting to, what cannot be changed.

Keeping these concerns in mind, let's look at some classic and current theories and research about aging well.

Normative Models

For normative theorists, adults age successfully when they complete the normal psychological tasks of each period of life in an emotionally healthy way. Erikson saw the critical tasks of middle and late adulthood as generativity and integration. Jung and Levinson spoke of a need to balance the masculine and feminine sides of one's nature and to turn from striving for worldly success to explore the inner life. Three classic models focus specifically on adaptation to aging.

PECK: PERSONALITY ADJUSTMENTS OF MIDDLE
AND LATE ADULTHOOD

One of the earliest attempts to specify factors in successful aging was that of Robert Peck (1955). Expanding on Erikson's concepts, Peck identified seven psychological developments he saw as necessary to healthful adaptation to aging: four in middle age and three in old age.

Peck's critical adjustments of middle age represent a shift from physical prowess to mental and emotional flexibility. None of these developments need wait until middle age; but according to Peck, if they do not take place by middle age, successful adjustment is doubtful.

- *Valuing wisdom versus valuing physical powers. Wisdom,* defined as the ability to make the best choices in life, depends on a broad range of life experience and more than makes up for diminished strength and stamina and the loss of youthful appearance.
- *Socializing versus sexualizing in human relationships.* People come to value the men and women in their lives as unique individuals, as friends, and as companions rather than primarily as sex objects.
- *Emotional flexibility versus emotional impoverishment.* As children grow up and become independent, and as parents, spouses, and friends die, the ability to shift emotional investment from one person to another and from one activity to another becomes crucial.
- *Mental flexibility versus mental rigidity.* By midlife, many people have worked out a set of answers to life's important questions. But unless they continue to seek new answers, they can become set in their ways and closed to new ideas.

Peck's necessary adjustments of late life allow people to move beyond concerns with work, physical well-being, and mere existence to a broader understanding of the self and of life's purpose.

- *Broader self-definition versus preoccupation with work roles.* As retirement approaches, people who have defined themselves by their work need to redefine their worth and give new structure and direction to their lives by exploring other interests and taking pride in personal attributes.
- *Transcendence of the body versus preoccupation with the body.* As physical abilities decline, people adjust better if they focus on relationships and activities that do not demand perfect health. Throughout life, adults need to cultivate mental and social powers that can grow with age.
- *Transcendence of the ego versus preoccupation with the ego.* Probably the hardest, and possibly the most crucial, adjustment for older people is to move beyond concern with themselves and their present lives to acceptance of the certainty of death. They need to recognize the lasting significance they have achieved through what they have done—children they have raised, contributions they have made to society, and personal relationships they have forged. Rather than becoming preoccupied with their own needs, they can continue to contribute to the well-being of others.

DISENGAGEMENT THEORY VERSUS ACTIVITY THEORY

Which is a healthier, or more adaptive, adjustment to aging: tranquilly watching the world go by from a rocking chair or keeping busy from morning till night? Two contrasting models have been proposed: disengagement theory and activity theory. According to **disengagement theory,** aging normally brings a gradual reduction in social involvement and greater preoccupation with the self. According to **activity theory,** the more active people remain, the better they age.

Disengagement theory was one of the first influential theories in gerontology. Its proponents (Cumming & Henry, 1961) argued that disengagement is a universal condition of aging—that declining physical functioning results in an inevitable, gradual withdrawal from social roles, ultimately leading to death. More than three decades later, there have been few independent empirical findings to support disengagement theory, and it has "largely disappeared from the empirical literature" (Achenbaum & Bengtson, 1994, p. 756). It is now viewed as fundamentally flawed. David Gutmann (1974, 1977, 1992), for example, has argued that "disengagement" in traditional cultures, such as Druze society (see Box 11.3 in Chapter 11), is only a transition between the roles of middle age and late adulthood, and that true disengagement occurs only in societies in which elderly people are left without established roles appropriate to their stage of life.

Activity theory arose as an alternative to disengagement theory. Bernice Neugarten and her associates (Neugarten, Havighurst, & Tobin, 1968), found that individuals whose social roles reflected high levels of activity had high life satisfaction. Individuals who had social roles reflecting disengagement also had high life satisfaction. According to activity theory, continued activity is crucial to successful aging. An adult's roles (worker, spouse, parent, and so on) are seen as the major source of satisfaction; the greater the loss of roles through retirement, widowhood, distance from children, or infirmity, the less satisfied a person will be. People who are aging successfully keep up as many activities as possible and find substitutes for lost roles.

When Neugarten and her associates looked at aging adults' personalities, activity, and satisfaction with life (Neugarten et al., 1968), they found four major styles of aging. (1) *Integrated* people were functioning well, with a complex inner life, intact cognitive abilities, and a high level of satisfaction. (Individuals with social roles high in levels of activity and disengaged individuals were both in this category.) (2) *Armor-defended* people were achievement-oriented, striving, and tightly controlled. (3) *Passive-dependent* people were apathetic or sought comfort from others. (4) *Unintegrated* people were disorganized, had little control over their emotions, showed poor cognitive and psychological functioning, and had problems coping. This research indicates that there are a number of social roles that can lead to life satisfaction.

Other studies found that activity in and of itself bears little relationship to satisfaction with life (Lemon, Bengtson, & Peterson, 1972). Later studies suggested that the *kind* of activity matters: informal activities with friends and family are more satisfying than formal, structured, group activities or solitary activities such as reading, watching television, and hobbies (Longino & Kart, 1982). But a subsequent analysis indicated that people's attitude about life is affected only slightly, if at all, by *any* kind of activity (Okun, Stick, Haring, & Witter, 1984). Further, an analysis of the effect of activity on mortality among 508 older Mexican Americans and "Anglos" over an 8-year period found that whether people died earlier or later was totally unrelated to how active they had been once other factors such as age, health, and gender were taken into account (Lee & Markides, 1990). Thus although activity theory has not, so far, been discarded (Marshall, 1994), some gerontologists have come to view it as simplistic.

Balance Models

According to normative models, people adapt to aging through a series of typical personality changes. But aging, particularly in developed societies, has lost some of its normative character, in part because of advances in health and fitness and wide variations in whether and when people retire. Two recent models emphasize interaction between individual and environment, suggesting that "successful aging" is a balance between stability and change, and that the right balance may not be the same for everyone.

ATCHLEY: CONTINUITY THEORY

According to **continuity theory**, which has been proposed by the gerontologist Robert Atchley (1989), people who age successfully are able to maintain some continuity, or connection with the past, in both internal and external structures of their lives. *Internal structures* include knowledge, self-esteem, and a sense of personal history, or what Erikson called "ego integrity." *External structures* include roles, relationships, activities, and sources of social support, as well as the physical environment.

It is normal, Atchley suggests, for aging adults to seek a satisfactory balance between continuity and change in their life structures. Too much change makes life too unpredictable; too little change makes life too dull. Thus although some change is both desirable and inevitable, there is an internal drive for consistency: a need to avoid a total break with the past. This drive is socially reinforced, since others tend to expect a person to think and act about the same as always.

"Successful aging," then, may mean different things to different people. In this view, activity is important not for its own sake, but to the extent that it represents a continuation of a person's lifestyle. For older adults who always have been active and involved in social roles, it may be important to continue a high level of activity. Others, who have been less active in the past, may be happier in the proverbial rocking chair. This idea gains support from research (reported in Chapter 8) showing that many retired people are happiest pursuing work or leisure activities similar to those they have enjoyed in the past.

When aging brings physical or cognitive changes, it may be hard to maintain continuity in the external environment. An older adult may become dependent on caregivers and may have to make new living arrangements. Successful adaptation may depend on support from family, friends, or social institutions to help compensate for losses and to minimize discontinuity. This idea is in line with the growing trend in many countries to try to keep older adults out of institutions and in the community, and to help them live as independently as possible (see Chapter 10).

Continuity theory may help explain findings that—contrary to widespread belief—homosexuals tend to adapt to aging with relative ease. It has been suggested that, since they have generally had practice in dealing with one kind of stigma, they may be better prepared to cope with another—the stigma of aging. And their sexual orientation may make them comfortable with flexible, androgynous roles (Berger & Kelly, 1986). Thus, shocks of aging may be cushioned by continuity in certain areas. Homosexuals who are best adjusted in the later years—most satisfied with their lives, least self-critical, and least prone to psychosomatic problems—are highly satisfied with their sexual orientation; they tend to have gone through a period of sexual experimentation earlier in life, which may have helped them adjust to the implications of being homosexual (Adelman, 1991).

WHITBOURNE: IDENTITY STYLES AND ADAPTATIONS TO AGING

According to Whitbourne's (1987; Whitbourne & Primus, 1996) model of personality development (introduced in Chapter 11), people cope with aging much as they have coped with earlier challenges. Physical, mental, and emotional changes associated with aging can be unsettling to the self-concept and must be assimilated, accommodated, or both. Identity style—how a person generally strikes a balance between assimilation (continuity) and accommodation (change)—is likely to determine how someone adapts to aging.

Both assimilation and accommodation have benefits and costs. People whose style is predominantly assimilative are likely to maintain a youthful, positive self-image and to deny any negative changes. They may deplete their psychological energy trying to keep up this optimistic outlook and may fail to take measures that might help compensate for losses. People whose style is predominantly accommodative are likely to see themselves—perhaps prematurely—as old. Although more secure in their definition of themselves, they may become overly preoccupied with symptoms of aging and disease. People with a more evenly balanced identity style may be able to make a more realistic adjustment. They can take steps to control what can be controlled and strive to accept what cannot.

Currently, in line with the growing recognition of both stability and change in personality throughout the adult life span, balance models—particularly continuity theory—are attracting more interest than the older normative models. It will be interesting to see whether these newer models can develop a stronger research base. Ultimately, theories of "successful aging" must stand or fall on how accurately they can describe "normal" behavior in late life. It may be, however, that no grand, universal theory can be devised to describe normal aging—that "successful aging" may be different for each society, each successive cohort, or even each individual.

Laypeople's Views About Successful Aging

How would *you* define "successful aging"? One researcher (Ryff, 1989) asked a group of middle-aged and older adults. Unlike theorists who emphasize self-oriented factors, such as self-knowledge and self-acceptance, participants in both age groups defined "successful aging" mostly in terms of relationships: caring about and getting along with others.

However, differences between the two age groups showed up when they were asked what they were unhappy about and what they would change if they could. Middle-aged people were most unhappy about family problems. They wished they could change some aspect of themselves or accomplish more in schooling or careers. Older people most commonly said that they were unhappy about nothing and would change nothing except health. The fact that middle-aged people emphasized continued growth and older people emphasized acceptance is reminiscent of Erikson and Peck, and suggests that "successful aging" may take on a different meaning near the end of life.

Unfortunately, not everyone at any age copes successfully with the many stresses of living. In the next section we'll deal with destructive behavior patterns. We'll conclude the chapter with a look at mental health in late life: how satisfied older adults are with their lives; mental disorders that sometimes occur; and inner strengths developed in the course of living that can be unique resources for coping with aging.

Destructive Behavior Patterns

When Nicole Simpson called the police in a frantic attempt to get her husband, O. J. Simpson, to stop beating her, the football hero told the officers to go home; he said it was just a private matter. But destructive behavior—whether directed at oneself or at others—is not just a private matter. People who abuse alcohol or drugs not only hurt themselves and those around them but often do irreparable damage to their children. People who abuse domestic partners or children do harm that can have long-lasting repercussions, even for future generations, since victims of abuse often become abusers themselves. And people who abuse the aged and infirm contribute to a climate in which everyone's safety and dignity are imperiled.

Substance Use Disorders

Elvis Presley, Janis Joplin, John Belushi, River Phoenix—there is a long list of celebrities who have succumbed to substance use disorders. **Substance abuse** means harmful use of alcohol or other drugs. It is defined as a maladaptive behavior pattern, consisting of one or more of the following criteria occurring in a 12-month period: failure to fulfill major role obligations, using the substance in hazardous situations, legal problems related to use of the substance, or social/interpersonal problems (DSM-IV). Abuse can lead to **substance dependence,** or addiction, which may be physiological, psychological, or both. A person who meets three of the following criteria is considered dependent: increased tolerance (needing more of the substance to achieve the same effect); experiencing withdrawal symptoms when taken off the substance; taking more of the substance, or for a longer time, than intended; wanting but being unable to cut down or control its use; spending a great deal of time and effort to obtain the substance or to recover from its effects; giving up or reducing important social, occupational, or recreational activities because of use of the substance; continuing to use it even though it is causing or worsening persistent or recurrent physical or psychological problems (APA, 1994). Substance use disorders tend to run in families and may result from a combination of genetic factors, vulnerable personality, and environmental influences (Irons, 1994).

The extent of substance problems among older adults is often underestimated. Since many older people live alone or have limited social contacts, a problem may go undetected. Family members sometimes ignore or cover up evidence of substance abuse. Even in hospitals, substance disorders in this age group are often unrecognized, unreported, or not referred for treatment, perhaps because of a mistaken notion that these are not problems of the elderly or that not much can be done about them (Atkinson, Ganzini, & Bernstein, 1992). Table 12.2 shows factors that increase the risk of substance abuse in an older adult.

CRITICAL THINKING

What destructive behavior patterns do you observe in our society, your peer group, and yourself? What would you recommend we do to reduce or eliminate these destructive patterns?

CRITICAL THINKING

Consider the people you know who abuse substances. Do genetic factors, personality, or environmental influences seem to act in concert or does one factor dominate over others? What individual differences are apparent?

TABLE 12.2

Factors Increasing Risk of Substance Abuse in Older Adults

Demographic Factors
    Male gender (alcohol, illicit substances)
    Female gender (sedative-hypnotics)

Substance-Related Factors
    Prior substance abuse
    Family history (alcohol)

Increased Biological Sensitivity
    Drug sensitivity
    Medical illnesses associated with aging
        Cognitive loss
        Cardiovascular disease
        Metabolic disorders

Medically Induced Factors
    Prescription-drug dependence
    Drug-drug and alcohol-drug interactions
    Caregiver overuse of *as needed* medication
    Physician advice or permission to use alcohol

Psychosocial Factors
    Loss and other major stresses
    Discretionary time, money
    Social isolation
    Family collusion

Psychiatric Factors
    Depression
    Dementia
    Subjective symptoms of chronic illness

SOURCE: Adapted from Atkinson et al., 1992, p. 520.

COHORT EFFECTS

Imagine what would happen if marijuana, cocaine, and heroin were legalized in the United States tomorrow, as they have already been in some countries. Almost overnight, you would begin to see advertisements for these products, and they would soon become readily available in many stores. If this happened, would your attitude toward the use of such drugs change? Would your children's attitudes be different from yours if they grew up in a society in which these drugs were legal?

One drug, alcohol, was illegal for a time in the United States but then was legalized again. Most readers of this text cannot remember a time when there were, for instance, no beer commercials, but many older adults can. People who grew up between 1920 and 1933, when it was illegal to sell or distribute alcohol (though the prohibition was widely disobeyed), may well have different attitudes toward drinking from younger age groups.

Use or abuse of specific substances has less to do with age than with cohort and context; and habits and attitudes are usually set by early adulthood (Atkinson et al., 1992). Middle-aged adults who grew up in the 1960s, when adolescents' use of marijuana and other illegal drugs was at its peak, are far more likely to use those drugs today than their parents were at the same time of life (SAMHSA, 2001). In one longitudinal study, when more than 1,000 high school sophomores and juniors were interviewed again at age 24 or 25, most of those who had begun using a certain drug in their teens were still using it (Kandel, Davies, Karus, & Yamaguchi, 1986).

As baby boomers age, the need for substance abuse treatment in older adults is likely to increase. Gfroerer, Penne, Pemberton, and Folsom (2003) predict that by 2020 the number of people over the age of 50 needing substance abuse treatment will increase from 1.7 million to 4.4 million. Baby boomers are more likely to use illicit drugs (including nonmedical use of prescription drugs) than previous generations—56 percent have used an illicit drug in their lifetime, compared to 26 percent of previous generations (SAMHSA, 2002). They also began using drugs early in life, which is associated with increased substance abuse and dependence later in life. In addition to higher rates of illicit drugs, baby boomers also have higher rates of heavy alcohol use than previous generations, with alcohol accounting for 74 percent of admissions to treatment centers in those 55 and over (SAMHSA, 2004).

ALCOHOL ABUSE AND DEPENDENCE

Alcoholism has been called the "major mental health problem of the century" (Horton & Fogelman, 1991, p. 302). Though it has seen a reduction in recent years due to education and awareness programs, 11 million Americans still abuse alcohol or are dependent on alcohol (SAMHSA, 2002). It has been estimated that 50 percent of homicides (CDC, 2004) and 40 percent of all rapes and automobile accidents involve alcohol (SAMHSA, 2005). Alcohol abuse is especially a male problem; it is the most commonly diagnosed mental illness among men age 18 to 64 and third most common among men age 65 and older, after affective disorders and other kinds of substance abuse (B. S. Grant, personal communication, July 6, 1995; Horton & Fogelman, 1991). Alcoholism is the leading mental health problem among Native Americans (Stanford & Du Bois, 1992).

Although older adults are less likely to abuse alcohol than other age groups, the most common substance problems in this age group involve alcohol. Older adults are more likely to abuse alcohol than other drugs, especially illegal drugs (Kopera-Frye, Wiscott, & Sterns, 1999). Some data suggest that about 1 in 10 older persons living in the community and 1 in 5 living in nursing homes are alcoholic (Horton & Fogelman, 1991). Other estimates for the institutionalized elderly range as high as 60 percent, though there are no studies on actual rates of alcohol abuse in long-term care (Lichtenberg, 1994). Older men are 2 to 6 times likelier than older women to have documented alcohol problems. Two clinical studies suggest that alcoholism may be more prevalent among older African Americans than among other racial or ethnic groups (Blum & Rosner, 1983; McCusker, Cherubin, & Zimberg, 1971).

Two-thirds of elderly alcoholics began drinking before or during their early twenties and typically showed a lifelong pattern of addictive behavior. However, some started drinking heavily after age 50, generally in response to stressors such as bereavement, retirement, loneliness, physical illness, or pain. Contrary to a common misconception, elderly alcoholics in both categories respond well to treatment (Horton & Fogelman, 1991; Lichtenberg, 1994)—sometimes even better than younger alcoholics (Atkinson et al., 1992). Table 12.3

TABLE 12.3

Common Beliefs About Alcohol Problems

Belief	True or False, and Why
"It is easier to detect an alcohol problem in an older adult than in a younger one."	*False.* Alcohol abuse in later life is often hidden and consequently overlooked. Older people's drinking isn't as likely to be detected through problems at work or arrests for drunk driving, and many drink only in private.
"Medications usually reduce effects of alcohol in older people."	*False.* Medications intensify alcohol's effects, thereby intensifying its dangers.
"Women with alcohol problems tend to be more secretive about their drinking than men."	*True.* Society places a greater stigma on women who abuse alcohol than on men, so women may hide their drinking more and feel greater shame and guilt.
"In older people, the central nervous system is very sensitive to the depressant effect of alcohol."	*True.* The central nervous system is quite sensitive to alcohol, and its effects may be mistaken for dementia.
"Signs of alcohol problems in older persons are easy to detect."	*False.* Alcohol dependence can resemble many medical conditions, and medical problems can mask alcohol dependence.
"Older adults are more likely than younger ones to admit to having an alcohol problem."	*False.* An alcohol problem is often a strong moral issue for older adults, and denial may be stronger in this group.
"Alcohol problems in later life increase the chance of suicide."	*True.* Risk of suicide is very high for older white males with a history of alcohol abuse who live alone.
"Alcohol is a stimulant and makes older persons feel younger and more energetic."	*False.* Alcohol is a depressant and impairs thinking, memory, judgment, and coordination.
"A person must want to stop drinking before he or she can be helped to stop."	*False.* Alcoholics usually cannot recognize the severity of their problem, but many can be persuaded to seek treatment.
"The same amount of alcohol has a greater effect on older adults than on younger ones."	*True.* Alcohol is metabolized and excreted more slowly in older adults, resulting in higher blood alcohol levels and more rapid intoxication.

SOURCE: Adapted from Pratt, Wilson, Benthin, & Schmall, 1992.

deals with other common beliefs and mistaken beliefs about alcohol problems, particularly in later life.

Alcohol is likely to become a more serious problem for older adults in the future (Kopera-Frye, Wiscott, & Sterns, 1999). Although cross-sectional research shows less alcohol use among older adults than among younger adults, this may well be a cohort effect limited to the generation that lived through Prohibition. Two large longitudinal studies (Dufour, Colliver, Stinson, & Grigson, 1988; Glynn, Bouchard, LoCastro, & Laird, 1985) found no change in use of alcohol for any age group. Thus future generations of older adults are likely to maintain their current higher levels of alcohol consumption.

Substance addiction is not just an individual problem. It can affect a whole family, and it is often associated with domestic violence and family conflict (Irons, 1994).

Intimate Partner Violence

The cases of Nicole Simpson's murder and of Lorena Bobbitt, who cut off her husband's penis with a kitchen knife after four years of alleged sexual and physical abuse, have focused public attention on intimate partner violence—violence against a spouse, former spouse or an intimate partner. **Intimate partner violence (IPV)** includes physical violence (intentional use of physical force with the potential for causing death, disability, injury or harm), sexual violence (use of physical force to compel a person to engage in a sexual act against his or her will, a sex act with someone who is unable to consent, or any abusive sexual contact), threats of physical or sexual violence (use of words, gestures or weapons to communicate intent), psychological or emotional abuse (trauma to the victim caused by acts, threats, or coercive tactics), and stalking (repeated behavior that leads victims to feel a high level of fear) (CDC, 2004).

According to the National Crime Victimization Survey, there are about one million incidences of IPV each year, and only about half of them get reported. Such violence generally occurs in private, and victims often do not report it because they are ashamed or afraid of reprisal. There were about 1,830 deaths from IPV in 1998 and 1,300 were women. The most likely victims of IPV are women who are young (ages 18–24), poor, uneducated, black, and divorced or separated (U.S. Bureau of Justice Statistics, 1994; CDC, 2006b).

IPV occurs in both heterosexual and same-sex couples. Although rates of IPV against women have decreased 21 percent since 1993, women are still the victims in 85 percent of cases. About half of these women sustain physical injury, and 4 in 10 of the victims receive medical treatment (CDC, 2006b).

Abuse typically begins with shoving or slapping and then escalates into beatings that leave some women living in terror, some critically injured, and some dead. In cases of homicide by an intimate partner, 44 percent of the victims had an emergency room visit related to abuse within the two years prior to her death (Crandall, 2004). Ninety-one percent of victims of attempted or completed murder by an intimate partner had reported being stalked within the previous year (Aldridge & Brown, 2003).

ABUSERS AND VICTIMS

Men who abuse women tend to be social isolates, to have low self-esteem, to be sexually inadequate, to be inordinately jealous, to minimize or deny the frequency and intensity of their violence, and to blame the woman (Bernard & Bernard, 1984; Bouza, 1990). Wife battering is most frequent in marriages with a dominant husband and least frequent in egalitarian marriages. It is fairly frequent in marriages with a dominant wife; a frustrated husband may see hitting his wife as the only way to exert power over her (Yllo, 1984).

©Stephen Agricola/Stock Boston

Shelters where battered women can go for refuge and counseling are one response to the problem of domestic violence.

Why do women stay with men who abuse them? Some have low self-esteem and feel that they deserve to be beaten. Also, victims of aggression often minimize its importance. They may attribute it to alcohol, frustration, and stress. They may interpret it as a sign of love or of masculinity and may deny that their mates really mean to hurt them. As many as one-fourth of women and one-third of men with aggressive spouses do not consider themselves unhappily married (O'Leary et al., 1989). Financially dependent wives are especially vulnerable; battered wives who return to their husbands are usually not employed and feel they have nowhere else to go (Kalmuss & Straus, 1982; Strube & Barbour, 1984). Some women are afraid to leave. Constant ridicule, criticism, threats, punishment, and psychological manipulation can undermine their self-confidence (NOW Legal Defense and Education Fund & Chernow-O'Leary, 1987). Also, their abusers isolate them from family and friends. If they try to end the relationship or call the police, they simply get more abuse (Geller, 1992).

Rates of IPV are highest among African Americans, and this group is also most likely to engage in mutual partner violence (both partners are violent toward each other). Researchers suggest this may occur because African American women have historically contributed significantly to the financial well-being of the household, which may make them "less likely to tolerate relationships with violent partners without retaliating or engaging in defensive violence" (Field & Caetano, 2004).

Cultural norms and expectations may explain why South Asian and Hispanic women are less likely to report IPV or use services such as women's shelters, counseling, and courts to get out of a violent situation. Gender roles of being a good wife and mother and strong feelings of loyalty, identification, and attachment to the family may prevent them from seeking help. South Asian women also cite the strong stigma associated with divorce in their culture, as well as the fear of appearing too "westernized" as reasons for not leaving a violent relationship. Cultural values of respect, family honor, and family solidarity are influential in Hispanic women's decision whether to report IPV or leave the relationship (Yoshioka, Gilbert, El-Bassel, & Baig-Amin, 2003).

The U.S. Violence Against Women Act, adopted in 1994, provides for tougher law enforcement, funding for shelters, a national domestic violence hotline, and educating judges and court personnel, as well as young people, about domestic violence (Walker, 1999). Shelters need to offer expanded employment and educational opportunities for abused women who are economically dependent on their partners, and health providers need to question women about suspicious injuries and tell them about the physical and mental health risks of staying with abusive partners (Kaukinen, 2004).

Abusers who recognize their problem the first or second time it arises and seek help are most likely to change. Also, many of those who get court-ordered treatment can be taught to modify their behavior. Men who are arrested for family violence are less likely to continue to abuse their families, and an increasing number of communities are adopting this approach (Bouza, 1990; Sherman & Berk, 1984; Sherman & Cohn, 1989). However, some hard-core abusers see nothing wrong with what they do. They are the ones least amenable to rehabilitation and most likely to kill (Geller, 1992). The federal Violence Against Women Act, passed in 1994, provides for tougher law enforcement, funding for shelters, a national domestic violence hotline, and educating judges and court personnel, as well as young people, about domestic violence.

ABUSED OLDER WOMEN

When we think of wife beating, we may think of a young woman, often with children. Yet studies show that about 1.4 million American women age 45 to 64 and an estimated 500,000 women age 65 and older are abused by a husband or male partner (Older Women's League, 1994). In interviews with a random sample of 2,000 older adults in the Boston area, 58 percent of women who had been subjected to violence accused their spouses (Pillemer & Finkelhor, 1988).

Why do older men abuse their mates? Conflict that has gone on throughout a marriage may break out more virulently when something happens to upset the equilibrium. A retired man who feels a loss of manhood may try to reassert it by striking his wife; a man who was abusive to co-workers and subordinates may now turn on his wife as the only handy target (AARP, 1993). If a woman becomes infirm, her partner may crack under the stress of caregiving.

Special pressures tend to keep an older abused wife in an abusive relationship. These women's values and behavioral norms were shaped at a time when women were not encouraged to be independent and women's roles were vastly different. Abuse of any kind was not talked about or recognized, and societal expectations dictated that women should preserve the institutions of marriage and family and make it work. The economic and psychological jolt of leaving a home of many years and disrupting long-established relationships with friends, family, and neighbors can be formidable. A woman may feel that she has more to lose by leaving because she has invested so much in these relationships. Furthermore, older women may lack the education or skills necessary to get a job and support themselves (Rhodes & McKenzie, 1998).

Child Abuse and Neglect

Partner abuse and **child abuse**—maltreatment of a child involving physical injury—often go together. In half of all American families in which women are beaten, children are beaten too (NOW Legal Defense and Education Fund & Chernow-O'Leary, 1987).

Since its peak in 1993, the rate of reported child abuse and **neglect**—failure to meet a dependent's basic needs—in the United States has declined by about 20 percent. Still, state and local child protective services agencies investigated and confirmed some 896,000 cases in 2002, and the actual number was undoubtedly far higher (USDHHS, 2004).

Children are abused and neglected at all ages, but the highest rates of *deaths* from maltreatment (76 percent) are for ages 3 and younger (USDHHS, 2004; see Figure 6.2; refer back to the discussion of shaken baby syndrome in Box 4.2.) An estimated 1,400 U.S. children died of abuse or neglect in 2002— 38 percent from neglect, 30 percent from physical abuse, and 29 percent from more than one type of maltreatment (USDHHS, 2004).

In more than 8 out of 10 cases of physical abuse or neglect, the perpetrators are the child's parents, usually the mother (USDHHS, 2004). Maltreatment by parents is a symptom of extreme disturbance in child rearing, usually aggravated by other family problems, such as poverty, lack of education, alcoholism, depression, or antisocial behavior. A disproportionate number of abused and neglected children are in large, poor, or single-parent families, which tend to be under stress and to have trouble meeting children's needs (Sedlak & Broadhurst, 1996; USDHHS, 2004). Yet what pushes one parent over the edge, another may take in stride. Although most neglect cases occur in very poor families, most low-income parents do not neglect their children.

The likelihood that a child will be physically abused has little to do with the child's own characteristics and more to do with the household environment, according to a nationally representative longitudinal study of twins (Jaffee et al., 2004). Abuse may begin when a parent who is already anxious, depressed, or hostile tries to control a child physically but loses self-control and ends up shaking or beating the child (USDHHS, 1999). Parents who abuse children tend to have marital problems and to fight physically. Their households tend to be disorganized, and they experience more stressful events than other families (Reid et al., 1982; Sedlak & Broadhurst, 1996).

Parents who are neglectful distance themselves from their children. They may be critical or uncommunicative. Many of the mothers were neglected themselves as children and are depressed or feel hopeless. Many of the fathers have deserted them or do not give enough financial or emotional support. The family atmosphere tends to be chaotic, with people moving in and out (Dubowitz, 1999).

Child abuse and neglect often occur in the same families. Such families tend to have no one to turn to in times of stress and no one to see what is happening (Dubowitz, 1999). Substance abuse is a factor in at least one-third of cases of abuse and neglect (USDHHS, 1999).

CRITICAL THINKING

What critical coping mechanisms and personal skills do abusers appear to be missing and nonabusers regularly implement?

Abuse may be followed by killing. According to the Department of Justice, parents were charged in 57 percent of murders of children under 12 years old in large urban areas in 1988; and in 8 out of 10 cases the parent had abused the child (Dawson & Langan, 1994). Sometimes a child's killer is the mother's boyfriend, and the mother fails to intervene or tries to cover up. Sometimes the woman is abused and is too intimidated to protect the child.

What makes one low-income neighborhood a place where children are highly likely to be maltreated and another, matched for ethnic population and income levels, safer? In one inner-city Chicago neighborhood, the proportion of children who died from maltreatment (1 death for every 2,541 children) was about twice the proportion in another inner-city neighborhood. In the high-abuse community, criminal activity was rampant, and facilities for community programs were dreary. In the low-abuse neighborhood, people described their community as a poor but decent place to live. They painted a picture of a neighborhood with robust social support networks, well-known community services, and strong political leadership. In a community like this, maltreatment is less likely to occur (Garbarino & Kostelny, 1993).

Two cultural factors associated with child abuse are societal violence and physical punishment of children. In countries where violent crime is infrequent and children are rarely spanked, such as Japan, China, and Tahiti, child abuse is rare (Celis, 1990). In the United States, homicide, domestic violence, and rape are common, and many states still permit corporal punishment in schools. According to a representative sampling, more than 9 out of 10 parents of preschoolers and about half of parents of school-age children report using physical punishment at home (Straus & Stewart, 1999).

Abuse of the Elderly

Consider the following scenario: a middle-aged woman drives up to a hospital emergency room in a middle-sized American city. She lifts a frail, elderly woman (who appears somewhat confused) out of the car and into a wheelchair, wheels her into the emergency room, and quietly walks out and drives away, leaving no identification (Barnhart, 1992). "Dumping" is one form of **elder abuse**—maltreatment or neglect of dependent older persons or violation of their personal rights.

Although an estimated 2.1 million incidents of elder abuse occur each year (American Psychological Association, 2005), only 1 in 14 cases comes to the attention of authorities (U.S. Department of Justice, 2001), mostly through physicians and other healthcare professionals. Contrary to popular belief, most elder abuse does not occur in institutions, where there are laws and regulations to prevent it. Elder abuse most often happens to frail and vulnerable elderly people living with spouses or adult children. In 90 percent of all cases the abuser is a family member, and in two-thirds of these cases is a spouse or adult child (Administration on Aging, 2005).

Neglect is the most common form of maltreatment (nearly 50 percent), followed by psychological abuse (about 35 percent), financial exploitation

(30 percent), and physical abuse (25 percent) (U.S. Department of Justice, 2001). Older women are more likely than men to be abused. Violence is especially likely to occur if the elder is suffering from dementia or depression, is otherwise mentally impaired, or has a physical disability or illness (American Psychological Association, 2005).

In the United States, the majority of reported victims of elder abuse are white. It is difficult to study elder abuse in minorities because people in various ethnic groups have different ideas as to what constitutes abuse or may, for cultural reasons, be less likely to complain about it or report it. In traditional Chinese and Japanese cultures, caring for elders is the responsibility of the family. As views on family and relationships change, younger generations are increasingly unwilling to assume this responsibility, and the concept of elder abuse has become a focus of study in recent years. In a study of older Chinese adults, verbal abuse was the most common type of abuse reported. Physical abuse and violation of personal rights were relatively rare (Chau-Wai Yan & So-Kum Tang, 2004). In a study of Japanese older adults, neglect was the most common type of abuse, and many cases involved a daughter-in-law who was responsible for the care of her husband's parents. Physical abuse was the second most common form of abuse, followed by psychological abuse (Shibusawa, Kodaka, Iwano, & Kaizu, 2005).

Elder abuse may arise from many situations: a history or continuation of violence in the relationship, a caregiver who tends to use violence to solve problems, caregiver stress, substance abuse, financial stress, lack of caregiving knowledge or skills, mental or emotional illness, or a caregiver who feels trapped and hopeless. More commonly, it occurs from a change in living situation. The addition of a dependent older adult to a household can be a great source of stress and, sometimes, a financial burden for families.

Elder abuse should be recognized as a type of domestic violence; both the abused and the abuser generally need treatment. Counseling can help families deal with personal and behavioral problems, as well as cope with stress. Social support and self-help groups may help victims acknowledge what is happening, recognize that they do not have to put up with mistreatment, and find out how to stop it or get away from it. Support groups for family members provide a way to discuss problems, share solutions, and relieve tension (American Psychological Association, 2005). Table 12.4 lists typical signs of various types of elder abuse.

Elder abuse should be recognized as a type of domestic violence. Both abused and abuser generally need treatment (Hooyman, Rathbone-McCuan, & Klingbeil, 1982; Pillemer & Finkelhor, 1988). Neglect by family caregivers is usually unintentional; many don't know how to give proper care or are in poor health themselves. Most physical abuse can be quickly resolved by counseling and provision of needed services (AARP, 1993). Abusers need treatment to recognize what they are doing and assistance to reduce the stress of caregiving. Self-help groups may help victims acknowledge what is happening, recognize that they do not have to put up with mistreatment, and find out how to stop it or get away from it.

TABLE 12.4

Signs of Elder Abuse

Type of Abuse	Specific Indications
Physical abuse	Willful infliction of pain or injury Pushing, hitting, pinching Force-feeding Improper use of restraints Improper use of medication
Physical neglect	Failure of caregiver to provide necessities (such as food, drinks, eyeglasses, and hearing aids)
Psychological abuse	Causing mental anguish through berating, intimidating, or threats of punishment or isolation
Psychological neglect	Failure to provide social stimulation Prolonged isolation Ignoring or giving silent treatment
Financial or material abuse	Stealing money or possessions Coercing signature on contracts Illegal or improper use of an elder's funds, property, or assets
Financial or material neglect	Failure to use available funds and resources to sustain or restore health and well-being
Violating personal rights	Denying right to privacy Denying right to make own personal and health decisions Forcible eviction or forcible placement in nursing home
Sexual abuse	Infliction of nonconsensual sexual contact of any kind
Self-neglect	Behavior of an elderly person that threatens his or her own health or safety
Abandonment	Desertion of an elderly person by an individual who has physical custody or has assumed responsibility for providing care

SOURCE: Administration on Aging, 2005.

Mental Health in Late Life: A Lifespan Developmental Approach

Contrary to stereotype, decline in mental health is not typical in late life. Most older adults enjoy good mental health, but nearly 20 percent of those who are 55 and older experience mental disorders that are not part of normal aging (Older Adults and Mental Health: Issues and Opportunities, 2001). In fact, mental illness is less common among older adults than among younger adults. In the United States, fewer than 14 percent of older women and fewer than 11 percent of older men have any mental disorders (Wykle & Musil, 1993), though among older people admitted to nursing homes, an estimated 43 to 60 percent do (Gatz & Smyer, 1992).

Emphasis on the multidirectionality of change—growth as well as decline—is an important feature of the lifespan development perspective. Adults become more different than alike as they age, and mental status is no exception. Other features of the lifespan approach—recognition of the context of development and its multiple causes—apply to mental health as well.

Mental disorders often have a physical basis. A person who has trouble getting around because of arthritis may become depressed unless special efforts are made to maintain social contact. A person who loves crossword puzzles but can no longer write without pain may need to look for new sources of intellectual stimulation. A person who has had a heart attack may be afraid to resume sexual activity, and if this concern is not communicated and dealt with, it may strain the marital relationship and affect the mental health of both spouses.

Personality can also play a role. People high in a dimension called *neuroticism* (see Chapter 11) may be vulnerable to mental disorders in old age. Common personality developments that have been identified with aging, such as interiority and preoccupation with bodily changes, may lead to disturbance if carried to extremes. Where a person lives and with whom—the presence or absence of a spouse or some other intimate companion—can make a difference (Lebowitz & Niederehe, 1992).

Plasticity is another feature of the lifespan approach. Contrary to Freud's belief that older people's mental processes are too rigid and that they have too little time left to make therapy worthwhile (Whitbourne, 1989), gerontologists find that the aged can respond successfully to treatment.

Let's look first at the positive side of mental health, then at mental disorders in late life, and finally at a way of assessing strengths and resources of older adults.

> **CRITICAL THINKING**
>
> What are the barriers associated with providing mental health services to aging adults in late life? Should these services be a part of end-of-life treatment?

Mental Health and Life Satisfaction

Many factors, including physical health, psychological adjustment, socioeconomic status, life events, and social support, can affect an older person's mental health (Wykle & Musil, 1993). Similar factors have been identified as important in life satisfaction (Schulz, 1985). A sense of personal control is vital (Hooker & Kaus, 1994; Lachman, 1986).

CRITICAL THINKING

How would you characterize an older person who has good psychological health?

MULTIPLE DIMENSIONS OF WELL-BEING

Well-being has many facets, and different researchers have used different criteria to measure it, making it difficult to compare results. Carol Ryff and her colleagues (Keyes & Ryff, 1999; Ryff, 1995; Ryff & Singer, 1998), drawing on a range of theorists from Erikson to Maslow, have developed a multifaceted model that includes six dimensions of well-being and a self-report scale to measure them. The six dimensions are *self-acceptance, positive relations with others, autonomy, environmental mastery, purpose in life,* and *personal growth* (see Table 12.5). According to Ryff, psychologically healthy people have positive attitudes toward themselves and others. They make their own decisions and regulate their own behavior, and they choose or shape environments compatible with their needs. They have goals that make their lives meaningful, and they strive to explore and develop themselves as fully as possible.

A series of cross-sectional studies based on Ryff's scale show midlife to be a period of generally positive mental health (Ryff & Singer, 1998). Middle-aged people expressed greater well-being than older and younger adults in some areas but not in others. They were more autonomous than younger adults but somewhat less purposeful and less focused on personal growth—future-oriented dimensions that declined even more sharply in late adulthood. Environmental mastery, on the other hand, increased between middle and late adulthood. Self-acceptance was relatively stable for all age groups. Of course, since this research was cross-sectional, we do not know whether the differences were due to maturation, aging, or cohort factors.

The studies also looked at influences of gender and class. Overall, men's and women's well-being were quite similar, but women had more positive social relationships. Well-being was greater for men and women with more education and better jobs (Ryff & Singer, 1998).

Indeed, paid work—long seen as central to men's well-being—is today being recognized as an important source of well-being for women as well, providing a sense of independence and competence apart from family duties. Despite the potential for stress, many middle-aged women seem to flourish best in multiple roles (Antonucci & Akiyama, 1997; Barnett, 1997).

Mental Disorders

Contrary to common belief, mental health tends to improve with age. Only 6 percent of older Americans report frequent mental distress (Moore, Moir, & Patrick, 2004). However, mental and behavioral disrtubances that do occur in older adults can result in functional impairment in major life activities as well as in cognitive decline (van Hooren, et al., 2005).

Disease, important social losses, and long-standing personality characteristics seem to be more important than age per se in causing depression or,

TABLE 12.5

Dimensions of Well-Being Used in Ryff's Scale

Self-Acceptance

High scorer: possesses a positive attitude toward the self; acknowledges and accepts multiple aspects of self including good and bad qualities; feels positive about past life.

Low scorer: feels dissatisfied with self, is disappointed with what has occurred in past life; is troubled about certain personal qualities; wishes to be different [from] what he or she is.

Positive Relations with Others

High scorer: has warm, satisfying, trusting relationships with others; is concerned about the welfare of others; [is] capable of strong empathy, affection, and intimacy; understands give and take of human relationships.

Low scorer: has few close, trusting relationships with others; finds it difficult to be warm, open, and concerned about others; is isolated and frustrated in interpersonal relationships; [is] not willing to make compromises to sustain important ties with others.

Autonomy

High scorer: is self-determining and independent; [is] able to resist social pressures to think and act in certain ways; regulates behavior from within; evaluates self by personal standards.

Low scorer: is concerned about the expectations and evaluations of others; relies on judgments of others to make important decisions; conforms to social pressures to think and act in certain ways.

Environmental Mastery

High scorer: has a sense of mastery and competence in managing the environment; controls complex array of external activities; makes effective use of surrounding opportunities; [is] able to choose or create contexts suitable to personal needs and values.

Low scorer: has difficulty managing everyday affairs; feels unable to change or improve surrounding context; is unaware of surrounding opportunities; lacks sense of control over external world.

Purpose in Life

High scorer: has goals in life and a sense of directedness; feels there is meaning to present and past life; holds beliefs that give life purpose; has aims and objectives for living.

Low scorer: lacks a sense of meaning in life; has few goals or aims, lacks sense of direction; does not see purpose in past life; has no outlooks or beliefs that give life meaning.

Personal Growth

High scorer: has a feeling of continued development; sees self as growing and expanding; is open to new experiences; has sense of realizing his or her potential; sees improvement in self and behavior over time; is changing in ways that reflect more self-knowledge and effectiveness.

Low scorer: has a sense of personal stagnation; lacks sense of improvement or expansion over time; feels bored [with] and uninterested [in] life; feels unable to develop new attitudes or behaviors.

SOURCE: Adapted from Keyes & Ryff, 1999, Table 1, p. 163.

other, mental illness. There is a growing interest by mental health professionals concerning the need for the clinical assessment of the aged. *Psychopathology* in older adults has been defined as occurring when an old person contemporaneously expresses distress, disturbs others, is incompetent, and shows a change from his or her previous state, especially when this change is rapid and marked; when the causes of these events are seen to originate in the individual rather than in his or her circumstances; when the events are judged to be maladaptive; and when a treatment is available to slow down, or reverse, the progress of these events. This definition allows one to view the characteristics of psychopathology along a continuum (Smyer & Qualls, 1999).

Adaptation may be defined as the process of meeting an individual's biological, psychological, and social needs in a continuously changing environment. *Pathology* is the result of failure on the part of the individual to adapt to the demands to meet basic needs or attempt to meet basic needs in ways that are maladaptive (e.g., at the expense of pain) through suffering and disorder within the individual or the environment.

Emotional health in old age often involves successful adaptation to a number of life tasks. A major task is the adaptation to losses of the older adult period, which can include loss of spouse, loss of social relationships and social roles, loss of job and related associates, declines in income, mobility, physical health, and loss of opportunity for meaningful work and recognition. Financial resources, housing, health, and social involvement are all interrelated with emotional responses and capacities. A positive response would include the replacement of some of the losses with new relationships and new roles or the retraining of lost capacities. When necessary, older adults may have to learn to make do with less (Butler, Lewis, & Sunderland, 1998).

Many older people and their families mistakenly believe that they can do nothing about mental and behavioral problems. Actually, some 100 such conditions—including about 15 percent of dementia cases—can be cured or alleviated. The most common, besides drug intoxication, are depression, delirium, metabolic or infectious disorders, malnutrition, anemia, alcoholism, low thyroid functioning, emotional problems, and minor head injuries (National Institute on Aging, 1980, 1993; Wykle & Musil, 1993). But many older adults, especially those in minority groups and those who live in rural areas, do not get the help they need (Fellin & Powell, 1988; Roybal, 1988), whether because they do not realize their symptoms are treatable, because they are too proud or too fearful to admit they need help, or because they think they cannot afford it. Private treatment can be expensive; not every community offers low-cost mental health services, and not enough programs reach out to find those in need. Although it has been estimated that close to 8 percent of non-institutionalized older adults need psychiatric services, only about 5 percent get treatment from either mental health professionals or primary physicians (Burns & Taub, 1990).

Older people may be afflicted with the same mental illnesses that strike younger people, except that **schizophrenia**—loss of contact with reality, involving hallucinations, delusions, and other thought disturbances—rarely begins in old age (Butler, 1987b). Let's look more closely at three mental disorders popularly believed to be most common in late life: depression, dementia, and hypochondriasis.* As we'll see, this seems to be true only of dementia.

DEPRESSION

Art Buchwald is a Pulitzer prize-winning author whose humorous columns appear in some 550 newspapers; he has made millions of Americans laugh for four decades. In private life, however, Buchwald has struggled for years with depression so serious that twice he came close to suicide (Buchwald, 1994). Barbara Bush, the former First Lady, has told of a 6-month episode she experienced in 1976, when she fought off depression that had led her to thoughts of suicide (Bush, 1994).

Everyone feels "blue" at times; an occasional low mood does not necessarily signify clinical depression. A **major depressive episode,** the most severe form of clinical depression, is one that continues for at least 2 weeks, during which a person shows extreme sadness or loss of interest or pleasure in life, as well as at least four other symptoms, such as changes in weight or appetite; insomnia; agitation; fatigue; feelings of worthlessness or inappropriate guilt; inability to think, concentrate, or make decisions; and thoughts of death or suicide. The symptoms must not be due to drug abuse, medication, a medical condition, or recent bereavement and must cause significant distress or impairment in social, occupational, or other functioning (APA, 1994). Other forms of clinical depression are either severe but transient, or continuing or chronic but milder ("Depression," 1995).

About 15 to 17 percent of Americans, two-thirds of them women, have experienced some form of clinical depression, 9.5 percent within a given year (NIMH, 2003). Anywhere from 50 to 65 percent of depressed people—including a disproportionate number of older adults—go untreated, in part because of a mistaken belief that depression is a sign of weakness or that it will lift by itself. Actually, in 1 out of 5 cases depression becomes chronic, and it may indeed lead to suicide ("Depression," 1995; "Listening to Depression," 1995).

© Stan Levy/Photo Researchers

Depression in older adults may be underdiagnosed because physicians attribute the symptoms to physical illness or to aging, or because older people tend not to complain of feeling depressed. Men are less likely than women to see doctors or report health problems.

---

*Diagnostic criteria for all three conditions come from the American Psychiatric Association's *Diagnostic and Statistical Manual of Mental Disorders, Fourth Edition* (APA, 1994).

Diagnosing Depression in Older Adults   A common belief is that older people, because of their physical and emotional losses, are particularly subject to depression. Older adults do show more symptoms of mood disturbances than younger ones. But, surprisingly, they are less likely to be diagnosed as depressed (Gallo, Anthony, & Methuen, 1994; Katona, 2000). Only an estimated 2 to 3 percent of noninstitutionalized elderly people meet the diagnostic criteria for depression, though 8 to 15 percent have some symptoms. Some who do not meet the criteria for depression most likely have minor depression or subsyndromal depression, both of which can result in impaired functioning, similar to that of major depression (Hinrichsen & Dick-Sisken, 2000).

Research findings on age-related prevalence of depression are inconsistent. Some studies find increases in depression, others find decreases, and still others find no changes across the life span. Another explanation may be that "age related changes in the somatic and psychological components of depression" may cause younger and older adults to experience depression differently. Also, older adults may be less able to realize, remember, and report changes related to depression (Snowdon, 2001).

One reason that depression may be underdiagnosed in older adults is that doctors may attribute its symptoms to physical illness or consider them a normal part of the aging process. According to U.S. Department of Health and Human Services (1999), 8 to 20 percent of older adults have depression. Symptoms of depression often overlap with normal changes associated with aging, such as thoughts about dying, change in sex drive, change in sleep pattern, and decreased energy (Katona, 2000). Depression in older adults is most likely to be recognized by a doctor when a patient has more concrete symptoms, such as weight gain or loss (Pfaff & Almeida, 2004). Because depression accompanies such medical conditions as Parkinson's disease, stroke, thyroid disorder, and certain vitamin deficiencies, it may be hard to sort out which is which (Jefferson & Greist, 1993; Knight, 2004).

Standard diagnostic criteria may fail to detect some cases of depression in older adults. This may also be true of members of racial and ethnic minorities whose poverty would seem to put them at high risk of depression but who do not seem to become clinically depressed any more frequently than white people do (George, 1993; Stanford & Du Bois, 1992). Perhaps the simplest explanation, which is supported by a large-scale study in Baltimore and the Durham-Piedmont region of North Carolina, is that older adults are less likely than younger ones to *say* they feel depressed (Gallo et al., 1994), and their symptoms may be described as physical complaints (NIMH, 2005).

One indication that depression may be underdiagnosed in older adults is the prevalence of suicide in this age group. Suicide rates are high among older adults (see Figure 13.3 in Chapter 13), particularly among white men and people with chronic ailments (Wykle, Segal, & Nagley, 1992). In 1988, 21 percent of suicides in the United States were committed by older people, although older people are only 12.4 percent of the population (McIntosh, 1992). Physicians often fail to identify suicidal older patients, because an older person may complain of physical symptoms rather than mental distress and is also less likely to discuss suicidal ideation (Katona, 2000; Wykle & Musil, 1993; we discuss suicide in more detail in Chapter 13).

According to national and international epidemiological studies, older women are almost twice as likely as older men to be clinically depressed (Bebbington, 1990; Regier et al., 1988). But other sources suggest that rates of depression among women and men even out after age 65 (Barefoot, Helms, Mortensen, Avlund, & Schroll, 2001; Jefferson & Greist, 1993). An explanation for this discrepancy may be that women are more likely to see doctors and to report physical problems, which often accompany depression (Wykle & Musil, 1993).

Causes of Depression   Depression can have various causes, which may act together. Some people may be genetically predisposed to it through a biochemical imbalance in the brain. Failure to maintain a healthful lifestyle with adequate exercise can contribute to it. Stressful events or loneliness can trigger it (Jefferson & Greist, 1993; "Listening to Depression," 1995). Conservative estimates show that during the first year following the death of a spouse, 10–20 percent of widows or widowers suffer from clinical depression (Vierck & Hodges, 2003). Nearly half of all caregivers of Alzheimer's patients suffer from it ("Alzheimer's and Stress," 1994). A strong network of family and friends can help older people ward off depression or cope with it.

Depression can be a side effect of certain medications, such as tranquilizers, sedatives, sleeping pills, and drugs prescribed for high blood pressure, especially when accompanied by excessive drinking (Jefferson & Greist, 1993). An older person may take a dozen or more different medicines, some of them nonprescription ("over the counter"). Because physicians do not always ask what medications a patient is already taking, they may prescribe drugs that interact harmfully. And because of age-related changes in metabolism, a dosage that would be right for a 40-year-old may be an overdose for an 80-year-old.

Treatments for Depression   **Antidepressant drugs** can treat depression by restoring the chemical balance of neurotransmitters in the brain, but they can have some unwanted side effects, which are 2 to 3 times more likely to occur in older adults. Older adults generally respond well to antidepressants, though more slowly than younger adults (up to 12 weeks, compared to 3–6 weeks in younger adults). They also have higher rates of noncompliance and are more likely to relapse if not monitored carefully (Karel & Hinrichsen, 2000).

Electroconvulsive Therapy (ECT), also called shock therapy, may be necessary to treat severe depression. Because it works more quickly than antidepressant drugs, ECT is sometimes preferred when there is a high risk of suicide. It has fewer side effects than antidepressants, but the side effects that do occur tend to be more severe, such as increased confusion, greater risk of falls, and cardiovascular and respiratory problems (van der Wuff, Stek, Hoogendijk, & Beekman, 2003).

Psychotherapies have also been effective in treating older persons with depression. **Cognitive therapy** (teaching patients to recognize and correct negative thinking) and **behavioral therapy** (using positive and negative reinforcement) have been shown to be very effective when used together and can be used in older adults with minimal modifications. These therapies assume that people—regardless of age—can learn and change, and they require the patient to take an active role in treatment (Karel & Hinrichsen, 2000). **Interpersonal therapy** targets interpersonal problems that interfere with well-being. Treatment lasts for 16 weeks and focuses on 1 of 4 conflicts: unresolved grief, interpersonal disputes, role transitions, or interpersonal deficits. This type of therapy readily applies to older adults and is particularly effective in those with a coexisting medical illness (Hinrichsen, 1999). **Brief dynamic therapy** creates a genuine, nonmanipulative working alliance between therapist and client and stresses the differences between younger and older adults. Older adults differ from younger ones in maturational level, cohort, and social context. The therapist must be adept at identifying where the patient fits in these categories and adapting the treatment accordingly (Kivnick & Kavka, 1999). A promising, cost-effective intervention is **music therapy**: learning how to reduce stress by listening to music. A homebound person can learn the techniques with only a weekly visit or phone call from a therapist (Hanser & Thompson, 1994).

DEMENTIA

Dementia—development of multiple cognitive deficits including memory impairment—is not one illness but a dozen or more that have similar symptoms but different causes. Dementias may be due to one or a combination of medical conditions, most commonly Alzheimer's disease. Dementia may also be caused by other conditions, such as cardiovascular disease, Parkinson's disease, and substance abuse; but not all people who have those conditions develop dementia.

Dementia can come on gradually or suddenly. People with dementia lose their ability to learn new information, remember old information, or both. In addition, they become impaired in at least one of the following areas: speech and writing; motor activities; recognition of objects and people; and planning, executing, and monitoring their own behavior (usually a function of the frontal lobes). To constitute dementia, these impairments must be severe enough to cause problems at work, in daily activities, or in social relationships. People with dementia may have trouble packing a suitcase; show poor judgment (for example, they may drive in a blizzard); become violent or suicidal; stumble and fall frequently; make crude jokes, stop bathing, and disregard other social conventions; or accuse family members of stealing their belongings. Often, they are oblivious of their condition and make plans that are completely unrealistic, such as deciding to run for president.

Dementia is uncommon even in late life, but (except for dementia caused by HIV, the AIDS virus) it is more likely to occur in late life than at any other time. A large British study (Paykel et al., 1994) found that the rate of dementia doubles approximately every 5 years after age 75, from slightly more than 2 percent of people age 75 to 79 to about 8.5 percent at ages 85 to 89. Minimal dementia, which involves milder impairment, rises more steeply, from about 3 percent at age 75 to almost 30 percent after age 90.

In the past, dementia was defined by a progressive pattern of deterioration. Today, diagnosis is based simply on the presence of the deficits described above, whether or not they get worse. Whether dementia can be arrested or reversed depends on the underlying cause and also on the timeliness and effectiveness of treatment.

The most common form of dementia among older adults is *dementia of the Alzheimer's type* (described in Chapter 4). The onset of this progressive, degenerative dementia is gradual. The next most common form among older adults is *vascular dementia* (formerly called *multi-infarct dementia*), a syndrome in which the brain is damaged by a series of small strokes or any of a wide variety of other vascular diseases, including arteriosclerosis. Chronic abnormalities of blood pressure—both low and high—can lead to vascular dementia and to cognitive impairment. Estimates of mixed dementia (Alzheimer's and vascular dementia combined) vary widely, from 9 to 39 percent of all dementia cases, as it is difficult to diagnose (Gold, 2003).

Vascular dementia is thought to be more prevalent in men than in women. In this type of dementia, rapid changes are more common than a slow progression, and the pattern of deficits may depend on what areas of the brain are affected. As with other irreversible dementias, treatment is aimed at arresting or controlling the progress of the disease or ameliorating its symptoms. Treatment for vascular dementia usually focuses on controlling hypertension and taking other steps to reduce the risk of a massive stroke.

In recent years, attention has focused on dementia with Lewy bodies (DLB). Lewy bodies are deposits in the brain that contain damaged nerve cells. DLB accounts for 15–25 percent of dementia cases and frequently co-occurs with Parkinson's disease, depression, and Alzheimer's. It is difficult to diagnose, as many of the features overlap with other dementia disorders. DLB is characterized by visual hallucinations, fluctuation in cognitive performance, and Parkinsonian symptoms (most commonly bradykinesia and postural instability). Two of these symptoms are required for a diagnosis of DLB; in addition the cognitive deficits must be severe enough to interfere with normal social and occupational activity (Rampello et al., 2004).

Parkinson's disease is a slowly progressive neurological disorder characterized by tremor, stiffness, slowed movement, and unstable posture. Patients also experience difficulty with cognitive and memory functions, and many have depression (Riley, 1999). Anywhere from 20 to 60 percent of people with Parkinson's disease suffer from dementia. The physical symptoms of the disease can be treated with drugs designed to increase the level of the neurotransmitter dopamine or to slow its loss.

Education and large head size seem to be protective against dementia (Mortimer, Snowdon, & Markesbery, 2002), as is having a challenging job (Seidler et al., 2004). Cognitive impairment is more likely in people in poor physical health, especially those who have had strokes or diabetes (Tilvis et al., 2004). The risk of cognitive impairment may be lessened by walking or by other long-term, regular physical activity (Abbott et al., 2004; van Gelder et al., 2004; Weuve et al., 2004) and possibly by nutritional supplements (Manders et al., 2004). In one study, older women who drank moderate amounts of alcohol each day had a 40 percent lower risk of cognitive impairment or dementia (Espeland et al., 2005). A longitudinal study of 354 adults ages 50 and older found that people who had large social networks or had frequent social contact or could rely on emotional support from family or friends were less likely to show cognitive decline 12 years later (Holtzman et al., 2004).

Since victims of major depression often show cognitive losses, including memory lapses and difficulty in thinking and concentrating, it can be difficult—particularly in older persons—to pinpoint the cause as dementia, depression, or both (see Table 12.6). The standard term for cognitive impairment due to major depression is **pseudodementia** (APA, 1994). This type of depression may occur as a result of lack of stimulation from the environment, or from being physically or mentally inactive. Stress and physical problems are also known to contribute to pseudodementia (Weiss, 1999). Some researchers prefer to use the term *transitory dementia* (Emery & Oxman, 1994), since people who are treated for depression sometimes improve for a while and then regress. In some longitudinal studies, dementia associated with depression has evolved into degenerative, or irreversible, dementia. This suggests that real deterioration does occur in depressive dementia, though at present the factors associated with such a progression are not known.

TABLE 12.6

Features That Are Helpful in Differentiating Alzheimer's Disease from Dementia Syndrome of Depression

Measure	Alzheimer's Disease	Dementia Syndrome of Depression
Symptom duration at time of seeking medical attention	Long	Short
Previous psychiatric history	Unusual	Usual
Progression of symptoms	Slow	Rapid
Patient complaint of deficit	Variable	Abundant
Emotional reaction	Variable	Marked distress
Patient valuation of accomplishments	Variable	Minimized
Behavior congruent with cognitive deficits	Usual	Unusual
Delusions	Mood independent	Mood congruent
Mood disorder	Environmentally responsive	Persistent

SOURCE: From Kaszniak & Ditraglia Christenson, 1994.

HYPOCHONDRIASIS

People who complain of aches and pains that seem to have no medical basis are often dismissed as hypochondriacs. Many laypersons and even some physicians do not realize that **hypochondriasis** is a mental illness, defined as "preoccupation with fears of having, or the idea that one has, a serious disease based on a misinterpretation of one or more bodily signs or symptoms" (APA, 1994, p. 462). This belief continues even though the patient is reassured that his or her concern is medically unwarranted or exaggerated. To be diagnosed as hypochondriasis, the condition must have lasted for at least 6 months; must not be limited to concerns about appearance; and must cause significant problems in social life, occupation, or other aspects of everyday living—for example, causing the person to stay home from work or to stay away from family gatherings. Cultural factors may need to be taken into consideration; in some cultural groups a physician's reassurances may not carry as much weight as the opinion of a traditional nonmedical healer.

The common belief that older people are more likely to be hypochondriacs is mistaken. Hypochondriasis can start at any age, and in fact it is believed to begin most often in young adulthood. Because it is a chronic condition, it becomes in effect part of the personality structure. Thus older adults who show such a "trait" may simply be acting as they have acted for years. People who have had (or whose family members have had) serious illnesses, particularly as children, are more likely to become hypochondriacs. So are people who have experienced severe psychosocial stress, such as bereavement. In some cases hypochondriasis accompanies other mental disorders, particularly anxiety and depression (APA, 1994).

Assessing Strengths

> Instead of thinking about old age primarily in terms of compensating for deficits, we must learn . . . to think also in terms of maximizing human resources. And we must broaden our notion of elders' resources to include the vitality, the grit, the underlying commitment to values that constitute the infinite resources of the human spirit. (Kivnick, 1993, p.13)

A 92-year-old woman—a descendant of a slave—with near-crippling arthritis keeps her longtime clerical job and remains active in her church. Two middle-aged professional women keep up their morale and that of the 85-year-old mother-in-law they care for, who has lost her eyesight and has had to be moved from her southern farm community to their northern city. How can people like these do what they do? According to Helen Q. Kivnick (1993), who worked extensively with Erik Erikson, the answer lies in the dynamics and strength of the human spirit.

According to Kivnick, those who deal with this age group should not focus merely on remediating or compensating for mental health problems. Rather, older people should be helped to identify, use, and build on the unique strengths they have displayed during the course of their lives, not only for

Life Strengths Interview Guide

Stage 1: Trust versus mistrust
1. What is it in your life that gives you hope?
2. How do moral beliefs and values fit into your life?
3. What is it in your life that gives you a sense of security?

Stage 2: Autonomy versus shame and doubt
1. What parts of your life is it most important that you stay in charge of?
2. Do you get to use the phone, listen to the radio, watch TV, decorate, spend money as you wish?

Stage 3: Initiative versus guilt
1. What do you do for fun these days?
2. What have you done, in your life, which makes you the proudest?
3. What do you want to do, most of all, with the rest of your life?

Stage 4: Industry versus inferiority
1. What have you worked hard at?
2. What kinds of things have you always been good at?

Stage 5: Identity versus confusion
1. When people describe you, what do they say? What would you like them to say?
2. What is the image that you carry around inside, about who you are to the world?

Stage 6: Intimacy versus isolation
1. Whom do you count on these days? Who counts on you?
2. Who, in which relationships, has brought out the best in you?

Stage 7: Generativity versus self-absorption
1. How do you show your caring?
2. What is there about yourself and your life that you want to make sure people remember?

Stage 8: Integrity versus despair
1. What strategies have you used for coping with fear?
2. Are you afraid of dying? Do you know what you are afraid of?
3. What are your thoughts about your own death? How you'd like to die? Where you'd like to die? Who should be there with you?

NOTE: Questions are grouped under the stages of Erikson's theory of personality development to which they relate.
SOURCE: Adapted from Kivnick, 1993, pp. 18–19.

their own benefit but also as resources for society. On the basis of Erikson's theory of personality development, Kivnick has created a guide for assessing "life strengths" of older adults. This guide can be used by care managers or family members in talking with older people about their needs and desires. It can also help older people reflect on their own situation and help younger people anticipate and prepare for old age.

The suggested questions are designed to discover individual strengths that have evolved out of Erikson's eight "crises," or stages of life. Table 12.7 offers a sampling of questions addressing issues of each stage. Three fundamental questions underlie all the others: *What is it about your life that is most worth living for? What makes you feel most alive? What makes you feel most like yourself?* As you read the questions, think about how you would answer them today. Do you think you are likely to answer them in the same way when you grow older? How would your parents and grandparents have answered these questions? (If you don't know, and if they are still alive, why not ask them?)

Many younger adults (and some older ones) may never have truly addressed the last group of questions—questions about their attitude toward their own death. This is, to a large extent, a reflection of the way American society deals with (or, more typically, refuses to deal with) death and dying. Yet living and dying are intertwined, and confronting death is a critical issue for mental health in adulthood. In Chapter 13, we discuss death and bereavement, and how people in various cultures cope with these inevitable events.

SUMMARY AND KEY TERMS

- Mental health can be defined in terms of self-concept, self-development, and satisfaction with life.
- Almost half of American adults have had a mental disorder, most commonly major depression.
- Young adults are more susceptible to emotional illness, anxiety, and substance abuse; older adults are more susceptible to severe cognitive impairment.

Models of Coping

- Three traditional approaches to the study of coping are environmental, behavioral, and coping-style models.
- Environmental models emphasize quantitative change based on the magnitude of environmental demands.
- Behavioral models place more emphasis on active responses to stress.
- Coping-style models emphasize individual strategies of problem solving.
- The cognitive-appraisal model views the choice of appropriate coping efforts as the result of constant reappraisal of a situation.

coping (p. 435)	**environmental-press model (p. 436)**
congruence model (p. 435)	**learned helplessness (p. 437)**

adaptive mechanisms (p. 437)
cognitive-appraisal model (p. 438)

problem-focused coping (p. 439)
emotion-focused coping (p. 439)

"Successful Aging"

- Three classic normative models of successful aging are Peck's personality adjustments of middle and late adulthood, disengagement theory, and activity theory.
- According to Atchley's continuity theory, aging adults seek a balance between continuity and change.
- According to Whitbourne's model of personality development, identity style can predict adaptation to aging.
- Research on ordinary adults' concepts of successful aging points to the importance of relationships, of growth for middle-aged people, and of acceptance for older people.

disengagement theory (p. 446)
activity theory (p. 446)

continuity theory (p. 447)

Destructive Behavior Patterns

- The extent of substance abuse among older adults is often underestimated.
- Habits and attitudes regarding substance use are generally established by young adulthood and have more to do with cohort than with age.
- Alcoholism is a major mental health problem, especially among men. Older adults are more likely to abuse alcohol than other drugs.
- The overwhelming majority of victims of partner abuse are women. Abused women often stay with their abusers out of vulnerability, fear, and a lack of alternatives. Older abused wives face special problems.
- Abusive and neglectful parents show specific characteristics and behavior patterns.
- Elder abuse, which may be significantly underreported, most often happens to a frail elderly person living with a spouse who is his or her caregiver.

substance abuse (p. 450)
substance dependence (p. 450)
intimate partner violence (IPV) (p. 454)

child abuse (p. 457)
neglect (p. 457)
elder abuse (p. 458)

Mental Health in Late Life: A Lifespan Developmental Approach

- Except among nursing home residents, mental illness is less common in late life than among younger adults.
- A lifespan developmental perspective on mental health emphasizes tendencies toward both growth and decline, the context and multiple causation of mental status, and responsiveness to treatment even in late life.
- Most older Americans seem to be fairly satisfied with life, although satisfaction is lower among some ethnic groups.
- Nearly half of older adults who need treatment for mental conditions that can be cured or alleviated do not get it.
- For many reasons, depression may be underdiagnosed in older adults and therefore go untreated.

- Dementias, which may be due to one or a combination of conditions, are most likely to occur in late life. Some dementias can be reversed with treatment.
- Common forms of progressive dementia are those caused by Alzheimer's disease, vascular disease, and Parkinson's disease.
- Hypochondriasis is a chronic condition that can begin at any age.
- Assessing the life strengths of older adults can help them and society to make the most of the inner resources they have developed.

schizophrenia (p. 464)

major depressive episode (p. 465)

antidepressant drugs (p. 467)

electroconvulsive therapy (ECT) (p. 467)

cognitive therapy (p. 468)

behavior therapy (p. 468)

interpersonal therapy (p. 468)

brief dynamic therapy (p. 468)

music therapy (p. 468)

Parkinson's disease (p. 469)

pseudodementia (p. 470)

hypochondriasis (p. 471)

Dealing with Death and Bereavement

◈ **FOCUS: LOUISA MAY ALCOTT**

The key to the question of death unlocks the door of life.
—Elisabeth Kübler-Ross, *Death: The Final Stage of Growth,* 1975

All the while I thought I was learning how to live, I have been learning how to die.
—*Notebooks of Leonardo da Vinci*

ONE OF THE MOST moving parts of Louisa May Alcott's classic nineteenth-century novel *Little Women* is the chapter recounting the last year in the life of gentle, home-loving Beth, the third of the March sisters (the others being Meg, Jo, and Amy). Beth's life and her death at age 18 are based on those of Alcott's own sister Elizabeth (Lizzie), who wasted away and died at 23 (Elbert, 1984; MacDonald, 1983; Stern, 1950). Despite its dated language and what some may consider sugar-coated sentimentality, Alcott's fictionalized account of her family's growing intimacy in the face of tragedy has struck an empathetic chord in generations of readers, and in viewers of

© Bettmann/Corbis Images

476

the four film versions of the book and a Broadway musical based on it, many of whom have never actually seen a person die.

In the novel, realizing that Beth's illness was terminal, "the family accepted the inevitable, and tried to bear it cheerfully. . . . They put away their grief, and each did his or her part toward making that last year a happy one.

"The pleasantest room in the house was set apart for Beth, and in it was gathered everything that she most loved. . . . Father's best books found their way there, mother's easy chair, Jo's desk, Amy's finest sketches; and every day Meg brought her babies on a loving pilgrimage, to make sunshine for Aunty Beth. . . .

"Here, cherished like a household saint in its shrine, sat Beth, tranquil and busy as ever. . . . The feeble fingers were never idle, and one of her pleasures was to make little things for the school-children daily passing to and fro . . ." (Alcott, 1929, pp. 533–534).

As Beth's illness progressed, the increasingly frail invalid put down the sewing needle that had become "so heavy." Now "talking wearied her, faces troubled her, pain claimed her for its own, and her tranquil spirit was sorrowfully perturbed by the ills that vexed her feeble flesh," while "those who loved her best were forced to see the thin hands stretched out to them beseechingly, to hear the bitter cry, 'Help me, help me!' and to feel that there was no help." But with "the wreck of her frail body, Beth's soul grew strong." Jo stayed with Beth constantly (as Alcott herself stayed with her sister Lizzie), sleeping on a couch by her side and "waking often to renew the fire, to feed, lift, or wait upon

the patient creature" (pp. 534–535). Beth finally drew her last quiet breath "on the bosom where she had drawn her first"; and "mother and sisters made her ready for the long sleep that pain would never mar again" (p. 540).

The sequence of events described in *Little Women* is strikingly close to reality, as outlined by one of Alcott's biographers: "In February, Lizzie began to fail rapidly from what Dr. Geist labeled consumption. With aching heart Louisa watched while her sister sewed or read or lay looking at the fire. . . . Father had come home from the West to hear from Dr. Geist that there was no hope. . . . Anna [Alcott's older sister] did the housekeeping so that Mother and Louisa could devote themselves to Lizzie. The sad, quiet days stretched on in her room, and during endless nights Louisa kindled the fire and watched her sister. . . . The farewells were spoken. . . . At last . . . Lizzie became unconscious, quietly breathing her life away. . . . With her mother, Louisa dressed Lizzie for the last time . . ." (Stern, 1950, pp. 856).

Alcott herself wrote at the time, "Our Lizzie is *well* at last, not in this world but another where I hope she will find nothing but rest from her long suffering. . . . Last Friday night after suffering much all day, she asked to lie in Father's arms & called us all about her holding our hands & smiling at us as she silently seemed to bid us good bye. . . . At midnight she said 'Now I'm comfortable & so happy,' & soon after became unconscious. We sat beside her while she quietly breathed her life away, opening her eyes to give us one beautiful look before they closed forever" (Myerson, Shealy, & Stern, 1987, pp. 32–33).

HUMAN BEINGS ARE INDIVIDUALS. THEY undergo different experiences and react to them in different ways. But one unavoidable part of everyone's life is its end. The better people can understand this inevitable event and the more wisely they can approach it, the more fully they can live until it comes.

People's attitudes toward death are shaped by the time and place in which they live. Louisa May Alcott's (and the fictional Jo's) tender care of a beloved, dying sister around whom the entire household revolved for a full year represents a common experience not only in the nineteenth-century United States but in many contemporary rural cultures. Looking death in the eye, bit by bit, day by day, Alcott and her family absorbed an important truth: that dying is part of living, and confronting the end of life can give deeper meaning to the whole of life. Such an experience is less common in American society today.

The stark biological fact of death, then, is far from the whole story. Its meaning and impact are profoundly influenced by what people feel and do, and people's feelings and behavior are greatly affected by how their culture deals with death.

In this chapter, we look at the intertwined biological, social, and psychological aspects of death (the state) and dying (the process), and at changing societal views and customs related to both. We note differences in how adults of different ages think and feel about dying. We examine changes adults undergo in the face of death and how they deal with the death of those they love. We compare mourning patterns in different cultures and various forms grief can take. We discuss such controversial issues as assisted suicide and euthanasia ("mercy killing"). Finally, we see how facing death can help people find meaning and purpose in life.

CHANGING PERSPECTIVES ON DEATH AND DYING

Before modern times, in a typical year some 50 people out of every 1,000 died; and during plagues or natural disasters, the death rate might reach 40 percent. More than one-third of all babies died in infancy, and half of all children died before their tenth birthday. People saw relatives and friends succumb to fatal illnesses at an early age, and they expected some of their own children to die young (Lofland, 1986). Death was a normal, expected event, sometimes even welcomed as a peaceful end to suffering.

CRITICAL THINKING

How does your perspective on death differ from that of your parents, grandparents, or a physician?

Reading *Little Women* is a vivid reminder of the great historical changes regarding death and dying that have taken place since the late nineteenth century, especially in developed countries. Advances in medicine and sanitation, new treatments for many once-fatal illnesses, and a better-educated, more health-conscious population have brought about a "mortality revolution." Women today are less likely to die in childbirth, infants are more likely to survive their first year, children are more likely to grow to adulthood, young adults like Alcott's sister Lizzie are more likely to reach old age, and older people often can overcome illnesses they grow up regarding as fatal.

The top causes of death in the United States in the 1900s were diseases that most often affected children and young people: pneumonia and influenza, tuberculosis, diarrhea, and enteritis. Today nearly three-quarters of all deaths in the United States occur among people ages 65 and over (NCHS, 2004). Young people may die, but at some point older adults must die. Older persons have been found to have chronic, life-threatening illnesses over larger and larger periods of time due to medical intervention that may prolong a person's life (Stillion, 2005).

As death increasingly became a phenomenon of late adulthood, it became "invisible and abstract" (Fulton & Owen, 1987–1988, p. 380). The urbanized "baby boom" generation born after World War II was the first to reach adulthood with only a 5 percent chance of having experienced the death of anyone in the immediate family. Care of the dying and the dead, a familiar aspect of family life in rural societies, became largely a task for professionals. People went to hospitals or nursing homes to die, and undertakers prepared their bodies for burial. More than 2 out of 3 deaths in the United States occurred somewhere other than at home. Many people went through most of their lives without thinking much about their own death (Fulton & Owen, 1987–1988; Lofland, 1986).

Today, though, things are again changing. Violence, drug abuse, poverty, and—above all—the spread of AIDS make it hard to deny the reality of death. Because of the prohibitive cost of extended hospital care that can do nothing to save the terminally ill, many more deaths are occurring at home (Techner, 1994). Hospice care is helping patients and their families face death and bereavement more openly and supportively. Still, it generally takes an airplane crash, a series of suicides, or an epidemic to bring death to the forefront of public awareness.

Biological, Social, and Psychological Aspects of Death

There are at least three aspects of death and dying: *biological, social,* and *psychological.*

Although the legal definition varies, *biological* death is generally considered to be the cessation of bodily processes. A person may be pronounced dead when breathing and heartbeat stop for a significant time or when all electrical activity in the brain ceases. Criteria for death have become more complex with the development of medical apparatus that can prolong basic signs of life, sometimes indefinitely. People in a deep coma can be kept alive for years. A person whose brain has completely stopped functioning—and who, therefore, is by definition dead—can be maintained by mechanical devices that artificially sustain heartbeat and respiration.

These medical developments have raised agonizing questions about whether or when life supports, such as respirators and feeding tubes, may be withheld or removed, and whose judgment should prevail. Sometimes humanitarian or practical considerations conflict with religious beliefs or professional standards. Many of these issues have ended up in court, and some are still unresolved.

Biological aspects of death are becoming harder to disentangle from some of its *social* aspects: attitudes toward death, care of and behavior toward the dying, where death takes place, and efforts to postpone or hasten it. Other social aspects of death include disposing of the dead, mourning customs and rituals, and the transfer of possessions and roles.

CRITICAL THINKING

Are your personal beliefs about biological, social, and psychological death and dying in agreement with the definitions presented in the text? Why or why not?

Many social aspects of death and dying are governed by religious or legal prescriptions that reflect a society's view of what death is and what happens afterward. In Malayan society, for instance (as in many other preliterate societies), death was seen as a gradual transition. A body was at first given only provisional burial. Survivors continued to perform mourning rites until the body decayed to the point where the soul was believed to have left it and to have been admitted into the spiritual realm. The ancient Egyptian *Book of the Dead* gave instructions for sacrifices and rituals to help a dying or deceased person achieve a rightful place in the community of the dead (Kastenbaum & Aisenberg, 1972).

In ancient Greece, bodies of heroes were publicly burned as a sign of honor. Cremation still is widely practiced by Hindus in India and Nepal. By contrast, cremation is prohibited under Orthodox Jewish law in the belief that the dead will rise again for a Last Judgment and the chance for eternal life (Ausubel, 1964).

In Japan, religious rituals encourage survivors to maintain contact with the deceased. Families keep an alter in the home dedicated to their ancestors; they talk to their dead loved ones and offer them food or cigars. In Gambia the dead are considered part of the community; among Native Americans, the Hopi fear the spirits of the dead and try to forget a deceased person as quickly as possible. Muslims in Egypt show grief through expressions of deep sorrow; Muslims in Bali are encouraged to suppress sadness, to laugh, and to be joyful (Stroebe, Gergen, Gergen, & Stroebe, 1992). All these varied customs and practices help people deal with death and bereavement through well-understood cultural meanings that provide a stable anchor amid the turbulence of loss.

Some modern social customs have evolved from ancient beliefs and practices. Embalming goes back to a practice common in ancient Egypt and China: mummification, preserving a body so the soul can return to it. A traditional Jewish custom is never to leave a dying person alone, even for an instant (Gordon, 1975; Heller, 1975). Anthropologists suggest that the original reason for this may have been a belief (widespread among ancient peoples) that evil spirits hover around a dying person, trying to enter the body (Ausubel, 1964).

Such social conventions, and the attitudes they reflect, are closely linked with *psychological* aspects of death: how people feel about their own death and about the death of those close to them. Rituals give people facing a loss something important to do at a time when they otherwise would feel helpless. Some rituals allow for extended interaction with the dying or dead person and affirm the strength and efficacy of the community (Kastenbaum & Aisenberg, 1972). The Jewish deathbed vigil not only provides spiritual solace to the dying but also helps alleviate any guilt survivors might feel (Gordon, 1975; Heller, 1975).

An Orthodox Jewish funeral is designed to help the bereaved confront the reality of death. The simple coffin (often a plain pine box) is kept closed. At the cemetery, mourners shovel dirt into the grave. After the funeral, all who attend are invited to the home of the nearest relative, where, throughout the week of *shiva*—a period of intense mourning following a death—mourners vent their feelings and share memories of the deceased. During the following year, the bereaved are gradually drawn back into the life of the community (Gordon, 1975; Heller, 1975).

By contrast, many people in contemporary American society have a great deal of trouble coming to terms with death. Avoidance or denial has been fostered by social conventions that contrast sharply with those of Orthodox Judaism and of Louisa May Alcott's era: isolation of dying persons in hospitals or nursing homes; refusal to openly discuss their condition with them; and reluctance to visit, thus leaving them to cope with dying alone.

The Study of Death: Thanatology and Death Education

Thanatology, the study of death and dying—or "the study of life with death left in" (Kastenbaum, 1993, p. 76)—is arousing a great deal of interest as people come to recognize the importance of integrating death into life.

How can people prepare for their own death, or the death of those they love? How much should terminally ill patients be told about their situation? These are among the questions dealt with in **death education:** programs to teach people about death and to help them deal with it personally and professionally. Such programs are offered to students, social workers, doctors, nurses, and other professionals who work with dying people and survivors and to the community. Goals include allaying death-related anxieties; helping people to develop their own belief systems, to see death as a natural end to life, and to prepare for their own death and the death of those close to them; teaching humane ways to treat the dying; providing a realistic view of health care workers and their obligations to the dying and their families; offering an understanding of the dynamics of grief; helping suicidal people and those around them; and helping consumers decide what kinds of funeral services they want (Leviton, 1977).

CRITICAL THINKING

What do you think about and how do you feel during academic discussions of death? Did you learn these responses by watching family members' responses to death or from some other experience?

Hospice Care

Along with the growing tendency to face death openly and honestly, movements have arisen to make dying more humane. These include hospice care and support groups for dying people and their families.

Hospice care is warm, personal, patient- and family-centered care for the terminally ill, focused on palliative care that aims toward the relief of pain, control of symptoms, and quality of life. It can be given in a hospital or another institution, at home, or through some combination of home and institution.

The hospice movement began in London in 1968 in response to a need for special facilities and special care for dying patients. A typical hospital is set up to treat acute illness, with the goal of curing patients and sending them home well. As a result, dying patients in a hospital often receive needless tests and useless treatments, are given less attention than patients with better chances of recovery, and are constrained by rules that are not relevant to them. And hospital care for an extended terminal illness has become enormously expensive.

Today there are about 3,300 hospice programs that provide service to an estimated 950,000 people. About half are cancer patients; other common illnesses are heart disease, dementia, lung disease, and kidney or liver disease. Hospice care is an affordable way to care for family members with a terminal illness. Many insurance policies will pay for hospice services. Patients over the age of 65 are entitled to the Medicare Hospice Benefit, and Medicaid covers hospice care in 45 states; both Medicare and Medicaid pay for nearly all of the services (National Hospice and Palliative Care Organization, 2005).

The hospice philosophy is summed up in the words of its founder, Cicely Saunders: "You matter to the last moment of your life, and we will do all we can, not only to help you die peacefully, but to live until you die" (National Hospice Organization, undated, p. 6). The emphasis is on **palliative care**, on relieving pain and suffering and allowing patients to die in peace and dignity. Doctors, nurses, social workers, psychologists, aides, clergy, friends, and volunteers work together to treat symptoms, to keep patients as comfortable and alert as possible, to show interest in and kindness to them and their families, and to help families deal with the illness and ultimately with bereavement.

What does it mean to preserve the dignity of a patient who is dying? One research team decided to ask patients themselves. From interviews with 50 Canadian patients with advanced terminal cancer, the researchers developed a list of dignity-related questions, concerns, and treatment guidelines (Chochinov, Hack, McClement, Harlos, & Kristjanson, 2002).

Above all, the researchers concluded, dignity-conserving care depends not only on how patients are treated, but also on how they are regarded: "When dying patients are seen, and know that they are seen, as being worthy of honor and esteem by those who care for them, dignity is more likely to be maintained" (Chochinov, 2002, p. 2259).

FACING DEATH

CRITICAL THINKING

Do you believe that at some point, everyone achieves peace about death? Or are you more likely to believe that most people ask, Why me? or Why now? Explain your answer.

All deaths are different, just as all lives are different. The experience of dying is not the same for an accident victim, a patient with terminal cancer, a person who commits suicide, and someone who dies instantaneously of a heart attack. Nor is the experience of loss the same for their survivors. The timing-of-events model (see Chapter 11) suggests why death does not mean the same thing to an 85-year-old man with excruciatingly painful arthritis, a 56-year-old woman at the height of a brilliant legal career who discovers she has leukemia, and a 20-year-old who dies of an overdose of drugs. Nor, as contextual theorists would point out, is death the same for a Brahman in India as for a homeless person in New York. Cohort also plays a role. Among older first-generation Japanese Americans, acceptance of the inevitable may reflect Buddhist teachings; but third-generation Japanese Americans have been found to be less accepting, not only because they are younger but also because they have grown up with the American belief in the ability to control one's destiny (Kalish & Reynolds, 1976).

Yet, all people are human, and just as there are commonalities in adults' lives, there are similarities in the way adults face death at different ages. Let's look first at how young, middle-aged, and older adults feel about dying, and then at changes that may occur as death approaches.

Attitudes Toward Death and Dying

Do you ever think about your own death? Do you think about it as much as your parents or grandparents? How do adults of different ages cope with the knowledge that they must die?

CRITICAL THINKING
Under what circumstances have you thought about your death? Was the thought serious enough to motivate you to change your behavior in any way?

YOUNG ADULTHOOD

Most young adults avoid thinking about death. Of course, they understand in an abstract way that it does occur. Adolescents are influenced by the *personal fable*—an egocentric belief that they are unique or special, are not subject to the natural rules that govern the rest of the world, and can take almost any kind of risk without danger (Elkind, 1984). This belief fades as young adults take on sobering occupational and family responsibilities, but young adults still do not like to think that death can happen to them (Kastenbaum, 1977).

Those who have finished their education or training and have embarked on careers, marriage, or parenthood are eager to live the lives they have been preparing for. If they are suddenly taken ill or badly injured, they are likely to feel more intensely emotional about imminent death than people in any other period of life (Pattison, 1977). They are extremely frustrated: they have worked terribly hard—for nothing. Their frustration turns to rage, and that rage often makes young adults troublesome hospital patients.

MIDDLE ADULTHOOD

It is in middle age that most people realize they are indeed going to die. As they read the obituary pages—which they are likely to do more regularly than before—they find more and more familiar names, and they may compare the ages with their own. Their bodies send them signals that they are not so young, agile, and hearty as they once were; and they may become more introspective (see Chapter 11). Often—especially after the death of both parents—there is a new awareness of being the "older generation" (Scharlach & Fredriksen, 1993).

Middle-aged people perceive time in a new way. Previously, they thought in terms of how many years they had been alive; now they think of how many years are left until death, and of how to make the most of those years (Neugarten, 1967). The realization that death is certain and that the time remaining is limited may be an impetus for a major life change. When Saul Alinsky, a community organizer in Chicago, was asked what had made him decide to devote his life to organizing working-class people, he recalled a time when he had been gravely ill: "I realized then that I was going to die. I had always known that in some abstract sense, of course, but for the first time I really knew it deep inside me. And I made up my mind that before I died I would do something that would really make a difference in the world" (S. Alinsky, personal communication, 1966).

Even people who outwardly continue their previous patterns of living often make subtle shifts and more conscious choices. Awareness that time is

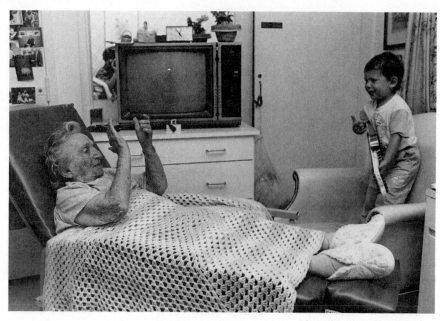

© Susan Woog Wagner/Photo Researchers

According to Erikson, people in the last stage of life must deal with the developmental stage: integrity versus despair. The outcome may be wisdom that enables them to accept their coming death, as well as the way they have lived their lives.

shortening may lead them to take stock of careers, marriages, relationships with children, friendships, values, and how they spend their time and energy (see Box 11.2 in Chapter 11).

LATE ADULTHOOD

In general, older people are less anxious about death than middle-aged people (Bengtson, Cuellar, & Ragan, 1975). They are more likely to use emotion-focused coping strategies (see Chapter 12). Through the years, as people lose friends and relatives, they gradually reorganize their thoughts and feelings to accept their own mortality. Physical losses and other problems of old age may diminish their pleasure in living. On the other hand, when 414 hospitalized patients in their eighties and nineties were asked how much time they would be willing to trade for excellent health, about 2 out of 3 were unwilling to give up more than a month of life (Tsevat et al., 1998).

According to Erikson (see Chapter 11), people in late adulthood must deal with the last of eight crises: *integrity versus despair.* Those who resolve this final crisis achieve a wisdom that enables them to accept both what they have done with their lives and their impending death. Peck's adjustments of old age (see Chapter 12) may help people cope. People who feel that their lives have been meaningful are usually better able to face death.

Some, though, have complex feelings—like 82-year-old Rita Duskin, the mother of one of the authors of this book, who wrote the following lines shortly before her second, fatal heart attack:

> I refuse to believe I am a piece of dust scuttering through uncaring space. I believe I count—that I have work to do—that there is need of me. I have a place. I want to live. The moment is Now—Now is my forever. I am still somebody—somebody on whom nothing is lost. With my last breath, I sing a psalm. (R. Duskin, personal communication, February 1986)

Thus, acknowledgment of death may be mixed with a poignant affirmation of the preciousness of the life that is slipping away.

Approaching Death

What kinds of changes do people undergo shortly before death? How do they come to terms with its imminence?

PHYSICAL AND PSYCHOLOGICAL CHANGES

Psychological changes often begin to take place even before there are overt physiological signs of dying. In Chapter 6, we noted that a terminal drop in intellectual functioning often appears at this time (Kleemeier, 1962; Riegel & Riegel, 1972). This effect has been found in longitudinal studies in various countries—not only of the very old (Johansson et al., 2004; Singer, Verhaeghen, Ghisletta, Lindenberger, & Baltes, 2003; Small, Fratiglioni, von Strauss, & Bäckman, 2003), but also of adults of a wide range of ages—and it operates regardless of apparent health status, gender, SES, or cause of death (Rabbitt et al., 2002; Small et al., 2003). Terminal declines have been found to predict death as much as 11 years later. A decline in verbal ability, which is normally least affected by increasing age, may be an especially important marker of terminal drop (Rabbitt et al., 2002). An English study of 3,572 active adults ages 49 to 93 in England suggests that depression, which can have negative effects on brain function, may help explain terminal drop (Rabbit et al., 2002). Terminal drop is sometimes attributed to chronic ailments that sap mental energy and motivation. It affects abilities that are relatively unaffected by age, such as vocabulary, and it is seen in people who die young as well as those who die at a more advanced age (Berg, 1996).

Terminal drop may predict which individuals in a tested group are within a few years of death (Berg, 1996). One research team (Siegler, McCarty, & Logue, 1982), using data from the Duke Longitudinal Study, compared scores on intelligence and memory tests of people who died within 1 year of testing with scores of people who died 8 to 13 years afterward and people who died 14 or more years afterward or were still alive. Those who survived longest, regardless of age, tended to have had the highest scores on both verbal and nonverbal items (see Figure 13.1).

Personality changes also show up during the terminal period. In one study, 80 people age 65 to 91 were given psychological tests. Afterward, the

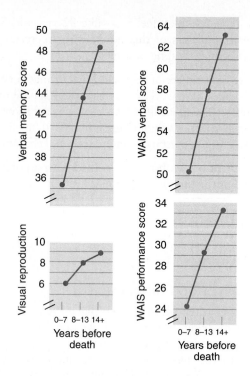

FIGURE 13.1 *Effects of terminal drop on memory and intelligence*. People closer to death performed worse on verbal and visual memory tests and on the verbal and nonverbal performance sections of the Wechsler Adult Intelligence Scale (WAIS). *SOURCE: Siegler et al., 1982, fig. 2.*

researchers compared the scores of those who died within 1 year with the scores of those who lived an average of 3 more years. The people who died within 1 year had lower scores on cognitive tests, indicating terminal drop; and on the whole, they also were less introspective and more docile. Individual differences had to do with what was going on in people's lives at the time of testing. Those who were dealing with a crisis and were close to death were more afraid of and more preoccupied with death than those facing similar crises who were not close to death; but those close to death whose lives were relatively stable at the time showed neither special fear of death nor preoccupation with it (Lieberman & Coplan, 1970). These observations suggest a psychosomatic relationship, in which psychological changes are related to physiological changes in the body, and vice versa. The changes cannot simply be effects of a single episode of disease, since people who later recovered from acute illnesses did not show the same pattern of decline as those who later died from the same kinds of illnesses.

Some people who have come close to death have had visions or other experiences that are sometimes interpreted as a result of physiological or psychological changes on the brink of death.

CRITICAL THINKING

What implications do lower cognitive scores and the effects of terminal drop have for the quality of life of older persons?

KÜBLER-ROSS: STAGES OF DYING

Elisabeth Kübler-Ross, a psychiatrist who worked with dying people, is widely credited with having inspired the current interest in the psychology of death and dying. She found that most patients welcome an opportunity to speak openly about their condition, and that most are aware of being close to death even when they have not been told how sick they are.

After speaking with some 500 terminally ill patients, Kübler-Ross (1969, 1970) outlined five stages in coming to terms with death (see Table 13.1 for a fuller description and illustration of each). The stages are (1) denial (refusal to accept the reality of what is happening); (2) anger; (3) bargaining for extra time (see Box 13.1 on page 490); (4) depression; and (5) ultimate acceptance. She also proposed a similar progression in the feelings of people facing imminent bereavement (Kübler-Ross, 1975).

Kübler-Ross's model has been criticized and modified by other professionals who work with dying patients. They point out that Kübler-Ross's "stages" are not true stages, as in organismic theories. Although the emotions that Kübler-Ross describes are common, not everyone goes through all five stages, and people may go through the stages in different sequences. A person may go back and forth between anger and depression, for example, or may feel both at once. Instead of the orderly progression in the theoretical model, dying people may show "a jumble of conflicting or alternating reactions running the gamut from denial to acceptance, with a tremendous variation affected by age, sex, race, ethnic group, social setting, and personality" (Butler & Lewis, 1982, p. 370). Unfortunately, some health professionals assume that these stages are inevitable and universal, and others feel that they have failed if they cannot bring a patient to "the ultimate goal, the big number 5—'acceptance' of death" (Leviton, 1977, p. 259).

Dying, like living, is an individual experience. For some people, denial or anger may be a healthier way to face death than calm acceptance. Thus, Kübler-Ross's description—useful as it is in helping us understand the feelings of people who are facing the end of life—should not be held up as a model or a criterion for a "good death."

FACING BEREAVEMENT

Bereavement is the loss of someone to whom one feels close, and the process of adjustment to it. Bereavement can affect practically all aspects of a survivor's life, often starting with a change in status and roles—for example, from a wife to a widow or from a son or daughter to an orphan. **Grief** is the emotional response experienced in the early phases of bereavement; it can take many forms, from rage to a feeling of emptiness. Although bereavement and grief are universal experiences, they also have a cultural context. **Mourning** refers not to feelings but to behavior—the ways, usually culturally accepted, in which the bereaved and the community act while adjusting to a death. Examples of mourning include the all-night Irish wake, at which

TABLE 13.1

Kübler-Ross's Stages of Dying

Stage	Explanation	Example
Denial	Most people respond with shock to the knowledge that they are about to die. Their first thought is, "Oh, no, this can't be happening to me." When people around the patient also deny reality, he or she has no one to talk to and, as a result, feels deserted and isolated. When allowed some hope along with the first announcement and given the assurance that they will not be deserted no matter what happens, people can drop the initial shock and denial rather quickly.	Mrs. K., 28, a mother of two young children, was hospitalized with a terminal liver disease. After visiting a faith healer, she told the hospital chaplain, "It was wonderful. I have been healed. I am going to show the doctors that God will heal me. I am all well now" (1970, p. 43). Eventually, she showed that she was no longer denying her illness when, holding the doctor's hand, she said, "You have such warm hands. I hope you are going to be with me when I get colder and colder" (1970, p. 45).
Anger	After realizing that they are dying, people become angry. They ask, "Why me?" They become envious of those around them who are young and healthy. They are really angry not at these people but at the youth and health they themselves do not have. They need to express their rage to get rid of it.	Mr. O., a successful businessman who had been a dominant, controlling person all his life, became enraged as Hodgkin's disease took away his control over his life. His anger dissipated somewhat after his wife and the hospital nurses gave him back a measure of control by consulting him on time and length of family visits and times for various hospital procedures.
Bargaining	The next thought may be, "Yes, it's happening to me—*but*." The *but* is an attempt to bargain for time. People may pray to God, "If you just let me live to see my daughter graduated . . . *or* my son married . . . *or* my grandchild born . . . I'll be a better person . . . *or* I won't ask for anything more . . . *or* I'll accept my lot in life." These bargains represent the acknowledgment that time is limited and life is finite. When people drop the *but*, they are able to say, "Yes, me."	A woman in great pain was very sad at the thought that she would not be able to attend the wedding of her oldest and favorite child. With the aid of self-hypnosis, she controlled her pain; and during the period before the wedding she promised that she would ask no more if she could live only long enough to be there. She did attend, a radiant mother of the groom, and when she returned to the hospital, despite her fatigue she told the doctor, "Now don't forget I have another son!" (1970, p. 83).

SOURCE: Kübler-Ross, 1969, 1970.

TABLE 13.1 *(continued)*

Kübler-Ross's Stages of Dying

Stage	Explanation	Example
Depression	In this stage, people need to cry, to grieve for the loss of their own life. By expressing the depths of their anguish, they can overcome depression much more quickly than if they feel pressured to hide their sorrow.	Mr. H., who had enjoyed singing in the choir, teaching Sunday school, and doing other church and community work, was no longer able to carry out these activities because of his illness. He said, "The one thing that makes life worthless right now is the fact that I look upon myself … as not ever being able to go back to these things" (1970, p. 103). Other elements in his depression were his feeling that his wife did not appreciate his involvement in these nonpaying activities that he considered valuable, and the fact that he had never completed the mourning process for his parents and a daughter who had died. After he reviewed his feelings with the doctor and the chaplain and his wife reassured him that she did appreciate him, his depression lifted.
Acceptance	Finally, people can acknowledge, "My time is very close now, and it's all right." This is not necessarily a happy time, but people who have worked through their anxieties and anger about death and have resolved their unfinished business end up with a feeling of peace with themselves and the world.	Mrs. W., 58, was facing the pain and the knowledge of abdominal cancer with courage and dignity—until her husband begged the surgeons to do an operation that could prolong her life. She changed radically, becoming restless and anxious, asking often for pain relief, and screaming and hallucinating in the operating room so that the surgery did not take place. After husband and wife spoke separately with the doctor, it became clear that Mrs. W. was ready to die but felt that she could not until her husband was able to accept her illness and let her go. When he finally saw that his need to keep her alive conflicted with her need to detach herself from the world (including him) and die, both partners were able to share their feelings and accept her death.

Postponing Death

President Thomas Jefferson died on the Fourth of July, the anniversary of the Declaration of Independence, of which he had been the principal author. Jefferson's last words were "Is it the Fourth?"

Is there such a thing as a will to live? Can people postpone their own death so that they can celebrate a birthday, an anniversary, a grandchild's wedding, or another significant event?

Studies have examined death rates around two important holidays—Passover and the Harvest Moon festival—each identified with, and meaningful to, a certain ethnic group and not to others, who thus can serve as comparison groups. On the Jewish feast of Passover, more than 75 percent of American Jews attend a *seder* (a ceremonial dinner), usually at home with close family members (Phillips & King, 1988). During the Chinese Harvest Moon festival, the senior woman of the house directs a ceremonial meal there (Phillips & Smith, 1990); this holiday emphasizes the symbolic

importance of older women and is more important to them than to young women or to men of any age. Passover usually falls near Easter (the last supper of Jesus and the disciples is said to have been a seder), and the Harvest Moon festival takes place in the autumn. But the date of each changes from year to year by as much as 4 weeks.

In two California studies, death rates from natural causes were found to be lower just before each of these two holidays for people of Jewish and Chinese extraction, respectively, and higher just afterward. For Jewish people, the "Passover effect" was strongest if the festival fell on a weekend, when more people tend to celebrate it; it was not affected by the specific date of the holiday. The effect was especially strong among Jewish men, who usually lead the seder. It was not found in African Americans, in Asians, or in Jewish infants, none of whom celebrate Passover (Phillips & King, 1988). Similarly, the "Harvest Moon effect" did not appear among Jewish people or the general population,

friends and family toast the memory of the dead person; and flying a flag at half-mast after the death of a public figure (Lund, 1993b).

Traditional cultures help people deal with bereavement through customs that have well-understood meanings and provide a reassuring anchor amid the turbulence of loss. These customs vary greatly from culture to culture. In Japan, religious rituals encourage survivors to maintain contact with the deceased. Families keep an altar in the home dedicated to their ancestors; they talk to their dead loved ones and offer them food or cigars (Stroebe, Gergen, Gergen, & Stroebe, 1992). Alex Haley, in *Roots* (1976), observed that in Gambia the dead were still considered part of the community. For example, at his graduation, 10-year-old Kunta Kinte felt proud not only of his family sitting in the front row but also of his ancestors buried beyond the village, especially his beloved grandmother. By contrast, among Native Americans, the

or among elderly Chinese men or younger Chinese women. It appeared only among Chinese women over age 75, the group to whom this holiday means the most. Their death rate was unusually low before the Harvest Moon festival and unusually high afterward. The pattern held for the three leading causes of death in the elderly: heart disease, cancer, and stroke (Phillips & Smith, 1990).

Research (O. Anson & J. Anson, 1997) from Israel focused on Muslims around major holidays for the years 1983–1992. During the fast month of Ramadan, women's mortality was greater than during the preceding month. In the two weeks leading up to the feast of 'Id el-Adhha, mortality was greater for women than in the two weeks after the festival. Men were found to show higher mortality in the two weeks after the feast of 'Id el-Fitr than in the two weeks preceding. It appears that the pattern of mortality for men and women is different and reflects their differing roles in the preparation and celebration of the holy days.

Recently, the same researchers (O. Anson & J. Anson, 2001) conducted research on the deaths of Jewish men and women aged 35–74 in Israel from 1983 to 1992. There was a consistent decline in mortality on the Sabbath (Saturday) for men and women, young and old. There was an increase in the number of deaths for men on Sundays and for younger women on Mondays. The Sabbath is considered the most important religious event that occurs regularly throughout the year. No consistent holy-day effect was found for the other major holidays.

How might such effects work? It is not likely that stress or overeating causes high death rates after these holidays; these factors would not explain the very much lower death rates before the holidays. Perhaps psychosomatic processes allow some people to postpone death until they have reached an occasion important to them. They may will themselves to live just a little while longer, putting forth every ounce of psychological and physical strength so as to experience just one more celebration.

Hopi try to forget a dead person as quickly as possible. They believe that death brings pollution and that the spirits of the dead are to be feared; therefore, they do not keep photos or other reminders of someone who has died. Muslims in Egypt express grief through deep sorrow; Muslims in Bali are encouraged to laugh, be joyful, and suppress sadness (Stroebe et al., 1992).

There is no one "best" way to cope with loss. What works for one culture or one family may not work for another. In helping people handle grief, counselors need to take both ethnic traditions and individual differences into account (Kastenbaum, 1999).

Let's look next at forms and patterns of grief. Then we'll focus on how people adjust to one kind of bereavement that happens to many adults, especially as they grow older: loss of a spouse. Finally, we'll discuss two other particularly difficult losses: death of a parent and death of a child.

© AP/Eduardo Verdugo/Wide World Photos

Mourning customs vary greatly across cultures. In Mexico, young and old alike sit on tombs of relatives, keeping an all-night vigil on the nationwide Day of the Dead. Family members clean the graves, plant flowers, light candles, and even offer the deceased person's favorite foods.

CRITICAL THINKING

Do you think it is easier to adjust to the death of someone who was ill for a period of time or to a sudden death? Why?

Forms and Patterns of Grief

Grief is a highly personal experience. Recent research has challenged earlier notions of a single, "normal" pattern of grieving and a "normal" timetable for recovery. For example, a widow talking to her late husband might once have been considered emotionally disturbed; now this is recognized as a very common and helpful behavior (Lund, 1993b). And while some people recover fairly quickly after bereavement, others never completely get over it.

ANTICIPATORY GRIEF

The family and friends of a person who has been ill for a long time often prepare themselves for the loss through **anticipatory grief**, symptoms of grief experienced while the person is still alive. Anticipatory grief may help survivors handle the actual death more easily (Brown & Stroudemire, 1983). Women who can prepare themselves for widowhood psychologically and in practical terms—for example, by discussing pensions and insurance with their husbands—may make a more positive adjustment, though they may be no less distressed after the loss (O'Bryant, 1990–1991). In other cases, however, preparation seems to have little impact on adjustment. One study found that elderly widows who had expected their husband's deaths and "rehearsed" for widowhood by thinking and talking about the future were no better or worse adjusted than women whose husbands had died unexpectedly (Hill, Thompson, & Gallagher, 1988).

GRIEF WORK: A THREE-STAGE PATTERN

Perhaps the most common and most widely studied pattern of grief after death is that the bereaved person accepts the painful reality of the loss, gradually lets go of the bond with the dead person, readjusts to life without that person, and develops new interests and relationships. This process of **grief work** generally takes place in three phases—though, as with Kübler-Ross's stages, they may vary (Brown & Stoudemire, 1983; Schulz, 1978).

1. *Shock and disbelief.* This first phase may last several weeks, especially after a sudden or unexpected death. Immediately following a death, survivors often feel lost and confused. Their shock, and their inability to believe in the death, may protect them from more intense reactions. Shortness of breath, tightness in the chest or throat, nausea, and a feeling of emptiness in the abdomen are common. As awareness of the loss sinks in, the initial numbness gives way to overwhelming feelings of sadness, which are commonly expressed by frequent crying.

2. *Preoccupation with the memory of the dead person.* The second phase may last 6 months or longer. The survivor tries to come to terms with the death but cannot yet accept it. Frequent crying continues, and often insomnia, fatigue, and loss of appetite. A widow may relive her hus-

band's death and their entire relationship. From time to time, she may be seized by a feeling that her dead husband is present: she will hear his voice, sense his presence in the room, even see his face before her. She may have vivid dreams of him. These experiences diminish with time, though they may recur—perhaps for years—on such occasions as the anniversary of the marriage or of the death.

3. *Resolution.* The final phase has arrived when the bereaved person renews interest in everyday activities. Memories of the dead person bring fond feelings mingled with sadness, rather than sharp pain and longing. A widower may still miss his dead wife; but he knows that life must go on, and he becomes more active socially. He gets out more, sees people, picks up old interests, and perhaps discovers new ones.

VARIED REACTIONS TO LOSS

How universal is the pattern described above? Recently, researchers have found that grieving does not necessarily follow a straight line from shock to resolution. Instead, it may be a succession of emotional ups and downs of varying lengths, which may eventually subside but never completely flatten out (Lund, 1993b). Furthermore, there are considerable differences in reactions to bereavement. Some people mourn intensely for a very long time: Queen Victoria of England wore black and mourned her husband, Prince Albert, for the last 40 years of her life. Others, apparently, hardly mourn at all.

One team of psychologists (Wortman & Silver, 1989) reviewed studies of reactions to major losses: in some cases, the death of a loved one; in other cases, loss of a person's own mobility as a result of spinal injury. The psychologists found some common assumptions to be more myth than fact. Five common beliefs about loss are (1) Everyone who suffers a severe loss will be distraught and probably depressed. (2) People who do not show such distress will have psychological problems later on. (3) A bereaved person has to "work through" a loss by focusing on it and trying to make sense of it. (4) The intense distress of mourning will come to an end within a fairly short time. (5) People will eventually accept a loss, both intellectually and emotionally. According to these researchers, none of these beliefs is valid for everyone.

First, they say, depression is far from universal. From 3 weeks to 2 years after their loss, only 15 to 35 percent of widows, widowers, and victims of spinal cord injury showed signs of depression. *Second*, failure to show distress at the outset does not necessarily lead to problems; in fact, the people who were most upset immediately after a loss or injury were likely to be most troubled up to 2 years later. *Third*, not everyone needs to work through a loss or will benefit from doing so; some of the people who did the most intense grief work had more problems later. *Fourth*, not everyone returns to normal quickly. Studies have found that parents of children killed by drunk drivers are likely to be functioning poorly up to 7 years later, and that more than 40 percent of widows and widowers show moderate to severe anxiety up to 4 years after the spouse's death, especially if it was sudden. *Fifth*, people cannot always resolve their grief and accept their loss. Parents and spouses of people who die in car accidents often have painful memories of the loved one

Ambiguous Loss

A woman whose husband was in the World Trade Center at the time of the terrorist attack on September 11, 2001, did not truly believe he was dead until months later, when clean-up workers turned up a shard of his bone. Survivors of the December 2004 tsunami in Southeast Asia grieve for partners, children, and parents swept away without a trace by the massive waves. Middle-aged women and men fly to Southeast Asia to search for the remains of husbands and fathers whose planes were shot down decades ago. A woman whose father committed suicide and who did not have an opportunity to view his body before burial has recurring dreams that he is still alive.

Dealing with the death of a loved one is difficult enough under normal circumstances. But when there is no body—no clear evidence of death—it can be harder to face the finality of loss. This is especially true in U.S. culture, with its tendency to deny the reality of death. "People yearn for a body," says the family therapist Pauline Boss (2002, p. 15), "because, paradoxically, *having* the body enables them to let go of it." Viewing the body overcomes confusion,

"provides cognitive certainty of death," and thus enables the bereaved to begin mourning. Without a body, survivors feel cheated out of the chance to say goodbye and to honor the loved one properly. Boss tells of a woman whose husband was missing in the World Trade Center, who wished for just a part of him to bury—even a fingernail.

Boss (1999, 2002, 2004; Boss, Beaulieu, Wieling, Turner, & LaCruz, 2003) applies the term **ambiguous loss** to situations in which loss is not clearly defined and therefore is confusing and difficult to resolve. Ambiguous loss is not a psychological disorder but a relational disorder in which grief remains frozen and resolution cannot occur. It is not an illness but a source of debilitating stress. When loss lacks tangible confirmation, people are denied ritual and emotional closure and may be immobilized—unable to go on with the necessary task of reorganizing family roles and relationships. The loss goes on and on, creating physical and emotional exhaustion, and the support of friends and family may drop away.

In New York, after the September 11 attack, thousands of families had to cope with this kind

even after many years (Wortman & Silver, 1989). Acceptance may be particularly difficult when a loss is *ambiguous*, as when a loved one is missing and presumed dead (see Box 13.2).

Rather than a single three-stage pattern, this research found three main patterns of grieving. In the expected pattern, the mourner goes from high to low distress. In a second pattern, the mourner does not experience intense distress immediately or later. In a third pattern, the mourner remains distressed for a long time (Wortman & Silver, 1989).

In the Changing Lives of Older Couples (CLOC) study, researchers interviewed 1,532 married older adults and then did follow-up interviews on 185 (161 women and 24 men) whose spouses had died. The interviews took place six months and again up to four years after the loss (Boerner, Wortman, & Bonanno, 2005; Bonanno, Wortman, & Nesses, 2004; Bonanno et al., 2002).

of loss. Giving the situation a name seems to alleviate the anguish of the bereaved, who otherwise may blame themselves for feeling confused, helpless, anxious, and unable to grieve normally. Boss also has applied the concept of ambiguous loss to situations in which the loved one is physically present but psychologically absent, as in Alzheimer's disease, drug addiction, and other chronic mental illnesses.

People who can best tolerate ambiguous loss tend to have certain characteristics: (1) They are deeply spiritual and do not expect to understand what happens in the world—they have faith and trust in the unknown. (2) They are optimistic by nature. (3) They can hold two opposite ideas at one time ("I need to reorganize my life but keep hope alive") and thus can live with uncertainty. (4) Often they grew up in a family or culture where mastery, control, and finding answers to questions was less important than learning to live with what is.

Some Native American cultures provide rituals, ceremonies, and symbols to mark ambiguous loss. An Anishinabe woman in northern Minnesota, who was taking care of her demented mother, held a "funeral" for her "because the woman that I knew was just not there anymore" (Boss, 1999, p. 17). In New York, Mayor Rudolph Guiliani offered official certificates of presumed death and an urn of ashes from Ground Zero. Some people accepted these tokens as evidence of death, allowing themselves to begin the grieving process, but others chose to wait for more solid proof. Different families, different cultures, and different people within a family may have different ways of coping.

Therapy can help people to "understand, cope, and move on after the loss, even if it remains unclear" (Boss, 1999, p. 7). Telling and hearing stories about the missing person may begin the healing process. Reconstructing family rituals can affirm that family life goes on.

Therapists working with people suffering from ambiguous loss need to be able to tolerate ambiguity themselves. They must recognize that the classic stages of grief work (described in this chapter) do not apply. Pressing for closure will bring resistance. Families can learn to manage the stress of ambiguous loss at their own pace and in their own way.

Common grief—depression that sets in immediately after bereavement and subsides over time, as in the classic three-stage grief work pattern, was surprisingly uncommon (11 percent of the sample). Also, there was no clear evidence of either absent or delayed grief—lack of overt grieving immediately after the death, which, in the delayed pattern, is thought to result in a later unhealthy eruption of distress. Instead, by far the most prevalent pattern (shown by 46 percent of the sample) was resilience: a low and gradually diminishing level of distress. The resilient mourners expressed acceptance of death as a natural process. After their loss, they spent relatively little time thinking and talking about it or searching for meaning in it, though the majority did report some yearning and emotional pangs during the first six months. These findings challenge the assumption that something is wrong if a bereaved person shows only mild distress and demonstrates that "'doing well' after a loss is not necessarily a cause for concern but rather a normal response for many older adults" (Boerner et al., 2005, p. P72).

Among those widowed persons who showed high long-term distress, the researchers distinguished between *chronic grievers* (16 percent), who became depressed following their loss, and the *chronically depressed* (8 percent), who had been depressed beforehand and became more so afterward. Chronic grievers tended to have been excessively dependent, both on their spouses and in general. They were most likely to keep thinking about, talking about, and searching for meaning in their loss, but they did "get over it" by the 48-month mark, whereas the chronically depressed did not. Thus, chronically depressed widows and widowers may be the most likely candidates for treatment. On the other hand, some mourners (10 percent) who had shown high levels of depression before their loss *improved during bereavement*. For this group, the death appeared to represent the end of a chronic stressor. They tended to have been negative or ambivalent about their marriages and many of their spouses had been seriously ill before death. The finding that grief takes varied forms and patterns has important implications for helping people deal with loss (Boerner et al., 2004, 2005; Bonanno et al., 2002). It may be unnecessary and even harmful to urge or lead mourners to "work through" a loss or to expect them to follow a set pattern of emotional reactions—just as it may be unnecessary and harmful to expect all dying patients to experience Kübler-Ross's stages. Respect for different ways of showing grief can help the bereaved deal with loss without making them feel that their reactions are abnormal. The finding that grief takes varied forms and patterns has important implications for helping people deal with loss (Boerner et al., 2004, 2005; Bonanno et al., 2002). It may be unnecessary and even harmful to urge or lead mourners to "work through" a loss, or to expect them to follow a set pattern of emotional reactions—just as it may be unnecessary and harmful to expect all dying patients to experience Kübler-Ross's stages. Respect for different ways of showing grief can help the bereaved deal with loss without making them feel that their reactions are abnormal. The finding that grief takes varied forms and patterns has important implications for helping people deal with loss. It may be unnecessary and even harmful to urge or lead mourners to "work through" a loss, or to expect them to follow a set pattern of emotional reactions—just as it may be unnecessary and harmful to expect all dying patients to experience Kübler-Ross's stages. Respect for differing patterns of grief can help the bereaved deal with loss without making them feel that their reactions are abnormal.

GRIEF THERAPY

Most bereaved people eventually are able to come to terms with their loss and resume normal lives, often with the help of family and friends. For some, however, **grief therapy**—treatment to help the bereaved cope with their loss—is indicated. Professional grief therapists help survivors express sorrow, guilt, hostility, and anger. They encourage clients to review the relationship with the deceased and to integrate the fact of the death into their lives. In helping people handle grief, counselors need to take into account ethnic and family traditions and individual differences.

Often, unfortunately, studies find that grief therapy is ineffectual or, in a disturbing proportion of cases (38 percent, according to one study), even harmful (Fortner, Neimeyer, Anderson, & Berman, reported in Neimeyer, 2000). The findings reported in the previous section (Boerner et al., 2005; Bonanno et al., 2002) suggest that many bereaved persons are unlikely to need or benefit from counseling. Typical assumptions of grief therapy—that "absent grief" represents unacknowledged problems related to the loss and that bereavement is one of the most stressful life events most people ever encounter—need to be reevaluated.

Chronic grievers are most likely to benefit from treatment that acknowledges the centrality of their loss and helps them to process it, build self-esteem, and restructure their lives. The chronically depressed might be helped more by interventions that focus on their ongoing emotional problems and assist them in dealing with the everyday strains of widowhood. If that approach is unsuccessful, some may need to be treated with antidepressant drugs (Boerner et al., 2005).

Surviving a Spouse

Widowhood is one of the greatest emotional challenges that can face any human being. It means not only the loss of a life partner but the disruption of virtually every aspect of the survivor's life. In a classic ranking of stressful life events, the event identified as requiring the most adjustment was death of a spouse (see Table 4.3 in Chapter 4). Yet widowhood can also be seen as a developmental experience.

Because women tend to live longer than men and to be younger than their husbands, they are more likely to be widowed. They also tend to be widowed at an earlier age. One-third of women lose their husbands by age 65, it is not until 75 that an equal proportion of men lose their wives (Atchley, 1997).

CRITICAL THINKING

What facilitates adjustment to loss of a spouse? How can family and friends help? How can they interfere?

ADJUSTMENTS

Aside from grieving, how does losing a husband or wife affect day-to-day life? A survivor of a long marriage generally faces many emotional and practical problems. A good marriage can leave a gaping emotional void: the loss of a lover, a confidant, a good friend, and a steady companion. Even with a bad marriage, a loss may be felt.

For one thing, the survivor no longer has the *role* of spouse. This loss may be especially hard for a woman who has structured her life and her identity around caring for her husband (Lucas, Clark, Georgellis, & Diener, 2003; Marks & Lambert, 1988; Saunders, 1981). It also affects working people of both sexes who no longer have a partner to come home to, and retirees who have no one to talk to—or argue with.

The quality of the marital relationship that has been lost affects the degree to which widowhood affects mental health. In the CLOC study discussed earlier, widowed persons who had been highly dependent on their spouses tended to become more anxious and yearned more for their partners six months

© PhotoDisc

Widowhood is a tremendous emotional challenge, not only because of the loss of a life partner but also because it changes almost all aspects of the survivor's life. Women, who tend to live longer than men, are more likely to be widowed.

after the death than did those who had not been so dependent. Not surprisingly, those who had been especially close to their spouses also reported greater yearning (Carr et al., 2000).

Social life changes, too. Friends and family usually rally to the mourner's side immediately after the death, but then they go back to their own lives. Married friends, uncomfortable with the thought that bereavement could happen to them too, may avoid the widowed person. Both widowed men and women often feel like a "fifth wheel" with couples who have been longtime friends (Brubaker, 1990). However, both widows and widowers see friends more often than married people do, perhaps because they have more time and more need for social contact; and, although most widowed people make new friends, most of their friends continue to be old ones (Field & Minkler, 1988). Widowed men are more likely to seek the companionship of women. Women—especially middle-aged and older ones—usually make friends with other widows but have a hard time meeting and forming relationships with men (Brecher & Editors of Consumer Reports Books, 1984; Lopata, 1977, 1979).

Economic hardship can be a major problem. On average, family income drops 44 percent after the death of a spouse (Healy, 1983; Hungerford, 2001). When the husband has been the main breadwinner, his widow is deprived of his income; when the husband is widowed, he has to buy many of the services his wife provided. When both spouses have been employed, the loss of one income can be a blow (Lopata, 1977, 1979).

The stress of widowhood may affect physical health. In a large-scale Finnish study, men who lost their wives within a 5-year period were 21 percent more likely to die within the same period than men who remained married, and widowed women were 10 percent more likely to die than nonwidowed women (Martikainen & Valkonen, 1996). Social relationships are related to good health. The loss of the protective "shield" of companionship may explain the strong likelihood that a widowed person will soon follow the spouse to the grave (Ray, 2004). However, the CLOC study suggests a more practical reason. After the death of a spouse, there may be no one to remind an older widow to take her pills or to make sure a widowed man adheres to a special diet. Those who received such reminders (say, from children or health workers) tended to improve in health habits and reported health (Williams, 2004).

Not surprisingly, widowed people of both sexes have higher rates of mental illness, especially depression, than married people (Balkwell, 1981). Widowed men tend to be more vulnerable to depression than widowed women, perhaps because they are less likely than women to have formed other intimate relationships. Among women, a primary factor in depression seems to be financial strain; among men, the stress of managing a household (Umberson et al., 1992).

Although it takes time for the pain of loss to heal, most bereaved spouses eventually rebuild their lives. They may not get over the loss, but they get used to it. Loneliness and sadness give way to confidence in the ability to manage on their own. The people who adjust best are those who keep busy, take on new roles (such as new paid or volunteer work), or become more deeply involved in ongoing activities. They see friends often (which helps more than frequent visits with their children), and they may take part in support groups for widows. Social support—including being encouraged to express feelings without being given unsolicited advice—is especially important in the first few months; survivors who cope well during that period usually do better than others in the long run. Quality of relationships may be more important than frequency of contact (Anderson, 1984; Balkwell, 1981; Barrett, 1978; Lund, 1989, 1993b; Vachon, Lydall, Rogers, Freedmen-Letofky, & Freeman, 1980).

Ultimately, for women especially, the distress of loss can be a catalyst for introspection and growth—for discovering submerged aspects of themselves and learning to stand on their own feet. More acutely aware of their own mortality, they may reevaluate their lives in a search for personal meaning. In the process, they may look back at their marriages more realistically. Some return to school or find new jobs (Lieberman, 1996).

Many studies have found older adults to be better adjusted to widowhood than younger adults. A common interpretation is that loss of a spouse is more traumatic in young adulthood, when it is less expected (DiGiulio, 1992). However, the reason may be that younger widowed people in these studies were more recently bereaved. One study did control for how long people had been widowed; it found that the age at which bereavement occurs has little long-term effect on morale: losing a husband or wife is no easier or harder at an earlier or a later age. Older widows and widowers did tend to have somewhat higher morale than younger ones; a crucial factor may be greater availability of companions, especially widowed peers (Balkwell, 1985).

In the short term, younger widows do have more psychological problems (Parkes & Weiss, 1983). Burdened with full responsibility for breadwinning and parenthood, and often with a drastically reduced standard of living, they may lack the time or energy to develop a new social life. They may find themselves resenting their children and feeling guilty about their resentment (DiGiulio, 1992). Physical health, however, is more likely to be adversely affected when loss occurs in middle age (Perkins & Harris, 1990; Wolinsky & Johnson, 1992a, 1992b).

In general, though, age is not a major factor in the grieving process; coping skills are. People who have had practice in coping with loss and have developed effective coping strategies are better able to deal with bereavement (Lund, 1993b).

REMARRIAGE

Elderly widowers are more likely to remarry than widows, much as men of any age are more likely to remarry after divorce (Kastenbaum, 1999). With available women greatly outnumbering available men, elderly widowers are four times as likely to remarry as elderly widows. Men usually feel more need to remarry; women usually can handle their household needs and may be

© Barbara Alper/Stock Boston

Late-life marriages can be very satisfying. Widowed older adults often remarry because of their previously successful marital relationship. People choose to marry late in life for the same reasons younger adults do, such as companionship, intimacy, and love.

reluctant to give up survivors' pension benefits or the freedom of living alone or to face the prospect of caring for an infirm husband, perhaps for the second time. An analysis of data from the CLOC study found that neither widows nor widowers are more likely to seek out a new romantic relationship if they have close, supportive friends, suggesting that the main benefit of many marriages in late life is companionship (Carr, 2004).

In one study of 24 older couples who had remarried when both partners were over 60, most had been widowed. Most of them had known each other during their first marriages or had been introduced by friends or relatives (Vinick, 1978). Why had they decided to marry again? Men tended to mention companionship and relief from loneliness; women tended to mention their feelings toward the new husband or his personal qualities. Almost all these people, who had been remarried for 2 to 6 years, were happy. Their marriages were calmer than marriages earlier in life; the partners had a "live and let live" attitude.

Losing a Parent

Problems of widowhood are much discussed; so are effects of caring for an aging parent (Chapter 10). Less attention has been paid to the impact on an adult child of the death of a parent. Yet that loss can be hard to bear: "Not only is there the loss of the oldest and one of the most important (yet ambivalent) relationships in one's life, but there [may be] the trauma of breaking up a household in which one may have grown up and of losing the older buffer between oneself and death" (Dainoff, 1989, p. 64). This connection may be stronger today than ever before, since, with longer life expectancies, it is not unusual for a parent to remain alive during the first 50 years or more of a child's life (Umberson & Chen, 1994). Thus, the loss of parents often occurs in middle age (Aldwin & Levenson, 2001), and the deaths of both parents in young adulthood is a nonnormative experience that may negatively affect mental or physical health (Marks, Bumpass, & Jun, 2004).

A survey of 220 bereaved adult children found that 1 out of 4 still suffered social and emotional problems 1 to 5 years after the parent's death (Scharlach, 1991). In-depth interviews with 83 volunteers, age 35 to 60, found a majority still experiencing emotional distress—ranging from sadness and crying to depression and thoughts of suicide—after 1 to 5 years, especially following loss of a mother. Close to half of those who had lost either parent reported continuing physical reactions, such as illness, fatigue, and a general decline in health (Scharlach & Fredriksen, 1993). While psychological distress generally surfaces quickly, health problems may show up considerably later (Umberson & Chen, 1994).

On a deeper level, the death of a parent can be a maturing experience. From an organismic perspective, it can push adults into resolving important midlife developmental issues: achieving a stronger sense of self and of personal choice, along with a greater sense of responsibility, commitment, and attachment to others and a more pressing, realistic awareness of their own mortality (Moss & Moss, 1989; Scharlach & Fredriksen, 1993). The 83 respondents mentioned above, while not a representative sample, reported changes dramatic enough to serve as "evidence of the potential importance of parental death as a developmentally significant event in midlife" (Scharlach & Fredriksen, 1993, p. 317). Let's look at some of those changes.*

CHANGES IN THE SELF

Eight years after the distinguished actor Michael Redgrave died, his daughter, the actress Lynn Redgrave (then 50), wrote and performed a one-woman show, *Shakespeare for My Father*. In it, she finally came to terms with the hurt and frustration her father's coldness had caused her as a child. "It was a privilege to be my father's daughter," she told an interviewer. "But with it went a great price. I paid that price, and I'm stronger for it" (Ryan, 1993).

Many middle-aged adults who lose a parent experience some effect—generally positive—on their sense of self (see Table 13.2). Many feel themselves becoming more self-assertive, autonomous, self-confident, and responsible—in short, more mature—when their parents die. As one adult who had lost a mother said, "I can't call her up if I need advice anymore" (Scharlach & Fredriksen, 1993, p. 310). Orphaned middle-aged adults often feel strengthened as they review the parent's life in relation to their own. For the first time they may be able to accept and forgive the parent's failures, especially toward themselves. They also may be prompted to review their own lives and to revise their goals and activities—change jobs, go back to school, or retire. Many now place more importance on personal relationships, simple pleasures such as enjoying nature, and personal happiness, and less emphasis on material possessions. Some experience a surge of creativity as they deal with the loss by editing a parent's diary or memoirs, or (like Lynn Redgrave) writing their own. But some, especially those whose identity has been intertwined with the parent, may worry about the future, despair over their lack of self-fulfillment, and shy away from responsibility for managing their own lives.

A parent's death is a reminder of one's own mortality. It removes a "buffer" against death and may leave the adult child feeling older and unprotected. Yet sometimes it brings a less anxious acceptance of death, along with a greater sense of purpose about the time remaining. Often the loss of a

---

*The discussion in the remainder of this section is largely indebted to Moss and Moss (1989) and Scharlach and Fredriksen (1993).

TABLE 13.2

Self-Reported Psychological Impacts of a Parent's Death

Impacts	Death of Mother (Percentage)	Death of Father (Percentage)
Self-Concept		
More adult	29	43
More self-confident	19	20
More responsible	11	4
Less mature	14	3
Other	8	17
No impact	19	12
Feelings About Mortality		
Increased awareness of own mortality	30	29
More accepting of own death	19	10
Made concrete plans regarding own death	10	4
Increased fear of own death	10	18
Other	14	16
No impact	17	23
Religiosity		
More religious	26	29
Less religious	11	2
Other	3	10
No impact	60	59
Personal Priorities		
Personal relationships more important	35	28
Simple pleasures more important	16	13
Personal happiness more important	10	7
Material possessions less important	5	8
Other	20	8
No impact	14	36
Work or Career Plans		
Left job	29	16
Adjusted goals	15	10
Changed plans due to family needs	5	6
Moved	4	10
Other	13	19
No impact	34	39

SOURCE: Scharlach & Fredriksen, 1993, table 1, p. 311.

parent leads people to prepare for death in concrete ways, such as making funeral arrangements or a will. Many people, especially those whose parents died young, consider the parents' age at death significant for their own life span. One man threw a large party for his fiftieth birthday, celebrating the fact that he had lived longer than his father. Some people make special plans for their "bonus" years. Some alter their lifestyle. "I don't want to die like my father," said one woman. "I'm on a stringent exercise program to make sure I stay healthy" (Scharlach & Fredriksen, 1993, p. 310).

CHANGES IN RELATIONSHIPS

The death of a parent often brings changes in other relationships—either more intimacy or more conflict. A bereaved adult child may assume more responsibility for the surviving parent and for keeping the family together (Aldwin & Levenson, 2001). The intense emotions of bereavement may draw siblings closer, or they may become alienated over differences that arose during the parent's final illness.

If an adult child has been taking care of a parent, the parent's death may free him or her to spend more time and emotional energy on relationships that have been temporarily neglected, such as those with a spouse or partner or with children or grandchildren. Or the death may free a middle-aged person to shed a relationship that was being maintained to meet the parent's expectations.

The death of a second parent can have especially great impact. The adult child may feel a sharpened sense of mortality now that the buffer of the older generation is gone (Aldwin & Levenson, 2001). This awareness can be an opportunity for growth, leading to a more mature outlook on life and a greater appreciation of the value of personal relationships (Scharlach & Fredriksen, 1993).

Recognizing the finality of death and the impossibility of saying anything more to the deceased parent, some people are motivated to resolve any conflicts in their ties to the living while there is still time. Sometimes siblings who have been estranged realize that the parent who provided a link between them is no longer there, and they try to mend the rift. People may also be moved to reconcile with their own adult children.

For many people, the bond between parent and child—powerful in life—persists after death. "Death ends a life but it does not end a relationship" (Anderson, 1980, p. 110). Even very old people often mention their parents as the most influential persons in their lives, and a dead parent can be an ongoing presence in a son's or daughter's life (Troll & Smith, 1976).

Losing a Child

When King David, in the Bible, hears that Absalom, the favorite son who has tried to dethrone him, is dead, the king weeps: "O my son Absalom, my son, my son Absalom! Would I had died for you, O Absalom, my son, my son!" (2 Samuel, 19:1).

There is no English word for a parent who has lost a child. A person who has lost a spouse is a *widow* or *widower;* a person who has lost both parents is an *orphan*. But a person whose child has died is bereft even of an identity. A person may be somewhat emotionally prepared for the death of a spouse or a parent, but not for the death of a child.

In earlier times, it was more common for a parent to bury a child. Today, with medical advances and the increase in life expectancy in industrialized countries, a child who survives the first year of life is far more likely to live to old age, and infant mortality has reached record lows—in the United States, 8.5 deaths per 1,000 live births (Centers for Disease Control and Prevention, 1994; USDHHS, 1995). The death of a child, therefore, no matter at what age, comes as a cruel, unnatural shock, an untimely event that, in the normal course of things, should not have happened (Raphael, 1983). The parents may feel they have failed, no matter how much they loved and cared for the child, and they may find it hard to let go.

If a marriage is strong, the couple may draw closer together, supporting each other in their shared loss. But the death of a child can weaken and destroy a marriage. One spouse may blame the other. Or the husband and wife may simply have different ways of grieving and of rebuilding their lives. Unresolved issues stemming from a child's death may lead to a divorce, even years later (Brandt, 1989).

Parents, especially mothers, who have lost a child are at heightened risk of being hospitalized for mental illness (Li, Laursen, Precht, Olsen, Mortensen, 2005). The stress of a child's loss may even hasten parents' death (Li, Precht, Mortensen, & Olsen, 2003).

Many parents hesitate to discuss a terminally ill child's impending death with the child, but those who do so tend to achieve a sense of closure that helps them cope after the loss. In 2001, a Swedish research team surveyed 449 Swedish parents who had lost a child to cancer four to nine years earlier. About one-third of the parents said they had talked with their children about their impending death, and none of these parents regretted having done so, whereas 27 percent of those who had not brought up the subjected regretted it. Most likely to have regrets were parents who had sensed that their child was aware of his or her imminent death but had not spoken to the child about it, and a disproportionate number of these parents were still suffering from depression and anxiety (Kreicbergs, Baldimarsdóttir, Onelöv, Henter, & Steineck, 2004).

Although each mourner must cope with grief in his or her own way, some bereaved parents have found that plunging into work, interests, and other relationships, or joining a support group of bereaved parents, helps ease their pain. Some well-meaning friends tell bereaved parents not to dwell on their loss. But remembering the child in a meaningful way may be exactly what parents need to do. At the 1992 Democratic National Convention, Elizabeth Glaser, the wife of the television actor and director Paul Michael Glaser, told how, in 1981, she had contracted the HIV virus from a blood transfusion and unknowingly passed it on to her infant daughter, Ariel, in her breast milk. After Ariel died of AIDS at age 7, Elizabeth Glaser launched a crusade to increase public awareness of pediatric AIDS. By the time of her own death in

1994 at the age of 47, the foundation she established had raised more than $30 million for research and education (Kennedy, 1994).

Mourning a Miscarriage

At a Buddhist temple in Tokyo, small statues of infants accompanied by toys and gifts are left as offering to Jizo, an enlightened being who is believed to watch over miscarried and aborted fetuses and eventually, through reincarnation, to guide them into a new life. The ritual of *mizuko kuyo*, a rite of apology and remembrance, is observed as a means of making amends to the aborted life (Orenstein, 2002).

The Japanese word *mizuko* means "water child." Japanese Buddhists believe that life flows into an organism gradually, like water, and a *mizuko* is somewhere on the continuum between life and death (Orenstein, 2002). In English, by contrast, there is no word for a miscarried or aborted fetus, or any ritual of mourning. Families, friends, and health professionals tend to avoid talking about such losses, because they are often considered insignificant compared with the loss of a living child (Van, 2001). Grief can be more wrenching without social support.

How do prospective parents cope with the loss of a child they never knew? Because each person's (or couple's) experience of loss is unique, it is hard to generalize (Van, 2001). In one small study, eleven men whose child had died in utero reported being overcome with frustration and helplessness during and after the delivery, but several found relief in supporting their partners (Samuelsson, Radestad, & Segesten, 2001). In another study, grieving parents perceived their spouses and extended families as most helpful and their doctors as least helpful. Some bereaved parents benefited from a support group, and some not (DiMarco, Menke, & McNamara, 2001). Differences in the ways men and women grieve may be a source of tension and divisiveness in a couple's relationship (Caelli, Downie, & Letendre, 2002). Couples who have gone through the loss of a pregnancy may need extra-compassionate care during a later pregnancy (Caelli et al., 2002).

CONTROVERSIAL ISSUES

Do people have a right to take their own life? If so, under what circumstances? What should be the legal liability, if any, of someone who helps a person commit suicide? Should a doctor prescribe a medicine for a terminally ill patient that will relieve pain but may shorten the patient's life? What about giving a lethal injection to end the patient's suffering? Who decides that a life is not worth prolonging? Who decides when to stop treatment?

These are only a few of the questions that face individuals, families, physicians, and society today—questions involving the quality of life and the nature and circumstances of death. The field of medical ethics is expanding rapidly, in large part because of questions raised by recent technological advances: antibiotics that enable older patients to survive one illness only to succumb to another; respirators that keep people breathing when they are in a

> CRITICAL THINKING
>
> Who should decide what choices a patient and physician can make about circumstances of death?

coma and show no brain activity or other physiological function; organ transplants that may achieve "miracles" at great risk and great cost. None of these questions has a simple answer. Each requires soul searching. Let's look at two subjects that have received much attention: suicide and euthanasia. Both involve the issue of the "right to die."

Suicide

CRITICAL THINKING

How would you describe the patterns of suicide across sexes, countries, and ethnic groups? Suggest why these patterns are evident.

Audience members at a Metropolitan Opera performance of Verdi's *Macbeth* were horrified when, during the intermission, an elderly man—Bantcho Bantchevsky—plunged to his death from a balcony. Bantchevsky was an 82-year-old vocal coach who had lived for his music and his friends. He had been lively and gregarious; but when his health began to deteriorate, he became depressed. His depression grew until he took his life, dying as theatrically as he had lived (Okun, 1988).

Many people find life so precious that they cannot understand why anyone would voluntarily end it. In most nations, suicide rates rise with age and are higher among men than among women (Kinsella & Velkoff, 2001). By far the highest rate of suicide is among white men over age 50, who account for 30 percent of all suicides (Harvard Medical School, 2003). The risk rises with age, particularly among men 85 and older (NCHS, 2004). Older people are more likely than younger people to be depressed and socially isolated, and if they try to commit suicide, they are more likely to succeed the first time (CDC, 2002b). Divorced and widowed men have high suicide rates at all ages. Suicide in older adults is associated with physical illness, family conflict, and financial troubles (Harvard Medical School, 2003). Although more women than men attempt suicide, men are four times more likely to succeed (NCHS, 2004). That is because they tend to use more reliable methods, such as firearms, whereas women are equally likely to choose poisoning. An estimated 60 percent of completed suicides are by gunshot (Harvard Medical School, 2003).

White and Native American men have the highest suicide rates. Members of these two groups are approximately twice as likely to commit suicide as Hispanic American, African American, or Asian American men (NCHS, 2004). Older African Americans are only one-third as likely to commit suicide as older white people (NCHS, 2004), perhaps in part because of religious commitment and in part because they may be accustomed to coping with hard knocks (NCHS, 1998b; NIMH, 1999a). A family history of suicide and suicide attempts greatly raises the risk of suicide. This apparent hereditary vulnerability may be related to low activity of the mood- and impulse-regulating brain chemical serotonin in the prefrontal cortex, the seat of judgment, planning, and inhibition (Harvard Medical School, 2003).

Statistically, it is not surprising that Bantcho Bantchevsky—an elderly white man—would commit suicide.

Although suicide is no longer a crime in modern societies, there is still a stigma against it, based in part on religious prohibitions and in part on society's interest in preserving life. A person who expresses suicidal thoughts may be considered—often with good reason—mentally ill. On the other hand, a growing number of people consider a mature adult's deliberate choice of a time to end his or her life a rational decision and a right to be defended.

However, even among supporters of the right to die, many people hold that family, friends, and others should try to thwart a suicide. According to this view, suicide is often not so much a wish for death as a desire to avoid unbearable pain, either physical or emotional. Finding ways to reduce pain (for example, through hospice care) may prevent a suicide.

Suicide rates in the United States began declining in the late 1990s after a 25 percent rise from 1981 to 1997 (Sahyoun, Lentzner, et al., 2001). Still, more than 30,000 people took their own lives in 2003, according to preliminary data, making suicide the eleventh leading cause of death and the third leading cause among 15- to 24-year-olds. The suicide rate in the United States—10.5 deaths per 100,000 population (Hoyert, Kung, & Smith, 2005)—is lower than in many other industrialized countries (Kinsella & Velkoff, 2001; see Table 13.3). Worldwide, suicide is the thirteenth leading cause of death (WHO, 2003).

As with Bantchevsky, suicide often occurs in conjunction with depression or debilitating physical illness. Nearly 9 out of 10 people who kill themselves have depression or another mental or substance use disorder (NIMH, 1999a). Other factors that increase the risk of suicide are being divorced, widowed, or unemployed; having relatives who attempted or committed suicide; having had psychiatric treatment; having undergone stressful life events; suffering from schizophrenia, substance abuse, or panic attacks; and keeping a handgun in the home. Personality factors associated with a high risk of suicide include dependence, helplessness, hopelessness, inability to accept help, difficulty in forming close relationships, poor problem-solving ability (especially under stress), extreme anxiety or irritability, difficulty in concentrating, and antisocial behavior (Boyer & Buthrie, 1985; Kellerman et al., 1992; Meehan, 1990; *Morbidity and Mortality Weekly Report*, 1985; "Suicide," 1986; USDHHS, 1990, 1992; Weissman, Klerman, Markowitz, & Ouelette, 1989).

Statistics probably understate the number of suicides, since many go unreported and some (such as traffic "accidents" and "accidental" medicinal overdoses) are not recognized as such. Also, the figures on suicides often do not include suicide *attempts*; an estimated 20 to 60 percent of people who commit suicide have tried before, and about 10 percent of people who attempt suicide will kill themselves within 10 years (Harvard Medical School, 2003). A national study found that 60 percent of nonfatal self-inflicted injuries treated in U.S. hospital emergency rooms, especially among teenage girls and young women, are probable suicide attempts and 10 percent are possible attempts (Ikeda et al., 2002).

PREVENTING SUICIDE: WARNING SIGNS

Although some people intent on suicide carefully conceal their plans, 8 out of 10 who kill themselves give warning signs. A person who is truly determined to end his or her life will probably find a way to do it. But sometimes an attempted suicide is a call for help.

TABLE 13.3

Suicide Rates for All Ages in Selected Countries

Country	Year	Males	Females
Hungary	1998	51.1	14.7
Germany	1998	21.5	7.3
China (mainland)	1994	14.3	17.9
Austria	1998	30.0	9.2
Denmark	1996	24.3	9.8
France	1997	28.4	10.1
Japan	1997	26.0	11.9
Czech Republic	1998	25.3	6.5
Switzerland	1996	29.2	11.6
Russian Federation	1997	66.4	12.3
Finland	1996	38.7	10.7
Argentina	1996	9.9	3.0
Israel	1996	8.2	2.6
United States	1997	18.7	4.4
Italy	1996	12.4	4.2
Netherlands	1997	13.5	6.7
Spain	1996	12.8	4.3
Australia	1995	19.0	5.1
Norway	1995	19.1	6.2
Canada	1997	19.6	5.1
Poland	1996	24.1	4.6
Venezuela	1994	8.3	1.9
United Kingdom	1997	11.0	3.2
Greece	1997	6.2	1.0
Colombia	1994	5.5	1.5

NOTE: Suicide Rates (per 100,000) (most recent year available, as of October 2000).
SOURCE: www.who.int-mental_health-Topic_Suicide-suicide_rates.html World Health Organization, Geneva, October 2000.

Warning signs of suicide include withdrawing from family or friends; talking about death, the hereafter, or suicide; giving away prized possessions; abusing drugs or alcohol; personality changes, such as unusual anger, boredom, or apathy.

People who are suicidal often show signs of depression, such as unusual difficulty concentrating, loss of self-esteem, and feelings of helplessness, hopelessness, extreme anxiety, or panic (Harvard Medical School, 2003; NIMH, 1999a&b).

Many suicides are impulsive; if a convenient means is not at hand, a suicidal person may desist or defer action long enough to get help. Psychotherapy, medication, or increased social contacts can often help to lessen feelings of isolation, lift depression, and restore interest in life.

Survivors of people who take their own lives have been called "suicide's other victims." Many of them blame themselves for failing to recognize the signs. They "obsessively replay the events leading up to the death, imagining how they could have prevented it and berating themselves for their failure to do so" (Goldman & Rothschild, in press). Because of the stigma attached to suicide, they often struggle with their emotions alone rather than sharing them with others who might understand.

A 45-year-old Israeli filmmaker shot a video in which his 83-year-old father and 82-year-old mother stated that they planned to kill themselves while they were still healthy, to avoid deteriorating, suffering, or becoming a burden on their children. Four days later, the couple carried out their plan by taking an overdose of sleeping pills. At the funeral, the son read a letter in which his parents had said they hoped what they were about to do would help "break the taboo" on suicide (Perry, 1995, p. 10).

In traditional Inuit (Eskimo) society, there is no such taboo. Given the belief that the personality survives death, an older man who feels that he can no longer be useful may ask his sons to help him strangle himself; and an older woman who feels that she cannot complete an arduous journey across the tundra may ask her children to leave her behind on the trail. Children usually attempt to change their parents' minds but soon grant this last wish (Guemple, 1983).

Aid in Dying: Euthanasia and Assisted Suicide

A 79-year-old man visited his 62-year-old wife in a nursing home. Once a successful businesswoman, the wife, now suffering from advanced Alzheimer's disease, screamed constantly and was unable or unwilling to speak. The man pushed his wife's wheelchair into a stairwell, where he killed her with a pistol shot. The district attorney who prosecuted the husband called his action "classic first-degree murder." But the grand jury refused to indict, and he went free (Malcolm, 1984).

This husband claimed to be practicing euthanasia ("good death"), sometimes called *mercy killing*. If so, his act was an example of **active euthanasia**, action taken deliberately to shorten a life, in order to end suffering or allow a terminally ill person to die with dignity. **Passive euthanasia** is deliberately withholding or discontinuing treatment that might extend the life of a terminally ill patient, such as medication, life-support systems, or feeding tubes. Active euthanasia is generally illegal; passive euthanasia, in some circumstances and in some places, is not. Recently, **assisted suicide**, in which a physician or someone else helps a person die, has become a controversial issue. All of these are forms of what is sometimes called aid in dying or hastening death, but their moral and ethical implications may differ and even their definitions are often debated.

CRITICAL THINKING

What are the benefits and potential dangers of legalizing euthanasia? Should active and/or passive euthanasia be openly discussed and legislated?

CHANGING ATTITUDES TOWARD EUTHANASIA

A change in attitudes toward euthanasia can be attributed to revulsion against technologies that keep patients alive indefinitely after the brain has, for all practical purposes, stopped functioning. But there are thorny ethical questions for society and for patients and their families.

The President's Commission for the Study of Ethical Problems in Medicine and Biomedical and Behavioral Research proposed that mentally competent patients, and families acting on behalf of incompetent patients, be allowed to halt medical treatment that keeps the patients alive without any hope of cure or improvement. The commission recommended that ending a life intentionally be forbidden, but that doctors should be allowed to give drugs that are likely to shorten life if the reason for administering the drugs is to relieve pain (Schmeck, 1983). However, the Harris poll conducted in December 1994 found that 70 percent of adults would "allow doctors to comply with the wishes of a dying patient in severe distress who asks to have his or her life ended" (Taylor, 1995).

ADVANCE DIRECTIVES

The United States Supreme Court has held that a person whose wishes are clearly known has a constitutional right to have life-sustaining treatment discontinued (*Cruzan v. Director, Missouri Department of Health*, 1990; Gostin, 1997). Since that decision, more people have specified in writing what measures they want—or do not want—taken if they become mentally incompetent or terminally ill, or if they are in a **persistent vegetative state**, a state in which, while technically alive, they have no awareness and only rudimentary brain functioning. The importance of putting these requests in legally enforceable form was highlighted by a survey of 1,400 doctors and nurses in five major hospitals around the United States. Nearly half of attending doctors and nurses and 70 percent of resident doctors reported prolonging life support for terminally ill patients—even though they knew the patients would not want such treatment—while failing to give them enough pain medication (Solomon, 1993).

A mentally competent person's wishes can be spelled out in advance in a document called an **advance directive**, which contains instructions for when and how to discontinue futile medical care. All 50 states have now legalized some form of advance directive or adopted other provisions governing the making of end-of-life decisions (APA Working Group on Assisted Suicide and End-of-Life Decision Making, 2005).

One type of directive is the **living will**. It may contain specific provisions with regard to circumstances in which treatment should be discontinued, what extraordinary measures—if any—should be taken to prolong life, and what kind of pain management is desired. A person also may specify, through a donor card or a signature on the back of his or her driver's license, that his or her organs be donated to someone in need of an organ transplant.

Some "living will" legislation applies only to terminally ill patients—not to patients who are incapacitated by illness or injury but may live many years in severe pain, or to patients in a coma, or to patients in some other extremely disabled state, such as a persistent vegetative state. Therefore, it may be advisable to draw up a **durable power of attorney**, which appoints another person to make decisions if someone becomes incapacitated. A number of states have enacted statutes expressly for decisions about health care, which provide for a simple form known as a *medical durable power of attorney expressly for decisions about health care*.

ACTIVE EUTHANASIA: THE NEXT STEP?

The case of Terri Schiavo—a young woman diagnosed in a persistent vegetative state who had not left a written advance directive—erupted into a seven-year legal battle culminating in an unprecedented Congressional intervention in the judicial process because of a bitter disagreement between her husband and her parents over what her wishes had been and whether her condition was truly irreversible (Annas, 2005). An autopsy, which took place after all legal efforts were exhausted and her feeding tubes were finally removed, revealed that her brain had atrophied to about half of what it should have been, and there were indications that her vision centers had been destroyed. This tends to support her husband's contention that she would *not* have recovered and that her suffering might have been prolonged by keeping her on life support for 15 years.

Even with advance directives, many patients have undergone protracted, fruitless treatment against their expressed wishes. In a 5-year study of some 9,000 critically ill patients at five U.S. teaching hospitals, doctors were frequently unaware of patients' request not to be resuscitated in the event of cardiac arrest (The SUPPORT Principal Investigators, 1995).

Such findings led the American Medical Association to form a Task Force on Quality Care at the End of Life. Many hospitals now have ethics committees that create guidelines, review cases, and help doctors, patients, and their families with decisions about end-of-life care (Simpson, 1996); and a smaller number of hospitals employ full-time ethics consultants. A prospective randomized controlled two-year study of 551 patients in intensive care suggests that ethics consultations in difficult, value-laden situations can help resolve conflicts that might otherwise prolong nonbeneficial or unwanted treatment (Schneiderman et al., 2003).

Assisted Suicide: Pros and Cons

In Michigan, when Jack Kevorkian—a retired pathologist—devised and used a machine to help terminally ill people commit suicide by inhaling a lethal gas, the state legislature banned it. Kevorkian remained defiant; and by December 1994, when the Michigan Supreme Court upheld the law, he had attended 21 deaths ("Michigan Court," 1994). A Harris poll of 1,200 adults found that, of those who knew about Kevorkian, 58 percent supported him (Taylor, 1995). In 1998, CBS aired a videotape of Kevorkian assisting a man named Thomas York, who had Lou Gehrig's disease, to administer a lethal injection. He was subsequently charged and found guilty of second degree murder and delivery of a controlled substance. He had also been charged with criminal assisted suicide, but the charge was dropped, leaving the testimony of York's family as to York's intent to die irrelevant during the trial.

© Hillary/Reuters/Corbis Images

Physician-assisted suicide for the terminally ill has become a controversial issue. Jack Kevorkian, M.D., defied Michigan's law banning the practice by aiding in the deaths of at least 21 people. The two women shown here, Marcella Lawrence (left) and Marguerite Tate (right), took their lives in Kevorkian's presence a few hours before the governor signed the bill into law.

Assisted suicide, called physician aid in dying when a doctor's help is involved, is still legal in most places but in recent years has come to the forefront of public debate. It may be similar in principle to voluntary active euthanasia, in which, for example, a patient asks for and receives a lethal injection; but in assisted suicide the person who wants to die performs the actual deed. The American Medical Association opposes physician aid in dying as contrary to a practitioner's oath to "do no harm." Doctors are permitted to give drugs that may shorten a life if the purpose is to relieve pain (Gostin, 1997; Quill, Lo, & Brock, 1997), but some physicians refuse for reasons of personal or medical ethics (APA, 2001).

The ethical arguments *for* assisted suicide are based on the principles of autonomy and self-determination: that mentally competent persons should have the right to control the quality of their own lives and the timing and nature of their death. Proponents of assisted suicide place a high value on preserving the dignity and personhood of the dying human being. *Medical* arguments hold that a doctor is obligated to take all measures necessary to relieve suffering. Besides, the patient is the one who takes the actual steps to end life. A *legal* argument is that legalizing assisted suicide would permit the regulation of practices that now occur anyway out of compassion for suffering patients. It is argued that adequate safeguards against abuse can be put in place through a combination of legislation and professional regulation (APA, 2001).

Some ethical and legal scholars go further: They favor legalizing *all* forms of *voluntary* euthanasia with safeguards against involuntary euthanasia. The key issue, according to these scholars, is not how death occurs but who makes the decision. They see no difference in principle between pulling the plug on a respirator or pulling out feeding tubes and giving a lethal injection or prescribing an overdose of pills at the patient's request. They maintain that aid in dying, if openly available, would reduce fear and helplessness by enabling patients to control their own fate (APA, 2001; Brock, 1992; R. A. Epstein, 1989; Orentlicher, 1996).

Ethical arguments *against* assisted suicide center on two principles: (1) the belief that taking a life, even with consent is wrong; and (2) concern for protection of the disadvantaged. Opponents of aid-in-dying point out that autonomy is often limited by poverty or disability or membership in a stigmatized social group, and they fear that persons in these categories may be subtly pressured into choosing suicide with cost containment as an underlying factor. Some patients may internalize this concern, insisting that they do not want their families to waste limited resources on their prolonged care. *Medical* arguments against assisted suicide include the possibility of misdiagnosis, the potential future availability of new treatments, the likelihood of incorrect prognosis, and the belief that helping someone die is incompatible with a physician's role as healer and that adequate safeguards are not possible. *Legal* arguments against assisted suicide include concerns about enforceability of such safeguards and also about lawsuits when family members disagree about the propriety of terminating a life (APA, 2001).

Because self-administered pills do not always work, some opponents contend that physician-assisted suicide would lead to voluntary active euthanasia (Groenewoud et al., 2000). The next step on the "slippery slope," some warn, would be involuntary euthanasia—not only for the terminally ill but also for others, such as people with disabilities, whose quality of life is perceived as diminished. They claim that people who want to die are often temporarily depressed and might change their minds with treatment or palliative care (APA, 2005; Butler, 1996; Hendin, 1994; Latimer, 1992; Quill et al., 1997; Simpson, 1996; Singer, 1988; Singer & Siegler, 1990).

Legalizing Physician Aid in Dying

In September, 1996, a 66-year-old Australian man with advanced prostate cancer was the first person to die legally by assisted suicide. Under a law passed in the Northern Territory, he pressed a computer key that administered a lethal dose of barbiturates. In 1997 the law was repealed ("Australian Man," 1996; Voluntary Euthanasia Society, 2002).

Since 1997, when a unanimous U.S. Supreme Court left regulation of physician aid in dying up to the states, measures to legalize assisted suicide for the terminally ill have been introduced in several states. So far Oregon is the only state to pass such a law, the Death with Dignity Act. In 1994, Oregonians voted to let mentally competent patients who have been told by two doctors that they have less than six months to live request a lethal prescription with strong safeguards to make sure that the request is serious and voluntary and that all other alternatives have been considered. The Oregon law survived a court challenge and a repeal referendum in 1997. In 2002 a federal district court overruled an attempt by U.S. Attorney General John Ashcroft to block the operation of the statute by making doctors criminally liable if they prescribe drugs to help patients end their lives. In January 2006 the U.S. Supreme Court issued a 6 to 3 decision (Gonzales v. Oregon) upholding Oregon's physician-assisted suicide law (Vollmar, 2006).

What has been the experience under the Oregon law? In its first seven years of operation, 238 terminally ill patients were reported to state health officials to have taken their lives under the act, 37 of them in 2004 (Schwartz, 2005). In an earlier study after two years of operation, physicians reported granting about one-sixth of the 221 requests for lethal prescriptions, but nearly half of these patients changed their minds and did not take the medications. Patients who received palliative interventions, such as control of pain or referral to a hospice program, were more likely to change their minds (Ganzini et al., 2000). Patients who requested and used lethal prescriptions tended to be more concerned about loss of autonomy or control of bodily functions than about fear of pain or financial loss (Chin, Hedberg, Higginson, & Fleming, 1999; Sullivan et al., 2000).

Active euthanasia remains illegal in the United States, even in Oregon, but not in the Netherlands, where in 2001 voluntary euthanasia was legalized for patients in a state of continuous, unbearable, and incurable suffering (Johnston, 2001; Osborn, 2002). In such cases, doctors can now inject a lethal dose of medication. Belgium followed suit the following year ("Belgium Legalises Euthanasia," 2002).

Before 2001, both assisted suicide and active euthanasia were technically illegal in the Netherlands, but physicians who engaged in these practices could avoid prosecution under strict conditions of reporting and government oversight (Simons, 1993). In 1995, 2.5 percent of deaths in the Netherlands resulted from euthanasia or assisted suicide (Van der Maas et al., 1996). Researchers found little evidence of a "slippery slope" and observed that Dutch doctors seemed to be practicing physician aid in dying "only reluctantly and under compelling circumstances" (Angell, 1996, p. 1677). Critics in the United States disagreed, claiming that doctors in the Netherlands had moved from assisted suicide for the terminally ill all the way to euthanasia for those with chronic illness or psychological distress and even, in some cases, to involuntary euthanasia (Hendin, Rutenfrans, & Zylicz, 1997).

END-OF-LIFE DECISIONS AND CULTURAL ATTITUDES

It is hard to compare the experience of the Netherlands, which has a homogeneous population and universal national health coverage, with that of such a large, diverse country as the United States (APA, 2001; Griffiths, Bood, & Weyers, 1998). Nevertheless, with increasing numbers of Americans—3 out of 4 in a 2005 Gallup poll (Moore, 2005)—favoring euthanasia for a patient who is incurably ill and wants to die, some U.S. doctors have acceded to patients' requests for assistance in hastening death. A nationwide survey of 1,902 physicians whose specialties involve care of dying patients found that, of those who had received requests for help with suicide (18 percent) or lethal injections (11 percent), about 7 percent had complied at least once (Meier et al., 1998). On the other hand, in a survey in the United Kingdom, 80 percent of geriatric physicians—but only 52 percent of intensive care physicians—considered active voluntary euthanasia *never* ethically justified (Dickinson, Lancaster, Clark, Ahmedzai, & Noble, 2002).

The first representative study of end-of-life decisions in six European countries (Belgium, Denmark, Italy, the Netherlands, Sweden, and Switzerland) found important cultural differences. Questionnaires to be completed anonymously were sent to attending physicians in a random sample of deaths during a six-month period. In all six countries, physicians reported withholding or withdrawing life-prolonging treatment—most typically medication, followed by hydration or nutrition—but the frequency varied greatly, from 41 percent of deaths in Switzerland to 6 percent in Italy (Bosshard et al., 2005). Active forms of physician-assisted death were most prevalent in the Netherlands and Belgium. In these two countries as well as in Switzerland, end-of-life decisions were more frequenlty discussed with patients and relatives than in the other three countries (van der Heide et al., 2003).

Special end-of-life issues concern treatment of newborns with incurable conditions or very poor prognoses for quality of life. Forgoing or withdrawing life-prolonging treatment for newborns with no chance of survival and those born with severe brain abnormalities or extensive organ damage is now widely accepted medical practice (Verhagen & Sauer, 2005). Yet, here, too, cultural differences appear. In a study of physicians' self-reported practices in France, Germany, Italy, the Netherlands, Spain, Sweden, and the United Kingdom, the vast majority of neonatal practitioners in all seven countries had been involved at least once in decisions to withhold or not institute treatment. French, British, Dutch, and Swedish doctors were more likely to report clear-cut decisions such as withdrawal of ventilators. Only French and Dutch physicians acknowledged with significant frequency having administered drugs to end a newborn's life (Cuttini et al., 2000).

Active euthanasia of infants who would otherwise survive with unbearable pain or suffering remains illegal in the Netherlands, as elsewhere. Yet, as was the case with assisted suicide before enactment of the 2001 law, such deaths do occur there with a form of legal endorsement. Since 1998, 22 cases of euthanasia in newborns with very severe forms of spina bifida have been reported to Dutch authorities without prosecution. Guidelines developed by Groninen Hospital in Amsterdam in 2002 in cooperation with a district attorney permit doctors, with parental approval, to end the lives of newborns deemed to be in great pain from incurable disease or extreme deformities when an infant's medical team and independent doctors agree that there is no prospect for improvement. Four such deaths were reported in 2003; again, none were prosecuted (Verhagen & Sauer, 2005).

One salutary result of the aid-in-dying controversy has been to call attention to the need for better palliative care and closer attention to patients' motivation and state of mind. A request for aid in dying can provide an opening to explore the reasons behind it. When doctors talk openly with patients about their physical and mental symptoms, their expectations, their fears and goals, their options for end-of-life care, their family concerns, and their need for meaning and quality of life, ways may be found to diminish these concerns without the taking of life (Bascom & Tolle, 2002). In terminally ill patients, the will to live can fluctuate greatly, so if aid in dying is contemplated, it is essential to ensure that the request is not just a passing one (Chochinov, Tataryn, Clinch, & Dudgeon, 1999). Sometimes a psychiatric consultation may discover an underlying disturbance masked by a seemingly rational request (Muskin, 1998). If lethal measures *are* taken, it is important that a physician be present to ensure that the death is as merciful and pain-free as possible (Nuland, 2000).

In the United States, with its ethnically diverse population, issues of social and cultural diversity need to be addressed in end-of-life decision making. Planning for death is inconsistent with traditional Navajo values, which avoid negative thinking and talk. Chinese families may seek to protect a dying person from unfavorable information, including knowledge of his or her impending death. Recent Mexican or Korean immigrants may believe less in individual autonomy than is customary in the dominant U.S. culture. Among some ethnic minorities, the value of longevity may take priority over health. African Americans and Hispanic Americans, for example, are more likely than European Americans to prefer life-sustaining treatment regardless of the state of the disease and of their educational level (APA Working Group on Assisted Suicide, 2005).

Issues of hastening death will become more pressing as the population ages. In years to come, both the courts and the public will be forced to come to terms with these issues as increasing numbers of people claim a right to die with dignity and with help.

FINDING MEANING AND PURPOSE IN LIFE AND DEATH

For most people, death comes at a time and in a way not of their choosing. As the end of their journey approaches, they look back over what they have made of themselves—how they have changed and grown. They ask themselves about the purpose of life and death and try to sum up what their lives have meant.

Reviewing a Life

In Ingmar Bergman's film *Wild Strawberries*, an elderly doctor dreams and thinks about his past and his coming death. Realizing how cold and unaffectionate he has been, he becomes warmer and more open in his last days. In

Charles Dickens's *A Christmas Carol*, Scrooge changes his greedy, heartless ways after seeing ghostly visions of his past, his present, and his future—his death. In Kurosawa's film *Ikiru* ("To Live"), a petty bureaucrat who discovers that he is dying of cancer looks back over the emptiness of his life and, in a final burst of energy, creates a meaningful legacy by pushing through a project for a children's park, which he has previously blocked. These three fictional characters make their remaining time more purposeful through **life review**, a process of reminiscence that enables a person to see the significance of his or her life as death draws nearer.

CRITICAL THINKING

As you talk with aging individuals, do they give you an impression of their ego integrity? What do they say or do to reveal the conclusions they have made about life and death?

Life review, which commonly occurs in old age, can foster *ego integrity*—according to Erikson, the final critical task of the life span. Awareness of mortality may be an impetus for reexamination of one's values. By going over their lives, people may see their experiences and actions in a new light. They may be able to complete unfinished tasks—such as reconciliation with estranged family members or friends—and thus achieve a satisfying sense of closure.

Not all memories are equally conducive to life review or to mental health. One research team (Sherman, 1991, 1993; Sherman & Peak, 1991) identified three types of reminiscences. *Reminiscences for pleasure* (the most frequent kind) enhance mood and self-image. *Reminiscences for self-understanding* (reported by about 1 out of 4 older adults) help people resolve past problems and find meaning in life. *Reminiscences to solve present problems and cope with losses* are predominant among about 1 in 10 older people. People who use reminiscence for self-understanding show the greatest ego integrity and positive mental health, although those actively engaged in a life review may temporarily experience lower morale. Those who shut out all but pleasurable memories have high spirits but less ego integrity. Then there is a group who keep recalling negative events and are obsessed with regret, hopelessness, and fear of death. These people, from Erikson's perspective, have given way to despair and may need treatment (Sherman, 1993; Walasky, Whitbourne, & Nehrke, 1983–1984).

Another team of researchers (Wong & Watt, 1991) found that people who are "aging successfully" (according to the measures used) have more integrative or instrumental reminiscences and fewer obsessive or escapist reminiscences than people who are "aging unsuccessfully." *Integrative* reminiscences help people accept their lives, resolve old conflicts, and reconcile their idealized version of the past with reality. *Instrumental* reminiscences allow them to draw on coping strategies that have worked in the past to deal with current problems. *Escapist* reminiscences glorify the past over the present. *Obsessive* reminiscences are colored by guilt, bitterness, or despair.

Life-review therapy can help focus the natural process of life review and make it more conscious, purposeful, and efficient (Butler, 1961; Lewis & Butler, 1974). Box 13.3 describes methods often used for uncovering memories in life-review therapy, which may also be used by older adults to facilitate their own life review. (The questions listed in Table 12.6 offer additional possibilities.)

Evoking Memories for a Life Review

The following methods for uncovering memories (adapted from Lewis & Butler, 1974) are often used in life-review therapy and can also be used fruitfully outside a therapeutic situation. By engaging in such projects with younger family members or friends, older adults can creatively order their lives, build a bridge between generations, and give younger people insights that may help them in their own old age.

- *Written or taped autobiographies.* What a person includes—or does not include—in an autobiography may be significant. One successful professional man put together an extensive record of his life, with practically no mention of his two middle-aged children. When the therapist explored this omission, the man revealed that he was estranged from both children—and was then able to use the therapy to examine his feelings about them.
- *Pilgrimages.* When possible, older people can make trips back to scenes of their birth, childhood, and young adulthood, taking photographs and notes to put their thoughts together. If they cannot do this in reality, they may be able to contact people still living in these places. Such pilgrimages can reawaken memories and provide new understanding. One woman, who was still angry with her parents for forbidding her to go into the attic and had for years fantasized about what they were hiding from her, discovered upon revisiting her childhood home that there were no stairs to the attic and that the prohibition had been simply for her safety.
- *Reunions.* Getting together with high school and college classmates, distant family members, or members of a religious or civic organization can give older adults a new view of themselves in relation to their peers and other important people in their lives.
- *Constructing a genealogy.* Developing a family tree can provide a sense of continuity. The search is interesting; it may include putting advertisements in newspapers, visiting cemeteries, and poring over town records, family documents, and records of churches, synagogues, or other religious institutions.
- *Scrapbooks, photo albums, old letters, and other memorabilia.* The items usually have a special, pleasurable meaning. By talking about them, older people can often recall forgotten events, acquaintances, and emotional experiences.
- *Focus on ethnic identity.* By describing special ethnic traditions they have enjoyed and valued, older persons can enhance their appreciation of their heritage and pass it on.
- *Summation of a life's work.* By summing up what they regard as their contributions to the world, older people can gain a sense of their meaningful participation in it. Some of these summations have grown into published books, poems, and music.

Overcoming Fear of Death

The central character in Leo Tolstoy's story "The Death of Ivan Ilyich" is racked by a fatal illness. But even greater than his physical suffering is his mental torment. He asks himself over and over what meaning there is to his agony, and he becomes more and more convinced that his life has been without purpose and his death will be equally pointless. At the last minute, though, he experiences a spiritual revelation, a concern for his wife and son, which gives him a final moment of integrity and enables him to conquer his terror.

What Tolstoy dramatized in literature is being confirmed by social scientists. A researcher who administered attitudinal scales to 39 women whose average age was 76 found that those who saw the most purpose in life had the least fear of death (Durlak, 1973). "There is no need to be afraid of death," Kübler-Ross wrote (1975, p.164); facing the reality of death is a key to growth:

> It is the denial of death that is partially responsible for [people's] living empty, purposeless lives; for when you live as if you'll live forever, it becomes too easy to postpone the things you know that you must do. In contrast, when you fully understand that each day you awaken could be the last you have, you take the time *that day* to grow, to become more of who you really are, to reach out to other human beings. (p. 164)

Consciousness of impending death, then, can give adults a last chance to express their best qualities and to savor the sweetness of life.

Development: A Lifelong Process

In his late seventies, the artist Pierre-Auguste Renoir had crippling arthritis and chronic bronchitis and had lost his wife; he was confined to a wheelchair and was so pain-wracked that he could not sleep through the night. He was unable to hold a palette and could no longer grip a brush: he had to have his brush tied to his right hand. Yet he continued to produce brilliant, youthful paintings, full of color and vibrant life. Finally, stricken by pneumonia, he lay in bed, gazing at some anemones his maid had picked. He gathered enough strength to sketch the form of these beautiful flowers, and then—just before he died—lay back and whispered, "I think I am beginning to understand something about it" (Hanson, 1968).

Even dying can be a developmental experience. As one health practitioner put it, ". . . there are things to be gained, accomplished in dying. Time with and for those whom we are close to, achieving a final and enduring sense of self-worth, and a readiness to let go are priceless elements of a good death" (Weinberger, 1999)—the kind of death Louisa May Alcott described in *Little Women*.

Within a limited life span, no person can realize all capabilities, gratify all desires, engage all interests, or experience all the richness that life has to offer. The tension between virtually infinite possibilities for growth and a finite time in which to grow defines human life, particularly during late adulthood. By choosing which possibilities to pursue and by continuing to follow them as far as possible, even up to the very end, each person contributes to the unfinished story of adult development.

Changing Perspectives on Death and Dying

- Dying has three interrelated aspects: biological, social, and psychological.
- Although denial of death has been characteristic of modern American society, there is now an upsurge of interest in understanding and dealing realistically and compassionately with death.

thanatology (p. 481)   **hospice care (p. 481)**

death education (p. 481)   **palliative care (p. 482)**

Facing Death

- Attitudes toward death are affected by culture and cohort and vary at different stages of adulthood.
- People often undergo cognitive and personality changes shortly before death.
- Elisabeth Kübler-Ross proposed five stages in coming to terms with death: denial, anger, bargaining, depression, and acceptance. These stages, and their sequence, are not universal.

Facing Bereavement

- Mourning customs vary greatly from one culture to another.
- Anticipatory grief may or may not help survivors handle actual bereavement.
- The most widely studied pattern of grief after a death moves from shock and disbelief to preoccupation with the memory of the dead person and finally to resolution. Research has found several variations: high to low distress, no intense distress, and prolonged distress.
- Being widowed has been found to be the most stressful life event. Women are more likely to be widowed than men. Older adults seem better adjusted to widowhood than younger ones. Men are more likely to remarry than women.
- Today, more people are losing parents later in life. Death of a parent can precipitate changes in the self and in relationships with others.
- The loss of a child can be especially difficult because it is no longer normative.

bereavement (p. 487)   **grief work (p. 492)**

grief (p. 487)   **ambiguous loss(p. 494)**

mourning (p. 487)   **grief therapy (p. 496)**

anticipatory grief (p. 492)

Controversial Issues

- Suicide is the ninth leading cause of death in the United States, is prevalent worldwide, and is often associated with depression or debilitating illness. The highest suicide rate in the United States is among elderly white men. The "right to die" and assisted suicide are controversial issues.
- Passive euthanasia is generally permitted with the patient's consent or with advance directives. Active euthanasia is generally illegal, but voluntary active euthanasia is tolerated in the Netherlands under strict conditions.

active euthanasia (p. 509)
passive euthanasia (p. 509)
assisted suicide (p. 509)
persistent vegetative state (p. 510)

advance directive (p. 510)
living will (p. 510)
durable power of attorney (p. 511)

Finding Meaning and Purpose in Life and Death

- Life review helps people prepare for death and gives them a last chance to complete unfinished tasks.
- The more purpose and meaning people find in their lives, the less they fear death.
- Development can continue up to the moment of death.

  life review (p. 517)

Epilogue

*To accept all experiences as raw material out of which the human
spirit distills meanings and values is a part of the meaning of maturity.*
—Howard Thurman, *Meditations of the Heart*, 1953

WE PROMISED AT THE BEGINNING of this book that the study of adult development and aging would be fascinating because it is the study of real lives. In earlier chapters we have focused on many issues and topics concerning young adulthood, middle adulthood, and later adulthood that affect each of us, our families, our friends, and our communities. We hope this book has stimulated your interest and has provided a solid basis for your personal and professional development.

The changing individual in a changing world has been a major theme of this book. Change results from both internal and external forces and affects us at personal, familial, cultural, national, and global levels. Lifespan developmental theory emphasizes that developmental change occurs on multiple dimensions, with both gains and losses on each dimension throughout life.

Aging, as you have learned, is not simply biological; it results from a complex interaction of biological, historical, and sociocultural influences. The relative contributions of these influences vary for different dimensions in different individuals at different points in the life span. In a way, aging is not fair. Some people renew their drivers' licenses at 100; others need long-term care in their sixties.

Bernice Neugarten, in the early 1970s, wrote about an "age irrelevant society," and in many respects age has lost much of its predictive power. Adults of all ages are returning to school, and young adults are taking on leadership roles in business and government. Lifespan theory emphasizes the changing ways in which people are growing older. An example is the concept of a second "middle age" between the sixties and the eighties (Sterns & Huyck, 2001). Even when health changes become more of an issue and individuals become more physically frail, there still is the desire for active and involved life styles.

However, there still are many conventional ideas regarding timing norms and expectancies about periods of adulthood and especially about the later part of life. Even seasoned professionals in gerontology have difficulty fully understanding the changing nature of the aging process. Others are raising serious questions about the issues of a society too focused on older adults (Dychtwald, 1999). Even with increasing knowledge of differences in people and of available options, we are trying to understand how people make their personal decisions.

To be an applied gerontologist is to be an interventionist (Sterns & Camp, 1998): to engage in programmatic approaches that modify the course of psychological aging (Baltes & Danish, 1980). Gerontologists are on a continuing quest for ways to facilitate optimal development and improved assessment and treatment approaches. Especially important is to improve the quality of life for adults of all ages by developing the interventions necessary to prevent, delay, or reverse disabilities that affect the functional capacity of adults (Ball & Rebok, 1994). At the same time, we need to be sensitive to meeting the needs and wants of adults on limited incomes. Housing, employment and skills training, nutrition services, health care, and many other services make it possible for these people to live more fulfilling lives. What knowledge and research will be needed to create supportive environments and services in the public sector and private sector so that more and more people can make meaningful choices?

It has taken many years for researchers, educators, policymakers, business leaders, governmental officials, and others to realize the implications of an aging society. New data from the 2000 census are having an impact in every community in the United States as each reviews the demographics and implications for the future. A number of years ago Robert Butler, first director of the National Institute on Aging, talked about 20/20 vision as we look ahead to the year 2020, when the peak of the baby boom reaches age 65 (Ferraro & Sterns, 1990).

Publicity about the aging of baby boomers has made people much more aware of the changes taking place at midlife and beyond in the United States and throughout the world. As we gain understanding of the middle years, it becomes apparent that midlife can be separated into early and later phases. Of current interest is the transition into midlife: how one becomes aware that one has become middle-aged and the issues (or crises) that this awareness engenders. Issues in the first portion of midlife often revolve around (1) recognizing the limits of career progress and deciding whether to shift gears or remain in place, and (2) rebalancing work and family needs as children become more independent. During the second phase of midlife, the career issues revolve increasingly around decisions about how much energy and ambition to invest in work and about withdrawal from paid employment (Sterns & Huyck, 2001).

As the number of older adults continues to increase, the demand for services that an aging population needs is creating challenges for public and private agencies. The ability to age in place and maintain the highest levels of independent functioning is directly related to the ability to go grocery shopping, access medical facilities, obtain community services, conduct personal business, and socialize (Sterns & Camp, 1998). We need to support the concept of "aging friendly communities" where people can live out their lives with the informal support of families and friends and when necessary with formal services provided by community agencies. In the next few years, we will be dealing with key policy issues of health insurance, social security, housing, mobility, and others.

The study of adult development and aging provides important background for our own growth, as well as sensitivity to our parents', grandparents', and friends' needs and wants. What is apparent is the need for a flexible approach to the future. How one plans one's work life, career updating, and the decision to work full time, part time, or any combination thereof are issues for many adults today, regardless of age.

What we call *retirement education*, which ideally begins in early adulthood, can help clarify life planning. Over the past thirty years we have come to realize that our concept of retirement needs to evolve. The issue in the 1970s was convincing people of the normalcy of retirement. Now individual differences play a major role. Whether, when, and how a person retires may be under that person's control. Current research indicates that more people will want to work longer, either full time or part time. On the other hand, changing circumstances may take away people's control, especially in mid and later life. Layoffs, downsizing, and changing economies have replaced the stable bedrock of social expectations (Sterns & Subich, 2005).

Self-management of our careers and life has become an obvious goal (Sterns & Gray, 1999). Choices regarding health care, wills, durable power of attorney for finances and/or health care, and decisions to be made regarding death are all examples. Each of us must be in a position to be able to make choices for ourselves, to offer suggestions to our loved ones, and, if part of our work, to apply lifespan developmental and gerontological knowledge to assist clients.

The quotation that opened this epilogue speaks of the fact that how we live our lives depends on how we see meanings in life and how we develop our personal values. Aging is in your future; what you do with it is largely up to you.

Glossary

A

achieving stage Second of Schaie's five cognitive stages, in which young adults use knowledge to gain competence and independence.

acquired immune deficiency syndrome (AIDS) Failure of the immune system due to a viral infection, which leaves the body vulnerable to fatal disease.

acquisitive stage First of Schaie's five cognitive stages, characterized by a child's or adolescent's learning of information and skills largely for their own sake or as preparation for participation in society.

active euthanasia Deliberate action to shorten the life of a terminally ill person in order to end suffering or allow death with dignity; also called *mercy killing*. Compare *passive euthanasia*.

activity theory Theory of aging, proposed by Neugarten and others, which holds that in order to age successfully a person must remain as active as possible. Compare *disengagement theory*.

adaptation Adjustment to changing events, circumstances, and conditions of life.

adaptive mechanisms Characteristic ways in which an individual copes or interacts with the environment.

advance directive Legal document written by an individual that contains instructions for future medical care in the event he or she becomes physically or mentally incapacitated.

age structure Percentages of various age groups in a given population.

age-differentiated Life structure in which primary roles—learning, working, and leisure—are based on age; typical in industrialized societies. Compare *age-integrated*.

age-integrated Life structure in which all roles—learning, working, and leisure—are open to adults of all ages and can be interspersed throughout the life span. Compare *age-differentiated*.

ageism Prejudice or discrimination (most commonly against older people) based on age.

ageless self Concept of remaining the same person regardless of age.

age-related macular degeneration Visual disorder in which the central part of the retina loses ability to distinguish fine details; common cause of functional blindness in older adults.

aging in place Remaining in one's own home, with or without assistance, during late life.

Alzheimer's disease (AD) Degenerative brain disorder characterized by irreversible deterioration in memory, awareness, and control of bodily functions, eventually leading to death.

ambiguous loss A loss which is not clearly defined.

androgynous Personality type integrating characteristics typically thought of as masculine with characteristics typically thought of as feminine.

anticipatory grief Grief that begins before an expected death in preparation for bereavement.

antidepressant drugs Drugs used to treat depression by restoring the chemical balance of neurotransmitters in the brain.

archetypes In Jung's terminology, images of ideas important in a culture's mythic tradition, which survive in the "collective unconscious."

arteriosclerosis Age-related condition in which walls of the arteries become thickened and more rigid; also called *hardening of the arteries*.

arthritis Group of disorders involving painful inflammation of joints.

articulatory loop (phonological loop) In information-processing models, component of working memory that allows information about sounds and language to be kept in consciousness.

artificial insemination Injection of sperm into a woman's cervix in order to enable her to conceive.

assisted suicide Suicide in which a physician or someone else helps a person take his or her own life.

assortative mating Tendency to fall in love with and marry a person similar to oneself.

atherosclerosis Buildup of fatty deposits on inner walls of arteries, obstructing the flow of blood; this can lead to heart attack. Also called *coronary artery disease*.

attentional resources In Craik's terminology, amount of mental energy a person has available to focus on a task.

autoimmunity Tendency of an aging body to mistake its own tissues for foreign invaders and to attack and destroy them.

B

balanced investment Pattern of retirement activity allocated among family, work, and leisure. Compare *family-focused lifestyle*.

behavior therapy Therapeutic method that uses positive and negative reinforcement to modify behavior.

bereavement Loss, due to death, of someone to whom one feels close and the process of adjustment to the loss.

bioecological approach Bronfenbrenner's system of understanding development, which identifies five levels of environmental influences, from most intimate to broadest.

biological age Measure of progress along the potential life span predicted by a person's physical condition.

biomarkers Specific biological measures of the rate at which a body is aging.

bisexual Sexually oriented toward both sexes.

blended family Family resulting from the marriage or cohabitation of an adult who already has children; also called *stepfamily, reconstituted family*, or *combined family*.

blood pressure Force of blood flow against arterial walls.

brief dynamic therapy Therapeutic method based on a genuine, nonmanipulative working alliance between therapist and client.

burnout Syndrome characterized by emotional exhaustion and a sense that one no longer can be effective on the job.

C

cancer Group of diseases involving uncontrolled growth of abnormal cells, which invade and destroy healthy tissue.

carcinogens Cancer-causing agents in the environment.

cardiac reserve Heart's ability to pump faster under stress.

caregiver burnout Condition of physical, mental, and emotional exhaustion affecting adults who care for other persons.

caregiving Informal or unpaid care of a person whose independence is physically, mentally, emotionally, or economically limited.

case study Research design covering a single case or life, based on observations, interviews, or biographical and documentary material.

cataracts Cloudy or opaque areas in the lens of the eye, which often cause blurring of vision in older adults.

central executive In information-processing models of memory, component of working memory that selects and processes sensory inputs and transforms them into meaningful mental representations; it also can retrieve information from long-term memory.

change Alteration or modification from one time to another.

child abuse Maltreatment of a child involving physical and mental injury.

chronological age Number of years a person has lived.

classic aging pattern On Wechsler Adult Intelligence Scale (WAIS), greater and sharper age-associated decline in performance IQ than in verbal IQ.

classical conditioning Form of unconscious learning in which a previously neutral stimulus (one that does not ordinarily elicit a particular involuntary response) comes to elicit the response as a result of repeated association with a stimulus that normally produces the response.

climacteric Period of 2 to 5 years during which a woman's body undergoes physiological changes that bring on menopause.

cochlear implants Electronic devices, useful for people with hearing impairment, which transform sound waves into electrical signals to be transmitted to the brain.

cognitive-appraisal model Model, proposed by Lazarus and colleagues, that views coping as dynamic interaction between individual and environment, in which an individual chooses effortful coping strategies on the basis of cognitive appraisal of a situation that taxes or exceeds his or her resources.

cognitive-developmental theory Theory, proposed by Kohlberg and others, that children learn about gender and other aspects of their world by actively thinking about their experience and then organize their behavior around these perceptions.

cognitive therapy Therapeutic method aimed at teaching patients to recognize and correct negative thinking.

cohabitation Living together and maintaining a sexual relationship without being legally married.

cohort Group of people with a common experience; often, people born at the same point in time.

commitment within relativism In Perry's terminology, final stage of college students' cognitive development, in which they commit themselves to self-chosen beliefs and values despite uncertainty and recognition of other valid possibilities.

compensation hypothesis Hypothesis that there is a negative correlation between intellectuality of work and of leisure activities because people seek leisure activities that make up for what they find missing in work. Compare *spillover hypothesis, resource provision-depletion hypothesis,* and *segmentation hypothesis.*

componential element In Sternberg's triarchic theory, the analytic aspect of intelligence, which determines how efficiently people process information and solve problems.

conductive hearing loss Hearing loss due to blockage of sound from ear wax buildup, abnormal bone growth, or an infection in the middle or outer ear.

congestive heart failure Inability of the heart to pump an adequate supply of blood, as a result of cardiovascular disease.

congruence model Model, proposed by Kahana, which holds that life satisfaction or stress depends on the match between an individual's needs and an environment's ability to meet those needs.

consolidation stage In Super's terminology, fifth stage of career exploration and development, in which people in their mid thirties strive for rapid advancement and consolidate gains.

construct validity Ability of a researcher to demonstrate that the manipulations and measures used in a study pertain to, or represent, the concept or phenomenon under study.

contextual element In Sternberg's triarchic theory, the practical aspect of intelligence, which determines how effectively people deal with their environment.

contextual perspective Metatheory that views development as the product of an ongoing process of interaction between an individual and the context within which the individual acts to achieve goals.

contingent career paths In Raynor's terminology, career paths in which workers are motivated by a perception that their future success hinges on their own actions. Compare *noncontingent career paths.*

continuity theory Theory of aging, proposed by Atchley, which holds that in order to age successfully people must maintain a balance of continuity and change in both the internal and the external structures of their lives.

control group In an experiment, a group of people who are similar to the people in the experimental group but who do not receive the treatment under study. Results obtained with the control group are compared with results obtained with the experimental group.

convergent thinking Thinking aimed at finding the single right answer to a problem, usually the conventional answer. Compare with *divergent thinking.*

convoy theory Theory, proposed by Kahn and Antonucci, that reduction of social contacts in outer circles after retirement may be offset by new contacts in those circles, as well as by maintenance of an inner core of close friends and family. Compare *selectivity theory.*

coping Adaptive thinking or behavior aimed at reducing or relieving stress that arises from harmful, threatening, or challenging conditions.

corneal disease Visual disorder characterized by clouding, scarring, or distortion of the cornea, the front surface of the eye.

correlational study Research design intended to discover whether a statistical correlation can be calculated showing the direction and strength of a relationship between variables.

cosmic perspective Viewpoint achieved in Kohlberg's proposed seventh stage of moral reasoning, characterized by a sense of unity with the cosmos, nature, or the divine.

cross-sectional study Quasi-experimental research design in which people of different ages are assessed on one occasion, providing comparative information about age differences. Compare with *longitudinal study*.

crystallization stage In Super's terminology, first stage of career exploration and development, in which younger adolescents develop a general concept of occupation as a defining feature of the self.

crystallized intelligence Type of intelligence, proposed by Horn, that involves remembering and applying learned information; it is relatively dependent on education and cultural background. Compare *fluid intelligence*.

cultural bias Tendency of psychometric intelligence tests to include questions involving content or skills more familiar and meaningful to some cultural groups than to others.

D

data Information gathered from research.

death education Programs to educate people about death and to help them deal with issues concerning dying and grief in their personal and professional lives.

deceleration stage In Super's terminology, seventh stage of career exploration and development, in which people in their late fifties begin to anticipate retirement and distance themselves from their work.

declarative memory In information-processing models, memory for facts and events that can be recalled or recognized and stated verbally or can cause feelings of familiarity; compare with *nondeclarative memory*.

dementia Deterioration in cognitive and behavioral functioning due to physiological causes; sometimes inaccurately called *senility*.

dependency ratio Comparative size of productive and dependent portions of a population.

dependent variable In an experiment, the variable that may or may not change as a result of manipulation of the independent variable. Compare *independent variable*.

development Systematic process of adaptive change in behavior in one or more directions.

developmental reserve In Baltes's terminology, extent to which memory can be improved with training.

deviation IQ Measurement of intelligence based on distribution of raw scores and standard deviation from the mean.

digit span Number of digits a person can remember at one time; it usually consists of 5 to 9 digits but can be increased by chunking.

disengagement theory Theory of aging, proposed by Cumming and Henry, which holds that successful aging is characterized by mutual withdrawal between the older person and society. Compare *activity theory*.

divergent thinking Thinking that produces a variety of novel possibilities; believed to be a factor in creativity. Compare with *convergent thinking*.

dream In Levinson's terminology, a vision of the future that spurs a young adult's personal and vocational development.

dual-process model Model of intellectual functioning in late adulthood, proposed by Baltes, which identifies and seeks to measure two dimensions of intelligence: mechanics and pragmatics.

durable power of attorney Legal instrument that appoints one person to make decisions in the event of another person's incapacitation.

dynamic visual acuity Ability to see moving objects clearly.

dysmenorrhea Menstrual cramps.

E

ecological validity Characteristic of adult intelligence tests that indicates competence in dealing with real problems or challenges faced by adults.

E-I-E-I-O model Camp's model for classifying mnemonic techniques according to type of processing (explicit or implicit) and initial site of storage (external or internal).

elaboration Encoding strategy or mnemonic device, consisting of making associations, often between new information and information already in memory.

elder abuse Maltreatment or neglect of dependent older people, or violation of their personal rights.

electroconvulsive therapy (ECT) Electric shocks administered to treat severe depression; also called *shock therapy*.

emphysema Irreversible disease, often caused by smoking, which destroys lung tissue, causing progressive difficulty in breathing.

emotion-focused coping In Lazarus's cognitive-appraisal model, coping strategy directed toward managing the emotional response to a stressful situation so as to lessen its physical or psychological impact; also called *palliative coping*. Compare *problem-focused coping*.

empty nest Transitional phase of parenting following the last child's leaving home.

encapsulation In Hoyer's terminology, progressive dedication of information processing and fluid thinking to specific knowledge systems, making knowledge more readily accessible and compensating for declines in cognitive machinery.

encoding In information-processing models of memory, the process by which information is prepared for long-term storage and later retrieval.

environment Totality of nongenetic stimuli influencing development.

environmental press model Model, proposed by Lawton, which holds that stress and adaptation depend on the fit between environmental demands and an individual's competence to meet them.

episodic buffer Allows retrieval of information, which has been stored in episodes, to be retrieved from multiple sources.

episodic memory In information-processing models, memory for personal experiences, activities, and events linked with specific times and places; compare with *semantic memory*.

erectile dysfunction (see impotence)

establishment stage In Super's terminology, fourth stage of career exploration and development, in which people in their late twenties seek advancement along a chosen career path, develop expertise, and see work as intrinsic to the self-concept.

estrogen-replacement therapy (ERT) Treatment with artificial estrogen, sometimes in combination with the hormone progesterone, to relieve or prevent symptoms caused by decline in estrogen levels after menopause. Also called *hormone-replacement therapy (HRT)*.

executive stage Fourth of Schaie's five cognitive stages, in which middle-aged people responsible for societal systems deal with complex relationships on several levels.

experiential element In Sternberg's triarchic theory, the insightful aspect of intelligence, which determines how effectively people process both novel and familiar tasks.

experiment Rigorously controlled, replicable (repeatable) procedure in which a researcher (experimenter) manipulates variables to assess the effect of one on the other.

experimental group In an experiment, the group receiving the treatment under study; any changes in these people are compared with any changes in the control group.

explanatory style Person's habitual way of explaining misfortune.

explicit memory In information-processing models of memory, processing that is intentional and conscious; compare with *implicit memory*.

extended family Multigenerational family made up of parents, children, and more distant relatives, sometimes living together in an *extended-family household*.

external validity Generalizability of experimental results beyond the study situation.

F

factor analysis Statistical method that seeks to identify underlying dimensions (factors) common to a group of tests on which the same people score similarly.

factorial invariance Issue of whether a dimension(s) represents or pertains to the same construct in all age groups.

family-focused lifestyle Pattern of retirement activity that revolves around family, home, and companions. Compare *balanced investment*.

five-factor model Costa and McCrae's model of personality, consisting of five dimensions: neuroticism, extraversion, openness to experience, conscientiousness, and agreeableness.

fluid intelligence Type of intelligence, proposed by Horn, that is applied to novel problems and is relatively independent of educational and cultural influences. Compare *crystallized intelligence*.

free radicals Unstable, highly reactive atoms or molecules formed during metabolism, which can cause bodily damage.

frontal lobes Front portions of the brain's cerebral cortex, or outer layer, which form and direct strategies for encoding, storage, and retrieval of memories.

functional age Measure of a person's ability to function effectively, in his or her physical and social environment, relative to chronological age.

fundamental pragmatics of life In Baltes's terminology, the area in which a wise person is expert, including knowledge of facts and procedures concerning the essence of the human condition.

G

gender identity Personal awareness of what it means to be male or female; includes gender roles and (sometimes) gender stereotypes.

gender roles Behaviors, interests, attitudes, abilities, and personality traits that a culture considers appropriate for men or women and expects them to display.

gender-schema theory Theory, proposed by Bem, that people develop gender schemas, patterns of behavior organized around gender, which help them sort out their observations of what it means to be male or female.

gender stereotypes Exaggerated generalizations about differences between men and women, which may form a part of a society's gender roles, though not all men and women conform to these generalizations.

gene therapy Experimental method of treating certain diseases by insertion of genetic material into the body to alter cellular composition or replace defective genes.

generativity In Erikson's terminology, middle-aged person's concern with establishing and guiding the next generation.

genes Basic functional units of heredity, composed of deoxyribonucleic acid (DNA), which determine inherited characteristics.

genetic-programming theories Theories that explain biological aging as resulting from a genetically determined developmental timetable; compare *variable-rate theories*.

geriatrics Branch of medicine concerned with processes of aging and age-related medical conditions and care.

gerontologists People engaged in gerontology, the study of the aged and processes of aging.

glaucoma Visual disorder caused by buildup of fluid pressure in the eye; it can cause blindness if not treated.

grief Emotional response experienced in the early phases of bereavement.

grief therapy Program of treatment to help the bereaved cope with loss.

grief work Common pattern of grief in which the bereaved person accepts the loss, releases the bond with the deceased, and rebuilds a life without that person.

H

Hayflick limit Limit, discovered by Hayflick, on the number of times an animal cell can divide (about 50 times for human cells).

heredity Inborn influences on development, carried on the genes.

heterosexual Sexually oriented toward the other sex.

hippocampus Structure in the medial temporal lobe of the brain, actively involved in initial encoding and storage and immediate retrieval of new information.

homeostasis Maintenance of vital functions within optimum range.

homosexual Sexually oriented toward the same sex.

hormone replacement therapy Estrogen, sometimes in combination with progestin, prescribed to treat the physical effects of menopause.

hospice care Warm, personal, patient- and family-centered care for a person with a terminal illness, focused on relieving pain, controlling symptoms, and maintaining quality of life.

hypertension High blood pressure.

hypochondriasis Mental disorder characterized by preoccupation with fear of having a serious disease; this fear is based on misinterpretation of physical symptoms.

I

ideal self Person's concept of who he or she would like to be. Compare with *real self*.

identity accommodation In Whitbourne's terminology, adjusting the self-concept to fit new experience. Compare with *identity assimilation*.

identity assimilation   In Whitbourne's terminology, effort to fit new experience into an existing self-concept. Compare with *identity accommodation*.

identity styles   In Whitbourne's terminology, characteristic ways of confronting, interpreting, and responding to experience.

implementation stage   In Super's terminology, third stage of career exploration and development, in which people in their early twenties try out entry-level jobs or start professional training and make a final choice of career.

implicit memory   In information-processing models, processing that is unintentional and unconscious; compare with *explicit memory*.

impotence (erectile dysfunction)   Inability of a man to achieve or maintain an erect penis sufficient for satisfactory sexual performance.

in vitro fertilization   Fertilization of an ovum outside the mother's body.

independent variable   In an experiment, the variable over which the experimenter has direct control; its manipulation is called the *treatment*. Compare *dependent variable*.

infertility   Inability to conceive after 12 to 18 months of trying.

information-processing theory   Study of mental processes that underlie intelligent behavior: these involve manipulation of symbols and perceptions to acquire, store, and retrieve information and solve problems.

integrated level   Third and final level in Labouvie-Vief's model of adult cognitive development, characterized by openness, flexibility, and autonomous choice of principles; integration of subjectivity with objectivity; and judgment of truth claims on the basis of rational, disciplined reflection and collective thought and discussion.

intelligence quotient (IQ)   Measurement of intelligence traditionally obtained by dividing a person's mental age by his or her chronological age and multiplying the result by 100.

intelligent behavior   Behavior that is goal-oriented (conscious and deliberate) and adaptive (used to identify and solve problems effectively).

interiority   In Neugarten's terminology, tendency toward introspection, or preoccupation with inner life, which usually appears in middle age.

internal validity   Assurance that the conclusions of an experiment are valid; in other words, that the treatment, and only the treatment, caused the result.

interpersonal therapy   Short-term psychotherapy that focuses on improving interpersonal and social functioning to treat mental illness; has proven to be very effective in treating depression.

interpersonal wisdom   According to Achenbaum and Orwoll, one of three facets of wisdom, characterized by empathy, understanding, and maturity in social relationships.

intersystemic level   Second level in Labouvie-Vief's model of adult cognitive development, characterized by awareness of multiple, contradictory systems of thought.

intrapersonal wisdom   According to Achenbaum and Orwoll, one of three facets of wisdom, characterized by self-examination, self-knowledge, and integrity.

intrasystemic level   First level in Labouvie-Vief's model of adult cognitive development, characterized by ability to reason only within a single system of thought.

intrinsic motivation   Urge to solve problems for the gains achieved in solving them, rather than for external rewards; believed to be a factor in creativity.

intrusion errors   "Remembering" information that was not originally presented, through associations retrieved from long-term memory.

L

laboratory observation   Research method in which the behavior of all participants is noted and recorded in the same situation, under controlled conditions. Compare *naturalistic observation*.

learned helplessness   Adaptive pattern in which an organism learns to cope with an extremely stressful and uncontrollable situation by doing nothing.

learning   Long-lasting change in behavior as a result of experience.

life expectancy   Age to which a person in a particular cohort is statistically likely to live; this age is based on average longevity of a population.

life review   Reminiscence about a person's life course in order to determine its significance.

life structure   In Levinson's terminology, the underlying pattern of a person's life at a given time; this structure is built around whatever aspects of life the person finds most important.

lifelong learning   Organized, sustained study by adults of all ages.

lifespan development   Concept of development as a lifelong process of adaptation.

lifespan developmental psychology   Branch of psychology whose primary task is the scientific study of lifespan development.

living will   Document specifying the type of care wanted by the maker in the event of terminal illness.

long-term memory   In information-processing models, storage of virtually unlimited capacity, which holds information for very long periods.

longevity   Length of an individual's life.

longitudinal study   Quasi-experimental research design in which data are collected about the same person or persons over a period of time, to assess developmental changes that occur with age. Compare with *cross-sectional study*.

lumpectomy   Surgical treatment for breast cancer involving removal of the tumor and a small amount of surrounding tissue; compare *mastectomy*.

M

maintenance stage   In Super's terminology, sixth stage of career exploration and development, in which people in their mid forties focus on maintaining rather than acquiring prestige, authority, and responsibility.

major depressive episode   Mental disorder lasting at least 2 weeks and not caused by substance abuse, medication, a medical condition, or recent bereavement, in which a person shows extreme sadness or loss of interest or pleasure in normal activities, as well as at least four of the following: change in weight or appetite; insomnia; agitation; fatigue; feelings of worthlessness or guilt; inability to think, concentrate, or make decisions; and thoughts of death or suicide.

male climacteric   Period of physiological, emotional, and psychological change involving a man's reproductive and other body systems.

mammography   Diagnostic X-ray examination of the breast to detect signs of breast cancer.

mastectomy   Surgical treatment for breast cancer involving removal of all or part of the breast; compare *lumpectomy*.

maturation   Unfolding of a biologically determined sequence of behavior patterns, including readiness to master new abilities.

mechanics of intelligence   In Baltes's dual-process model, basic physiological functions or procedures used to process information (similar to fluid intelligence); the dimension of intellect in which there is often an age-related decline. Compare with *pragmatics of intelligence*.

mechanistic perspective   Metatheory, based on the machine as a metaphor, that views development as a response to internal and external stimuli and studies phenomena by analyzing the operation of their component parts.

menopause   Cessation of menstruation and of ability to bear children, typically around age 50.

mentor   In Levinson's terminology, a slightly older person whose guidance and advice in both career and personal matters strongly influence a young adult's prospects for success.

metacognition   Knowledge about what one knows and about one's own thinking processes.

metamemory   Knowledge or beliefs about how one's own memory works.

metatheory   Hypothesis about the operation of the universe, which embraces a group of theories having similar assumptions and values.

method of loci   Mnemonic technique in which a series of places (loci) are associated with items to be remembered and then mentally revisited during recall.

midlife crisis   In some stage models, potentially stressful life period precipitated by review and reevaluation of one's past, typically occurring in the early to middle forties.

mixed hearing loss   Hearing loss that is a combination of sensorineural and conductive hearing loss.

mnemonics   Strategies for enhancing memory.

model   Concrete image or other representation of a theory, which helps in understanding meaningful relationships among data.

morality of autonomous moral principles   Kohlberg's third level of moral reasoning, in which morality is fully internal and principled. Also called *postconventional morality*.

morality of conventional role conformity   Kohlberg's second level of moral reasoning, in which standards of authority figures are internalized. Also called *conventional morality*.

mourning   Behavior of the bereaved and the community, including culturally accepted customs and rituals.

multidirectional In the lifespan developmental approach, descriptive of development that involves both growth and decline.

music therapy Therapeutic method used to treat depression by teaching the patient how to reduce stress by listening to music.

myocardial infarction Damage to part of the heart muscle due to stoppage of blood circulation through a coronary artery; also called *heart attack*.

N

naturalistic observation Method of research in which people's behavior is noted and recorded in natural settings without the observer's intervention or manipulation. Compare *laboratory observation*.

necessary subjectivity In Sinnott's terminology, characteristic of social interactions in which each person's view of the situation inevitably affects the other's and the situation as a whole.

neglect Withholding of adequate care; usually refers to physical needs, such as food, clothing, and supervision.

nondeclarative memory In information-processing models, memory for procedures, habits, skills, or other types of information that generally do not require effort to recall; also called *procedural memory*. Compare with *declarative memory*.

nonnormative life events In the timing-of-events model, life experiences which are unusual and thus not normally anticipated, or are ordinary but come at unexpected times, and which may have a major impact on development. Compare with *normative life events*.

normative age-graded influences Biological and environmental influences on development that are highly similar for people in a given age group.

normative history-graded influences Biological and environmental influences on development that are common to a particular cohort.

normative life events In the timing-of-events model, commonly expected life experiences that occur at customary times. Compare with *nonnormative life events*.

normative personality change Age-related patterns of personality development that occur in most members of a population.

nuclear family Two-generational family made up of parents and growing children related by blood or adoption and living together.

O

obesity Overweight condition defined as skinfold measurement in the 85th percentile.

observer bias Tendency of an observer to misinterpret or distort data to fit his or her expectations.

orchiectomy Hormone treatment for prostate cancer in which the testicles are removed to prevent male hormones from reaching cancer cells.

organismic perspective Metatheory that views development as internally initiated and controlled and as occurring in a universal sequence of qualitatively different stages culminating in full maturation.

organization Encoding strategy or mnemonic device, consisting of arranging or categorizing material to be remembered.

osteoporosis Condition, most often affecting postmenopausal women, in which the bones become extremely thin, porous, and susceptible to fractures, and posture typically becomes stooped owing to compression and collapse of vertebrae.

ovum transfer Method of conception in which a woman who cannot produce normal ova receives an ovum donated by a fertile woman.

P

palliative care Care aimed at relieving pain and suffering and allowing the terminally ill to die in peace, comfort, and dignity.

Parkinson's disease Slowly progressive neurological disorder characterized by tremor, rigidity, slowed movement, and unstable posture.

passive euthanasia Deliberate withholding or discontinuation of life-prolonging treatment of a terminally ill person in order to end suffering or allow death with dignity. Compare *active euthanasia*.

passive smoking Inhaling smoke as a result of being in the presence of someone who is smoking.

periodontitis Gum disease.

persistent vegetative state State in which a patient, while technically alive, has lost all but the most rudimentary brain functioning.

personality Distinctive patterns of characteristic behavioral, mental, and emotional adaptations—that is, a person's unique and relatively consistent way of thinking, feeling, and behaving.

personality dimensions   Groupings or categories of related personality traits, devised for research purposes.

personality inventory   Instrument that yields psychometric ratings of personality traits or categories of traits.

plasticity   In the lifespan developmental approach, modifiability of skills with training and practice, even in late life.

postformal thought   Mature thinking which relies on experience and intuition as well as logic, can transcend particular systems, and can deal with ambiguity, uncertainty, inconsistency, contradiction, imperfection, and compromise.

pragmatics of intelligence   In Baltes's dual-process model, processes that involve application of the contents of the mind—an accumulation of culture-based factual and procedural knowledge; the dimension of intellect that tends to grow with age. Compare with *mechanics of intelligence*.

preconventional morality   Kohlberg's first level of moral reasoning, in which right conduct is based on external control or self-interest.

premenstrual syndrome (PMS)   Disorder producing physical discomfort and emotional tension before a menstrual period.

presbycusis   Gradual loss of hearing, beginning with sounds at upper frequencies.

presbyopia   Age-related decline in near vision, stemming from loss of elasticity of the lens of the eye.

primary aging   Gradual, genetically based process of bodily change throughout the life span.

priming   Increase in ability to do a task or remember information as a result of a previous encounter with the task or information.

problem finding   Ability to identify and formulate novel and important problems to be solved; believed to be a characteristic of creativity and postformal thought.

problem-focused coping   In Lazarus's cognitive-appraisal model, coping strategy directed toward eliminating, managing, or improving a stressful situation. Compare *emotion-focused coping*.

production deficiency   Failure to generate efficient encoding strategies in working memory.

productive aging   Concept that older persons are potentially unlimited contributors to the goods, services, and products available for themselves and for society.

prospective memory   Remembering to perform future actions.

pseudodementia   Cognitive impairment due to major depression; sometimes called *transitory dementia*.

psychological age   Measure of how effectively a person can adapt to environmental challenges.

psychometric approach   Study of intelligence through quantitative measurements of intellectual functioning.

Q

Q-sort   Instrument that yields distribution of self-descriptive statements or characteristics.

qualitative development   Changes, occurring at successive times of life, in kind, nature, structure, or organization of phenomena, such as stages of development. Compare *quantitative development*.

qualitative research   Research that focuses on changes in kind, such as new behaviors or new stages. One example would be moving from preoperational stage to concrete operational stage.

quantitative development   Changes, occurring with age, in number or amount of something, such as how many items can be remembered. Compare *qualitative development*.

quantitative research   Research that focuses on change in degree or amount, such as numbers of learning experiences.

quasi experiment   Study which resembles an experiment in that it attempts to measure change or to find differences among groups, but which lacks control based on random assignment.

R

radical prostatectomy   Treatment for prostate cancer in which the entire prostate is removed.

random assignment   Technique used in assigning members of a study sample to experimental and control groups, in which each member of the sample has an equal chance to be assigned to each group and to receive or not receive the treatment.

random sample   Type of study sample in which representativeness is ensured through random selection.

random selection   Technique used to ensure representativeness of a sample by giving each member of a population an equal chance to be selected. Compare *random sample*.

real self Person's concept of who he or she actually is. Compare with *ideal self*.

reflective thinking Complex abstract thinking that constantly reevaluates facts and ideas, and the subsequent conclusions.

rehearsal Conscious repetition of information to keep it in working memory or transfer it to long-term memory.

reintegrative stage Fifth of Schaie's five cognitive stages, in which older adults choose to focus limited energy on tasks that have meaning for them.

reliable With regard to a research method or tool, consistent in measuring performance.

reserve capacity Ability of body organs and systems to put forth 4 to 10 times as much effort as usual under stress; also called *organ reserve*.

resource provision-depletion hypothesis Hypothesis that work and leisure activities may be either positively or negatively related because work either promotes or constrains leisure activities by providing or depleting the resources (time, energy, and money) needed for those activities. Compare *spillover hypothesis, compensation hypothesis*, and *segmentation hypothesis*.

responsible stage Third of Schaie's five cognitive stages, in which middle-aged people are concerned with long-range goals and practical problems related to their responsibility for others.

retirement stage In Super's terminology, eighth stage of career exploration and development, in which people formally separate from their work, usually at age 65, and adjust their self-concept to lack of a career.

retrieval In information-processing models of memory, the process by which information is accessed or recalled from storage.

revolving door syndrome Adult children returning to their parents' home.

S

sample Group of research participants chosen to represent a population under study.

sandwich generation Adult generation who is trying to raise their children while caring for elderly parents, and must devote time, energy, and resources to both.

schemas Working conceptual models, or constructs of reality, around which behavior is organized.

schizophrenia Group of mental disorders involving loss of contact with reality and such symptoms as delusions, hallucinations, and thought disturbances.

scientific method System of established principles and processes of scientific inquiry, including careful observation and recording of data, testing of alternative hypotheses, and widespread dissemination of findings and conclusions so that other scientists can check, analyze, repeat, learn from, and build on the results.

secondary aging Bodily changes that result from disease, abuse, and disuse and are often preventable.

segmentation hypothesis Hypothesis that there is no correlation between work and leisure activities. Compare *spillover hypothesis, compensation hypothesis*, and *resource provision-depletion hypothesis*.

selective optimization with compensation In Baltes's dual-process model, strategy for maintaining or enhancing overall intellectual functioning by careful choice of tasks, increased practice, and use of stronger abilities to compensate for those that have weakened.

selectivity theory Theory proposed by Carstensen, that reduction of social contacts directed toward information gathering and identity formation is adaptive to aging, while contacts that fulfill emotional needs become central. Compare *convoy theory*.

self-concept One's sense of self.

self-in-relation theory Theory proposed by Jean Baker-Miller, that men develop gender identity by distancing from the mother, while women develop gender identity within the relationship with the mother.

semantic memory In information-processing models, memory for general factual knowledge about the world, social customs, and language; compare with *episodic memory*.

senescence Period of the life span during which adults experience decrements in bodily functioning associated with aging; begins at different ages for different people.

sensorineural hearing loss Loss of hearing due to damage to the nerves in the inner ear, auditory nerve, or hearing pathways in the brain.

sensory memory In information-processing models, initial storage facility where sensory information registers but decays rapidly without attention.

sequential designs   Research designs that combine two or all three of the simple quasi-experimental designs (cross-sectional, longitudinal, and time-lag) to clarify causes of developmental change.

serial monogamy   Pattern of involvement in a succession of sexually exclusive relationships.

serious leisure   Leisure activity requiring skill, attention, and commitment.

sexual orientation   Tendency to be consistently attracted to members of the other sex (heterosexual orientation), the same sex (homosexual orientation), or both sexes (bisexual orientation).

short term memory   Temporary storage for information.

sleep apnea   Disorder in which breathing stops for 10 seconds or more at a time, causing frequent awakening.

social age   Measure of conformity to an expected progression of social roles at various phases of life.

social clock   Set of cultural norms or expectations for the times of life when important events such as marriage, parenthood, work, and retirement should occur.

social-learning theory   Theory, proposed chiefly by Bandura, which holds that behaviors, including gender roles, are learned by observing and mutating models and through reinforcement of socially approved behavior.

spaced retrieval   Mnemonic technique involving priming or classical conditioning, in which people are trained to recall information for an increasingly long time.

specification stage   In Super's terminology, second stage of career exploration and development, in which older adolescents or college-age adults gain information about occupations and working conditions and begin to focus on specific vocations.

spillover hypothesis   Hypothesis that there is a positive correlation between intellectuality of work and of leisure activities because of a carryover of learning from work to leisure. Compare *compensation hypothesis*, *resource provision-depletion hypothesis*, and *segmentation hypothesis*.

stage   Specific pattern of behavior typical of a certain period of development, which leads to a qualitatively different, usually more advanced pattern of behavior.

stepfamily   Family resulting from the marriage or cohabitation of an adult who already has children.

storage   In information-processing models, the process by which, or location in which, memories are retained for future use.

stress   Organism's physiological and psychological reaction to difficult demands made on it.

stroke   Cessation of blood flow to the brain, or hemorrhage in the brain, causing damage to brain cells and sometimes paralysis or death.

substance abuse   Maladaptive behavior pattern, lasting more than 1 month, in which a person continues to use a substance after knowingly being harmed by it or uses it repeatedly in a hazardous situation.

substance dependence   Physiological or psychological addiction to a substance.

substantive complexity   Degree to which a person's work requires thought and independent judgment.

surrogate motherhood   Method of conception in which a woman who is not married to a man agrees to bear his baby and then give the child to the father and his wife.

survival curves   Curves, plotted on a graph, showing percentages of a population who survive at each age level.

T

tacit knowledge   In Sternberg's terminology, information that is not formally taught or openly expressed but is necessary to get ahead; includes self-management and management of tasks and of others.

temperament   Characteristic, biologically based emotional style with which a person approaches and reacts to people and situations. Also called *disposition*.

terminal drop   Sudden decrease in intellectual performance shortly before death.

thanatology   Study of death and dying.

theory   Coherent set of related concepts that seeks to organize and explain data.

time-lag study   Quasi-experimental research design in which data are collected about different age cohorts on two or more occasions when the groups of people being studied are the same chronological age.

timing-of-events model   Theoretical model, supported by Neugarten and others, that describes adult personality development as a response to whether the occurrence and timing of important life events are expected or unexpected.

tinnitus   Hearing disorder characterized by persistent ringing or buzzing in the ears.

Torrance Tests of Creative Thinking   Widely used psychometric tests of creativity.

transpersonal wisdom   According to Achenbaum and Orwoll, one of three facets of wisdom, characterized by capacity for self-transcendence.

transurethral resection   Surgical removal of prostate gland or bladder lesions by means of an endoscope inserted through the urethra, usually for the relief of prostate obstruction or for treatment of bladder malignancies.

treatment   Manipulation of an independent variable whose effects an experiment is designed to study.

triangular theory of love   Sternberg's theory that the relative presence or absence of three elements of love—intimacy, passion, and commitment—affects the nature and course of a relationship.

Type I diabetes (formerly called juvenile onset or insulin dependent)   The pancreas does not produce enough insulin for the body to use sugar, which is critical to the proper functioning of cells.

Type II diabetes (formerly called mature onset or noninsulin dependent)   The pancreas produces sufficient insulin but the body does not use it properly. Type II is the most common form of diabetes.

U

undifferentiated   Personality type consisting of low degrees of traits typically thought of as masculine and feminine.

V

valid   With regard to research, yielding conclusions appropriate to the phenomena and population under study.

variable-rate theories   Theories explaining biological aging as a result of processes that vary from person to person and are influenced by both the internal and the external environment; compare *genetic-programming theories*.

variables   Phenomena that change or vary among members of a group, or can be varied for purposes of research.

visual acuity   Ability of the eye to distinguish visual details.

visual (or spatial) scratch pad   In information-processing models of memory, component of working memory that allows information about the shape and location of visual images to be kept in consciousness.

vital capacity   Amount of air that can be drawn in with a deep breath and expelled; may be a biomarker of aging.

W

Wechsler Adult Intelligence Scale (WAIS)   Intelligence test for adults, consisting of eleven subtests that yield verbal IQ, performance IQ, and total IQ scores.

working memory   In information-processing models of memory, intermediate storage where information from sensory memory or from long-term memory is consciously manipulated or reorganized.

References

AARP. (1999). Modern maturity sexuality survey—summary of findings. [Online]. Available: http://research.aarp.org/health/mmsexsurvey_1.html. Access date: October 10, 2003.

AARP. (2000). AARP survey on lifelong learning. Washington, DC: Author.

AARP. (2003). A new definition for volunteering and giving among the 45+ population finds thirty percent are more inclined to volunteer since 9/11. [Online]. Available: www.AARP.org/research/press-center/presscurrentnews/a2003-11-14multicultural.html.

AARP. (2006). *Keeping safe: Helping your parents stay mobile*. [Online]. Available: http://www.aarp.org/families/driver_safety/driver_safetyissues/a2004-06-22-mobileparents.html

AARP. 40+ singles ISO love on the Internet? [Online]. Available: www.aarp.org/press/2003/nr092903.hml. Access date: October 10, 2003.

AARP. Facts about grandparents raising grandchildren. [Online]. Available: www.aarp/confacts/grandparents/grandfacts.html. Access date: October 10, 2003.

Abbey, A., Andrews, F. M., & Halman, J. (1992). Infertility and subjective well being: The mediating roles of self-esteem, internal control, and interpersonal conflict. *Journal of Marriage and the Family*, 54, 408–417.

Abbot, R.D., White, L.R., Ross, G.W., Masaki, K.H., Curb, J.D., & Petrovitch, H. (2004). Walking and dementia in physically capable elderly men. *Journal of the American Medical Association*, 292, 1447–1453.

Abel, E. K. (1991). *Who cares for the elderly?* Philadelphia: Temple University Press.

Abraham, Sheila. (1998). Satisfaction of participants in university-administered elderhostel programs. *Educational Gerontology*, 24, 6, 529–536.

Abrahams, B., Feldman, S. S., & Nash, S. C. (1978). Sex role self-concept and sex role attitudes: Enduring personality characteristics or adaptations to changing life situations? *Developmental Psychology*, 14, 393–400.

Achenbaum, W. A., & Bengtson, V. L. (1994). Re-engaging the disengagement theory of aging: On the history and assessment of theory development in gerontology. *The Gerontologist*, 34, 756–763.

Achenbaum, W. A., & Orwoll, L. (1991). Becoming wise: A psychogerontological interpretation of the Book of Job. *International Journal of Aging and Human Development*, 32, 21–39.

Adamchak, D. J. (1993). Demographic aging in the industrialized world: A rising burden? *Generations*, 17(4), 6–9.

Adamchak, D. J., & Friedmann, E. A. (1983). Societal aging and generational dependency relationships: Problems of measurement and conceptualization. *Research on Aging*, 5, 319–338.

Adams, D. (1985). *So long and thanks for all the fish*. New York: Harmony.

Adams, R. G. (1986). Friendship and aging. *Generations*, 10(4), 40–43.

Adams, R., & Laursen, B. (2001). The organization and dynamics of adolescent conflict with parents and friends. *Journal of Marriage and the Family*, 63, 97–110.

Adelman, M. (1991). Stigma, gay lifestyles, and adjustment to aging: A study of later-life gay men and lesbians. *Gay Midlife and Maturity, 4,* 7–32.

Adler, N.E., & Newman, K. (2002). Socioeconomic disparities in health: Pathways and policies. *Health Affairs, 21,* 60–76.

Administration on Aging. (1998). The national elder abuse incidence study. [Online]. Available: http://www.aoa.gov/eldfam/Elder_Rights/ Elder_Abuse/ABuseReport_Full.pdf. Access date: July 19, 2005.

Administration on Aging. (2001). *A profile of older American: 2001.* Washington, DC: author.

Administration on Aging. (2005). Elder rights and resources. [Online]. Available: www.aoa.gov/ eldfam/Elder_Rights/Elder_Abuse_/Elder_Abuse_ pf.asp. Access date: June 13, 2005.

Age Discrimination in Employment Act (ADEA) of 1967. (1978 and 1986). 29 U.S.C. Sec. 621 et seq. (1976 & Supp V. 1978 & 1986).

Ageworks. (2000). Gero 513. [Online]. Available: http://www.ageworks.com/course_demo/513/ module3/pages/immune.html

Aggarwal, S., Gollapudi, S., & Gupta, S. (1999). Increased TNF-alpha-induced apoptosis in lymphocytes from aged humans: Changes in TNF-alpha receptor expression and activation of caspases. *Journal of Immunology, 162,* 2154–2161.

Aging and cholesterol. (1995, February). *University of California at Berkeley Wellness Letter,* pp. 4–5.

Agoda, L. (1995). Minorities and ESRD. Review: African American study of kidney disease and hypertension clinical trials. *Nephrology News & Issues, 9,* 18–19.

Akutsu, H., Legge, G. E., Ross, J. A., & Schuebel, K. J. (1991). Psychophysics of reading: Effects of age-related changes in vision. *Journal of Gerontology: Psychological Sciences 46*(6), P325–331.

Alcott, L. M. (1929). *Little women.* New York: Saalfield. (Original work published 1868).

Aldous, J. J. (1987). Family life of the elderly and near-elderly. *Journal of Marriage and the Family, 49*(2), 227–234.

Aldridge, M.L., & Browne, K.D. (2003). Perpetrators of spousal homicide. A review. *Trauma, Violence & Abuse, 4*(3), 265–276.

Aldwin, C.M., & Levenson, M.R. (2001). Stress, coping, and health at midlife: A developmental perspective. In M. E. Lachman (Ed.), *Handbook of midlife development* (pp. 188–214). New York: Wiley.

Alexander, B. B., Rubinstein, R. L., Goodman, M., & Luborsky, M. (1992). A path not taken: A cultural analysis of regrets and childlessness in the lives of older women. *The Gerontologist, 32*(5), 618–626.

Alexander, C. N. (1982). Ego development, personality and behavioral change in inmates practicing the Transcendental Meditation technique or participating in other programs: A cross-sectional and longitudinal study (Doctoral dissertation, Harvard University). *Dissertation Abstracts International, 43*(2), 539B.

Alexander, C. N., Kurth, S. C., Travis, F., Warner, T., & Alexander, V. K. (1991). Cognitive stage development in children practicing the Transcendental Meditation program: Acquisition and consolidation of conservation. In R. A. Chalmer, G. Clements, H. Schenkluhn, &M. Weinless (Eds.), *Scientific research on Maharishi's Transcendental Meditation and TM-Sidhi programme: Collective papers* (Vol. 4, pp. 2352–2370). Vlodrop, Netherlands: MERU Press.

Alexander, C. N., Swanson, G., Rainforth, M., Carlisle, T., & Todd, C. (1991). The Transcendental Meditation program and business: A prospective study. In R. K. Wallace, D. W. Orme-Johnson, & M. C. Dillbeck (Eds.), *Scientific research on Maharishi's Transcendental Meditation and TM-Sidhi program: Collected papers* (Vol. 5, pp. 3141–3149). Fairfield, IA: MIU Press.

Allan, R & Scheidt, S. (1996). *Heart & mind: The practice of cardiac psychology.* Washington, DC: American Psychological Association.

Allen, K. A., Blieszner, R., & Roberto, K. A. (2000). Families in the middle and later years: A review and critique in the 1990s. *Journal of Marriage and the Family, 62,* 911–926.

Altman, L. K. (1992, July 21). Women worldwide nearing higher rate for AIDS than men. *New York Times,* pp. C1, C3.

Alzheimer's and stress: Caregivers at risk. (1994, Fall). *Alzheimer's Association Newsletter,* pp. 1, 9.

Alzheimer's Association. (1998b, Fall). When the diagnosis isn't Alzheimer's. *Advances: Progress in Alzheimer Research and Care,* p. 23.

Alzheimer's Association. (2003). Alzheimer's disease fact sheet. [Online]. Available: www.alzheimers.org/pubs/adfact.html. Access date: March 3, 2004.

Alzheimer's Association. (2004). Statistics about Alzheimer's disease. [Online]. Available: www.alz.org/aboutad/statistics.asp. Access date: April 1, 2004.

Amaducci, L., Maggi, S., Langlois, J., Minicuci, N., Baldereschi, M., DiCarlo, A., & Grigoletto, F. (1998). Education and the risk of physical disability and morality among men and women aged 65 to 84: The Italian longitudinal study on aging. *Journals of Gerontology: Series A: Biological Sciences and Medical Sciennces, 53,* M484–M490.

Amato, P. R. (2000). The consequences of divorce for adults and children. *Journal of Marriage and the Family, 49,* 327–337.

American Academy of Ophthalmology. Basik Lasik: Tips on Lasik Surgery. [Online]. Available: www.ftc.gov/bcp/conline/pubs/health/lasik.htm. Access date: April 21, 2004.

American Academy of Otolaryngology-Head and Neck Surgery. (1986). *Smell and taste disorders.* Alexandria, VA: Author.

American Academy of Pediatrics (AAP) Committee on Bioethics. (1992, July). Ethical issues in surrogate motherhood. *AAP News,* pp.14–15.

American Academy of Pediatrics Committee on Psychological Aspects of Child and Family Health. (2002). Co-parent or second-parent adoption by same sex parent. *Pediatrics, 109,* 339–340.

American Association of Retired Persons (AARP). (1993). *Abused elders or battered women?* Washington, DC: Author.

American Association of Retired Persons (AARP). (1994). *A profile of older Americans.* Washington, DC: Author.

American Association of Retired Persons (AARP). (1999). *A profile of older Americans.* Washington, DC: Author.

American Association of Retired Persons. (2002). Facts about grandparents raising grandchildren. [Online]. Available: http://www.aarp.org/confacts/grandparents/grandfacts.html. Access date: December 18, 2002.

American Cancer Society. (2000). *Cancer facts and figures 2000.* Atlanta: Author.

American Cancer Society. (2003). Cigarette smoking. [Online]. Available: www.cancer.org/docroot/PED/content/PED_10_2x_CIgarette_Smoking.asp?sitearea=PED. Access date: March 18, 2004.

American Cancer Society. (2003). Secondhand smoke. [Online]. Available: www.cancer.org/docroot/RED/content/PED_10_2x_Secondhand_Smoke–Clean_Indoor_Air.aps. Access date: March 18, 2004.

American Cancer Society. (2003a). Overview: Breast cancer. [Online]. Available: www.cancer.org/docroot/CRI/CRI_2x.asp?sitearea=LRN&dt=5. Access date: March 18, 2004.

American Cancer Society. (2003b). Overview: Prostate Cancer. [Online]. Available: www.cancer.org/docroot/CRI/CRI_2_1x.asp?rnav=criov7dt=36. Access date: March 18, 2004.

American Cancer Society. (2004). *Cancer facts and figures.* Atlanta, GA: American Cancer Society, Inc.

American Cancer Society (2005a). Cigarette smoking. [Online]. Available: www.cancer.org/docroot/PED/content/PED_10_2x_Cigarette_Smoking.asp? Access date: January 30, 2006.

American Dental Association. (2004). At my age, why should I bother with oral hygiene, such as brushing and flossing? [Online]. Available: www.ada.org/public/topics/oral_changes_faq.asp. Access date: April 9, 2004.

American Diabetes Association. (1992). *Diabetes facts.* Alexandria, VA: Author.

American Diabetes Association. (2000). *Diabetes facts.* Alexandria, VA: Author.

American Diabetes Association. (2006*). Direct and indirect costs of diabetes in the United States.* [Online]. Available: http://www.diabetes.org/diabetes-statistics/cost-of-diabetes-in-us.jsp

American Diabetes Association. National diabetes fact sheet. [Online]. Available: www.diabetes.org/diabetes-statistics/national-diabetes-fact-sheet.jsp. Access date: March 26, 2004.

American Heart Association. (1990). *The healthy American diet.* Dallas: Author.

American Heart Association. (1992). *Silent epidemic: The truth about women and heart disease.* Dallas: Author.

American Heart Association (AHA). (1995). *Silent epidemic: The truth about women and heart disease.* Dallas: Author.

American Heart Assocation. (2003). *Heart disease and stroke statistics–2004* Update. Dallas.

American Heart Association. (2004a). Risk factors and coronary heart disease. [Online]. Available: www.americanheart.org/presenter.jhtms?identifier=235. Access date: March 23, 2004.

American Heart Association. (2004b). Am I at risk? [Online]. Available: www.americanheart.org/presenter.jhtml?identifier=1520. Access date: April 5, 2004.

American Heart Association. (2004c). What are healthy levels of cholesterol? [Online]. Available: www.americanheart.org/presenter.jhtml?identifier=183. Access date: April 5, 2004.

American Heart Association. A special message for women. [Online]. Available: www.americanheart.org/presenter.jhtml?identifier=2123. Access date: March 15, 2004.

American Lung Association. (2003). Sleep apnea (sleep–disordered breathing). [Online]. Available: www.lungusa.org/diseases/sleepapnea.html. Access date: March 30, 2004.

American Lung Association (2005a). Smoking 101 fact sheet. [Online]. Available: www.lungusa.org/site/pp.asp?c=dvluk90oe&b=39853. Access date: January 30, 2006.

American Lung Association. (2005b). Quit smoking. [Online]. www.lungusa.org/site/pp.asp?c=dvluk90oe&b=33484. Access date: January 30, 2006.

American Medical Association. (1998). *Essential guide to menopause.* New York: Simon & Schuster, Inc.

American Medical Association. (2002). Bone loss common in men as well as women. *American Medical News*, Nov. 18, 2002.

American Medical Association. (2004). Bad to the bone: The risk of osteoporosis. *American Medical News*, Jan. 19, 2004.

American Medical Association. Report 6 of the council on scientific affairs (A-97). [Online]. Available: www.ama-assn.org/ama/pub/article/2036-2520.html. Access date: March 3, 2004.

American Psychiatric Association. (1994). *Diagnostic and statistical manual of mental disorders* (4th ed.). Washington, DC: Author.

American Psychological Association. (2000). Guidelines for psychotherapy with lesbian, gay, and bisexual clients. *American Psychologist, 57,* 1060-1073.

American Psychological Association. (2000). Guidelines for psychotherapy with lesbian, gay, and bisexual clients. *American Psychologist, 57,* 1060–1073.

American Psychological Association (2001). answers to your questions about sexual orientation and homosexuality. APA Public Communications. Available: http://www.apa.org/pubinfo/orient.html.

American Psychological Association (APA) (2002). *APA ethical principles of psychologists and code of conduct.* [Online]. Available: http://www.apa.org/ethics/code2002.html

American Psychological Association. (2005). Elder abuse and neglect: in search of solutions. [Online]. Available: www.apa.org/pi/aging/eldabuse.html. Access date: June 7, 2005.

American Psychological Association Working Group on Assisted Suicide and End-of- Life Decisions. (2005). Formation of APA working group on assisted suicide and end-of-life decisions. [Online]. Available: www.apa.org/pi/aseol/introduction.html.

American Sleep Apnea Association. Information about sleep apnea. [Online]. Available: www.sleepapnea.org/geninfo.html. Access date: March 26, 2004.

American Speech-Language Hearing Association. Cochlear implants fact sheet. [Online]. Available: www.asha.org/about/news/tipsheets/cochlear_facts.htm. Access date: April 30, 2004.

Americans on Values Follow-up Survey, 1998. (1999). Washington, DC: Kaiser Family Foundation/Washington Post/Harvard University.

Amory, M. (1987). The author. In G. O'Connor (Ed.), *Olivier: In celebration.* (p.187–191). New York: Dodd, Mead.

Amyotrophic Lateral Sclerosis Association. (undated). Profiles in courage: Three stories of determination and hope. Woodland Hills, CA: Author.

Anastasi, A. (1988). *Psychological testing* (6th ed.). New York: Macmillan.

Anastasi, A., & Urbana, S. (1997). *Psychological testing* (7th ed.). Upper Saddle River, NJ: Prentice Hall.

Anders, T. R., Fozard, J. L., & Lillyquist, T. D. (1972). Effects of age upon retrieval from short-term memory. *Developmental Psychology*, 6(2), 214–217.

Anderson, M. (1956). *My Lord, what a morning*. New York: Viking.

Anderson, M. (1992). *My Lord, what a morning*. Madison: University of Wisconsin Press.

Anderson, R. (1980). I never sang for my father. In R. G. Lyell (Ed.), *Middle age, old age* (pp. 55–110). New York: Harcourt Brace Jovanovich.

Anderson, R.N. (2001). Deaths: Leading causes for 1999. *National Vital Statistics Reports, 49*(11).

Anderson, S. A., Russell, C. S., & Schumm, W. R. (1983). Perceived marital quality and family life-cycle categories: A further analysis. *Journal of Marriage and the Family, 45*, 127–139.

Anderson, T. B. (1984). Widowhood as a life transition: Its impact on kinship ties. *Journal of Marriage and the Family, 46*, 105–114.

Anderson, W. F. (1998). Human gene therapy. *Nature, 392 (Suppl.)*, 25–30.

Anderssen, N., Amlie, C., & Ytteroy, E. A. (2002). Outcomes for children with lesbian or gay parents: A review of studies from 1978 to 2000. *Scandinavian Journal of Psychology, 43*, 335–351.

Angell, M. (1996). Euthanasia in the Netherlands—Good news or bad? *New England Journal of Medicine, 335*, 1676–1678.

Angier, N. (1990, April 17). Diet offers tantalizing clues to long life. *New York Times*, pp. C1–C2.

Angier, N. (1993, March 4). Scientists find long-sought gene that causes Lou Gehrig's disease. *New York Times*, pp. A1, B8.

Annas, G. J. (2005). "Culture of life" politics at the bedside—The case of Terri Schiavo. *New England Journal of Medicine*. [Online]. Available: www.nejm.org.

Anschutz, L., Camp, C. I., Markley, R. P., & Kramer, J. J. (1985). Maintenance and generalization of mnemonics for grocery shopping by older adults. *Experimental Aging Research, 11*, 157–160.

Anschutz, L., Camp, C. I., Markley, R P., & Kramer, J. J. (1987). Remembering mnemonics: A 3-year follow-up on the effects of mnemonics training in elderly adults. *Experimental Aging Research, 13*, 141–143.

Anson, O. (1989). Marital status and women's health revisited: The importance of a proximate adult. *Journal of Marriage and the Family, 51*, 185–194.

Anson, O. & Anson, J. (1997). Suriving the holidays: Gender differences in mortality in the context of three Moslem Holidays. *Sex Roles, 37*, 381–399.

Anson, O. & Anson, J. (2001). Death rests a while: Holy day and Sabbath effects on Jewish mortality in Israel. *Social Science and Medicine, 52*, 83–97.

Antonucci, T.C. & Akiyama, H. (1995). Convoys of social relations: family and friendships within a life span context. In R. Blieszner & V. Hilkevitch (Eds.), *Handbook of aging and the family* (pp. 355–371). Westport, CT: Greenwood Press.

Antonucci, T. C. & Akiyama, H. (1997). Concern with others at midlife: Care, comfort, or compromise? In M. E.Lachman & J. B. James (Eds.), *Multiple paths of midlife development* (pp. 145–169). Chicago: University of Chicago Press.

Antonucci, T. C., Akiyama, H., Merline, A. (2001). Dynamics of social relationships in midlife. In M. E. Lachman (Ed.), *Handbook of midlife development* (pp. 571–598). New York: Wiley.

Aquilino, W. S. (1996). The returning adult child and parental experience at midlife. In C. Ryff & M. M. Seltzer (Eds.), *The parental experience in midlife* (pp. 423–458). Chicago: University of Chicago Press.

Aquilino, W. S., & Supple, K. R. (1991). Parent-child relations and parent's satisfaction with living arrangements when adult children live at home. *Journal of Marriage and the Family, 53*, 13–27.

Arlin, P. K. (1975). Cognitive development in adulthood: A fifth stage? *Developmental Psychology, 11*, 602–606.

Arlin, P. K. (1984). Adolescent and adult thought: A structural interpretation. In M. L.Commons, F. A. Richards, & C. Armon (Eds.), *Beyond formal operations* (pp. 258–271). New York: Praeger.

Arthritis Foundation (1993). Arthritis information. Basic facts: Answers to your questions. Atlanta: Author.

Ashcraft, M. H. (1994). *Human memory and cognition* (2nd ed.). New York: HarperCollins.

Ashe, A., & Rampersad, A. (1993). *Days of grace: A memoir*. New York: Ballantine.

Atchley, R. C. (1985). *Social forces and aging* (4th ed.). Belmont, CA: Wadsworth.

Atchley, R. C. (1989). A continuity theory of normal aging. *The Gerontologist, 29*, 183–190.

Atchley, R. C. (1991, November). *Detachment and disengagement: Vedantic perspectives on wisdom*. Paper presented at the meeting of the Gerontological Society of America, San Francisco.

Atchley, R. C. (1997). *Social forces and aging: An introduction to social gerontology* (8th ed.). Belmont, CA: Wadsworth.

Atchley, R.C. (1999). Continuity and adaptation in aging: Creating positive experiences. Baltimore, MD: Johns Hopkins University Press.

Atkins Nutritionals. What is the Atkins Nutritional Approach? [Online]. Available: http://atkins.com/Archive/2001/11/11/29-367514.printable.html? Access date: April 7, 2004.

Atkinson, R. M., Ganzini, L., & Bernstein, M. J. (1992). Alcohol and substance use disorders in the elderly. In J. E. Birren, R. Sloane, & G. D. Cohen (Eds.), *Handbook of mental health and aging* (2nd ed., pp. 515–555). New York: Academic.

Atoh, M. (1998). *"Who takes care of children and the elderly in an aging society?",* Paper prepared fo rhte Rencontres Sauvy International Seminar, Institut National d'Etude Demographique, Paris, 14-15 October.

Aube, J. & Koestner, R. (1995). Gender characteristics and relationship adjustment: Another look at similarity complementarity hypothesis. *Journal of Personality, 63*(4), 879–904.

August, M. (1995, January 12). Compound may ease pains of growing old. *Chicago Sun-Times,* p. 48.

Ausbel, N. (1964). *The book of Jewish knowledge.* New York: Crown.

Australian man first in world to die with legal euthanasia. (1996, September 26). *New York Times* (International ed.), p. A5.

Austrom, D., & Hanel, K. (1985). Psychological issues of single life in Canada: An exploratory study. *International Journal of Women's Studies, 8,* 12–23.

Ausubel, N. (1964). *The book of Jewish knowledge.* New York: Crown.

Avis, N.E. (1999). Women's health at midlife. In S.L. Willis and J.D. Reid (Eds.), *Life in the middle: psychological and social development in middle age* (pp.105-146). San Diego: Academic Press.

Ayya, N. (1994, November–December). AIDS is of growing concern to professionals in aging. *Aging Today,* pp. 1, 4.

Babchuk, N. (1978–1979). Aging and primary relations. *International Journal of Aging and Human Development, 9*(2), 137–151.

Bachrach, C. A., London, K. A., & Maza, P. L. (1991). On the path to adoption: Adoption seeking in the United States, 1988. *Journal of Marriage and the Family, 53,* 705–718.

Backman, L., Small, B. J., Wahlin, A. (2001). Aging and memory: Cognitive and biological perspectives. In Birren, J. E. (Ed.), *Handbook of the psychology of aging* (5th ed.). San Diego: Academic Press.

Baddeley, A. D. (1981). The concept of working memory: A view of its current state and probable future development. *Cognition, 10,* 17–23.

Baddeley, A.D. (1986). *Working memory.* London, Oxford University Press.

Baddeley, A. D. (2002). Is working memory still working? *European Psychologist, 7*(2), 85–97.

Bailey, A., Le Couteur, A., Gottesman, I., & Bolton, P. (1995). Autism as a strongly genetic disorder: Evidence from a British twin study. *Psychological Medicine, 25,* 63–77.

Bailey, J.M., Bobrow, D., Wolfe, M & Mikach, S. (1995). Sexual orientation of adult sons of gay fathers. *Developmental Psychology, 31,* 124-129.

Bailey, J.M., & Zucker, K.J. (1995). Childhood sex-type behavior and sexual orientation: A conceptual analysis and quantitative review. *Developmental Psychology, 31,* 43–55.

Baker-Miller, J. (1976). *Toward a new psychology of women.* Boston: Beacon.

Balk, J.L., Whiteside, D.A., Naus, G., Defarrari, E., & Roberts, J.M (2002). A pilot study of the effects of phytoestrogen supplementation on postmenopausal endometrium. *Journal of the Society of Gynecologic Investigation, 9,* 238–242.

Balkwell, C. (1981). Transition to widowhood: A review of the literature. *Family Relations, 30,* 117–127.

Balkwell, C. (1985). An attitudinal correlate of the timing of a major life event: The case of morale in widowhood. *Family Relations, 34,* 577–581.

Baltes, P. B. (1983). Life span developmental psychology: Observations on history and theory revisited. In R. M. Lerner (Ed.), *Developmental psychology: Historical and developmental perspectives* (pp. 79–111). Hillsdale, NJ: Erlbaum.

Baltes, P. B. (1985). *The aging of intelligence: On the dynamics between growth and decline.* Unpublished manuscript.

Baltes, P. B. (1987). Theoretical propositions of life-span development psychology: On the dynamics between growth and decline. *Developmental Psychology, 23*(5), 611–626.

Baltes, P. B. (1993). The aging mind: Potential and limits. *The Gerontologist, 33,* 580–594.

Baltes, P. B., & Baltes, M. M. (1980). Plasticity and variability in psychological aging. Methodological and theoretical issues. In G. E. Gurski (Ed.), *Determining the effects of aging on the central nervous system* (pp. 41–66). Berlin: Schering.

Baltes, P. B., & Baltes, M. M. (1990). Psychological perspectives on successful aging: The model of selective optimization with compensation. In P. B. Baltes & M. M. Baltes (Eds.), *Successful aging: Perspectives from the behavioral sciences* (pp. 1–34). New York: Cambridge University Press.

Baltes, P. B., & Graf, P. (1996). Psychology aspects of aging: Facts and frontiers. In D. Magnusson (Ed.), *The lifespan development of individuals: Behavioral, neurobiosocial and psychosocial perspectives* (pp. 427–460). Cambridge, UK: Cambridge University Press.

Baltes, P. B., & Kliegl, R. (1992). Further testing of limits of cognitive plasticity: Negative age differences in a mnemonic skill are robust. *Developmental Psychology, 28,* 121–125.

Baltes, P. B., & Schaie, K. W. (1974). Aging and IQ: The myth of the twilight years. *Psychology Today, 7*(10), 35–38.

Baltes, P. B., & Schaie, K. W. (1976). On the plasticity of intelligence in adulthood and old age: Where Horn and Donaldson fail. *American Psychologist, 31,* 720–725.

Baltes, P. B. & Smith, J. (2004). Lifespan psychology: From developmental contextualism to developmental biocultural co-constructionism. Research in *Human Development, 1*(3), 123–144.

Baltes, P. B., & Willis, S. L. (1982). Enhancement (plasticity) of intellectual functioning in old age: Penn State's Adult Development and Enrichment Project (ADEPT). In F. I. M. Craik & S. Trehub (Eds.), *Aging and cognitive processes* (pp. 353–389). New York: Plenum.

Baltes, P. B., Dittman-Kohli, F., & Dixon, R. A. (1984). New perspectives in the development of intelligence in adulthood: Toward a dual-process conception and a model of selective optimization with compensation. In P. B.

Baltes & O. G. Brim, Ir. (Eds.), *Life-span development and behavior* (Vol. 6, pp. 33–76). New York: Academic Press.

Baltes, P. B., Reese, H. W., & Lipsitt, L. (1980). Life-span developmental psychology. *Annual Review of Psychology, 31,* 65–110.

Baltes, P. B., Reese, H. W., & Nesselroade, I. R. (1977). *Life-span developmental psychology: Introduction to research methods.* Pacific Grove, CA: Brooks/Cole.

Banks, D.A. & Fossel, M. (1997). Telomeres, cancer and aging: Altering the human life span. *Journal of the American Medical Association, 278,* 1345-1348.

Banner, C. (1992). Recent insights into the biology of Alzheimer's disease. *Generations, 16*(4), 31–35.

Barager, J. R. (Ed.). (1968). *Why Perón came to power: The background to Peronism in Argentina.* New York: Knopf.

Barchillon, J. (1961). Creativity and its inhibition in child prodigies. In *Personality dimensions of creativity.* New York: Lincoln Institute of Psychotherapy.

Barefoot, J. C., Helms, M. J., Mortensen, E. L., Avlund. K., & Schroll, M. (2001). A longitudinal study of gender differences in depressive symptoms from age 50–80. *Psychology and Aging, 16*(2), 342–345.

Barfield, R. E., & Morgan, J. N. (1974). *Early retirement: The decision and the experience and a second look.* Ann Arbor, MI: Institute for Social Research.

Barfield, R. E., & Morgan, J. N. (1978). Trends in satisfaction with retirement. *The Gerontologist, 18,* 19–23.

Barnett, R. (1985, March 2). *We've come a long way–but where are we and what are the rewards?* Paper presented at the conference on Women in Transition, New York University School of Continuing Education, Center for Career and Life Planning, New York.

Barnett, R. C. (1997). Gender, employment, and psychological well-being: Historical and life-course perspectives. In M.E. Lachman & J. B. James (Eds.), *Multiple paths of midlife development* (pp. 325–343). Chicago: University of Chicago Press.

Barnett, R. C., & Hyde, J. S. (2001). Women, men, work, and family. *American Psychologist, 56,* 781–796.

Barnett, R. C., Kibria, N., Baruch, G. K., & Pleck, J. H. (1991). Adult daughter-parent relationships and their association with daughters' subjective well-being and psychological distress. *Journal of Marriage and the Family, 53*, 29–42.

Barnett, R. C., Marshall, N. L, & Pleck, J. H. (1992). Men's multiple roles and their relationship to men's psychological distress. *Journal of Marriage and the Family, 54*, 358–367.

Barnhart, M. A. (1992, Fall). Coping with the Methuselah syndrome. *Free Inquiry*, pp. 19–22.

Barrett, C. J. (1978). Effectiveness of widows' groups in facilitating change. *Journal of Counseling and Clinical Psychology, 46*(1), 20–31.

Bartlett, F. (1958). *Thinking*. New York: Basic Books.

Bartlett, F. C. (1932). *Remembering*. Cambridge, England: Cambridge University Press.

Barton, P., & Lapointe, A. (1995). Learning by degrees: Indicators of performance in higher education. Princeton, NJ: ETS Policy Information Center.

Baruch, G., Barnett, R., & Rivers, C. (1983). *Lifeprints*. New York: McGraw-Hill.

Barzel, U. S. (2001). Osteoporosis. In G. L. Maddox (Ed.), *The encyclopedia of aging* (3rd ed.). New York: Springer Publishing Company.

Bascom, P. B., & Tolle, S.W. (2002). Responding to requests for physician assisted suicide: "These are uncharted waters for both of us..."*Journal of the American Medical Association, 288*, 91–98.

Basinger, K.S., Gibbs, J.C., Fuller, D. (1995). Context and the measurement of moral judgment. *International Journal of Behavioral Development, 18*(3), 537–556.

Bates, J. E., & Wachs, T. D. (Eds.). (1994). *Temperament: Individual differences at the interface of biology and behavior*. Washington, DC: American Psychological Association.

Bateson, G. (1982). Totemic knowledge in New Guinea. In U. Neisser (Ed.), *Memory observed: Remembering in natural contexts* (pp. 269–273). San Francisco: Freeman.

Baumeister, R. F., & Leary, M. R. (1995). The need to belong: Desire for interpersonal attachments as a fundamental human motivation. *Psychological Bulletin, 117*(3), 497–529.

Bayley, N., & Oden, M. (1955). The maintenance of intellectual ability in gifted adults. *Journal of Gerontology, 10*, 91–107.

Beard, G. M. (1874). *Legal responsibility in old age*. New York: Russell.

Bebbington, P. (1990). Population surveys of psychiatric disorder and the need for treatment. *Social Psychiatry and Psychiatric Medicine, 25*, 33–40.

Beck, S. H. (1982). Adjustment to and satisfaction with retirement. *Journal of Gerontology, 37*, 616–624.

Becker, G. S. (1992, December 7). Finding fault with no-fault divorce. *BusinessWeek*, p. 23.

Becker, P. E., & Moen, P. (1999). Scaling back: Dual-earner couples' work-family strategies. *Journal of Marriage and the Family, 61*, 995–1007.

Bedford, V. H. (1995). Sibling relationships in middle and old age. In R. Blieszner & V. Hilkevitch (Eds.), *Handbook of aging and the family* (pp. 201–222). Westport, CT: Greenwood Press.

Belgium legalises euthanasia. (2002, May 16). BBC-News Online. Available: www.nvve.nl.

Bell, J. (1992). In search of a discourse on aging: The elderly on television. *The Gerontologist, 32*(3), 305–311.

Belsky, J., & Rovine, M. (1990). Patterns of marital change across the transition to parenthood: Pregnancy to three years postpartum. *Journal of Marriage and the Family, 52*, 5–19.

Belsky, J., Lang, M., & Huston, T. L. (1986). Sex typing and division of labor as determinants of marital change across the transition to parenthood. *Journal of Personality and Social Psychology, 50*, 517–522.

Bem, S. L. (1974). The measurement of psychological androgyny. *Journal of Consulting and Clinical Psychology, 42*, 155–162.

Bem, S. L. (1976). Probing the promise of androgyny. In A. G. Kaplan & J. P. Bean (Eds.), *Beyond sex-role sterotypes: Readings toward a psychology of androgyny*. Boston: Little, Brown.

Bem, S. L. (1981). Gender schema theory: A cognitive account of sex typing. *Psychological Review, 88*, 54–369.

Bem, S. L. (1983). Gender schema theory and its implications for child development: Raising gender-aschematic children in a gender-schema society. *Sign, 8*, 598–616.

Bem, S. L. (1985). Androgyny and gender schema theory: A conceptual and empirical investigation.

In T. B. Sondregger (Ed.), *Nebraska Symposium on Motivation, 1984: Psychology and gender.* Lincoln: University of Nebraska Press.

Bemon, P., & Sharma, A. S. (1994). *Growing up adopted: A portrait of adolescents and their families.* Minneapolis: Search Institute of Minnesota.

Bengston, V. L. (2001). Beyond the nuclear family: The increasing importance of multigenerational bonds. *Journal of Marriage and the Family, 63,* 1–16.

Bengston, V. L., Rosenthal, C. J., & Burton, L. M. (1990). Families and aging: Diversity and heterogeneity. In R. Bingstock & L. K. George (Eds.), *Handbook of aging and the social sciences* (pp. 263–287). San Diego: Academic Press.

Bengston, V. L., Rosenthal, C. J., & Burton, L. M. (1996). Paradoxes of families and aging. In R. H. Binstock & L. K. George (Eds.), *Handbook of aging and the social sciences* (pp. 253–282). San Diego: Academic Press.

Bengtson, V., Cuellar, J. A., & Ragan, P. (1975, October 29). *Group contrasts in attitudes toward death: Variation by race, age, occupational status and sex.* Paper presented at the annual meeting of the Gerontological Society, Louisville, KY.

Benner, P. (1984). *From novice to expert: Excellence and practice in clinical nursing practice.* Reading, MA: Addison-Wesley.

Benson, M. (1986). *Nelson Mandela: The man and the movement.* New York: Norton.

Benzing, W. C., & Squire, L. R. (1989). Preserved learning and memory in amnesia: Intact adaptation–level effects and learning of stereoscopic depth. *Behavioral Neuroscience, 103,* 538–547

Berardo, D. H., Sheehan, C. L., & Leslie, G. R. (1987). A residue of tradition: Jobs, careers, and spouses' time in housework. *Journal of Marriage and the Family, 49,* 381–390.

Berg, C.A., & Klaczynski, P.A. (1996). Practical intelligence and problem solving: Search for perspectives. In F. Blanchard-Fields & T. M. Hess (Eds.). *Pespectives on cognitive change in adulthood and aging* (pp. 323–357). New York: McGraw Hill.

Berger, R. M. (1982). *Gay and gray: The older homosexual male.* Urbana: University of Illinois Press.

Berger, R. M. (1984, January–February). Realities of gay and lesbian aging. *Social Work,* pp. 57–62.

Berger, R. M., & Kelly, J. J. (1986). Working with homosexuals of the older population. *Social Casework, 67,* 203–210.

Bergman, I., & Burgess, A. (1980). *Ingrid Bergman: My story.* New York: Delacorte.

Bergman, S. J. (1991). Men's psychological development: A relational perspective (Work in Progress No. 48). Wellesley, MA: The Stone Center, Wellesley College.

Berkowitz, G. S., Skovron, M. L., Lapinski, R. H., & Berkowitz, R. L. (1990). Delayed childbearing and the outcome of pregnancy. *New England Journal of Medicine, 322,* 659–664.

Bernard, J. L., & Bernard, M. L. (1984). The abusive male seeking treatment: Jekyll and Hyde. *Family Relations, 33,* 543–547.

Bernstein, J. (1995). *Where's the payoff?* Washington, DC: Economic Policy Institute.

Berrios, J. (1993, June–July). Partners in progress: Gannett Company profits from workplace diversity. *The National Voter,* pp. 12–13.

Berscheid, E., & Campbell, B. (1981). The changing longevity of heterosexual close relationships. In M. J. Lerner & S. C. Lerner (Eds.), *The justice motive in social behavior.* New York: Plenum.

Beyette, B. (1998, November 29). Carter keeps zest for life. *Chicago Sun-Times,* pp. A6-A7.

Bianchi, S. M. (1995). The changing demographic and socioeconomic characteristics of single-parent families. *Marriage and Family Review, 20*(1–2), 71–97.

Bianchi, S. M., & Spain, D. (1986). *American women in transition.* New York: Russell Sage Foundation.

Biegel, D. E. (1995). Caregiver burden. In G. E. Maddox (Ed.), *The encyclopedia of aging* (2nd ed., pp. 138–141). New York: Springer.

Bielby, D., & Papalia, D. (1975). Moral development and perceptual role-taking egocentrism: Their development and interrelationship across the life span. *International Journal of Aging and Human Development, 6*(4), 293–308.

Bigger, J. T., Jr. (1985). Heart and blood vessel disease. In D. F. Tapley, R. J. Weiss, & T. Q. Morris (Eds.), *The Columbia University College* of *Physicians and Surgeons complete home medical guide* (pp. 386–394). New York: Crown.

Binet, A., & Simon, T. (1905). Application des méthodes nouvelles au diagnostic du niveau intellectuel chez des enfants normaux et anormaux d'hospice et d'ecole primaire. *L'Année Psychologique, 11*, 245–336.

Binet, A., & Simon, T. (1908). Le développement de l'intelligence chez les enfants. *L'Année Psychologique, 14*, 1–94.

Binstock, R. H. (1993). Healthcare costs around the world: Is aging a fiscal "blackhole"? *Generations, 17(4)*, 37–42.

Bird, K. (1990, November 12). The very model of an ex-president. *The Nation*, pp. 545, 560–564.

Biringer, F., Anderson, J.R., Strubes, D. (1980). Self recognition in senile dementia. *Experimental Aging Research, 14*, 177–180.

Birren, J. E., & Cunningham, W. R. (1985). Research on the psychology of aging. In J. E. Birren & K. W. Schaie (Eds.), *Handbook of the psychology of aging* (2nd ed., pp. 3–34). New York: Van Nostrand Reinhold.

Birren, J. E., & Morrison, D. F. (1961). Analysis of the WAIS subtests in relation to age and education. *Journal of Gerontology, 16*, 363–369.

Birren, J. E., & Renner, V. J. (1977). Research on the psychology of aging: Principles and experimentation. In J. E. Birren & K. W. Schaie (Eds.), *Handbook of the psychology of aging* (pp. 3–38). New York: Van Nostrand Reinhold.

Birren, J. E. & Schroots, J. J. F. (1996). *A history of geropsychology in autobiography.* Washington, DC: American Psychological Association.

Birren, J. E. & Woodruff, D.S. (1972). Age changes and cohort difference in personality. *Developmental Psychology, 6(2)*, 252-259.

Birren, J. E., Woods, A. M., & Williams, M. V. (1980). Behavioral slowing with age: Causes, organization and consequences. In L. W. Poon (Ed.), *Aging in the 1980s.* Washington, DC: American Psychological Association.

Blackburn, J. A. (1984). The influence of personality, curriculum, and memory correlates on formal reasoning in young adults and elderly persons. *Journal of Gerontology, 39*, 207–209.

Blackburn, J.A., Papalia-Finlay, D., Foye, B.F., & Serlin, R.C. (1988). Modifiability of figural relations performance among elderly adults.

Journal of Gerontology: Psychological Sciences 43(3), 87–89.

Blair, S. N., Kohl, H. W., Paffenbarger, R. S., Clark, D. G., Cooper, K. H., & Gibbons, L. W. (1989). Physical fitness and all-cause mortality: A prospective study of healthy men and women. *Journal of the American Medical Association, 262*, 2395–2401.

Blanchard-Fields, F., & Abeles, R. P. (in press). Social structural influences on behavior. In J. E. Birren & K., Schaie (Eds.), *Handbook of the psychology of aging* (4th ed.). San Diego: Academic.

Blanchard-Fields, F., & Irion, J. (1987). Coping strategies from the perspective of two developmental markers: Age and social reasoning. *Journal of Genetic Psychology, 149*, 141–151.

Blanchard-Fields, F., & Norris, L. (1994). Casual attributions from adolescence through adulthood: Age differences, ego level, and generalized response style. *Aging and Cognition, 1*, 67–86.

Blanchard-Fields, F., & Abeles, R.A. (1996). Social cognition and aging. In J. E. Birren & K. W. Schaie (Eds.), *Handbook of the psychology of aging* (4th ed., pp. 150–161). New York: Academic Press.

Blanchard-Fields, F., Brannan, J. R., & Camp, C. I. (1987). Alternative conceptions of wisdom: An onion-peeling exercise. *Educational Gerontology, 13*, 497–503.

Blanchard-Fields, F., Jahnke, H. C., & Camp, C. J. (1995). Age differences in problem solving style: The role of emotional salience. *Psychology and Aging, 10*, 173–180.

Blanchard-Fields, F., Suhrer-Roussel, L., & Hertzog, C. (1994). A confirmatory factor analysis of the Bern Sex Role Inventory: Old questions, new answers. *Sex Roles, 30*, 423–457.

Blanksten, G. I. (1953). *Perón's Argentina.* Chicago: University of Chicago Press.

Blazer, D. G., Kessler, R. C., McGonagle, K. A., & Swartz, M. S. (1994). The prevalence and distribution of major depression in a national community sample: The National Comorbidity Survey. *American Journal of Psychiatry, 151*, 979–986.

Blieszner, R., & Shifflett, P. A. (1990). The effects of Alzheimer's disease on close relationships between patients and caregivers. *Family Relations, 39,* 57–62.

Blieszner, R., Willis, S. L., & Baltes, P. B. (1981). Training research on induction ability: A short-term longitudinal study. *Journal of Applied Developmental Psychology, 2,* 247–265.

Block, J. (1981). Some enduring and consequential structures of personality. In A. I. Rabin et al. (Eds.), Further explorations in personality. New York: Wiley.

Block, J. (1993). Studying personality the long way. In D. C. Funder, R. D. Parke, C. Tomlinson-Keasey, & K. Widaman (Eds.), *Studying lives through time: Personality and development* (pp. 9–44). Washington, DC: American Psychological Association.

Bloom, D. E., & Pebley, A. R. (1982). Voluntary childlessness: A review of the evidence and its implications, *Population Research and Policy Review, 1,* 203–234.

Bureau of Labor Statistics (BLS). (2003). *Volunteering in the United States: 2003.* Washington, DC: United States Department of Labor.

Bureau of Labor Statistics (BLS). (2004). *The employment situation: March 2004.* Washington, DC: United States Department of Labor.

Blum, L., & Rosner, F. (1983). Alcoholism in the elderly: An analysis of 50 patients. *Journal of the National Medical Association, 75,* 489–495.

Blumstein, P. W., & Schwartz, P. (1983). *American couples.* New York: Morrow.

Boerner, K., Schulz, R., & Horowitz, A. (2004). Positive aspects of caregiving and adaptation to bereavement. *Psychology and Aging, 19,* 668–675.

Boerner, K., Wortman, C.B., & Bonanno, G.A. (2005). Resilient or at risk? A 4 year study of older adults who initially showed high or low distress following conjugal loss. *Journal of Gerontology: Psychological Sciences, 60B,* 67–73.

Bogerts, B. (1993). Images in psychiatry: Alois Alzheimer. *American Journal of Psychiatry, 150,* 1868.

Bogg, T., & Roberts, B.W. (2004). Conscientiousness and health-related behaviors: A meta-analysis of the leading behavioral contributors to mortality. *Psychological Bulletin, 130,* 887–919.

Bograd, R., & Spilka, B. (1996). Self-disclosure and marital satisfaction in midlife and late-life remarriages. *International Journal of Aging and Human Development, 42*(3), 161–172.

Bolger, N., DeLongis, A., Kessler, R. C., & Schilling, E. A. (1989). Effects of daily stress on negative mood. *Journal of Personality and Social Psychology, 57,* 808–818.

Bolles, R. N. (1979). *The three boxes of life.* Berkeley, CA: Ten Speed.

Bonanno, G.A., Wortman, C.B, & Ness, R.M. (2004). Prospective patterns of resilience and maladjustment during widowhood. *Psychology and Aging, 19,* 260–271.

Bonanno, G.A., Wortman, C.B., Lehman, D.R., Tweed, R.G., Haring, M., Sonnega, J., Carr, D., & Nesse, R.M. (2002). Resilience to loss and chronic grief: A prospective study from preloss to 18 month post loss. *Journal of Personality and Social Psychology,* 1150–1164.

Bond, J. T., & Galinsky, E. (1998). *1997 National Study of the Changing Workforce.* New York: Families and Work Institute.

Bonder, B.R., & Wagner, M.B. (2001). *Functional performance in older adults.* Philadelphia, PA: F.A. Davis Comapny.

Booth, A., & Edwards, J. N. (1992). Starting over: Why remarriages are more unstable. *Journal of Family Issues, 13,* 179–194.

Borges, J. L. (1964). *Labyrinths: Selected stories and other writings.* New York: New Directions.

Borkowski, A., & Ozanne, E. (1993). New directions in aging policy in Australia. *Generations, 17*(4), 55–60.

Boss, P. (1999). *Ambigious loss: Learning to live with unresolved grief.* Cambridge, MA: Harvard University Press.

Boss, P. (2002). Ambigous loss: Working with families of the missing. *Family Processes, 41,* 14–17.

Boss, P., Beaulieu, L., Wieling, E., Turner, W., & LaCruz, S. (2003). Healing loss, ambiguity, and trauma: A community based interventiom with families of union workers missing after the 9/11 attacks in New York City. *Journal of Marriage and Family Therapy, 29,* 455–467.

Bossé, R., Aldwin, C. M., Levenson, M. R., & Ekerdt, D. J. (1987). Mental health among retirees and workers: Findings from the

Normative Aging Study. *Psychology and Aging*, 2, 383–389.

Bossé, R., Aldwin, C. M., Levenson, M. R., & Workman–Daniels, K. (1991). How stressful is retirement? Findings from the Normative Aging Study. *Journal of Gerontology: Psychological Sciences*, 46, P9–14.

Bossé, R., Aldwin, C. M., Levenson, M. R., Spiro, A., & Mroczek, D. K. (1993). Change in social support after retirement: Longitudinal findings from the normative aging study. *Journal of Gerontology: Psychological Sciences*, 48, P210–217.

Bosshard, G., Nilstun, T., Bilsen, J., Norup, M., Miccinesi, G., vanDelden, J.J.M., Faisst, K., van der Heide, A., for the European End of Life Consortium (2005). Forgoing treatment at the end of life in 6 European countries. *Archives of Internal Medicine*, 165, 401–407.

Botwinick, J. (1978). *Aging and behavior* (2nd ed.). New York: Springer.

Botwinick, J. (1984). *Aging and behavior* (3rd ed.). New York: Springer.

Bouvier, L. F., & Simcox, D. (1994). *Foreign born professionals in the U.S.* Washington, DC: Center for Immigration Studies.

Bouza, A. V. (1990). *The police mystique: An insider's look at cops, crime, and the criminal justice system.* New York: Plenum.

Bowlby, J. (1973). *Separation: Anxiety and anger.* New York: Basic Books.

Boyer, J. L., & Guthrie, L. (1985). Assessment and treatment of the suicidal patient. In E. E. Beckham & W. R. Leber (Eds.), *Handbook of depression.* Homewood, IL: Dorsey.

Brabant, S. (1994). An overlooked AIDS affected population: The elderly parent as caregiver. *Journal of Gerontological Social Work*, 22, 131–145.

Brabeck, M.M., & Shore, E.L. (2003). Gender differences in intellectual and moral develoment? The evidence refutes the claims. In. J. Demick and C. Andreoletti (Eds.), *Handbook of adult development.* New York: Plenum Press.

Bradford, J., & Ryan, C. (1991). Who are we: Health concerns of middle-aged lesbians. In J. W. B. Sang & A. Smith (Eds), *Lesbians at midlife: The creative transition* (pp.147–163). San Francisco: Spinsters.

Bramlett, M. D., & Mosher, W. D. (2001). *First marriage dissolution, divorce and remarriage: United States.* (Advance data from vital and national health statistics, no. 323). Hyattsville, MD: National Center for Health Statistics.

Bramlett, M. D., & Mosher, W. D. (2002). Cohabitation, marriage, divorce, and remarriage in the United States. *Vital Health Statistics*, 23(22). Hyattsville, MD: National Center for Health Statistics.

Brandt, B. (1989). A place for her death. *Humanistic Judaism*, 17(3), 83–85.

Braungart, J. M., Plomin, R., DeFries, J. C., & Fulker, D. W. (1992). Genetic influence on tester-rated infant temperament as assessed by Bayley's Infant Behavior Record: Nonadoptive and adoptive siblings and twins. *Developmental Psychology*, 28, 40–47.

Brave new biology: Granny gives birth. (1993, February 13). *Science News*, p. 100.

Braveman, N. S. (1987). Immunity and aging: Immunologic and behavioral perspectives. In M. W. Riley, J. D. Matarazzo, & A. Baum (Eds.), *Perspectives in behavioral medicine: The aging dimension* (pp. 93–124). Hillsdale, NJ: Erlbaum.

Bray, D. W., & Howard, A. (1983). The AT&T longitudinal study of managers. In K. W. Schaie (Ed.), *Longitudinal studies on adult psychological development* (pp. 266–312). New York: Guilford.

Bray, J.H., & Hetherington, E.M. (1993). Families in transition: Introduction and overview. *Journal of Family Psychology*, 7, 3–8.

Brecher, E., & the Editors of Consumer Reports Books. (1984). *Love, sex, and aging: A Consumers Union report.* Boston: Little, Brown.

Bremner, W. J., Vitiello, M. V., & Prinz, P. N. (1983). Loss of circadian rhythmicity in blood testosterone levels with aging in normal men. *Journal of Clinical Endocrinology and Metabolism*, 56, 1278–1281.

Brenner, M. H. (1991). Health, productivity, and the economic environment: Dynamic role of socio-economic status. In G. Green & F. Baker (Eds.), *Work, health, and productivity* (pp. 241–255). New York: Oxford University Press.

Brickfield, C. F. (1984). Attitudes and perceptions of older people toward technology. In P. K. Robinson & J. E. Birren (Eds.), *Aging and technological advances* (pp. 31–38). New York: Plenum.

Brigham, M. C., & Pressley, M. (1988). Cognitive monitoring and strategy choice in younger and older adults. *Psychology and Aging, 3,* 249–257.

Briley, M. (1980, July–August). Burnout stress and the human energy crisis. *Dynamic Years,* pp. 36–39.

Brim, O. G. (1977). Theories of male midlife crisis. In N. Schlossberg & A. Entine (Eds.), *Counseling adults.* Monterey, CA: Brooks/Cole.

Brint, S. F. (1989). *Sight for a lifetime.* Metairie, LA: Plantain.

Brocas, A., Cailloux, A., & Oget, V. (1990). Women and social security: Progress towards equality of treatment. Geneva: International Labour Office.

Brock, D. W. (1992, March–April). Voluntary active euthanasia. *Hastings Center Report,* pp. 10–22.

Brody, E. B., & Brody, N. (1976). *Intelligence: Nature, determinants, and consequences.* New York: Academic.

Brody, E. M. (1978). Community housing for the elderly. *The Gerontologist, 18*(2), 121–128.

Brody, H. (1955). Organization of the cerebral cortex: 3. A study of aging in the cerebral cortex. *Journal of Comparative Neurology, 102,* 511–556.

Brody, H. (1970). Structural changes in the aging nervous system. In H. T. Blumenthal (Ed.), *The regulatory role of the nervous system in aging: 7. Interdisciplinary topics in gerontology* (pp. 9–21). Basel, Switzerland: Karger.

Brodzinsky, D. (1997). Infertility and adoption adjustment: Considerations and clinical issues. In S. R. Leiblum (Ed.), *Infertility: Psychological issues and counseling strategies* (pp. 246–262). New York: Wiley.

Bronfenbrenner, U. (1979). *The ecology of human development.* Cambridge, MA: Harvard University Press.

Bronstein, P., Clauson, J., Stoll, M.E. & Abrams, C. L. (1993). Parenting behavior and children's social, psychological, and academic adjustment in diverse family structures. *Family Relations, 42,* 268–276.

Bronte, L. (1993). *The longevity factor: The new reality of long careers and how it can lead to richer lives.* New York: HarperCollins.

Brooks-Gunn, J., Klebanov, P., Smith, J., Duncan, G. J., Lee, K. (2003). *Applied Developmental Science, 7*(4), 239–252.

Brown, J. T., & Stoudemire, A. (1983). Normal and pathological grief. *Journal of the American Medical Association, 250,* 378–382.

Brown, M. B., & Tedrick, T. (1993). Outdoor leisure involvements of black older Americans: An exploration of ethnicity and marginality. In *Activities, adaptation, and aging* (pp. 55–65). New York: Haworth.

Brown, N. M. (1990). Age and children in the Kalahari.

Brown, N. M. (1993). Singular women. *Health and Human Development Research, 3,* 16–21.

Brown, P. (1993, April 17). Motherhood past midnight. *New Scientist,* pp. 4–8.

Browning, C. R. (2002). The span of collective efficacy: Extending social disorganization theory to partner violence. *Journal of Marriage and the Family, 64,* 833-850.

Brubaker, T. H. (1983). Introduction. In T. H. Brubaker (Ed.), *Family relationships in later life.* Beverly Hills, CA: Sage.

Brubaker, T. H. (1990). Families in later life: A burgeoning research area. *Journal of Marriage and the Family, 52,* 959–981.

Brubaker, T. H. (Ed.). (1993). *Family relationships; Current and future directions.* Newbury Park, CA: Sage.

Bruce, J., Lloyd, C. B., & Leonard, A. (1995). *Families in focus; New perspectives on mothers, fathers, and children.* New York: Population Council.

Brumberg, E. (1993, August–September). What price beauty? *Modern Maturity,* p. 74.

Buchwald, A. (1994). *Leaving home.* New York: Putnam.

Bühler, C. (1933). *Der menschliche lebenslauf als psychologisches problem.* Leipzig: Verlag von S. Hirzel.

Bühler, C. (1968a). The developmental structure of goal setting in group and individual studies. In C. Bühle & F. Massarik (Eds.), *The course of human life* (pp. 27–54). New York: Springer.

Bühler, C. (1968b). The general structure of the human life cycle. In C. Bühle & F. Massarik (Eds.), *The course of human life* (pp. 12–26). New York: Springer.

Bulcroft, K., & O'Conner, M. (1986). The importance of dating relationships on quality of life for older persons. *Family Relations, 35,* 397–401.

Bulcroft, R. A., & Bulcroft, K. A. (1991). The nature and function of dating in later life. *Research on Aging, 13,* 244–260.

Bumpass, L.L., & Lu, H.H. (2000). Trends in cohabitation and implications for children's family contexts in the United States. *Population Studies, 54,* 29–41.

Bumpass, L. L., & Sweet, J. A. (1988). *Preliminary evidence on cohabitation* (NSFH Working Paper No. 2). Madison: University of Wisconsin, Center for Demography and Ecology.

Bumpass, L.L. , Sweet, J., & Martin, T. C. (1990). Changing patterns of remarriage. *Journal of Marriage and the Family, 52,* 747–756.

Bureau of Justice Statistics. (2000). Intimate partner violence. *Bureau of Justice Statistics Special Report,* May.

Bureau of Labor Statistics (BLS). (1999). Employment characteristics of families in 1998. [Online]. Available: http://www.bls.gov/ news.release/famee.nws.htm.

Bureau of Labor Statistics (BLS). (2001). Industry at a glance. [Online]. Available: http//www.bls.gov/ iag/iaghome/htm.

Bureau of Labor Statistics (BLS). (2003). *Volunteering in the United States: 2003.* Washington, DC: United States Department of Labor.

Bureau of Labor Statistics (BLS). (2004). *The employment situation: March 2004.* Washington, DC: United States Department of Labor.

Burke, D.M., & Shafto, M.A. (2004). Aging and language production. *American Psychological Society, 13(1),* 21–24.

Burkhauser, R. V., & Quinn, J. (1989). Work and retirement: The American experience. In W. Schmahl (Ed.), *Redefining the process of retirement: An international perspective.* Berlin: Springer-Verlag.

Burkhauser, R. V., Holden, K. C., & Feaster, D. (1988). Incidence, timing, and events associated with poverty: A dynamic view of poverty in retirement. *Journal of Gerontology: Social Sciences, 43,* S546–52.

Burns, A. (1992). Mother-headed families: An international perspective and the case of Australia. *Social Policy Report of the Society for Research Child Development, 6(1).*

Burns, B., & Taub, C. (1990). Mental health services in general medical care and nursing homes. In B. Fogel, A. Furino, & G. Gottlieb (Eds.), *Mental health policy for older Americans: Protecting minds at risk* (pp. 63–83). Washington, DC: American Psychiatric Press.

Burns, G. (1983). *How to live to be 100 or more: The ultimate diet, sex, and exercise book.* New York: Putnam.

Burtless, G., Quinn, J.F. (December, 2002). *Is working longer the answer for an aging workforce? An issue in brief.* Center for Retirement Research, 11.

Burton, L. M. (1992). Black grandparents rearing children of drug-addicted parents: stressors, outcomes, and social service needs. *The Gerontologist, 32,* 744–751.

Bush, B. (1994). *Barbara Bush: A memoir.* New York: Scribner's.

Busse, E. W. (1987). Primary and secondary aging. In G. L. Maddox (Ed.), *The encyclopedia of aging* (p. 534). New York: Springer.

Butler, R. (1961). Re-awakening interests. Nursing Homes. *Journal of American Nursing Home Association, 10,* 8–19.

Butler, R. N. (1987b). Mental health and illness. In G. L. Maddox (Ed.), *The encyclopedia of aging* (pp. 439–440). New York: Springer.

Butler, R. N. (1996). The dangers of physician assisted suicide. *Geriatrics, 51,* 7.

Butler, R. N., & Lewis, M. (1982). *Aging and mental health* (3d ed.). St. Louis: Mosby.

Butler, R. N., Lewis, M. I., & Sunderland, T. (1991). *Aging and mental health: Positive psychosocial and biomedical approaches* (4th ed.). New York: Merrill.

Butler, R. N., Lewis, M. I., Sunderland, T. (1998). *Aging and mental health.* Boston, MA: Allyn Bacon Publishing.

Butrica, B.A. & Uccello, C.E. (2004). How will boomers fare at retirement? Final report. Washington, DC: AARP.

Caelli, K., Downie, J., Letendre, A. (2002). Parents' experiences of midwife-managed care following the loss of a baby in a previous pregnancy. *Journal of Advanced Nursing, 39,* 127–136.

Call, V., Sprecher, S., & Scwartz, P. (1995) The incidence and frequency of marital sex in a national sample. *Journal of Marriage and the Family*, 57, 639–652.

Callan, V. (1986). The impact of the first birth: Married and single women preferring childlessness, one child, or two children. *Journal of Marriage and the Family*, 48, 261–269.

Camp, C. J. (1988). In pursuit of trivia: Remembering, forgetting, and aging. *Gerontological Review*, 1, 37–42.

Camp, C. J. (1989). World-knowledge systems. In L. W. Poon, O. C. Rubin, & B. A. Wilson (Eds.), *Everyday cognition in adulthood and late life* (pp. 457–482). Cambridge: Cambridge University Press.

Camp, C. J., & McKitrick, L. A. (1989). The dialectics of remembering and forgetting across the adult lifespan. In D. Kramer & M. Bopp (Eds.), *Dialectics and contextualism in clinical and developmental psychology: Change, transformation, and the social context* (pp. 169–187). New York: Springer.

Camp, C. J., & McKitrick, L. A. (1992). Memory interventions in Alzheimer's-type dementia populations: Methodological and theoretical issues. In R. L. West & J. D. Sinnott (Eds.), *Everyday memory and aging: Current research and methodology* (pp. 155–172). New York: Springer-Verlag.

Camp, C. J., & Pignatiello, M. F. (1988). Beliefs about fact retrieval and inferential reasoning across the adult lifespan. *Experimental Aging Research*, 14, 89–98.

Camp, C. J., & Stevens, A. B. (1990). Spaced-retrieval: A memory intervention for dementia of the Alzheimer's type (DAT). *Clinical Gerontologist*, 10, 58–61.

Camp, C. J., Foss, J. W., Stevens, A. B., Reichard, C. C., McKitrick, L. A., & O'Hanlon, A. M. (1993). Memory training in normal and demented populations: The E-I-E-I-O model. *Experimental Aging Research*, 19, 277–290.

Camp, C. J., Markley, R. P., & Kramer, J. J. (1983). Spontaneous use of mnemonics by elderly individuals. *Educational Gerontology*, 9, 57–71.

Camp, C. J., Markley, R. P., & Spenser, M. (1987, May). *Directed forgetting and aging.* Paper presented at the first annual Cognition and Aging Conference, Atlanta.

Camp, C., Doherty, K., Moody-Thomas, S., & Denney, N. W. (1989). Practical problem solving in adults: A comparison of problem types and scoring methods. In J. D. Sinnott (Ed.), *Everyday problem solving: Theory and applications* (pp. 211–228). New York: Praeger.

Campbell, J., & Moyers, W. (1988). *The power of myth with Bill Moyers.* New York: Doubleday.

Caraballo, R. S., Giovino, G. A., Pechacek, T. F., Mowery, P. D., Richter, P. A., Strauss, W. J., Sharp, D. J., Erikensen, M. P., Pirkle, J. L., & Maurer, K. R. (1998). Racial and ethnic differences in serum cotinine levels of cigarette smokers. *Journal of the American Medical Association*, 280, 135-139.

Cargan, L. (1981). Singles: An examination of two stereotypes. *Family Relations*, 30, 377–385.

Carlson, E., & Crowley, S. L. (1992, September). The Friedan mystique. *AARP Bulletin*, pp. 20, 15.

Carr, D. (2004). The desire to date and remarry among older widows and widowers. *Journal of Marriage and Family*, 66, 1951–1968.

Carr., D., House, J. S., Kessler, R. C., Nesse, R. M., Sonnege, J., & Wortman, C. (2000). Marital quality and psychological adjustment to widowhood among older adults: A longitudinal analysis. *Journal of Gerontology: Social Sciences*, 55B, S197–S207.

Carroll, J. B. (1991a). No demonstration that g is not unitary, but there's more to the story: Comment on Kranzler and Jensen. *Intelligence*, 15, 423–436.

Carroll, J. B. (1991b). Still no demonstration that g is not unitary, but there's more to the story: Comment on Kranzler and Jensen. *Intelligence*, 15, 449–453.

Carson, A. D., & Mowsesian, R. (1993). Self-monitoring and private self-consciousness: Relations to Holland's vocational personality types. *Journal of Vocational Behavior*, 42, 2, 212–222.

Carstensen, L. L. (1991). *Selectivity theory: Social activity in life-span context. In annual review of gerontology and geriatrics* (Vol. 11, pp. 195–217). New York: Springer.

Carstensen, L. L. (1993). Women of a certain age. In S. Matteo (Ed.), *Critical issues facing women in the '90s* (pp .66–78). Boston: Northeastern University Press.

Carstensen, L. L. (1995). Evidence for a life span theory of socioemotional selectivity. *Current Directions in Psychological Science, 4,* 150–156.

Carstensen, L. L. (1996). Socioemotional selectivity: A life span developmental account of social behavior. In M. R. Merrens & G. C. Brannigan (Eds.), *The developmental psychologists: Research adventures across the life span* (pp. 251–272). New York: McGraw-Hill.

Carter Center. (1995, Winter). *Carter Center News,* pp. 1, 3, 4–6, 9.

Carter, J. (1975). *Why not the best?* Nashville: Broadman.

Casper, L. M., & Bryson, K. R. (1998). *Co-resident grandparents and their grandchildren: grandparent maintained families* (Population Division Working Paper No. 26). Washington, DC: U.S. Bureau of the Census.

Caspi, A. (1993). Why maladaptive behaviors persist: Sources of continuity and change across the life course. In D. C. Funder, R. D. Parke, C. Tomlinson-Keasey, & K. Widaman (Eds.), *Studying lives through time: Personality and development* (pp. 343–376). Washington, DC: American Psychological Association.

Catania, J. A., Coates, T. J., Stall, R., Turner, H., et al. (1992). Prevalence of AIDS-related risk factors and condom use in the United States. *Science, 258*(5085), 1101–1106.

Cattell, R B. (1965). *The scientific analysis of personality.* Baltimore: Penguin.

Cavanaugh, J. C., & Morton, K. R. (1989). Contextualism, naturalistic inquiry, and the need for new science: A rethinking of everyday memory aging and childhood sexual abuse. In D. A. Kramer & M. Bopp (Eds.), *Transformation in clinical and developmental psychology* (pp. 89–114). New York: Springer-Verlag.

Cavanaugh, J. C., Kramer, D. A., Sinnott, J. D., Camp, C. J., & Markley, R. P. (1985). On missing links and such: Interfaces between cognitive research and everyday problem solving. *Human Development, 28,* 146–168.

Ceci, S., & Liker, J. (1986). A day at the races: A study of IQ, expertise, and cognitive complexity. *Journal of Experimental Psychology: General, 114,* 255–266.

Celis, W. (1990). More states are laying school paddle to rest. *New York Times,* p. A1, p. B12.

Center on Addiction and Substance Abuse at Columbia University (CASA). (1996, June). *Substance Abuse and the American Woman.* New York: Author.

Center on Elderly People Living Alone. (1995, January). *Medicaid and long-term care for older people* (Public Policy Institute Fact Sheet FSI8R). Washington, DC: American Association of Retired Persons.

Centers for Disease Control and Prevention. (1994). Annual summary of births, marriages, divorces, and deaths: United States, 1993. *Monthly Vital Statistics, 42*(13), 18–20.

Centers for Disease Control and Prevention. (1995). Differences in maternal mortality among black and white women: United States, 1990. *MMWR, 44*(1), 6–7, 13–14.

Centers for Disease Control and Prevention (2001). *Assisted reproductive technology success rates: National summary and fertility clinic reports.* Atlanta, GA: Author.

Centers for Disease Control and Prevention. (2001a). HIV/AIDS Surveillance Report, 2001; 13.

Centers for Disease Control and Prevention. (2001b). HIV testing among pregnant women—United States and Canada, 1998–2001. *MMWR, 2002;51.*

Centers for Disease Control and Prevention (2001c). *The oral health of older Americans: United States, 2001.* Aging Trends, March, No. 3.

Centers for Disease Control and Prevention. (2002). The national breast and cervical cancer early detection program. [Online]. Available: www.cdc.gov/cancer/nbccedp/about2002.htm. Access date: March 19, 2004.

Centers for Disease Control and Prevention. (2002b). Suicide in the United States. [Online]. Available: www.cdc.gov/ncipc/factsheets/suifacts.htm.

Centers for Disease Control and Prevention. (2003). Hypertension. [Online]. Available: www.cdc.gov/nchs/fastats/hypertens.htm. Access date: March 3, 2004.

Centers for Disease Control and Prevention. (2003a). Prostate cancer: The public health perspective. [Online]. Available: www.cdc.gov/cancer/prostate.htm. Access date: March 19, 2004).

Centers for Disease Control and Prevention (2003b). Heart disease. [Online]. Available: www.cdc.gov/nchs/fastats/heart.htm.

Centers for Disease Control and Prevention. (2003c). Tobacco use in the United States. [Online]. Available: www.cdc.gov/tobacco/overview/tobus_us.htm. Access date: March 23, 2004.

Centers for Disease Control and Prevention. (2003e). U.S. pregnancy rate down from peak; Births and abortions on the decline. [Online]. Available: www.cdc.gov/nchs/releases/03facts/pregbirths.htm. Access date: January 26, 2004.

Centers for Disease Control and Prevention (2003f). New report looks at latest mortality trends. [Online]. Available: www.cdc.gov/nchs/releases/03facts/mortalitytrends.htm. Access date: January 26, 2004.

Centers for Disease Control and Prevention. (2004a). Defining overweight and obesity. [Online]. Available: www.cdc.gov/nccdphp/dnpa/obesity/defining.htm. Access date: March 10, 2004.

Centers for Disease Control and Prevention. (2004b). Deaths: Final for 2002. *National Vital Statistics Reports, 53*(5).

Centers for Disease Control and Prevention. (2005a). Falls and hip fractures among older adults [Online]. Available: www.cdc.gov/ncipc/factsheets/falls.htm. Access date: January 30, 2006.

Centers for Disease Control and Prevention. (2005b). Deaths—leading causes. [Online]. Available: www.cdc.gov/nchs/faststats/lcod.htm. Access date: January 30, 2006.

Centers for Disease Control and Prevention (2006a). *Deaths/mortality.* [Online]. Available: www.cdc.gov/nchs/fastats/deaths.htm

Centers for Disease Control and Prevention (2006b). *Intimate partner violence: Fact sheet.* [Online]. Available: http://www.cdc.gov/ncipc/factsheets/ipvfacts.htm

Centers for Disease Control and Prevention. Basic statistics. [Online]. Available: www.cdc.gov/hiv/stats.htm. Access date: January 5, 2004.

Centers for Disease Control and Prevention. Preventing injuries at home and in the community. [Online]. Available: www.cdc.gov/ncipc/pub-res/research_agenda/04_home.htm. Access date: March 26, 2004.

Centers for Disease Control and Prevention. Noise and hearing loss prevention. [Online]. Available: www.cdc.gov/niosh/topics/noise/abouthlp/workerhl.html. Access date: April 30, 2004.

Centers for Disease Control and Prevention. Child maltreatment: Fact sheet. [Online]. Available: www.cdc.gov/ncipc/factsheets/cmfacts.htm. Access date: June 16, 2005.

Centers for Disease Control and Prevention. Intimate partner violence: Overview. [Online]. Available: www.cdc.gov/ncipc/factsheets/ipvoverview.htm. Access date: June 7, 2005.

Centers for Disease Control and Prevention. General alcohol information. [Online]. Available: www.cdc.gov/alcohol.factsheets/general_information.htm. Access date: July 2, 2005.

Centers for Disease Control and Prevention. Hospice care. [Online]. Available: www.cdc.gov/nchs/fastats/hospicecare.htm. Access date: July 5, 2005.

Centers for Disease Control and Prevention. Intimate partner violence: Fact sheet. [Online]. Available: www.cdc.gov/ncipc/factsheets/ipvfacts.htm. Access date: July 7, 2005.

Central Bureau of Statistics. (1992). *Statistical pocket book 1992.* Kathmandu, Nepal: Ratna Offset Press.

Chafetz, M. D. (1992). *Smart for life.* New York: Penguin.

Chalfie, D. (1994). *Going it alone: A closer look at grandparents parenting grandchildren.* Washington, DC: AARP Women's Initiative.

Chalfonte, B., & Johnson, M. K. (1996). Feature memory and binding in younger and older adults. *Memory and Cognition, 26,* 403–416.

Chambre, S. M. (1993). Volunteerism by elders: Past trends and future prospects. *The Gerontologist, 33,* 221–227.

Chan, R.W., Raboy, B., Patterson, C. J. (1998). Psychosocial adjustment among children conceived via donor insemination by lesbian and heterosexual mothers. *Child Development, 69,* 443–457.

Chandra, A., Abma, J., Maza, P., Bachrach, C. (1999). *Adoption, adoption seeking and relinquishment for adoption in the United States* (Advance data from Vital and Health Statistics No. 306). Hyattsville, MD: National Center for Health Statistics.

Chappell, N. L. (1991). Living arrangements and sources of caregiving. *Journal of Gerontology: Social Sciences, 46*(1), S1–8.

Charness, N., Schumann, C. E., & Boritz, G. M. (1992). Training older adults in word processing: Effects of age, training technique, and computer anxiety. *International Journal of Technology and Aging, 5*, 79–106.

Charness, N., Kelley, C. L., Bosman, E. A., Mottram, M. (2001). Word-processing training and retraining: Effects of adult age, experience, and interface. *Psychology and Aging, 16*(1) 110–127.

Chatters, L. M., & Taylor, R. J. (1989). Age differences in religious participation among black adults. *Journal of Gerontology: Social Sciences, 44*(5), S183–189.

Chau-Wai Yan, E., So-Kum Tang, C. (2004). Elder abuse by caregivers: A study of prevalence and risk factors in Hong Kong Chinese Families. *Journal of Family Violence, 19*(5), 269–277.

Chawla, S. (1993). Demographic aging and development. *Generations, 17*(4), 20–23.

Checkoway, B. (1992). Empowering the elderly: Gerontological health promotion in Latin America. Unpublished manuscript.

Cherlin, A., & Furstenberg, F. F. (1986a). Grandparents and family crisis. *Generations, 10*(4), 26–28.

Cherlin, A., & Furstenberg, F. F., Jr. (1986b). *The new American grandparent.* New York: Basic Books.

Cherry, K E., & Park, D. C. (1993). Individual differences and contextual variables influence spatial memory in younger and older adults. *Psychology and Aging, 8*, 517–526.

Children's Defense Fund. (2001). *The state of America's children yearbook 2001.* Washington DC: Author.

Chin, A. E., Hedberg, K., Higginson, G. K., & Fleming, D. W. (1999). Legalized physician assisted suicide in Oregon: the first year's experience. *New England Journal of Medicine, 340*, 577–583.

Chinen, A. B. (1985). Fairy tales and transpersonal development in later life. *Journal of Transpersonal Psychology, 17*, 99–122.

Chiriboga, D. (1982). Adaptation to marital separation in later and earlier life. *Journal of Gerontology, 37*, 109–114.

Chiriboga, D. (1989). Mental health at the midpoint: Crisis, challenge, or relief? In S. Hunter & M. Sundel (Eds.), *Midlife myths.* Newbury Park, CA: Sage.

Chiriboga, D. (1997). Crisis, challenge and stability in the middle years. In M. E. Lachman & J. B. James (Eds.), Multiple paths of midlife development (pp. 293–322). Chicago: University of Chicago Press.

Chiriboga, D., & Thurnher, M. (1975). Concept of self. In M. F. Lowenthal, M. Thurnher, & D. A. Chiriboga (Eds.), *Four stages of life: A comparative study of women and men facing transitions.* San Francisco: Jossey-Bass.

Chochinov, H. M. (2002). Dignity-conserving care: A new model for paliative care: Helping the patient feel valued. *Journal of the American Medical Association, 287*, 2253–2260.

Chochinov, H. M., Hack, T., McClement, S., Harlos, M., Kristjanson, L. (2002). Dignity in the terminally ill: A developing empirical model. *Social Science Medicine, 54*, 433–443.

Chochinov, H. M., Tataryn, D., Clinch, J. J., & Dudgeon, D. (1999). Will to live in the terminally ill. *Lancet, 354*, 816–819.

Cholesterol: Can you stop worrying? (1995, February), *The John Hopkins Medical Letter*, pp. 1–2.

Chumlea, W. C. (1982). Physical growth in adolescence. In B. B. Wolman (Ed.). Handbook of developmental psychology. Englewood Cliffs, NJ: Prentice-Hall.

Cicirelli, V. G. (1977). Relationship of siblings to the elderly person's feelings and concerns. *Journal of Gerontology, 12*(3), 317–322.

Cicirelli, V. G. (1980, December). *Adult children's views on providing services for elderly parents.* Report to the Andrus Foundation.

Cicirelli, V. G. (1989a). Feelings of attachment to siblings and well-being in later life. *Psychology and Aging, 4*(2), 211–216.

Cicirelli, V. G. (1989b). Helping relationships in later life: A reexamination. In J. A. Mancini (Ed.), *Aging parents and adult children.* Lexington, MA: Heath.

Cicirelli, V.G. (1995). *Sibling relationships across the life span.* New York: Plenum Press.

Clark, L. F., & Collins, J. E. (1993). Remembering old flames: How the past affects assessment of the present. *Personality and Social Psychology Bulletin, 19*, 399–408.

Clarke, C. J., & Neidert, L. J. (1992). Living arrangements of the elderly: An examination of differences according to ancestry and generation. *The Gerontologist, 32*(6), 796–804.

Clausen, I. A. (1993). *American lives*. New York: Free.

Clay, R. A. (1995, November). Social forces workplace violence. *APA Monitor*, p. 37.

Clayton, V. (1975). Erikson's theory of human development as it applies to the aged: Wisdom as contradictory cognition. *Human Development, 18*, 119–128.

Clayton, V. (1982). Wisdom and intelligence: The nature and function of knowledge in the later years. *International Journal of Aging and Development, 15*, 315–321.

Cleiren, M. P., Diekstra, R. F., Kerkhof, A. D., & Van der Wal, J. (1994). Mode of death and kinship in bereavement: Focusing on "who" rather than "how." *Crisis, 14*, 22–36.

Clements, M.L., Stanely, S.M., & Markman, H.J. (2004). Before they said "I do": Discriminating among marital outcomes over 13 years. *Journal of Marriage and the Family, 66*, 613–626.

Cm. 849. (1989). *Caring for people: Community care in the next decade and beyond*. London: HMSO.

CNN. (1998). An overlooked part of the AIDS epidemic: Older adults. [Online]. Available: http://www.cnn.com/HEALTH/9801/22/older.aids/

Cochran, S. D. (2001). Emerging issues in research on lesbians' and gay men's mental health: Does sexual orientation really matter? *American Psychologist, 56*, 169–179.

Cochran, W. G., Mosteller, F., & Tukey, I. W. (1953). Statistical problems of the Kinsey report. *Journal of the American Statistical Association, 48*, 674–716.

Cohan, C. L., & Kleinbaum, S. (2002). Toward a greater understanding of the cohabitation effect: Premarital cohabitation and marital communication. *Journal of Marriage and the Family, 64*, 180–192.

Cohen, G., & Faulkner, D. (1989). Age differences in source forgetting: Effects on reality monitoring and on eyewitness testimony. *Psychology and Aging, 4*, 10–17.

Cohen, N. L, Waltzman, S. B., Fisher, S. G., Tyler, R., and Department of Veterans Affairs Cochlear Implant Study Group. (1993). A prospective randomized study of cochlear implants. *New England Journal of Medicine, 328*(4), 233–237.

Coke, M. M., & Twaite, J. A. (1995). *The black elderly: Satisfaction and quality of later life*. New York: Haworth.

Coke, M. M. (1992). Correlates of life satisfaction among elderly African-Americans. *Journal of Gerontology: Psychological Sciences, 47*(5), P316–320.

Colby, A. (1978). Evolution of a moral development theory. In W. Damon (Ed.), *New directions for child development* (No.2). San Fransisco, CA: Jossey-Bass.

Colby, A., & Damon, W. (1992). Gaining insight into the lives of moral leaders. *Chronicle of Higher Education, 39*(20), 83–84.

Colby, A., Kohlberg, L., Gibbs, J., & Lieberman, M. (1983). A longitudinal study of moral development. *Monographs of the Society for Research in Child Development, 48*(1–2, Serial No. 200).

Cole, M., & Cole, S. R. (1989). *The development of children*. New York: Freeman.

Cole, M., & Scribner, S. (1974). *Culture and thought: A psychological introduction*. New York: Wiley.

Coleman, M., Ganong, L., & Fine, M. (2000). Reinvestigating marriage: Another decade of progress. *Journal of Marriage and the Family, 62*, 1288–1307.

Coles, R. (1970). Erik H. Erikson: The growth of his work.

Coley, R. L. (2001). (In)visible men: Emerging research on low income, unmarried and minority fathers. *American Psychologist, 56*, 743–753.

Collins, N. L., & Miller, L. C. (1994). Self-disclosure and liking: A meta-analytic review. *Psychological Bulletin, 116*, 457–475.

Commonwealth Fund Commission on Elderly People Living Alone. (1992). *Study of elderly people in five countries—U.S., Canada, Germany, Britain, and Japan: Key findings*. New York: Harris & Associates.

Conference Board. (1999, June 25). *Workplace education programs are benefiting U.S. corporation and workers* [Online.] Available: http://www.newswise.com/articles/1999/6/WEP.TCB.html.

Conger, R. D., Rueter, M. A., Elder, G. H., Jr., (1999). Couple resilience to economic pressure. *Journal of Personality and Social Psychology, 76,* 54–71.

Connidis, I. A. (1992). life transitions and the adult sibling tie: A qualitative study. *Journal of Marriage and the Family, 54,*972–982.

Conway, M. A. (1991). In defense of everyday memory. *American Psychologist, 46*(1), 19–26.

Cooper, K. L., & Gutmann, D. L. (1987). Gender identity and ego mastery style in middle-aged, pre- and post-empty nest women. *The Gerontologist, 27*(3), 347–352.

Cornelius, S. W., & Caspi, A. (1987). Everyday problem solving in adulthood and old age. *Psychology and Aging, 2,* 144–153

Costa, P. T., Jr., & McCrae, R. R. (1980). Still stable after all these years: Personality as a key to some issues in adulthood and old age. In P. B. Baltes & O. G. Brim, Jr. (Eds.), *Life-span development and behavior* (Vol. 3, pp. 65–102). New York: Academic.

Costa, P. T., Jr., & McCrae, R. R. (1988). Personality in adulthood: A six–year longitudinal study of self-reports and spouse ratings on the NEO Personality Inventory. *Journal of Personality and Social Psychology, 54,* 853–863.

Costa, P. T., Jr., & McCrae, R. R. (1994a). Set like plaster? Evidence for the stability of adult personality. In T. F. Heatherton & J. L. Weinberger (Eds.), *Can personality change?* (pp. 21–41). Washington, DC: American Psychological Association.

Costa, P. T., Jr., & McCrae, R. R. (1994b). Stability and change in personality from adolescence through adulthood. In C. F. Halverson, G. A. Kohnstamm, & R. P. Martin (Eds.), *The developing structure of temperament and personality from infancy to adulthood.* Hillsdale, NJ: Erlbaum.

Costa, P. T., Jr., McCrae, R. R., Zonderman, A. B., Barbano, H. E., Lebowitz, B., & Larson, D. M. (1986). Cross-sectional studies of personality in a national sample: 2. Stability in neuroticism, extraversion, and openness. *Psychology and Aging, 1,* 144–149.

Council of Europe. (1993). *Recent demographic developments in Europe and North America: 1992.* Strasbourg: Council of Europe Press.

Craik, F. I. M. (1977). Age differences in human memory. In J. E. Birren & K. W. Schaie (Eds.), *Handbook of the psychology of aging* (pp. 384–420). New York: Van Nostrand Reinhold.

Craik, F. I. M. (1994). Memory changes in normal aging. *Current Directions in Psychological Science, 5,* 155–158.

Craik, F. I. M., & Byrd, M. (1982). Aging and cognitive deficits: The role of attentional resources.

Craik, F. I. M., & Jennings, J. M. (1992). Human memory. In F. I. M. Craik & T. A. Salthouse (Eds.), *The handbook of aging and cognition* (pp. 51–110). Hillsdale, NJ: Erlbaum.

Craik, F. I. M., Morris, L. W., Morris, R. G., & Loewen, E. R. (1990). Aging, source amnesia, and frontal lobe functioning. *Psychology and Aging, 5,* 148–151.

Cramer, J. A. & Rosenheck, R. (1998). Compliance with medication regimens for mental and physical disorders. *Psychiatric Services, 49*(2), 196-201.

Crandall, M., Nathens, A.B., Kernic, M.A., Hot, V.L., Rivara, F.P. (2004). Predicting future injury among women in abusive relationships. *Journal of Trauma–Injury Infection and Critical Care, 56*(4), 906–912.

Crimmins, E. M., Reynolds, S. L., & Saito, Y. (1999). Trends in health and stability to work among the older working-age population. *Journal of Gerontology: Psychological Sciences, 54B,* S31–S40.

Crisp, A. H., Queenan, M., & D'Souza, M. F. (1984, March 17). Myocardial infarction and the emotional climate. *Lancet,* pp. 616–618.

Crouter, A. C., & Manke, B. (1994). The changing American workplace: Implications for individuals and families. *Family Relations, 43,* 117–124.

Crowley, S. L. (1993, October). Grandparents to the rescue. *AARP Bulletin,* pp. 1, 16–17.

Crowley, S. L. (1994, May). Much ado about menopause: Plenty of information but precious few answers. *AARP Bulletin, 2,*7.

Crown, W. H. (1993). Projecting the costs of aging populations. *Generations, 17*(4),32–36.

Crutchfield, R. S. (1962). Conformity and creative thinking. In H. E. Gruber, G. Terrell, & M. Wertheimer (Eds.), *Contemporary approaches to creative thinking* (pp.120–140). New York: Atherton.

Cruzan v. Director, Missouri Department of Health, 110 S. Ct. 2841 (1990).

Csikszentmihalyi, M., & Rathunde, K. (1990). The psychology of wisdom: An evolutionary interpretation. In R. J. Stemberg (Ed.), *Wisdom: Its nature, origins, and development* (pp. 25–51). Cambridge: Cambridge University Press.

Cumming, E., & Henry, W. (1961). *Growing old*. New York: Basic Books.

Cutler, N. E., Whitelaw, N. A., & Beattie, B. L. (2002). *American perception of aging in the 21st century: A myths and realities of aging chartbook*. Washington, DC: National Council on Aging.

Cuttini, M., Nadai, M., Kaminski, M., Hansen, G., de Leeuw, R., Lenoir, S., Persson, J., Rabagliato, M., Reid, M., de Vonderweid, U., Lenard, H.G., Orzalesi, M., & Saracci, R., for the EURONIC study group. End of life decisions in neonatal intensive care: Physicians' self-reported practices in 7 European countries. *Lancet, 355*, 2112–2118.

Cvetanovski, J., & Jex, S. (1994). Locus of control of unemployed people and its relationship to psychological and physical well-being. *Work and Stress, 8(1)*, 60–67.

Cytrynbaum, S., Bluum, L., Patrick, R., Stein, J., Wadner, D., & Wilk, C. (1980). Midlife development: A personality and social systems perspective. In L. Poon (Ed.), *Aging in the 1980s*. Washington, DC: American Psychological Association.

Czaja, S.J. (2001). Technological change and the older worker. In J. E. Birren & K. W. Schaie (Eds.), *Handbook of the Psychology of Aging* (pp. 547–568). San Diego: Academic Press.

Czaja, S. J., Sharit, J. (1998). Ability-performance relationships as a function of age and task experience for a data entry task. *Journal of Experimental Psychology: Applied, 4(4)*, 332–351.

Czaja, S.J., & Sharit, J. (1999). Age differences in a complex information search and retrieval task. Annual Meeting of the American Psychological Association, Boston.

Czaja, S. J., Sharit, J., Ownby, R., Roth, D. L., & Nair, S. (2001). Examining age differences in performance of a complex information search and retrieval task. *Psychology and Aging, 16(4)*, 564–579.

Dainoff, M. (1989). Death and other losses. *Humanistic Judaism, 17(3)*, 63–67.

Daniel, M. H. (1997). Intelligence testing: Status and trends. *American Psychologist, 52*, 1038–1045.

Daniels, D., & Plomin, R. (1985). Origins of individual differences in infant shyness. *Developmental Psychology, 21*, 118–121.

Darley, J., & Fazio, R. H. (1980). Expectancy confirmation processes arising in the social interaction sequence. *American Psychology, 35*, 867–881.

Datan, N., Rodeheaver, D., & Hughes, F. (1987). Adult development and aging. *Annual Review of Psychology, 38*, 153–180.

Davidson, G. P. (1985). Family law and family therapy: A New Zealand history of convergent development. Paper presented at the conference of the California Chapter of the Association of Family and Conciliation Courts, Anaheim.

Davidson, N. E. (1995). Hormone-replacement therapy—Breast versus heart versus bone. *New England Journal of Medicine, 332*, 1638–1639.

Davies, B. (1993). Caring for the frail elderly: An international perspective. *Generations, 17(4)*, 51–54.

Davies, C., & Williams, D. (2002). *The grandparent study 2020 report*. Washington, DC: AARP.

Davis, K. E. (1985, February). Near and dear: Friendship and love compared. *Psychology Today*, pp. 22–30.

Davis, K. L. et al. (1992). A double-blind placebo controlled multicenter study of tacrine for Alzheimer's disease. *New England Journal of Medicine, 327*, 1253–1259.

Davis-Friedmann, D. (1985). Chinese retirement: Policy and practices. In Z. S. Blau (Ed.), Current perspectives on aging and the life cycle (Vol. 1). Greenwich, CT: JAI.

Dawson, D. A. (1991). Family structure and children's health and well being: Data from the 1988 National Health Interview Survey on Child Health. *Journal of Marriage and the Family, 53*, 573–584.

Dawson, J. M., & Langan, P. A. (1994, July). Murder in families (Bureau of Justice Statistics Special Report). Washington, DC: U.S. Government Printing Office.

Dawson-Hughes, B., Harris, S. S., Krall, E. A., & Dallal, G. E., (1997). Effect of calcium and vitamin D supplementation on bone density in men and women 65 years of age and older. *New England Journal of Medicine, 337,* 670–676.

de Lafuente, D. (1994, September 11). Fertility clinics: Trying to cut the cost of high-tech baby making. *Chicago Sun-Times,* p. 4C.

de Vaus, D. (2002, winter). Marriage and mental health. *Family Matters* 62, 26-32.

de Vos, S. (1990). Extended family living among older people in six Latin American countries. *Journal of Gerontology: Social Sciences, 45,* S87–94.

DeAngelis, T. (1994, October). Loving styles may be determined in infancy. *American Psychological Association Monitor,* p. 21.

DeCarlo, D., & Gruenfeld, D. (1989). *Stress in the American workplace.* Horsham, PA: LRP.

Delany, E., Delany, S., & Hearth, A. H. (1993). *The Delany sisters first 100 years.* New York: Kodansha America.

Denney, N. W. (1974). Classification ability in the elderly. *Journal of Gerontology, 29,* 309–314.

Denney, N. W., & Palmer, A. M. (1981). Adult age differences on traditional and practical problem-solving measures. *Journal of Gerontology, 36(3),* 323–328.

Denney, N. W., & Pearce, K. A. (1989). A developmental study of practical problem solving in adults. *Psychology and Aging, 4(4),* 438–442.

Depression. (1995, March). *Harvard Women's Health Watch,* pp. 2–3.

Dewey, J. (1910/1991). *How we think.* Amherst, NY: Prometheus Books

Dewey, J. & Tufts, J. (1908). *Ethics.* New York: Herny Holt & Co.

Dickinson, G.E., Lancaster, C.J., Clark, D., Ahmedzai, S.H., & Noble, W. (2002). U.K. physicians' attitudes toward active voluntary euthanasia and physician-assisted suicide. *Death Studies, 26,* 479–490.

Dien, D. S. F. (1982). A Chinese perspective on Kohlberg's theory of moral development. *Developmental Review, 2,* 331–341.

Diener, E., & Suh, E. (1998). Age and subjective well-being: An international analysis. *Annual Review of Gerontology and Geriatrics, 17,* 304–324.

Diener, E., Suh, E. M., Lucas, R. E., & Smith, H. L. (1999). Subjective well being: Three decades of progress. *Psychological Bulletin, 125(2),* 276–302.

DiGiulio, J. F. (1992). Early widowhood: An atypical transition. *Journal of Mental Health Counseling, 14,* 97–109.

DiMarco, M.A., Menke, E.M., & McNamara, T. (2001). Evaluating a support group for perinatal loss. 135–140.

Dittmann-Kohli, F., & Baltes, P. B. (1990). Toward a neofunctionalist conception of adult intellectual development: Wisdom as a prototypical case of intellectual growth. In C. N. Alexander & E. J. Langer (Eds.), *Higher stages of human development: Perspectives on adult growth* (pp. 54–78). New York: Oxford University Press.

Divorce Magazine. Percentage of divorces in selected countries. [Online]. Available: www.divorcemagazine.com/statistics/statsWorld.shtml. Access date: November 17, 2003.

Dixon, R. A., & Baltes, P. B. (1986). Toward life-span research on the functions and pragmatics of intelligence. In R. J. Sternberg & R. K. Wagner (Eds.), *Practical intelligence: Nature and origins of competence in the everyday world* (pp. 203–235). New York: Cambridge University Press.

Dixon, R. A. & Hultsch, D. F. (1999). Intelligence and cognition potential in late life. In J. C. Cavanaugh and S. K. Whitbourne (Eds.). *Gerontology: An interdisciplinary perspective.* (pp. 213–237). New York: Oxford University Press.

Dixon, R. A., Hultsch, D. F., & Hertzog, C. (1988). The metamemory in adulthood (MIA) questionnaire. *Psychopharmocology Bulletin, 24,* 671–688.

Dixon, R. A., Kurzman, D., & Friesen, I. C. (1993). Handwriting performance in younger and older adults: Age, familiarity, and practice effects. *Psychology and Aging, 8,* 360–370.

Dobbs, A. R., & Rule, B. G. (1987). Prospective memory and self-reports of memory abilities in older adults. *Canadian Journal of Psychology, 41,* 209–222.

Doherty, W. J., & Jacobson, N. S. (1982). Marriage and the family. In B. Wolman (Ed.), *Handbook of developmental psychology.* Englewood Cliffs, NJ: Prentice-Hall.

Doka, K. J., & Mertz, M. E. (1988). The meaning and significance of great-grandparenthood. *The Gerontologist, 28(2),* 192–197.

Dorris, M. (1989). *The broken cord.* New York: Harper and Row.

Douglas, D. (2004). *Mortality rates low when HIV therapy begins early.* [Online]. Available: www.nlm.nih.gov/medlineplus/news/fullstory_16120.html.

Dreyfus, H. L. (1993–1994, Winter). What computers still can't do. *The Key Reporter*, pp. 4–9.

Drinka, P., Jaschob, K., Schultz, S., & Rudman, D. (1992). Is male hip fracture a marker for low testosterone in elderly male nursing home residents? *Journal of the American Geriatrics Society, 41*(2), 192, 199.

Dube, E. F. (1982). Literacy, cultural familiarity, and "intelligence" as determinants of story recall. In H. C. Trandis & A. Heron (Eds.), *Handbook of cross-cultural psychology: Developmental psychology* (pp. 274–292). Boston: Allyn & Bacon.

Dubin, R. (1956). Industrial workers' worlds: A study in the central life interests of industrial workers. *Social Problems, 4*, 131–142.

Dubowitz, H. (1999). The families of neglected children. In M. E. Lamb (Ed.), *Parenting and child development in "nontraditional" families* (pp. 327–345). Mahwah, NJ: Erlbaum.

Dudukovic, N.M., Marsh, E.J., Tversky, B. (2004). Telling a story or telling it straight: The effects of entertaining versus accurate retellings on memory. *Applied Cognitive Psychology, 18*(2), 125–143.

Dufour, M., Colliver, J., Stinson, F., & Grigson, B. (1988, November). *Changes in alcohol consumption with age: NHANES I epidemiologic followup.* Paper presented at the 116th annual meeting of the American Public Health Association, Boston.

Duncan, G. J., & Hoffman, S. D. (1985). Economic consequences of marital instability. In M. David & T. Smeeding (Eds.), *Horizontal equity, uncertainty, and economic well-being* (pp. 427–467). Chicago: University of Chicago Press.

Dunlosky, J., & Hertzog, Z. (1998). Aging and deficits in associative memory: What is the role of strategy production? *Psychology and Aging, 13*, 597–607.

Dunson, D. (2002). *Late breaking research session. Increasing fertility with increasing age: good news and bad news for older couples.* Paper presented at 18th Annual Meeting of the European Society of Human Reproduction and Embryology, Vienna.

Dunson, D.B., Colombo, B., & Baird, D.D. (2002). Changes with age in the level and duration of fertility in the menstrual cycle. *Human Reproduction, 17*, 1399–1403.

Durlak, J. A. (1973). Relationship between attitudes toward life and death among elderly women. *Developmental Psychology, 8*(1),146.

Dustman, R. E., Emmerson, R. Y., Steinhaus, L. A., Shearer, D. E., & Dustman, T. J. (1992). The effects of videogame playing on neuropsychological performance of elderly individuals. *Journal of Gerontology: Psychological Sciences, 47*(3), P168–171.

Dutta, R., Schulenberg, E., & Lair, T. J. (1986, April). *The effect of job characteristics on cognitive abilities and intellectual flexibility.* Paper presented at the annual meeting of the Eastern Psychological Association, New York.

Dychtwald, K. (1999). *Age Power.* New York, New York: Penguin Putnam.

Dychtwald, K. & Flower, J. (1990). *Age wave: How the most important trend of our time will change your future.* New York: Bantam.

Dykstra, P.A. (1995). Loneliness among the never and formerly married: The importance of supportive friendships and a desire for independence. *Journal of Gerontology: Social Sciences, 50B*, S321–329.

Eastell, R. (1998). Treatment of postmenopausal osteoporosis. *New England Journal of Medicine, 338*, 736–746.

Eastman, F. (1965). John H. Glenn. In The World Book Encyclopedia (vol 8, pp.214-214d). Chicago: Field Enterprises Educational Corporation.

Eaves, L. J., Eysenck, H. J., & Martin, N. G. (1989). *Genes, culture, and behavior: An empirical approach.* San Diego: Academic.

Economist. (12/20/03). *Japanese pension reform.* [Online]. Available: http://economist.com/finance/displaysotry.cfm?story_id=E1_NPDQGRC

Economist. (3/27/04). *Don't go yet.* [Online]. Available: http://economist.com/displaystory.cfm?story_id=E1_NVTGRPO

Edson, L. (1968, August 18). To hell with being discovered when you're dead. *New York Times Magazine*, pp. 26–27, 29–31, 34–36, 41, 44–46.

Edwards, C. P. (1977). The comparative study of the development of moral judgment and reasoning. In R. Monroe, R. Monroe, & B. B. Whiting (Eds.), *Handbook of cross-cultural human development*. New York: Garland.

Effective solutions for impotence. (1994, October). *Johns Hopkins Medical Letter: Health after 50*, pp. 2–3.

Eichenbaum, H., & Fortin, N. (2003). Episodic memory and the hippocampus: It's about time. *American Psychological Society*, 12(2), 53–57.

Eichorn, D. H., Clausen, J. A., Haan, N., Honzik, M. P., & Mussen, P. H. (Eds.). (1981). *Present and past in middle life*. New York: Academic.

Einstein, A., & Infeld, L. (1938). *The evolution of physics*. New York: Simon & Schuster.

Einstein, G. (1992, April). *Aging and prospective memory: Examining the influence of self-initiated retrieval*. Paper presented at the Cognitive Aging Conference, Atlanta.

Einstein, G. O., & McDaniel, M. A. (1990). Normal aging and prospective memory. *Journal of Experimental Psychology: Learning, Memory, and Cognition*, 16, 717–726.

Einstein, G. O., Smith, R. E., McDaniel, M. A., & Shaw, P. (1997). Aging and prospective memory: The influence of increased task demands at encoding and retrieval. *Psychology and Aging*, 12, 479-488.

Eisenberg, L. (1995, Spring). Is the family obsolete? *The Key Reporter*, pp. 1–5.

Ekerdt, D. (1986). The busy ethic: Moral continuity between work and retirement. *The Gerontologist*, 26, 239–244.

Elbert, S. E. (1984). *A hunger for home: Louisa May Alcott and "Little Women."* Philadelphia: Temple University Press.

Elder, G. H., Jr., & Pavalko, E. K. (1993). Work careers in men's later years: Transitions, trajectories, and historical change. *Journal of Gerontology: Social Sciences*, 48, S180–191.

Elderhostel (2006). What is Elderhostel? [Online.] Available at: http://www.elderhostel.org/about/what_is.asp. Access date: April 15, 2006.

Elderly driving poses challenges for families. (1994, February). *The Menninger Letter*, p. 6.

Elias, P. K., Elias, M. F., Robbins, M. A., & Gage, P. (1987). Acquisition of word-processing skills by younger, middle-age, and older adults. *Psychology and Aging*, 2, 340–348.

Elkind, D. (1984). *All grown up and no place to go.* Reading, MA: Addison-Wesley.

Emde, R. N., Plomin, R., Robinson, J., Corley, R., DeFries, J., Fulker, D. W., Reznick, J. S., Campos, J., Kagan, J., & Zahn-Waxler, C. (1992). Temperament, emotion, and cognition at 14 months: The MacArthur longitudinal twin study. *Child Development*, 63, 1437–1455.

Emery, R. E. (1988). *Marriage, divorce, and children's adjustment*. Newbury Park, CA: Sage.

Emery, V. O. B., & Oxman, T. E. (1994). *Dementia presentations, differential diagnosis, and nosology*. Baltimore: Johns Hopkins University Press.

Epstein, E., & Gutmann, R. (1984). Mate selection in man: Evidence, theory, and outcome. *Social Biology*, 31, 243–278.

Epstein, R. A. (1989, Spring). Voluntary euthanasia. *The Law School Record* (University of Chicago), pp. 8–13.

Epstein, S. (1990). Cognitive-experiential self-theory. In L. A. Pervin (Ed.), *Handbook of personality theory and research* (pp. 165–192). New York: Guilford.

Epstein, W. (1977). Mechanisms of directed forgetting. In G. H. Bower (Ed.), *The psychology of learning and motivation: Advances in research and theory* (Vol. 6, pp. 147–191). New York: Academic.

Equal Employment Opportunity Commision. (2004). Sexual harassment charges EEOC & FEPAs combined: FY 1992–FY 2002. Washington, DC: Office of Research, Information, and Planning, Equal Employment Opportunity Commission.

Equal Employment Opportunity Commission. (2004). Sexual Harassment. Washington, DC: Equal Employment Opportunity Commission.

Equal Employment Opportunity Commission (EEOC). (1994). Enforcement guidance on *Harris v. Forklift Systems. Fair Employment Practices*, No. 743 (Bureau of National Affairs, 405), 7165–7170.

Erber, J. T., & Prager, I. G. (1999). Age and memory: Perceptions of forgetful young and older adults. In F. Blanchard-Fields & T. M. Hess

(Eds.), *The cognitive perspective and the study of aging*. California: Academic Press.

Erdrich, L. (1984). *Love medicine*. New York: Holt Rinehart & Winston.

Erikson, E. H. (1950). *Childhood and society*. New York: Norton.

Erikson, E. H. (1985). *The life cycle completed*. New York: Norton.

Erikson, E. H., Erikson, J. M., & Kivnick, H. Q. (1986). *Vital involvement in old age: The experience of old age in our time*. New York: Norton.

Espeland, M.E., Rapp, S.R., Shumaker, S.A., Brunner, R., Manson, J.E., Sherwin, B.B., Hsia, Margolis, K.L., Hogan, P.E., Wallace, R., Dailey, M., Freeman, R., Hays, J. for the Women's Health Initiative Memory Study Investigators. (2004). Conjugated equine estrogens and global cognitive function in postmenopausal women: Women's health initiative memory study. *Journal of the American Medical Association, 21*, 2959–2968.

Essex, M. J., & Nam, S. (1987). Marital status and loneliness among older women: The differential importance of close family and friends. *Journal of Marriage and the Family, 49*, 93–106.

Estés, C. P. (1992). *Women who run with the wolves: Myths and stories of the wild woman*. New York: Ballantine.

Evans, G. W., & Stecker, R. (2004). Motivational consequences of environmental stress. *Journal of Enviomental Psychology, 24*, 143–465.

Evans, J. (1994). *Caring for the caregiver: Body, mind and spirit*. New York: American Parkinson Disease Association.

Evans-Pritchard, E. E. (1970). Sexual inversion among the Azande. *American Anthropologist, 72*, 1428–1433.

Eveleth, P. B., & Tanner, J. M. (1976). *Worldwide variation in human growth*. London: Cambridge University Press.

Faber, S.D., & Burns, J.W. (1996). Anger management style, degree of expressed anger, and gender influence: Cardiovascular recovery from interpersonal harassment. *Journal of Behavioral Medicine, 19*(1), 31–53.

Fackelmann, K. A. (1993, December 11). Nabbing a gene for colorectal cancer. *Science News*, p. 388.

Farina, E., Fioravanti, R., Chiavari, L., Imbourne, E., Alberoni, M., Pomati, S., Pinardi, G., Pignatti, R., & Mariani, C. (2002). Comparing two programs of cognitive training in Alzheimer's disease: a pilot study. *ACTA Neurologica Scandinavica, 105*, 365–371.

Farr, J. L., Tesluk, P. E., & Klein, S. R. (1998). Organizational structure of the workplace and the older worker. In K. W. Schaie & C. Schooler Eds.), *Impact of work on older individuals* (pp. 143–185). New York: Springer.

Farrell, C., Palmer, A. T., Atchison, S., & Andelman, B. (1994, September 12). The economics of aging: Why the growing number of elderly won't bankrupt America. *Business Week*, pp. 60–68.

Farrell, M. P., & Rosenberg, S. D. (1981). *Men at midlife*. Boston: Auburn.

Farrer, L. A., Myers, R. H., Cupples, L. A., St. George-Hyslop, P. H., Bird, T. D., Rossor, M. N., Mullan, M. J., Polinsky, R., Nee, L., Heston, L., Van Broeckhoven, C., Martin, J. J., Crapper-McLachlan, D., & Growdon, J. H. (1990). Transmission and age at onset patterns in familial Alzheimer's disease: Evidence for heterogeneity. *Neurology, 40*, 395–403.

Farrer, L.A., Cupples, L.A., Haines, J.L., Hyman, B., Kukull, W.A., Mayeux, R.., Myers, R.H., Pericak-Vance, M.A., Risch, N., & van Duijn, C.M. (1997). Effects of age, sex, and ethinicity on the assoiation between apolipoprotein E genotype and Alzheimer disease meta analysis consortium. *Journal of the American Medical Association, 278*(16).

Feazell, C. S., Mayers, R. S., & Deschner, J. (1984). Services for men who batter: Implications for programs and policies. *Family Relations, 33*, 217–223.

Federal Glass Ceiling Commission. (1995). *Good for business: Making full use of the nation's human capital: The environmental scam*. Washington, DC: U.S. Department of Labor.

Federal Interagency Forum on Aging-Related Statistics (Forum). (2004). Older Americans 2004: Key Indicators of Well-Being. Washington, DC: U.S. Government Printing Office.

Federal Trade Commission (FTC) (2000). Basik Lasik: Tips on Lasik Eye Surgery. [Online]. Available: www.ftc.gov/bcp/conline/pubs/health/lasik.htm Access date: January 23, 2006.

Feinleib, J. A., & Michael, R. T. (2000). Reported changes in sexual behavior in response to AIDS in the United States. In E. O. Laumann & R. T. Michael (Eds.), *Sex, love and health in America: Private choices and public policies* (pp. 302–326). Chicago: University of Chicago Press.

Feldman, H.A., Goldstein, I., Hatzichristou, D.G., Krane, R.J., & McKinlay, J.B. (1994). Impotence and its medical and psychosocial correlates: Results of the Massachusetts male aging study. *Journal of Urology, 151,* 54–61.

Feldman, R. D. (1982). *Whatever happened to the Quiz Kids? Perils and profits of growing up gifted*. Chicago: Chicago Review Press.

Feldman, R. D. (1985, August 6). Libraries open the books on local adult illiteracy. *Chicago Sun-Times* School Guide, pp. 10–11.

Feldman, R. S. (1993). *Understanding Psychology* (3rd ed.). New York: McGraw-Hill.

Feldman, S. S., Biringen, Z. C., & Nash, S. C. (1981). Fluctuations of sex-related self-attributions as a function of stage of family life cycle. *Developmental Psychology, 17,* 24–35.

Fellin, P. A., & Powell, T. J. (1988). Mental health services and older adult minorities: An assessment. *The Gerontologist, 28*(4), 442–446.

Ferrante, L. S., & Woodruff-Pak, D. S. (1995). Longitudinal investigation of eyeblink classical conditioning in elderly human subjects. *Journal of Gerontology: Psychological Sciences, 50,* P42–50.

Ferraro, K. F., & Su, Y. (1999). Financial strain, social relations, and psychological distress among older people: A cross-cultural analysis. *Journal of Gerontology: Psychological Sciences, 54B,* P3–P15.

Ferstenberg, R. L. (1992). Mediation versus litigation in divorce and why a litigator becomes a mediator. *American Journal of Family Therapy, 20,* 266–273.

Field, C.A. & Caetano, R. (2004). Ethnic differences in intimate partner violence in the U.S. general population. *Trauma, Violence and Abuse, 5*(4), 303–317.

Field, D., & Millsap, R. E. (1991). Personality in advanced old age: Continuity or change? *Journal of Gerontology: Psychological Sciences, 46,* P299–308.

Field, D., & Minkler, M. (1988). Continuity and change in social support between young-old and old-old or very-old age. *Journal of Gerontology: Psychological Sciences, 43(4),* P100–106.

Field, D., Minkler, M., Falk, R. F., & Leino, E. V. (1993). The influence of health on family contacts and family functioning in advanced old age: A longitudinal study. *Journal of Gerontology: Psychological Sciences, 48*(1), P18–28.

Fields, J. (2003). *Children's living arrangements and characteristics: March 2002.* (Current Population Reports, P20–547). Washington, DC: U.S. Census Bureau.

Fields, J., & Casper, L. (2001). *America's families and living arrangements: March 2000.* (Current population reports, P20–537). Washington, DC: U.S. Census Bureau.

Fiest, G.J. & Barron, F.X. (2003). Predicting creativity from early to late adulthood: Intellect, potential, and personality. *Journal of Research in Personality, 37,* 62–88.

Finn, R. (1993, February 8). Arthur Ashe, tennis champion, dies of AIDS. *New York Times*, pp. B1, 843.

Fiore, M. C., Novotny, T. E., Pierce, J. P. et al., (1990). Methods used to quit smoking in the United States: Do cessation programs help? *Journal of the American Medical Association, 263,* 2760–2765.

Fischer, K.W. & Pruyne, E. (2003). Reflective thinking in adulthood. In J. Demick & C. Andreoletti (Eds.), *Handbook of adult development*. New York: Plenum Press.

Fisher, L., & Lieberman, M. (1994, September). Alzheimer's disease: The impact of the family on spouses, offspring, and in-laws. *Family Process, 33*(3), 305–325.

Fleeson, W. & Heckhausen, J. (1997). More or less "me" in past, present, and future: Perceived lifetime personality during adulthood. *Psychology and Aging, 12*(1), 125–136.

Flores, J. (1952). *The woman with the whip: Eva Peron*. Garden City, NY: Doubleday.

Folkman, S., & Lazarus, R. S. (1980). An analysis of coping in a middle-aged community sample. *Journal of Health and Social Behavior, 21,* 219–239.

Folkman, S., Lazarus, R. S., Pimley, S., & Novacek, J. (1987). Age differences in stress and coping processes. *Psychology and Aging, 2,* 171–184.

Food and Drug Administration (FDA). (2003). FDA approves Memantine (Namenda) for Alzheimer's Disease. [Online]. Available: www.fda.gov/bbs/topics/NEWS/2003/NEW00961.html. Access date: April 1, 2004

Food and Drug Administration (FDA). (2004). LASIK eye surgery. [Online]. Available: www.fda.gov/cdrh/lasik/. Access date: May 21, 2004.

Ford, C. S., & Beach, F. A. (1951). *Patterns of sexual behavior*. New York: Harper Torchbooks.

Ford, P. (April 10, 2002). In Europe, marriage is back. *Christian Science Monitor*, p.1.

Foreman, J. (1994, May 16). Brain power's sliding scale. *Boston Globe*, pp. 25, 29.

Fortner, Neimeyer, Anderson & Berman, reported in Neimeyer, 2000

Foster, D. (1991, May–June). Double vision: An interview with the authors. *Mother Jones*, pp. 26, 78, 80.

Fowler, J. (1981). *Stages of faith: The psychology of human development and the quest for meaning*. New York: Harper & Row.

Foy, K. (1987, Fall). Family and divorce mediation: A comparative analysis of international programs. *Mediation Quarterly*, pp. 83–96.

Frank, S. J., Avery, C. B., & Laman, M. S. (1988). Young adults' perception of their relationships with their parents: Individual differences in connectedness, competence, and emotional autonomy. *Developmental Psychology, 24,* 729–737.

Freiberg, P. (1998, July). Bullying in the workplace is a violence warning sign [Online]. *APA Monitor, 29*(7), 1–2. Available: http://www.apa.org/monitor/jul98/bully.html.

Freud, S. (1947). *Leonardo da Vinci: A study in psychosexuality*. New York: Random House. (Original work published 1910.)

Freud, S. (1949). *The unconscious*. In Collected Papers (Vol. 4). London: Hogarth. (Original work published 1915.)

Freud, S. (1957). Leonardo da Vinci and a memory of his childhood. In J. Strachey, A. Freud, A. Strachey, and A. Tyson (Eds., Trans.), *The standard edition of the complete psychological works of Sigmund Freud* (Vol. 11, pp. 59–138). London: Hogarth and Institute of Psycho Analysis. (Original work published 1910.)

Freund, A. M., & Baltes, P. B. (2002). Life-management strategies of selection, optimization, and compensation: Measurement by self-report and and construct validity. *Journal of Personality and Social Psychology, 82*(4), 642–662.

Friedan, B. (1963). *The Feminine Mystique*. New York: Norton.

Friedan, B. (2000). *Life So Far*. New York: Simon & Schuster.

Friedman, H. S. & Markey, C. N. (2003). Paths to longevity on the highly intelligent Terman cohort. In C. E. Finch, J. Robine, J., & Y. Christen (Eds.), *Brain and longevity* (p. 165-175). New York: Springer.

Friedman, H. S., Tucker, J. S., Schwartz, J. E., Tomlison-Keasy, C., Martin, L. R., Wingard, D. L., & Criqui, M. H. (1995). Psychological and behavioral predictors of longevity? *Journal of Personality and Social Psychology, 65,* 176–185.

Friedman, H. S., Tucker, J. S., Schwartz, J. E., Tomlison-Keasy, C., Martin, L. R., Wingard, D. L., & Criqui, M. H. (1995). Childhood conscientiousness and longevity: Health behaviors and cause of death. *Journal of Personality and Social Psychology, 68,* 696–703.

Friedman, H. S., Tucker, J.S., Schwartz, J. E., Tomlison-Keasey, C., Martin, L. R., Wingard, D. L., Criqui, M. H. (1993). Does childhood personality predict longevity? *Journal of Personality and Social Psychology, 65,* 176–185.

Friedman, H. S., & Markey, C. N. (2003). Paths to longevity on the highly intelligent Terman cohort. In C. E. Finch, J. Robine, J., & Y Christen (Eds.), *Brain and longevity* (p. 165–175). New York: Springer.

Friedman, M., & Rosenman, R. H. (1974). Type A behavior and your heart. New York: Knopf.

Friend, R. A. (1991). Older lesbians and gay people: A theory of successful aging. In J. A. Lee (Ed), *Gay midlife and maturity* (pp. 99–118). New York: Haworth.

Fries, J. F., & Crapo, L. M. (1981). *Vitality and aging*. San Francisco: W. H. Freeman.

Frieze, I. H., Parsons, J. E., Johnson, P. B., Ruble, D. N., & Zellman, G. L. (1978). *Women and sex roles: A social psychological perspective*. New York: Norton.

Frone, M. R., Russell, M., Barnes, G. M. (1996). Work-family conflict, gender, and health-related outcomes: A study of employed parents in two community samples. *Journal of Occupational Health Psychology, 1*(1), 57–69.

Fulton, R., & Owen, G. (1987–1988). Death and society in twentieth-century America: Special issue–Research in thanatology. *Omega: Journal of Death and Dying, 18,* 379–395.

Funder, D. C. (1993). Judgments as data for personality and developmental psychology: Error versus accuracy. In D. C. Funder, R. D. Parke, C. Tomlinson-Keasey, & K. Widaman (Eds.), *Studying lives through time: Personality and development* (pp. 121–146). Washington, DC: American Psychological Association.

Fuwa, K. (2001). Lifelong education in Japan, a highly school-centered society: Educational opportunities and practical education activities for adults. *International Journal of Lifelong Education, 20,* 127–136.

Gagné, J. P. (1992). Ancillary aural rehabilitation services for adult cochlear implant recipients: A review and analysis of literature. *Journal of Speech, Language Pathology and Audiology, 16,* 121–128.

Gagné, J. P., Parnes, L. S., LaRocque, M., Hassan, R., & Vidas, S. (1991). Effectiveness of an intensive speech perception training program for adult cochlear implant recipients. *Annals of Otorhinolaryngology, 100,* 700–707.

Galea, S., Arhen, J., Resnick, H., Kilpatrick, D., Bucuvalas, M., Gold, J., & Vlahov, D. (2002). Psychological sequel of the September 11 terrorist attacks in New York City. *New England Journal of Medicine, 346,* 982–987.

Gallo, J. J., Anthony, J. C., & Muthen, B. O. (1994). Age differences in the symptoms of depression: A latent trace analysis. *Journal of Gerontology: Psychological Sciences,49,* P251–264.

Gallup, G. H. (1984). *The Gallup Poll: Public opinion 1983.* Wilmington, DE: Scholarly Resources.

Gallup. (2003). Teen career picks: The more things change…[Online]. Available: http://poll.gallup.com/content/default.aspx?ci=8371&pg=1.

Ganzini, L., Nelson, H.D., Schmidt, T.A., Kraemer, D.F., Delorit, M.A., & Lee, M.A. (2000). Physicians' experiences with the Oregon Death with Dignity Act. *New England Journal of Medicine, 342-557–563.*

Garasky, S. & Meyer, D. R. (1996). Reconsidering the increase in father-only families. *Demography, 22,* 285–393.

Garbarino, J., & Kostelny, K. (1993). Neighborhood and community influences on parenting. In T. Luster & L. Okagaki (Eds.), *Parenting: An ecological perspective* (pp. 203–226). Hillsdale, NJ: Erlbaum.

Gardiner, H. W., Mutter, J. D., & Kosmitzki, C. (1998*). Lives across cultures: Cross-cultural human development.* Boston: Allyn and Bacon.

Gardner, H. (1981, July). Breakaway minds. *Psychology Today,* pp. 64–71.

Gardner, H. (1983). *Frames of mind: The theory of multiple intelligences.* New York: Basic Books.

Gardner, H. (1986, Summer). Freud in three frames. *Daedalus,* 105–134.

Gardner, H. (1988). Creative lives and creative works: A synthetic scientific approach. In R. J. Sternberg (Ed.), *The nature of creativity: Contemporary psychological perspectives* (pp. 298–321). Cambridge: Cambridge University Press.

Gardner, H. (1999). *Intelligence reframed.* New York: Basic Books.

Garfein, A. J., Schaie, K. W., & Willis, S. L. (1988). Micro-computer proficiency in later-middle-aged and older adults: Teaching old dogs new tricks. *Social Behavior, 3,* 131–148.

Garwick, A. W. et al. (1994, September). Family perceptions of living with Alzheimer's disease. *Family Process, 33*(3), 327–340.

Gatz, M., & Smyer, M. (1992). The mental health system and older adults in the 1990's. *American Psychologist, 47,* 741–751.

Gelfand, D. E. (1982). *Aging: The ethnic factor.* Boston: Little Brown.

Geller, J. A. (1992). *Breaking destructive patterns: Multiple strategies for treating partner abuse.* New York: Free Press.

Gelles, R. J., & Maynard, P. E. (1987). A structural family systems approach to intervention in cases of family violence. *Family Relations, 36,* 270–275.

Geneva Association. (2003). Public policy, aging and work—An International Symposium, St. Catherine's College, Cambridge, December 17-19, 2002.

Genevay, B. (1986). Intimacy as we age. *Generations, 10*(4), 12–15.

George, L. K. (1980). *Role transitions in later life.* Monterey, CA: Brooks/Cole.

George, L. K. (1993). Depressive disorders and symptoms in later life. *Generations, 17*(1), 35–38.

Gerhard, G. S., & Cristofalo, V. J. (1992). The limits of biogerontology. *Generations, 16*(4), 55–59.

Getzels, J. W. (1964). Creative thinking, problem-solving, and instruction. In *Yearbook of the National Society for the Study of Education* (Part 1, pp. 240–267). Chicago: University of Chicago Press.

Getzels, J. W. (1984, March). *Problem finding and creativity in higher education.* Boston: Boston College, School of Education.

Getzels, J. W., & Csikszentmihalyi, M. (1968). The value orientations of art students as determinants of artistic specialization and creative performance. *Studies in Art Education, 10*(1), 5–16.

Getzels, J. W., & Csikszentmihalyi, M. (1975). From problem solving to problem finding. In J. A. Taylor & J. W. Getzels (Eds.), *Perspectives in creativity* (pp. 90–116). Volente, TX: Aldine.

Getzels, J. W., & Csikszentmihalyi, M. (1976). *The creative vision: A longitudinal study of problem finding in art.* New York: Wiley.

Getzels, J. W., & Jackson, P. W. (1962). *Creativity and intelligence: Explorations with gifted students.* New York: Wiley.

Geyer, G. A. (1983). *Buying the night flight.* New York: Delacorte/Seymour Lawrence.

Gfroerer, J., Penne, M., Pemberton, M., & Folsom, R. (2003). Substance abuse treatment need among older adults in 2020: the impact of the aging baby-boom cohort. *Drug and Alcohol Dependence, 69,* 127–135.

Giambra, L. M., & Arenberg, D. (1993). Adult age differences in forgetting sentences. *Psychology and Aging, 8,* 451–462.

Gibbs, J.C., Basinger, K.S., & Fuller, D. (1992). *Moral maturity: Measuring the development of sociomoral reflection.* Hillsdale, NJ: Lawrence Erlbaum Associates.

Gibson, R. C. (1986). Older black Americans. *Generations, 10*(4), 35–39.

Gilbert, L. A. (1994). Current perspectives in dual-career families. *Current Directions in Psychological Science, 3,* 101–105.

Gilford, R. (1984). Contrasts in marital satisfaction throughout old age: An exchange theory analysis. *Journal of Gerontology, 39,* 325–333.

Gilford, R. (1986). Marriages later in life. *Generations, 10*(4), 16–20.

Gilford, R., & Bengtson, V. (1979). Measuring marital satisfaction in three generations: Positive and negative dimensions. *Journal of Marriage and the Family, 41,* 387–398.

Gilliand, P. (1989). Evolution of family policy in light of development in western European countries. *International Social Security Review, 42,* 395–426.

Gilligan, C. (1982). *In a different voice: Psychological theory and women's development.* Cambridge, MA: Harvard University Press.

Gilligan, C. (1987a). Adolescent development reconsidered. In E. E. Irwin, (Ed.), *Adolescent social behavior and health.* San Francisco: Jossey-Bass.

Gilligan, C. (1987b). Moral orientation and moral development. In E. F. Kittay & D. T. Meyers (Eds.), *Women and moral theory* (pp. 19–33). Totowa, NJ: Rowman & Littlefield.

Gilligan, C., Murphy, J. M., & Tappan, M. B. (1990). Moral development beyond adolescence. In C. N. Alexander & E. J. Langer (Eds.), *Higher stages of human development* (pp. 208–228). New York: Oxford University Press.

Gist, M., Rosen, B., & Schwoerer, C. (1988). The influence of training method and trainee age on the acquisition of computer skills. *Personnel Psychology, 41,* 255–265.

Gladue, B. A. (1994). The biopsychology of sexual orientation. *Current Directions in Psychological Science, 3,* 150–154.

Glasheen, L. K. (1993, September). A place to call your own. *AARP Bulletin,* pp. 1, 10–14.

Glenn, N. D. (1987, October). Marriage on the rocks. *Psychology Today,* pp. 20–21.

Glenn, N. D. (1991). The recent trend in marital success in the United States. *Journal of Marriage and the Family, 53,* 261–270.

Glick, J. (1975). Cognitive development in cross-cultural perspective. In F. Horowitz (Ed.), *Review of child development research* (Vol. 4, pp. 595–654). Chicago: University of Chicago Press.

Glick, J. E., & Van Hook, J. (2002). Parents' correspondence with adult children: Can immigration explain racial and ethnic variation? *Journal of Marriage and the Family, 64,* 240–253.

Glick, P. C. (1989). Remarried families, stepfamilies, and stepchildren: A brief demographic profile. *Family Relations, 38,* 24–27.

Glynn, R. J., Bouchard, G. R., LoCastro, J. S., & Laird, N. M. (1985). Aging and generational effects on drinking behaviors in men: Results from the Normative Aging Study. *American Journal of Public Health, 75,* 1413–1419.

Goddard, I. (2002). Less calories more life. *Goddard's Journal.*

Gold, G. (2003). Vascular dementia: A diagnostic challenge. *International Psychogeriatrics, 15*(1), 111–114.

Golden, D. (1994, July). Building a better brain. *Life,* pp. 63–70.

Goldman, L. L., & Rothschild, J. (in press). Healing the wounded with art therapy. In B. Danto (Ed.), *Bereavement and suicide.* Philadelphia: Charles.

Goldstein, I., Padma-Nathan, H., Rosen, R.C., Steers, W.D., & Wickler, P.A. for the Sildenafil Study group. (1998). Oral sildenafil in the treatment of erectile dysfunction. *New England Journal of Medicine, 338,* 1397–1404.

Golombok, S., & Tasker, F. (1996). Do parents influence the sexual orientation of their children? Findings from a longitudinal study of lesbian families. *Developmental Psychology, 32,* 3–11.

Gonyea, J. G., Hudson, R. B., & Seltzer, G. B. (1990). Housing preferences of vulnerable elders in suburbia. *Journal of Housing for the Elderly, 7,* 79–95.

Goodman, C., & Silverstein, M. (2002). Grandmothers raising grandchildren: Family structure and well-being in culturally diverse families. *The Gerontologist, 42*(5), 676–689.

Goodman, G. S., Emery, R. E. & Haugaard, J. J. (1998). Developmental psychology and law: Divorce, child maltreatment, foster care, and adoption. In W. Damon (Series Ed.), I. E. Sigel, & K. A. Renninger (Vol. Eds.), *Handbook of child psychology* (Vol. 4, pp. 775–874). New York: Wiley.

Goodrich, C. (1995, January 18). Mandela tells the story of his monumental life. *Chicago Sun-Times,* p. 45.

Goodwin, J. (1994). *Akira Kurosawa and intertextual cinema.* Baltimore: Johns Hopkins University Press.

Gordon, A. (1975). The Jewish view of death: Guidelines for mourning. In E. Kübler-Ross (Ed.), *Death: The final stage of growth.* Englewood Cliffs, NJ: Prentice-Hall.

Gorman, C. Why so many of us are getting diabetes. *Time,* December 8, 2003.

Gorman, M. (1993). Help and self-help for older adults in developing countries. *Generations, 17*(4),73–76.

Gostin, L. O. (1997). Deciding life and death in the courtroom: From Quinlan to Cruzan, Glucksberg and Vacco—A brief history and analysis of constitutional protection of the right to die. *Journal of the American Medical Association, 278,* 1523–1528.

Gottfredson, L. S., & Deary, I. J. (2004). Intelligence predicts health and longevity, but why? *American Psychological Society, 13*(1), 1–4.

Gottman, J. M., & Krokoff, L. J. (1989). Marital interaction and satisfaction: A longitudinal view. *Journal of Consulting and Clinical Psychology, 57,* 47–52.

Granger, D. (1987). The Granada factor. In G. O'Connor (Ed.), *Olivier: In Celebration.* New York: Dodd, Mead.

Greenberg, J., & Becker, M. (1988). Aging parents as family resources. *The Gerontologist, 28*(6), 786–790.

Greenhouse, L. (February 23). Justices accept Oregon case weighing assisted suicide. *New York Times,* p. A1.

Greenstein, T. N. (1995). Gender ideology, marital disruption, and the employment of married women. *Journal of Marriage and the Family, 57,* 31–42.

Greenwald, A. G. (1980). The totalitarian ego: Fabrication and revision of personal history. *American Psychologist, 35,* 603–618.

Greenwell, I. (2001, August). DHEA: Anti-aging hormone. *Life Extension Magazine.*

Gribbin, K., Schaie, K. W., & Parham, I. A. (1980). Complexity of lifestyle and maintenance of intellectual abilities. *Journal of Social Issues, 36,* 47–61.

Grieder, L. (2001, December). Hard times drive adults kids "home"; Parents grapple with rules for "boomerangers."*AARP Bulletin,* pp. 3, 14.

Griffiths, J., Bood, A., & Weyers, H. (1998). *Euthanasia & law in the Netherlands.* Amsterdam: Amsterdam University Press.

Groenwoud, J.H., van der Heide, A., Onwuteaka-Philipsen, B.D., Willems, D.L., van der Maas, P.J., & van der Wal, G. (2000). Clinical problems with the performance of euthanasia and physician assisted suicide in the Netherlands. *New England Journal of Medicine, 342,* 551–556.

Gruber, A., & Schaie, K. W. (1986, November 21). *Longitudinal-sequential studies of marital assortativity.* Paper presented at the annual meeting of the Gerontological Society of America, Chicago.

Gruber, H. (1981). *Darwin on man.* Chicago: University of Chicago Press.

Gruber-Baldini, A. L. (1991). *The impact of health and disease on cognitive ability in adulthood and old age in the Seattle Longitudinal Study.* Unpublished doctoral dissertation, Pennsylvania State University.

Guemple, L. (1983). Growing old in Inuit society. In J. Sokolovsky (Ed.), *Growing old in different societies* (pp. 24–28). Belmont, CA: Wadsworth.

Guilford, J. P. (1956). Structure of intellect. *Psychological Bulletin, 53,* 267–293.

Guilford, J. P. (1959). Three faces of intellect. *American Psychologist, 14,* 469–479.

Guilford, J. P. (1960). Basic conceptual problems of the psychology of thinking. Proceedings of the New York Academy of Sciences, 91, 6–21.

Guilford, J. P. (1967). *The nature of human intelligence.* New York: McGraw-Hill.

Guilford, J. P. (1982). Cognitive psychology's ambiguities: Some suggested remedies. *Psychology Review, 89,* 48–59.

Guilford, J. P. (1986). *Creative talents: Their nature, uses and development.* Buffalo, NY: Bearly.

Gupta, S. (2004, February 2). Hope for Alzheimer's. *Time.*

Gutman, A. (2000). *EEO Law and Personnel Practices* (2nd ed.). Thousand Oaks, CA: Sage.

Gutmann, D. (1975). Parenting: A key to the comparative study of the life cycle. In N. Datan & L. H. Ginsberg (Eds.), *Life-span developmental psychology: Normative life crises.* New York: Academic.

Gutmann, D. (1977). The cross-cultural perspective: Notes toward a comparative psychology of aging. In J. Birren & K. W. Schaie (Eds.), *Handbook of the psychology of aging* (pp. 302–326). New York: Van Nostrand Reinhold.

Gutmann, D. (1985). The parental imperative revisited. In J. Meacham (Ed.), *Family and individual development.* Basel, Switzerland: Karger.

Gutmann, D. (1992). Culture and mental health in later life. In J. E. Birren, R. Sloane, & G. D. Cohen (Eds.), *Handbook of mental health and aging* (2nd ed., pp. 75–96). New York: Academic.

Gutmann, D. L. (1974). Alternatives to disengagement: Aging among the highland Druze. In R. LeVine (Ed.), *Culture and personality: Contemporary readings* (pp. 232–245). Chicago: Aldine.

Haan, N. (1990). Personality at midlife. In S. Hunter & M. Sundel (Eds.), *Midlife myths.* Newbury Park: Sage.

Haan, N., & Day, D. (1974). A longitudinal study of change and sameness in personality development: Adolescence to later adulthood. *International Journal of Aging and Human Development, 5,* 11–39.

Haas, A. D. (1989, Winter). Adults in college. *Women's American ORT Reporter,* pp. 7, 14.

Haas, S. M., & Stafford, L. (1998). An initial examination of maintenance behaviors in gay and lesbian relationships. *Journal of Social and Personal Relationships, 15,* 846–855.

Hagestad, G. O. (1978). *Patterns of communication and influence between grandparents and grandchildren in a changing society.* Paper presented at the meeting of the World Conference of Sociology, Uppsala, Sweden.

Hagestad, G. O. (1982). *Issues in the study of intergenerational continuity.* Paper presented at the National Council on Family Relations Theory and Methods Workshop, Washington, DC.

Hagestad, G.O. (2000). *Intergenerational relations.* Paper prepared for the United Nations Economic Commission for Europe Conference on Generations and Gender, Geneva, July 3–5.

Haley, A. (1976). *Roots.* Garden City, NY: Doubleday.

Hall, C., & Lindzey, G. (1978). *Personality* (3rd ed.). New York: Wiley.

Hall, D. R., & Zhao, J. Z. (1995). Cohabitation in Canada: Testing the selectivity hypothesis. *Journal of Marriage and the Family, 57,* 421–427.

Hall, D. T., & Mirvis, P. H. (1995a). The new career contract: Developing the whole person at midlife and beyond. *Journal of Vocational Behavior, 47,* 269–289.

Hall, D. T., & Mirvis, P. H. (1995b). Careers as lifelong learning. In A. Howard (Ed.), *The changing nature of work* (pp. 323–361). San Francisco: Jossey-Bass.

Hall, D. T., & Mirvis, P H. (1996). The new protean career: Psychological success and the path with a heart. In D. T. Hall and associates (Eds.), *The career is dead—Long live the career: A relational approach to careers.* San Francisco: Jossey-Bass Publishers.

Hall, G. S. (1922). *Senescence: The last half of life.* New York: Appleton.

Hamer, D. H., Hu, S., Magnuson, V. L., Hu, N., & Pattatucci, A. M. L. (1993) A linkage between DNA markers on the X chromosome and male sexual orientation. *Science, 261,* 321–327.

Hamilton, B. E., Martin, J. A., & Sutton, P. D. (2003). Births: Preliminary data for 2003. *National Vital Statistics Reports, 51,* 11.

Hamon, R. R., & Blieszner, R. (1990). Filial responsibility expectations among adult child-older parent pairs. *Journal of Gerontology: Psychological Sciences, 45*(3), P110–112.

Han, K.K., Soares, J.M., Jr., Haidar, M.A., de Lima, G.R., & Baracat, E.C. (2002). Benefits of soy isoflavene therapeutic regimen on menopausal symptoms. *Obstetrics & Gynecology, 99,* 389–394.

Handy, C. (1991, October–November). Building small fires: Keep life sizzling–diversify! *Modern Maturity,* pp. 35–39.

Hankinson, S. E., Stampfer, M. J., Seddon, J. M., Colditz, G. A., Rosner, B., Speizer, F. E., & Willett, W. C. (1992). Nutrient intake and cataract extraction in women: A prospective study. *British Medical Journal, 305*(6849), 335–339.

Hanley, R. (1988a, February 4). Surrogate deals for mothers held illegal in Jersey. *New York Times,* pp. A1, B6.

Hanley, R. (1988b, February 4). Legislators are hesitant on regulating surrogacy. *New York Times,* p. B7.

Hanser, S. B., & Thompson, L. W. (1994). Effects of a music therapy strategy on depressed older adults. *Journal of Gerontology: Psychological Sciences, 49,* P265–269.

Hanson, L. (1968). *Renoir: The man, the painter, and his world.* New York: Dodd, Mead.

Hargrove, J. (1989). *Nelson Mandela: South Africa's silent voice of protest.* Chicago: Children's Press.

Harkins, S. W. (1995). Pain. In G. Maddox (Ed.), *The encyclopedia of aging* (pp. 725–726). New York: Springer.

Harper, S., & Lund, D. (1990). Wives, husbands, and daughters caring for institutionalized and noninstitutionalized dementia patients: Toward a model of caregiving burden. *International Journal of Aging and Human Development, 30,* 241–262.

Hartley, A. A., Hartley, J. T., & Johnson, S. A. (1984). The older adult as computer user. In P. K. Robinson & J. E. Birren (Eds.), *Aging and technological advances* (pp. 347–348). New York: Plenum.

Hartup, W.W., & Stevens, N. (1999). Friendships and adaptation across the life span. *Current Directions in Psychological Science, 8,* 76–79.

Harvard Medical School. (2003, June). Confronting suicide, Part II. *Harvard Mental Health Letter, 19*(12), 1–5.

Harvard Medical School. (2006). Alcohol. [Online]. Available: http://www.hsph.harvard.edu/ nutritionsource/alcohol.html

Harvey, J. H., & Pauwels, J. (1997). Recent developments in close relationships theory. *Current Directions in Psychological Science, 8*(3), 93–95.

Harvey, J. H., & Omarzu, J. (1997). Minding the close relationship. *Personality and Psychology Review, 1,* 224–240.

Hasher, L. (1992, April). *Inhibitory mechanisms: Overview.* Paper presented at the Fourth Cognitive Aging Conference, Atlanta.

Hasher, L., & Zacks, R. T. (1988). Working memory, comprehension, and aging: A review and a new view. In G. H. Bower (Ed.), *The psychology of learning and motivation: Advances in research and theory* (Vol. 22, pp. 193–225). New York: Academic.

Haugaard, J. J. (1998). Is adoption a risk factor for the development of adjustment problems? *Clinical Psychology Review, 18,* 47–69.

Hawking, S. W. (1988). *A brief history of time: From the Big Bang to black holes*. New York: Bantam.

Hayflick, L. (2003). Living forever and dying in the attempt. *Experimental Gerontology, 38,* 1231–1241.

Hayslip, B., & Goldberg-Glen Hayslip, R. G. (2000). *Grandparents raising grandchildren: Theoretical, empirical, and clinical perspectives.* New York: Springer.

He, J., Vupputuri, S., Allen, K., Prerost, M. R., Hughes, J., & Whelton, P. K. (1999). Passive smoking and the risk of coronary heart disease—a meta-analysis of epidemiologic studies. *New England Journal of Medicine, 340,* 920–926.

Health Care Finance Administration. (1981). *Long-term care: Background and future directions.* Washington, DC: U.S. Department of Health and Human Services.

Health Systems Trust (HST). (2004). AIDS is world's fourth leading cause of death. [Online]. Available: http://new.hst.org.za/news/index.php/20020102/. Access date: March 15, 2004.

Healy, J. (1983). Bereavement issues and anticipatory grief. In Symposium on death and dying: The role of the family and estate planner. New York: Foundation of Thanatology.

Heath, S. B. (1989). Oral and literate tradition among black Americans living in poverty. *American Psychologist, 44,* 367–373.

Heckhausen, J., & Krueger, J. (1993). Developmental expectations for the self and most other people: Age grading in three functions of social comparisons. *Developmental Psychology, 29,* 539–548.

Heindel, W. C., Butters, N., & Salmon, D. P. (1988). Impaired learning of a motor skill in patients with Huntington's disease. *Behavioral Neuroscience, 102,* 141–147.

Heindel, W. C., Salmon, D. P., & Butters, N. (1989). Neuropsychological differentiation of memory impairments in dementia. In G. C. Gilmore, P. J. Whitehouse, & M. L. Wykle (Eds.), *Memory, aging, and dementia; Theory, assessment, and treatment* (pp. 112–139). New York: Springer.

Heindel, W. C., Salmon, D. P., & Butters, N. (1991). The biasing of weight judgments in Alzheimer's and Huntington's disease: A priming or programming phenomenon? *Journal of Clinical and Experimental Neuropsychology, 13,* 189–203.

Heinonen, K., Raikkonen, K., Keltikangas–Jarvinen, L. (2005). Dispositional optimism: Development over 21 years from the perspectives of perceived temperament and mothering. *Personality and Individual Differences, 38,* 425–435.

Heller, R. B., & Dobbs, A. R. (1993). Age differences in word finding in discourse and nondiscourse situations. *Psychology and Aging, 8,* 443–450.

Heller, Z. I. (1975). The Jewish view of dying: Guidelines for dying. In E. Kübler–Ross (Ed.), *Death: The final stage of growth.* Englewood Cliffs, NJ: Prentice-Hall.

Helms, J. E. (1992). Why is there no study of cultural equivalence in standardized cognitive ability testing? *American Psychologist, 47,* 1083–1101.

Helson, R. (1992). Women's difficult times and the rewriting of the life story. *Psychology of Women Quarterly, 16,* 331–347.

Helson, R. (1993). Comparing longitudinal studies of adult development: Toward a paradigm of tension between stability and change. In D. C. Funder, R. D. Parke, C. Tomlinson-Keasey, & K. Widaman (Eds.), *Studying lives through time: Personality and development* (pp. 93–120). Washington, DC: American Psychological Association.

Helson, R. (1997). The self in middle age. In M. E. Lachman & J. B. James (Eds.), *Multiple paths of midlife development* (pp. 93–120). Chicago: University of Chicago Press.

Helson, R., & Moane, G. (1987). Personality change in women from college to midlife. *Journal of Personality and Social Psychology, 53,* 176–186.

Helson, R., & Picano, J. (1990). Is the traditional role bad for women? *Journal of Personality and Social Psychology, 59,* 311–320.

Helson, R., & Wink, P. (1992). Personality change in women from the early 40s to the early 50s. *Psychology and Aging, 7*(1), 46–55.

Henderson, V. W., & Finch, C. E. (1989). The neurobiology of Alzheimer's disease. *Journal of Neurosurgery, 70,* 335–353.

Hendin, H. (1994, December 16). Scared to death of dying. *New York Times,* p. A369.

Hendin, H., Rutenfrans, C., & Zylicz, Z. (1997). Physician assisted suicide and euthanasia in the Netherlands: Lessons from the Dutch. *Journal of the American Medical Association, 277,* 1720–1722.

Henke, K., Treyer, V., Nagy, E., Kneifel, S., Dursteler, Nitsch, R., Buck, A. (2003). Active hippocampus during nonconscious memories. *Consciousness and Cognition, 12,* 31–48.

Henker, F. O. (1981). Male climeractic. In J. G. Howells (Ed.), *Modern perspectives in the psychiatry of middle age.* New York: Brunner/Mazel.

Herbst, J. H., McCrae, R. R., Costa, P. T., Feaganes, J. R., Siegler, I. C. (2000). Self-perceptions of stability and change in personality at midlife: The UNC alumni heart study. *Assessment, 7*(4), 379–388.

Herdt, G. (1981). *Guardians of the flutes.* New York: McGraw-Hill.

Herdt, G. (1987). *Sambia: Ritual and gender in New Guinea.* New York: Harcourt Brace.

Hertzog, C. (1989). Influences of cognitive slowing on age differences in intelligence. *Developmental Psychology, 25*(4), 636–651.

Hertzog, C., & Dixon, R. A. (1994). Metacognitive development in adulthood and old age. In J. Metcalfe & A. P. Shimamura (Eds.), *Metacognition: Knowing about knowing* (pp. 221–251). Cambridge, MA: MIT Press.

Hertzog, C., Dixon, R. A., & Hultsch, D. F. (1990). Relationships between metamemory, memory predictions, and memory task performance in adults. *Psychology and Aging, 5*(2), 215–227.

Hertzog, C., Saylor, L. L., Fleece, A. M., & Dixon, R. A. (1994). Metamemory and aging: Relations between predicted, actual and perceived memory task performance. *Aging and Cognition, 1,* 203–237.

Hertzog, C., Schaie, K. W., & Gribbin, K. (1978). Cardiovascular disease and changes in intellectual functioning from middle to old age. *Journal of Gerontology, 33,* 872–883.

Herzog, A. R., House, J. S., & Morgan, J. N. (1991). Relation of work and retirement to health and well-being in older age. *Psychology and Aging, 6,* 202–211.

Hess, T. C., & Pullen, S. M. (1996). Memory in context. In F. Blanchard-Fields & T. M. Hess (Eds.), *Perspectives on cognitive change in adulthood and aging.* New York: McGraw-Hill.

Hetherington, E. M. (1989). Coping with family transitions: Winners, losers and survivors. *Child Development, 60,* 1–4.

Hetherington, E. M., Bridges, M., & Insabella, G. M. (1998). What matters? What does not? Five perspectives on the association between marital transitions and children's adjustment. *American Psychologist, 44,* 303–312.

Heymann, S. J. (2000). *The widening gap: Why American working families are in jeopardy and what can be done about it.* New York: Basic Books.

Hiedemann, B., Suhomilinova, O., & O'Rand, A. M. (1998). Economic independence, economic status, and empty nest in midlife marital disruption. *Journal of Marriage and the Family, 60,* 219–231.

Hill, C. D., Thompson, L. W., & Gallagher, D. (1988). The role of anticipatory bereavement in older women's adjustment to widowhood. *The Gerontologist, 28*(6), 792–796.

Hill, P. C., & Pargament, K. I. (2003). Advances in the conceptualization and measurement of religion and spirituality: Implications for physical and mental health research.

Hill, T.D., Angel, J.L., Ellison, C.G., & Angel, R.J. (2005). Religious attendance and mortality: An 8-year follow-up of older Mexican Americans. *Journal of Gerontology: Social Sciences, 60B,* S102–S109.

Hines, A. M. (1997). Divorce-related transitions, adolescent development, and the role of the parent-child relationship: A review of the literature. *Journal of Marriage and the Family, 59,* 375–388.

Hinrichsen, G.A. (1999). Interpersonal psychotherapy for late-life depression. In M. Duffy (Ed.), *Handbook of counseling and psychotherapy with older adults.* Hoboken, NJ: John Wiley & Sons, Inc.

Hinrichsen, G. A. & Dick-Sisken, L. P. (2000). General principles of therapy. In S.K. Whitbource (Ed.), *Psychopathology in later adulthood.* Hoboken, NJ: John Wiley & Sons.

Hjelle, L. A., & Ziegler, D. J. (1992). *Personality theories* (3rd ed.). New York: McGraw-Hill.

Hochanadel, G. A. (1991). *Neuropsychological changes in aging: A process-oriented error analysis*. Dissertation Abstracts International, 52(4–B), 2347.

Hofstede, G., & McCrae, R. R. (2004). Personality and culture revisited: Linking traits and dimensions of culture. *Cross-Culture Research: The Journal of Comparative Social Science*, *38(1)*, 52–88.

Holden, A. (1988). *Laurence Olivier*. New York, Atheneum.

Holland, J. (1985). *Professional manual for the self-directed search*. Odessa, FL: Psychological Assessment Resources.

Holland, J. L. (1996). Exploring careers with a typology: What we have learned and some new directions. *American Psychologist, 51*, 397–406.

Holland, M. J. (1990). No sweat: How heat and stress affect the elderly. *Health and Human Development Research, 1*, 31–33.

Holliday, S. G., & Chandler, M. J. (1986). *Wisdom: Explorations in adult competence*. Basel, Switzerland: Karger.

Holmes, T. H., & Rahe, R. H. (1976). The social readjustment rating scale. *Journal of Psychosomatic Research, 11*, 213.

Holstein, M. B., & Minkler, M. (2003). Self, society, and the "new gerontology". *Gerontologist, 43(6)*, 787-796.

Holtzman, N. A., Murphy, P. D., Watson, M. S., & Barr, P. A. (1997). Predictive genetic testing: From basic research to clinical practice. *Science, 278*, 602–605.

Holtzman, N. A., Rebok, G. W., Saczynski, J. S., Kouzis, A. C., Doyle, K. W., & Eaton, W. W. (2004). Predictive genetic testing: From basic research to clinical practice. *Science, 278*, 602–605.

Honigmann, J. J. (1967). *Personality in culture*. New York: Harper & Row.

Hooker, K., & Kaus, C. R. (1994). Health-related possible selves in young and middle adulthood. *Psychology and Aging, 9*, 126–133.

Hooker, K., Monahan, D., Shifren, K., & Hutchinson, C. (1992). Mental and physical health of spouse caregivers: The role of personality. *Psychology and Aging, 7(3)*, 367–375.

Hooyman, N. R., Rathbone-McCuan, E., & Klingbeil, K. (1982). Serving the vulnerable elderly. *Urban and Social Change Review, 15(2)*, 9–13.

Hopper, J. L., & Seeman, E. (1994). The bone density of female twins discordant for tobacco use. *New England Journal of Medicine, 330*, 387–392.

Hormone therapy: When and for how long? (1997, March 25). *HealthNews, 3(4)*, 12.

Horn, J. C., & Meer, J. (1987, May). The vintage years. *Psychology Today*, pp. 76–90.

Horn, J. L. (1967). Intelligence–Why it grows, why it declines. *Transaction, 5(1)*, 23–31.

Horn, J. L. (1968). Organization of abilities and the development of intelligence. *Psychological Review, 75*, 242–259.

Horn, J. L. (1970). Organization of data on life-span development of human abilities. In L. R. Goulet & P. B. Baltes (Eds.), *Life-span developmental psychology: Theory and research* (pp. 424–466). New York: Academic.

Horn, J. L. (1982a). The aging of human abilities. In B. B. Wolman (Ed.), *Handbook of developmental psychology* (pp. 847–870). Englewood Cliffs, NJ: Prentice-Hall.

Horn, J. L. (1982b). The theory of fluid and crystallized intelligence in relation to concepts of cognitive psychology and aging in adulthood. In F. I. M. Craik & S. Trehub (Eds.), *Aging and cognitive processes* (Vol. 8, pp. 237–278). New York: Plenum.

Horn, J. L., & Cattell, R. B. (1966). Age differences in primary mental ability factors. *Journal of Gerontology, 21*, 210–220.

Horn, J. L., & Donaldson, G. (1976). On the myth of intellectual decline in adulthood. *American Psychologist, 31*, 701–719.

Horn, J. L., & Donaldson, G. (1977). Faith is not enough: A response to the Baltes–Schaie claim that intelligence does not wane. *American Psychologist, 32*, 369–373.

Horn, J. L., & Donaldson, G. (1980). Cognitive development: 2. Adulthood development of human abilities. In O. G. Brim & I. Kagan (Eds.), *Constancy and change in human development*. Cambridge, MA: Harvard University Press.

Horton, A. M., & Fogelman, C. J. (1991). Behavioral treatment of aged alcoholics and drug addicts. In P. A.Wisocki (Ed.), *Handbook of clinical behavioral therapy with the elderly client* (pp. 299–316). New York: Plenum.

Horwitz, A. V., White, H. R., & Howell-White, S. (1996). Becoming married and mental health: A longitudinal study of a cohort of young adults. *Journal of Marriage and the Family, 58,* 895–907.

Hosaka, T., & Sugiyama, Y. (2003). Structured intervention in family caregivers of the demented elderly and changes in their immune function. *Psychiatry and Clinical Neurosciences, 57,* 147–151.

House, S. J., Landis, K. R., & Umberson, D. (1988). Social relationships and health. *Science, 241,* 540–544.

Howard, D. V. (1991). Implicit memory: An expanding picture of cognitive aging. In K. W. Schaie & M. P. Lawton (Eds.), *Annual review of gerontology and geriatrics* (pp. 1–22). New York: Springer.

Howard, D. V. (1996). The aging of implicit and explicit memory. In H. Blanchard-Fields & T. M. Hess, *Perspectives on cognitive change in adulthood and aging.* New York: McGraw-Hill.

Hoyer, W. J., & Ingolfsdottir, D. (2003). Age, skill, and contextual cuing in target detection. *Psychology and Aging, 18*(2), 210–218.

Hoyer, W. J., & Rybash, J. M. (1994). Characterizing adult cognitive development. *Journal of Adult Development, 1*(1), 7–12.

Hoyer, W. J., & Verhaeghen, P. (2006). Memory aging. In J. E. Birren & K. W. Scheia (Eds.), *Handbook of the Psychology of aging.* New York: Elsevier.

Hoyert, D. L., & Rosenberg, H. M. (1999). Mortality from Alzheimer's Disease: An update. *National Vital Statistics Reports, 47*(20). Hyattsville, MD: National Center for Health Statistics.

Hoyert, D. L., Kung, H.-C., & Smith, B. L. (2005). Deaths: Preliminary data for 2003. *National Vital Statistics Reports, 53*(15). Hyattsville, MD: National Center for Health Statistics.

Hu, S., Pattatucci, A.M.L., Patterson, C., Li, L., Fulker, D. W., Cherney, S. S., Kruglyak, & Hamer, D. H (1995). Linkage between sexual orientation and chromosome q28 i males but not in females. *Nature Genetics, 11,* 248–256.

Hu, Y., & Goldman, N. (1990). Mortality differentials by marital status: An international comparison. *Demography, 27*(2), 233–250.

Hudnall, C. E. (2001, November). "Grand" parents get help: Programs aid aging caregivers and youngsters. *AARP Bulletin,* pp. 9, 12–13.

Hull, R. H. (1980). Talking to the hearing impaired older person. *ASHA, 22,* 194.

Hultsch, D. F. (1971). Organization and memory in adulthood. *Human Development, 14,* 16–29.

Human Genome Program. (2000). U.S. Department of Energy, *Human Genome News, 11,* 1–2.

Human Genome Project. (2004). Human genome project goal and completion dates. [Online]. Available:http://www.ornl.gov/sci/techresources/Human_Genome/project/50yr/goals_complete.shtml

Human Genome Project. (2005). Gene Therapy. [Online]. Available: www.ornl.gov.sci/techresources/Human_Genome/medicine/genetherapy.shtml. Access Date: January 23, 2006.

Human Genome Project. (2006). *Genetics privacy and legislation.* [Online]. Available: http://www.ornl.gov/sci/techresources/Human_Genome/elsi/legislat.shtml#III

Hungerford, T. L. (2001). The economic consequences of widowhood on elderly women in the United States and Germany. *The Gerontologist, 41,* 103–110.

Hunt, B., & Hunt, M. (1974). *Prime time.* New York: Stein & Day.

Hurd, M. D. (1989). The economic status of the elderly. *Science, 244,* 659–664.

Hurley, D. (1994, May 11). Pump better than CPR for heart attack: Study. *Chicago Sun-Times,* p. 5.

Huyck, M. H. (1990). Gender differences in aging. In J. E. Birren & K. W. Schaie (Eds.), *Handbook of the psychology of aging* (3rd ed., pp. 124–132). San Diego: Academic.

Huyck, M. H. (1995). Marriage and close relationships of the marital kind. In R. Blieszner & V. Hilkevitch (Eds). *Handbook of aging and the family* (pp. 181–200). Westport, CT: Greenwood Press

Hyde, J. S. (1986). *Understanding human sexuality* (3rd ed.). New York: McGraw-Hill.

Hyde, J. S., Krajnik, M., & Skuldt-Niederberger, K. (1991). Androgyny across the life span: A replication and longitudinal follow-up. *Developmental Psychology, 27,* 516–519.

Ickovics, J. R., et al. (1994). Limited effects of HIV counseling and testing for women: A prospective study of behavioral and psychological consequences. *Journal of the American Medical Association*, 272(6), 443–448.

Ikeda, R., Mahendra, R., Saltzman, L., Crosby, A., Willis, L., Mercy, J., Holmgreen, P., & Annest, J. L. (2002). Nonfatal self-inflicted injuries treated in hospital departments. United States, 2000. *MMWR*, 51, 436–438.

Illinois Task Force on Gender Bias in the Courts. (1990). Executive summary with status of recommendations.

Innocenti, G. M. (1994). Some new trends in the study of the corpus callosum. *Behavioral and Brain Research*, 64, 1–8.

Irons, R. R. (1994, December 1). Addiction affects all members of family. *The Menninger Letter*, p. 3.

Irving, H. H., & Benjamin, M. (1988). Divorce mediation in a court-based fee for service agency: An empirical study. *Conciliation Courts Review*, 26(1), 43–47.

Isaacowits, D. M., Charles, S. T., & Carstensen, L. L. (2000). Emotion and cognition. In F. I. M. Craik & T. A. Salthouse (Eds.) *The handbook of aging and cognition* (2nd ed., pp. 593–632), Mahway, NJ: Erlbaum Associates.

Ivy, G. O., MacLeod, C. M., Petit, T. L., & Markus, E. J. (1992). A physiological framework for perceptual and cognitive changes in aging. In F. I. M. Craik & T. A. Salthouse (Eds.), *The handbook of aging and cognition* (pp. 273–314). Hillsdale, NJ: Erlbaum.

Jacques, E. (1967). The midlife crisis. In R. Owen (Ed.), *Middle age*. London: BBC.

Jaffe, I. M. D. (1985). Arthritis. In D. F. Tapley, R. J. Weiss, & T. Q. Morris (Eds.), *The Columbia University College of Physicians and Surgeons complete home medical guide* (pp. 564–587). New York: Crown.

Jaffe, S., & Hyde, J. S. (2000). Gender differences in moral orientation: A meta-analysis. *Psychological Bulletin*, 126, 703–725.

Jaffee, S. R., Caspim, A., Moffit, T. E., Polo-Thomas, M., Price, T. S., & Taylor, A. (2004). The limits of child effects: Evidence for genetically mediated child effects on corporal punishment but not on physical maltreatment. *Developmental Psychology*, 40, 1047–1058.

Jahoda, M. (1958). *Current concepts of positive mental health*. New York: Basic Books.

Jallinoja, J. (1989). Women between the family and employment. In K. Boh et al. (Eds.), *Changing patterns of European family life* (pp. 95–122). London: Routledge.

Japanese Social Welfare Association. (1990). *The conditions of caring for the elderly*. Tokyo: Author.

Jaroff, L. (1992, June 8). Einstein's inspiring heir. *Time*, pp. 88–89.

Jay, G. M., & Willis, S. L. (1992). Influence of direct computer experience on older adults' attitudes toward computers. *Journal of Gerontology: Psychological Sciences*, 47, P250–257.

Jefferson, J. W., & Greist, J. H. (1993). *Depression and older people: Recognizing hidden signs and taking steps toward recovery*. Madison, WI: Pratt Pharmaceuticals.

Jendrek, M. P. (1994). Grandparents who parent grandchildren: Circumstances and decisions. *The Gerontologist*, 34, 206–216.

Jensen, A. R. (1969). How much can we boost IQ and scholastic achievement? *Harvard Educational Review*, 39, 1–123.

Jensen, A. R. (1993). Test validity: g versus "tacit knowledge." *Current Directions in Psychological Science*, 2(1), 9–10.

Johansson, B., Hofer, S. M., Allaire, J. C., Maldonado,-Molina, M. M., Piccinin, A. M., Berg, S., Pedersen, N. L., & McClearn, G. E. (2004). Change in cognitive capabilities in the oldest old: The effects of proximity to death in genetically related individuals over a 6 year period. *Psychology and Aging*, 19, 145–156.

Johnson, C. L. (1995). Cultural diversity in the late-life family. In R. Blieszner & V. Hilkevitch (Eds.), *Handbook of aging and the family* (pp. 307–331).

Johnson, C. L., & Catalano, D. J. (1981). Childless elderly and their family supports. *The Gerontologist*, 21(6), 610–618.

Johnson, C. L., & Troll, L. (1992). Family functioning in late late life. *Journal of Gerontology: Social Sciences*, 47(2), S66–72.

Johnson, C. L., & Troll, L. E. (1994). Constraints and facilitators to friendships in late late life. *The Gerontologist*, 34, 79–87.

Johnson, F. L., Foxall, M. J., Kelleher, E., Kentopp, E., Mannlein, E. A., & Cook, E. (1986). Life satisfaction of the elderly American Indian.

International Journal of Nursing Studies, 23, 265–273.

Johnson, F. L., Foxall, M. J., Kelleher, E., Kentopp, E., Mannlein, E. A., & Cook, E. (1988). Comparison of mental health life satisfaction of five elderly ethnic groups. *Western Journal of Nursing, 10,* 613–628.

Johnson, L. (1991). Bridging paradigms: The role of a change agent in an international technical transfer project. In J. D. Sinnott & J. C. Cavanaugh (Eds.), *Bridging Paradigms* (pp. 59–71). New York: Praeger.

Johnson, N. J., Backlund, E., Sorlie, P. D., Loveless, C.A. (2000). *Marital status and mortality: The National Longitudinal Mortality Study. Ann Epidemiol* ,10, 224-238.

Johnson, S. J., & Rybash, J. M. (1993). A cognitive neuroscience perspective on age-related slowing: Developmental changes in the functional architecture. In J. Cerella, J. M. Rybash, W. J. Hoyer, & M. Lo Commons (Eds.), *Adult information processing: Limits on loss* (pp. 143–175). San Diego: Academic.

Johnson, T. E. (1990). Age–1 mutants of Caenorhabditis elegans prolong life by modifying the Gompertz rate of aging. *Science, 229,* 908–912.

Johnston, L. D., O'Malley, P. M., Bachman, J. G., & Schulenberg, J. E. (2003, December 19). National press release, "Teen smoking continues to decline in 2003, but declines are slowing." University of Michigan News and Information Services, Ann Arbor, 15 pp.

Johnston, P. (2001, April 10). Dutch make euthanasia legal. *Chicago Sun-Times,* p. 22.

Jones, E. (1961). The life and work of Sigmund Freud. New York: Basic Books.

Jones, H. W, & Toner, J. P. (1993). The infertile couple. *New England Journal of Medicine, 329,* 1710–1715.

Jones, J. H. (1981). *Bad blood: The Tuskegee syphilis experiment.* New York: Free Press.

Jones, X., McGrattan, E., Manuelli, R. (2002, January). *Why are married women working so much?* Paper presented at the American Economic Association annual meeting in Atlanta. *Journal of Gerontology: Social Sciences, 53(B)6,* S324–S335.

Jung, C. G. (1933). *Modern man in search of a soul.* New York: Harcourt Brace & World.

Jung, C. G. (1953). The stages of life. In H. Read, M. Fordham, & G. Adler (Eds.), *Collected works* (Vol. 2). Princeton, NJ: Princeton University Press. (Original work published 1931.)

Jung, C. G. (1966). Two essays on analytic psychology. In *Collected works* (Vol. 7). Princeton, NJ: Princeton University Press.

Jung, C. G. (1969). *The structure and dynamics of the psyche.* Princeton, NJ: Princeton University Press.

Kabanoff, B. (1980). Work and nonwork: A review of models, methods, and findings. *Psychological Bulletin, 88,* 60–77.

Kagan, J. (1989). *Unstable ideas: Temperament, cognition, and self.* Cambridge, MA: Harvard University Press.

Kahana, B., & Kahana, E. (1970). Grandparenthood from the perspective of the developing grandchild. *Developmental Psychology, 3,* 98–105.

Kahana, E. (1982). A congruence model of person-environment interaction. In M. P. Lawton & T. O. Byerts (Eds.), *Aging and the environment: Theoretical approaches* (pp. 97–121). New York: Springer.

Kahana, E., Lovegreen, L., Kahana, B., Kahana, M. (2003). Person, environment, and person–environment fit as influences on residential satisfaction of elders. *Environment and Behavior, 35*(3), 434–453.

Kahn, R. L., & Antonucci, T. C. (1980). Convoys over the life course: Attachment, roles, and social support. In P. B. Baltes & O. G. Brim, Jr. (Eds.), *Life-span development and behavior* (Vol. 3, pp. 253–286). New York: Academic.

Kahn, S., Zimmerman, G., Csikszentmihalyi, M., & Getzels, J. W. (1985). Relations between identity in young adulthood and intimacy at midlife. *Journal of Personality and Social Psychology, 49,* 1316–1322.

Kai-Ming, C., Xinhou, J., & Xiaobo, G. (1999). From training to education. Lifelong learning in China. *Comparative Education, 35,* 119–129.

Kaiser, M. A. (1993). The productive roles of older people in developing countries: What are the implications of economic, social, and cultural participation? *Generations, 17*(4), 65–69.

Kalat, J. W. (1992). *Biological psychology.* Pacific Grove, CA: Brooks/Cole.

Kalish, R. A., & Reynolds, D. K. (1976). *Death and ethnicity: A psychocultural study*. Los Angeles: University of Southern California, Ethel Percy Andrus Gerontology Center.

Kalmuss, D. S., & Straus, M. A. (1982). Wife's marital dependency and wife abuse. *Journal of Marriage and the Family, 44,* 277–286.

Kamin, L. J. (1974). *The science and politics of IQ.* Potomac, MD: Erlbaum.

Kamin, L. J. (1981). Commentary. In S. Scarr (Ed.), *Race, social class, and individual differences in I.Q.* Hillsdale, NJ: Erlbaum.

Kandel, D. B., Davies, M., Karus, D., & Yamaguchi, K. (1986). The consequences in young adulthood of adolescent drug involvement. *Archives of General Psychiatry, 43,* 746–754.

Karel, M. J., & Hinrichsen, G. (2000). Treatment of depression in late life: Psychotherapeutic interventions. *Clinical Psychology Review, 20*(6), 707–729.

Karlinsky, H., Lennox, A., & Rossor, M. (1994). Alzheimer's disease and genetic testing. *Alzheimer's Disease and Associated Disorders, 8*(2), 63–65.

Karni, A., Tanne, D., Rubenstein, B. S., Askenasy, J. J., & Sagi, D. (1994). Dependence on REM sleep for overnight improvement of a perceptual skill. *Science, 2655*(5172), 679–682.

Kastenbaum, R. (1977). The kingdom where nobody dies. In S. Zarit (Ed.), *Readings in aging and death: Contemporary perspectives.* New York: Harper & Row.

Kastenbaum, R. (1993). Reconstructing death in postmodern society. *Omega, 27,* 75–89.

Kastenbaum, R. (1999). Dying and bereavement. In J. C. Cavanaugh (Ed.), *Gerontology: An interdisciplinary perspective,* pp. 155–185. New York: Oxford University Press.

Kastenbaum, R., & Aisenberg, R. (1972). *The psychology of death.* New York: Springer.

Kaszniak, A. W., Christenson, G. D. (1994). Differential diagnosis of dementia and depression. In M. Storandt & G. R. VandenBos (Eds.), *Neuropsychological assessment of demenia and depression in older adults: A clinician's guide.* Washington, DC: American Psychological Association.

Katchadourian, H. (1987). *Fifty: Midlife in perspective.* New York: Freeman.

Katona, C. (2000). Managing depression and anxiety in the elderly patient. *European Neuropsychopharmacology, 10,* S427–432.

Katzman, R. (1993). Education and prevalence of dementia and Alzheimer's disease. *Neurology, 43,* 13–20.

Kaufman, A. S. (2001). WAIS–III, Horn's theory, and generational changes from young adulthood to old age. *Intelligence, 29,* 131–167.

Kaufman, S. R. (1986). *The ageless self: Sources of meaning in late life.* Madison: University of Wisconsin Press.

Kaufman, T. S. (1993). *The combined family: A guide to creating successful step-relationships.* New York: Plenum.

Kaukinen, C. (2004). Status compatibility, physical violence, and emotional abuse in intimate relationships. *Journal of Marriage and the Family, 66,* 452-471.

Kausler, D. H. (1990). Automaticity of encoding and episodic memory processes. In E. A. Lovelace (Ed.), *Aging and cognition: Mental processes, self-awareness and interventions* (pp. 29–67). Amsterdam: North-Holland, Elsevier.

Kay, B., & Neelley, J. N. (1982). Sexuality and aging: A review of the current literature. *Sexuality and Disability, 5,* 38–46.

Keegan, R. T. (1996). Creativity from childhood to adulthood: A difference of degree and not of kind. *New Directions for Child Development, 72,* 57–66.

Keith, P. M. (1983). A comparison of the resources of parents and childless men and women in very old age. *Family Relations, 32,* 403–409.

Kellermann, A. L., Rivara, F. P., Somes, G., Reay, D. T., Francisco, J., Banton, J. G., Prodzinski, J., Flinger, C., & Hackman, B. B. (1992). Suicide in the home in relation to gun ownership. *New England Journal of Medicine, 327,* 467–472.

Kelly, J. R. (1987). *Peoria winter: Styles and resources in later life.* Lexington, MA: Lexington.

Kelly, J. R. (1994). Recreation and leisure. In A. Monk (Ed.), *The Columbia retirement handbook* (pp. 489–508). New York: Columbia University Press.

Kelly, J. R., Steinkamp, M., & Kelly, J. (1986). Later life leisure: How they play in Peoria. *The Gerontologist, 26,* 531–537.

Kelly, R. C. (1976). Witchcraft and sexual relations: An exploration in the social and semantic implications of the structure of belief. In P. Brown & G. Buchbinder (Eds.), *Man and woman in the New Guinea highlands* (pp. 36–53). Washington, DC: American Anthropological Association.

Kemper, T. L. (1994). Neuroanatomical and neuropathological changes during aging and dementia. In M. L. Albert & J. E. Knoefel (Eds.), *Clinical neurology of aging* (p. 367). New York: Oxford University Press.

Kennedy, R. (1994, December 5). Elizabeth Glaser dies at 47; crusader for pediatric AIDS. *New York Times*, p. A12.

Kenrick, D. T., & Funder, D. C. (1988). Profiting from controversy: Lessons from the person-situation debate. *American Psychologist, 43*, 23–34.

Keppel, K. G., Pearcy, J. N., Wagener, D. K. (2002). Trends in racial and ethnic-specific rates for the health status indicators: United States, 1990–1998. *Statistical Notes*, No. 23. Hyattsville, MD: National Center for Health Statistics.

Kernan, M. (1993, June). The object at hand. *Smithsonian*, pp.14–16.

Kerschner, H. K. (1992). *An incumbent versus a new candidate paradigm in aging*. Washington, DC: American Association for International Aging.

Kessler, R. C., McGonagle, K. A., Nelson, C. B., Hughes, M., Swartz, M., & Blazer, D. G. (1994). Sex and depression in the National Comorbidity Survey: 2. Cohort effects. *Journal of Affective Disorders, 30*, 15–26.

Kiefe, C.I., Williams, O. D., Weissman, N. W., Schreiner, P. J., Sidney, S., & Wallace, D. D. (2000). Changes in US health care access in the 90s: Race and income differences from the CARDIA study. Coronary Artery Risk Development in Young Adults. *Ethnicity and Disease, 10*, 418–431.

Kiernan, T. (1981). *Sir Larry: The life of Laurence Olivier*. New York: Times.

Kihlstrom, J. F. (1983). Instructed forgetting: Hypnotic and nonhypnotic. *Journal of Experimental Psychology: General, 112*, 73–79.

Kim, J. E., & Moen, P. (2000). Retirement transitions, gender, and psychological well-being in late midlife.

Kim, J. E., & Moen, P. (2001). Moving into retirement: Preparation and transitions in late midlife. In M. Lachman (Ed.), *Handbook of Midlife Development*. New York: John Wiley and Sons.

Kim, N. W., Piatyszek, M. A., Prowse, K. R., Harley, C. B., West, M. D., Ho, P. L. C., Coviello, G. M., Wright, W. E., Weinrich, S. L., & Shay, J. W. (1994). Specific association of human telomerase activity with immortal cells and cancer. *Science, 266*, 2011–2015.

Kimmel, D. (1990). *Adulthood and aging: An interdisciplinary, developmental view*. New York: Wiley.

Kimmel, D. C. (1988). Ageism, psychology, and public policy. *American Psychologist, 43*(3), 175–178.

King, B. M. (1996). *Human sexuality today*. Englewood Cliffs, NJ: Prentice-Hall.

King, B. M., Camp, C. J., & Downey, A. M. (1991). *Human sexuality today*. Englewood Cliffs, NJ: Prentice-Hall.

King, D. (1993, March). Age-old questions [Letter to the Editor]. *New Woman*, p. 14.

Kinsella, K. & Gist, Y. J. (1995). *Older workers, retirement, and pensions: A comparative international chartbook* (International Population Center Report IPC/95-2). Washington, DC: U.S. Bureau of the Census.

Kinsella, K., & Velkoff, V. A. (2001). *An aging world: 2001*. U.S. Census Bureau, Series P95/01-1. Washington, DC: U.S. Government Printing Office.

Kirby, S. E., Coleman, P. G., Daley, D. (2004). Spirituality and well-being in frail and nonfrail older adults. *Journal of Gerontology: Psychological Sciences, 59B*, P123–P129.

Kirsch, I. S., Jenkins, L., Jungeblut, A., & Kolstad, A. (1993). *Adult literacy in America: A first look at the results of the National Adult Literacy Survey*. Princeton, NJ: Educational Testing Service.

Kirschenbaum, M. J. (1994, August). Breaking the cycle of domestic violence. *The Menninger Letter*, pp. 1–2.

Kirschenbaum, R. J. (1990, November–December). An interview with Howard Gardner. *The Gifted Child Today*, pp. 26–32.

Kite, M. E., & Johnson, B. T. (1988). Attitudes toward older and younger adults: A meta-analysis. *Psychology and Aging, 3*(3), 232–244.

Kite, M. E. (1996). Age, gender, and occupational label: A test of social role theory. *Psychology of Women Quarterly, 20*(3), 361–374.

Kitson, G. C., & Morgan, L. A. (1990). The multiple consequences of divorce: A decade review. *Journal of Marriage and Family Therapy, 52*, 913–924.

Kitson, G. C., & Roach, M. J. (1989). Independence and social and psychological adjustment in widowhood and divorce. In D. A. Lund (Ed.), *Older bereaved spouses: Research with practical implications*. New York: Hemisphere.

Kivett, V. R. (1991). Centrality of the grandfather role among older rural black and white men. *Journal of Gerontology: Social Sciences, 46*(5), S250–258.

Kivett, V. R. (1993). Racial comparisons of the grandmother role: Implications for strengthening the family support system of older Black women. *Family Relations, 42*, 165–172.

Kivett, V. R. (1996). The saliency of the grandmother-granddaughter relationship: Predictors of association. *Journal of Women and Aging, 8*, 25–39.

Kivnick, H. (1982). *The meaning of grandparenthood*. Minneapolis: UMI Research.

Kivnick, H. Q. (1993). Everyday mental health: A guide to assessing life strengths. *Generations, 17*(1), 13–20.

Kivnick, H. Q. & Kavka, A. (1999). It takes two: Therapeutic alliance with older clients. In M. Duffy (Ed.), *Handbook of counseling and psychotherapy with older adults*. Hoboken, NJ: John Wiley & Sons, Inc.

Klagsbrun, F. (1993, November). Marching in front. *Hadassah*, pp. 24–25.

Klass, D. (1986, November). *When is forgetting cognitive decline?* Paper presented at the annual meeting of the Gerontological Society of America, Chicago.

Klatzky, R. L. (1991). Let's be friends. *American Psychologist, 46*(1), 43–45.

Kleemeier, R. W. (1962). Intellectual changes in the senium. *Proceedings of the American Statistical Association, 1*, 181–190.

Kliegl, R., & Lindenberger, U. (1993). Modeling intrusions and correct recall in episodic memory: Adult age differences in encoding of list context.

Journal of Experimental Psychology: Learning, Memory, and Cognition, 19, 617–637.

Kline & Schneber, F. (1985). Vision and aging. In J. E. Birren and K. W. Schaie (Eds.), *Handbook of psychology and aging* (2nd ed, pp. 296–331). New York: Van Nostrand Reinhold.

Kline, D. W. & Scialfa, C. T. (1996) Visual and auditory aging. In J. E.Birren & K. W. Schaie (Eds.), *Handbook of the psychology of aging* (pp. 181–203). San Diego, CA: Academic Press.

Kline, D. W., Kline, T. J. B., Fozard, J. L., Kosnik, W., Schieber, F., & Sekuler, R. (1992). Vision, aging, and driving: The problems of older drivers. *Journal of Gerontology, 47*(1), P27–34.

Kobayashi, M. K. (1996). Adult business education programmes in private educational institutions in Japan. *Journal of Management Development, 15*, 30–37.

Koenig, H. G., George, L. K., & Siegler, I. C. (1988). The use of religion and other emotion-regulating coping strategies among older adults. *The Gerontologist, 28*(3), 303–310.

Koenig, H. G., Kvale, J. N., & Ferrel, C. (1988). Religion and well-being in later life. *The Gerontologist, 28*(1), 18–28.

Kohlberg, L. (1966). A cognitive-developmental analysis of children's sex-role concepts and attitudes. In E. E. Maccoby (Ed.), *The development of sex differences* (pp. 82–173). Stanford, CA: Stanford University Press.

Kohlberg, L. (1969). Stage and sequence: The cognitive-developmental approach to socialization. In D. A. Goslin (Ed.), *Handbook of socialization theory and research*. Chicago: Rand McNally.

Kohlberg, L. (1973). Continuities in childhood and adult moral development revisited. In P. Baltes & K. W. Schaie (Eds.), *Life-span developmental psychology: Personality and socialization* (pp. 180–207). New York: Academic.

Kohlberg, L. (1974b, March 24). More authority [Letter to the Editor]. *New York Times*, VII, p. 42.

Kohlberg, L., & Ryncarz, R. A. (1990). Beyond justice reasoning: Moral development and consideration of a seventh stage. In C. N. Alexander & E. J. Langer (Eds.), *Higher stages of human development* (pp. 191–207). New York: Oxford University Press.

Kohn, M. L. (1980). Job complexity and adult personality. In N. J. Smelser & E. H. Erikson (Eds.), *Themes of work and love in adulthood.* Cambridge, MA: Harvard University Press.

Koivula, I., Sten, M., & Makela, P. H. (1999). Prognosis after community-acquired pneumonia in the elderly. *Archives of Internal Medicine, 159,* 1550–1555.

Kopera-Frye, K., Wiscott, R., Sterns, H. L. (1999). Can the drinking problem index provide valuable therapeutic information for recovering alcoholic adults? *Aging & Mental Health, 3,* 246–256.

Kopka, T. L. C., Schantz, N. B., and Korb, R. A. (1998). *Adult Education in the 1990s: A Report on the 1991 National Household Education Survey* (NCES 98–03). Washington, DC: U.S. Department of Education, National Center for Education Statistics.

Kopp, C. B., & McCall, R. B. (1982). Predicting later mental performance for normal, at-risk, and handicapped infants. In P. B. Baltes & O. G. Brim (Eds.), *Life-span development and behavior* (Vol. 4). New York: Academic.

Kornhaber, A. (1986). *Between parents and grandparents.* New York: St. Martin's.

Kornhaber, A., & Forsyth, S. (1994). *Grandparent power: How to strengthen the vital connection among grandparents, parents and children.* New York: Crown.

Kornhaber, A., & Woodward, K. L. (1981). *Grandparents/grandchildren: The vital connection.* Garden City, NY: Anchor/Doubleday.

Kosnik, W., Winslow, L., Kline, D., Rasinski, K., & Sekuler, R. (1988). Visual changes in daily life throughout adulthood. *Journal of Gerontology, 43*(3), P63–70.

Kottak, C. P. (1994). *Cultural anthropology.* New York: McGraw-Hill.

Koutstaal, W., Reddy, C., Jackson, E. M., Prince, S., Cendan, D. L., Schacter, D. L. (2003). False recognition of abstract versus common objects in older and younger adults: Testing the semantic categorization account. *Journal of Experimental Psychology, 29*(4), 449-510.

Koustaal, W., Schacter, D. L., Galluccio, L., Stofer, K. A. (1999). Reducing gist-based false recognition in older adults: Encoding and retrieval manipulations. *Psychology and Aging, 14*(2), 220–237.

Kraaykamp, G. (2002). Trends and countertrends in sexual permissiveness: Three decades of attitude change in the Netherlands 1965–1995. *Journal of Marriage and the Family, 64,* 225–239.

Kramarow, E., Lentzner, H., Rooks, R., Weeks, J. & Saydah, S. (1999). *Health and Aging Chartbook for Health, United States, 1999.* Hyattsville, MD: National Center for Health Statistics.

Kranzler, J. H., & Jensen, A. R. (1991a). The nature of psychometric g: Unitary process or a number of independent processes? *Intelligence, 15,* 397–422.

Kranzler, J. H., & Jensen, A. R. (1991b). Unitary g: Unquestioned postulate or empirical fact? *Intelligence, 15,* 437–448.

Krause, N. (2004a). Common facets of religion, unique facets of religion, and life satisfaction among older African Americans. *Journal of Gerontology: Social Sciences, 59B,* S109-117.

Krause, N., & Shaw, B. A. (2000). Role-specific feelings of control and mortality. *Psychology and Aging, 15,* 617–626.

Kraut, R., Kiesler, S., Boneva, B., Cummings, J., Helgeson, V., & Crawford, A. (2002). Internet paradox revisited. *Journal of Social Issues, 58,* 49–74.

Kraut, R., Lundmark, V., Patterson, M., Kiesler, S., Mukopadhyay, R., & Sherlis, W. (1998). Internet paradox: A social technology that reduces social involvement and psychological well-being? *American Psychologist, 53,* 1017–1031.

Kreicsbergs, U., Valdimarsdottir, U., Onelov, E., Henter, J., & Steineck, G. (2004). Talking about death with children who have severe malignant disease. *New England Journal of Medicine, 351,* 1175–1253.

Kreider, R. M., & Fields, J. M. (2002). Number, timing, and duration of marriages and divorces: Fall 1996. *Current Population Reports,* pp. 70–80. Washington, DC: U.S. Census Bureau.

Krieger, D. (1982). Cushing's syndrome. *Monographs in Endocrinology, 22,* 1–142.

Krishna, D. (2000). Telomerase: cancer detection and therapy. *Indian Journal of Pharmaceutical Sciences, 62*(1), 9–15.

Kristof, N. D. (1990, December 6). At 102, he's back in school, with many like him. *New York Times*, p. A4.

Kroenke, K. & Spitzer, R. L. (1998). Gender differences in the reporting of physical and somatoform symptoms. *Psychosomatic Medicine, 60*, 50–155.

Kubie, L. S. (1958). *The neurotic distortion of the creative process*. Lawrence: University of Kansas Press.

Kübler-Ross, E. (1969). *On death and dying*. New York: Macmillan.

Kübler-Ross, E. (1970). *On death and dying*. (paperback ed.). New York: Macmillan.

Kübler-Ross, E. (Ed.). (1975). *Death: The final stage of growth*. Englewood Cliffs, NJ: Prentice-Hall.

Kumar, C., & Puri, M. (1983). *Mahatma Gandhi: His life and influence*. New York: Franklin Watts.

Kurdek, L. A. (1995). Assessing multiple determinants of relationship: Commitment in cohabiting gay, cohabiting lesbian, dating heterosexual, and married heterosexual couples. *Family Relations, 44*, 249–261.

Kurosawa, A. (1981). *Something like an autobiography* (A. E. Bock, Trans.). New York: Knopf.

La Sala, M. C. (1998). Coupled gay men, parents, and in-laws: Intergenerational approval and the need for thick skin. *Families in Society, 79*, 585–595.

Labouvie-Vief, G. (1982). Dynamic development and mature autonomy: A theoretical prologue. *Human Development, 25*, 161–191.

Labouvie-Vief, G. (1985). Intelligence and cognition. In J. E. Birren & K. W. Schaie (Eds.), *Handbook of the psychology of aging* (pp. 500–530). New York: Van Nostrand Reinhold.

Labouvie-Vief, G. (1986). Modes of knowledge and the organization of development. In M. Commons, L. Kohlberg, F. Richards, & J. Sinnott (Eds.), *Beyond formal operations: 3, Models and methods in the study of adult and adolescent thought*. New York: Praeger.

Labouvie-Vief, G. (1990a). Modes of knowledge and the organization of development. In M. L. Commons, L. Kohlberg, R. Richards, & J. Sinnott (Eds.), *Beyond formal operations: 2, Models and methods in the study of adult and adolescent thought*. New York: Praeger.

Labouvie-Vief, G. (1990b). Wisdom as integrated thought: Historical and development perspectives. In R. J. Sternberg (Ed.), *Wisdom: Its nature, origins, and development* (pp. 52–83). Cambridge: Cambridge University Press.

Labouvie-Vief, G. (1997). Cognitive-emotional integration in adulthood. In K. W. Schaie & M. P. Lawton (Eds.), *Annual review of gerontology and geriatrics* (Vol. 17, pp. 203–237). New York: Springer.

Labouvie-Vief, G., & Hakim-Larson, J. (1989). Developmental shifts in adult thought. In S. Hunter & M. Sundel (Eds.), *Midlife myths*. Newbury Park, CA: Sage.

Labouvie-Vief, G., Adams, C., Hakim-Larson, J., Hayden, M., & DeVoe, M. (1987). *Modes of text processing from preadolescence to mature adulthood*. Unpublished manuscript, Wayne State University, Detroit.

Labouvie-Vief, G., Hakim-Larson, J., & Hobart, C. J. (1987). Age, ego level, and the life-span development of coping and defense processes. *Psychology and Aging, 2*, 286–293.

Labouvie-Vief, G., Hakim-Larson, J., DeVoe, M., & Schoeberlein, S. (1989). Emotions and self-regulation: A life-span view. *Human Development, 32*, 279–299.

Labouvie-Vief, G., Schell, D. A., & Weaverdyck, S. E. (1982). *Recall deficit in the aged: A fable recalled*. Unpublished manuscript, Wayne State University, Detroit.

Lachman, J. L., & Lachman, R. (1980). Age and the actualization of knowledge. In L. W. Poon, J. L. Fozard, L. S. Cermak, D. Arenberg, & L. W. Thompson (Eds.), *New directions in memory and aging* (pp. 313–343). Hillsdale, NJ: Erlbaum.

Lachman, M. E. (1986). Locus of control in aging research: A case for multidimensional and domain-specific assessment. *Psychology and Aging, 1*, 34–40.

Lachman, M. E., & Bertrand, R. M (2001). Introduction. In M.E. Lachman (Ed.), *Handbook of midlife development*. New York: Wiley.

Lachman, M. E., & Weaver, S. L. (1998). Sociodemographic variations in the sense of control by domain: Findings from the MacArthur Studies of Midlife. *Psychology and Aging, 13*, 553–562.

Lachman, R., Lachman, J. L., & Taylor, D. W. (1982). Reallocation of mental resources over the productive life-span: Assumptions and task analyses. In F. I. M. Craik & S. Trehub (Eds.), *Aging and cognitive processes* (pp. 279–307). New York: Plenum.

Lacy, W. B., & Hendricks, J. (1980). Developmental model of adult life: Myth or reality? *Aging and Human Development, 11,* 89–110.

Lakatta, E. G. (1990). Changes in cardiovascular function with aging. *European Heart Journal, 11c,* 22–29.

Lakoff, R. T., & Coyne, I. C. (1993). *Father knows best: The use and abuse of power in Freud's case of Dora.* New York: Teacher's College Press.

Lamb, M. E. (1987). *The father's role: Cross-cultural perspectives.* Hillsdale, NJ: Erlbaum.

Lambeth, G. S., & Hallett, M. (2002). Promoting healthy decision making in relationships: Developmental interventions with young adults on college and university campuses. In C. L. & D. R. Atkinson (Eds.), *Counseling across the lifespan: Prevention and treatment* (pp. 209–226). Thousand Oaks, CA: Sage.

Lamy, M., Mojon, P., Kalykakis, G., Legrand, R., Butz-Jorgensen, E. (1999). Oral status and nutrition in the institutionalized elderly. *Journal of Dentistry, 27, 6,* 443–448.

Lancy, D. F. (1977). Studies of memory in culture. *Annals of the New York Academy of Science, 285,* 297–307.

Landers, S. (1992, March). Family "kin care" trend increasing. *National Association of Social Workers News,* p. 5.

Landy, F. J. (1992, February 19). *Research on the use of fitness tests for police and fire fighting jobs.* Presentation at the Second Annual Scientific Psychology Forum of the American Psychological Association, Washington, DC.

Landy, F. J. (1994, July–August). Mandatory retirement age: Serving the public welfare? *Psychological Science Agenda: American Psychological Association,* pp. 10–11, 20.

Lansford, J. E., Sherman, A. M., & Antonucci, T. C. (1998). Satisfaction with social networks: An examination of socioemotional selectivity. *Psychology and Aging, 13(4),* 544–552.

Lapham, E. V., Kozma, C., & Weiss, J. O. (1996). Genetic discrimination: Perspectives of consumers. *Science, 274,* 621–624.

Larsen, D. (1990, December–1991, January). Unplanned parenthood. *Modern Maturity,* pp. 32–36.

Larson, A. (1989). Social context of human immunodeficiency virus transmission in Africa: Historical and cultural bases of east and central African sexual relations. *Review of Infectious Diseases, 11,* 713–731.

Larson, R., Mannell, R., & Zuzanek, J. (1986). Daily well-being of older adults with friends and family. *Psychology and Aging, 1(2),* 117–126.

Larson, R., Zuzanek, J., & Mannell, R. (1985). Being alone versus being with people: Disengagement in the daily experience of older adults. *Journal of Gerontology, 40,* 375–381.

Latimer, E. J. (1992, February). Euthanasia: A physician's reflections. *Ontario Medical Review,* pp. 21–29.

Laudenslager, M. L., Ryan, S. M., Drugan, R. C., Hyson, R. L., & Maier, S. F. (1983). Coping and immunosuppression: Inescapable but not escapable shock suppresses lymphocyte proliferation. *Science, 221,* 568–570.

Lauer, J., & Lauer, R. (1985). Marriages made to last. *Psychology Today, 19(6),* 22–26.

Laumann, E. O., & Michael, R. T. (Eds.). (2000). *Sex, love, and health in America: Private choices and public policies.* Chicago: University of Chicago Press.

Laumann, E. O., Gagnon, J. H., Michael, R. T., & Michaels, S. (1994). *The social organization of sexuality: Sexual practices in the United States.* Chicago: University of Chicago Press.

Launer, L. J., Andersen, K., Dewey, M. E., Letenneur, L., Ott, A., Amaducci, L. A., Brayne, C., Copeland, J. R. M., Dartigues, J.-F., Kragh-Sorensen, P., Lobo, A., Martinez-Lage, J. M., Stijnen, T., & Hofman, A. (1999). Rates and risk factors for dementia and Alzheimer's disease: Results from EURODEM pooled analyses. *Neurology, 52,* 78–84. *Gerontology: Social Sciences, 48,* S9–16.

Lawton, M. P. (1982). Competence, environmental press, and the adaptation of old people. In M. P. Lawton & T. O. Byerts (Eds.), *Aging and the environment: Theoretical approaches* (pp. 33–59). New York: Springer.

Lawton, M. P., & Nahemow, L. (1973). Ecology and the aging process. In C. Eisdorfer &

M. P. Lawton (Eds.), The psychology of adult development and aging. Washington, DC: American Psychological Association.

Lawton, M. P. (2001). Quality of life and the end of life. In J. E. Birren, & K. W. Schaie (Eds.), *Handbook of the psychology of aging,* p. 592–616. San Diego, CA: Academic Press.

Lazarus, R. S. (1981, July). Little hassles can be hazardous to health. *Psychology Today,* pp. 58–62.

Lazarus, R. S. (2003). Does the positive psychology movement have legs? *Psychological Inquiry,* 14(2), 93–109.

Lazarus, R. S., & Folkman, S. (1984). *Stress, appraisal, and coping.* New York: Springer.

Lebowitz, B. D., & Niederehe, G. (1992). Concepts and issues in mental health and aging. In J. E. Birren, R. B. Sloane, & G. D. Cohen (Eds.), *Handbook of mental health and aging* (2nd ed., pp. 3–26). San Diego: Academic.

Lee, D. J., & Markides, K. S. (1990). Activity and mortality among aged people over an eight-year period. *Journal of Gerontology: Social Sciences,* 45(1), S539–542.

Lee, G. R., Dwyer, J. W., & Coward, R. T. (1993). Gender differences in parent care: Demographic factors and some gender preferences. *Journal of Gerontology: Social Sciences,* 48, S9–16.

Lee, G. R., Netzer, J. K., Coward, R. T. (1995). Depression among older parents: The role of intergenerational exchange. *Journal of Marriage and the Family,* 57, 823–833.

Lee, I.-M., & Paffenbarger, R. S. (1992). Changes in body weight and longevity. *Journal of the American Medical Association,* 268, 2045–2049.

Lee, P. R., Franks, P., Thomas, G. S., & Paffenbarger, R. S. (1981). *Exercise and health: The evidence and its implications.* Cambridge, MA: Oelgeschlager, Gunn, & Hain.

Lee, T. R., Mancini, J. A., & Maxwell, J. W. (1990). Sibling relationships in adulthood: Current patterns and motivations. *Journal of Marriage and the Family,* 52, 431–440.

Lefrancois, G. R. (1982). *Psychology for teaching: A bear rarely faces the front.* Belmont, CA: Wadsworth.

Lehrman, S. (2002, March). The topic in-depth. *Genetics of Aging and Longevity.*

Lemmon, J. A. (1983). Divorce mediation: Optimal scope and practical issues. *Mediation Quarterly,* 1, 45–61.

Lemon, B., Bengtson, V., & Peterson, J. (1972). An exploration of the activity theory of aging: Activity types and life satisfaction among movers to a retirement community. *Journal of Gerontology,* 27(4), 511–523.

Lemonick, M. D. (2001, November 5). Beyond the theoretical. *Time.*

Lengua, L. J., & Kovacs, E. A. (2005). Bidirectional associations between temperament and parenting and the prediction of adjustment problems in middle childhood. *Applied Developmental Psychology,* 26, 21–38.

Lennox, A., Karlinsky, H., Meschino, J., Buchanan, J. A., Percy, M. E., & Berg, J. M. (1994). Molecular genetic predictive testing for Alzheimer's disease: Deliberations and preliminary recommendations. *Alzheimer Disease and Associated Disorders,* 8, 126–147.

Lenz, E. (1993, August–September). Mirror, mirror...: One woman's reflections on her changing image. *Modern Maturity,* pp. 24, 26–28, 80.

Lerner, M. J., Somers, D. G., Reid, D., Chiriboga, D., & Tierney, M. (1991). Adult children as caregivers: Egocentric biases in judgments of sibling contributions. *The Gerontologist,* 31(6), 746–755.

Lesgold, A. M. (1983). *Expert systems.* Paper presented at the Cognitive Science Meetings, Rochester, NY.

LeVay, S. (1991). A difference in hypothalamic structure between heterosexual and homosexual men. *Science,* 253, 1034–1037.

Levin, J. S., & Taylor, R. J. (1993). Gender and age differences in religiosity among black Americans. *The Gerontologist,* 33(1), 16–23.

Levin, J. S., Taylor, R. J., & Chatters, L. M. (1994). Race and gender differences in religiosity among older adults: Findings from four national surveys. *Journal of Gerontology: Social Sciences,* 49, S137–145.

Levine, R. (1980). Adulthood among the Gusii of Kenya. In N. J. Smelser & E. H. Erikson (Eds.), *Themes of work and love in adulthood* (pp. 77–104). Cambridge, MA: Harvard University Press.

Levinson, D. (1978). *The seasons of a man's life.* New York: Knopf.

Levinson, D. (1980). Toward a conception of the adult life course. In N. J. Smelser & E. H. Erikson (Eds.), *Themes of work and love in adulthood* (pp. 265–290). Cambridge, MA: Harvard University Press.

Levinson, D. (1986). A conception of adult development. *American Psychologist, 41,* 3–13.

Levinson, D. J., & Levinson, J. D. (1996). *The seasons of a woman's life.* New York: Ballantine Books

Levinson, W., & Altkorn, D. (1998). Primary prevention of postmenopausal osteoporosis. *Journal of the American Medical Association, 280,* 1821–1822.

Leviton, D. (1977). Death education. In H. Feifel (Ed.), *New meanings of death* (pp. 253–272). New York: McGraw-Hill.

Levron, J., Aviram. A., Madgar, I., Livshits, A., Raviv, G., Bider, D., Hourwitz, A., Bakari, G., Goldman, B., Mashiach, S. (1998, October). *High rate of chromosomal neupoloidies in testicular spermatozoa retrieved from azoospermic patients undergoing testicular sperm extraction for in vitro fertilization.* Paper presented at the 16th World Congress on Fertility and Sterility and the 54th annual meeting of the American Society for Reproductive Medicine, San Francisco, CA.

Levy, B., & Langer, E. (1994). Aging free from negative stereotypes: Successful memory in China and among the American deaf. *Journal of Personality and Social Psychology, 66,* 989–997.

Levy-Cushman, J., & Abeles, N. (1998). Memory complaints in the able elderly. *Clinical Gerontologist, 19,* 3–24.

Lewis, D. B. W. (1968). *The World of Goya.* New York: Potter.

Lewis, M. I., & Butler, R. N. (1974). Life-review therapy: Putting memories to work in individual and group psychotherapy. *Geriatrics, 29,* 165–173.

Li, J., Laursen, T. M., Precht, D. H., Olsen, J., & Mortensen, P. B. (2005). Hospitalization for mental illness among parents after the death of a child. *New England Journal of Medicine, 352,* 1190–1196.

Li, J., Precht, D. H., Mortensen, P. B., & Olsen, J. (2003). Mortality in parents after death of a child in Denmark: A nationwide follow-up study. *The Lancet, 361,* 363–367.

Li, S., Lindenberger, U., Hommel, B., Aschersleben, G., Prinz, W., & Baltes, P. (2004). Transformations in the couplings among intellectual abilities and constituent cognitive processes across the lifespan. *American Psychological Society, 15*(30), 155–163.

Lichtenberg, P. A. (1994). *A guide to psychological practice in geriatric long-term care.* Binghampton, NY: Haworth.

Lickona, T. (Ed.). (1976). *Moral development and behavior.* New York: Holt.

Lieberman, M. (1996). *Doors close, doors open: Widows, grieving and growing.* New York: Putnam.

Lieberman, M., & Coplan, A. (1970). Distance from death as a variable in the study of aging. *Developmental Psychology, 2*(1), 71–84.

Liebman, B. (1995, June). A meat and potatoes man. *Nutrition Action Health Letter, 22*(5), 6–7.

Light, L. L. (1990). Interactions between memory and language in old age. In J. E. Birren & K. W. Schaie (Eds.), *Handbook of the psychology of aging* (3rd ed., pp. 275–290). San Diego: Academic.

Lindeman, R. D., Tobin, J., & Shock, N. (1985). Longitudinal studies on rate of decline in renal function with age. *Journal of the American Geriatrics Society, 33,* 278–285.

Linder, K. (1990). *Functional literacy projects and project proposals: Selected examples.* Paris: United Nations Educational, Scientific, and Cultural Organization.

Lino, M. (2001). *Expenditures on children by families, 2000 annual report* (Misc. Publication No. 1528–2000). Washington, DC: U.S. Department of Agriculture, Center for Nutrition Policy and Promotion.

Lipid Research Clinics Program. (1984a). The lipid research clinic coronary primary prevention trial results: 1. Reduction in incidence of coronary heart disease. *Journal of the American Medical Association, 251,* 351–364.

Lipid Research Clinics Program. (1984b). The lipid research clinic coronary primary prevention trial results: 2. The relationship of reduction in incidence of coronary heart disease to cholesterol lowering. *Journal of the American Medical Association, 251*, 365–374.

Listening to depression: The new medicines. (1995, January). *Johns Hopkins Medical Letter: Health after 50*, pp. 4–5.

Livson, F. (1976, November). *Sex differences in personality development in the middle adult years: A longitudinal study*. Paper presented at the annual meeting of the Gerontological Society, Louisville, KY.

Lock, M. (1994). Menopause in cultural context. *Experimental Gerontology, 29*, 307-317.

Lock, M. (1998). Deconstructing the change: Female maturation in Japan and North America. In R. A. Shweder (Ed.), *Welcome to middle age (and other cultural fictions)* (pp.45-74). Chicago: University of Chicago Press.

Lofland, L. H. (1986). When others die. *Generations, 10*(4), 59–61.

Loftus, E. F. (1991). The glitter of everyday memory ... and the gold. *American Psychologist, 46*(1), 16–18.

Longino, C. F., & Earle, J. R. (1996). Who are the grandparents at century's end? *Generations, 20*(1), 13–16.

Longino, C. F., & Kart, C. S. (1982). Explicating activity theory: A formal replication. *Journal of Gerontology, 37*(6), 713–721.

Lopata, H. (1977, September–October). Widows and widowers. *The Humanist*, pp. 25–28.

Lopata, H. (1979). *Women as widows*. New York: Elsevier.

Lord, A. B. (1982). Oral poetry in Yugoslavia. In U. Neisser (Ed.), *Memory observed: Remembering in natural contexts* (pp. 243–257). San Francisco: Freeman.

Louis Harris & Associates. (1995). *Women's issues* (Survey conducted for Families and Work Institute and the Whirlpool Foundation). New York: Author.

Lovelace, E. A. (1990). Basic concepts in cognition and aging. In E. A. Lovelace (Ed.), *Aging and cognition: Mental processes, self-awareness, and interventions* (pp. 1–28). Amsterdam: North-Holland, Elsevier.

Lowenthal, M., & Haven, C. (1968). Interaction and adaptation: Intimacy as a critical variable. *American Sociological Review, 33*, 20–30.

Luborsky, M. R., & McMullen, C. K. (1999). Culture and aging. In J. Cavanaugh, Whitbourne, & S. Krauss (Eds.), *Gerontology: An interdisciplinary perspective* (pp. 65–90). New York: Oxford University Press.

Lucas, R. E., Clark, A. E., Georgellis, Y., Diener, E. (2004). *American Psychological Society, 15*(1), 8–13.

Ludmer-Gliebe, S. (1994, Spring). Can Johnny read? The American illiteracy crisis. *The Reporter (Women's American ORT)*, pp. 18–20.

Lund, D. A. (1993a). Caregiving. In R. Kastenbaum (Ed.), *Encyclopedia of adult development* (pp. 57–63). Phoenix: Oryx.

Lund, D. A. (1993b). Widowhood: The coping response. In R. Kastenbaum (Ed.), *Encyclopedia of adult development* (pp. 537–541). Phoenix: Oryx.

Lund, D. A. (Ed.). (1989). *Older bereaved spouses: Research with practical applications*. Washington, DC: Hemisphere.

Luria, A. R. (1968). *The mind of a mnemonist*. New York: Basic Books.

Luria, A. R. (1976). *Cognitive development: Its cultural and social foundations*. Cambridge, MA: Harvard University Press.

Lutjen, P., Trounson, A., Leeton, J., Findlay, J., Wood, C., & Renou, P. (1984). The establishment and maintenance of pregnancy using in vitro fertilization and embryo donation in a patient with primary ovarian failure, *Nature, 307*, 174–175.

Lytton, H. (1990). Child and parent effects in boys' conduct disorder: A reinterpretation. *Developmental Psychology, 26*, 683–697.

MacAdam, M. (1993). Review of Caring for an Aging World: International models for long-term care, financing, and delivery. *Generations, 17*(4), 77–78.

MacDonald, R. K., (1983). *Louisa May Alcott*. Boston: Twayne.

Mackay, J. & Ericksen, M. (2002). *The tobacco atlas*. Geneva, Switzerland: World Health Organization.

MacKinnon, D. W. (1962). The nature and nurture of creative talent. *American Psychologist, 7*, 488–495.

Main, M. (1987). *Working models of attachment in adolescence and adulthood*. Symposium presented at the Society of Research in Child Development, Baltimore.

Maitland, S. B., Interieri, R. C., Schaie, K. W., Willis, S. L. (2000). Gender differences and changes in cognitive abilites across the adult life span. *Aging, Neuropsychology, and Cognition, 7*(1), 32–53.

Malcolm, A. H. (1984, September 23). Many see mercy in ending lives. *New York Times*, pp. 1, 56.

Mandela, N. (1994). *Long walk to freedom: The autobiography of Nelson Mandela.* Boston: Little, Brown.

Manders, M., deGroot, L.C.P.G.M., van Staveren, W. A., Woulters-Wessling, W., Mulders, A. J. M. J., & Hoefnaagels, W. H. L. (2004). Effectiveness of nutritional *of Gerontology: Medical Sciences, 59A*, 1041–1049.

Mannell, R. (1993). High investment activity and life satisfaction: Commitment, serious leisure, and flow in the daily lives of older adults. In J. Kelly (Ed.), *Activity and aging.* Newbury Park, CA: Sage.

Manning, C. A., Hall, J. L., & Gold, P. E. (1990). Glucose effects on memory and other neuropsychological tests in elderly humans. *Psychological Science, 1*(5), 307–311.

Mansfield, R. S., & Busse, T. V. (1981). *The psychology of creativity and discovery: Scientists and their work.* Chicago: Nelson-Hall.

Manton, K. G., Siegler, I. C., & Woodbury, M. A. (1986). Patterns of intellectual development in later life. *Journal of Gerontology, 41*, 486–499.

Manuelidis, E. E., deFigueiredo, J. M., Kim, J. H., Fritch, W. W., & Manuelidis, L. (1988). Transmission studies from blood of Alzheimer's patients and healthy relatives. *Proceedings of the National Academy of Science, USA, 85*, 4898–4901.

Markman, H. J., Renick, M. J., Floyd, F. J., Stanley, S. M., & Clements, M. (1993). *Journal of Consulting and Clinical Psychology, 61*, 70–77.

Marks, N. (1998). Does it hurt to care? Caregiving, work-family conflict, and midlife well-being. *Journal of Marriage and the Family, 60*, 951–956.

Marks, N. F. & Lambert, J. D. (1998). Marital status continuity and change among young and midlife adults: Longitudinal effects on psychological well being. *Journal of Family Issues, 19*(6), 652–686.

Marks, N.F, Bumpass, L. L, & Jun, H. (2004). Family roles and well-being during the middle life course. In O. G. Brim, C. D. Ryff, and R. C. Kessler (Eds.), *How healthy are we? A national study of well-being at midlife* (pp. 514–549). Chicago: University of Chicago Press.

Markus, H. (1977). Self-schemata and processing information about the self. *Journal of Personality and Social Psychology, 35*, 63–78.

Markus, H., & Cross, S. (1990). The interpersonal self. In L. Pervin (Ed.), *Handbook of personality: Theory and research* (pp. 576–608). New York: Guilford.

Markus, H., & Nurius, P. (1986). Possible selves. *American Psychologist, 41*, 954–969.

Marshall, E. (1993). A tough line on genetic screening. *Science, 262*, 984–985.

Marshall, V. W. (1994). Sociology, psychology, and the theoretical legacy of the Kansas City studies. *The Gerontologist, 34*, 768–774.

Martikainen, P. & Valkonen, T. (1996). Mortality after the death of a spouse: Rates and causes of death in a large Finnish cohort. *American Journal of Public Health, 86*, 1087–1093.

Martin, J. A., Hamilton, B. E., Ventura, S. J., Menacker, F., Park, M. M., & Sutton, P. D. (2002). Births: Final data for 2001, *National Vital Statistics Reports, 51*, 2.

Martin, L. G. (1988). The aging of Asia. *Journal of Gerontology: Social Sciences, 43*(4), S599–113.

Martin, L. R., Friedman, H. S., Tucker, J. S., Tomlison-Keasey, C., Criqui, M. H., & Schwartz, J. E. (2002). A life course perspective on childhood cheerfulness and its relation to mortality risk. *Personality and Social Psychology Bulletin, 28*, 1155–1165.

Martin, P., Hagberg, B., Poon, L. W. (1997). Predictors of loneliness in centenarians: A parallel study. *Journal of Cross-Cultural Gerontology, 12*, 203–224.

Martino-Salzman, D., Blasch, B. B., Morris, R. D., & McNeal, L. W. (1991). Travel behavior of nursing home residents perceived as wanderers and nonwanderers. *The Gerontologist, 31*, 666–672.

Marvell, T. B. (1989). Divorce rates and the fault requirement. *Law and Society Review, 23*, 543–567.

Maslach, C., & Jackson, S. E. (1985). Burnout in health professions: A social psychological analysis. In G. Sanders & J. Suls (Eds.), *Social psychology of health and illness*. Hillsdale, NJ: Erlbaum.

Masoro, E. J. (1985). Metabolism. In C. E. Finch & E. L. Schneider (Eds.), *Handbook of the biology of aging* (2nd ed., pp. 540–563). New York: Van Nostrand Reinhold.

Masters, W. H., & Johnson, V. E. (1966). *Human sexual response*. Boston: Little, Brown.

Masters, W. H., & Johnson, V. E. (1970). *Human sexual inadequacy*. Boston: Little, Brown.

Masters, W. H., & Johnson, V. E, (1981). Sex and the aging process. *Journal of the American Geriatrics Society, 29*, 385–390.

Masters, W. H., Johnson, V. E., & Kolodny, R. C. (1988). *Human sexuality* (3rd ed.). Glenview, IL: Scott, Foresman.

Matlin, M. M. (1987). *The psychology of women*. New York: Holt.

Matthews, A. M., & Brown, K. H. (1988). Retirement as a critical life event: The differential experience of women and men. *Research on Aging, 9*, 548–551.

Mays, V. M., Chatters, L. M., Cochran, S. D., Mackness, J. (1998). African American families in diversity: Gay men and lesbians as participants. *Journal of Comparative Family Studies, 29*(1), 73-87.

Mazel, A. (1984). Reforme legislative et sociologie judiciaire: Le nouveau divorce [Legislative reform and judicial sociology: The new divorce]. *Informatica e diritto, 10*, 383–408.

Mazzuca, J. (2003). Teen career picks: The more things change … The Gallup Poll Tuesday Briefing, 05/13/2003. The Gallup Organization. Available: www.gallup.com/poll/tb/educaYouth/20030513.asp. Access date: January 31, 2004.

McArdle, J. J., Prescott, C. A., Hamagamie, F., & Horn, J. L. (1998). A contemporary method for developmental–genetic analyses of age changes in intellectual abilites. *Developmental Neuropsychology, 14*(1), 69–114.

McCann, I. L., & Holmes, D. S. (1984). Influence of aerobic exercise on depression. *Journal of Personality and Social Psychology, 46*(5), 1142–1147. *Clinical Pediatrics, 25*(2, 3, 4), 65–71.

McCartney, N., Hicks, A.L, Martin, J., & Webber, C. E. (1996). A longitudinal trial of weight

training in the elderly: Continued improvements in year 2. *The Journals of Gerontology: Series A: Biological Sciences and Medical Sciences, 51*, B425–B433.

McClelland, D. C. (1993). Intelligence is not the best predictor of job performance. *Current Directions in Psychological Science, 2*(1), 5–6.

McCrae, R. R., & Costa, P. T. (1984). *Emerging lives, enduring dispositions*. Boston: Little, Brown.

McCrae, R. R., & Costa, P. T. (1997). Personality trait structure as a human universal. *American Psychologist, 52*(5), 509–516.

McCrae, R. R., Costa, P. T., Jr., & Busch, C. M. (1986). Evaluating comprehensiveness in personality system: The California Q-set and the five factor model. *Journal of Personality, 54*, 430–446.

McCrae, R. R., Costa, P. T., Martin, T. A., Oryol, V. E., Rukavishnikov, A. A., Senin, I. G., Hrebickova, M., & Urbanek, T. (2004). Consensual validation of personality traits across cultures. *Journal of Research in Psychology, 38*, 179–201.

McCrae, R. R., Costa, P. T., Ostendorf, F., Angleitner, A., Hrebickova, M., Avia, M. D., Sanz, M. D., Sanchez-Bernardos, M. L., Kusdil, M. E., Woodfield, R., Saunders, P. R., Smith, P. B. (2000). Nature over Nurture: Temperament, personality and life span development. *Journal of Personality and Social Psychology, 78*(1), 173–186.

McCusker, J., Cherubin, C. F., & Zimberg, S. (1971). Prevalence of alcoholism in general municipal hospital population. *New York State Journal of Medicine, 71*, 751–754.

McFall, S., & Miller, B. H. (1992). Caregiver burden and nursing home admission of frail elderly patients. *Journal of Gerontology: Social Sciences, 47*, S73–79.

McGue, M., Bacon, S., & Lykken, D. T, (1993). Personality stability and change in early adulthood: A behavioral genetic analysis. *Developmental Psychology, 21*, 96–109.

McKay, N. Y. (1992). *Introduction*. In M. Anderson, *My Lord, what a morning* (pp. ix–xxxiii). Madison: University of Wisconsin Press.

McKitrick, L. A., Camp, C. J., & Black, F. W. (1992). Prospective memory intervention in

Alzheimer's disease. *Journal of Gerontology*, 47(5), 337–343.

McIntosh, J. L. (1992). Epidemiology of suicide in the elderly. *Suicide and Life-Threatening Behavior*, 22, 15–35.

McMullen, R. (1984). *Degas: His life, times, and work*. Boston: Houghton Mifflin.

McNally, J. W., & Mosher, W. D. (1991, May 14). AIDS-related knowledge and behavior among women 15–44 years of age: United States, 1988. *Advance Data*, 200.

Meacham, J. A. (1982). Wisdom and the context of knowledge: Knowing that one doesn't know. In D. Kuhn & J. A. Meacham (Eds.), *On the development of developmental psychology* (pp. 111–134). Basel, Switzerland: Karger.

Meacham, J. A. (1990). The loss of wisdom. In R. J. Sternberg (Ed.), *Wisdom: Its nature, origins, and development* (pp. 181–211). Cambridge: Cambridge University Press.

MedlinPlus Medical Ecycolpedia. (2004). *Medical encyclopedia: Aging changes in immunity*. [Online]. Available: http://www.nlm.nih.gov/medlineplus/ency/article/004008.htm

Meehan, P. J. (1990). Prevention: The endpoint of suicidology. *Mayo Clinic Proceedings*, 65, 115–118.

Meer, F. (1988). *Higher than hope: The authorized biography of Nelson Mandela*. New York: Harper & Row.

Meer, J. T. (1987, May). The oldest old: The years after 85. *Psychology Today*, p. 82.

Meier, D. E., Emmons, C. A., Wallenstein, S., Quill, T., Morrison, R. S., & Cassel, C. (1998). A national survey of physician-assisted suicide and euthanasia in the United States. *New England Journal of Medicine*, 338, 1193–1201.

Menken, J., Trussell, J., & Larsen, U. (1986). Age and infertility. *Science*, 233, 1389–1394.

Menninger Foundation. (1994, March). Grandparenting after divorce still a key role for older persons. *The Menninger Letter*, p. 3.

Mergler, N. L., & Goldstein, M. D. (1983). Why are there old people: Senescence as biological and cultural preparedness for the transmission of information. *Human Development*, 26, 72–90.

Merrill, S. S. & Verbrugge, L. M. (1999). Health and disease in midlife. In S. L. Willis & J. D. Reid (Eds.), *Life in the middle: Psychological and social development in middle age* (pp.78-103). San Diego: Academic Press.

Merva, M., & Fowles, R. (1992). *Effects of diminished economic opportunities on social stress: Heart attacks, strokes, and crime* [Briefing paper]. Washington, DC: Economic Policy Institute.

Meyers, H. (1989). The impact of teenaged children on parents. In J. M. Oldham & R. S. Liebert (Eds.), *The middle years*. New Haven, CT: Yale University Press.

Mezger, R. (2000, July 11). Condition affects millions of Americans, but it's not a 'sentence to blindness'. *Akron Beacon Journal*.

Michael, R. T., Gagnon, J. H., Laumann, E. O., & Kolata, G. (1994). *Sex in America: A definitive survey*. Boston: Little, Brown.

Michigan court upholds ban on assisted suicide. (1994, December 14). *Chicago Sun-Times*, p. 28.

Milgram, S. (1963). *Obedience to authority; An experimental view*. New York: Harper & Row.

Milkie, M. A., & Peltola, P. (1999). Playing all the roles: Gender and the work-family balancing act. *Journal of Marriage and the Family*, 61, 476–490.

Miller, G. A. (1956). The magical number seven, plus or minus two: Some limits on our capacity to process information. *Psychological Review*, 63, 81–97.

Miller, J. (1987). Aboard the victory O. In G. O'Connor (ed), Olivier: In Celebration. (pp. 125–129). New York: Dodd, Mead.

Miller, J. B. (1991). The development of women's sense of self. In J. V. Jordan, A. G. Kaplan, J. B. Miller, I. P. Stiver, & J. L. Surrey (Eds.), *Women's growth in connection; Writings from the Stone Center*. New York: Guilford.

Miller, K., & Kohn, M. (1983). The reciprocal effects of job condition and the intellectuality of leisure-time activities. In M. L. Kohn & C. Schooler (Eds.), *Work and personality: An inquiry into the impact of social stratifications* (pp. 217–241). Norwood, NJ: Ablex.

Miller, N., & Rockwell, R. C. (Eds). (1988). *AIDS in Africa: The social and policy impact*. Lewiston, PA: Mellen.

Miller, P. H. (1983). *Theory of developmental psychology*. San Francisco: Freeman.

Miller, W. R., & Thoresen, C. E. (2003). Spirituality, religion, and health: An emerging research field. *American Psychologist, 58*(1), 24–35.

Miller-Jones, D. (1989). Culture and testing. *American Psychologist, 44*, 360–366.

Mind and body. (1993, April 17). *New Scientist-Supplement*, p. 10.

Mindel, C. H. (1983). The elderly in minority families. In T. H. Brubaker (Ed.), *Family relationships in later life* (pp. 193–208). Beverly Hills, CA: Sage.

Minino, A. M., Arias, E., Kochanek, K. D., Murphy, S. L., Smith, B. L. (2002). Deaths: Final data for 2000. *National Vital Statistics Reports, 50*(15). Hyattsville, MD: National Center for Health Statistics.

Minkler, H., & Roe, K. (1992). *Forgotten caregivers: Grandmothers raising the children of the crack cocaine epidemic*. Newbury Park, CA: Sage.

Minkler, H., & Roe, K. (1996). Grandparents as surrogate parents. *Generations, 20*(1), 34–38.

Mirvis, P. H., & Hall, D. T. (1996). Career development for the older worker. In D. T. Hall and associates (Eds.), *The career is dead – Long live the career: A relational approach to careers.* (pp. 278–296). San Francisco: Jossey-Bass Publishers.

Mishel, L., & Bernstein, J. (1994). *The state of working America 1994–1995*. Armonk, NY: Sharp.

Mischel, W. (1986). *Introduction to personality* (4th ed.). New York: Holt Rinehart & Winston.

Mitchell, B. A., Wister, A. V., & Burch, T. K. (1989). The family environment and leaving the parental home. *Journal of Marriage and the Family, 51*, 605–613.

Mitchell, D. B., Brown, A. S., & Murphy, D. R. (1990). Dissociations between procedural and episodic memory: Effects of time and aging. *Psychology and Aging, 5*, 264–276.

Mitchell, V., & Helson, R. (1990). Women's prime of life: Is it the 50s? *Psychology of Women Quaterly, 16*, 331–347

Monat, A., & Lazarus, R. S. (Eds.). (1985). *Stress and coping: An anthology*. New York: Columbia University Press.

Monk, A. (1994). Retirement and aging: An introduction to the Columbia retirement handbook. In A. Monk (Ed.), *The Columbia retirement handbook* (pp. 3–11). New York: Columbia University Press.

Monnier, A., & de Guibert-Lamoine, C. (1993). La conjoncture démographique: L'Europe et les developpés d'outre–mer. *Population, 48*(4), 1043–1067.

Montepare, J. M., & Lachman, M. E. (1989). "You're only as old as you feel": Self-perceptions of age, fears of aging, and life satisfaction from adolescence to old age. *Psychology and Aging, 4*(1), 73–78.

Mooney-Somers, J., & Golombok, S. (2000). Children of lesbian mothers: From the 1970's to the new millennium. *Sexual and Relationship Therapy, 15*, 121–714.

Moore, M. (2000). *The only menopause guide you'll need*. Baltimore: The John Hopkins University Press.

Moore, M. J., Moir, P., & Patrick, M. M. (2004). *The state of aging and health in America 2004*. Washington, DC: Centers for Disease Control and Prevention and Merck Institute of Aging & Health.

Morbidity and Mortality Weekly Report (MMWR). (1985, June 21). Suicide–U.S., 1970–1980.

Morrison, D. R., & Cherlin, A. J. (1995). The divorce process and young children's well-being: A prospective analysis. *Journal of Marriage and the Family, 57*, 800–812.

Morse, J. M., & Field, P. A. (1995). *Qualitative research methods for health professionals*. Thousand Oak, CA: Sage.

Mortimer, J. A., Snowdon, D. A, & Markesbery, W. R. (2002). Head circumference, education, and risk of dementia: Findings from the Nun study. *Journal of Clinical and Experimental Neuropsychology, 25*, 671–679.

Morton, J. (1991). The bankruptcy of everyday thinking. *American Psychologist, 46*(1), 32–33.

Morton, K. R., Worthley, J. S., Nitch, S. R., Lamberton, H. H., Loo, L. K., & Testerman, J. K. (2000). Integration of cognition and emotion: A postformal operations model of physician-patient interaction. *Journal of Adult Development, 7*, 151–160.

Moscovitch, M., & Winocur, G. (1992). The neuropsychology of memory and aging. In F. I. M. Craik & T. A. Salthouse (Eds.), *The handbook of aging and cognition* (pp. 315–372). Hillsdale, NJ: Erlbaum.

Moskow-McKenzie, D., & Manheimer, R. J. (1994). *A planning guide to organize educational programs for older adults*. Asheville, NC: University Publications, UNCA.

Moss, M. S., & Moss, S. Z. (1989). The death of a parent. In R. A. Kalish (Ed.), *Midlife loss: Coping strategies*. Newbury Park, CA: Sage.

Moye, J. (1999). Assessment of competency and decision making capacity. In P.A. Lichtenberg (Ed.), *Handbook of assessment in clinical gerontology*, pp. 488–528. Hoboken, NJ: John Wiley & Sons, Inc.

Mui, A. C. (1992). Caregiver strain among black and white daughter caregivers: A role theory perspective. *The Gerontologist, 32*(2), 203–212.

Munck, A., Guyre, P., & Holbrook, N. (1984). Physiological functions of glucocorticoids in stress and their relation to pharmacological actions. *Endocrine Reviews, 5*, 25–44.

Murstein, B. I. (1980). Mate selection in the 1970s. *Journal of Marriage and the Family, 42*, 777–792.

Muskin, P.R. (1998). The request to die. Role for a psychodynamic perspective on physician-assisted suicide. *Journal of the American Medical Association, 279*, 323–328.

Mutran, E. J., Reitzes, D. J., Bratton, K. A., & Fernandez, M. E. (1997). Self-esteem and subjective responses to work among mature workers: Similarities and differences by gender. *Journal of Gerontology: Social Sciences, 52B*, S89–S96.

Mutran, E.J., Reitzes, D.C., & Fernandez, M.E. (1997). Factors that influence attitudes toward retirement. *Research on Aging, 19*, 251–273.

Muuss, R. E. H. (1988). *Theories of adolescence* (5th ed.). New York: Random House.

Myers, D. G. (2000). The funds, friends, and faith of happy people. *American Psychologist, 55*, 56–57.

Myers, D., & Diener, E. (1995). Who is happy? *Psychological Science, 6*, 10–19.

Myers, J. E., & Perrin, N. (1993). Grandparents affected by parental divorce: A population at risk? *Journal of Counseling and Development, 72*, 62–66.

Myerson, J., Shealy, D., & Stern, M. B. (Eds.). (1987). *The selected letters of Louisa May Alcott*. Boston: Little, Brown.

Nash, S. C., & Feldman, S. S. (1981). Sex role and sex-related attributions: Constancy and change across the family life cycle. In M. E. Lamb & A. L. Brown (Eds.), *Advances in developmental psychology* (Vol. 1, pp. 137–147). Hillsdale, NJ: Erlbaum.

National Cancer Institute. (2002). What you need to know about prostate cancer. [Online]. Available: www.nci.nih.gov/cancerinfo.wyntk/prostate. Access date: March 22, 2004.

National Cancer Institute. (2004). Colon cancer genes. [Online]. Available: www.cancer.gov/cancerinfo/pdq/genetics/colorectal. Access date: April 8, 2004.

National Cancer Institute. (2004). Genetics of breast and ovarian cancer. [Online]. Available: www.nci.nih.gov/cancerinfo/pdq/genetics/breast-and-ovarian. Access date: March 22, 2004.

National Cancer Institute. Understanding breast changes: A health guide for all women. [Online]. Available: www.cancer.gov/cancerinfo/understanding-breast-changes/page3. Access date: March 19, 2004.

National Center for Education Statistics (NCES). (1989). *National higher education statistics: Fall, 1989*. (Publication No. NCES-90-379). Washington, DC: U.S. Department of Education.

National Center for Education Statistics (NCES). (1991). *National higher education statistics: Fall, 1991*. (Publication No. NCES 92-038). Washington, DC: U.S. Department of Education, Office of Educational Research and Improvement.

National Center for Education Statistics (NCES). (2002). *The condition of education: 2002*. (NCES 2002-025). Washington, DC: Author.

National Center for Education Statistics (NCES). (2005a). *Digest of education statistics, 2004*. (NCES 2006-005), *Chapter 3*. Washington, DC: Author.

National Center for Education Statistics (NCES). (2005b). *The condition of education: 2005*. (NCES 2005-031). Washington, DC: Author.

National Center for Health Statistics (NCHS). (1990). *Health, United States, 1998 with socioeconomic status and health chartbook*. Hyattsville, MD: Author.

National Center for Health Statistics (NCHS). (2003). *Health, United States, 2003*. Hyattsville, MD: Author.

National Center for Health Statistics (NCHS). (1990). *Health, United States, 1989 and prevention profile.* (DHHS Publication No. 90-1232). Washington, DC: U.S. Government Printing Office.

National Center for Health Statistics (NCHS). (1992). *Statistics on suicide rates in the United States, 1935–1989.* Washington, DC: U.S. Government Printing Office.

National Center for Health Statistics (NCHS). (1993). *Health, United States, 1992 and prevention profile.* Washington, DC: U.S. Public Health Service.

National Center for Health Statistics (NCHS). (1994). *Health, United States.* Hyattsville, MD: Author.

National Center for Health Statistics (NCHS). (1998a). *Health, United States, 1998 with socioeconomic status and health chartbook.* Hyattsville, MD: Author.

National Center for Health Statistics (NCHS). (2004). *Health, United States, 2004 with chartbook on trends in the health of Americans.* (DHHS Publication No. 2004-1232). Hyattsville, MD: National Center for Health Statistics.

National Council on Aging. (1981). *Aging in the eighties: America in transition.* Washington, DC: Author.

National Council on Aging (2002). *American perceptions of aging in the 21st century: The NCOA's continuing study of the myths and realities of aging* (2002 update). Washington, DC: Author.

National Eye Institute. (2001). Facts about the cornea and corneal disease. [Online]. Available: www.nei.nih.gov/health/cornealdisease/index.htm. Access date: April 30, 2004.

National Eye Institute. (2004a). Age-related macular degeneration: What you should know. [Online]. Available: www.nei.nih.gov/health/maculardegeneration_armd_facts.htm. Access date: April 27, 2004.

National Eye Institute. (2004b). Glaucoma: What you should know. [Online]. Available: www.nei.nih.gov/health/glaucoma/glaucoma_facts.htm. Access date: April 27, 2004.

National Eye Institute. (2005). Cataract: What you should know. [Online]. Available: www.nei.nih.gov/health/cataract/cataract_facts.asp. Access date: January 23, 2006.

National Hospice and Palliative Care Organization. Hospice and palliative care information. [Online]. Available: www.nhpco.org/i4a/pages/index.cfm?pageid=3306. Access date: July 5, 2005.

National Hospice and Palliative Care Organization. Hospice facts and figures. [Online]. Available: www.nhcpo.org/files/public/hospice_facts_110104.pdf. Access date: July 5, 2005.

National Hospice Organization (undated). *Hospice: A special kind of caring.* Arlington, VA: Author.

National Institute for Occupational Health and Safety. (2001). *Women's safety and health issues at work.* Washington, DC: U.S. Department of Health and Human Services, Public Health Services, Centers for Disease Control and Prevention, National Institute for Occupational Health and Safety, DHHS (NIOSH) Publication No. 2001–123.

National Institute for Occupational Health and Safety (NIOSH). (2002). The changing organization of work and the safety and health of working people: Knowledge gaps and research direction, by S. L. Sauter, W. S. Brightwell, M. J. Colligan, J. J. Hurrell, Jr., T. M. Katz, D. E. LeGrande, N. Lessin, R. A. Lippin, J. A. Lipscomb, L. R. Murphy, R. H. Peters, G. P. Keita, S. R. Robertson, J. M. Stellman, N. G. Swanson, L. E. Tetrick. Cincinnati, OH.

National Institute of Allergy and Infectious Diseases. (2004). HIV/AIDS statistics. [Online]. Available: www.niaid.nih.gov/factsheets/aidsstat.htm. Access date: January 26, 2004.

National Institute of Health. (2001). Depressive disorders. [Online]. Available: www.nimh.nih.gov/publicat/womensoms.cfm. Access date: January 23, 2006.

National Institute of Mental Health (NIMH). (1999). Suicide facts. [Online]. Available: www.nimh.nih.gov/research/suifact.htm.

National Institute of Mental Health. (2003). Older adults: Depression and suicide facts. [Online]. Available: www.nimh.nih.gov/publicat/elderlydepsuicide.cfm?. Access date: June 7, 2005.

National Institute on Aging (NIA). (1980). *Senility: Myth or madness.* Washington, DC: U.S. Government Printing Office.

National Institute on Aging (NIA). (1993). *Bound for good health: A collection of Age Pages.* Washington, DC.: U.S. Government Printing Office.

National Institute on Aging. (1999). HIV, AIDS, and older people. [Online]. Available: www.niapublications.org.engagepages/aids.asp. Access date: March 15, 2004.

National Institute on Aging. (2000). Skin care and aging. [Online]. Available: www.naipublications.org/engagepages/skin.asp. Access date: April 26, 2004.

National Institute on Aging. (2002). Alcohol use and abuse. [Online]. Available: www.niapublications.org/engagepages/alcohol.asp. Access date: June 2, 2005.

National Institute on Aging. (2002). Osteoporosis: The bone thief. [Online]. Available: www.niapublications.org/engagepages/osteo.asp. Access date: March 3, 2004.

National Institute on Aging. (2002). Sexuality later in life. [Online]. Available: www.niapublications.org/engagepages/sexuality.asp. Access date: April 28, 2004.

National Institute on Aging (NIA). (2003). *Alzheimer's information.* [Online]. Available: http://www.nia.nih.gov/Alzheimers/AlzheimersInformation/Diagnosis/

National Institute on Aging. (2004). Depression: Don't let the blues hang around. [Online]. Available: www.niapublications.org/engagepages/depression.asp. Access date: July 19, 2005.

National Institute on Deafness and Other Communication Disorders. (2001). Hearing loss and older adults. [Online]. Available: www.nidcdc.nih.gov/.health/hearing/older.asp. Access date: January 23, 2006.

National Institute on Deafness and Other Communication Disorders. (2004). Hearing aids. [Online]. Available: www.nidcd.nih.gov/health/hearing/hearingaid.asp. Access date: April 30, 2004.

National Institutes of Health (NIH). (1984). *Osteoporosis.* [1984-421-132:4652, Consensus Development Conference Statement, 5(3)]. Bethesda, MD: U.S. Government Printing Office.

National Institutes of Health (NIH). (1992, December 7–9). *Impotence.* NIH Consensus Statement, 10(4), 1–31. Washington, DC: U.S. Government Printing Office.

National Institute of Health. (2001). Depressive disorders. [Online]. Available: www.nimh.nih.gov/publicat/womensoms.cfm. Access date: January 23, 2006.

National Institutes of Health. (2002). Aging changes in immunity. [Online]. Available: www.nlm.nih.gov/medlineplus/ency/article/004008.htm. Access date: March 29, 2004.

National Institutes of Health. (2002). NHLBI stops trial of estrogen plus progestin due to increased breast cancer risk, lack of overall benefit. [Online]. Available: www.nhlbi.nih.gov.new/press/02-07-09.htm. Access date: June 3, 2004.

National Institute of Health (NIH). (2003). Prostate cancer. [Online]. Available: http://nihseniorhealth.gov/prostatecancer/causesandriskfactors/05.html

National Institutes of Health. (2003). Rates of dementia increase among older women on combination hormone therapy. [Online]. Available: www.nih.gov/news/pr/may2003/nia–27.htm. Access date: June 3, 2004.

National Institutes of Health. (2003a). Alzheimer's disease. [Online]. Available: http://nihseniorhealth.gov/alzheimersdisease/toc.html. Access date: April 1, 2004.

National Institutes of Health. (2003b). Prostate cancer. [Online]. Available: http://nihseniorhealth.gov/prostatecancer/toc.html. Access date: March 22, 2004.

National Institutes of Health (NIH). (2004). Gastrointestinal surgery for severe obesity. [Online]. Available: http://win.niddk.nih.gov/publications/gastric.htm

National Institutes of Health. (2004). NIH asks participants in women's health initiative estrogen-alone study to stop study pills, begin follow-up phase. [Online]. Available: www.nhlbi.nih.gov/new/press/04-03-02.htm. Access date: June 3, 2004.

National Institutes of Health. (2004a). Researchers study long-term AIDS drugs use. [Online]. Available: www.nlm.nih.gov/medlineplus/news/fullstory_16147.html. Access date: March 10, 2004.

National Institutes of Health. Emerging and re-emerging infectious diseases. [Online]. Available: http://science.education.nih.gov/supplements/nih1/diseases/activites/activity5_ai ds-–database.htm. Access date: March 10, 2004.

National Institutes of Health. Mortality rates low when HIV therapy begins early. [Online]. Available: www.nlm.nih.gov/medlineplus/news/fullstory_16120.html. Access date: March 10, 2004

National Institutes of Health/National Institute on Aging (NIH/NIA). (1993, May). *In search of the secrets of aging.* (NIH Publication No. 93–2756). Washington, DC: Department of Health and Human Services, Public Health Service, National Institutes of Health.

National Sleep Foundation. (2005). Sleep apnea. [Online]. Available: www.sleepfoundation.org/sleeptionary/index.php?id=10. Access date: January 30, 2006.

Naveh-Benjamin, M. (2000). Adult age differences in memory performance: Tests of an associative deficit hypothesis. *Journal of Experimental Psychology: Learning, Memory, and Cognition, 26*, 1170–1188.

Neff, W. S. (1985). *Work and human behavior.* New York: Aldine.

Negative stereotypes still plague older workers on the job. (1995, April). *AARP Bulletin,* p. 3.

Neimeyer, R.A. (2000). Searching for the meaning of meaning: Grief therapy and the process of reconstruction. *Death Studies, 24,* 541–558.

Neisser, U. (1991). A case of misplaced nostalgia. *American Psychologist, 46*(1), 34–36.

Neisser, U., Boodoo, G., Bouchard, T. J., Jr., Boykin, A.W., Brody, N., Ceci, S. J., Halpern, D. F., Lochlin, J. C., Perloff, R., Sternberg, R. J., Urbaina, S. (1996). Intelligence: Knowns and unknowns. *American Psychologist, 51*(2), 11–101.

Nelan, B. W. (1994, May 9). Time to take charge. *Time,* pp. 27–28.

Nelson, E. N. P. (1954). Persistence of attitudes of college students fourteen years later. *Psychological Monographs, 68,* 1–13.

Nelson, J. (1994, December 18). Motive behind Carter's missions sparks debate. *Chicago Sun-Times,* p. 40.

Neugarten, B. L. (1967). The awareness of middle age. In R. Owen (Ed.), *Middle age.* London: BBC.

Neugarten, B. L. (1968). Adult personality: Toward a psychology of the life cycle. In B. Neugarten (Ed.), *Middle age and aging.* Chicago: University of Chicago Press.

Neugarten, B. L. (1977). Personality and aging. In J. E. Birren & K. W. Schaie (Eds.), *Handbook of*

the psychology of aging (pp. 626–649). New York: Van Nostrand Reinhold.

Neugarten, B. L., & Hagestad, G. (1976). Age and the life course. In H. Binstock & E. Shanas (Eds.), *Handbook of aging and the social sciences.* New York: Van Nostrand Reinhold.

Neugarten, B. L., & Neugarten, D. A. (1987, May). The changing meanings of age. *Psychology Today,* pp. 29–33.

Neugarten, B. L., Havighurst, R., & Tobin, S. (1968). Personality and patterns of aging. In B. Neugarten (Ed.), *Middle age and aging.* Chicago: University of Chicago Press.

Neugarten, B. L., Moore, J. W., & Lowe, J. C. (1965). Age norms, age constraints, and adult socialization. *American Journal of Sociology, 70,* 710–717.

Newsweek Poll. (2000). *Post super Tuesday gays and lesbians (United States).* Storrs, CT: Roper Center for Public Opinion Research.

Nickerson, R. S. (1981). Why interactive computer systems are sometimes not used by people who might benefit from them. *International Journal of Man-Machine Studies, 15,* 469–507.

Nickerson, R. S., & Adams, M.J. (1979). Long-term memory for a common object. *Cognitive Psychology, 11,* 287–307.

NIOSH. (2002). The changing organization of work and the safety and health of working people: Knowledge gaps and research direction, by S. L. Sauter, W. S. Brightwell, M. J. Colligan, J. J. Hurrell, Jr., T. M. Katz, D. E. LeGrande, N. Lessin, R. A. Lippin, J. A. Lipscomb, L. R. Murphy, R. H. Peters, G. P. Keita, S. R. Robertson, J. M. Stellman, N. G. Swanson, L. E. Tetrick. Cincinnati, OH.

Nisan, M., & Kohlberg, L. (1982). Universality and variation in moral judgment: A longitudinal and cross-sectional study in Turkey. *Child Development, 53,* 865–876.

Nishio, H. K. (1994). Japan's welfare vision: Dealing with a rapidly increasing elderly population. In L. K. Olson (Ed.), *The graying of the world: Who will care for the frail elderly?* (pp. 233–260). New York: Haworth.

No reference for this appears in the original bibliography: Erikson's obituary in the *New York Times,* May 13, 1994, p. C16.

Noberini, M., & Neugarten, B. (1975, November). A follow-up study of adaptation in middle-aged women. Paper presented at the annual meeting of the Gerontological Society, Portland, OR.

Nock, S. L. (1995). Commitment and dependency in marriage. *Journal of Marriage and the Family, 57*, 503–514.

Nojima, M. (1994). Japan's approach to continuing education for senior citizens. *Educational Gerontology, 20*, 463–471.

Notelovitz, M., & Ware, M. (1983). *Stand tall: The informed woman's guide to preventing osteoporosis.* Gainesville, FL: Triad.

NOW Legal Defense and Education Fund, & Chernow-O'Leary, R. (1987). *The state-by-state guide to women's legal rights.* New York: McGraw-Hill.

Nuland, S. B. (2000). Physician-assisted suicide and euthanasia in practice. *New England Journal of Medicine, 342*, 583–584.

Nuss, S., Denti, E., & Viry, D. (1989). *Women in the world of work: Statistical analyses and projections to the year 2000.* Geneva: International Labor Office.

O'Bryant, S. L. (1988). Sibling support and older widows' well-being. *Journal of Marriage and the Family, 50*, 173–183.

O'Bryant, S. L. (1990–1991). Forewarning of a husband's death: Does it make a difference for older widows? *Omega, 22*, 227–239.

O'Connor, B. P., & Vallerand, R. J. (1998). Psychological adjustment variables as predictors of mortality among nursing home residents. *Psychology and Aging, 13(3)*, 368–374.

O'Grady-LeShane, R. (1993). Changes in the lives of women and their families: Have old age pensions kept pace? *Generations, 17(4)*, 27–31.

O'Leary, K. D., Barling, J., Arias, I., Rosenbaum, A., Malone, J., & Tyree, A. (1989). Prevalence and stability of physical aggression between spouses: A longitudinal analysis. *Journal of Consulting and Clinical Psychology, 57(2)*, 263–268.

Offer, D. (1982). Adolescent turmoil. *New York University Education Quarterly, 13*, 29–32.

Offer, D. (1987). In defense of adolescents. *Journal of the American Medical Association, 25*, 3407–3408.

Offer, D., & Schonert-Reichl, K. A. (1992). Debunking the myths of adolescence: Findings from recent research. *Journal of the Academy of Child and Adolescent Psychiatry, 31*, 1003–1014.

Okie, S. (2001, December). Media coverage of anti-aging breakthroughs. *Life Extension Magazine.*

Okun, M. A., Stick, W. A., Haring, M. J., & Witter, R. A. (1984). The social activity/subjective well-being relation: A quantitative synthesis. *Research on Aging, 6*, 45–65.

Okun, S. (1988, January 29). Opera coach died in his "house of worship." *New York Times*, pp. B1, B3.

Older Adults and Mental Health: Issues & Opportunities, 2001, a report by the Administraion on Aging, U.S. Department of Health and Human Services. Available: http://www.aoa.dhhs.gov/mh/report2001.

Older Americans 2000: Key Indicators of Well-being, a report by the Federal Interagency Forum on Aging Related Statistics. Washington, DC: The Data Dissemination Branch of the National Center on Health Statistics. Available: www.agingstats.gov.

Older Women's League. (1994). *Ending violence against midlife and older women.* Washington, DC: Author.

Older workers: The good, the bad, and the truth. (1993, April–May). *Modern Maturity*, p. 10.

Olmsted, P. P., & Weikart, D. P. (Eds.). (1994). *Family speak: Early childhood care and education in eleven countries.* Ypsilanti, MI: High/Scope.

Omnibus Budget Reconciliation Act, 1987 (Public Law 100–203), Omnibus Budget Reconciliation Act, 1990 (Public Law 101–508).

Ong, A. (1987). *Spirits of resistance and capitalist discipline: Factory women in Malaysia.* Albany: State University of New York Press.

Orbuch, T. L., House, J. S., Mero, R. P., & Webster, P. S. (1996). Marital quality over the life course. *Social Psychology Quarterly, 59*, 162–171.

Orenstein, P. (2002, April, 12). *Mourning my miscarriage.* Available: NY Times.com.

Orentlicher, D. (1996). The legalization of physician assisted suicide. *New England Journal of Medicine, 335*, 663–667.

Osborn, A. (2002, April 1). Mercy killing now legal in Netherlands. *The Guardian.* [Online]. Available: www.nvve.ni/english/info/euth. legal_guardian01–04–02. Access date: July 31, 2002.

Otten, M. W., Teutsch, S. M., Williamson, D. F., & Marks, J. S. (1990). The effect of known risk factors on the excess mortality of black adults in the United States. *Journal of the American Medical Association, 263*(6), 845–850.

Owens, J. F., Matthews, K. A., Wing, R., & Kuller, L. H. (1992). Can physical activity mitigate the effects of aging in middle-aged women? *Circulation, 85*(3), 1265–1270.

Owens, W. A. (1966). Age and mental abilities: A second adult follow-up. *Journal of Educational Psychology, 57*(6), 311–325.

Paden, S. L., & Buehler, C. (1995). Coping with the dual-income lifestyle. *Journal of Marriage and the Family, 57*, 101–110.

Paes, A. H. P., Bakker, A., & Soe-Agnie, C. J. (1997). Impact of dosage frequency on patient compliance. *Diabetes Care, 20*, 1512-1517.

Palaniappan, L., Anthony, M.N., Mahesh, C., Elliot, M., Killeen, A., Giacherio, D., & Rubenfire, M. (2002). Cardiovascular risk factors in ethnic minority women aged less-than-or-equal 30 years. *American Journal of Cardiology, 89*, 524–529.

Palmore, E. B. (1982). Predictors of the longevity difference. *The Gerontologist, 22*, 513–518.

Palmore, E. B., Burchett, B. M., Fillenbaum, G. G., George, L. K., & Wallman, L. M. (1985). *Retirement: Causes and consequences.* New York: Springer.

Palmore, E. B., Fillenbaum, G. G., & George, L. K. (1984). Consequences of retirement. *Journal of Gerontology, 39*, 109–116.

Pamuk, E., Makuc, D., Heck, K., Reuben, C., & Lochner, K. (1998). Socioeconomic status and health chartbook. In *Health, United States, 1998.* Hyattsville, MD: National Center for Health Statistics.

Papalia, D. (1972). The status of several conservation abilities across the lifespan. *Human Development, 15*, 229–243.

Papalia, D., & Bielby, D. (1974). Cognitive functioning in middle and old age adults: A review of research on Piaget's theory. *Human Development, 17*, 424–443.

Papalia, D., Wendkos, S., Duskin Freedman, R. (2001). *Human development.* 8th ed. New York: McGraw Hill.

Park, D. C., Puglisi, J. T., & Smith, A. D. (1986). Memory for pictures: Does an age-related decline exist? *Psychology and Aging, 1*, 11–17.

Park, D. C., Royal, D., Dudley, W., & Morrel, R. (1988). Forgetting of pictures over a long retention interval in young and older adults. *Psychology and Aging, 3*, 94–95.

Park, D. C., Smith, A. D., & Cavanaugh, J. C. (1990). Metamemories of memory researchers. *Memory and Cognition, 18*, 321–327.

Park, R. D., & Buriel, R. (1998). Socialization in the family: Ethnic and ecological perspectives. In W. Damon (Series Ed.) & N. Eisenberg (Vol. Ed.), *Handbook of child psychology: Vol. 3. Social, emotional, and personality development* (5th ed., pp. 463–552). New York: Wiley

Parkes, C. M., & Weiss, R. S. (1983). *Recovery from bereavement.* New York: Basic Books.

Parkin, A. J., & Walter, B. M. (1992). Recollective experience, normal aging, and frontal dysfunction. *Psychology and Aging, 7*(2), 290–298.

Parlee, M. B. (1983). Menstrual rhythms in sensory processes: A review of fluctuations in vision, olfaction, audition, taste, and touch. *Psychological Bulletin, 93*(3), 539–548.

Parnes, H. S., & Sommers, D. G. (1994). Shunning retirement: Work experience of men in their seventies and early eighties. *Journal of Gerontology: Social Sciences, 49*, S117–124.

Parsons, F. (1909). *On choosing a vocation.* Boston: Houghton Mifflin.

Passaro, V. (1991, April 21). Tales from a literary marriage. *New York Times Magazine*, pp. 34–36.

Patterson, C. J. (1992). Children of gay and lesbian parents. *Child Development, 63*, 1025–1042.

Patterson, C. J. (1995a). Lesbian mothers, gay fathers, and their children. In A. R. D'Augelli and C. J. Patterson (Eds.), *Lesbian, gay and bisexual identities over the lifespan: Psychological perspectives* (pp. 293–320). New York: Oxford University Press.

Patterson, C. J. (1995b). Sexual orientation and human development: An overview. *Developmental Psychology, 31*, 3–11.

Patterson, C. J. (1997). Children of gay and lesbian parents. In T. H. Ollendick & R. J. Prinz (Eds.), *Advances in clinical child psychology* (Vol. 19, pp. 81–105). New York: Cambridge University Press.

Pattison, E. M. (Ed.). (1977). *The experience of dying.* Englewood Cliffs, NJ: Prentice-Hall.

Paul, E. L. (1997). A longitudinal analysis of midlife interpersonal relationships and well-being. In M. E. Lachmann & J. B. James (Eds.), *Multiple paths of midlife development* (pp. 171–206). Chicago: University of Chicago Press.

Paveza, G. J., Cohen, D., Eisdorfer, C., Freels, S., Semla, T., Ashford, J. W., Gorelick, P., Hirschman, R., Luchins, D., & Levy, P. (1992). Severe family violence and Alzheimer's disease: Prevalence and risk factors. *The Gerontologist, 32*(4), 493–497.

Pavur, E. J., Comeaux, J. M., & Zeringue, J. A. (1984). Younger and older adults' attention to relevant and irrelevant stimuli in free recall. *Experimental Aging Research, 11*, 207–213.

Paykel, E. S., et al. (1994). Incidence of dementia in a population older than 75 in the United Kingdom. *Archives of General Psychiatry, 51*, 325–332.

Payne, J. D., & Overend, E. (1990). Divorce mediation: Process and strategies—an overview. *Family and Conciliation Courts Review, 28*, 27–34.

Pear, J. (2001). *The science of learning.* Philadelphia, PA: Psychology Press/Taylor & Francis.

Pearlin, L. I. (1980). Life strains and psychological distress among adults. In N. J. Smelser & E. H. Erikson (Eds.), *Themes of work and love in adulthood.* Cambridge, MA: Harvard University Press.

Pearlin, L. I., Lieberman, M. A., Menaghan, E. G., & Mullan, J. T. (1981). The stress process. *Journal of Health and Social Behavior, 22*, 337–356.

Peck, R. C. (1955). Psychological developments in the second half of life. In J. E. Anderson (Ed.), *Psychological aspects of aging.* Washington, DC: American Psychological Association.

Penick, S., & Solomon, P. R. (1991). Hippocampus, context, and conditioning. *Behavioral Neuroscience, 105*, 611–617.

Penning, M.J. (1998). In the middle: Parental caregiving in the context of other roles. *Journal of Gerontology: Social Sciences, 53B*, S188–S197.

Pepper, S. C. (1942). *World hypotheses.* Berkeley: University of California Press.

Pepper, S. C. (1961). *World hypotheses.* Berkeley: University of California Press.

Perez-Stable, E.J., Herrera, B., Jacob, P., III, & Benowitz, N.L. (1998). Nicotine metabolism and intake in black and white smokers. *Journal of the American Medical Association, 280*, 152–156.

Perkins, H. W., & Harris, L. B. (1990). Familial bereavement and health in adult life course perspective. *Journal of Marriage and the Family, 52*, 233–241.

Perón, E. (1951). La razón de mi vida. Buenos Aires: Ediciones Peuser.

Perrin, E.C. and the Committee on Psychosocial Aspects of Child and Family Health. (2002). Technical report: Coparent or second parent adoption by same-sex parents. *Pediatrics, 109*(2), 341–344.

Perrucci, C. C., Perrucci, R., & Targ, D. B. (1988). *Plant closings.* New York: Aldine.

Perry, D. (1995, March 3–9). Merciful end? Couple's suicide raises profound questions. *Chicago Jewish News*, p. 10.

Perry, E. L., Simpson, P. A., NicDomhnaill, O. M., & Siegel, D. M. (2003). Is there a technology age gap? Associations among age, skills, and employment outcomes. *International Journal of Selection & Assessment, 11*(2–3), 141–149.

Perry, W. G. (1970). *Forms of intellectual and ethical development in the college years.* New York: Holt.

Pfaff, J. J., & Almeida, O. P. (2005). A cross-sectional analysis of factors that influence the detection of depression in older primary care patients. *Australian and New Zealand Journal of Psychiatry, 39*, 262–265.

Phillips, D.F. (1998). Reproductive medicine experts will an increasingly fertile field. *Journal of the American Medical Association, 280*, 1893–1895.

Phillips, D. P., & King, E. W. (1988, September 24). Death takes a holiday: Mortality surrounding major social occasions. *Lancet*, pp. 728–732.

Phillips, D. P., & Smith, D. G. (1990). Postponement of death until symbolically meaningful occasions. *Journal of the American Medical Association, 263*, 1947–1951.

Phillips, D. P., Ruth, T. E., & Wagner, L. M. (1993, November 6). Psychology and survival. *Lancet*, pp. 1142–1145.

Phillips, S. M., & Sherwin, B. B. (1992). Effects of estrogen on memory function in surgically menopausal women. *Psychoneuroendocrinology, 17*, 485–495.

Pillemer, K., & Finkelhor, D. (1988). The prevalence of elder abuse: A random sample survey. *The Gerontologist, 28*(1), 51–57.

Pillemer, K., & Suitor, J. J. (1991). "Will I ever escape my child's problems?": Effects of adult children's problems on elderly parents. *Journal of Marriage and the Family, 53*, 585–594.

Planned Parenthood (2003). Perimenopause is unpredictable. [Online]. Available: www.planned parenthood.org/pp2/portal/files/portal/medicalinfo/femalesexualhealth

Pleck, J. H. (1975). Masculinity-femininity: Current and alternative paradigms. *Sex Roles, 1,* 161–178.

Plemons, J., Willis, S., & Baltes, P. (1978). Modifiability of fluid intelligence in aging: A short-term longitudinal training approach. *Journal of Gerontology, 33*(2), 224–231.

Plomin, R., & Rutter, M. (1998). Child development, molecular genetics, and what to do with genes once they are found. *Child Development, 69* (4), 223–242.

PMS: It's real. (1994, July). *Harvard Women's Health Watch,* pp. 2–3.

Pompi, K. F., & Lachman, R. (1967). Surrogate processes in the short-term retention of connected discourse. *Journal of Experimental Psychology, 75*, 143–150.

Poon, L. W. (1985). Differences in human memory with aging. Nature, causes, and clinical implications. In J. Birren & K. W. Schaie (Eds.), *Handbook of the psychology of aging* (2nd ed., pp. 427–462). New York: Van Nostrand Reinhold.

Popenoe, D., & Whitehead, B.D. (1999). *Should we live together? What young adults need to know about cohabitation before marriage.* New Brunswick: National Marriage Project, Rutgers, State University of New Jersey.

Porcino, J. (1983). *Growing older, getting better: A handbook for women in the second half of life.* Reading, MA: Addison-Wesley.

Porcino, J. (1991). *Living longer, living better: Adventures in community housing for the second half of life.* New York: Continuum.

Porcino, J. (1993, April–May). Designs for living. *Modern Maturity,* pp. 24–33.

Porterfield, J. D., & St. Pierre, R. S. (1992). *Wellness: Healthful aging.* Guilford, CT: Dushkin.

Post, S. G. (1994). Ethical commentary: Genetic testing for Alzheimer's disease. *Alzheimer Disease and Associated Disorders, 8,* 66–67.

Powell, L. H., Shahabi, L., Thoresen, C. E. (2003). Religion and spirituality: Linkages to physical health. *American Psychologist, 58*(1), 36–52.

Pratt, C. C., Wilson, W., Benthin, A., & Schmall, V. (1992). Alcohol problems and depression in later life: Development of two knowledge quizzes. *The Gerontologist, 32*, 175–183.

Pratt, M. (1999). Benefits of lifestyle activity vs. structured exercise. *Journal of the American Medical Association, 281*, 375–376.

Prestwood, K. M., Pilbeam, C. C., Burleson, J. A., Woodiel, F. N., Delmas, P. D., Deftos, L. J., & Raisz, L. G. (1994). The short-term effects of conjugated estrogen on bone turnover in older women. *Journal of Clinical Endocrinology and Metabolism, 79*, 366–371. 691–694.

Prevention Research Center. (1992). *Prevention index '92: A report on the nation's health.* Emmaus, PA: Rodale.

Prinz, P. (1987). Sleep disorders. In G. Maddox (Ed.), *The encyclopedia of aging* (pp. 615–617). New York: Springer.

Prohaska, T. R., Leventhal, E. A., Leventhal, H., & Keller, M. L. (1985). Health practices and illness cognition in young, middle-aged, and elderly adults. *Journal of Gerontology, 40,* 569–578.

Putney, N. M., & Bengston, V. L. (2001). Families, intergeneration relationships, and kinkeeping in midlife. In M.E. Lachman (Ed.), *Handbook of midlife development* (pp. 528–570).

Quill, T. E., Lo, B., & Brock, D. W. (1997). Palliative options of the last resort. *Journal of the American Medical Association, 278*, 2099–2104.

Quinby, N. (1985, October) On testing and teaching intelligence: A conversation with Robert Sternberg. *Educational Leadership,* pp. 50–53.

Quinn, J. F. (1993). Is early retirement an economic threat? *Generations, 17*(4), 10–14.

Rabbitt, P., Watson, P., Donlan, C., McInnes, L., Horan., M., Pendleton, N., Clague, J. (2002) Effects of death within 11 years on cognitive performance in old age. *Psychology and Aging 17*, 468–481.

Rampello, L., Cerasa, S., Alvano, A., Butta, V., Raffaele, R., Veccio, I., Cavallaro, T., Cimino, E., Incognito, T., Nicoletti, F. (2004). Dementia with

Lewy bodies: A review. *Archives of Gerontology and Geriatrics, 39*, 1–14.

Raphael, B. (1983). *The anatomy of bereavement.* New York: Basic Books.

Raven, J. C. (1983). *Raven progressive matrices test.* San Antonio, TX: Psychological Corp.

Ray, O. (2004). How the mind hurts and heals the body. *American Psychologist, 59*, 29–40.

Raymo, J.M., Liang, J., Sugisawa, H., Kobayashi, E., Sugihara, Y. (2004). Work at older ages in Japan: Variation by gender and employment status. *Journals of Gerontology: Series B: Psychological Sciences and Social Sciences, 59*(B), S154–S163.

Read, P. P. (1974). *Alive: The story of the Andes survivors.* New York: Lippincott.

Rebecca, M., Hefner, R., & Oleshansky, B. (1976). A model of sex-role transcendence. *Journal of Social Issues, 32*, 197–206.

Ree, M. J., & Earles, J. A. (1992). Intelligence is the best predictor of job performance. *Current Directions in Psychological Science, 1*(3), 86–89.

Ree, M. J., & Earles, J. A. (1993). g is to psychology what carbon is to chemistry: A reply to Sternberg and Wagner, McClelland, and Calfee. *Current Directions in Psychological Science, 2*(1), 11–12.

Regier, D. A., Boyd, J. H., Burke, J. D., Locke, B. Z., Rae, D. S., Myers, J. K., Kramer, M., Robins, L. N., George, L. K., Karno, M., & Locke, B. Z. (1988). One-month prevalence of mental disorders in the U.S.: Based on five epidemiologic catchment area sites. *Archives of General Psychiatry, 45*, 977–986.

Reid, J. D. (1995). Development in late life: Older lesbian and gay life. In A. R. D'Augelli & C. J. Patterson (Eds.), *Lesbian, gay and bisexual identities over the lifespan: Psychological perspectives* (pp. 215–240). New York: Oxford University Press.

Reijo, R., Alagappan, R. K., Patrizio, P., & Page, D. C. (1996). Severe oligozoospermia resulting from deletions of azoospermia factor gene on Y chromosome. *Lancet, 347*, 1290–1293.

Reis, H.T., & Patrick, B.C. (1996). Attachment and intimacy: Component process. In E. T. Higgins & A. Kruglanski (Eds.), *Social psychology: Handbook of basic principles* (pp. 523–563). New York: Guilford.

Rempel, J. (1985). Childless elderly: What are they missing? *Journal of Marriage and the Family, 47*(2), 343–348.

Rennie, J. (1994, June). Grading the gene tests. *Scientific American*, pp. 86–97.

Research to Prevent Blindness. (1994). *Progress report, 1994.* New York: Author.

Research Update: The more were learn, the more questions there are to be answered. (1995, Winter). *LINK* (Newsletter of Amyotrophic Lateral Sclerosis Association), p. 1–2.

Revicki, D., & Mitchell, J. (1990). Strain, social support, and mental health in rural elderly individuals. *Journal of Gerontology: Social Sciences, 45*, S267–274.

Rexroat, C., & Shehan, C. (1987). The family life cycle of spouses' time in housework. *Journal of Marriage and the Family, 49*, 737–750.

Reynolds, C. R. (1988, Winter). Race differences in intelligence: Why the controversy? *Mensa Research Journal*, pp. 4–7.

Rhodes, N. R., & McKenzie, E. B. (1998). Why do battered women stay? Three decades of research. *Aggression and Violent Behavior, 3*(4), 391–406.

Rhodes, S. R. (1983). Age-related differences in work attitudes and behaviors. A review and conceptual analysis. *Psychological Bulletin, 93*(2), 328–367.

Ribot, T. (1906). *Essays on the creative imagination.* London: Routledge & Kegan Paul.

Rice, G., Anderson, C., Risch, N., & Ebers, G. (1999). Male homosexuality: Absence of linkage to microsatellite markers at Xq28. *Science, 284*, 665–667.

Richardson, V. E. (1993). *Retirement counseling: A handbook for gerontology practitioners.* New York: Springer.

Richie, D. (1965). *The films of Akira Kurosawa.* Berkeley: University of California Press.

Riegel, K. F. (1977). History of psychological gerontology. In J. E. Birren & K. W. Schaie (Eds.), *Handbook of the psychology of aging* (pp. 70–102). New York: Van Nostrand Reinhold.

Riegel, K. F., & Riegel, R. M. (1972). Development, drop, and death. *Developmental Psychology, 6*, 309–316.

Rifkin, J. (1998, May 5). Creating the "perfect" human. *Chicago Sun-Times*, p. 29.

Riley, K.P. (1999). Assessment of dementia in the older adult. In P. A. Lichtenberg (Ed.), *Handbook of assessment in clinical gerontology*, pp. 134–166. Hoboken, NJ: John Wiley & Sons, Inc.

Riley, M. (1992). Aging in the twenty-first century. In Cutler, N. E., Gregg, D. W. & Lawton, M. P. (Eds.), *Aging, money, and life satisfaction: Aspects of financial gerontology,* p. 23-36.

Riley, M. W. (1994). Aging and society: Past, present, and future. *The Gerontologist, 34,* 436–444.

Rilke, R. M. (1984). The notebooks of Malte Laurids Brigge. In E. Schwarz (Ed.), *Rainer Maria Rilke: Prose and poetry* (pp. 12–13). New York: Continuum.

Rindfuss, R. R., & St. John, C. (1983). Social determinants of age at first birth. *Journal of Marriage and the Family, 45,* 553–565.

Rindfuss, R. R., Morgan, S. P., & Swicegood, G. (1988). *First births in America.* Berkeley: University of California Press.

Rix, S. E. (1994). Older workers: How do they measure up? (Pub. No. 9412). Washington, DC: AARP Public Policy Institute.

Roazen, P. (1976). *Erik H. Erikson; The power and limits of a vision.* New York: Macmillan.

Robbins, T. (1984). *Jitterbug perfume.* New York: Bantam.

Roberts, B. W., Helson, R., Klohnen, E.C. (2002). Personality development and growth in women across 30 years: Three perspectives. *Journal of Personality, 70(1),* 79–102.

Roberts, P., Papalia-Finlay, D., Davis, E. S., Blackburn, J., & Dellman, M. (1982). "No two fields ever grow grass the same way": Assessment of conservation abilities in the elderly. *International Journal of Aging and Human Development, 15(3),* 185–195.

Robins, L. N., Helzer, J. C., Weissman, M. M., Owaschel, H., Bruenberg, E., Burke, J. O., & Regier, D. A. (1984). Lifetime prevalence of specific psychiatric disorders in three sites. *Archives of General Psychiatry, 41,* 949–958.

Robinson, B., & Thurnher, M. (1981). Taking care of aged parents: A family cycle transition. *The Gerontologist, 19(6),* 586–593.

Robinson, L. C., & Blanton, P. W. (1993). Marital strengths in enduring marriages. *Family Relations, 42,* 38–45.

Rodehoffer, R. J., Gerstenblith, G., Becker, L. C., Fleg, J. L., Weisfeldt, M. L., & Lakatta, E. G. (1984). Exercise cardiac output is maintained with advancing age in healthy human subjects: Cardiac dilation and increased stroke volume compensate for a diminished heart rate. *Circulation, 69,* 203–213.

Rodin, J. & Ickovics, J. (1990). Women's health: Review and research agenda as we approach the 21st century. *American Psychologist, 45,* 1018–1034.

Rodin, J., Timko, C., & Harris, S. (1985). The construct of control: Biological and psychological correlates. *Annual Review of Gerontology and Geriatrics, 5,* 3–55.

Roediger, H. L. (1990). Implicit memory: Retention without remembering. *American Psychologist, 45,* 1043–1056.

Roediger, H. L. (1991). They read an article? A commentary on the everyday memory controversy. *American Psychologist, 46(1),* 37–38.

Roff, L. C., & Atherton, C. R. (1989). *Promoting successful aging.* Chicago: Nelson-Hall.

Rogers, W. A., & Fisk, A. D. (2000). Human factors, applied cognition, and aging. In F. I. Draik & T. A. Salthouse (Eds.), *The handbook of aging and cognition.* Mahwah, NJ: Lawrence Erlbaum Associates.

Rogoff, B., & Morelli, G. (1989). Perspectives on children's development from cultural psychology. *American Psychologist, 44(2),* 343–348.

Roosa, M. W. (1988). The effect of age in the transition to parenthood: Are delayed childbearers a unique group? *Family Relations, 37,* 322–328.

Rosen, D. R. et al. (1993). Mutations in Cu/Zn superoxide dismutase gene are associated with familial amyotrophic lateral sclerosis. *Nature, 362,* 59–62.

Rosen, M. I., Rigsby, M. O., Salahi, J. T., Ryan, C. E., & Cramer, J. A. (2004). Electronic monitoring and counseling to improve medication adherence. *Behaviour Research and Therapy, 42(4),* 409-422.

Rosenberg, L., Palmer, J. R., & Shapiro, S. (1990). Decline in the risk of myocardial infarction among women who stop smoking. *New England Journal of Medicine, 322,* 213–217.

Rosenbluth, S.C., & Steil, J.M. (1995). Predictors of intimacy for women in heterosexual and homosexual couples. *Journal of Social and Personal Relationships, 12(2),* 163–175.

Rosenburg, H. (in press). The elderly and the use of illicit drugs: Sociological and epidemiological considerations. *International Journal of Addictions.*

Rosenfeld, D. (1999). Identity work among lesbian and gay elderly. *Journal of Aging Studies, 13,* 121–144.

Rosenfeld, I. (2002, February 14). The silent vision thief. *Parade Magazine.*

Rosenthal, C. J., Martin-Matthews, A., & Matthews, S. H. (1996). Caught in the middle? Occupancy in multiple roles and help to parents in a national probability sample of Canadian adults. *Journal of Gerontology: Social Sciences, 51B,* S274–S283

Roses, A. D. (1994, September). *Apolipoprotein E affects Alzheimer's disease expression.* Paper presented at workshop on Alzheimer's Disease: Advances in Understanding and Treatment, Philadelphia.

Ross, C. E., Mirowsky, J., & Goldsteen, K. (1990). The impact of the family on health: A decade in review. *Journal of Marriage and the Family, 52,* 1059–1078.

Ross, H. G., Dalton, M. J., & Milgram, J. I. (1980, November). *Older adults' perceptions of closeness in sibling relationships.* Paper presented at the annual meeting of the Gerontological Society of America, San Diego.

Ross, L. (1977). The intuitive psychologist and his shortcomings. In L. Berkowitz (Ed.), *Advances in experimental social psychology* (Vol. 10, pp. 174–214). San Diego: Academic.

Ross, L., & Nisbett, R. E. (1991). *The person and the situation: Perspectives of social psychology.* New York: McGraw-Hill.

Rossi, A. S. (1980). Aging and parenthood in the middle years. In P. B. Baltes & O. G. Brim (Eds.), *Life-span development and behavior* (Vol. 3). New York: Academic.

Rossi, A. S., & Rossi, P. H. (1990). *Of human bonding: Parent-child relations across the life course.* New York: Aldine de Gruyter.

Rothenberg, K., Fuller, B., Rothstein, M., Duster, T., Kahn, M. J. E., Cunningham, R., Fine, B., Hudson, K., King, M. C., Murphy, P., Swergold, G., & Collins, F. (1997). Genetic information and the workplace: Legislative approaches and policy challenges. *Science, 275,* 1755–1757.

Rowe, J. W. et al. (1976). The effect of age on creatine clearance in men: A cross-sectional and longitudinal study. *Journal of Gerontology, 31,* 184–189.

Rowe, John W., & Kahn, Robert L. (1998). *Successful Aging.* New York: Random House.

Roybal, E. R. (1988). Mental health and aging. *American Psychologist, 43*(3), 184–189.

Ruberman, W., Weinblatt, E., Goldberg, J. D., & Chaudhary, B. S. (1984). Psychosocial influences on mortality after myocardial infarction. *New England Journal of Medicine, 311,* 552–559.

Rubin, K. H. (1973, August). *Decentration skills in institutionalized and noninstitutionalized elderly.* Paper presented at the annual meeting of the American Psychological Association.

Rubin, K. H., Attewell, P., Tierney, M., & Tumulo, P. (1973). Development of spatial egocentrism and conservation across the lifespan. *Developmental Psychology, 9*(3), 432.

Rubinstein, A. (1980). *My many years.* New York: Knopf.

Rubinstein, R. L., Alexander, B. B., Goodman, M., & Luborsky, M. (1991). Key relationships of never married, childless older women: A cultural analysis. *Journal of Gerontology: Social Sciences, 46,* S270–277.

Runco, M. A., & Albert, R. S. (Eds.). (1990). *Theories of creativity.* Newbury Park, CA: Sage.

Ryan, M. (1993, September 26). I couldn't bear the silence. *Parade,* p. 14.

Rybash, J. M., Hoyer, W. J., & Roodin, P. A. (1986). *Adult cognition and aging: Developmental changes in processing, knowing and thinking.* New York: Pergamon.

Ryff, C. D. (1989). In the eye of the beholder: Views of psychological well-being among middle-aged and older adults. *Psychology and Aging, 4*(2), 195–210.

Ryff, C.D., & Seltzer, M.M. (1995). Family relations and individual development in adulthood and aging. In R. Blieszner & V. Hilkevitch (Eds.), *Handbook of Aging and the Family* (pp. 95–113). Westport, CT: Greenwood Press.

Ryff, C. D., & Singer, B. (1998). Middle age and well-being. *Encyclopedia of Mental Health, 2,* 707–719.

Sabatelli, R. M., Meth, R. L., & Gavazzi, S. M. (1988). Factors mediating the adjustment to involuntary childlessness. *Family Relations, 37,* 338–343.

Sagan, C. (1977). *The dragons of Eden: Speculations on the evolution of human intelligence.* New York: Random House.

Sagan, C. (1988). Introduction. In S. W. Hawking, *A brief history of time: From the Big Bang to black holes* (pp. ix–x). New York: Bantam.

Sahyoun, N. R., Pratt, L. A., Lentzer, H., Dey, A., & Robinson, K. N. (2001). Trends in causes of death among the elderly. *Aging Trends,* No. 1. Hyattsville, MD: National Center for Health Statistics.

Sahyoun, N. R., Pratt, L. A., Lentzner, H., Dey, A., & Robinson, K. N. (2001). The changing profile of nursing home residents: 1985–1997. *Aging Trends,* No. 4. Hyattsville, MD: National Center for Health Statistics.

Salthouse, T. A. (1985). Anticipatory processing in transcription typing. *Journal of Applied Psychology, 70,* 264–271.

Salthouse, T. A. (1991). *Theoretical perspectives on cognitive aging.* Hillsdale, NJ: Erlbaum.

Salthouse, T. A., & Maurer, T. J. (1996). Aging, job performance, and career development. In J. E. Birren & K. W. Schaie (Eds.), *Handbook of the psychology of aging* (pp. 353–364). San Diego: Academic Press.

Salthouse, T. A., Kausler, D. H., & Saults, J. S. (1988). Utilization of path–analytic procedures to investigate the role of processing resources in cognitive aging. *Psychology and Aging, 3,* 158–166.

Sammartino, F. J. (1987, January). The effect of health on retirement. *Social Security Bulletin,* pp. 31–47.

Samuelsson, M., Radestad, L., & Segesten K. (2001). A waste of life: Fathers' experiences of losing a chld before birth. *Birth, 28,* 124–130.

Sanchez, C. (1992). Mental health issues: The elderly Hispanic. *Journal of Geriatric Psychiatry, 25,* 69–84.

Sanders, S., Laurendeau, M., & Bergeron, J. (1966). Aging and the concept of space: The conservation of surfaces. *Journal of Gerontology, 21,* 281–285.

Sansone, C., & Berg, C. A. (1993). Adapting to the environment across the life span: Different process or different inputs? *International Journal of Behavioral Development, 16,* 215–241.

Sapolsky, R. M. (1992). Stress and neuroendocrine changes during aging. *Generations, 16*(4), 35–38.

Sattler, J. M. (1988). *Assessment of children* (3rd ed.). San Diego: Author.

Sauer, M. V., Paulson, R. J., & Lobo, R. A. (1990). A preliminary report on oocyte donation extending reproductive potential to women over 40. *New England Journal of Medicine, 323,* 1157–1160.

Sauer, M. V., Paulson, R. J., & Lobo, R. A. (1993, March). *Pregnancy after age 50: Applying oocyte donation to women following natural menopause.* Paper presented at the 40th annual meeting of the Society for Gynecological Research, Toronto.

Saunders, J. (1981). A process of bereavement resolution: Uncoupled identity. *Western Journal of Nursing Research, 3,* 319–332.

Saxon, S. V., & Etton, M. J. (2002). *Physical change and aging.* New York: The Tiresias Press, Inc.

Scandinavian Simvastatin Survival Study Group. (1994). Randomized trial of cholesterol lowering in 4444 patients with coronary heart disease: The Scandinavian simvastatin survival study (45). *Lancet, 344,* 1383–1389.

Schacter, D. L. (1992). Understanding implicit memory: A cognitive neuroscience approach. *American Psychologist, 47,* 559–569.

Schafer, R. (1980). *Narrative action in psychoanalysis.* Worchester, MA: Clark University Press.

Schaie, K. W. (1965). A general model for the study of developmental problems. *Psychological Bulletin, 64,* 91–107.

Schaie, K. W. (1977–1978). Toward a stage theory of adult cognitive development. *Journal of Aging and Human Development, 8*(2), 129–138.

Schaie, K. W. (1978). External validity in the assessment of intellectual development in adulthood. *Journal of Gerontology, 33,* 696–701.

Schaie, K. W. (1979). The primary mental abilities in adulthood: An exploration in the development of psychometric intelligence. In P. B. Baltes & O. G. Brim (Eds.), *Life-span development and behavior* (Vol. 2, pp. 67–115). New York: Academic.

Schaie, K. W. (1983). The Seattle longitudinal study: A twenty-one-year investigation of psychometric intelligence. In K. W. Schaie (Ed.), *Longitudinal studies of adult personality development* (pp. 64–155). New York: Guilford.

Schaie, K. W. (1984). Midlife influences upon intellectual functioning in old age. *Journal of Behavioral Development, 7,* 463–478.

Schaie, K. W. (1988a). Ageism in psychological research. *American Psychologist, 43,* 179–183.

Schaie, K. W. (1988b). The delicate balance: Technology, intellectual competence, and normal aging. In G. Lesnoff-Caravaglia (Ed.), *Aging in a technical society* (Vol. 7, pp. 155–166). New York: Human Sciences Press.

Schaie, K. W. (1989). The hazards of cognitive aging. *The Gerontologist, 29*(4), 484–493.

Schaie, K. W. (1990). Intellectual development in adulthood. In J. E. Birren & K. W. Schaie (Eds.), *Handbook of the psychology of aging* (pp. 291–309). San Diego: Academic.

Schaie, K. W. (1994). The course of adult intellectual development. *American Psychologist, 49*(4), 304–313.

Schaie, K. W. (2000). The impact of longitudinal studies on understanding development from young adulthood to old age. *International Journal of Behavioral Development, 24*(3), 257–266.

Schaie, K. W. (2001). *Intelligence.* In G. L. Maddox (Ed.), *Encyclopedia of Aging* (3rd ed.). New York: Springer.

Schaie, K.W. (2005). *Developmental influences on adult intelligence*: The Seattle Longitudinal Study. New York: Oxford University Press.

Schaie, K. W., & Baltes, P. B. (1977). Some faith helps to see the forest: A final comment on the Horn-Donaldson myth of the Baltes-Schaie position on adult intelligence. *American Psychologist, 32,* 1118–1120.

Schaie, K. W., & Hertzog, C. (1983). Fourteen-year cohort sequential analyses of adult intellectual development. *Developmental Psychology, 19*(4), 531–543.

Schaie, K. W., & Hertzog, C. (1986). Toward a comprehensive model of adult intellectual development: Contributions of the Seattle Longitudinal Study. In R. J. Sternberg (Ed.), *Advances in human intelligence* (Vol. 3, pp. 79–118). Hillsdale, NJ: Erlbaum.

Schaie, K. W., & Strother, C. (1968). A cross-sequential study of age changes in cognitive behavior. *Psychological Bulletin, 70,* 671–680.

Schaie, K. W., & Willis, S. L. (1986). Can decline in adult intellectual functioning be reversed? *Developmental Psychology, 22,* 223–232.

Schaie, K. W., & Willis, S. L. (1991). Adult personality and psychomotor performance: Cross-sectional and longitudinal analysis. *Journal of Gerontology: Psychological Sciences, 46,* P275–284.

Schaie, K. W., & Willis, S. L. (1996). Psychometric intelligence and aging. In F. Blanchard-Fields & T. M. Hess (Eds.), *Perspectives on cognitive change in adulthood and aging.* New York: McGraw-Hill.

Schaie, K. W., & Willis, S. L. (2000). A stage theory model of adult cognitive development revisited. In B. Rubinstein, M. Moss, & M. Kleban (Eds.), *The many dimensions of aging: Essays in honor of M. Powell Lawton* (pp. 173–191). New York: Springer.

Schardt, D. (1995, June). For men only. *Nutrition Action Health Letter, 22*(5), 4–7.

Scharlach, A. E. (1987). Relieving feelings of strain among women with elderly mothers. *Psychology and Aging, 2*(1), 9–13.

Scharlach, A.E. (1991). Factors associated with filial grief following the death of an elderly parent.

Scharlach, A. E., & Fredriksen, K. I. (1993). Reactions to the death of a parent during midlife. *Omega, 27,* 307–319. *American Journal of Orthopsychiatry, 61,* 307–313.

Schellenberg, G. D., Bird, T., Wijsman, E., et al. (1992). Genetic linkage evidence for a familial Alzheimer's disease locus on chromosome 14. *Science, 258,* 668–671.

Scherer, M. (1985, January). How many ways is a child intelligent? *Instructor,* pp. 32–35.

Schick, F. L. (Ed.). (1986). *Statistical handbook on aging Americans.* Phoenix: Oryx.

Schieber, F. & Baldwin, C. L. (1996). Vision, audition, and aging research. In F. Blanchard-Fields & T. M. Hess (Eds.), *Perspectives on cognitive change in adulthood and aging* (pp. 122–162). New York: McGraw Hill.

Schieffelin, E. (1976). The sorrow of the lonely and the burning of the dancers. New York: St. Martin's.

Schiffman, S. S. (1995). In G. Maddox (Ed.), *The encyclopedia of aging* (pp. 920–922). New York: Springer.

Schlossberg, N. K. (1987, May). Taking the mystery out of change. *Psychology Today,* pp. 74–75.

Schmeck, H. M. (1983, March 22). U.S. panel calls for patients' right to end life. *New York Times,* pp. A1, C7.

Schmeck, H. M. (1995, June 24). Jonas Salk, whose polio drug altered life in U.S., dies at 80. *New York Times*, pp. A1, A10.

Schmidt, W. E. (1988, April 6). Graying of America prompts new highway safety efforts. *New York Times*, pp. A1, A17.

Schneider, B. A., & Pichora-Fuller, M. K. (2000). Implications of perceptual deterioration for cognitive aging research. In F. I. M. Craik & T. A. Salthouse (Eds.), *The handbook of aging and cognition* (pp. 155–219). Hillsdale, NJ: Lawrence Erlbaum Associates.

Schneider, E. L. (1992). Biological theories of aging. *Generations*, 16(4), 7–10.

Schneider, E. L., & Guralnik, J. M. (1990). The aging of America: Impact on health care costs. *Journal of the American Medical Association*, 263(17), 2335–2340.

Schneiderman, L.J., Gilmer, T., Teetze, H.D., Dugan, D.O, Blustein, J., Cranford, R., Briggs, K.B., Komatsu, G.I., Goodman-Crews, P., Cohn, F., Young, E.W.D. (2003). Effects of ethics consultations on nonbeneficial life-sustaining treatments in the intensive care setting: A randomized controlled trial. *Journal of the American Medical Association*, 290, 1166–1172.

Schoen, R. (1992). First unions and the stability of first marriages. *Journal of Marriage and the Family*, 54, 281–284.

Schoenborn, C., Adams, P., Barnes, P., Vickerie, L., & Schiller, J. (2004). Health behaviors of adults: United States, 1999–2001. National Center for Health Statistics. Vital Health Statistics. 10(219).

Schonberg, H. C. (1992). *Horowitz: His life and music*. New York: Simon & Schuster.

Schonfield, D. (1974). Translations in gerontology–from lab to life: Utilizing information. *American Psychologist*, 29, 228–236.

Schonfield, D., & Robertson, E. A. (1968). The coding and sorting of digits and symbols by an elderly sample. *Journal of Gerontology*, 23, 318–323.

Schulz, J. H. (1993a). Why the "welfare state"' will continue to spread around the world. *Generations*, 17(4).

Schulz, J. H. (1993b). Introduction: And then Chicken Little said, "The sky is falling!" *Generations*, 17(4), 5.

Schulz, J. H. (1993c). Should developing countries copy Chile's pension system? *Generations*, 17(4), 70–72.

Schulz, R. (1978). *The psychology of death, dying, and bereavement*. Reading, MA: Addison-Wesley.

Schulz, R. (1985). Emotion and affect. In J. E. Birren & K. W. Schaie (Eds.), *Handbook of the psychology of aging* (2nd ed., pp. 531–543). New York: Van Nostrand Reinhold.

Schulz, R., & Heckhausen, J. (1996). A lifespan model of successful aging. *American Psychologist*, 51, 702–714.

Schumacher, M. (1991, June). Louise Erdrich and Michael Dorris: A marriage of minds. *Writer's Digest*, pp. 28–31, 59.

Schwartz, J. (2005, March 21). New openness in deciding when and how to die. *New York Times*, P.A1.

Scogin, F., & Bienias, J. L. (1988). A three-year follow-up of older adult participants in a memory-skills training program. *Psychology and Aging*, 3, 334–337.

Scott, C. (1993). *Decade of the executive woman*. New York: Korn/Ferry International.

Scott, J. (1998). Changing attitudes to sexual morality: A cross-cultural comparison. *Sociology*, 32, 815–845.

Scott, J. P., & Roberto, K. A. (1981, October). *Sibling relationships in late life*. Paper presented at the annual meeting of the National Council on Family Relations, Milwaukee.

Scribner, S. (1979). Modes of thinking and ways of speaking: Culture and logic reconsidered. In R. O. Freedle (Ed.), *New directions in discourse processing* (Vol. 2). Norwood, NJ: Ablex.

Seccombe, K. (1991). Assessing the costs and benefits of children: Gender comparisons among childfree husbands and wives. *Journal of Marriage and the Family*, 53, 191–202.

Secter, B. (1995, January 1). Some stats count for nothing: Surveys often produce "data"from thin air. *Chicago Sun-Times*, p. 17.

Sedlak, A. J., & Broadhurst, D. D. (1996). *Executive summary of the third national incidence study of child abuse and neglect* (NIS–3). Washington, DC: U.S. Department of Health and Human Services.

Seeman, T. E., Dubin, L. F., Seeman, M. (2003). Religiosity/spirituality and health: A critical review of the evidence for biological pathways. *American Psychologist, 58*(1), 53–63.

Seidler, R., Neinhaus, A., Bernhardt, T., Kauppinen, T., Elo, A.L., & Frolich, L. (2004). Psychological work factors and dementia. *Occupational and Environmental Medicine, 61,* 962–971.

Selkoe, D. J. (1992). Aging brain, aging mind. *Scientific American, 267,* 135–142.

Sellers, E.M. (1998). Pharmogenetics and ethnoracial differences in smoking. *Journal of the American Medical Association, 280,* 179–180.

Seltzer, J. A. (2000). Families formed outside of marriage. *Journal of Marriage and the Family, 62,* 1247–1268.

Seltzer, J. A., & Garfinkel, I. (1990). Inequality in divorce settlements: An investigation of property settlements and child support awards. *Social Science Research, 19,* 82–111.

Selye, H. (Ed.) (1980). *Selye's guide to stress research* (Vol.1). New York: Van Nostrand Reinhold.

Seybold, K.S. & Hill, P.C. (2001). The role of religion and spirituality in mental and physical health. *Current Directions in Psychological Science, 10,* 21–24.

Shadish, W.R., Cook, T. D., Campbell, D.T. (2002). *Experimental and quasi-experimental designs for generalized causal inference.* Boston, MA: Houghton Mifflin, Co.

Shapiro, P. (1994, November). My house is your house: Advance planning can ease the way when parents move in with adult kids. *AARP Bulletin,* p. 2.

Sharf, R. S. (1992). *Applying career development theory to counseling.* Pacific Grove, CA: Brooks/Cole Publishing Company.

Sharp, D., Cole, M., & Lave, C. (1978). *Education and cognitive development: The evidence from experimental research.* Chicago: University of Chicago Press.

Shaw, M. P. (1989). The eureka process: A structure for the creative experience in science and engineering. *Creativity Research Journal, 2,* 286–298.

Shaw, M. P. (1992a). Affective components of scientific creativity. In M. P. Shaw & M. A. Runco (Eds.), *Creativity and affect.* Norwood, NJ: Ablex.

Shaw, M. P. (1992b). Reason, emotionality, and creative thinking. *Humanistic Judaism, 20*(4), 42–44.

Sheehy, G. (1992). *The silent passage: Menopause.* New York: Random House.

Sheehy, G. (1995). *New passages: Mapping your life across time.* New York: Random House.

Sherman, E. (1991). *Reminiscence and the self in old age.* New York: Springer.

Sherman, E. (1993). Mental health and successful adaptation in late life. *Generations, 17*(1), 43–46.

Sherman, E., & Peak, T. (1991). Patterns of reminiscence and the assessment of late life adjustment. *Gerontological Social Work, 16,* 59–74.

Sherman, L. W., & Berk, R. A. (1984, April). The Minneapolis domestic violence experiment. *Police Foundation Reports,* pp. 1–8.

Sherman, L. W., & Cohn, E. G. (1989). The impact of research on legal policy: The Minneapolis domestic violence experiment. *Law and Society Review,* pp. 118–144.

Shibusawa, T., Kodaka, M., Iwano, S., Kaizu, K. (2005). Interventions for elder abuse and neglect with frail elders in Japan. *Brief Treatment and Crisis Intervention, 5*(2), 203–211.

Shier, A. (1992). *Oh, Utopia, how we miss you.* Livonia, MI: Mini-Lectures Press.

Shimamura, A. P., Janowsky, J. S., & Squire, L. R. (1991). What is the role of frontal lobe damage in memory disorders? In H. D. Levine, H. M. Eisenberg, & A. L. Benton (Eds.), *Frontal lobe functioning and dysfunction* (pp. 173–195). New York: Oxford University Press.

Shipp, E. R. (1988, February 4). Decision could hinder surrogacy across nation. *New York Times,* p. B6.

Siano, B. (1993, July–August). False history, gas chambers, blue smoke, and cracked mirrors. *The Humanist,* pp. 31–33.

Siegler, I., McCarty, S. M., & Logue, P. E. (1982). Wechsler Memory Scale scores, selective attribution, and distance from death. *Journal of Gerontology, 37,* 176–181.

Siegler, R. S. (1998). *Children's thinking* (3rd ed.). Upper Saddle River, NJ: Prentice Hall.

Silverstein, M., & Long, J. D. (1998). Trajectories of grandparents' perceived solidarity with adult grandchildren: A growth curve analysis over 23 years. *Journal of Marriage and the Family, 60,* 912–923.

Silverstein, M., Giarrusso, R., & Bengston, V. L. (1998). Intergenerational solidarity and the grandparent role. In M. Szinovacz (Ed.), *Handbook on grandparenthood* (pp. 144–158). Westport, CT: Greenwood.

Simons, M. (1993, February 10). Dutch parliament approves law permitting euthanasia. *New York Times,* p. A10.

Simonton, D. K. (1985). Quality, quantity, and age: The careers of 10 distinguished psychologists. *International Journal of Aging and Human Development, 21,* 241–254.

Simonton, D. K. (1989). The swan-song phenomenon: Last-works effects for 172 classical composers. *Psychology and Aging, 4,* 42–47.

Simonton, D. K. (1990). Creativity and wisdom in aging. In J. E. Birren & K. W. Schaie (Eds.), *Handbook of the psychology of aging* (pp. 320–329). New York: Academic.

Simonton, D.K. (1998). Career paths and creative lives: A theoretical perspective on late life potential. In C. E. Adams-Price (Ed.), *Creativity and Successful Aging.* New York: Springer.

Simonton, D.K. (2000a). Creative development as acquired expertise: Theoretical issues and an empirical test. *Developmental Review, 20,* 283–318.

Simonton, D.K. (2000b). Creativity: Cognitive, personal, developmental and social aspects. *American Psychologist, 55*(1), 151–158.

Simpson, K.H. (1996). Alternatives to physician-assisted suicide. *Humanistic Judaism, 24*(4), 21–23.

Sinclair, A.J. (2001). Diabetes mellitus. In G.L. Maddox (Ed.) *The encyclopedia of aging.* (3rd ed.). New York: Springer Publishing Company.

Singer, P. A. (1988, June 1). Should doctors kill patients? *Canadian Medical Association Journal, 138,* 1000–1001.

Singer, T., Verhaeghen, P., Ghisletta, P., Lindernberger, U., Baltesm P. B. (2003). The fate of cognition in very old age: Six-year longitudinal findings in the Berlin Aging Study. *Psychology and Aging, 18*(2), 318–331.

Sinnott, J. D. (1984). Postformal reasoning: The relativistic stage. In M. L. Commons, F. A. Richards, & C. Armon (Eds.), *Beyond formal operations: Late adolescence and adult cognitive development* (pp. 357–380). New York: Praeger.

Sinnott, J. D. (1989). Prospective memory and aging: Memory as adaptive action. In L. W. Poon, D. C. Rubin, & B. A. Wilson (Eds.), *Everyday cognition in adulthood and old age* (pp. 352–372). New York: Cambridge University Press.

Sinnot, J. D. (1989a). A model for solution of ill-structured problems: Implications for everyday and abstract problem solving. In J. D. Sinnot (Ed.), *Everyday problem solving: Theory and applications* (pp. 72–99). New York: Praeger.

Sinnnot, J. D. (1989b). Life-span relativistic postformal thought: Methodology and data from everyday problem-solving studies. In M. L. Commons, J. D. Sinnot, F. A. Richards, & C. Armon (Eds.), *Adult development: Vol 1. Comparison and application of developmental models* (pp. 239–278). New York: Praeger.

Sinnot, J. D. (1991). Limits to problem solving: Emotion, intention, goal clarity, health and other factors in postformal thought. In J. D. Sinnot & J. C. Cavanaugh (Eds.), *Bridging paradigms: Positive development in adulthood and cognitive aging* (pp. 169–202). New York: Praeger.

Sinnot, J. D. (1994). The relationship of postformal thought, adult learning, and lifespan development. In J. D. Sinnot (Ed.), *Interdisciplinary handbook of adult lifespan learning* (pp. 105–119). Westport, CT: Greenwood Press.

Sinnot, J. D. (1996). The developmental approach: Postformal thought as adaptive intelligence. In F. Blanchard-Fields & T. M. Hess (Eds.), *Perspectives on cognitive change in adulthood and aging* (pp. 358–383.). New York: McGraw-Hill.

Sinnot, J. D. (1998). *The development of logic in adulthood: Postformal thought and its applications.* New York: Plenum.

Sinnot, J. D. (2003). Postformal thought and adult development. In J. Demick and C. Andreoletto

(Eds.), *Handbook of adult development*. New York: Plenum Press.

Sitarz, D. (1990). *Divorce yourself*. Carbondale, IL: Nova.

Skaff, M. M., & Pearlin, L. I. (1992). Caregiving: Role engulfment and the loss of self. *The Gerontologist, 32*(5), 656–664.

Sleep: From apnea to zzzz's. (1995, March). *University of California at Berkeley Wellness Letter*, pp. 4–5.

Sloan, R. P., & Bagiella, E. (2002). Claims about religious involvement and health outcomes. *Annals of Behavioral Medicine, 24*, 14–21.

Small, B. J., Fratiglioni, L., von Strauss, E., Backman, L. (2003). Terminal decline and cognitive performance in very old age: Does cause of death matter? *Psychology and Aging, 18*(2), 193–202.

Small, G. W., Rabins, P. V., Barry, P. P., Buckholtz, N. S., DeKosky, S. T., Ferris, S. H., Finkel, S. I., Gwyther, L. P., Khachaturian, Z. S., Lebowitz, B. D., McRae, T. D., Morris, J. C., Oakley, F., Schneider, L. S., Streim, J. E., Sunderland, T., Teri, L. A., & Tune, L. E. (1997). Diagnosis and treatment of Alzheimer Disease and related disorders: Consensus statement of the American Association for Geriatric Psychiatry, the Alzheimer's Association, and the American Geriatrics Society. *Journal of the American Medical Society, 278*, 1363–1371.

Smedley, B.D., Stith, A.Y., & Nelson, A.R. (Eds.). (2002). Unequal treatment: Confronting racial and ethnic disparities in healthcare. Washington, DC: National Academy Press.

Smith, A. D., & Earles, J. L. (1996). Memory changes in normal aging. In F. Blanchard-Fields & T. M. Hess (Eds.), *Perspectives on cognitive change in adulthood and aging* (pp. 165–191). New York: McGraw-Hill.

Smith, D. (2003). The older population in the United States: March 2002. U.S. Census Bureau Current Population Reports, P20-546. Washington, DC.

Smith, D. W., & Brodzinsky, D. M. (1994). Stress and coping in adopted children: A developmental study. *Journal of Clinical Child Psychology, 23*(1), 91–99.

Smith, J., & Baltes, P. B. (1990). Wisdom-related knowledge: Age/cohort differences in response to life planning problems. *Developmental Psychology, 26*(3), 494–505.

Smith, J. P. (2005). Unraveling the SES-health connection. *Aging, Health and Public Policy, 30*, 108–132.

Smith, K. (2002). Who's minding the kids? Child care arrangements: Spring 1997. *Current Population Reports*, pp. 70–86. Washington, DC: U.S. Census Bureau.

Smith, K. E., & Bachu, A. (1999). *Women's labor force attachment patterns and maternity leave: A review of the literature. Population Division Working Paper No. 32*. Washington, DC: U.S. Census Bureau.

Smith, R. B., & Brown, R. A. (1997). The impact of social support on gay male couples. *Journal of Homosexuality, 33*, 39–61.

Smith, T. (1999). *The emerging 21st-century American family*. Chicago: National Opinion Research Center, University of Chicago.

Smith, T. W. (1994). *The demography of sexual behavior*. Menlo Park, CA: Henry J. Kaiser Family Foundation.

Smith, T. W. (1995). *Holocaust denial: What the survey data reveal*. New York: American Jewish Committee, Institute of Human Relations.

Smyer, M. A., & Qualls, S. H. (1999). *Aging and mental health*. Massachusetts: Blackwell Publishers.

Snarey, J. R. (1985). Cross-cultural universality of social-moral development: A critical review of Kohlbergian research. *Psychological Bulletin, 97*, 202–232.

Snowdon, J. (2001). Is depression more prevalent in old age? *Australian and New Zealand Journal of Psychiatry, 35*, 782–787.

Snyder, C. J., & Barrett, G. V. (1988). The Age Discrimination in Employment Act: A review of court decisions. *Experimental Aging Research, 14*, 3–47.

Snyder, M. (1987). *Public appearance/private realities: The psychology of self-monitoring*. New York: Freeman.

Snyderman, M., & Rothman, S. (1987). Survey of expert opinion on intelligence and aptitude testing. *American Psychologist, 42*, 137–144.

Society for Assisted Reproductive Technology, & the American Society for Reproductive Medicine. (2002). Assisted reproductive technology in the

United States: 1998 results generated from the American Society for Reproductive Medicine/ Society for Assisted Reproductive Technology Registry. *Fertility and Sterility, 77*(1), 18–31.

Society for Assisted Reproductive Technology, & the American Fertility Society. (1993). Assisted reproductive technology in the United States and Canada: 1991 results from the Society for Assisted Reproductive Technology generated from the American Fertility Society Registry. *Fertility, 59,* 956–962.

Solomon, M. (1993). Report of survey of doctors and nurses about treatment of terminally ill patients. *American Journal of Public Health, 83*(1), 23–25.

Solomon, P. R., Pomerleau, D., Bennett, L., James, J., & Morse, D. L. (1989). Acquisition of the classically conditioned eyeblink response in humans over the life span. *Psychology and Aging, 4*(1), 34–41.

Spearman, C. E. (1927). *The abilities of man.* New York: Macmillan.

Spearman, C. E. (1930). *Creative mind.* Cambridge: Cambridge University Press.

Spence, A. P. (1989). *Biology of human aging.* Englewood Cliffs, NJ: Prentice-Hall.

Spence, J. T. (1993). Women, men and society. In Oskamp, S., & Costanzo, M. (Eds.), *Gender issues in contemporary society,* p. 3-17. Thousand Oaks, CA: Sage Publications.

Spilich, G. W., June, L., & Renner, J. (1992). Cigarette smoking and cognitive performance. *British Journal of Addiction, 87,* 1313–1326.

Spirduso, W. W., & MacRae, P. G. (1990). Motor performance and aging. In J. E. Birren & K. W. Schaie (Eds.), *Psychology of aging* (3rd ed., pp. 183–200). New York: Academic.

Spitze, G., & Miner, S. (1992). Gender differences in adult child contact among elderly black parents. *The Gerontologist, 32,* 213–218.

Spoto, D. (1992). *Laurence Olivier: A biography.* New York: Harper Collins.

Spoto, D. (1997). *Notorious: The life of Ingrid Bergman.* New York: Harper Collins.

Sprott, R. L., & Roth, G. S. (1992). Biomarkers of aging: Can we predict individual life span? *Generations, 16,* 11–14.

Spurlock, J. (1990). Single women. In J. Spurlock & C. B. Robinowitz (Eds.), *Women's progress:*

Promises and problems (pp. 23–33). Washington, DC: American Psychiatric Association.

Squire, L. R. (1992). Memory and the hippocampus: A synthesis of findings with rats, monkeys, and humans. *Psychological Review, 99,* 195–231.

Squire, L. R. (1994). Declarative and nondeclarative memory: Multiple brain systems supporting learning and memory. In D. L. Schacter & E. Tulving (Eds.), *Memory systems 1994* (pp. 203–232). Cambridge, MA: MIT Press.

St. George-Hyslop, P. H., Tanzi, R. E., Polinsky, et al. (1987). The genetic defect causing familial Alzheimer's disease maps on chromosome 21. *Science, 235,* 885–890.

Stadtman, E. R. (1992). Protein oxidation and aging. *Science, 257,* 1220–1224.

Staines, G. L. (1980). Spillover versus compensation: A review of the literature on the relationship between work and nonwork. *Human Relations, 33,* 111–129.

Stanford, E. P., & Du Bois, B. C. (1992). Gender and ethnicity patterns. In J. E. Birren, R. B. Sloane, & G. D. Cohen (Eds.), *Handbook of mental health and aging* (pp. 99–119). San Diego: Academic.

Starkweather, E. K. (1976). Creativity research instruments designed for use with preschool children. In A. M. Biondi & S. J. Parnes (Eds.), *Assessing creative growth: The tests–Book 1* (pp. 79–90). Buffalo, NY: Creative Education Foundation.

Starr, B. D., & Weiner, M. B. (1981). *The Starr-Weiner report on sex and sexuality in the mature years.* New York: Stein & Day.

Statistics Canada. (1996). 1996 Census Nation tables [Online]. Available: http://www.statcan.ca/english/Pgdb/People/Families/famil5a.html.

Staudinger, U. M., & Bluck, S. (2001). A view of midlife development from life span theory. In M. E. Lachman (Ed.), *Handbook of midlife development* (pp. 3–39). New York: Wiley.

Staudinger, U. M., Smith, J., & Baltes, P. B. (1992). Wisdom-related knowledge in a life review task: Age differences and the role of professional specialization. *Psychology and Aging, 7,* 271–281.

Steinbach, U. (1992). Social networks, institutionalization, and mortality among elderly people in the United States. *Journal of Gerontology: Social Sciences, 47*(4), S183–190.

Steinberg, L., & Silverberg, S. B. (1987). Influences on marital satisfaction during the middle stages of the family life cycle. *Journal of Marriage and the Family, 49*, 751–760.

Steinberg, S., Javitt, J. C., et al. (1993). The content and cost of cataract surgery. *Archives of Ophthalmology, 111*, 1041–1049.

Stengel, R. (1994, May 9). The making of a leader. *Time*, pp. 36–38.

Stephens, M. P., & Franks, M. M. (1999). Parent care in the context of women's multiple roles. *Current Directions in Psychological Science, 8*(5), 149–152.

Stephens, M.A.P., Franks, M., & Townsend, A.L. (1994). Stress and rewards in women's multiple roles: The case of women in the middle. *Psychology and Aging, 9*(1), 45–52.

Stern, M. B. (1950). *Louisa May Alcott*. Norman: University of Oklahoma Press.

Sternbach, H. (1998). Age-associated testosterone decline in men: Clinical issues for psychiatry. *American Journal of Psychiatry, 155*, 1310-1318.

Sternberg, R. J. (1985a). *Beyond IQ: A triarchic theory of human intelligence*. New York: Cambridge University Press.

Sternberg, R. J. (1985b, August). *A triangular theory of love*. Paper presented at the annual meeting of the American Psychological Association, Los Angeles.

Sternberg, R. J. (1986). *Intelligence applied: Understanding and increasing your intellectual skills*. San Diego: Harcourt Brace.

Sternberg, R. J. (1987, September 23). The uses and misuses of intelligence testing: Misunderstanding meaning, users overrely on scores. *Education Week*, pp. 28, 22.

Sternberg, R. J. (1990). Wisdom and its relations to intelligence and creativity. In R. J. Sternberg (Ed.), *Wisdom: Its nature, origins, and development* (pp. 142–159). Cambridge: Cambridge University Press.

Sternberg, R. J. (1995). A broad view of intelligence. *Consulting Psychology Journal: Practice and Research, 55*(3), 139–154.

Sternberg, R. J. (1997). The concept of intelligence and its role in lifelong learning and success. *American Psychologist, 52*, 1030-1037.

Sternberg, R. J. (2003a). Our research program validating the triarchic theory of successful intelligence: Reply to Gottsfredson. *Intelligence, 31*, 399-413.

Sternberg, R. J. (2003b). *Wisdom, intelligence, and creativity synthesized*. Cambridge: Cambridge University Press.

Sternberg, R. J., & Barnes, M. L. (1985). Real and ideal other in romantic relationships: Is four a crowd? *Journal of Personality and Social Psychology, 49*, 1586–1608.

Sternberg, R. J., & Detterman, D. K. (1986). *What is intelligence?* Norwood, NJ: Ablex.

Sternberg, R. J., & Grajek, S. (1984). The nature of love. *Journal of Personality and Social Psychology, 47*, 312–329.

Sternberg, R. J., & Horvath, J. A. (1998). Cognitive conceptions of expertise and their relations to giftedness. In R. C. Friedman & K. B. Rogers (Eds.), *Talent in context: Historical and social perspectives on giftedness* (pp. 177–191).

Sternberg, R. J., & Lubart, T. I. (1995). *Defying the crowd: Cultivating creativity in a culture of conformity*. New York: Free Press.

Sternberg, R.J. & Lubart, T. I. (2001). Wisdom and creativity. In J. E. Birren, & K. W. Scheia (Eds.), *Handbook of the psychology of aging*, p. 500–522. San Diego, CA: Academic Press.

Sternberg, R. J., & Wagner, R. K. (1993). The g-centric view of intelligence and job performance is wrong. *Current Directions in Psychological Science, 2*(1), 1–4.

Sterns, H. L., & Gray, J. H. (1999). Work, leisure, and retirement. In J. Cavanaugh & S. Whitbourne (Eds.), *Gerontology* (pp. 355–390). Oxford University Press.

Sterns, H. L., & Huyck, M. H. (2001). Midlife and work. In M. E. Lachmann (Ed.), *Handbook of midlife development* (pp. 447–486). New York: Wiley.

Sterns, H. L., & Kaplan, J. (2003). Self-management of career and retirement. In G. A. Adams & T. A. Beehr (Eds.), *Retirement: Reasons, processes, and results* (pp. 188–213). New York: Springer Publishing.

Sterns, H. L., & Miklos, S. M. (1995). The aging worker in a changing environment: Organizational and individual issues. *Journal of Vocational Behavior, 47*, 248–268.

Sterns, H. L., & Sterns, A.A. (1995). Health and the employment capability of older Americans. In

S. A. Bass, (Ed.), *Older and active: How Americans over 55 are contributing to society.* Chelsea, MI: Yale University Press.

Sterns, H. L., Barrett, G. V., & Alexander, R. A. (1985). Accidents and the aging individual. In J. E. Birren & K. W. Schaie (Eds.), *Handbook of the psychology of aging* (2nd ed., pp. 703–724). New York: Van Nostrand Reinhold.

Sterns, H. L., Junkins, M. P., & Bayer, J. (2001). Work and retirement. In B. R. Bonder & M. B. Wagner (Eds.), *Functional performance in older adults* (2nd ed., pp. 179–195). Philadelphia: F. A. Davis Company.

Sterns, H. L., Matheson, N. K., & Park, L. S. (1997). Work and retirement. In K. Ferrar (Ed.), *Gerontology: Gerontology Perspectives and issues* (2nd ed.), pp. 171–192. New York: Springer.

Sterns, H.L., Doverspike, D., & Lax, G.A. (2005). The Age Discrimination in Employment Act. In F. J. Landy (Ed.), *Employment discrimination litigation: Behavioral, quantitative and legal perspectives.* San Francisco, CA: Jossey-Bass.

Stevens, J. C. (1992). Aging and spatial activity of touch. *Journal of Gerontology and Psychological Sciences, 47*(1), 35–40.

Stevens, J. C., Cain, W. S., Demarque, A., & Ruthruff, A. M. (1991). On the discrimination of missing ingredients: Aging and salt flavor. *Appetite, 16,* 129–140.

Stevens, J. C., Cruz, L. A., Hoffman, J. M., & Patterson, M. Q. (1995). Taste sensitivity and aging: High incidence of decline revealed by repeated threshold measures. *Chemical Senses, 20,* 451–459.

Stevens, R. (1983). *Erik Erikson: An introduction.* New York: St. Martin's.

Stewart, M. A., & Olds, S. W. (1973). *Raising a hyperactive child.* New York: Harper & Row.

Sticht, T. G., & McDonald, B. A. (1990). Teach the mother and reach the child: Literacy across generations—literacy lessons. Geneva: International Bureau of Education.

Stillion, J. M. (2005). Understanding the end of life: An overview. In J. L, Werth, & D. Blevins (Eds.), *Psychosocial issues near the end of life: A resource for professional care providers.* Washington, DC: American Psychological Association.

Stine-Morrow, E. A., & Miller, L. M. (1999). Basic cognitive processes. In J. C. Cavanaugh and S. K. Whitbourne (Eds.), *Gerontology: An interdisciplinary perspective* (pp. 186–212). New York: Oxford University Press.

Stoppard, M. (1999). *HRT: Hormone Replacement Therapy.* New York: DK Publishing, Inc.

Storandt, M. (1976). Speed and coding effects in relation to age and ability level. *Developmental Psychology, 12,* 177–178.

Straus, M. A., & Stewart, J. H. (1999). Corporal punishment by American parents: National data on prevalence, chronicity, severity, and duration, in relation to child and family characteristics. *Clinical Child and Family Psychology Review, 2*(2), 55–70.

Strawbridge, W. J., & Wallhagen, M. I. (1991). Impact of family conflict on adult child caregivers. *The Gerontologist, 31*(6), 770–777.

Stroebe, M., Gergen, M. M., Gergen, K. J., & Stroebe, W. (1992). Broken hearts or broken bonds: Love and death in historical perspective. *American Psychologist, 47*(10), 1205–1212.

Strom, R., Collinsworth, P., Strom, S., & Griswold, D. (1992–1993). Strengths and needs of black grandparents. *International Journal of Aging and Human Development, 36,255–268.*

Strong, M. (1988). *Mainstay.* Boston: Little, Brown.

Strube, M. J., & Barbour, L. S. (1984). Factors related to the decision to leave an abusive relationship. *Journal of Marriage and the Family, 46,* 837–844.

Stuck, A. E., Egger, M., Hammer, A., Minder, C. E., & Beck, J. C. (2002). Home visits to prevent nursing home admission and functional decline in elderly people. *Journal of the American Medical Association, 287,* 1022–1028.

Stuen, C., & Faye, E. (2003). Vision loss: Normal and not normal changes among older adults. *Generations,* Spring.

Substance Abuse and Mental Health Services Administration (SAMHSA). Substance use among older adults: 2002 and 2003 update. [Online]. Available: http://oas.samhsa.gov/2k5/olderadults/olderadults.pdf. Access date: July 19, 2005.

Substance Abuse and Mental Health Services Administration (SAMHSA) (1998). *Preliminary results from the 1997 National Household Survey on Drug Abuse.* Washington,DC: Author.

Substance Abuse and Mental Health Services Administration (SAMHSA) (2001). *Summary of findings from the 2000 National Household Survey on Drug Abuse*. NHSDA Series H-13, DHHS Publication No. (SMA) 01-3549. Rockville, MD: Office of Applied Studies.

Substance Abuse and Mental Health Services Administration (SAMHSA). (2001). Older adults in substance abuse treatment: [Online]. Available: http://www.oas.samhsa.gov/2k4/olderAdultsTX/olderAdultsTX.htm. Access date: July 19, 2005.

Substance Abuse and Mental Health Services Administration (SAMHSA). (2002). Characteristics of primary alcohol admissions by age of first use of alcohol: [Online]. Available: http://oas.samhsa.gov/2k5/alcAgeTX/alcAgeTX.pdf. Access date: July 19, 2005.

Substance Abuse and Mental Health Services Administration (SAMHSA). (2002). Substance use by older adults: Estimates of future impact on the treatment system. [Online]. Available: http://www.oas.samhsa.gov/analytic.htm

Substance Abuse and Mental Health Services Administration (SAMHSA). (2004). *Results from the 2003 National Survwey on Drug Use and Health: National Findings*. NSDUH Series H-25, DHHS Publications No. SMA04-3964. Rockville: MD: Office of Applied Studies.

Substance Abuse and Mental Health Services Administration (SAMHSA). Alcohol dependence or abuse and age at first use. [Online]. Available: http://oas.samhsa.gov/2k4/ageDependence/ageDependence.pdf. Access date: July 19, 2005.

Substance Abuse and Mental Health Services Administration (SAMHSA). Older adults in substance abuse treatment. [Online]. Available: http://oas.samhsa.gov/2k5/olderAdultsTX/olderAdultsTX.pdf. Access date: July 19, 2005.

Substance Abuse and Mental Health Services Administration (SAMHSA). Preventing problems related to alcohol availability: Environmental approaches. [Online]. Available: www.health.org/govpubs/PHD822/acc.aspx. Access date: June 2, 2005.

Substance Abuse and Mental Health Services Administration. Substance abuse or dependence. [Online]. Available: http://www.drugabusestatistics.samhsa.gov/2k2/dependence/dependence.pdf. Access date: July 19, 2005.

Substance Abuse and Mental Health Services Administration (SAMHSA). Substance use among older adults. Online]. Available: http://www.oas.samhsa.gov/2k1/olderadults/olderadults.pdf. Access date: July 19, 2005.

Sugarman, J. (1999). Ethical considerations in leaping from bench to bedside. *Science, 285,* 2071–2072.

Suicide: Part 1. (1986, February). *Harvard Medical School Health Letter*, pp. 1–4.

Suitor, J. J., & Pillemer, K. (1987). The presence of adult children: A source of stress for elderly married couples? *Journal of Marriage and the Family, 49,* 717–725.

Suitor, J. J., & Pillemer, K. (1988). Explaining intergenerational conflict when adult children and elderly parents live together. *Journal of Marriage and the Family, 50,* 1037–1047.

Suitor, J. J., & Pillemer, K. (1993). Support and interpersonal stress in the social networks of married daughters caring S1–8.

Suitor, J. J., Pillemer, K., Keeton, S., & Robinson, J. (1995). Aged parents and aging children: Determinants of relationship quality. In R. Blieszner & V. Hilkevitch (Eds.), *Handbook of aging and the family* (pp. 223–242). Westport, CT: Greenwood Press.

Sullivan, A. D., Hedberg, K., & Fleming, D. W. (2000). Legalized physician-assisted suicide in Oregon: The second year. *New England Journal of Medicine, 342,* 598–604.

Sullivan, R. (2001). Cardiovascular disease. In G. L. Maddox (Ed.) The encyclopedia of aging (3rd ed.). New York: Springer Publishing Company.

Suls, A. & Swain, J. (1996). Reproducibility of blood pressure and heart rate reactivity: A meta analysis. *Psychophysiology, 33*(2), 162-174.

Super, D. E. (1957). *The psychology of careers*. New York: Harper & Row.

Super, D. E. (1985). Coming of age in Middletown: Careers in the making. *American Psychologist, 40,* 405–414.

Susman, E. (2004, February 19). Researchers study long-term AIDS drugs use. *Science News.*

Swann, W. B. (1983). Self-verification: Bringing social reality into harmony with the self. In J. Suls & A. B. Greenwald (Eds.), *Psychological perspectives of the self* (Vol. 2, pp. 33–66). Hillsdale, NJ: Erlbaum.

Swann, W. B. (1987). Identity negotiations: Where two roads meet. *Journal of Personality and Social Psychology, 53,* 1038–1051.

Szinovacz, M. E. (1998). Grandparents today: A demographic profile. *The Gerontologist, 38,* 37–52.

Talbott, M. M. (1998). Older widows' attitudes towards men and remarriage. *Journal of Aging Studies, 12,* 429–449.

Tamir, L. M. (1989). Modern myths about men at midlife: An assessment. In S. Hunter & M. Sundel (Eds.), *Midlife myths.* Newbury Park, CA: Sage.

Tanfer, K., & Horn, M. C. (1985). Contraceptive use, pregnancy and fertility patterns among single American women in their 20s. *Family Planning Perspectives, 17*(1), 10–19.

Taniguchi, H. (1999). The timing of childbearing and women's wages. *Journal of Marriage and the Family, 61,* 1008–1019.

Taylor, H. (1995, January 30). *Doctor-assisted suicide: Support for Dr. Kevorkian remains strong, and 2-to-1 majority approves Oregon-style assisted suicide bill.* New York: Harris and Associates.

Taylor, I. A. (1959). The nature of the creative process. In P. Smith (Ed.), *Creativity* (pp. 51–82). New York: Hastings House.

Taylor, J. M. (1979). *Eva Peron: The myths of a woman.* Chicago: University of Chicago Press.

Taylor, P. (1994, May 11). Mandela's moment comes: Inauguration draws crush of foreign leaders. *Chicago Sun-Times,* p. 3.

Taylor, R. J., & Chatters, L. M. (1991). Extended family networks of older Black adults. *Journal of Gerontology: Social Sciences, 46*(4), 5210–5217.

Taylor, S. C. (1993, October–November). The end of retirement. *Modern Maturity,* pp. 32–39.

Teachman, J. (2003). Premarital sex, premarital cohabitation, and the risk of subsequent marital dissolution. *Journal of Marriage and the Family, 65,* 444–455.

Teachman, J. D., Tedrow, L. M., Crowder, K. D. (2000). The changing demography of America's families. *Journal of Marriage and the Family, 58,* 1234–1246.

Techner, D. (1994, February 6). *Death and dying.* Seminar presentation for candidates in Leadership Program, International Institute for Secular Humanistic Judaism, Farmington Hills, MI.

Tellegren, A., Lykken, D. T., Bouchard, T, J., Wilcox, K. J., Segal, N. L., & Rich, S. (1988). Personality similarities in twins reared apart and reared together. *Journal of Personality and Social Psychology, 54,* 1031–1039.

Testing awareness of the Holocaust. (1993, May 5). *Christian Century,* p. 481. U.S. Government Printing Office.

Thabes, V. (1997). A survey analysis of women's long-term, post-divorce adjustment. *Journal of Divorce and Remarriage, 27,* 163–175.

The aging eye. (1994, December). *Harvard Women's Health Watch,* pp. 4–5.

The new genetic screens for cancer. (1995, January). *Johns Hopkins Medical Letter: Health after 50,* pp. 1–2.

The SUPPORT Principal Investigators. (1995). A controlled trial to improve care for seriously ill hospitalized patients: The study to understand prognoses and preferences for outcomes and risks of treatment (SUPPORT). *Journal of the American Medical Association, 274,* 1591–1598.

Thomas, A., & Chess, S. (1984). Genesis and evolution of behavioral disorders: From infancy to early adult life. *American Journal of Orthopsychiatry, 141,* 1–9.

Thomas, J. L. (1986). Gender differences in satisfaction with grandparenting. *Psychology and Aging, 1*(3), 215–219.

Thomas, S. P. (1997). Psychosocial correlates of women's self-rated physical health in middle adulthood. In M. E. Lachman & J. B. James (Eds.), *Multiple paths of midlife development* (pp. 257–291). Chicago: University of Chicago Press.

Thompson, L., & Walker, A. J. (1989). Gender in families: Women and men in marriage, work, and parenthood. *Journal of Marriage and the Family, 51,* 845–871.

Thomson, E., & Colella, U. (1992). Cohabitation and marital stability: Quality or commitment? *Journal of Marriage and the Family, 54,* 259–267.

Thornton, A. (1989). Changing attitudes toward family issues in the United States. *Journal of Marriage and the Family, 51,* 873–893.

Thurstone, L. L. (1938). *Primary mental abilities. Psychometric Monographs* (No. I).

Thurstone, L. L. (1952). Creative talent. In L. L. Thurstone (Ed.), *Applications of psychology* (pp. 18–37). New York: Harper & Row.

Tideiksaar, R. (2002). Falls in older people: Prevention & management. Baltimore, MD: Health Professions Press, Inc.

Tiger, L., & Shepher, J. (1975). *Women in the kibbutz*. New York: Harcourt Brace.

Tilvis, R.S., Kahonen-Vare, M.H., Jolkkonen, J., Valvanne, J., Pitkala, K.H., & Stradnberg, T.E. (2004). Predictors of cognitive decline and mortality of aged people over a 10-year period. *Journal of Gerontology: Medical Sciences, 59A*, 268–274.

Tomkins, S. (1986). Script theory. In J. Aronoff, A. Rabin, & R. A. Zucker (Eds.), *The emergence of personality* (pp. 147–216). New York: Springer.

Tomlinson-Keasey, C. (1982). Structures, functions, and stages: A trio of unresolved issues in formal operations. In S. Modgil & C. Modgil (Eds.), *Jean Piaget: Consensus and controversy*. New York: Holt, Rinehart, & Winston.

Tonna, E. A. (2001). Arthritis. In G.L. Maddox (Ed.) *i*(3rd ed.). New York: Springer Publishing Company.

Torrance, E. P. (1957). *Psychology of survival.* Unpublished manuscript, Air Force Personnel Research Center, Lackland Air Force Base, TX.

Torrance, E. P. (1966). *The Torrance Test of Creative Thinking: Technical-norms manual (research ed.).* Princeton, NJ: Personnel Press.

Torrance, E. P. (1972a). Career patterns and peak creative experiences of creative high school students 12 years later. *Gifted Child Quarterly, 16*, 75–88.

Torrance, E. P. (1972b). Predictive validity of the Torrance Test of Creative Thinking. *Journal of Creative Behavior, 6*, 236–252.

Torrance, E. P. (1974). *The Torrance Tests of Creative Thinking: Technical-norms manual.* Bensenville, IL: Scholastic Testing Service.

Torrance, E. P. (1981). Predicting the creativity of elementary school children (1958–1980)–and the teacher who made a "difference."*Gifted Child Quarterly, 25*, 55–62.

Torrance, E. P. (1988). The nature of creativity as manifests in its testing. In R. J. Sternberg (Ed.), *The nature of creativity: Contemporary psychological perspectives* (pp. 43–75). Cambridge: Cambridge University Press.

Torrance, E. P., & Ball, O. E. (1984). *The Torrance Test of Creative Thinking: Streamlined (revised) manual, Figural A and B.* Bensenville, IL: Scholastic Testing Service.

Tracy, M. B., & Pampel, F. C. (Eds.) (1991). *International handbook on old-age innocence.* Westport, CT: Greenwood.

Treas, J. (1995, May). *Older Americans in the 1990's and beyond. Population Bulletin, 50*(2). Washington, DC: Population Reference Bureau.

Troll, L. E. (1980). Grandparenting. In L. W. Poon (Ed.), Aging in the 1980s. Washington, DC: American Psychological Association.

Troll, L. E. (1983). Grandparents: The family watchdogs. In T. H. Brubaker (Ed.), *Family relationships in later life*. Beverly Hills, CA: Sage.

Troll, L. E. (1985). Early and middle adulthood. Monterey, CA: Brooks/Cole.

Troll, L. E. (1986). Parents and children in later life. *Generations, 10(4)*, 23–25.

Troll, L. E. (1989). Myths of midlife intergenerational relationships. In S. Hunter & M. Sundel (Eds.), *Midlife myths*. Newbury Park, CA: Sage.

Troll, L.E., & Fingerman, K.L. (1996). Connections between parents and their adult children. In C. Magai & S. H. McFadden (Eds.), *Handbook of emotion, adult development and aging* (pp.185–205). San Diego: Academic Press.

Troll, L. E., & Smith, J. (1976). Attachment through the life span. *Human Development, 3*, 156–171.

Troll, L. E., Miller, S., & Atchley, R. (1979). *Families in later life*. Belmont, CA: Wadsworth.

Trotter, R. J. (1986, August). Profile: Robert J. Sternberg: Three heads are better than one. *Psychology Today*, pp. 56–62.

Truehart, C. (1999, October 14). France gives right to unwed couples. *Boston Globe*, p.A4.

Truschke, E. F. (1998, Fall). Message from the president. *Advances: Progress in Alzheimer Research and Care*, p.1.

Tschann, J., Johnston, J. R., & Wallerstein, J. S. (1989). Resources, stressors, and attachment as predictors of adult adjustment after divorce: A longitudinal study. *Journal of Marriage and Family Therapy, 51,* 1033–1046.

Tsevat, J., Dawson, N.V., Wu, A.W., Lynn, J., Soukup, J.R., Cook, E., Francis, E., Vidaillet, H., Phillips, R.S. (1998). Health values of hospitalized patients 80 years or older. *Journal of the American Medical Association, 279*(5), 371–375.

Tucker, J. S., & Friedman, H. S. (1996). Emotion, personality and health. In C. Magai & S. H. McFadden (Eds.), *Handbook of emotion, adult development and aging.* San Diego: Academic Press.

Tucker, M.B., & Mitchell-Kernan, C. (1998). Psychological well-being and perceived marital opportunity among single African American, Latina, and White women. *Journal of Comparative Family Studies, 29,* 57–72.

Tucker, M. B., Taylor, R. J., & Mitchell–Kernan, C. (1993). Marriage and romantic involvement among aged African Americans. *Journal of Gerontology: Social Sciences, 48,* S123–132.

Tulving, E. (1991). Memory research is not a zero–sum game. *American Psychologist, 46*(1), 41–42.

Turiel, E. (1998). The development of morality. In W. Damon (Series Ed.), & N. Eisenberg (Vol. Ed.), *Handbook of child psychology: Vol 3. Social, emotional and personality development* (4th ed, pp. 863–932). New York: Wiley.

Twain, M. (1963). How to make history dates stick. In C. Neider (Ed.), *The complete essays of Mark Twain* (pp. 495–516). Garden City, NY: Doubleday.

U.S. Bureau of Justice Statistics. (1994, November). *Selected findings: Violence between intimates.* Washington, DC: U.S. Government Printing Office.

U.S. Bureau of the Census. (1991). *Household and family characteristics, March 1991* (Publication No. AP-20-458). Washington, DC: U.S. Government Printing Office.

U.S. Bureau of the Census. (1991a). *Household and family characteristics, March 1991* (Publication No. AP-20-458). Washington, DC: U.S. Government Printing Office.

U.S. Bureau of the Census. (1991b). *1990 census of population and housing.* Washington, DC: U.S. Government Printing Office.

U.S. Bureau of the Census. (1992b). *Marital status and living arrangements: March 1991* (Current Population Reports, Series P-20, No. 461). Washington, DC: U.S. Government Printing Office.

U.S. Bureau of the Census. (1993). *Sixty-five plus in America.* Washington, DC: U.S. Government Printing Office.

U.S. Bureau of the Census (1995). *Sixty-five plus in the United States.* Washington, DC: U.S. Government Printing Office.

U.S. Bureau of the Census. (1998). *Household and family characterstics: March 1998 (Update)* (Current Population Reports, P20–514). Washington, DC: U.S. Government Printing Press.

U.S. Bureau of the Census. (1999). Report WP/98, *World Population Profile:* 1998, U.S. Government Printing Office, Washington, DC.

U.S. Bureau of the Census. (2000). Marital status by sex, unmarried-partners households, and grandparents and caregivers: 2000. [Online]. Available: http://factfinder.census.gov/servlet/QTTable?_ts=82376307031. Access date: September 23, 2003.

U.S. Bureau of the Census. (2000). *Older Americans 2000.* Washington, DC: U.S. Government Printing Office.

U.S. Bureau of the Census. (2001). *The 65 years and over population: 2000.* Washington, DC: Author.

U.S. Bureau of the Census (2002). *The big payoff: Educational attainment and synthetic estimates of work-life earnings.* (Publication No. P23-210). Washington, DC: Author.

U.S. Bureau of the Census (2004). *Educational attainment in the United States: 2003.* (Publication No. P20-550). Washington, DC: U.S. Government Printing Office.

U.S. Bureau of the Census (2005). Educational attainment in the United States. Table A-2. Percent of people 25 year and over who have completed high school or college, by race, Hispanic origin and sex: Selected years 1940-2004. [Online]. Available: http://www.census.gov/population/www/socdemo/ educ-attn.html. Access date: April 15, 2006.

U.S. Bureau of the Census, Decennial Census Data and Population Projections, 2000.

U.S. Bureau of the Census, International Programs Center, International Data Base

U.S. Bureau of the Census, Official Statistics, 1999.

U.S. Department of Commerce (2002). A nation online: How Americans are expanding their use of the internet. [Online.] Available: http://www.ntia.doc.gov/ntiahome/dn/nationonline_020502.htm. Access date: April 15, 2006.

U.S. Department of Education (1986). *Participation in adult education, May 1984* (Office of Educational Research and Improvement Bulletin CS 86-308B). Washington, DC: Center for Educational Statistics.

U.S. Department of Education, National Center for Education Statistics. (2001). *Adult Literacy and education in America: Four studies based on the National Adult Literacy Survey, NCES 1999-469*, by Carl F. Kaestle, Anne, Campbell, Jeremy Finn, Sylvia, T. Johnson, and Larry H. Mikulecky. Project Officer: Andrew Kolstaf. Washington, DC.

U.S. Department of Health and Human Services (USDHHS). (1984). *Child sexual abuse prevention: Tips to parents*. Washington, DC: Office of Human Development Services, Administration for Children, Youth, and Families, and National Center on Child Abuse and Neglect.

U.S. Department of Health and Human Services (USDHHS). (1987). *Smoking and health: A national status report* (DHHS/PHS/Child Development Publication No. 87-8396). Washington, DC: U.S. Government Printing Office.

U.S. Department of Health and Human Services (USDHHS). (1988). *Social security programs throughout the world–1987* (Report No. 61). Washington, DC: U.S. Government Printing Office.

U.S. Department of Health and Human Services (USDHHS). (1990). *Health, United States, 1989* (DHHS Publication No. PHS 90–1232). Washington, DC: U.S. Government Printing Office.

U.S. Department of Health and Human Services (USDHHS). (1992). *Health, United States, 1991, and Prevention Profile* (DHHS Publication No. PHS 92–1232). Washington, DC: U.S. Government Printing Office.

U.S. Department of Health and Human Services (USDHHS). (1993a). *A cataract patient's guide* (Publication No. PHS A93-0544). Washington, DC: U.S. Government Printing Office.

U.S. Department of Health and Human Services (USDHHS). (1993b). *Monthly vital statistics report*, 42(3), supplement.

U.S. Department of Health and Human Services (USDHHS). (1995). *Health, United States, 1994* (DHHS Publication No. PHS 95–1232). Washington, DC: U.S. Government Printing Office.

U.S. Department of Health and Human Services (USDHHS) (1996). *Health, United States, 1995* (DHHS Publication No. PHS 96-1232). Washington, DC: U.S. Government Printing Office.

U.S. Department of Health and Human Services (USDHHS). (1999). *Blending perspectives and building common ground: A report to Congress on substance abuse and child protection*. Washington, DC: U.S. Government Printing Office.

U.S. Department of Health and Human Services (USDHHS) (1999). *Mental Health: A Report of the Surgeon General-Executive summary*. Rockville, MD: U.S. Department of Health and Human Services, Substance Abuse and Mental Health Services Administration, Center for Mental Health Services, National Institutes of Health, National Institute of Mental Health.

U.S. Department of Health and Human Services (USDHHS). (2003). Child maltreatment 2003. [Online]. Available: http://www.acf.hhs.gov/programs/cb/publications/cm03/cm2003.pdf. Access date: July 19, 2005.

U.S. Department of Health and Human Services (USDHHS). (2004). Child abuse and neglect fatalities: Statistics and interventions. [Online]. Available: http://nccanch.acf.hhs.gov/pubs/factsheets/fatality.pdf. Access date: July 19, 2005.

U.S. Department of Justice (2001). Elder abuse and neglect. [Online]. Available: www.ojp.usdoj.gov/ovc/nvcrw/2001/stat_over_7.htm. Access date: June 7, 2005.

U.S. Department of Justice (2004). Homicide trends in the U.S: Intimate homicide. [Online]. Available: www.ojp.usdoj.gov/bjs/homicide/intimates.htm. Access date: June 7, 2005.

U.S. Department of Labor. (1992). Statistics on employed civilians detailed by occupation, sex, race, and Hispanic origin. *Handbook of labor statistics*. Washington, DC: U.S. Government Printing Office.

U.S. Department of Labor. (2004). 20 Leading occupations of employed women full-time wage and salary workers: 2002 Annual averages. [Online]. Available: www.dol.gov/wb/factsheets,20lead2002.htm

U.S. Department of Labor, Bureau of Labor Statistics, Office of Employment and Unemployment Statistics, *Current Population Survey, 2001*.

U.S. Department of Labor—Women's Bureau. (1994). *Working women count*. Washington, DC: U.S. Government Printing Office.

U.S. Office of Technology Assessment. (1992). *The menopause, hormone therapy, and women's health*. Washington, DC: U.S. Government Printing Office.

Uhlenberg, P. (1988). Aging and the social significance of cohorts. In J. E. Birren & V. L. Bengtson (Eds.), *Emergent theories of aging* (pp. 405–425). New York: Springer.

Uhlenberg, P., & Myers, M. A. P. (1981). Divorce and the elderly. *The Gerontologist, 21*(3), 276–282.

Uhlenberg, P., Cooney, T., & Boyd, R. (1990). Divorce for women after midlife. *Journal of Gerontology, 45*(1), 53–11.

Umberson, D. (1992). Relationships between adult children and their parents: Psychological consequences for both generations. *Journal of Marriage and the Family, 54*, 664–674.

Umberson, D., & Chen, M. D. (1994). Effects of a parent's death on adult children: Relationship to salience and reaction to loss. *American Sociological Review, 59*, 152–168.

Umberson, D., Wortman, C. B., & Kessler, R. C. (1992). Widowhood and depression: Explaining long-term gender differences in vulnerability. *Journal of Health and Social Behavior, 33*, 10–24.

United Nations. (1991). *The world's women 1970–1990: Trends and statistics*. New York: Author.

United Nations. (1992a). *Developmental implications of population aging: Preliminary results of multi-country study*. Paper presented at meeting of the U.N. Expert Group on Population Growth and Demographic Structure.

United Nations (UN). (1999). International year of older persons. [Online]. Available: www.un.og/NewLinks/older/99.htm. Access date: September 12, 2003.

United Nations Economic Commission for Europe (UNECE). (2003). Trends in Europe and North America. [Online]. Available: www.unece.org/stats/trend/contents.htm. Access date: November 17, 2003.

United Nations Educational, Scientific, and Cultural Organization (UNESCO). (1989). *International Literacy Year (ILY), 1990*. Paris: Author.

United Nations Educational, Scientific, and Cultural Organization (UNESCO). (2004). Education for all global monitoring report- The quality imperactive. [Online]. Available: http://www.unesco.org/education/GMR2005/press. Access date: November 10, 2004.

United Nations General Assembly. (1992). International Year of Older Persons General Assembly resolution 47/5.

United Nations International Labor Organization (UNILO). (1993). *Job stress: The 20th-century disease*. New York: United Nations.

Ursin, H. (1980). Personality, activation and somatic health. In S. Levine & H. Ursin (Eds.), *Coping and health*. New York: Plenum.

Usui, C. (1998). Gradual retirement: Japanese strategies for older workers. In K. W. Schaie, & C. Schooler (Eds.), *Impact of work on older adults*. New York: Springer Publishing Co.

Vachon, M., Lyall, W., Rogers, J., Freedmen-Letofky, K., & Freeman, S. (1980). A controlled study of self-help intervention for widows. *American Journal of Psychiatry, 137*(11), 1380–1384.

Vaillant, G. E. (1977). *Adaptation to life*. Boston: Little, Brown.

Vaillant, G. E. (1989). The evolution of defense mechanisms during the middle years. In J. M. Oldham & R. S. Liebert (Eds.), *The middle years*. New Haven, CT: Yale University Press.

Vaillant, G. E. (2002). *Aging Well*. New York: Little Brown and Company.

Vaillant, G. E., & Vaillant, C. O. (1990). Natural history of male psychological health: 12. A 45-year study of predictors of successful aging. *American Journal of Psychiatry, 147,* 31–37.

Van, P. (2001). Breaking the silence of African American women: Healing after pregnancy loss. *Health Care Women International, 22,* 229–243.

van Baal, J. (1966). *Demo, description and analysis of Marindanim culture (South New Guinea).* The Hague: Nijhoff.

van der Heide, A., Deliens, L., Faisst, K., Nilstun, T., Norup, M., Paci, E., van der Wei, G., & van der Maas, P. J. on behalf of the EURELD consortium. (2003). End of life decision making in 6 European countries: A descriptive study. *Lancet, 362,* 345–350.

Van der Maas, P. J., Van der Wal, G., Haverkate, I., De Graeff, C. L. M., Kester, J. G. C., Onwuteaka-Philipsen, B. D., Van der Heide, A., Bosma, J. M., & Willems, D. L. (1996). Euthanasia, physician-assisted suicide, and other medical practices involving the end of life in the Netherlands. *New England Journal of Medicine, 35,* 1699–1705.

van der Wuff, F. B., Stek, M. L., Hoogendijk, W. J. G., & Beekman, A. T. F. (2003). The efficacy and safety of ECT in depressed older adults, a literature review. *International Journal of Geriatric Psychiatry, 18,* 894–904.

van Eijken, M., Tsang, S., Wensing, M., de Smet, P. A. G. M., Grol, R. P. T. M. (2003). Interventions to improve medication compliance in older patients living in the community: A systematic review of the literature. *Drugs and Aging, 29*(3), 229-240.

van Gelder, B.M., Tijhuis, M.A.R., Kalmijn, S., Giampaoli, S., Nissinen, A., & Krombout, D., (2004). Physical activity in relation to cognitive decline in elderly men. *American Academy of Neorology, 63,*2316–2321.

van Hooren, S.A.H., Valentijn, S.A.M., Bosma, H., Ponds, R.W.M, van Boxtel, M.P.J., & Jolles, J. (2005). Relation between health status and cognitive functioning: A 6-year followup of the Maastricht Aging Study. *Journal of Gerontology: Psychological Sciences, 60B,* P57–P60.

van Noord-Zaadstra, B. M., Looman, C. W., Alsbach, H., Habbema, J. D., te Velde, E. R., & Karbaat, J. (1991). Delayed childbearing: Effect of age on fecundity and outcome of pregnancy. *British Medical Journal, 302,*1361–1365.

Vargha-Khadem, F., Gadian, D. G., Watkins, K. E., Connelly, A., Van Paesschen, W., & Mishkin, M. (1970). Differential effects of early hippocampal pathology on episodic and semantic memory. *Science, 277,* 376–380.

Vaupel, J. W., Carey, J. R., Christensen, K., Johnson, T. E., Yashin, A. I., Holm, N. V., Iachine, I. A., Kannisto, V., Khazaeli, A. A., Liedo, P., Longo, V. D., Zeng, Y., Manton, K. G., & Curtsinger, J. W. (1998). Biodemographic trajectories of longevity. *Science, 280,* 855-860.

Veninga, R. L. (1998, January 15). Stress in the workplace: How to create a productive and healthy work environment. *Vital Speeches, 64,* 217–219.

Verbrugge, L.M., Gruber-Baldini, A.L., & Fozard, J.L. (1996). Age differences and age changes in activities: Baltimore Longitudinal Study of Aging. *Journal of Gerontology: Social Sciences, 51B,* S30–41.

Vercruyssen, M. (1997). Movement control and speed of behavior. In A. D. Fisk & W. A. Rogers (Eds.), *Handbook of human factors and the older adult* (pp. 55–86). San Diego, CA: Academic Press.

Verhaeghen, P., Marcoen, A., & Goossens, L. (1992). Improving memory performance in the aged through mnemonic training: A meta-analytic study. *Psychology and Aging, 7*(2), 242–251.

Verhagen, E., & Saur, P.J.J. (2005). The Groningen Protocol—Euthanasia in severely ill newborns. *New England Journal of Medicine, 352,* 959–962.

Vierck, E. & Hodge, K. (2003). Aging: Demographics, health, and health services. Westport, CT: Greenwood Press.

Vinick, B. (1978). Remarriage in old age. *Family Coordinator, 27,* 359–363.

Visher, E. B., & Visher, J. S. (1991). *How to win as a step family* (2nd ed.). New York: Brunner/Mazel.

Visser, A., van Leeuwen, A.F., Voogt, E., van der Heide, A., van der Rijt, K. (2003). *Patient Education and Counseling, 50*(3), 263–264.

Vlahov, D., Galea, S., Resnick, H., Ahern, J., Boscarino, J. A., Bucuvalas, M., Gold., J., & Kilpatrick, D. (2002). Increased use of cigarettes, alcohol, and marijuana among Manhattan, New York, residents after the September 11th terrorist attacks. *American Journal of Epidemiology, 155,* 988-996.

Voelker, R. (1993). The genetic revolution: Despite perfection of elegant techniques, ethical answers still elusive. *Journal of the American Medcial Association, 270,* 2273–2277.

Voluntary Euthanasia Society. (2002). In depth: Factsheets. [Online]. Available: www.ves.org.uk/DpFS_Aust.html.

Voydanoff, P. (1987). *Work and family life.* Newbury Park, CA: Sage.

Voydanoff, P. (1990). Economic distress and family relations: A review of the eighties. *Journal of Marriage and the Family, 52,* 1099–1115.

Wagner, D. A. (1978). Memories of Morocco: The influence of age, schooling and environment on memory. *Cognitive Psychology, 10,* 1–28.

Wagner, D. A. (1981). Culture and memory development. In H. C. Triandis & A. Heron (Eds.), *Handbook of cross-cultural psychology: Developmental psychology* (Vol. 4, pp. 187–232). Boston: Allyn & Bacon.

Wagner, R. K., & Sternberg, R. J. (1986). Tacit knowledge and intelligence in the everyday world. In R. J. Sternberg & R. K. Wagner (Eds.), *Practical intelligence: Nature and origins of competence in the everyday world.* Cambridge: Cambridge University Press.

Waite, L. J., & Joyner, K. (2000). Emotional and physical satisfaction with sex in married, cohabiting, and dating sexual unions: Do men and women differ? In E. O. Laumann, & R. T. Michael (Eds.), *Sex, love, and health in America: Private choices and public policies* (pp. 239–269). Chicago: University of Chicago Press.

Walasky, M., Whitbourne, S. K., & Nehrke, M. F. (1983–1984). Construction and validation of an ego–integrity status interview. *International Journal of Aging and Human Development, 81,* 61–72.

Walford, R. L. (1986). *The 120-year-diet.* New York: Simon & Schuster.

Walker, A. J., Martin, S. S. K., & Jones, L. L. (1992). The benefits and costs of caregiving and care receiving for daughters and mothers. *Journal of Gerontology, 47*(3), S130–139.

Walker, L. E. (1999). Psychology and domestic violence around the world. *American Psychologist, 54,* 21-29.

Walker, L. J. (1984). Sex differences in the development of moral reasoning: A critical review. *Child Development, 55,* 677–691.

Wallace, D. C. (1992). Mitochondrial genetics: A paradigm for aging and degenerative diseases? *Science, 2,* 56, 628–632.

Wallach, M. A., & Kogan, N. (1967). Creativity and intelligence in children's thinking. *Transaction, 4*(1), 38–43.

Wallas, G. (1926). *The art of thought.* New York: Harcourt Brace.

Wallechinsky & Wallace (1993, September 26). Achievers after the age of 90. *Parade,* p. 17.

Walls, C., & Zarit, S. (1991). Informal support from black churches and well-being of elderly blacks. *The Gerontologist, 31,* 490–495.

Walter, H., Gutierrez, K., Ramskogler, K., Hertling, I., Dvorak, A., Lesch, O. M. (2003). Gender-specific differences in alcoholism: Implications for treatment. *Archives of Women's Mental Health, 6,* 253–258.

Ward, R. A., & Kilbum, H. (1983). Community access and satisfaction: Racial differences in later life. *International Journal of Aging and Human Development, 16,* 209–219.

Warren, J. A., & Johnson, P. (1995). The impact of workplace support on work-family role strain. *Family Relations, 44,* 163–169.

Wassertheril-Smoller, S., Hendrix, S. L., Lomacher, M., Heiss, G., Kooperberg, C., Baird, A., Kotchen, T., Curb, J. D., Black, H., Rossouw, J. E., Aragaki, A., Safford, M., Stein, E., Laowattana, S., Mysiw, W. J., for the WHI Investigators. (2003). Effects of estrogen plus progestin on stroke in post-menopausal women: The Women's Health Initiative: A randomized trial. *Journal of the American Medical Association, 289,* 2673–2684.

Watson, R. (1994, October 25). Ever the best of enemies. *Newsweek,* pp. 35–36.

Wayler, A. H., Kapur, K. K., Feldman, R. S., & Chauncey, H. H. (1982). Effects of age and dentition status on measures of food acceptability. *Journal of Gerontology, 37*(3), 294–299.

Webb, W. B. (1987). Disorders of aging sleep. *Interdisciplinary Topics in Gerontology, 22*, 1–12.

Wechsler, D. (1939). *The measurement of adult intelligence.* Baltimore: Williams & Wilkins.

Wechsler, D. (1997). *Wechsler Adult Intetlligence Scale* (3rd ed.). San Antonio, TX: Psychological Corporation.

Weg, R. B. (1989). Sensuality/sexuality of the middle years. In S. Hunter & M. Sundel (Eds.), *Midlife myths.* Newbury Park, CA: Sage.

Weinberger, J. (1999, May 18). Enlightening conversation. [Letter to the editor]. *The New York Times*, p.F3.

Weindruch, R., & Walford, R. L. (1988). *The retardation of aging and disease by dietary restriction.* Springfield, IL: Thomas.

Weinstein, B. (2003). A primer on hearing loss in the elderly. *Aging and the Senses, Spring.*

Weiss, G. (1994, January). Women and psychotherapy. *The Lilac Tree Newsletter*, pp. 2–4. (Reprinted from Health Resources for Women, April 1990, newsletter of Illinois Masonic Medical Center's Women's Health Resources).

Weiss, M.J. (2002). Chasing youth. *American Demographics, 9*, 35-42.

Weiss, M. J. (2003, September). To be about to be. *American Demographics*, pp. 29–36.

Weiss, R. (1994, March 17). Second colon cancer gene identified. *Chicago Sun-Times*, p. 36.

Weissman, M. M., Klerman, G. L., Markowitz, J. S., & Ouelette, R. (1989). Suicidal ideation and suicide attempts in panic disorders and attacks. *New England Journal of Medicine, 32*, 11209–1214.

Weitzman, L. J. (1985). *The divorce revolution: The unexpected social and economic consequences for women and children in America.* New York:

Wertz, D. C., Fanos, J. H., & Reilly, P. R. (1994). Genetic testing for children and adolescents: Who decides? *Journal of the American Medical Association, 272*, 875–881.

West, R. L. (1985). *Memory fitness over 40.* Gainsville, FL: Triad.

Wethington, E., & Kessler, R. C. (1989). Employment, parental responsibility and psychological distress: A longitudinal study of married women. *Journal of Family Issues, 10*, 527–546.

Weuve, J., Kang, J.H., Manson, J.E., Breteler, M.M.B., Ware, J.H., & Grodstein, F. (2004). Physical activity, including walking, and cognitive function in older women. *Journal of the American Medical Association, 292*, 1454–1461.

Wharton, D. (1993, June–July). Through the glass ceiling: Minorities, women, and corporate America's human resource needs. *The National Voter*, pp. 10–11.

Which living arrangement is right for you? (April–May, 1993). *Modern Maturity*, pp. 32–33.

Whitbourne, S. K. (1987). Personality development in adulthood and old age: Relationships among identity style, health, and well-being. In K. W. Schaie (Ed.), *Annual review of gerontology and geriatrics* (Vol. 7, pp. 189–216). New York: Springer.

Whitbourne, S. K. (1989). Psychological treatment of the aging individual. *Journal of Integrative and Eclectic Psychotherapy, 8*, 161–173.

Whitbourne, S. K. (1999). Physical changes. In J. C. Cavanaugh & S. K. Whitbourne (Eds.). *Gerontology: An interdisciplinary perspective* (pp. 91–122). New York: Oxford University Press.

Whitbourne, S. K. & Connolly, L. A. (1999). The developing self in midlife. In S. L. Willis & J. D. Reid (Eds.), *Life in the middle: Psychological and social development in middle age* (pp. 25-45). San Diego: Academic Press.

Whitbourne, S. K., & Primus, L. A. (1996). Physical identity in later adulthood. In J. E. Birren (Ed.), *Encyclopedia of gerontology.* San Diego: Academic.

Whitbourne, S. K., & Primus, L. A. (in press). Physical identity in later adulthood. In J. E. Birren (Ed.), *Encyclopedia of gerontology.* San Diego: Academic.

White, J. M. (1992). Marital status and well-being in Canada: An analysis of age group variations. *Journal of Family Issues, 13*, 390–409.

White, L. K. (1990). Determinants of divorce: A review of research in the eighties. *Journal of Marriage and the Family, 52*, 904–912.

White, L., & Edwards, J. N. (1990). Emptying the nest and parental well-being: An analysis of national panel data. *American Sociological Review, 55*, 235–242.

White, N., & Cunningham, W. R. (1988). Is terminal drop pervasive or specific? *Journal of Gerontology, 43*(6), 141–144.

Who's Who in America. (2002). Providence, NJ: Marquis Who's Who.

Wiggins S., Whyte, P., Higgin, M., Adams, S., et al. (1992). The psychological consequences of predictive testing for Huntington's disease. *New England Journal of Medicine, 327,* 1401–1405.

Wilensky, H. L. (1960). Work, careers, and social integration. *International Social Science Journal, 12,* 543–560.

Willett, W. C., Stampfer, M. J., Colditz, G. A., Rosner, B. A., & Speizer, F. E. (1990). Relation of meat, fat, and fiber intake to the risk of colon cancer in a prospective study among women. *New England Journal of Medicine, 323,* 1664–1672.

Williams, G.J. (2001). The clinical significance of visual-verbal processing in evaluating children with potential learning-related visual problems. *Journal of Optometric Vision Development, 32*(2), 107–110.

Williams, J. E., & Best, D. L. (1982). *Measuring sex stereotypes: A thirty-nation study.* Beverly Hills, CA: Sage.

Williams, K. (2004). The transition to widowhood and the social regulation of health: Consquences of health and health risk behavior. *Journal of Gerontology, Social Sciences, 59B,* S343–349.

Williams, M.E. (1995). *The American Geriatric Society's complete guide to aging and health.* New York: Harmony.

Williams, T. F. (1992). Aging versus disease: Which changes seen with age are the result of "biological aging"? *Generations, 16*(4), 21–25.

Williamson, D. F., Kahn, H. S., Remington, P. L., & Anda, R. F. (1990). The 10-year incidence of overweight and major weight gain in U.S. adults. *Archives of Internal Medicine, 150,* 665–672.

Willis, S. L. (1985). Towards an educational psychology of the older learner: Intellectual and cognitive bases. In J. E. Birren & K. W. Schaie, (Eds.), *Handbook of the psychology of aging* (2nd ed., pp. 818–847). New York: Van Nostrand Reinhold.

Willis, S. L. (1990). Current issues in cognitive training research. In E. A. Lovelace (Ed.), *Aging and cognition: Mental processes, self-awareness, and intervention* (pp. 263–280). Amsterdam: North-Holland, Elsevier.

Willis, S. L., & Baltes, P. B. (1980). Intelligence in adulthood and aging: Contemporary issues. In L. W. Poon et al. (Eds.), *Aging in the 1980s* (pp. 260–272). Washington, DC: American Psychological Association.

Willis, S. L., & Nesselroade, C. S. (1990). Long-term effects of fluid ability training in old-old age. *Developmental Psychology, 26,* 905–910.

Willis, S. L., Blieszner, R., & Baltes, P. B. (1981). Intellectual training research in aging: Modification of performance on the fluid ability of figural relations. *Journal of Educational Psychology, 73,* 41–50.

Willis, S. L., Jay, G. M., Diehl, M., & Marsiske, M. (1992). Longitudinal change and prediction of everyday task competence in the elderly. *Research on Aging, 14,* 68–91.

Wilson, R. C. (1956). The program for gifted children in Portland, Oregon, schools. In C. W. Taylor (Ed.), *The 1955 University of Utah research conference on the identification of creative scientific talent* (pp. 14–22). Salt Lake City: University of Utah Press.

Wilson, R.S., Mendes de Leon, C.F., Bienias, J.L., Evans, D.A., & Bennet, D.A. (2004). Personality and mortality in old age. *Journal of Gerontology: Psychological Sciences, 59B,* P110–116.

Wingfield, A., & Stine, E. A. L. (1989). Modeling memory processes: Research and theory on memory and aging. In G. C. Gilmore, P. J. Whitehouse, & M. L. Wykle (Eds.), *Memory, aging, and dementia: Theory, assessment, and treatment* (pp. 4–40). New York: Springer.

Wingo, P. A., Ries, L. A. G., Giovino, G. A., Miller, D. S., Rosenberg, H. M., Shopland, D. R., Thun, M. J., & Edwards, B. K. (1999). Annual report to the nation on the status of cancer,1973–1996. *Journal of the National Cancer Institute, 91,* 675–690.

Wink, P. (1991). Self- and object-directedness in adult women. *Journal of Personality, 59,* 769–791.

Wink, P. (1992). Three types of narcissism in women from college to midlife. *Journal of Personality, 60,* 7–30.

Wink, P. & Dillon, M. (2003). Religiousness, spirituality, and psychosocial functioning in late adulthood: Findings from a longitudinal study. *Psychology and Aging, 18*(4), 916–924.

Wink, P., & Helson, R. (1993). Personality change in women and their partners. *Journal of Personality and Social Psychology, 65,* 597–606.

Winkler, A.E. (1998). Earnings of husbands and wives in dual-earner families. *Monthly Labor Review, 121,* 42–48.

Witteman, P. A. (1993, February 15). A man of fire and grace: Arthur Ashe, 1943–1993. *Time,* p. 70.

Willis, S. L., & Schaie, K. W. (1986). Training the elderly on the ability factors of spatial orientation and inductive reasoning. *Psychology and Aging,* 22, 39–247.

Willis, S. L., & Schaie, K. W. (1999). Intellectual functioning in midlife. In S. L. Willis & J. D. Reid (Eds.), *Life in the middle: Psychological and social development in middle age* (pp. 233–247). San Diego: Academic Press.

Wolf, M. (1968). *The house of Lim.* Englewood Cliffs, NJ: Prentice-Hall.

Wolinsky, F. D., & Johnson, R. J. (1992a). Perceived health status and mortality among older men and women. *Journal of Gerontology: Social Sciences,* 47(6), S304–312.

Wolinsky, F. D., & Johnson, R. J. (1992b). Widowhood, health status, and the use of health services by older adults: A cross-sectional and prospective approach. *Journal of Gerontology: Social Sciences,* 47(1), S8–16.

Wong, P. T. P., & Watt, L. M. (1991). What types of reminiscences are associated with successful aging? *Psychology and Aging,* 6(2), 272–279.

Woodruff, D. S. (1985). Arousal, sleep and aging. In J. E. Birren & K. W. Schaie (Eds.), *Handbook of the psychology of aging* (2nd ed., pp. 261–295). New York: Van Nostrand Reinhold.

Woodruff-Pak, D. S. (1987). Sleep apnea. In G. L. Maddox (Ed.), *The encyclopedia of aging* (pp. 614–615). New York: Springer.

Woodruff-Pak, D. S. (1990). Mammalian models of learning, memory, and aging. In J. E. Birren & K. W. Schaie (Eds.), *Handbook of the psychology of aging* (3rd ed., pp. 234–257). San Diego: Academic.

Woodruff-Pak, D. S., & Jaeger, M. (1998). Declarative and nondeclarative learning and memory across the adult age life span.

Woods, M. N. (1996, November). Department of Family Medicine and Community Health, Tufts University School of Medicine, personal communication.

Woodward, C. V. (1989, February 20). The noble dream: The "objectivity question" and the American historical profession. *The New Republic,* p. 40.

Wooten, J. (1995, January 29). The conciliator. *New York Times Magazine,* pp. 28–33.

Working Women Education Fund. (1981). *Health hazards for office workers.* Cleveland: Author.

World Book Yearbook. (1977). (Vol 3, p. 53). Chicago: World Book.

World Health Organization. (1991). *World health statistics annual, 1990.* Geneva: Author.

World Health Organization. (1999). AIDS Epidemic Update. [Online]. Available: http://www.unaids.org.

World Health Organization. (2000, June 4). *WHO issues new healthy life expectancy ratings: Japan number one in new "healthy life" system.* (Press release). Washington, DC: Author.

World Health Organization. (2002). AIDS epidemic update: December 2002. [Online]. Available: www.who.int/hiv/pub/epidemiology/epi2002/en/print.html. Yahoo! Health. Access date: March 8, 2004.

World Health Organization. (2003). Causes of death: Global regional and country specific estimates of death by cause, age, and sex. [Online]. Available: www.who.int/mip/2003/other_documents/en/causeofdeath.pdf.

World Health Organization. (2004). Healthy Life Expectancy. [Online]. Available: www.3.who.int/whosis/hale/hale.cfm?path+whosis,bod,hale&language=english. Access date: January 23, 2006.

Wortman, C. B., & Silver, R. C. (1989). The myths of coping with loss. *Journal of Consulting and Clinical Psychology,* 57(3),349–357.

Wright, G. C., & Stetson, D. M. (1978). The impact of no-fault divorce law reform on divorce in American states. *Journal of Marriage and the Family, 40,* 575–585.

Wright, V.C., Schieve, L.A., Reynolds, M.A., & Jeng, G. (2003). Assisted reproductive technology surveillance—United States, 2000. Division of Reproductive Health, National Center for Chronic Disease Prevention and Health Promotion. [Online]. Available: www.cdc.gov/reprod.

Writing Group for the Women's Health Initiative Investigators. (2002). Risks and benefits of estrogen plus progestin in healthy post-menopausal women: Principal results from the Women's Health Initiative randomized controlled trial. *Journal of the American Medical Association, 288,* 321–333.

Wu, Z. (1999). Premarital cohabitation and the timing of first marriage. *Canadian Review of Sociology and Anthropology, 36,* 109–127.

Wu, Z., & Pollard, M.S. (1998). Social support among unmarried childless elderly persons.

Wu, Z., Penning, M. J., Pollard, M. S., Hart, R. (2003). "In sickness and in health": Does cohabitation count? *Journal of Family Issues, 24*(6), 811–838.

WuDunn, S. (1996, March 23). Japan's single mothers face discrimination. *Cleveland Plain.*

Wurtman, R. J., & Wurtman, J. J. (1989). Carbohydrates and depression. *Scientific American, 260*(1), 68–75.

Wykle, M. L., & Musil, C. M. (1993). Mental health of older persons: Social and cultural factors. *Generations, 17*(1), 7–12.

Wykle, M. L., Segal, N., & Nagley, S. (1992). Mental health and aging: Hospital care–a nursing perspective. In J. E. Birren, R. B. Sloan, & G. Cohen (Eds.), *Handbook of mental health and aging* (pp. 815–831). San Diego: Academic.

Wysocki, C. J., & Gilbert, A. N. (1989). The National Geographic smell survey: Effects of age are heterogenous. *Annals for the New York Academy of Sciences, 56,* 112–28.

Yahoo! Health. (2003). Osteoporosis health center. [Online]. Available: http://health.yahoo.com/

Yeung, W. J., Sandberg, J. F., Davis-Kean, P. E., & Hofferth, S. L. (2001). Children's time with fathers in intact families. *Journal of Marriage and Family, 63,* 136–154.

Yllo, K. (1984). The status of women, marital equality, and violence against women: A contextual analysis. *Journal of Family Issues, 5,* 307–320.

Yoder, J.D. (1999). *Women and gender: Transforming psychology.* Upper Saddle River, NJ: Prentice Hall.

Yoshioka, M.R., Gilber, L., El-Bassel, Baig-Amin, M. (2003). Social support and disclosure of abuse: Comparing South Asian, African American, and Hispanic battered women. *Journal of Family Violence, 18*(3), 171–180.

Zacks, R. T., Hasher, L., & Li, K. Z. H. (2000). Human memory. In F. I. M. Craik, & T. A. Salthouse, *Handbook of aging and cognition* (2nd ed.). New Jersey: Erlbaum.

Zandri, E., & Charness, N. (1989). Training older and younger adults to use software. *Educational Gerontology, 15,* 61–639.

Zanjani, E.D., & Anderson, F. (1999). Prospects for in utero human gene therapy. *Science, 285,* 2084–2088.

Zimmer, H. (1956). *Philosophies of India.* New York: Meridian.

Zoglin, R. (1994, February 28). Murder, they wheezed. *Time,* pp. 60–62.

Zube, M. (1982). Changing behavior and outlook of aging men and women: Implications for marriage in the middle and later years. *Family Relations, 31*(1), 147–156.

Zuckerman, M. (1994). Impulsive unsocialized sensation seeking: The biological foundation of a basic dimension of personality. In J. E. Bates & T. D. Wachs (Eds.), *Temperament: Individual differences at the interface of biology and behavior* (pp. 219–255). Washington, DC: American Psychological Association.

Credits

Chapter 1

Figure 1.1   From *The Development of Children* by Michael Cole and Sheila Cole, © 1989, 1993, 1996, 2001 by Michael Cole and Sheila Cole. Used with the permission of W. H. Freeman and Company.

Table 1.1   Baltes, adapted from "Theoretical propositions of life-span development psychology: on the dynamics between growth and decline," from *Developmental Psychology,* Vol. 23, pp. 611–626. Copyright © 1987 by the American Psychological Association. Reprinted with permission.

Chapter 2

Figure 2.1   P. B. Baltes, H. W. Reese and J. R. Nesselroade, from "Cross-culture differences in hearing loss," *Life-Span Developmental Psychology: Introduction to Research Methods,* 1977. Used by permission.

Table 2.3   Source: Diane Papalia and Sally Olds, from *Human Development,* 6th Edition. Reprinted by permission of The McGraw-Hill Companies.

Chapter 3

Figure 3.2   From *Fifty: Midlife in Perspective* by Herant Katchadourian, © 1987 by Herant Katchadourian. Used with the permission of W. H. Freeman and Company.

Chapter 4

Figure 4.1   From *Fifty: Midlife in Perspective* by Herant Katchadourian, © 1987 by Herant Katchadourian. Used with the permission of W. H. Freeman and Company.

Figure 4.2   Map, "Adults and children estimated to be living with HIV/AIDS as of end 2002" from World Health Organization, http://www.who.int

Table 4.2   Adapted from "Hormone Therapy: When and for How long?, pp. 1–2 from *Healthnews,* March 25, 1997, 3 (4). Copyright © 1997 Massachusetts Medical Society. All rights reserved. Reprinted by permission of the publisher.

Table 4.4   Reprinted from Merrill and Verbrugge, "Health & Disease in Midlife," in S. L. Willis & J. D. Reid, eds., *Life in the Middle: Psychological & Social Development in Middle Age,* p. 87. Copyright © 1999. Reprinted with permission of Elsevier.

Table 4.5   T. H. Holmes and R. H. Rahe, from "Social Readjustment Rating Scale." Reprinted from the *Journal of Psychosomatic Research,* Vol. 11, copyright © 1967, with permission from Elsevier.

Chapter 5

Figure 5.2   Nickerson & Adams, from "Long-term memory for a common object," in *Cognitive Psychology,* Vol. 11, pp. 287–307, copyright © 1979. Reprinted with permission from Elsevier.

Figure 5.3   C. Sagan, from "The Brain and the Chariot," *The Dragons of Eden: Speculations on the Evolution of Human Intelligence*. Copyright © 1977 by Carl Sagan. Reprinted with permission from Democritus Properties, LLC.

Table 5.3   C. J. Camp et al, from "Memory training in normal and demented populations: The E-I-E-I-O model" from *Experimental Aging Research*, Vol. 19, pp. 177–290. Taylor & Francis, Inc., 1993.

Chapter 6

Figure 6.1   R. S. Feldman, from *Understanding Psychology*, 3rd Edition. Copyright © 1993. Reprinted by permission of The McGraw-Hill Companies.

Figure 6.2   R. S. Feldman, from *Understanding Psychology*, 3rd Edition. Copyright © 1993. Reprinted by permission of The McGraw-Hill Companies.

Figure 6.3   J. Botwinick, from *Aging and Behavior*, 3rd Edition. Springer Publishing Company, Inc., New York 10012. Used by permission of the publisher.

Figure 6.4   Simulated item similar to those in the Raven's Progressive Matrices. Copyright © 1994 by Harcourt Assessment, Inc. Reproduced with permission. All rights reserved.

Table 6.1   K. W. Schaie, republished with permission of *The Gerontologist* from K. W. Schaie, "The Hazards of Cognitive Aging," Vol. 29, pp. 484–493, 1989. Reprinted by permission of *The Gerontologist* via Copyright Clearance Center.

Chapter 7

Figure 7.1   K. W. Schaie and S. L. Willis, "A stage theory model of adult cognitive development revisited" from *The Many Dimensions of Aging: Essays in Honor of M. Powell Lawton*, pp. 173–191. Copyright © 2000. Springer Publishing Company, Inc., New York 10012. Used by permission.

Figure 7.2   Baltes, from "The aging mind: potential and limits," *The Gerontologist*, Vol. 33, pp. 580–594, 1993. Copyright © The Gerontological Society of America.

Table 7.1   R. J. Sternberg, from "Wisdom and Its Relation to Intelligence and Creativity," from *Wisdom: Its Nature, Origins, and Development*, 1990, pp. 142–159. Reprinted with permission of Cambridge University Press.

Table 7.2   Table, "Kohlberg's Levels and Stages of Moral Reasoning Typically Seen in Adults" from *Higher Stages of Human Development: Perspectives on Adult Growth*, edited by Ellen Langer, copyright © 1990 by Charles N. Alexander and Ellen Langer. Used by permission of Oxford University Press, Inc.

Chapter 8

Figure 8.1   Riley, from "Aging and society: Past, present, and future," *The Gerontologist*, Vol. 33, pp. 436–444, 1994. Copyright © 1994 The Gerontological Society of America.

Figure 8.2   Graph, "Female civilian employment as % of total, 1961–2001" from OECD Labour Force Statistics. Reprinted by permission of OECD.

Figure 8.3   Reprinted by permission of the National Council on Aging.

Figure 8.4   Reprinted by permission of the National Council on Aging.

Figure 8.5   Reprinted by permission of the National Council on Aging.

Chapter 9

Figure 9.1   From *The Social Organization of Sexuality*, by E. O. Laumann, H. Gagnon, R. T. Michael, and S. Michaels. Copyright © 1994. Reprinted by permission of the University of Chicago Press.

Table 9.1   From "A Triangular Theory of Love." Paper presented at the annual meeting of the American Psychological Association, Los Angeles, 1985. Reprinted by permission of R. J. Sternberg.

Chapter 10

Figure 10.1   From *The New American Grandparent* by A. Cherlin and E. F. Furstenberg, Jr., Basic Books, 1986, p 74. Reprinted by permission of the authors.

Figure 10.2   American Association of Retired Persons, 1993. From *A Profile of Older Americans: 1993*. Reprinted with permission.

Table 10.1 Hamon & Blieszner, from "Filial responsibility expectations among adult child-older parent pairs", *Journal of Gerontology,* Vol. 45, p. 110–112, 1990. Coyright © The Gerontological Society of America.

Table 10.3 From M. A. P. Stephens, M. M. Franks, & A. L. Townsend (1994). "Stress and rewards in women's multiple roles: The case of women in the middle." *Psychology and Aging,* Vol. 9, pp. 45–52. Copyright © 1994 by the American Psychological Association. Reprinted with permission of the publisher.

Table 10.4 From M. A. P. Stephens, M. M. Franks, & A. L. Townsend (1994). "Stress and rewards in women's multiple roles: The case of women in the middle." *Psychology and Aging,* Vol. 9, pp. 45–52. Copyright © 1994 by the American Psychological Association. Reprinted with permission of the publisher.

Chapter 11

Figure 11.1 Costa & McCrae, from "Personality in adulthood: A six-year longitudinal study of self-reports and spouse ratings on the NEO Personality Inventory," *Journal of Personality and Social Psychology,* Vol. 54, 1988, pp. 853–63. Reprinted by permission of Robert McCrae.

Table 11.2 R. Helson and P. Wink from "Personality change in women from the early 40s to the early 50s", *Psychology and Aging,* Vol. 7, 1992, pp. 45–55. Copyright © 1992 by the American Psychological Association. Reprinted with permission.

Chapter 12

Figure 12.1 M. P. Lawton and L. Nahemow from "Ecology and the aging process," in *The Psychology of Adult Development and Aging,* edited by C. Eisdorter and M. P. Lawton, p. 661.

Copyright © 1973 by the American Psychological Association. Reprinted with permission.

Table 12.1 Koenig, George, & Siegler, from "The use of religion and other emotion-regulating coping strategies among older adults," *The Gerontologist,* Vol. 28, pp. 303–310, 1988. Copyright © The Gerontological Society of America.

Table 12.2 Atkinson, Ganzini & Bernstein. From "Alcohol and substance-use disorders in the elderly," in *Handbook of Mental Health and Aging,* 2nd Edition, edited by J. E. Birren, R. Sloane and G. D. Cohen, pp. 515–555. Copyright © 1992 by Academic Press, reproduced by permission of the publisher.

Table 12.3 Pratt, Wilson, Benthin, & Schmall, adapted from "Alcohol problems and depression in later life: Development of two knowledge quizzes," *The Gerontologist,* Vol. 32, pp. 175–183, 1992. Copyright © The Gerontological Society of America.

Chapter 13

Figure 13.1 Signer, McCarthy, & Logue, from "Wechsler Memory Scale scores, selective attribution, and distance from death," *Journal of Gerontology,* Vol. 37, pp. 176–181, 1982. Copyright © The Gerontological Society of America.

Table 13.1 "The Five Stages of Death," adapted with the permission of Scribner, an imprint of Simon & Schuster Adult Publishing Group, from *On Death and Dying* by Elisabeth Kubler-Ross. Copyright © 1969 by Elisabeth Kubler-Ross. Copyright renewed © 1997 by Elisabeth Kubler-Ross.

Table 13.2 A. E. Scharlach and K. I. Frederiksen, reprinted from *Omega,* Vol. 27, "Reactions to the death of a parent during midlife," p. 311, copyright © 1993, with permission from Elsevier Science.

Name Index

Hodges, 26, 73, 385, 467
Hofferth, S. L., 348
Hoffman, J. M., 95
Hoffman, S. D., 336
Hofstede, 403
Holbrook, N., 146
Holden, 153
Holden, K. C., 304
Holland, John, 280
Holland, M. J., 96
Holliday, S. G., 248
Holmes, D. S., 150
Holmes, T. H., 145, 435
Holstein, 444
Holtzman, N. A., 114
Holzman, 470
Honzik, M. P., 396
Hoogendijk, W. J. G., 467
Hooker, K., 352, 462
Hooyman, N. R., 459
Hope, Bob, 85
Hopper, J. L., 144
Horn, 164, 172f, 200
Horn, J. C., 83
Horn, John L., 207, 209, 210,
    211, 216
Horowitz, 92
Horowitz, Vladimir, 96, 165,
    213–214
Horton, A. M., 452
Horvath, J. A., 219, 222
Horwitz, A. V., 141
House, J. S., 304, 305
Howard, D. V., 162, 185
Howell-White, H. R., 141
Hoyer, William, 233, 234
Hoyert, D. L., 132, 138, 140, 507
Hu, N., 319
Hu, Y., 141
Huang, 289
Hudnall, C. E., 373
Hudson, K., 260
Hudson, R. B., 375, 379
Hull, R. H., 95
Hultsch, David F., 158, 181–182, 182,
    196, 198, 213, 217, 227
Hungerford, 498
Hurd, M. D., 24
Hurley, D., 68
Huston, T. L., 351
Hutchinson, C., 352
Huyck, M. H., 325, 413, 417, 420
Hyde, J. S., 264, 318, 330, 331, 421

I

Ickovics, J. R., 139
Ikeda, R., 507
Imbourne, E., 134
Infeld, L., 226
Ingolfsdottir, 234
Irion, J., 441
Irons, R. R., 450, 454
Irving, Amy, 335
Irving, H. H., 336
Isaacowitz, 253
Ishii, 75
Ivy, G. O., 172
Iwano, S., 459
Izumi, Shigechiyo, 75

J

Jackson, P. W., 220, 290
Jacobson, N. S., 142
Jaeger, 166
Jaffee, 264, 457
Jahnke, H. C., 439
Jahoda, M., 433
James, J., 166
James, William, 392
Janowsky, 173
Jaroff, L., 111
Javits, Jaboc K., 111
Jay, 277
Jay, G. M., 217
Jefferson, J. W., 466, 467
Jefferson, Thomas, 490
Jendrek, M. P., 373
Jeng, G., 345
Jennings, J. M., 158, 159, 160,
    176, 178
Jensen,, A. R., 198, 203, 204
Jex, S., 291
Johansson, 485
Johnson, 98, 158, 316, 372
Johnson, C. L., 17, 315, 352, 357,
    366, 376
Johnson, Earvin "Magic", 127, 129
Johnson, L., 241, 243
Johnson, M. K., 163
Johnson, P., 330
Johnson, R. J., 499
Johnson, S. A., 276
Johnson, Samuel, 337
Johnson, T. E., 75, 76
Johnson, Virginia E., 46, 47, 103,
    106, 141

Johnston, J. R., 144, 289, 337
Johnston, P., 514
Jolkkonen, J., 469
Jones, Ernest, 222
Jones, H. W., 344
Jones, J. H., 67
Jones, L. L., 384
Jones, X., 330
Jordan, 106
Joyner, K., 329
Jun, H., 500
June, J., 170
Jung, Carl, 248, 254, 420
Junkins, M. P., 285

K

Kabanoff, B., 292
Kagan, J., 398
Kahana, 370
Kahana, B., 435
Kahana, E., 370, 435
Kahn, M. J. E., 260
Kahn, Robert L., 18, 74, 85, 97, 103,
    112, 115, 117, 133, 155, 283,
    305–306, 314, 444
Kahn, S., 414
Kahonen-Vare, M. H., 469
Kaiser, M. A., 30
Kaizu, K., 459
Kalat, J. W., 53
Kalish, R. A., 482
Kalmuss, D. S., 455
Kalykakis, 148
Kamarow, 122
Kamin, L. J., 198
Kaplan, J., 283, 292, 293, 294, 295,
    306
Kapur, K. K., 148
Karbaat, J., 344
Karel, M. J., 467, 468
Karlinsky, H., 134
Karni, Avi, 170
Kart, 447
Kastenbaum, Robert, 60, 480, 483,
    491, 499
Katchadourian, H., 18, 77f, 78, 85,
    92, 96, 97, 101, 144
Katona, C., 466, 467
Katzman, R., 54
Kaufman, A. S., 216
Kaufman, S. R., 302
Kaufman, T. S., 371
Kaus, C. R., 462

McDaniel, 178
McEnroe, John, 432
McFall, S., 380
McGonagle, K. A., 433
McGrattan, E., 330
McGue, M., 398
McGuire, 289
McIntosh, 277, 466
McKay, N. Y., 357
McKenzie, E. B., 456
McKitrick, L. A., 134, 158, 167, 186, 187, 188, 189
McMullen, R., 92, 357
McNally, J. W., 322
McNamara, T., 505
McNeal, L. W., 50
Meacham, John A., 250
Meehan, P. J., 507
Meer, F., 230
Meer, J., 26, 83
Meier, D. E., 515
Meir, Golda, 311
Menacker, F., 341, 396
Menaghan, 435
Mendes de Leon, C. F., 397
Menke, E. M., 505
Mergler, N. L., 164, 176
Merrill, 101, 103
Mertz, M. E., 372
Merva, M., 291
Methuen, 466
Meyer, D. R., 341
Meyers, H., 349
Mezger, R., 91
Michael, R. T., 319, 320, 321, 329
Michaels, 321
Mikach, 342
Miklos, S. M., 283
Milgram, Stanley, 68, 364
Milkie, M. A., 330
Miller, 359, 362, 419
Miller, B. H., 380
Miller, G. A., 159
Miller, J., 153, 154
Miller-Jones, 199
Miller, L. C., 314
Miller, S., 292
Millsap, R. E., 403
Mindel, C. H., 23
Minder, C. E., 380
Miner, S., 362
Mingus, Charles, 111
Miniño, A. M., 139

Minkler, H., 362, 363, 370, 373, 444, 498
Minkler, M., 316
Mirowsky, 141, 329
Mirvis, P. H., 283
Mischel, W., 395
Mishkin, M., 163
Mitchell, 98, 424
Mitchell, B. A., 314
Mitchell, D. B., 168
Mitchell, V., 349
Mitchell-Kernan, C., 323
Moane, G., 420, 424, 427, 428
Moen, P., 303, 305, 306, 330
Moir, P., 462
Monahan, D., 352
Monat, A., 439
Moody-Thomas, S., 236
Mooney-Somers, J., 342
Moore, 416, 514
Moore, M. J., 462
Mor, 97
Morelli, G., 15
Morgan, J. N., 303, 304, 305
Morgan, L. A., 336, 337, 343
Morgan, S. P., 343f
Morrel, R., 157
Morris, L. W., 173
Morris, R. D., 50
Morris, R. G., 173
Morrison, D. F., 215
Morrison, D. R., 336
Morrison, Toni, 218, 443
Morse, D. L., 166
Morse, J. M., 43, 44
Mortensen, E. L., 467
Mortensen, P. B., 504
Mortimer, J. A., 469
Morton, K. R., 201, 241
Moscovitch, M., 170, 173, 175
Mosher, W. D., 322, 327, 333, 337, 339
Moss, M. S., 501
Moss, S. Z., 501
Mosteller, F., 46
Mowesian, Richard, 281
Moye, J., 388
Moyers, W., 258
Mpomati, 134
Mroczek, D. K., 305, 315
Mui, A. C., 384
Mullan, M. J., 435
Munck, A., 146
Murphy, 264
Murphy, D. R., 168

Murphy, P., 260
Murphy, P. D., 114
Murray, 198
Murstein, B. I., 318
Musil, C. M., 433, 434, 461, 464, 467
Muskin, P. R., 516
Mussen, P. H., 396
Muthen, B. O., 466
Mutran, E. J., 305
Muuss, R. E. H., 258
Myers, J. E., 337, 371
Myers, R. H., 315
Myerson, J., 477

N

Nagley, S., 466
Nagy, E., 170
Nahemow, 436, 436f
Nair, 97
Nash, S. C., 421
National Institute on Alcohol Abuse and Alcoholism, 145
National Organization for Women, Legal Defense Fund, 455
Naus, 105
Naveh-Benjamin, M., 163
Neff, W. S., 282
Neimeyer, 497
Neisser, U., 198, 199
Nelan, B. W., 230
Nelson, 289
Nelson, A. R., 141
Nelson, Erland, 61, 62, 63
Nelson, J., 269
Nesselroade, I. R., 48, 49f, 216
Nesses, 495
Netzer, J. K., 363
Neugarten, Bernice, 5, 10, 396, 416, 417, 420, 446, 446–447, 483
Newman, 139
Newton, Sir Isaac, 111
Nickerson, R. S., 161f
Niederehe, G., 461
Nilstun, T., 515
Nisan, M., 258
Nisbett, R. E., 398
Niven, David, 111
Nixon, Richard M., 270
Noble, 515
Nock, S. L., 338
Norris, 241
Norup, M., 515
Notelovitz, M., 150

Wolinsky, F. D., 499
Wong, P. T. P., 517
Woodbury, 200
Woodruff, D. S., 125, 170, 404
Woodruff-Pak, D. S., 126, 166
Woods, A. M., 96
Woods, Margo N., 105
Woodward, C. Vann, 368, 427
Wooten, J., 269
Workman-Daniels, K., 303
Wortman, C. B., 493, 494, 495
Wright, 105
Wright, Frank Lloyd, 218
Wright, V. C., 345
Wu, A. W., 484
Wu, Z., 328, 352
WuDunn, S., 341
Wurtman, R. J., 100, 142

Wykle, M. L., 433, 434, 461, 464, 466, 467
Wysocki, C. J., 95

Y

Yamomoti, Kajiro, 192
Yeung, W. J., 348
Yllo, K., 455
Yoder, J. D., 417
Yoshioka, M. R., 456
Young, E. W. D., 511
Yrbask, 98
Ytteroy, E. A., 342

Z

Zacks, R. T., 156, 161, 176
Zahn-Waxler, C., 398
Zandri, E., 277

Zanjani, E. D., 114
Zappa, Frank, 136
Zarit, S., 443
Zeringue, J. A., 188
Zhao, J. Z., 327
Zhu, 97
Ziegler, D. J., 395, 398
Zimberg, S., 452
Zimmer, H., 414
Zimmerman, G., 414
Zoglin, R., 17
Zube, M., 351
Zuckerman, M., 318
Zuzanek, J., 254
Zylicz, Z., 514

Subject Index

Alzheimers Association, 132, 133t
Alzheimer's disease (AD), 112, **131**,
   131–134, 469
  causes of, 133–134
  differentiating from depression,
    470, 470t
  disease progression, 132, 133
  Familial Alzheimer's Disease (FAD),
    132, 134
  memory in, 187
  prevalence, United States, 132
  Sporadic Alzheimer's Disease (SAD),
    132, 134
  treatment for, 134
  warning signs, 133t
Ambiguous loss, 494
Ambiguous loss, 495
American Academy of
    Otolaryngology, 95
American Academy of Pediatrics, 346
    Committee on Psychosocial Aspects
    of Child and Family Health,
    326, 342, 342–343
American Association of Retired
    Persons (AARP), 22, 23, 24,
    121–122, 273, 276, 278, 286,
    295, 301, 321, 362, 367, 370,
    380, 456, 459
American Cancer Society, 102,
    134, 135, 135–136, 136, 137,
    144, 147
American Dental Association
    (ADA), 149
American Diabetes Association, 127
American Heart Association, 123,
    144, 148, 149
American Indians
  death beliefs, 480, 491
  and grief, 495
  and health status, 141
  suicide rate, 506
American Jewish Committee, 48
American Lives, 63
American Lung Association, 126, 144
American Medical Association
    (AMA), 100, 101, 118, 120, 512
    Task Force on Quality Care at the
    End of Life, 511
American Psychiatric Association
    (APA), 67, 100, 131, 319, 450,
    465, 470, 471, 512, 513, 514
    Working Group on Assisted Suicide
    and End-of-Life Decision
    Making, 510, 516

American Psychological Association,
    319, 458, 459
American Sleep Apnea
    Association, 126
American Speech-Language-Hearing
    Association (ASHA), 89
Americans with Disabilities Act
    (ADA), 115
Amyloid plaques, 132
Amyotrophic lateral sclerosis (ALS),
    79, 110–111, 112
Anal stage, 39t
Anastasia (film), 311
Androgynous, 418
Anger stage, of dying, 488t
Anorexia, 84
Anticipatory grief, 492
Antidepressants, 467
Archetypes, 248
Argentina, suicide rate, 508t
Aricept, 134
Arteriosclerosis, 123
Arthritis, 121–122
Arthritis Foundation, 121, 122
Articulatory loop, 159
Artificial insemination, 345
Asian Americans
  and domestic violence, 455
  and education, 24–25, 25, 274
  and health status, 141
  and lifelong learning, 275
  as percentage of elders, 22
  suicide rate, 506
Asian cultures, 27–29
  child abuse in, 458
  elder care, 388–390
  families in, 340, 368
  life satisfaction, 29
  living arrangements, for elders,
    28–29, 380
  moral development in, 259
  population control in, 28
  women in, 102
Assisted living facilities, 379
Assisted suicide, 509. *see also*
    Euthanasia
  vs. active euthanasia, 511–514
Assortative mating, 318
Atherosclerosis, 123
Atkins diet, 148
Attentional resources, 161
Australia
  elder care, 388
  euthanasia, 513

  life expectancy, 77f
  suicide rate, 508t
Austria, suicide rate, 508t
Autoimmune theory of aging, 126
Autoimmunity, 126
Autonomy vs. shame and doubt, 39t
Autumn Sonata (film), 311
AZT (Zidovudine), 128

B

Baby boomers, 18
Baby M case, 346
Bad Sleep Well, The (film), 192
Balance models, coping, 447–449
Balanced investment, 303
Baltimore Longitudinal Study of
    Aging, 113, 114, 116, 402
Bargaining stage, of dying, 488t
Bariatric surgery (stomach stapling), 148
Beauty products, 18
Behavioral models, coping, 437
Behavioral psychology, 395
Behavioral therapy, 468
Belgium, end-of-life decisions in,
    514, 515
Beloved (Morrison), 218
Bem's Sex Role Inventory, 419, 421
Bereavement, 487, 490, 491–505
Berkeley Growth Study, 5
Berkeley Longitudinal Studies, 62, 63
Bible, The, 248, 503
Bioecological approach, to
    development, 14
Biographical approach, to study of
    creativity, 222–223, 224–225
Biological age, 10
Biological aging, theories of, 80–83
Biological approach, to memory, 169,
    170, 171–174
Biological death, 479
Biomarkers, 83–84
Birth defects, 515
Birthrates, by mother's age, 343f
Bisexual, 318
Blastocyst transfer, 345
Blindness, 91
Blood pressure, 123
Body Mass Index (BMI), 147
Bogotá, Colombia, 30
Bone loss (osteoporosis), 85, 117,
    118–120
Book of the Dead, 480
Boston Normative Aging Study, 305
Botswana, age in, 12–13

Brain scans, 169
Brain, structure, 169, 170, 171–174, 172f
Breast cancer, 135–136
Brief dynamic therapy, 468
Brief History of Time (Hawking), 111
Buddhism, 505
Bulimia, 84
Bureau of Labor Statistics (BLS), 283, 284, 285, 290, 330
Bureau of the Census, 24, 272, 274, **282**, 296, 297, 323, 328, 332, 337, 367, 376
Burnout
  caregiver, 383
  workplace, 290

C

California Psychological Inventory (CPI), 424
Calorie restriction (CR), 76, 79
Camaroon, retirement in, 302
Cambridge University, 111
Canada
  divorce rates, 333f
  family support in, 28
  life satisfaction, 29
  single parents, 341
  suicide rate, 508t
Cancer, 134, 134–137
  breast, 135–136
  causes of, 135, 136, 137, 144
  deaths from, 134–135, 135, 136
  incidence, 134–135, 135, 136
  prostate, 136–137
  treatment for, 136, 137
Carcinogens, 135
Cardiovascular system, 122–125
Career patterns, changing, 282–285
Career selection, 279–282
  and personality, 280–281
  vocational guidance, 279, 280
Caregiver burnout, 383
Caregivers
  for elderly, 362, 363–364, 365, 382–390
  elderly as, 363
Caregiving
  definition, 382
  legal intervention and, 387–388
  rewards of, 386t
  and stress, 383–387
  worldwide, 388–390
Carousel (broadway musical), 218

Carter Center, 270
Casablanca (film), 311
Case studies, 51–52, 52–53, 52t
Cataracts, 90
Celebratory Centenarians, 18
Centenarians, population of, 19–20
Center for Elderly People Living Alone, 380
Center of Addiction and Substance Abuse (CASA), 139
Centers for Disease Control and Prevention (CDC), 118, 127, 129, 130, 135, 136, 137, 147, 149, 322, 344, 416, 452, 454, 504, 506
Centers for Medicare and Medicaid Services, 115
Chad, 77f
Change, 4
Change of life, 100–102
Changing Lives of Older Couples (CLOC) study, 494, 495, 497, 498
Child abuse, 457–458
Childlessness, 352–353
Chile, retirement in, 297
Chinese Americans, 118, 119
Chinese culture
  and bereavement, 490
  child abuse in, 458
  elder care, 389, 390
  elderly, as percentage of population, 28
  lifelong learning, 274
  nursing home placement, 28
  population control, 28
  sexual mores, 320
  suicide rate, 508t
Cholesterol, 148
Christmas Carol (Dickens), 517
Chronicle of Higher Education, 273
Chronological age, 10
Chronosystem, in bioecological approach, 14, 15
Cigarette smoking, 135, 140, 142–143, 143t, 144
Civil Rights Act, 290
Classic aging pattern, of IQ scores, 208
Classical conditioning, 166, 186
Climacteric, 100
Cochlear implants, 89
Cognex, 134
Cognitive appraisal model, coping, 438–439
Cognitive appraisal model, coping, 441

Cognitive development, 7
  lifespan model of, 244–245
Cognitive-developmental theories, 419–420
Cognitive stages, of Piaget's theory, 39t, 40t
Cognitive therapy, 468
Cohabitation, 326–327
Cohort, 11, 59
Cohort-sequential design, 64, 65f
College education, 272–274
Colombia, 358
  social programs, 30
  suicide rate, 508t
Commitment within relativism, 239–240
Commonwealth Fund Commission on Elderly People Living Alone, 28
Compensation hypothesis, 292
Componiential element of intelligence, 204
Computer training, 276, 277
Conditioned responses, 166
Conductive hearing loss, 94
Confounding, of variables, 59
Congestive heart failure, 124
Congregate housing, 379
Congruence model, 435
Consolidation stage, of career development, 282
Construct validity, 57–58, 58
Consumer Reports Books, 106, 498
Contextual element of intelligence, 205
Contextual perspective, 41
Contextual perspective, 41–42
  applying, 42
Continuing care retirement communities, 379
Continuity theory, 447–448
Control group, 56
Convergent thinking, 220
Convoy theory, 305–306, 314
Coordination, and aging, 98–99
Coping, 435
Coping, models of, 435–444
  behavioral, 437
  cognitive appraisal, 438–439, 441
  coping-style, 437–438
  environmental-press, 437
  normative, 445–447
Coping-style models, 437–438
Corneal disease, 92
Correlational studies, 52t, 54–55
Cosmetic surgery, 18

Friendship, 315–316
Friendship 7 space capsule, 72
Frontal lobes, brain, 172, 173
Functional age, 10
Fundamental pragmatics of life, 251

G

Gallup polls, 281, 514
Gamete intrafallopian transfer (GIFT), 346
Gaslight (film), 311
Gastric bypass surgery, 148
Gays. *see* Homosexuality
Gender
    and aging, 17–18, 18
    and caregiving, 363, 382
    and depression, 467
    and education, 272–273, 273, 274
    and friendship, 315
    and grandparenting, 370–371
    and health status, 138–139
    and income, 24, 274, 284
    and intelligence, 215
    and life expectancy, 75, 77f, 140f
    and lifelong learning, 275, 276
    and longevity, 20, 22t, 26
    and moral development, 264–265
    and nursing home placement, 23
    and osteoporosis, 120
    and personality development, 414, 415, 417–428
    and poverty, 303–304, 337
    and retirement, 300
    and suicide, 28
    and work, 23–24
    in the workplace, 283–284, 289–290
Gender identity, 417
Gender roles, 417, 418, 419–421
Gender-schema theory, 420
Gender stereotypes, 17–18, 18, 417
Gene therapy, 80, 81, 114
Generation Y, 18
Generativity, 412
Generativity vs. stagnation, 40t, 407, 408t, 409
Genes, genetics
    and Alzheimer's disease, 134
    and cancer, 135, 136
    and lifespan, 75
    and personality, 398–399
Genetic engineering, 114, 115
Genetic-programming theories, of aging, 80, 82–83
Genetic testing, 114, 115

Geneva Association, 298, 299
Genital stage, 40t
Germany
    end-of-life decisions, 515
    sexual mores, 320
    suicide rate, 508t
Gerontological Society of America, 78
Gerontologists, 10
GIFT (gamete intrafallopian transfer), 346
Glaucoma, 91
Gonzales v. Oregon, 514
Grandparents, role of, 367–371
    gender and race differences, 370–371
    raising grandchildren, 372–373
Grant Study of Adult Development, 5, 437
Gray Power, 28
Graying of America, 18–20
Graying of population, worldwide, 25, 27
Great Britain
    care, of elderly, 382
    cohabitation, 327
    divorce rates, 333f
    elder care, 388
    life expectancy, 77f
    sexual mores, 320
    suicide rate, 508t
Great-grandparents, 371–372
Greece, suicide rate, 508t
Grief, 487
Grief
    anticipatory, 492
Grief, patterns of, 492–497
    ambiguous loss, 494, 495
    three-stage model, 492–493
Grief therapy, 496–497
Grief work, 492
Groningen Hospital, Amsterdam, 515
Gusii people, 415

H

Habitat for Humanity, 270
Hamon Filial Responsibility Scale, 364t
Harcourt Assessment, Incorporated, 208f
Hardening of the arteries, 123
Harris polls, 510, 511
Harvard Medical School, 506, 507, 508
Harvard University, 203, 239, 437
    Grant Study of Adult Development, 5
Harvest Moon effect, 490, 491

Hayflick limit, 75
Health and aging, 112
Health care, 113
    cost of, 26
    long-term, 304
Health Care Finance Administration, 376
Health Insurance Portability and Accountability Act (HIPAA), 115
Health status, 25
    and activities of daily living, 113t
    and age, 138–139
    and alcohol, 145
    declining, 113, 114
    and dental care, 148–149
    and diet, 147–148
    and exercise, 149–150
    and gender, 138–139
    and IQ scores, 200
    and lifestyle factors, 142–150
    and marriage, 141–142
    mental health, 304–305
    of old-old, 26
    and personality, 396, 397
    and race, 25, 139–141
    and relationships, 141–142
    in retirement, 304–305
    and socioeconomic status, 139–140
    and stress, 145–147, 289, 291
Hearing, changes in, 89, 92, 93–95
    causes of, 93–94
    coping with, 94–95
    correcting, 89
Heart attack, 123–124
Heart disease, 115, 116, 123–125
    and personality, 124–125
    and race, 140–141
Heinz's dilemma, 254–255, 259, 262
Heredity, 11
Heterosexual, 318
Hinduism, 414–415
Hippocampus, 169, 170
Hispanic cultures
    and Alzheimer's disease, 134
    and domestic violence, 455, 456
    and education, 22, 24–25, 273
    elder care, 388
    extended families, 358–359, 368
    health issues, 25, 91
    and health status, 140
    kinship networks, 23
    as percentage of elders, 22
    in retirement, 303, 304

Portugal, nursing home placement, 380
Post-traumatic stress disorder
    (PTSD), 147
Postformal thought, 237–244, **238**
    and cultural change, 241–242
    development of, 239–240
    and social reasoning, 240–241
Poverty
    and divorce, 337
    and gender, 24, 303–304, 337
    and health status, 139
    and race, 24, 303, 304
    in retirement, 303–304
Pragmatics of intelligence, 211
Preconventional morality, 255
Premarital sex, 320
Premenstrual syndrome (PMS), 100
Presbycusis, 94
Presbyopia, 87f, 89–90
President's Commission on the Study
    of Ethical Problems in Medicine
    and Biomedical and Behavioral
    Research, 510
Primary aging, 83
Priming, memory, 167
Principles of Psychology (James), 392
Problem finding, and creativity, 226
Problem-focused coping, 439, 441
Problem solving, 235–236
Production deficiency, in
    memorization, 178–179
Productive aging, 30–31
Profession, definition, 279
Programmed senescence, 80, 81t
Prospective memory, 177–178
Prostate cancer, 136–137
Pseudodementia, 470
Psychoanalysis, 34
Psychological age, 10–11
Psychometric approach, 194
Psychometric tests, creativity, 220–222
Psychometric tests, intelligence, 194,
    195–201
    and statistical analysis, 202–203
Psychometric tests, personality, 396,
    397–398
Psychopathology, definition, 464
Psychosexual stages, of Freud's
    theory, 39
Psychosocial stages, of Erikson's
    theory, 40t
    and adult personality, 407, 408t, 409
Psychotherapy, 468
Public Health Service, U.S., 66–67

Q

Q-sort, 398
Q'ran, 180
Qualitative development, 36
Qualitative research, 43, 43–44
Quantitative development, 35–36, 37–38
Quantitative research, 43
Quantitative research, 44
Quasi-experiment, 58
Quasi-experimental designs, 58–66
    cross-sectional studies, 59–60, 64t
    longitudinal studies, 60–61, 61f, 62,
        63, 64t
    sequential designs, 63, 64–65
    time-lag studies, 61, 61f, 62, 63, 64t
Quiz Kids (TV show), 51, 52–53

R

Race, 22
    and depression, 467
    discrimination, 355–357
    and domestic violence, 455
    and education, 273, 284
    and family networks, 23
    and health status, 140–141
    and income, 24
    and life expectancy, 75, 140f
    and lifelong learning, 275
    and longevity, 20, 22
    and poverty, 24, 303, 304
    and retirement, 300, 301, 303, 304
    and suicide, 506
    in the workplace, 284–285
Racism, 432
    and intelligence testing, 198–199
Radcliffe College, 239
Radical prostatectomy, 137
Ramadan, 491
Random assignment, 56
Random assignment, 56
Random assignment, 56–57
Random sampling, 44, 44–45
Random selection, 44
Rashomon (film), 191
Rate-of-living theory of aging, 81t, 82
Raven's Progressive Matrices, 208f,
    209, 209f
Reaction time, and aging, 98–99
Real self, 398
Red Beard (film), 192
Reflective thinking, 237–238
Reintegrative stage, of cognitive
    development, **244–245**

Relationships. *see also* Families
    cohabitation, 326–327
    and health status, 141–142
    homosexual, 324–326
    single lifestyle, 322–324
Reliable, 43
Religion
    and coping, 258, 441, 441t,
        442–443
    and death, 480
    and morality, 258
REM sleep, 170
Reminiscence, 517
    evoking, 518
Reminyl, 134
Reorganizational stage, of cognitive
    development, **244**
Reproductive systems, 99–107
    changes, in human, 99t
    female, 99, 99t, 100–102
    male, 103, 106
Research designs, 51–66
    case studies, 51–52
Research designs, basic, 52t
Research ethics, 66–69
Research methods, 43–51
Research to Prevent Blindness, 90
Reserve capacity, 117
**Resource provision-depletion
    hypothesis, 292**
Respect, for elders, 358
Respect for the Aged Day, Japan, 28
Respiratory disorders, 125–126
Respiratory system, 125–126
Responsible stage, of cognitive
    development, **244**
Retirement, 269–272, 292–308
    and age-differentiated life structures,
        271–272
    decisions about, 294–296
    financing, 296–297, 298–300
    and gender, 300
    health issues, 304–305
    history of, 292–294
    in Japan, 298, 299
    leisure during, 302–303
    paid work after, 301
    and poverty, 303–304
    preparing for, 300–301
    and race, 300, 301, 303
    reasons given for, 296f
    self-concept in, 306
    and social isolation, 314
    social support in, 305–306

and society, 306–308
sources of income in, 300f
volunteerism, 301–302
worldwide, 297, 302
Retirement communities, 378
Retirement hotels, 378
Retirement stage, of career
development, **282**
Retirement status, of elderly
population, 295f
Revolving door syndrome, 373–374
Rhapsody in August (film), 192
Rheumatoid arthritis, 122
Rights of Passage (Golding), 224
Robie House, Chicago, 218
Role differentiation, by age, 271–272
Roles, new, 30–31
Russia (former USSR)
life expectancy, 77f
suicide rate, 508t

S

Safety checklist, 93t
Same-sex partners. *see* Homosexuality
SAMHSA, 145, 452
Sampling methods, 44–45
Sandwich generation, 385
Sanshiro Sugata (film), 192
Satisfaction, life, by country, 29
Scandinavia
care, of elderly, 382
marriage in, 328
Scandinavian Simvastatin Survival
Study Group, 148
Schemas, 405
Schizophrenia, 464–465
Scientific method, 43
Seattle Longitudinal Study, 5,
199–200, 211–214, 244
tests given in, 213t
Secondary aging, 83
Secondhand smoke, 144
Segmentation hypothesis, 292
**Selective optimization with
compensation, 212**
Selectivity theory, 306, 314–315
Self, and death, 501, 503
Self-concept, 398, 400
in retirement, 306
Self-concept models, of personality,
400, 405–407
Self-in-relation theory, 419
Self-reports, 45
Semantic memory, 163–164

Senescence, 80
Senescence (Hall), 5
Senses, five, changes in, 85–92
Sensorineural hearing loss, 93–94
Sensorimotor functioning, 85–99
Sensory memory, 158, 159
September 11, 2001, 44–45, 147,
494, 495
Sequential research designs, 63, 64–65
Serene Sixties, 18
SERM (selective estrogen receptor
modulator), 121
Sexual attitudes, 320, 321
Sexual behavior, 320, 321f
and AIDS, 321–322
marital, 329
Sexual Behavior in the Human Female
(Kinsey), 46
Sexual Behavior in the Human Male
(Kinsey), 46
Sexual dysfunction, 103
Sexual function, 99–107
Sexual harassment, 290
Sexual orientation, 318, 318–320
Sexuality, and aging, 106–107
Shakespeare for My Father (play), 501
Shame and the Search for Identity
(Lynd), 355
Shared housing, 378
Short-term memory, 158
Sibling relationships, 364–367
in later life, 366
in middle age, 365–366
stepfamilies, 364–365
Sight, changes in. *see* Vision changes
Singapore
elderly, as percentage of
population, 28
life expectancy, 27
nursing home placement, 28
Single lifestyle, 322–324
Single parents, 341
Skeletal system, 117, 119–122
Sleep, and memory, 170
Sleep apnea, 125–126
Smell, sense of, 95
Smoking, cigarette, 135, 140,
142–143, 143t, 144
Social age, 11
Social clock, 415
Social convoy theory, 305–306, 314
Social development, 7
Social insurance, 297. *see also* Social
Security

Social-learning theory, 419
Social Security, 299
advent of, 293
eligibility, 297
as percentage of income, 24
and remarriage, 338
Society for Assisted Reproductive
Technology, 346
Socioeconomic status, 23–24
and health status, 139–140
Socioemotional selectivity theory, 306,
314–315
Somalia, life expectancy, 77f
Somatic-mutation theory of aging,
81t, 82
South American Indians, 176–177
South Asia, women in, 102
South Beach Diet, 147–148
South Korea, retirement in, 297
Soviet Union (Russia). *see* Russia
(former USSR)
Spain, suicide rate, 508t
Spatial scratch pad, 159
Specification stage, of career
planning, **281**
Spillover hypothesis, 292
Spirituality, and death, 480
Sporadic Alzheimer's Disease (SAD),
132, 134
Sri Lanka
economic development in, 30
elderly, as percentage of
population, 28
Stage models, personality, 400, 407–415
evaluating, 413–415
Stage, of development, 38–39
Stage theories, of development, 38–40
Stalking, 454–455
Stanford Studies of Gifted Children, 5
Stanford University, 5
Stepfamilies, 341–342
Stepfamilies
sibling relationships, 364–365
Stereotypes, 16–17
combatting, 18
gender, 17–18, 18, 417, 418
and work, 23, 287–288
Stomach stapling, 148
Stratified random sample, 45
Strength, and aging, 97–98
Stress, 145–147
Stress, caregiver, 383–387
reducing, 386, 387
stressors, 383t